D0020757

Tahiti &
French Polynesia

Celeste Brash
Jean-Bernard Carillet

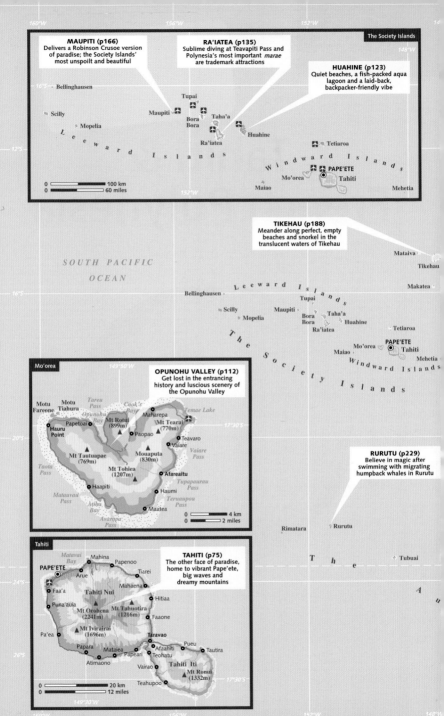

The Society Islands

MAUPITI (p166)
Delivers a Robinson Crusoe version of paradise; the Society Islands' most unspoilt and beautiful

RA'IATEA (p135)
Sublime diving at Teavapiti Pass and Polynesia's most important *marae* are trademark attractions

HUAHINE (p123)
Quiet beaches, a fish-packed aqua lagoon and a laid-back, backpacker-friendly vibe

Tupai
Maupiti
Bora Bora
Taha'a
Scilly
Mopelia
Bellinghausen
Ra'iatea
Huahine
Tetiaroa
L e e w a r d   I s l a n d s
W i n d w a r d   I s l a n d s
Mo'orea **PAPE'ETE**
Tahiti
Maiao
Mehetia

0 ——— 100 km
0 ——— 60 miles

TIKEHAU (p188)
Meander along perfect, empty beaches and snorkel in the translucent waters of Tikehau

Mataiva
Tikehau
Makatea

SOUTH PACIFIC OCEAN

L e e w a r d   I s l a n d s
Bellinghausen
Tupai
Scilly
Mopelia
Maupiti
Bora Bora
Taha'a
Huahine
Ra'iatea
Tetiaroa
T h e
Mo'orea **PAPE'ETE**
Tahiti
Maiao
Mehetia
S o c i e t y   I s l a n d s
W i n d w a r d   I s l a n d s

Mo'orea

OPUNOHU VALLEY (p112)
Get lost in the entrancing history and luscious scenery of the Opunohu Valley

Motu Fareone
Motu Tiahura
Tareu Pass
Opunohu Bay
Cook's Bay
Maharepa
Temae Lake
Papetoai
Mt Rotui (899m)
Mt Tearai (770m)
Hauru Point
Paopao
Teavaro
Vaiare
Mt Tautuapae (769m)
Mouaputa (830m)
Vaiare Pass
Mt Tohiea (1207m)
Afareaitu
Haapiti
Haumi
Tupapaurau Pass
Matauvau Pass
Atiha Bay
Maatea
Teruaupou Pass
Taota Pass
Asaropa Pass

0 ——— 4 km
0 ——— 2 miles

RURUTU (p229)
Believe in magic after swimming with migrating humpback whales in Rurutu

Rimatara
Rurutu

Tahiti

TAHITI (p75)
The other face of paradise, home to vibrant Pape'ete, big waves and dreamy mountains

Matavai Bay
Mahina
Papenoo
PAPE'ETE
Arue
Tiarei
Faa'a
Mahaena
Tahiti Nui
Hitiaa
Puna'auia
Mt Orohena (2241m)
Mt Tahuotira (1216m)
Faaone
Mt Ivirairai (1696m)
Pa'ea
Taravao
Pueu
Papara
Mataiea
Afaahiti
Tautira
Atimaono
Papeari
Teohatu
Vairao
Tahiti Iti
Teahupoo
Mt Ronui (1332m)

T h e
Tubuai
A
u

0 ——— 20 km
0 ——— 12 miles

Bora Bora

Motu Mute

BORA BORA (p150)
A temple to high-octane hedonism, it's ultra-gorgeous and over-the-top luxurious

Taihi Pt

Hitian Bay

Motu Tevairoa

Faanui

Vaitape   727m   Anau

Motu Toopua

Povai Bay

Motu Piti Aau

Paoaoa Pt

Kofai Bay

Fareone Pt

0   4 km
0   2 miles

151°40'W

The Marquesas

Motu One
Hatutu

Nuku Hiva

'Ua Huka

'Ua Pou

Hiva Oa

Tahuata

Fatu Hiva

NUKU HIVA (p201)
Hike the desert coasts and fecund valleys of Nuku Hiva

HIVA OA (p217)
Walk in Gauguin's footsteps and ponder eery, mossy archaeological sites

SOUTH PACIFIC OCEAN

Disappointment Islands

Tepoto Nord   Napuka

Puka Puka

Manihi

Ahe   Takaroa

Takapoto

Rangiroa
Arutua   Apataki
Kaukura   Aratika   Tikei
Toau   Taiaro
Kauehi

Niau   Raraka
Fakarava
Katiu
Faaite
Tahanea
Motutunga
Anaa

The Tuamotus

Takume   Fangatau
Fakahina

Taenga   Raroia

Nihiru   Rekareka
Makemo   Tauere
Marutea Nord
Tekokota   Tatakoto
Haraiki   Hikueru
Reitoru   Amanu
Marokau   Hao
Ravahere   Akiaki
Nengonengo   Vahitahi   Pukarua
Paraoa   Reao
Manuhangi   Vairaatea   Nukutavake
Pinaki

RANGIROA (p176)
Dive the sharky Tiputa and Avatoru passes and explore one of the world's most vast atoll lagoons

Ahunui

Hereheretue

Duke of Gloucester Islands

Anuanuraro
Anuanurunga
Nukutepipi

Vanavana   Tureia

Tematangi
Tenararo   Tenarunga
Vahanga   Marutea Sud
Matureivavao
Moruroa   Maria Island

Fangataufa   **The Gambier Archipelago**

Tropic of Capricorn

Morane   Mangareva   Temoe

THE GAMBIER ARCHIPELAGO (p238)
Enjoy white-sand beaches along the bluest lagoon in French Polynesia

Raivavae

SOUTH PACIFIC OCEAN

Rapa Iti (Rapa)

ELEVATION

2000m
1000m
500m
200m
0

LEGEND

Primary
Secondary
Unsealed

0   200 km
0   120 miles
Atolls not to scale

On the Road

CELESTE BRASH Coordinating Author

From the top of Mt Hiro, the highest summit of Raivavae (p234), there's a 360-degree view over the lagoon and its myriad of blues. The wind was pounding this day and we had a small flock of goats follow us up the crater. While the coastal areas of Raivavae are astoundingly lush, the hillsides are covered only in dry grass and a few struggling guava trees. What you can scarcely tell from this photo is that I'm sitting at the edge of a sheer cliff! I was not as comfortable here as I look.

JEAN-BERNARD CARILLET Here I'm just back from diving on Manihi (p192). The dive instructor told me that manta ray sightings are guaranteed on a site called The Circus (Le Cirque), which is a cleaning station for rays. I wanted to check it out. Indeed, there were five of them. There are few sights more surreal for scuba divers than watching these majestic creatures performing their loops and lining up to wait their turn for a skin-care treatment, as if they were in a merry-go-round. I positioned myself along the bottom to observe them up close, almost gasping in awe in my regulator.

For full author biographies see p276.

PARADISE FOUND

If paradise exists, this just might be it. The biggest decision you'll have to make is whether to do something really fun or nothing at all. By day you might dive or surf in translucent seas, hike through emerald waterfall valleys or simply crash out on a palm-fringed beach. And as the sun sets, be serenaded by ukulele riffs and the sounds of waves lapping on the shore, before the sky puts on its star-and-light show. When it comes time to go home, you'll be kicking and screaming.

Atolls, Lagoons & Beaches

Powder-white, sparkling-pink and graphite-black sands grace blue lagoons. But don't expect sweeping expanses with volleyball courts and drink vendors – French Polynesia's beaches are slim, intimate and often empty. The best of the best are found on the atolls and *motu* (fringing islets) of the high islands.

❶ Bora Bora

Nothing beats the iconic South Seas view of square-topped Bora Bora (p150) from its white-sand *motu*. Whether you're staying at a chic *motu* resort or spending the day on the lagoon with an excursion, you'll understand the hype.

❷ Maupiti

Don't want to understand Bora Bora's hype? Head next door to quiet, petite Maupiti (p166), where the white-sand *motu* and views of the island are nearly as grand, but the resorts and crowds are not.

❸ Tikehau

The atoll of choice if you're looking for pink sand. From white to rose to swirls of both, Tikehau's (p188) beaches wind past lagoon nooks and warm, blue-water delight.

❹ Raivavae

With dazzling, white-sand *motu* fringing its vast aquamarine lagoon, Raivavae (p234) has some of the best secret-spot beaches in the country. But the water temperature is, should we say, 'refreshing' compared to the other archipelagos.

❺ Rangiroa

The remote Lagon Bleu, a mini lagoon within Rangiroa's (p176) immense turquoise lagoon, has to be seen to be believed. This is the image you might have in your head when hearing the word paradise.

❻ Tahiti

While black volcanic-sand beaches such as Tahiti's Point Vénus (p100) rarely make it into the brochures, they are worth a stop for their dark, unpretentious beauty and a slice of the local beach scene.

Diving & Snorkelling

With 4 million sq km of water and only 4000 sq km of land, it makes sense that a good chunk of French Polynesia's action is below sea level. Whether you choose to strap on a bottle or a snorkel, be prepared for big fauna and incredible visibility.

③

Author Tip

You'll find decent snorkelling anywhere there's coral, so look for a calm spot and plunge in. All beaches in French Polynesia are public property but don't even think about going through someone's private property to get to the shore.

① Tiputa Pass, Rangiroa

Sharks anyone? Drift the Tiputa Pass (p69) currents and encounter hammerheads, grey and reef sharks, as well as a smattering of rays, tuna and frolicking dolphins. Add a rainbow of reef fish and you have underwater paradise.

② Teavapiti Pass, Ra'iatea

Teavapiti Pass (p68) claims to be the most fish-dense pass in the Society Islands and we're not going to argue. All the colourful little fish draw in the bigger players: reef sharks, rays and occasionally some big Napoleons.

③ Manta Point, Maupiti

Hang out quietly at the bottom at Manta Point (p69) as graceful manta rays fly by to be cleaned by resident wrasses. If you're lucky a few stingrays might turn up too.

④ Garuae Pass, Fakarava

Floating out with the current to the cobalt-blue drop-off and thriving corals of Garuae Pass (p71) is enough to make any diver kick for joy. Expect lots of fish as well as the Tuamotus' signature grey reef sharks.

⑤ Taiohae, Nuku Hiva

Nuku Hiva (p205) is an extraordinary place to snorkel with pods of rarely seen melon-headed whales. You might even get close enough to see the whites of their lips (one of the dolphin-like creature's defining features).

⑥ Rurutu

Rurutu has no barrier reef and water as clear as air. Dive in (see the boxed text, p231) to watch migrating humpbacks, often with their calves, peacefully glide by. To see the magnificent mammals breach from the surface is equally thrilling.

Hiking

Hiking along deep river valleys to vistas on crater ridges is an unsung high-light of French Polynesia. The largest islands with diverse topography, such as Tahiti, Mo'orea, Ra'iatea and Nuku Hiva, have the most exhilarating trails and on Tahiti you can even rappel down waterfalls and explore ravines while canyoning.

Author Tip
If you don't hire a guide, pay very close attention to the trail and consider leaving a Hansel and Gretel–type trail of rocks or such to mark your path. Even locals get lost regularly on French Polynesia's poorly marked tracks.

❶ Te Pari, Tahiti
It's hard to believe that Te Pari (p104), Tahiti's eastern-most coast, is only accessible by boat or on foot. This trail is dripping with waterfalls, archaeological sites, caves and empty beaches, but you'll need to have perfect weather conditions to go.

❷ Temehani Plateau, Ra'iatea
Search for the rare white-petalled flower *tiare tahiti* on the Temehani Plateau (p140) before reaching vista peaks with views of Bora Bora. This mountain is the legendary birthplace of 'Oro, the Polynesian god of war.

❸ Mt Hiro, Raivavae
Raivavae is so tiny that you can see the whole island and sweep of aquamarine lagoon from atop the island's highest peak, Mt Hiro (p235). Look down the precipices to tiny villages and herds of wild goats.

❹ Three Coconut Trees Pass, Mo'orea
Hike past dark, mossy rivers, fern-clad valleys and gnarled *mape* (chestnut) forests before reaching Three Coconut Trees Pass (p114) – which only has one coconut tree on it today. Views span over vertical mountaintops and out to sea.

❺ Hitiaa Lava Tubes, Tahiti
This 'hike' up-river through the cavernous Hitiaa Lava Tubes (p99) is about 50% swimming and 50% scrambling. It's also a popular place for canyoning, an even soggier option, which will get you on the faces of cliff-steep waterfalls.

❻ Nuku Hiva
There are so many different landscapes on Nuku Hiva (p201) that you'll be spoiled with diversity. From waterfalls and shady forests to vast expanses of steep, barren mountains, you'll only share the trail with your guide and wild goats.

Archaeology

Who were these seafaring geniuses who crossed the Pacific and populated even the most miniscule islands? Chances are we'll never know all of their secrets, but visiting Polynesian ancient *marae* (temples) sure can make the head reel with ideas. The locations of these sites are usually stunning.

Author Tip

Bring mosquito repellent! French Polynesia's archaeological sites all seem to have uncommonly abundant mosquito populations.

❶ Omoa Petroglyphs, Fatu Hiva

Find your favourite sea critters etched onto ancient slabs of volcanic rock at the remote Omoa petroglyphs (p226). Trek through exotically lush bush and feel like you're the first ones to see them in hundreds of years.

❷ Marae Taputapuatea, Ra'iatea

Considered to be the spiritual centre of Polynesia, Marae Taputapuatea (p138) is the queen of French Polynesia's archaeological sites. Experience the heat and energy of this place before taking a dip at the adjacent white-sand beach.

❸ Iipona, Hiva Oa

Five eerie *tiki* (sacred statues), including the tallest one in the country, make Iipona's (p222) mossy jungle enclave feel like you've gone back in time several hundred years. It's one of the best preserved sites in French Polynesia and an experience just getting there.

❹ Maeva, Huahine

The sprawling seaside part of Maeva (p126) is lovely, but it's the crumbling gems up the hill that make for a more Indiana Jones experience. Slather on the mosquito repellent and don't be afraid to get lost.

'Haere maru haere papu –
Take it slow, take it steady.'
Tahitian proverb

Polynesian Culture

Bursting with flowers, smiles, fast drums and shaking hips, Polynesian culture is experiencing a sensational renaissance after being stifled by religion and government for several generations. Polynesians are proud of their roots and the gorgeous cultural manifestations that visitors see aren't packaged for tourism – this is the real deal.

❶ Ukulele Music, Tikehau

Ukulele music provides the soundtrack to French Polynesia, particularly on Tikehau (p188). You can expect sunset serenades that lead you into perfect lagoonside starry nights. If these happy songs don't bring a smile to your face, nothing will.

❷ Heiva Dance Competitions, Tahiti

The missionaries were shocked by the sexiness of Polynesian dance and most folks today are just as dazzled by the dance's masculine and feminine gestures and sultry grace. The Heiva dance performances (p48) are the pinnacle of this spectacular art.

❸ Tahitian Pearls, Ahe

Forget diamonds, black pearls are a Tahitian gal's best friend and a must-buy souvenir. Don't miss visiting a farm (Ahe atoll, p193, has the most) to learn about the culturing process and to drool over these lustrous gems.

❹ Tattoos, the Marquesas

Both aesthetically beautiful and inexplicably raw, dark geometric patterns against bronze skin are making a huge comeback all over Polynesia. It's the artists of the Marquesas (p225), however, who are renowned for having perfected Polynesia's ancient designs.

❺ Flower Garlands, Tahiti

Flowers and garlands are welcome gifts, as well as a way to get gussied up local-style. Tuck that perfumed *tiare* (p50) you're given on arrival at Tahiti's Faa'a International Airport behind your ear and suddenly feel much more attractive.

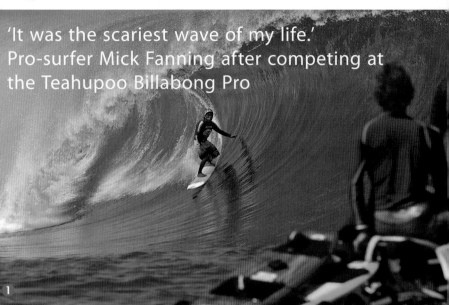

'It was the scariest wave of my life.'
Pro-surfer Mick Fanning after competing at
the Teahupoo Billabong Pro

Surfing

With warm, clear water, swell from all directions and innumerable breaks, it's no wonder that Polynesia has become a surf mecca. Beginners can paddle out to shore breaks while more advanced surfers will be spoiled with hollow reef waves year-round. Secret spots are everywhere if you're willing to look.

❶ Teahupoo, Tahiti

This is the big one. Whether you have the guts to surf the Teahupoo (p80) monster yourself or not, you can still hire a boat to take you out for fantastic views of pro-surfers riding the tube.

❷ Papara, Tahiti

When the waves are small, the Papara (p80) shore break is good for beginners and is also fun when it's bigger – if you know what you're doing. It's on a sweeping black-sand beach that's good for boogie-boarding or picnicking.

❸ Haapiti, Mo'orea

Haapiti (p111) is Mo'orea's excellent hollow and barrelling, intermediate to advanced wave that's good year-round. Rent a kayak or find someone with a boat to avoid the long paddle out.

Contents

On the Road 4

Paradise Found 5

Destination Tahiti &
French Polynesia 20

Getting Started 22

Itineraries 26

History 31

The Culture 41

Food & Drink 53

Environment 59

Diving 64

Tahiti 75
PAPE'ETE 82
History 82
Orientation 82
Information 83
Sights 83
Walking Tour 88
Festivals & Events 89
Sleeping 89
Eating 91
Drinking 92
Entertainment 93
Shopping 94
Getting There & Away 95
Getting Around 95
AROUND TAHITI NUI 96
West Coast 96
South Coast 98
East Coast 99
Inland 100

TAHITI ITI 102
Sights 102
Activities 103
Festivals & Events 104
Sleeping & Eating 104

Mo'orea 106
History 107
Geography & Geology 107
Orientation 107
Information 107
Sights 109
Activities 112
Courses 115
Mo'orea for Children 115
Tours 115
Sleeping 115
Eating 119
Drinking & Entertainment 121
Shopping 121
Getting There & Away 121
Getting Around 122

Huahine 123
History 124
Orientation 124
Information 124
Huahine Nui 124
Huahine Iti 128
Activities 129
Tours 130
Sleeping 130
Eating 133
Drinking & Entertainment 133
Getting There & Away 134
Getting Around 134

Ra'iatea & Taha'a 135
RA'IATEA 136
History 136
Orientation 136
Information 136
Sights 138
Activities 139
Tours 140
Sleeping 141
Eating 142
Drinking & Entertainment 143
Shopping 143

Getting There & Away 144
Getting Around 144
TAHA'A **145**
History 145
Orientation 145
Information 145
Sights 145
Activities 146
Tours 146
Sleeping 147
Eating & Drinking 148
Getting There & Away 148
Getting Around 148

Bora Bora 150
History 151
Orientation 151
Information 151
Sights 151
Activities 155
Bora Bora for Children 157
Sleeping 157
Eating 161
Drinking 163
Entertainment 163
Shopping 163
Getting There & Away 164
Getting Around 164

Maupiti 166
History 167
Orientation & Information 167
The Motu 167
The Main Island 167
Activities 169
Maupiti for Children 170
Sleeping 170
Eating 172
Shopping 172
Getting There & Away 172
Getting Around 172

The Tuamotus 173
RANGIROA **176**
History 177
Orientation 178
Information 178
Sights 178
Activities 180
Tours 180
Sleeping 181
Eating 183

Drinking & Entertainment 184
Getting There & Away 185
Getting Around 185
NORTHERN TUAMOTUS **185**
Fakarava 185
Tikehau 188
Mataiva 191
Manihi 192
Ahe 193
Takaroa 194
Takapoto 194
Makemo 196
Anaa 197
SOUTHERN & EASTERN TUAMOTUS **197**
Hao 197
Moruroa 198

The Marquesas 199
NUKU HIVA **201**
Taiohae 202
Hakaui Valley 206
Toovii Plateau 207
Taipivai 207
Hooumi 207
Hatiheu 208
Anaho & Haatuatua 209
Getting There & Away 209
Getting Around 210
'UA HUKA **211**
Information 211
Sights 211
Activities 213
Sleeping & Eating 213
Getting There & Away 214
Getting Around 214
'UA POU **214**
Hakahau 215
Hakanai 216
Hakahetau 216
Haakuti 216
Hakamaii 216
Hohoi 217
Getting There & Away 217
Getting Around 217
HIVA OA **217**
Atuona & Around 217
Taaoa 222
Puamau 222
Hanapaaoa & Surrounding Hamlets 223
Hanaiapa 223
Getting There & Away 223
TAHUATA **224**

Sights 224
Activities 225
Sleeping & Eating 225
Getting There & Away 225
Getting Around 225
FATU HIVA **225**
Information 226
Sights 226
Activities 226
Sleeping & Eating 226
Getting There & Away 227
Getting Around 227

The Australs 228
Rurutu 229
Tubuai 232
Raivavae 234
Rimatara 236
Rapa Iti (Rapa) 236

The Gambier Archipelago 238
Mangareva 240
Taravai & Aukena 241
Akamaru & Temoe 241

Directory 242
Accommodation 242
Activities 244
Business Hours 245
Children 245
Climate Charts 246
Customs 246
Dangers & Annoyances 246
Discount Cards 247
Embassies & Consulates 247
Festivals & Events 247
Food 248
Gay & Lesbian Travellers 248
Holidays 248
Insurance 248
Internet Access 248
Legal Matters 248
Maps 249
Money 249
Post 250
Shopping 250
Telephone 251
Time 251
Tourist Information 251

Travellers with
Disabilities 252
Visas 252
Volunteering 252
Women Travellers 253
Work 253

Transport 254
**GETTING THERE &
AWAY** 254
Entering the Country 254
Air 254
Sea 257
GETTING AROUND 257
Air 258
Bicycle 260
Boat 260
Local Transport 262

Health 264
BEFORE YOU GO 264
Insurance 264
Recommended
Vaccinations 264
Medical Checklist 264
Internet Resources 265
Further Reading 265
IN TRANSIT 265
Deep Vein
Thrombosis (DVT) 265
Jet Lag & Motion
Sickness 265
IN FRENCH POLYNESIA 265
Availability & Cost of
Health Care 265
Infectious Diseases 266
Traveller's Diarrhoea 267

Environmental Hazards 267
Travel with Children 269
Women's Health 269

Language 270

Glossary 273

The Authors 276

Behind the Scenes 277

Index 282

Map Legend 288

Regional Map Contents

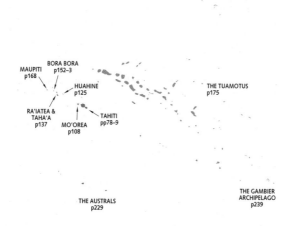

THE MARQUESAS
p200

MAUPITI
p168
BORA BORA
p152–3
HUAHINE
p125
THE TUAMOTUS
p175
RA'IATEA &
TAHA'A
p137
MO'OREA
p108
TAHITI
pp78–9

THE AUSTRALS
p229

THE GAMBIER
ARCHIPELAGO
p239

Destination Tahiti & French Polynesia

Raise your hand, who wants to go to Tahiti? We thought so. With a name synonymous with paradise, French Polynesia has the quandary of having to live up to expectations fuelled by hundreds of years of hype and lifetimes of daydreams. Paul Gauguin painted brown-skinned beauties wearing little more than content expressions on their faces and flowers behind their ears; Herman Melville went AWOL in the Marquesas; the *Bounty* mutineers risked their lives to stay on the 'Island of Love'; and Marlon Brando, while portraying mutineer Fletcher Christian, fell in love with his Tahitian co-star and settled here. With its history of seduction and romance it's no wonder French Polynesia has become a favourite with honeymooners.

But is French Polynesia still the new Cythera, as it was dubbed by French explorer Louis-Antoine de Bougainville back in 1768? The islands are blessed with some of the most stunning scenery in the world – just as you've seen in the brochures – from surreal geometric peaks to endless blue lagoons. What visitors do complain about, however, is the lack of beaches. Don't expect sweeping swaths of sand; instead, you'll have to be content with little strips of white or black where you have just enough room to plop down before plunging into the lagoon. Besides resorts and hotels there is little in the way of traditional Polynesian architecture or even colonial structures – houses today are modern, practical, made from cheap materials and boxlike – but the people inside them still wear the same smiles that have been greeting foreigners for generations.

Though the French Polynesia of today isn't exactly the same scene that inspired Gauguin, the ubiquitous scent of gardenias, the warm damp breezes and ukulele riffs by starlight still make plenty of modern visitors want to move here and devote their lives to love and art. Gauguin also showed up poor, and today that's not recommended. While prices have hardly gone up over the last few years, this still isn't a budget destination and most visitors arrive on luxury itineraries to five-star hotels. Yet the budget-minded will be happy to find that daily expenses in French Polynesia can be considerably lower than in most major cities in Europe, especially if you can forgo that fancy French restaurant or take the bus or bike instead of renting a car. It'll still leave an impact on your credit card bill, but nothing that will take a lifetime to pay back.

While tourists are looking for spacious beaches and baulking at the price of their lunch, French Polynesians are griping about politics. The country is technically part of France but for the most part it's self-governing. Since 2004 the country's government has been at a standstill as the main political parties battle it out, call each other names, and try to woo members of the assembly to flip-flop the balance of power. While democratic elections decide how many assembly seats go to each party, once there the members can switch parties. When there is a fragile majority, which is always the case, one or two allegiance changes can overturn the entire government. From 2004 to 2008 this happened seven times. Since French Polynesia is socialist and modelled on the French system, nearly everything, from applications for low-income housing to taxation, goes through several layers of functionaries. When the government flips, everything stops and goes back to zero, making it impossible for folks to get things done. Add the requisite strikes, and trying to do day-to-day things can become very frustrating (port strikes that block petrol are the worst). Rose, a local Tahitian fish-seller, sums up most people's attitude by saying: 'All I want is for our politicians to do their job and take care of us but that seems like a dream these days. I wish they'd just get it together and give our country some stability.' And Tahitians have the perfect word for how everyone is feeling about local politics: *fiu,* meaning sick and tired of it, worn out or just plain over it.

But Polynesians are happy people and don't like to whinge for long. When locals aren't talking politics they're usually talking about the season's events. Chinese New Year in late January or early February gets everyone discussing their Chinese horoscope and the year to come; in May everyone flocks to see surfing at the Billabong Pro in Teahupoo (p104) and the big beauty pageants (p44) around the islands; in July it's all about the Heiva (p48); and in October and November the Hawaiki Nui (p45) is the favourite topic of conversation. By December, Christmas and New Year's plans dominate the social scene. Between all this folks discuss how it's too hot or too rainy, gossip about the neighbours, and talk about how well their fruit trees are producing or what the fishing's been like. If you happen to pass by a group of Polynesians chatting together take notice of how much they laugh.

So is this paradise? If you're looking for clear-blue lagoons, laid-back people, fresh fish and a seriously slow pace of life, and have more than a few bucks in your pocket, it's hard to do much better than this; just remember, you're still in the modern world.

Getting Started

French Polynesia thrives on tourism, and the only thing difficult about travelling here is parting with the small fortune it's costs for a burger and Coke. That said, French Polynesia is a destination that benefits from planning. Start thinking about your trip around three to six months out; this will allow you enough time to scour the web for the best deals or book your dream honeymoon bungalow before someone else does. Definitely devote some serious hours to online research – from complete honeymoon packages to discounts on budget-oriented family guesthouses to internet-only deals on luxury resorts, there are thousands of sites out there offering everything French Polynesia related on sale. Once you arrive, an efficient and fast system of ferries, planes and taxis whisks you from destination to destination.

WHEN TO GO

French Polynesia is an outdoor destination, so the timing of your trip will probably be influenced by the weather. The dry winter period from May to October is the best time to go; the weather is cooler and there is much less rainfall during this time. Temperatures rise during the November to April summer rainy season when it's humid and cloudy. Three-quarters of the annual rainfall occurs during this period, generally in the form of brief, violent storms, although torrential rains lasting several days are not uncommon.

French Polynesia is south of the equator, but school holidays fall in line with those of the northern hemisphere. This means that the peak season is July and August; during this period it's no mean feat getting flights and accommodation. Christmas to early January, late February and early March, the Easter period, early May and early October are also quite busy times (which almost covers the entire year!). The peak July to August season coincides with the Heiva festival (p247), held throughout July, when the region comes to life. Unfortunately this is no secret, so plan ahead if July interests you.

See Climate Charts (p246) for more information.

Diving is popular year-round, and each season brings its share of discoveries (see the Diving chapter, p64). Surfing is also a year-round activity. If you are sailing, avoid the November to March tropical depressions – they can be depressing! Walking is best in the dry season, as some of the trails are simply impassable when it's wet.

COSTS & MONEY

French Polynesia is expensive, with travel costs on par with Europe or Australia. Flights alone tend to be a substantial cost, but once you arrive you may be shocked to find that even the cheapest meal, bought from a street vendor, will set you back around 1200 CFP. Backpackers who cook all their own meals and stay in the cheapest rooms possible can skimp by on 6000 to 8000 CFP per day depending on the island. Midrange-budget travellers, looking for more comfortable beds and wanting to enjoy a few restaurant meals and perhaps an organised excursion, can count on paying around 20,000 CFP per day. Top-end-budget visitors will find the sky is the limit when it comes to posh lodging and dining options and watery excursions. Over-water bungalows start at around US$500 per night, and a stay on a private island can cost as much as US$10,000. To score the best deals, try to book in advance. If you're travelling with kids, many places offer half-price discounts for children under the age of 12.

DON'T LEAVE HOME WITHOUT...

Imported goods are expensive in French Polynesia – and most goods are imported – so bring enough everyday essentials to last for your entire trip. The following are must-haves.

- Sunscreen: the sun can be devilishly scorching
- Raincoat: it can rain at any time, even during the supposedly dry season
- First-aid kit: be sure to pack the basics – aspirin, sticking plasters, antiseptic cream and anti-diarrhoea pills
- Insect repellent: French Polynesia doesn't have malaria, but the mosquitoes still bite hard and fast
- Plastic bags: keep your camera and other valuables protected from the elements
- International dive card: you won't want to miss French Polynesia's magnificent underwater worlds
- Snorkel, mask and flippers: the lagoons resemble personal aquariums, free to anyone carrying the right equipment
- Patience: island life moves slowly, so don't try to speed it up or you'll just be disappointed

---

Taxation is another bugbear here: a TVA (*taxe sur la valeur ajoutée;* value-added tax), which was introduced in 1998, currently adds 5% to your hotel bill, and that's not including the 5% government tax and the accommodation tax (*taxe de séjour;* daily tax) which top off the bill. We've included all taxes in our listed prices.

TRAVELLING RESPONSIBLY

Probably the best thing you can do to travel responsibly in Tahiti and French Polynesia is to stay at a locally run *pension* (guesthouse) rather than at a big resort. These small businesses have been hit the hardest with the drop in tourism and desperately need your business. Some travellers are afraid that family-run places won't offer the comforts they are looking for, but many up-scale *pensions* are stylish and plush, offering much better hospitality than you'll find at some multinational hotels. For recommended places see p30, or for booking ideas and packages go to http://english.islandsadventures.com.

When swimming remember not to walk on the coral (which are living organisms); for tips on responsible diving, see p71. To minimise the number of plastic bottles (for drinking water) you leave behind, consider bringing along a small water filter.

TRAVEL LITERATURE

Pulitzer-winning writer Tony Horwitz follows the voyages of Captain Cook and his beer-swilling friend Williamson in *Blue Latitudes: Boldly Going Where Captain Cook Has Gone Before* (2002). It's a frustrating, funny and insightful read.

The congenitally acerbic Paul Theroux was at his sourest when he visited *The Happy Isles of Oceania* (1992), describing Tahiti as 'a paradise of fruit trees, brown tits and kiddie porn'. Crossing the Pacific from Australia and New Zealand to Hawaii, he didn't find much of it very happy, but the insights are up to his usual high standards. His fellow passengers are prodded unmercifully with his sharpest pen and the beautiful, gloomy Marquesas are the perfect site for a Theroux visit. The French don't come out of it very well, but neither do the Polynesians, who are presented as eagerly embracing their own decline. This is a book to read after your trip. If you read it before

HOW MUCH?

Burger, fries and Coke at a *roulotte:* 1500 CFP

Dinner for two at a midrange restaurant: 6000 CFP

Simple bungalow with fan: 6000 to 10,000 CFP

Night in an over-the-water bungalow: 60,000 to 100,000 CFP

Five-island airpass: 26,500 CFP

TOP 10

OVER-THE-TOP LUXE RESORTS

If you're going to really splurge, French Polynesia just might be the best place in the world to do it. The following places are the best of the best.

1 Intercontinental Resort & Thalasso Spa Bora Bora (p160), Bora Bora

2 Four Seasons Resort Bora Bora (p160), Bora Bora

3 Le Taha'a Private Island & Spa (p148), Taha'a

4 Tikehau Pearl Beach Resort (p190), Tuamotus

5 Saint Régis Resort (p160), Bora Bora

6 Bora Bora Nui Resort & Spa (p160), Bora Bora

7 Le Méridien Bora Bora (p160), Bora Bora

8 Te Tiare Beach Outrigger Resort (p132), Huahine

9 Legends Resort (p117), Mo'orea

10 Bora Bora Pearl Beach Resort (p160), Bora Bora

BEST-VALUE ACCOMMODATION

The following are our top picks for good value – they are not necessarily the cheapest places, they simply have the best cost-to-worth ratio.

1 Sofitel Maeva Beach (p90), Tahiti

2 Taaroa Lodge (p97), Tahiti

3 Raiatea Lodge (p142), Ra'iatea

4 Pension Motu Iti (p116), Mo'orea

5 Novotel Bora Bora Beach Resort (p158), Bora Bora

6 Maupiti Residence (p170), Maupiti

7 Paahatea Nui (p205), Nuku Hiva

8 Pension Ariiheevai (p192), Mataiva

9 Pension Meherio (p131), Huahine

10 Pension Bounty (p182), Rangiroa

READS

For a bit of armchair-travel, try the following titles.

1 *Mutiny on the Bounty* by Charles Nordhoff and James Hall

2 *The Moon and Sixpence* by W Somerset Maugham

3 *Breadfruit* by Celestine Hitiura Vaite

4 *To Live in Paradise* by Reneé Roosevelt Denis

5 *Tales of the South Pacific* by James Michener

6 *Piracy in the Pacific* by Henri Jacquier

7 *Blue Latitudes: Boldly Going Where Captain Cook Has Gone Before* by Tony Horwitz

8 *Typee* by Herman Melville

9 *In the South Seas* by Robert Louis Stevenson

10 *Henderson's Spear* by Ronald Wright

or during you'll look at French Polynesia more cynically and Polynesia isn't very welcoming to cynics.

Much more upbeat is Gavin Bell's award-winning *In Search of Tusitala* (1994), which traces the Pacific wanderings of Robert Louis Stevenson. Like a number of other writers, Bell finds the Marquesas fascinating, beautiful and deeply depressing. 'How long has it been raining?' Bell asks the first Marquesan he meets. 'About one year,' comes the reply.

In *Kon-tiki: Across the Pacific by Raft* (1953), Norwegian explorer Thor Heyerdahl recounts his epic voyage to try to prove his (now discounted) theory that Polynesia was populated by Incas from South America. It is a great adventure read.

White Savages in the South Seas (1995) by Mel Kernahan is a witty collection of experiences, accumulated by the author during years of studying and travelling as a solo woman in French Polynesia. It provides a candid look at the not-so-swanky lives of real people living in Tahiti.

For an unabashed look at the history of travel and sex, check out *Sultry Climates: Travel and Sex Since the Grand Tour* (2002) by Ian Littlewood, which pays particular attention to the attitude of many early explorers towards Tahitian women. It also examines the myth of Tahiti as a place linked with the lure of uninhibited sex.

Reneé Roosevelt Denis writes the fabulously adventurous story of her life and how she came to live on the island of Mo'orea (where she still lives) in her book *To Live in Paradise* (1996). The story takes us from Haiti to Los Angeles and finally to Tahiti and Mo'orea where we meet Marlon Brando and members of the Roosevelt family and partake in Club Med romances.

INTERNET RESOURCES

Easy Tahiti (www.easytahiti.com) Create custom packages with resorts or family *pensions*.

Haere Mai (www.haere-mai.pf) Lists small hotels and family *pensions*.

Island Adventures (http://english.islandsadventures.com) Air Tahiti's site with great-value air and lodging packages in small hotels and *pensions* throughout French Polynesia.

Lonely Planet (www.lonelyplanet.com) Provides summaries on travelling to most places on earth; includes the all-important Thorn Tree travel forum, where you can ask questions of travellers who've been to Tahiti recently.

Tahiti Explorer (www.tahitiexplorer.com) Discounts on lodging, customised honeymoon packages and destination descriptions.

Tahiti Nui Travel (www.tahiti-nui.com) Aimed at travel agents but packed with loads of useful information.

Tahiti Tourisme (www.tahiti-tourisme.com) Official Tahiti Tourism website, in English.

SPECIALTY WEBSITES

News: www.tahitipresse.pf

Polynesian weddings: www.tahitianwedding.com

Pearls: www.perlesdetahiti.com

Itineraries
CLASSIC ROUTES

Experience some of the most beautiful islands in French Polynesia. Let your jaw drop at the majesty of Mo'orea, live it up on glitzy Bora Bora, then relax in the Polynesian calm of Huahine.

A GLIMPSE OF PARADISE   Six Days / Mo'orea, Bora Bora & Huahine

After arriving in Pape'ete, go straight to ultra-gorgeous **Mo'orea** (p106), where you'll want to stay for at least two nights. Boasting soaring peaks, verdant foliage and aqua waters, Mo'orea is considered by many to be the most beautiful isle in the Society Islands. Cycle around magnificent **Cook's Bay** (p109) and **Opunohu Bay** (p110), explore the island's **archaeological sites** (p112) or simply soak up the sun and splash around in the lagoon. From Mo'orea, fly to **Bora Bora** (p150). Live it up for a night or more (depending on your budget) in an over-water bungalow or partake in a variety of water excursions on the picture-perfect lagoon. From Bora Bora, it's a short flight to much more low-key **Huahine** (p123), where you can end your holiday with two days of complete relaxation and a taste of authentic Polynesian culture. Go diving or snorkelling, take an island tour and don't miss trying *ma'a Tahiti* (traditional-style food) at **Restaurant Mauarii** (p133).

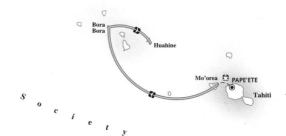

LAGOON SPECTACULAR   One Week to 10 Days / Tahiti to the Tuamotus

French Polynesia is more of a lagoon destination than a beach destination, and the best lagoons are found in the Tuamotus group. With a week to 10 days, water-lovers can get a taste of the Society Islands before taking off to the more remote atolls. Start with a day on **Tahiti** (p75), where you can take an island tour or hire a car to explore **Marché de Pape'ete** (p84) and the waterfalls, roadside caves and hidden beaches around the island. At night, catch a dance performance at one of the resorts or (if it's a Friday or Saturday) go out for a wild night in **Pape'ete** (p82). Next, spend at least two nights on **Mo'orea** (p106) and one on **Bora Bora** (p150) – see the previous itinerary for more details. From here it's time to explore the otherworldly atolls of the **Tuamotus** (p173). Head to **Rangiroa** (p176), the biggest and most developed of the archipelago, and spend at least two days exploring the atoll's immense, mostly untouched, lagoon, or diving and snorkelling in its sharky passes. Don't miss a chance to taste the only wine produced in the country at **Vin de Tahiti** (boxed text, p179) tasting room or take a tour of the bizarrely out-of-place vineyards. If you have time left after exploring Rangiroa, spend a few days checking out the white-sand beaches and outrageously fauna-rich pass of the prettiest atoll in the Tuamotus, **Tikehau** (p188). Alternatively you could visit the biosphere reserve of **Fakarava** (p185) with its two famous diving passes and pink-sand beaches.

Prepare to get wet. This itinerary gives you a taste of the high islands before leaving life as you know it for the otherworldly atolls. It's all about pink- and white-sand beaches and underwater action.

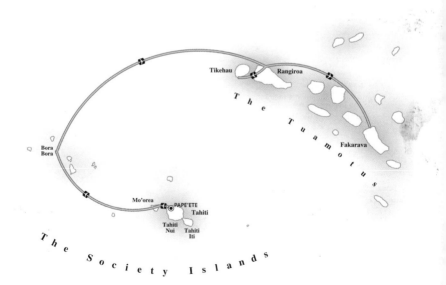

ROADS LESS TRAVELLED

ROOTS & RECLUSE

Two Weeks to Two Months / Tahiti, Gambier Archipelago & the Australs

Anywhere outside the Society Islands is well off the beaten track, and French Polynesia offers some really 'out there' options where you can live out your Robinson Crusoe dreams or simply get away from modern life and into the heart of Polynesian culture. Head first to the **Gambier Archipelago** (p238), which boasts one of the bluest lagoons you'll ever see, hills perfect for long, lonely walks, intensely colourful pearls and a unique history involving the over-zealous Catholic missionary Honoré Laval. Flights only leave once to twice a week (see p257), so be prepared to be stuck here awhile and make friends with the locals. Next go to the **Australs** (p228), your first stop being idyllic **Raivavae** (p234). Here you'll eat *ma'a Tahiti* nonstop and feel like you know half the people on the island after a day or two. Hike up Mt Hiro, bike around the island and boat out to one of the rustic, paradisaical *motu* cabins (p235) where you'll be left alone, with meals ferried out to you three times a day. Next make a quick stop on **Tubuai** (p232) to visit the remarkable archaeological sites before going to **Rurutu** (p229) to ramble through limestone caves, ride horses through the abundantly fertile interior and dive with whales and dolphins with the local dive club. Those with more time should visit **Rimatara** (p232), where you'll search for the rare Rimatara lorikeet and experience a culture that's had very little European contact. Alternatively, catch the cargo ship to **Rapa Iti** (p236) – but you'll be stuck on the island for a month at least!

So you really want to get away from it all? Visiting the Gambier and Austral Archipelagos gives you a glimpse into traditional Polynesian life and offers experiences of a lifetime. Go with an open mind and a big smile.

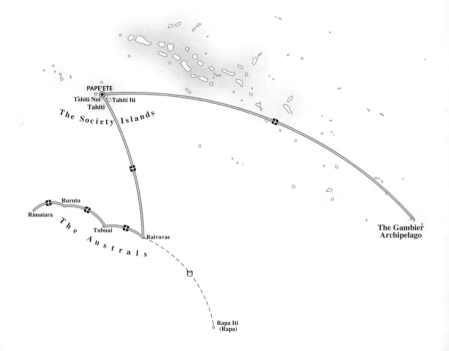

PAPE'ETE
Tahiti Nui   Tahiti Iti
Tahiti
The Society Islands

Rurutu
Rimatara
The Australs
Tubuai   Raivavae

The Gambier Archipelago

Rapa Iti
(Rapa)

TAILORED TRIPS

THE ULTIMATE HONEYMOON

While many people are happy to take a classic route for their honeymoon, such as our 'A Glimpse of Paradise' itinerary (p26), the ultimate honeymoon skips the main islands and brings you to our favourite spots for privacy and romance. Start at one of **Taha'a's** (p145) *motu* resorts, all which look out over the turquoise lagoon on one side and the awe-inspiring outline of Bora Bora on the other. Kayak, take an island tour to visit pearl farms and vanilla plantations, and lounge in your own private paradise. Next fly to **Maupiti** (p166), which is a more isolated and rustic version of Bora Bora. Digs are Polynesian-style bungalows on the beach – nothing fancy, but perfect for snuggling. From here you'll want to catch a flight to **Tikehau** (p188) to pamper yourselves at the secluded **Tikehau Pearl Beach Resort** (p190), or go more rustic and even more private on **Fakarava** (p185) at **Raimiti** (p188). Get the best tan you ever had, virtually live in the glass-clear lagoon, dive, snorkel, frolic, then dine on fabulous food and drink cocktails as the sun sets. Of course, you could pick just one of these islands and chill for a whole week.

TOO HOT FOR THE BEACH

Lounging around on a beach not your *maitai*? French Polynesia has plenty to offer the energetic crowd. Start off in **Tahiti** (p75) where your choices include canyoning through the **Hitiaa Lava Tubes** (p99) or hiking the wild coast of **Te Pari** (p104). Check out the **Billabong Pro Surf Competition** (p104) at Teahupoo in May, where you can watch the world's best surfers attack massive waves as you sit in a boat hovering in front of the tube. Try surfing for the first time on softer waves at **Papenoo** (p100) or if you're a seasoned surfer explore the breaks around the island. Next go to **Mo'orea** (p106) for **kite-surfing** (p113) lessons in the swimming-pool-blue lagoon and visit **Stingray World** (p115) to feed the stingrays by hand as you're circled by black-tip reef sharks. Take another day on the island to sign up for a **whale-watching tour** (p113) where, if you're lucky, you might get to swim with whales or dolphins. Fly then to **Rangiroa** (p69), one of the best-known dive areas in the world, home to lots of toothy sharks and powerfully strong currents. After all this, you'll *need* to lie on a beach!

ANCIENT POLYNESIAN MYSTERIES

One of French Polynesia's unsung attributes is its array of ancient sites that are intensely mysterious and vastly under visited. Your trip will start in **Tahiti** (p75), where you'll get into a 4WD and head to **Relais de la Maroto** (p102) at the island's centre. Visit the *marae* (traditional temples) in the cool mountains

and hike to waterfalls and jungle vistas. Next get on a plane to **Huahine** (p123) for one or two nights to visit the lovely **Maeva** (p126) archaeological area and enjoy the island's white-sand beaches. Then fly to **Ra'iatea** (p136) to see the impressive **Taputapuatea** (p138), one of the most important spiritual sites of ancient Polynesia. You'll change cultures entirely when you next go to the **Marquesas** (p199). Travelling here is like stepping back in time. Follow Gauguin's trail to **Hiva Oa** (p217) and don't miss the **Iipona** (p222) archaeological site and several others on the island. Next go to **Nuku Hiva** (p201), where you can hike across windswept ridges into ancient volcanic craters before checking out the island's array of archaeological sites, including **Hikokua** (p208) and **Kamuihei and Tahakia** (p208).

Alternatively, you could visit all of the Marquesas Islands by taking the **Aranui** (p203) cargo/cruise ship for one of the world's most unique cruises focusing on culture and archaeology.

IT'S NOT EASY BEING GREEN

The word 'eco' is only just becoming a part of French Polynesia's tourism vocabulary. The best thing you can do if you want to make less of an impact is to stay at locally run family *pensions* (guesthouses), which create little waste, sometimes run on solar power (particularly in the Tuamotus) and

are exceedingly better for the local economy than multinational-owned resorts. Don't assume that these places will be uncomfortable: many are stacked with amenities and are run like boutique bed and breakfasts. Start your trip at **La Maison de la Nature du Mou'a Roa** (p118) in Mo'orea, where you can learn about local flora, eat organic meals and enjoy fabulous hiking to lush vistas with views of knife-edged peaks. Next head to the Tuamotus where, if your budget is big enough, you can stay at **Kia Ora Sauvage** (p183) on Rangiroa or **Raimiti** (p188) on Fakarava – both small resorts were built with local materials and use minimal solar electricity. Those on a tighter budget should try **Relais Royal Tikehau** (p190) on Tikehau, which is run entirely on wind and solar power with

rubbish packed responsibly to Tahiti, or **Cocoperle Lodge** (p194) on Ahe, which runs on solar power and is part of the Reefwatch Foundation.

History

The idyllic, isolated islands of Polynesia were among the last places on earth to be settled by humans and, a thousand or so years later, were also some of the last places to be colonised by Europeans. Without written language, little is known of the islands' history before the first Europeans arrived.

GETTING THERE IS HALF THE FUN

The Great Polynesian Migration is one of the world's most outlandish yet mysterious historical events. No one knows why, but early Polynesians (hailing, it is now believed, from either Taiwan or Southeast Asia) some three to four thousand years ago tossed chickens, dogs, pigs, vegies and the kids into canoes and sailed into the wild blue yonder. And they found islands, lots of them. Remember, this was well over a thousand years before the Vikings, the greatest navigators of the West, had even made it to Iceland. Using celestial navigation as well as now-forgotten methods of reading cloud reflections, wave formations and bird flight patterns, Polynesians could find islands in the vast Pacific far better than you or I could find a last-minute seat on Air Tahiti Nui during Christmas holidays.

Nothing remains of the boats used to make these voyages, so we have to make do with descriptions given by 18th-century Europeans. Forerunners of the catamaran, the canoes had two parallel hulls fused together by cross beams or platforms; they could be driven by sail, paddle or both. They could

The locals' favourite text on pre-European French Polynesian culture is *Ancient Tahiti* by Teuira Henry. The text was translated into English, but the French version is much easier to find.

TOP 10 HISTORICAL PLACES TO VISIT

- Marae Taputapuatea, Ra'iatea (p138)
- Opunohu Valley *marae*, Mo'orea (p112)
- Maeva archaeological site, Huahine (p126)
- Paul Gauguin's tomb, Hiva Oa (p219)
- Iipona, Hiva Oa (p222)
- Hikokua, Kamuihei and Tahakia, Nuku Hiva (p208)
- Cathédrale Saint-Michel, Mangareva (p240)
- Paumotu *marae* of Takapoto (p194)
- *Marae* around the Relais de la Maroto, Tahiti (p101)
- James Norman Hall's House, Tahiti (p86)

TIMELINE

1500 BC	200 BC–AD 400	1520
Polynesia's westernmost islands of Samoa and Tonga are populated, probably via Melanesia. This Great Polynesian Migration is believed to have originally begun in Taiwan or Southeast Asia.	Eastern islands, including French Polynesia, Hawaii and Easter Island, are populated. It is also theorised that during this time there was trade between these islands and South America.	Ferdinand Magellan (Spanish), the first European to sail across the Pacific Ocean, sights Puka Puka in the northeast Tuamotus but manages to miss the rest of French Polynesia.

MYSTERIOUS SWEET POTATOES & PRE-COLUMBIAN CHICKENS

Current genetic and linguistic evidence has proved Thor Heyerdahl's Kon Tiki theory that the first Polynesians came from South America, to be incorrect. That doesn't mean that South America is completely out of the picture, however. All of the plant species introduced by the first Polynesians were of Southeast Asian origin save one, the sweet potato, which hails from Peru and Columbia. Studies show that this wily tuber arrived first to the Marquesas Islands sometime around AD 300. The Peruvian word for sweet potato is *kumar*. The Polynesian word is *umara* or *kumara*. You do the math.

Then there's the chicken. Chickens are originally from Asia and until recently it was believed that Europeans were the first to introduce poultry to South America. But in late 2006 chicken bones found in south-central Chile were carbon dated to be from over 100 years before the first European explorers arrived on the continent. DNA testing has proved that these pre-Columbian chickens are nearly identical to those found on Easter Island.

---

carry up to 70 people, and the plants, seeds and animals needed to colonise the new land were carried on the connecting platform.

The first settlers in French Polynesia landed in the Marquesas, having journeyed via Samoa, sometime around 200 BC. From here they went on to discover the Society Islands around AD 300. It would be over a thousand years before anyone else in the world would have the sailing technology to find these small specks of paradise.

Polynesian Interconnections: Samoa to Tahiti to Hawaii by Peter Leiataua AhChing has a young-adult reading level but accurately discusses the inter-relatedness of Polynesian peoples.

PARADISE: BEHIND THE SCENES

The Polynesian islands, and thus French Polynesia, were blessed with a situation unique in history: habitable, fertile islands where the pioneers could create their own society and religion in a place nearly devoid of danger. What this society was like before European contact is up to speculation but for most of their island history Polynesians would have lacked very little. Music, dance and the arts were revered and a big part of island life. It's easy to overly idealise what it must have been like, but no matter how cynically you look at it, Tahiti must have had one of the most paradisaical ways of life on earth.

Check out www.tahiti1 .com, a good, practical site with information about Tahitian ancient history, art and legends, as well as maritime history, tattooing and more.

But it wasn't free from problems. Overpopulation eventually caused shortages of farming areas, particularly for taro, and wars frequently broke out between clans. The outcome of these wars was cruel: the defeated were often massacred and their *marae* (traditional temples) destroyed. The victors would then take possession of the defeated clan's lands.

Society also wasn't as sweet and naive as European explorers perceived it. Underneath the smiles was an extremely hierarchical, structured and aristocratic system that was nearly feudal in nature and heavily ritualised. High chiefs known as *ari'i* ran the show and their positions were inherited,

1567	1615–16	1767
Alvaro de Mandaña (also Spanish) comes across the most northeast of the Polynesian islands and names them Las Marquesas de Mendoza after the viceroy of Peru. His visit is bloody and without cultural connection.	Dutch captain Jacob Le Maire sails through the Tuamotus. It isn't until 1722 that the Society Islands are sighted by another Dutchman, Jacob Roggeveen, who 'discovers' Maupiti but amazingly misses the rest of the archipelago.	Samuel Wallis arrives in Matavai Bay, Tahiti, on the *Dolphin*, kills many Tahitians and names the island 'King George's Land'. He sets up the first trade with the islanders and claims the island for England.

usually from their fathers; *tahua* were the priests (see p45 for more about ancient Tahitian religion); middle-class landowners were called *raatira*; the *arioi* were a group of itinerant artist-troubadours whose role it was to entertain everyone and who were considered to be descended from the god of war, 'Oro; and last were the lower classes, called *manahune*, which consisted of the bulk of the population including fishermen, farmers and servants. Human sacrifices were occasionally needed in religious rituals and these would invariably come from the *manahune*. Infanticide was also practised in circumstances where a girl of lower stature got pregnant by an *ari'i*. The *arioi* were not allowed to have children at all so would practise infanticide if primitive birth-control or abortion methods didn't work.

Despite this dark side, the unanimous reports from the first European explorers told of an exceptionally happy population who were uninhibited in showing their emotions; they were as quick to cry as they were to laugh.

The Word, the Pen and the Pistol by Robert Nicole examines mythical values attributed to Polynesians and recent history with the French.

THE NEW CYTHERA & ITS DROLL, WANTON TRICKS

Imagine months at sea in cramped, squalid quarters, with many of the crew suffering from scurvy, and happening upon a mountainous isle exploding with fruit, water and women. It was in these circumstances that, around 1500 years after the islands were settled, the first European explorers ventured into the region. Most of what we know about early Polynesia and the myths that evolved of nymphlike women comes from this very limited male perspective.

First came Captain Samuel Wallis on his ship the *Dolphin,* which he anchored at Matavai Bay in Tahiti's lagoon in late June 1767. A quarter of the

The most famous voyage of the Hokule'a (a modern replica of a traditional Polynesian canoe), from Hawaii to Tahiti in 1976, was completed using entirely traditional Polynesian navigation techniques.

WHAT'S A MARAE?

Scattered throughout the islands, mostly forgotten and few restored, the most visible remains of ancient Tahitian culture are in its *marae,* open-air places of worship. Today Polynesians have fully embraced Christianity and many of these temples have been destroyed in the name of agriculture, dismantled to construct churches, used as house foundations or simply left to become engulfed by vines and weeds. Accounts from early European explorers are the only insight we have into what these once vibrant and sacred sites must have been like.

Births, deaths and family events were celebrated at simple family *marae*; larger *marae* were temples of chiefs where village meetings, sacrifices and wider religious ceremonies were practised. The largest and most important temples were the royal *marae,* such as Ra'iatea's Taputapuatea, which had influence over the whole of Polynesia, attracting chiefs from afar who would pledge allegiance to the kings.

Visitors today will find the most comprehensive and well-restored *marae* in Opunohu Valley (p112) on Mo'orea; at Taputapuatea (p138) on Ra'iatea, the most important remaining *marae* in French Polynesia and the most impressive to visit; and on the principal islands of the Marquesas. Of course the mystery and feeling of discovery you'll experience finding an old *marae* tangled in the bush can make these lost gems equally interesting.

1768	1769	1772
Louis-Antoine de Bougainville visits Tahiti, ogles the women and begins the myth of 'New Cythera'; he also coins the expression 'Noble Savage'. Not knowing that Wallis had already been there, Bougainville claims Tahiti for France.	Captain James Cook makes his first voyages to Tahiti to observe and record the transit of Venus, but his equipment proves unworthy for the job.	Don Domingo de Boenechea dispatches missionaries at Tautira – the missionaries, fearing the Tahitians, lock themselves inside and scarcely come out again till their boat arrives in 1775 to return them to Peru.

crew was down with scurvy and Wallis himself was incapacitated during most of his visit. Initially the arrival was greeted with fascination as hundreds of canoes surrounded the ship, including canoes carrying young women 'who played a great many droll wanton tricks'. But the locals' fascination turned to fear and they attacked the *Dolphin*. Wallis retaliated by firing grapeshot at the Tahitians and then sending a party ashore to destroy homes and canoes. Following this a trade relationship somehow developed: the crew was desperate for fresh supplies and the Tahitians, who had not yet discovered metals, were delighted to receive knives, hatchets and nails in exchange.

When the *Dolphin* returned to Europe, Wallis wrote his official report describing Tahiti. This earnest, dull report, which focused on the geographical beauty of the region, was soon overshadowed by gleeful rumours of uninhibited and beautiful women greeting the sailors with 'lascivious gestures'.

With his ships *La Boudeuse* and *L'Etoile*, Louis-Antoine de Bougainville arrived on Tahiti in April 1768, less than a year after Wallis. At this time Wallis was still homeward bound, so Bougainville was completely unaware that he was not the first European to set eyes on the island. His visit only lasted nine days, but unlike Wallis, Bougainville had no unfriendly clashes with the Tahitians.

Bougainville explained that the Tahitians 'pressed us to choose a woman and come on shore with her; and their gestures, which were not ambiguous, denoted in what manner we should form an acquaintance with her'. Bougainville's reports of Venus-like women with 'the celestial form of that goddess', and of the people's uninhibited attitude towards sexual matters, swept through Paris like wildfire.

Bougainville more than compensated for Wallis' bland report with his tales of a new Cythera and his companion Dr Commerçon's gushing avowals that the Tahitians knew 'no other god than love'. Captain James Cook, who arrived a year after Bougainville, was less florid, but his reports confirmed the view that Tahitian women would 'dance a very indecent dance' while 'singing most indecent songs'.

In reality, Polynesian women were probably not hanging around waiting to seduce a shipload of uncouth and strange white men. Sex was a natural part of everyday life, so it wouldn't have been surprising that Polynesian women wanted to check whether these funny-looking guys had all the right bits and pieces. Serge Tcherkézoff in his book *Tahiti 1768: Jeunes Filles en Pleur* (Young Girls in Tears) theorises that the girls sent to the ships were not seducing sailors for their own curiosity, but had been given orders by Tahitian priests to become pregnant by the strangers in order to capture their essence. Alexander H Bolyanatz in his book *Pacific Romanticism: Tahiti and the European Imagination* takes another angle and says that the women's overtly sexual behaviour was defensive since the Tahitians had learned early on to fear European weaponry; by seducing the sailors the islanders would have more power over their often violent visitors.

For a good read, pick up *Piracy in the Pacific* by Henri Jacquier, a riveting, true story about the Rorique brothers, French pirates in Polynesia.

Pacific Romanticism: Tahiti and the European Imagination by Alexander H Bolyanatz explores misconceptions of Tahitian sexuality from first contact to today.

1772–75	1776–80	1789
On Cook's second expedition to Tahiti he picks up Omai, a Huahine islander and brings him to London. Omai, the first Polynesian to visit Europe, becomes a popular socialite.	On his last visit to Tahiti, Cook brings Omai back to Huahine, leaves many gifts that ultimately estrange Omai from his people, then later 'discovers' the Hawaiian Islands where he is killed and possibly eaten.	Fletcher Christian sets Captain Bligh adrift in a small boat then returns to Tahiti on the *Bounty*. The mutineers separate in two groups: some remain on Tahiti while the rest sail away to Pitcairn Island.

Whatever the case, this uninhibited approach to sex was soon exploited by sex-starved sailors, whalers and traders, who began buying sex with nails (coveted by the locals for making fish hooks), clothes and alcohol, creating a demand for prostitution, spreading European diseases and palpably contributing to the rapid decline of the Polynesian culture. The missionaries, whose impact would be just as strong, stamped out all the perceived lasciviousness that they could, and today Tahiti isn't really any more sexually liberal than most Western countries.

David Howarth's *Tahiti: A Paradise Lost* is a readable but idealistic account of Tahitian history from pre-European times to the French takeover.

DON'T MESS WITH CAPTAIN COOK

History depicts Captain James Cook as one of the greatest explorers of all time. Indeed, Cook's navigational and surveying skills, his ability to control unruly crews and keep them healthy and, above all, his cultural understanding, did set him apart. He is described as having been a dispassionate and tolerant man; it's often claimed he did not want to harm or offend the islanders, and that he made concerted efforts to befriend them.

In three great expeditions between 1769 and 1779, Cook filled out the map of the Pacific so comprehensively that future expeditions were reduced to joining the dots. Cook had been sent to the Pacific with two ambitious tasks. One, which was for the Royal Society, was to observe the transit of Venus as it passed across the face of the sun. By timing the transit from three very distant places it was hoped that the distance from the earth to the sun could be calculated. Tahiti was selected as one of the three measuring points (the other two were in Norway and Canada). Cook's second objective was to hunt for the mythical great continent of the south.

The instruments of the time proved to be insufficiently accurate to achieve Cook's first objective, but Cook's expeditions did yield impressive scientific work. As a result Cook's voyages communicated the wonders not only of Tahiti but also of New Zealand and Australia to an appreciative European audience.

The two most well-known archaeologists to conduct surveys in French Polynesia are Kenneth P Emory and Yosihiko Sinoto, both from the Bishop Museum in Honolulu.

But Cook's composure was far from impenetrable. All European explorers observed that the Polynesians were somewhat light-fingered. Having no concept of property or wealth – or the inextricable link European society had constructed between the two – the islanders would help themselves to the white men's odd and plentiful possessions. In the beginning at least, this was probably more a game than any real coveting of European possessions.

According to diary entries, by Cook's third and final voyage in the late 1770s some of the crew were feeling uncomfortable with Cook's treatment of those locals caught stealing. There are stories of an irate Cook wreaking havoc, burning houses and smashing canoes in anger at having had something stolen. David Howarth, a respected historian and author of *Tahiti: A Paradise Lost,* recounts the time when a Polynesian took a sextant. When the culprit confessed and the instrument was returned, Cook had the man's ears cut off.

1790	1797	1819
The British navy arrives in Tahiti to pick up the mutineers who stayed on the island – the mutineers who ended up on Pitcairn don't get caught.	The London Missionary Society arrives with 25 missionaries at Point Vénus in Tahiti – the Tahitians are welcoming but hard to convert so only a few of the missionaries stay.	The Code of Pomare is established, forming a Christian alliance between the Leeward Islands; governing is based entirely on the scriptures establishing an unofficial missionary rule.

THE MUTINY ON THE BOUNTY

There had been some colourful chapters in the history of European exploration in the Pacific, but none captured the imagination like the mutiny on the *Bounty*. It all started when Captain Bligh, an expert navigator who had learnt his trade under James Cook and had already visited Tahiti, was sent off to convey breadfruit from Tahiti to the Caribbean after someone had the bright idea that breadfruit would be a good food source for slaves in the Caribbean.

Bligh's expedition started late in 1787. After an arduous 10-month voyage, he arrived at a time when breadfruit-tree saplings could not be transplanted. The crew remained on Tahiti for six long, languorous months. Eventually, with the breadfruit trees loaded on board, the *Bounty* set sail, westbound, for the Caribbean. Three weeks later, on 28 April 1789, when passing by Tonga, the crew, led by first mate Fletcher Christian, mutinied and took over the ship.

Bligh was pushed onto the *Bounty's* launch with 18 faithful crew members and set adrift. Proving his unmatched skill as a champion navigator, Bligh sailed his overloaded little boat across the Pacific and amazingly made landfall in Timor after a 41-day, 5823km voyage that was promptly written into the record books. By early 1790 Bligh was back in England; an inquiry quickly cleared him of negligence and a ship was dispatched to carry British naval vengeance to Tahiti.

Meanwhile, Christian and his mutineers returned to Tahiti before sailing off to find a more remote hideaway. Ultimately 16 mutineers decided to stay on Tahiti while a smaller group left with Christian and the *Bounty* to inhabit Pitcairn Island. Today, thanks to Fletcher Christian's mutiny, the odd Tahitian-British colony still on Pitcairn Island is one of the last vestiges of the British Empire.

Vengeance arrived for the mutineers on Tahiti in 1791 in the shape of Captain Edward Edwards, who made Bligh look like a thoroughly nice guy. He quickly rounded up the mutineers and informed the men's new Tahitian wives that the men were going back to Britain to get their just deserts.

Bligh himself was back on Tahiti in 1792, this time in command of HMS *Providence* and with 19 marines to ensure there was no repeat performance. Bligh duly picked up his breadfruit saplings and transported them in record time to the Caribbean. As it turned out, the slaves never developed a taste for the fruit.

GUNS, DISEASE, WHISKY & GOD

Once the Europeans came on the scene, traditional Polynesian society took a beating. It was a three-pronged affair: a jab to the ribs with high-tech European weaponry, a blow to the head by an influx of diseases and hard liquor and, finally, a kick in the groin by some Old World Christianity.

First enter the guns. At the time of first contact, islands consisted of chiefdoms that warred with each other over resources. This was quick to change once the Tahitians realised the power of European weaponry. Most explorers resisted when clans pressed them to take sides in local conflicts, but the *Bounty* mutineers, along with whalers and traders, were happy to offer themselves as mercenaries to the highest bidder. The highest bidders were the Pomares, one of a number of important families, but by no means the most important at that time.

1842	1842	1864
Herman Melville deserts his whaling ship on Nuku Hiva and spends three weeks in remote Taipivai Valley – his book about the escapade, *Taipi*, is published in 1846.	The French take power and disperse Catholic missionaries. Queen Pomare IV pleads for British intervention to no avail. She flees to Ra'iatea then returns to Tahiti in 1847 as a mere figurehead.	The first 329 Chinese immigrants arrive to work at American-run cotton fields on Tahiti. Workers continue to arrive from China through the 20th century and eventually the group becomes the country's most successful merchants.

The mutineers and their weapons helped create the political environment where one group could feasibly control all of Tahiti. Pomare I, the nephew of Obarea, the 'fat, bouncing, good looking dame' who Wallis had assumed was the island's chief back in 1767, already controlled most of Tahiti when he died in 1803. His son, Pomare II, took over from there and today the Pomares still consider themselves the royal family of French Polynesia.

But guns weren't the only problem. Whalers and traders began frequenting Tahiti from England and the USA in the 1790s, escaping their harsh shipboard life, buying supplies, introducing alcohol and spreading diseases. These men were rough, hard-drinking and looking for sex (see p33). Traders also started to appear from the convict colonies in Australia; they exchanged weapons for food supplies, encouraged prostitution and established stills to produce alcohol.

Listless and plagued by diseases against which it had no natural immunity, the Polynesian population plummeted. The population of Tahiti in the late 1760s was estimated around 40,000; in 1800 another estimate put the population at less than 20,000; by the 1820s it was down to around 6000. In the Marquesas the situation was even worse: it has been estimated the population dropped from 80,000 to 2000 in one century.

French Polynesia's conversion to Christianity really started in March 1797, when 25 members of the London Missionary Society (LMS) landed at Point Vénus. While the new religion wasn't quick to catch on, the missionaries were able to closely associate themselves with King Pomare II and Christianity was established as the dominant religion in 1815. The king died soon after in 1821, probably after drinking himself to death. In 1827 his successor Pomare III also died and was succeeded by the young Queen Pomare IV who continued to be strongly 'advised' by the missionaries throughout her 50-year reign.

The missionaries were an unyielding bunch, and although they had the best intentions, they made no attempt to combine the best elements of traditional Polynesian beliefs with Christianity, but rather smothered many important, ancient customs with a rigid interpretation of Protestantism. A century later,

Tahitians: Mind and Experience in the Society Islands by Robert I Levy and Pierre Heyman is a well-respected, holistic anthropological work published in 1973.

In 1918 an influenza epidemic wiped out approximately 20% of Tahiti's population. There were so many dead the bodies were burned in great pyres.

BOENECHEA & THE FIRST MISSIONARIES

In 1772 Don Domingo de Boenechea, a Spaniard, sailed the *Aguilla* from Peru and anchored in the lagoon off Tautira on Tahiti Iti. Boenechea installed two missionaries and established Tautira as the first long-term European settlement on the island.

In 1775 the *Aguilla* again returned from Peru. The two Spanish missionaries, who had been spectacularly unsuccessful at converting 'the heathen', and who from all reports were terrified of the islanders, were more than happy to scuttle back to Peru. Boenechea died on Tahiti during this visit, and thus ended the Spanish role on Tahiti. He is buried by the Catholic church that today bears his name in Tautira on Tahiti Iti.

1877	1891	1911
Queen Pomare IV is succeeded by King Pomare V, who has little interest in the job and effectively abdicates power to the French four years later; then he drinks himself to death.	Post-Impressionist painter Paul Gauguin sails from France to Tahiti. He moves to the Marquesas in 1897 and dies there in 1903 of syphilis at age 54.	Phosphate mining begins on Makatea in the Tuamotu Archipelago and becomes a major component of the economy, which before was based on agriculture and fishing; mining continues till the supplies are exhausted in 1966.

the English writer Robert Keable, who had been a vicar with the Church of England, commented about pioneering missionary William Ellis that 'it was a thousand pities that the Tahitians did not convert Mr Ellis'.

Although the missionaries get a bad rap for destroying so much of the beauty of the Polynesian culture, in certain ways they very much helped the Polynesians by creating a spiritual framework in which to deal with all the new challenges (such as alcohol and prostitution) that were being introduced by less savoury Europeans. Today, Christianity is the country's best advocate and tool in the fight against alcoholism, domestic violence and incest, as well as providing exceptionally strong support for community.

A fire tragically destroyed half of the town of Pape'ete in 1884. After the disaster it became illegal to use local building materials within city limits.

ENTER THE FRENCH & THE NUCLEAR ERA

The French takeover of what is now French Polynesia was essentially a war of the missionaries. British clergy were an unofficial colonial power via the Pomare clan in the Society Islands, the Australs and the Tuamotus, but the French Catholic missionaries were in firm control in the Gambier Archipelago from 1834 and the Marquesas from 1838. In 1836 two French missionaries from the Gambier Archipelago were quietly dropped off near Tautira at the eastern extremity of Tahiti Iti; they were promptly arrested and deported by the British.

The deportation of the two French missionaries was considered a national insult to the French. Demands, claims, counterclaims, payments and apologies shuttled back and forth until 1842, when Rear Admiral Dupetit-Thouars arrived in *La Reine Blanche,* pointed his guns at Pape'ete and took power. Queen Pomare IV was forced to yield to the French, and soldiers and Catholic missionaries were promptly landed.

TV wasn't in French Polynesian homes until the early 1980s, when RFO (Radio France Overseas) began the first local broadcasts.

The queen, still hoping for British intervention, fled to Ra'iatea in 1844 and a guerrilla rebellion against the French broke out on Tahiti and other islands. The presence of French forts around Tahiti confirms that it was a fierce struggle, but eventually the rebels were subdued, and by 1846 France had control over Tahiti and Mo'orea. In 1847 Queen Pomare was persuaded to return to Tahiti, but she was now merely a figurehead.

Queen Pomare died in 1877 and was succeeded by her son, Pomare V. He had little interest in the position and effectively abdicated power in 1881; in true Pomare fashion he drank himself to death in 1891.

French Polynesia continued to be a valuable strategic port for the French, especially when the islands' economies of vanilla, cotton, copra and mother of pearl were flourishing during WWI, and during WWII, when American forces used Bora Bora as a military base. But postwar, as the territory's exports declined, a more practical usage of it was devised. In 1963 Moruroa and Fangataufa, atolls in the Tuamotus, were announced the 'lucky winners' to become France's nuclear test sites. Atmospheric nuclear explosions began in 1966. The Centre d'Expérimentation du Pacifique (CEP; Pacific

1942	1957–58	1961
Five thousand American soldiers descend on Bora Bora to build the territory's first airstrip. The American military use the island as their supply base through WWII.	The territory is officially named French Polynesia and votes to remain part of the French Republic amid riots in Pape'ete. Pouvana'a a Oopa, leader of Polynesia's popular separatist movement, is exiled to France.	Faa'a International Airport is constructed on landfill covering a coral reef. French Polynesia is opened up to the world and the tourism industry takes off.

THE RAINBOW WARRIOR

In 1985 French secret-service agents bombed and sank the Greenpeace ship *Rainbow Warrior* (which was preparing for a protest voyage to Moruroa) in Auckland Harbour, New Zealand, killing an onboard photographer. Captain Dominique Prieur and Major Alain Mafart, the only two of the French team that the New Zealand police were able to capture, were tried, found guilty (on reduced charges of manslaughter) and sentenced to 10 years' imprisonment. The French government then pressured New Zealand to allow Prieur and Mafart to be transferred to serve reduced sentences on Hao in the Tuamotus. France soon reneged on the agreement, the Club Med–style prison sentence was ended, and the two agents were returned to France to a hero's welcome (at least by the government – many French nationals were very opposed to France's involvement in the fiasco).

Experimentation Centre) soon became a major component of the French Polynesian economy.

Over the next 30 years, 193 tests were performed on the two atolls and more than 130,000 people worked for the CEP. In 1981, 17 years after the USA, Britain and the USSR agreed to halt atmospheric testing, the French drilled bomb shafts under the central lagoons of the atolls and finally moved the tests underground. In 1995, five years after former French president François Mitterrand had placed a one-year moratorium on the testing, the new French president Jacques Chirac announced a new series of underground tests, and a storm of protest erupted worldwide. Rioting broke out in Pape'ete but fell on deaf ears in France. The final round of tests were concluded in early 1996, and it was announced there would be no further testing in the Pacific.

For many years the French government denied that the tests posed any ecological threat to the region. Finally, in 1999 a French study reported that there had been radioactive leakage into underground water, and later that same year the existence of cracks in the coral cones of Moruroa and Fangataufa were also acknowledged. These cracks could cause leakage into the ocean, so, while the issue may be off the international stage, it is an ongoing debacle for those living in the region. A 2006 study conducted by the French Polynesian Territorial Assembly concluded that Tureia in the eastern Tuamotus and the Gambier Archipelago would have been exposed to nuclear fallout during atmospheric testing; but because there were never any dosimeter measurements taken on these islands, what the levels of radiation would have been has not been proved.

As of 2008 little more had been disclosed about the ongoing environmental impacts of the testing, but hundreds of French and Polynesians who worked at the test sites are now suffering from serious health problems. The French Defence Department continues to state that the radiation exposure would have been weak even in the worst-case scenarios and is not the

Income tax was only introduced to French Polynesia in 1994, although it is still very low compared to France or even the US.

Read the account of David McTaggart, Greenpeace International's first chairman, of sailing into the Moruroa nuclear test zone in 1972 at www.greenpeace.org/international/about/history/moruroa-journey-into-the-bomb.

1963	1963–64	1984
French Centre d'Expérimentation du Pacifique for nuclear testing opened on Moruroa and Fangataufa. The first atmospheric tests begin in 1966; in 1981, underground shafts are dug and the tests are moved underground.	Jean Domard, associated with an Australian company, seeds the first pearl oysters on Hikueru Atoll. The first farm opens on Manihi in 1968, but it isn't until the 1980s that the pearl-farming industry booms.	French Polynesia gains internal autonomy from France, which is later expanded in 1990 and again in 1996. In 2004 it gains the unique French status of 'Overseas Collectivity'.

root of these people's health troubles. Two associations, the Association of Nuclear Test Veterans (AVEN), which is made up of former French military personnel, and Moruroa e Tatou, which has over 4000 French Polynesian members, have been lobbying the French government for compensation for over a decade. In November 2008 the French defence minister announced a bill setting the standards for nuclear test workers' compensation that would be set to pass in early 2009. While members of the test veteran associations claim that the bill's purpose is to confuse public opinion and will not ease their quest in getting health compensation, they concede that any step towards recognition can be considered positive.

Travellers to this region can rest assured that radiation threat (which was only ever present in remote areas of the Tuamotu and Gambier Archipelagos) has long since passed.

FLOSSE, TEMARU, TONG SONG & POLITICAL CHAOS

Ever since Gaston Flosse lost the 2004 presidential elections, French Polynesia has been in political upheaval. Flosse was the elected president of the country for over twenty years and had become so powerful that he had gained an authority usually reserved only for dictators. Change was needed. In 2004 Flosse lost to long-time rival and Independentist Party leader Oscar Temaru. In the following four years the president and consequently the government of French Polynesia changed seven times, mostly flip-flopping back and forth between Flosse and Temaru.

The problem is in the system. The people of French Polynesia vote for a party, not a person, and how many votes that party gets decides how many seats they will get in the assembly. The head of the party with the majority becomes president. But assembly members can change parties midterm and often get bought out or just get mad at other members of their party then change sides. This flips the balance of power and the constant change makes it impossible for anyone to get on with actual governing. While it's a big hassle for the country's residents, it's nonviolent and shouldn't affect visitors in any way.

In February 2008 this political capriciousness was hoped to have ended with the election of a new guy in a new party, Gaston Tong Song. Unfortunately, at the time of writing Tong Song held a fragile majority and Flosse and Temaru had teamed up to consolidate power and were courting Tong Song's party members *en force*.

Although independence from France is a possibility in the future, it is unlikely to happen any time soon. For now, French Polynesia is the only French colony to enjoy the relatively autonomous status of 'Overseas Country', rather than the more common 'Overseas Territory'.

Since independentist Oscar Temaru was first elected president of French Polynesia in 2004 there have been serious motions to change the name of French Polynesia to Tahiti Nui.

For well-presented online daily news about French Polynesia in French and English, surf to www .tahitipresse.pf.

1995–96	2004	2008
Rioting against nuclear testing breaks out in Pape'ete and at Faa'a International Airport. The testing continues despite worldwide criticism until the series is complete in 1996.	Oscar Temaru's pro-independence party is elected to power, temporarily ending Gaston Flosse's 20-year reign. For the next four years the government changes seven times, mostly between Flosse and Temaru.	Gaston Tong Song is elected president after winning once in 2007 and being ousted by the unlikely union of Flosse and Temaru. His majority power remains unstable particularly when Flosse wins a French senatorial seat.

The Culture

THE NATIONAL PSYCHE

If French Polynesia had a national slogan it might be *haere maru* (take it slow), words that often fall from the lips of Tahitians to their busy French and Chinese cohabitants. It's hard not to take it slow on the islands. With one road encircling the main island of Tahiti, it's easy to get caught driving behind an old pick-up truck at 50km/h with no chance of passing; national holidays seem to close up the shops and banks once every week or so; and getting served in a restaurant can take an eternity. This can be frustrating to anyone in a hurry, but somehow it all works out: you make it to wherever you were going even if it does take twice as long, the bank can wait till tomorrow and your food arrives once you are really, really hungry. The Tahitian people know this and always seem slightly amused by anyone who tries to break the rhythm of calm.

Regardless of 'Tahiti time', Pape'ete manages to move at a pace fitting for a capital: there are traffic jams, everyone is on a mobile phone and the nightlife shakes on till 5am. The modern world is quickly infiltrating the slow pace of life and this is most evident in the younger generations.

LIFESTYLE
Family

The traditional Tahitian family is an open-armed force that is the country's backbone. Although modern girls are increasingly less likely to stay home and have baby after baby, an accidental pregnancy is considered more of a blessing than a hindrance, and babies are passed along to another eager, infant-loving family member. *Faamu* (adopted children) are not thought of as different from blood brothers and sisters by either the parents or siblings, although the birth mother, and occasionally the father, sometimes remain a peripheral part of the child's life. Once a child is in a family they are in no way obligated to stay; children move about to aunties, uncles and grandparents as they wish.

This family web is vitally important to an individual. When people first meet, the conversation usually starts with questions about family and most people are able to find a common relative between themselves within minutes. This accomplished, they are 'cousins' and fast friends.

But it's not all roses in what appears to be such a warm, fuzzy family framework. Domestic violence and incest are prevalent. This is closely connected with high rates of alcoholism. The government has launched numerous programs addressing these issues but little progress has been made.

Despite these domestic problems, women do hold a strong position in French Polynesian society. It was a woman whom Samuel Wallis met in his first encounter with what he believed to be a Tahitian chief. Today Nicole Bouteau, one of Tahiti's newest political stars, has started her own centrist political party that is rapidly gaining popularity. Many village mayors and high-powered politicians and business people in Tahiti are women. In the household, women are most often the homemaker but they don't wear this role lightly. They permeate a strength and dignity that set them in charge of everything domestic and sometimes more. Men (particularly those who don't drink) often share in the chores of cooking, cleaning and baby rearing; it's not uncommon to see massive, muscular, tattooed men nuzzling with an infant or holding hands with a toddler to cross the road.

Although religion has been teaching people to think otherwise, in French Polynesia homosexuality is generally viewed as a natural part of human

Go to www.tahiti.tv to watch video clips about all aspects of French Polynesia.

GENDER BENDER

You'll find that some women serving food in restaurants or working in hotels or boutiques, aren't actually women at all. *Mahu,* males who are raised as girls and continue to live their lives as women, were present when Europeans first arrived in the islands. Although the missionaries did their darndest to halt this 'unnatural crime', *mahu* are still an accepted part of the community today. In today's lingo, another category of *mahu,* called *raerae,* refers to more flamboyant transvestites who sometimes turn to prostitution and can often be found frequenting Pape'ete's nightspots. These people face more discrimination than their *mahu* counterparts who act more like very effeminate men.

It remains unclear whether this practice has a sexual or social origin, but it is generally assumed to be the latter as *mahu* don't necessarily have sex with men. *Raerae,* however, do prefer men and can be drop-dead gorgeous as well as convincingly feminine – watch out!

existence. This tolerance is displayed most strongly by the presence of *mahu* (and the more flamboyant *raerae*), men who dress and live their lives as women (see the boxed text, above). Lesbians are more rare but also quietly accepted. The discotheques of Pape'ete, particularly the Piano Bar (p93), are real hotspots for the gay community.

Pakalolo (marijuana), and the associated music-and-smoking lifestyle, have been thoroughly embraced in French Polynesia, but harder drugs are rare. The exception is 'ice', a highly addictive methamphetamine that has rapidly gained popularity among the upper classes of Pape'ete. The government has responded with an impressive effort that will hopefully curb the problem before it becomes too serious. In the meantime violent crime, almost entirely drug related, has been on the rise in Pape'ete. This shouldn't be much of an issue for travellers, but it's a good idea to take care when walking in Pape'ete late at night, especially on Friday and Saturday.

Education

The education system in French Polynesia is identical to that of France. School is compulsory from age five to 16. Teaching is in French; only a few hours of Tahitian a week are offered in primary and secondary schools. This tends to disadvantage Polynesian children, who have greater difficulty working in French and following the French education system than *demi* (Polynesian-European or Polynesian-Chinese), *popaa* (European) and Chinese children.

Most small islands do not have schools offering education beyond primary school (fifth grade) and the only high schools are on Tahiti and Ra'iatea. Because education is mandatory, most children living outside the main islands have to board on Tahiti to complete their studies. This is hard on both the parents and the children, especially those from far-away archipelagos like the Australs, the Tuamotus or the Marquesas, where the culture and language are very different from Tahiti. Some of these students get hooked on the buzz of Pape'ete city life and never want to return to their sleepy islands, while others can't wait to finish or fail so they can go home.

The Malay-Polynesian language group spreads from Madagascar in the east to Easter Island in the west.

School holidays are excessive: one month from mid-December to mid-January, six weeks in July and August, two weeks in October, three weeks in March and ten days in May. Other three- and four-day weekends are scattered throughout the year. Children boarding in Pape'ete often cannot afford to return home for all of these holidays.

The Université de Polynésie Française (UPF; University of French Polynesia) is steadily growing, but because it does not offer a wide range of disciplines many students go to university in France.

ECONOMY

With a per-capita GNP comparable to that of Australia, French Polynesia is one of the richest countries in the South Pacific. This elevated standard of living is, of course, somewhat artificial since it depends on lots of input from France. Unemployment is officially 13.2% of the active population, but this figure is virtually meaningless in the local context. On some atolls there is really no job market at all and the population is primarily self-sufficient. Combine that with the *fetii* (extended family) concept, and employment levels don't have the same impact as they do in the industrialised nations of the West. Pape'ete is the one exception, where unemployment has brought the same social problems experienced in other urban centres worldwide.

The primary industry of tourism has been seeing hard times for the last few years. Airfare hikes and a fluctuating dollar make this expensive destination that much more costly and the government seems mysteriously uninterested on courting midrange or budget travellers to fill the gaps.

Black-pearl production, which takes second rank to tourism, is looking even bleaker. A combination of little professional organisation among farmers, naive marketing, overproduction, and worldwide economic problems have made the industry workable only to small family-run farms that keep under the tax and social-security radar. See p176 for more details.

There are articles about nearly all of the islands of French Polynesia in the archives of www .airtahitimagazine.com.

Agriculture moves with fads; vanilla was sure to be the next 'black pearl', and the government offered great start-up packages for anyone with some land and a strong back. The price dropped radically before many began seriously harvesting, and the people turned to *noni* (see the boxed text, p62). *Noni* prices dropped and now islanders are returning to copra (see p178). All islands produce some crops for local consumption, but the Australs have become the primary producer of local produce for the country.

POPULATION

Paralleling worldwide patterns of urbanisation, French Polynesia's people have migrated towards the capital city and main island: 69% of the population currently make their home on Tahiti and 75% of those on Tahiti live in Pape'ete or its suburbs. While a few atolls in the Tuamotus continue to pull in new residents for work in the Tahitian pearl industry, most islands in the Tuamotu, Gambier, Marquesas and Austral Archipelagos have dismal growth rates below 1%. The Leeward Islands, especially the ones with a bigger tourist industry such as Bora Bora, Huahine and Ra'iatea, are growing at the same steady rate as the Windward Islands. The birth rates throughout the islands are dropping steadily, although they are still relatively high at 16.5 births per 1000 population (it's around 12 births per 1000 population in Australia and France), down from 20.4 in 2001.

On all of the islands the majority of the population lives in coastal zones. The rugged interior is virtually uninhabited, but archaeological evidence indicates that this wasn't always the case. Only in the Marquesas do people live mostly in the valleys; this is a habit left over from times when living near the beach left people more vulnerable to warring neighbouring tribes.

MULTICULTURALISM

From the times of the first European ships, Tahitians have been incredibly tolerant of the many races and cultures that have arrived at their ports. Whether as a symbol of welcome or as acts of free-spirited curiosity, girls descended upon the ships, arms open to what must have been a bunch of scabby, bony sailors. Babies born from these encounters were raised as any other Tahitian child would have been and thus the mix of genes began.

Today, most islanders have a surprisingly rich genealogical background ranging from European to American Indian to Asiatic.

Europeans came and went but, early on, very few stayed. In the last few decades, most French immigrants were in the military or on lucrative four- to six-year teaching contracts; when the contract was up most chose to leave. Some Americans and a handful of other nationalities bought land or moved to Tahiti in the 1970s, but soon stricter laws were put in place making it very difficult for non-French nationals to immigrate to Tahiti. Because of this, Tahiti is very much its own country even if its government is not entirely its own. Unlike Hawaii or New Zealand, land has remained primarily in the ownership of the population that can claim Polynesian ancestry.

Typee: A Peep at Polynesian Life (1846) is Herman Melville's idealistic account of three weeks spent with the Typee tribe of Nuku Hiva.

This is changing. French Polynesia is now a part of the EU and Europeans, still predominantly the French, are catching on that this is a really great place to live. Most choose to reside on Tahiti or Mo'orea where they mix very little with the locals. The few that choose to live on the outer islands integrate more with islanders although tension is sometimes created if locals feel that newcomers are taking away business opportunities. In general, those immigrants that are sensitive to local culture have little problems assimilating.

Chinese, who make up about 5% of the population of French Polynesia, have done a splendid job of integrating into Polynesian culture and filling in the commercial cracks. Shipped to Tahiti during the 19th century as cheap labour for soon-to-be-defunct cotton plantations, the Chinese began as the most underprivileged members of society to become some of the strongest business people in the country. Nearly every shop in French Polynesia is Chinese owned, and the biggest names in the pearl industry are also Chinese. Some Chinese still speak their ancestral language (Hakka) and most have excelled in learning Tahitian.

In between the three dominant cultures (particularly European and Tahitian) are the *demi,* those of mixed Polynesian-European and Polynesian-Chinese descent. *Demi* occupy some of the most important positions in public life, dominate the political sphere and, in many cases, drive nice cars, wear big sunglasses and own small dogs.

Very few French Polynesians choose to leave their country long-term. Some go to university in France or marry foreigners, but nearly all of them come back if they can. When Tahitians do expatriate it is usually to France or the USA.

Racial tension is rare but does exist. A few unsavoury insults have been created for each race although they are usually only uttered on drunken binges or in schoolyards. Outward displays of racism are usually from Polynesians to French while the more insidious kind goes from the French

---

DON'T MISS THE MISS

Beauty pageants are a national pastime in French Polynesia and none of the country's variety of lovelies are left out. Some of the bigger competitions are Miss Dragon for the Chinese community, Miss Popa'a for girls of European descent and Miss Vahine Tane (literally 'Miss Woman-Man') for all those leggy transvestites (see p42). But the one that makes front-page news for weeks is the spectacular Miss Tahiti pageant in May. To be Miss Tahiti in French Polynesia is to be the country's number-one celebrity for a whole year, and then some. The Miss Tahiti winners who go on to win the Miss France competition (and there have been several) become living legends. It's many a local girl's dream.

Ladies will be happy to know that the Mr Tahiti pageant is also rapidly gaining popularity and takes place in October ever year.

HAWAIKI NUI CANOE RACE

The sporting spectacular that has French Polynesians glued to their TV sets and talking passionately about favourites and challengers is indeed a canoe race. The three-day, four-island, Hawaiki Nui *va'a* race pits around 60 of the islands' best six-man *pirogue* teams against each other and against anyone who is brave enough to turn up from overseas.

The 116km race, held in November, starts on Huahine. The brawny paddlers, who often sport vivid Tahitian tattoos, head across the open sea to Ra'iatea, from there to Taha'a, and then finally on to Bora Bora. The canoes are a superb sight, with men paddling three on each side for about 10 strokes before switching sides with precise timing and lightning speed.

There's also a women's Hawaiki Nui race, known as the Va'a Hine, a play on words (*va'a* is Tahitian for 'canoe' and *vahine* is Tahitian for 'woman'). The Va'a Hine is usually held in October.

Check out www.hawaikinuivaa.pf (in French) for more details.

---

to the Polynesians. The Chinese make an impressive effort to stay out of it as they sell everyone their morning baguette.

SPORT

The national sport is, without dispute, *va'a* (*pirogue*, or outrigger-canoe) racing. You can admire the *pirogue* teams training on the lagoon, and if you are on Tahiti in late October or early November, you can catch the Hawaiki Nui canoe race (see the boxed text, above).

Surfing was an ancient Tahitian sport that is gaining strongly in popularity. The Billabong Pro international surf competition, held every May at the nearly mythically scary wave at Teahupoo on Tahiti Iti, brings worldwide coverage to Tahitian surfing. Slowly more and more surfers are travelling to French Polynesia to tempt fate at crystal-clear waves breaking inches over razor-sharp reef.

During the Heiva and a few scattered cultural festivals, Polynesians pull some very interesting traditional sports out of their hats. *Amoraa ofae* (rock lifting), which originated in the Australs, consists of lifting a rock weighing between 90kg and 145kg, then hoisting it onto the shoulders.

From the Tuamotus, *patia fa* (javelin throwing), comes to life at the Heiva (see p48). The object is to hit a coconut tied to the top of a 7.5m pole from a distance of 22m. Individuals or two-person teams compete in this event.

Coconut-husking competitions are also held at the Heiva and at many community events. Each team of three competitors has to split open and scoop out the insides of between 150 and 200 coconuts in the shortest possible time and place the meat in a sack.

There are two fruit-bearing races during the Heiva over a distance of about 2km. The first is run with a burden of 30kg and the second with a load of 50kg carried on a stick that rests on the shoulders.

RELIGION

The Polynesians were polytheistic, worshipping *atua* (gods) who were surrounded by a pantheon of secondary gods. The main gods were Ta'aroa (god of creation), Tu (man god), Tane (god of craftsmen), 'Oro (god of war) and Hiro (god of thieves and sailors). Their power was fought for and geographically limited. Tane, for instance, was ousted by Ta'aroa, who was in turn replaced by his son 'Oro, whose cult never extended beyond the limits of the Society Islands. Hiro was worshipped on Ra'iatea and Huahine.

Central to Polynesian beliefs, and notions that still linger on today, are *mana* and *tapu*. *Mana* is a supernatural force that can be transmitted between objects or persons. A *tiki* (sacred statue) or a *marae* (traditional temple)

Hardcore foot races, the Raid Tahiti, which traverses Tahiti Iti from Teahupoo to Tautira, and the Raid Painapo, which traverses the mountains of Mo'orea, are held in March and September respectively.

In pre-European Tahitian surfing (*fa'ahe'e*), only chiefs stood up on their surfboards; the rest of the population were more like ancient boogie boarders.

Teahupoo Tahiti's Mythic Wave is a coffee-table book of local expat surf photographer Tim McKenna's best shots of the mega wave.

might emanate great *mana* – a spiritual energy that is almost palpable. A person with good *mana* is someone who emits 'good vibes'; someone with bad *mana* makes the skin crawl.

Tapu is what modern English has adopted as the word 'taboo'. Basically, anything that is *tapu* is forbidden, and grave and mysterious consequences befall anyone who breaks the rules. Ancient Polynesian society was governed and kept in check by many *tapu* such as fishing restrictions, limitations on who could enter certain religious sites and even on who was high ranked enough to eat special foods such as turtle meat.

The arrival of Protestant missionaries at the end of the 18th century, followed soon after by the Catholics, marked the suppression of traditional religious beliefs. The missionaries changed the religious and cultural landscape forever, and even today French Polynesia has a surprising number and variety of churches relative to its population. Around half of the population is Protestant, particularly in the Society Islands and the Australs. Catholics make up around 30% of the population and live mostly in the Marquesas, the eastern Tuamotus and the Gambier Archipelago, but also on Tahiti (many of the *demi* and Chinese are Catholic). The balance is made up of Mormons, Seventh-Day Adventists, Sanitos (the local name for the reorganised Church of Jesus Christ of Latter-Day Saints, a dissident branch of the Mormons), Jehovah's Witnesses and Jews (Pape'ete has a synagogue). Most Chinese converted to Catholicism in the 1950s and '60s, although there are three Chinese temples in Pape'ete.

A few pre-Christian rituals and superstitions still survive alongside Christianity. Christian Polynesians continue to respect and fear ancient *tapu* sites, and nothing would persuade a Polynesian to move a *tiki* or *marae* stone. On occasion, a *tahua* (faith healer) is still consulted and *raau tahiti* (traditional herbal medicine) is making a comeback.

ARTS

The zealous missionaries endeavoured to wipe out all forms of 'primitive' Polynesian art and culture. They destroyed temples and carvings, banned tattooing and dancing, and generally took a lot of the joy out of life. Fortunately some traditions survived this period of cultural censorship, and in recent years there has been a revival of Polynesian culture, particularly in music, dance and tattooing.

Dance

Tahitian dance is not just a tourist attraction, it's one of the most vibrant forms of expression underlying Maohi (Polynesian) culture. The dances that

---

Polynesians are great believers in *tupapau* (ghosts) and most people will have a good story to tell about the supernatural if you ask them.

Grab a free copy of *Hiro'a*, a small magazine in French on everything cultural that's going on in French Polynesia. It's available at many *pensions* and restaurants.

SOCIAL GRACES

French Polynesians are generally very easygoing, and there are few social pitfalls for the unwary visitor. Nonetheless, it's worth remembering that religion permeates everyday life. Grace often precedes a meal and the churches are jammed on Sunday mornings. Given how religious the Polynesians are, it's wise to avoid criticism of the missionaries.

The most important thing to remember is to smile and say *bonjour* or *ia orana* to everyone you meet. Citylike habits of not acknowledging people can be interpreted as outright unfriendliness. When you are introduced to people, women are greeted with a kiss on each cheek and men with a handshake. Occasionally men greet women with a handshake instead of kisses and men who are good friends or family or want to show deep respect for each other will kiss each other on the cheeks. Women nearly always greet women with kisses *(bisous)*.

If visiting a Polynesian home, take your shoes off at the front door.

TYPES OF DANCE

There are five types of dance in French Polynesia, which are seldom performed on their own but instead integrated into a broad program. Note that the *tamure,* a term of recent origin, refers to the nightclub, hip-jiggling form of Tahitian dance that has no traditional cultural basis but is a whole lot of fun to try on a night out after you've had a few.

Otea Fast gyrating hip action for the women and scissorlike leg movements for the men – this is the classic Tahitian dance.

Aparima Free-flowing and graceful dance that tells a story using hand movements and song.

Hivinau Inspired by English sailors hoisting the anchor, this dance takes its name from the phrase 'heave now'.

Paoa Seated male and female choirs form a semicircle, in the centre of which a male soloist recites a legend. The members of the choir respond while slapping their thighs in rhythm.

Fire Dance A man juggles a flaming torch alight at both ends against a background of drums.

Marquesan Dance The most famous is the Haku Manu (Bird Dance), modelled on the movements of a bird. The Pig Dance mimics the symbolic phases of a hog's life.

visitors see performed in French Polynesia are not created for tourists – they are authentic performances, and they play a major part in spreading the influence of Tahitian culture abroad. Behind every performance lies months of rehearsals, rigorously standardised choreography and a specific legend that is acted out. In this land of oral traditions, dance is not merely an aesthetic medium but also a means of preserving the memory of the past.

The luxury hotels offer quality dance shows about twice a week. On Tahiti and Mo'orea they are performed by semiprofessional groups and range from small groups dancing to piped-in music (in the worst cases) to theatrical extravaganzas with live orchestras (the show at the Intercontinental Resort Tahiti, p91, is arguably the best); on other islands the companies are rather more amateur but it will never be a typically 'touristy' show. These shows come with a buffet (costing around 8000 CFP) and are open to all. If you only wish to attend the show, enquire about the hotel's policy.

From the accounts of early European visitors, we know that entertainment, especially dancing, held an important place in ancient Polynesian society. Deemed to be both pagan and lewd, dancing was officially forbidden in 1819. In 1895, a number of tightly controlled performances were allowed at the 14th of July festival (Bastille Day) called Tiurai (now known as the Heiva). It wasn't until 1956 that traditional dancing was modernised by Madeleine Moua, a former primary-school teacher, and was given a new image free of demonic overtones. She created Heiva, the first professional dance group, perfected the costumes and made choreography more straightforward, while still drawing on the rich Maohi cultural heritage. Many other dance companies have since appeared on the scene, and Tahitian dance has become vibrant once again.

Warning! At a local dance performance, prepare to shake your hips: tourists are often asked up to the stage to dance once the show is over.

Music

Traditional Polynesian music, usually performed as an accompaniment to dance, is heard reverberating through the islands. Ukuleles and percussion instruments dominate, and the music is structured by a fast-paced and often complex drum beat. Traditional, modern and religious song is also popular. Sunday *himene* (hymns) feature wonderful harmonies.

Drums are the Maohi instruments par excellence and the most used one is called a *toere*. The *toere* is a cylindrical, hollowed-out piece of wood with a narrow slit down the whole of its length. The *fa'atete* is a drum with a single skin and is played with two sticks and rests on a support. *Pahu,* or *tari parau,* is a drum with two skins, rather like a bass drum.

Rock concerts by international artists are often held at the Toata Amphitheatre. Most acts are reggae or French groups and you can usually buy a ticket at the door.

THE HEIVA

Each year for a month, from late June to late July, islanders from all the archipelagos join together for a full program of festivities in Pape'ete and on some of the other islands. The emphasis is on traditional dance contests (both professional and amateur) and singing competitions, but there is a huge amount of other activities on offer. Craft aficionados will love the demonstrations of *niau*-making (woven coconut-palm leaves), *tifaifai*-making (appliqué) and *tapa*-making (paperlike cloth), as well as a stone-carving competition. For entertainment there's a procession of floral floats, a vote for Miss Heiva and Mr Heiva, a funfair, firework displays, fire walking and tattoo displays. Meanwhile, for sports enthusiasts there's an outrigger-canoe race, an *amoraa ofae* (rock lifting) competition, *patia fa* (javelin throwing), coconut-husking races and fruit-carrying competitions; see p45.

The Heiva is organised by **Tahiti Nui 2000** (☎ 50 31 00). Reservations for the evening dance contests can be made from May onwards at the kiosk at Place Toata in Pape'ete. You can also enquire at the tourist office. The evening will set you back between 1000 and 2500 CFP. Dance performances take place at the Toata Amphitheatre.

String instruments are of European origin, though the ukulele, a mini-guitar with four strings, comes by way of Hawaii. Guitars are also now an integral part of the orchestra.

Modern Polynesian music by local artists is the blaring soundtrack to everyday life, whether it's in a bus, at a cafe or on the radio – some groups also perform in hotels and bars.

Literature

Polynesia has been getting the Western pen flowing since the first European explorers returned with accounts of paradise islands and beautiful people. But oral recitation was the fountain pen of the Pacific, and the written word only came into being after the missionaries began producing texts in Tahitian in the 19th century. This dependence on the spoken word has meant that Polynesia's history has been re-created out of European observations, and the Polynesian experience constructed out of European suppositions. It also means that literature written by Polynesians has only started to grace the bookshelves relatively recently.

Si Loin du Monde (2003) by 'Tavae' (in French) is the true, heroic story of a local Tahitian fisherman who survived 118 days lost at sea in his tiny fishing boat.

There are a number of interesting Polynesian writers who are slowly changing the literary landscape, but few have been translated into English. If you read French, writers such as Henri Hiro, Turo Raapoto, Hubert Bremond, Charles Manutahi, Michou Chaze, Chantal Spitz and Louise Peltzer are all of interest. A search on the internet, or at Pape'ete book-shops, will turn up info on any of these authors.

The *Materena* series, by Celestine Hitiura Vaite, a Tahitian living in Australia, are a trilogy of novels available in English that are set in contemporary Tahiti. The poverty and social problems facing many Tahitians are not glossed over; the dialogue is garnished with Tahitian and French (don't worry, a glossary is provided). The first book of the series, *Breadfruit*, is the most widely read book in Tahiti.

Architecture

Apart from the naturalistic, rustic-chic style popular with hotels and *pensions* (guesthouses), today's Tahitian architecture veers towards square, white and bland. Due to threat of cyclones, traditional *fare* (pronounced 'far-ay'), made of wood beams, thatched coconut fronds and plaited bamboo, are rare. Even most of the colonial-era buildings have been supplanted by the ubiquitous cement block. Government-aid housing, available to low-income residents and cyclone victims, can be purchased by any paying party and is the most affordable housing option in French Polynesia. These unsightly structures, with their particle-board walls and corrugated-iron roofing, have few windows and lack the aesthetic qualities of their forbears. Even with basic housing, Tahitians like to dress up their homes with turquoise or pink paints, brightly coloured fabrics, shells and year-round Christmas decorations; this is particularly true in the outer islands.

Painting

Even today, well over a hundred years after his arrival on Tahiti, painting in the South Pacific is synonymous with Paul Gauguin, the French post-Impressionist painter. Gauguin spent much of his later life in Polynesia, and presented Europe with images of the islands that moulded the way Europeans viewed (and, arguably, continue to view) Polynesia. In his wake a number of predominantly European artists – working in media ranging from watercolour to line drawing – have also sought inspiration in the region. These artists have contributed to the very characteristic painting style of the region, which is largely representational.

Adorning the World: Art of the Marquesas Islands, published by the Metropolitan Museum of Art, is a gorgeous coffee-table book that explores Marquesan art from collections around the world.

Matisse made a short visit to Tahiti, but his work on Polynesia is eclipsed by Jacques Boullaire's. Boullaire, a French artist who first travelled to Tahiti in the 1930s, produced magnificent watercolours; reproductions of his work are readily available today.

Other artists of French and Polynesian descent who have influenced the art scene locally and internationally include Christian Deloffre, François Ravello, Michèle Dallet, Bobby (also a singer and musician; he died in 1991), André Marere, Jean Masson, Garrick Yrondi, Maryse Noguier and Erhard Lux.

Sculpture & Woodcarving

Traditionally the best sculptures and woodcarvings have come out of the Marquesas, where fine *tiki,* bowls, mortars and pestles, spears and clubs are carved from rosewood, *tou* wood or stone. You can find these pieces in the market of Pape'ete, as well as gift shops around the islands, but the best deals are had in the Marquesas themselves.

Some woodwork sold in French Polynesia is actually made elsewhere (usually Indonesia), so if you see several of the same item, chances are it wasn't made in the country. Ask around to ensure you are getting the real thing.

Clothing & Decoration

Dress in French Polynesia is an odd combination of the very dowdy, inspired by the missionaries, and the very sexy, inspired by *Baywatch,* Brazilian soap operas and practicality – it's a hot country!

RECOMMENDED LISTENING

Angelo Neuffer Highly political and poetic lyrics have made Angelo one of the most popular Tahitian artists of all time. One of his best albums is *Nuna'a no Ananahi.*

Ester Tefana For old-fashioned, ukulele-accompanied, Tahitian mood music, Ester is your best bet.

Tapuarii Laughlin Most modern classics are written by 'Tapu' who mixes surfer cool with the traditional.

Bobby Very listenable, almost dreamy Polynesian music. His album with Angelo, titled *Bobby & Angelo,* is one of the most listened-to albums in Tahiti.

Te Ava Piti This is your classic Polynesian music with plenty of fast ukulele riffs.

Trio Kikiriri Perhaps a bit cheesy to Western ears, this synth/ukulele group is an all-time favourite for weddings and parties where people dance the Tahitian foxtrot.

Fenua Bringing Tahitian music into the future, this group fuses the traditional with techno for an explosive sound.

For day-to-day wear, T-shirts and surf shorts are the most popular for men and women, along with the traditional *pareu* which, like the Southeast Asian sarong, is a cool, comfortable, all-purpose piece of fabric. Men don't wear *pareu* out in public much these days but often wrap them around their waists like a skirt to wear around the house. Women have a variety of ways of wearing *pareu*: it can be worn as a skirt, tied above the breasts to make a dress or worn with two corners tied behind the neck as a halter neck. It's considered casual wear, appropriate for the store or beach, but is not worn for dressier occasions such as church or eating out at a nice restaurant.

Go to www.ica.pf (Institut de la Comminication Audiovisuelle, in French) for podcasts and videos of everything cultural in French Polynesia. Download or buy old films, and watch music videos, Tahitian news, clips of Tahitian dance and much, much more.

On the more remote islands, local women usually wear shorts and T-shirts in the water, although the bikini is unlikely to shock. French and Tahitian women sometimes go topless, particularly near Pape'ete and at hotel beaches. Elsewhere, use your common sense: if you are the only person on the beach over 12 baring your breasts, best to cover up.

MONOI
What can't it do? This local concoction, made from coconut oil and *tiare* flowers, is deliciously perfumed with sandalwood, vanilla, coconut or jasmine. It's used liberally as hair oil, ointment, sunscreen and even mosquito repellent. It costs from 400 to 600 CFP a bottle, is great on the skin after a day of sizzling in the sun and makes a great gift (although it does solidify in cooler climates).

TAPA
Traditionally made throughout the Pacific, *tapa* (paperlike cloth) is a non-woven fabric made from the bark of *uru* (breadfruit), banyan or *aute* (paper mulberry) trees. It was the semi-disposable clothing fabric of pre-European Polynesia. The colour depends upon the wood used, and varies from white to chestnut. The bark of young trunks or branches is removed then soaked in water to soften. The outer layer is scraped away, leaving just the sapwood. The sheets of bark, about 15cm wide, are spread out on a flat, elongated stone then pounded repeatedly for several hours. At this point the bark becomes thinner and gradually stretches.

When the piece is finished, it is dried and then dyed with the sap of various plants or decorated with traditional art work. Today, designs are sometimes just drawn on with ink.

Pacific Arts of Polynesia and Micronesia (2008) published by Oxford University Press includes contemporary as well as ancient art and covers everything from tattooing to musical instruments and sculpture.

The making of *tapa* rapidly declined when European cloth became available in the region, but it is still produced, particularly on Fatu Hiva in the Marquesas, for ceremonial use and for collectors. Gift cards and small pieces of *tapa* are found in most gift shops.

PLAITING & BASKETWORK
Baskets, hats and the panels used for roofing and the walls of houses are all made by women. Coconut-palm leaves are used for the more rough-and-ready woven work, while pandanus leaves or thin strips of bamboo are used for finer hats, bags and mats, which are often decorated with flowers or shells.

Some of the finest work comes from the Australs, where hillside pandanus (rather than common lagoonside pandanus) is used.

FLOWERS & SHELLS
Flowers are omnipresent in French Polynesia. From the moment you arrive at the airport, where you'll be presented with a *tiare* (Tahiti's national flower) to sniff as you brave the customs queues, to hotel rooms and even public toilets, flowers are displayed, offered and worn. Both men and women

tuck a *tiare* or other flower behind their ear in the world's most simple yet graceful gesture of physical adornment. Traditionally, a flower behind the left ear meant you were taken or married while a blossom tucked behind your right ear meant you were available; while Tahitians love to tell tourists about this practice, in reality no one will try and deduce your relationship status in this way anymore.

Flower crowns or necklaces are given as gifts on arrival while shell necklaces are given on departure. Engraved mother-of-pearl is now a favourite medium of some very creative local jewellery.

Tattoos

Another good reason for Tahitians to show some skin is the resurgence of tattooing. Since the early 1980s, tattooing has enjoyed a strong revival, becoming one of the most expressive and vibrant vehicles of Polynesian culture.

With encouragement from the great Samoan masters, young Tahitians have delved into their ancient traditions and have brought this ancestral form of bodily adornment, with its undisputed artistic qualities, completely up to date. Today many Polynesian men and women sport magnificent tattoos as symbols of their identity.

Modern tattooing is completely for the sake of style or beautification; in ancient times it was a highly socially significant and sophisticated art. Firstly, it was a symbol of community or clan membership and geographic origin. Each island group had their own style of tattoo: the Tuamotu Islands used simple, geometric shapes, while the Marquesan designs were the most intricate and elaborate and are the inspiration for contemporary tattoos. It was also an initiation rite: in the Marquesas, the onset of adulthood was marked by a ceremony during which young men would display their tattoos as symbols of bravery; women were not allowed to help with the cooking until they passed a rite of having their hands tattooed. Social status was also displayed through tattooing: as people progressed through different stages of life, they covered their bodies with more tattoos. This aesthetic adornment played a part in the seduction process as well. Finally, tattooing served to

Tattoo aficionados will love Tattoonesia (www .tattoonesia.com), the tattoo festival held in November every year.

MUTINY IN THE CINEMA

The story of the famous uprising aboard the *Bounty* has been embellished by big-budget film-makers three times in 50 years. If another version is ever made, audiences could be forgiven for having a mutiny of their own.

The original *Mutiny on the Bounty* epic was made in 1935. It was directed by Frank Lloyd and starred Charles Laughton as Captain Bligh and Clark Gable as Fletcher Christian. Although critics insist that this is the classic *Bounty* film, it certainly played fast and loose with history. Bligh flogs, keelhauls, lies and cheats his way through the entire film, while Christian is a charming, brave, purposeful aristocrat. Very little of the film was actually shot on Tahiti.

The lavish three-hour 1962 remake, *Mutiny on the Bounty,* was directed by Lewis Milestone, and stars Trevor Howard as Bligh and Marlon Brando as Christian. This film is a much more extravagant affair than the black-and-white original and was filmed on Tahiti and Bora Bora, to the great benefit of the local economy. Bligh is again portrayed as a monster, while Christian is a sort of simpering fop who clearly would have driven any captain nuts.

The third and final remake of the now-familiar tale, *Bounty,* produced by Dino de Laurentiis and directed by Roger Donaldson, is surprisingly respectable. Most of the location filming was done on Mo'orea, and 1980s' cinematic freedom meant that Polynesian nudity, and those goddesslike 'celestial forms' Bougainville so enthusiastically described, finally made it onto the big screen. Anthony Hopkins plays the not-quite-so-bad-and-mad Bligh and Mel Gibson is the more-handsome-than-ever Christian.

intimidate: in the Marquesas, warriors tattooed their faces to make themselves look terrifying to enemies.

Cinema

Tahiti's role as a movie backdrop is almost exclusively tied up with the *Bounty* (see the boxed text, p51). James Michener's *South Pacific* may have been about Polynesia, but it certainly wasn't filmed there.

Tabu, released in 1931, was filmed on Bora Bora. This work of fiction explores the notions of *tapu* (see p46), and when one of the directors was killed in an accident shortly after finishing filming, there was plenty of speculation that his death may have been the result of including *tapu* parts of the island in the film.

In 1979 a big-budget remake of *Hurricane*, the 1937 classic based on a Nordhoff and Hall novel, was filmed on Bora Bora. The film was a major flop, despite an all-star cast; for TV it was retitled *Forbidden Paradise*.

The five-day FIFO (Festival International du Film Documentaire Océanien; www.filmfestival eceanie.org, in French) in January screens the best documentary films (often in English) from around the Pacific.

Food & Drink

Polynesians like to eat and they like it when you eat. Luckily, the food on offer is a pleasure to the palate. Fish and seafood lovers may well mistake French Polynesia for nirvana; vegetarians can happily pick through the available produce; and even carnivores hunting down a good steak can come away satiated.

Modern Tahitian food is a fairly balanced melange of French, Chinese and Polynesian influence; béchamel, soy sauce or coconut milk all have an equal chance of topping your meal.

STAPLES & SPECIALITIES

Ma'a Tahiti, traditional Tahitian food, is a heavy mix of starchy taro and *uru* (breadfruit), raw or cooked fish, fatty pork, coconut milk and a few scattered vegetables. On special occasions, the whole lot is neatly prepared and placed in a *hima'a* (cooking pit) where a layer of stones and banana leaves separate the food from the hot coals beneath. The food is covered with more banana leaves then buried so all the flavours and juices can cook and mingle for several hours. The result is a steamy, tender ambrosia of a meal.

Ma'a Tahiti is most often served in restaurants and snack (snack bars) for lunch on Fridays and Sundays.

Main Dishes

Open-sea fish (tuna, bonito, wahoo, swordfish and *mahi mahi*) and lagoon fish (parrotfish, jackfish and squirrrelfish) feature prominently in traditional cuisine. *Poisson cru* (raw fish in coconut milk) is the most popular local dish, though fish is also served grilled, fried or poached. Lobster is not plentiful but is usually available at finer restaurants; *chevrettes* (freshwater shrimps) however, often served in curry, are farmed locally and can sometimes be found even at budget restaurants. Salmon and trout generally come from Australia or New Zealand, and prawns may be imported or farmed locally.

Cuisine Chinoise de Tahiti (in French) is the reference for Chinese Tahitian cooking, from the simple to the exceedingly difficult.

Pua (pork) is the preferred meat for the traditional underground oven. Although chickens run wild everywhere, most of what is consumed is imported frozen from the US and is of low quality. Lamb and beef, from New Zealand, make regular appearances on menus and are as good as you'll find anywhere in the world. In the Marquesas, goat meat takes pride of place, and dog is still eaten on the remote atolls of the Tuamotus. Although it is

---

TRAVEL YOUR TASTEBUDS

A distinctive feature of French Polynesian cooking is its usage of fermentation. In most cases this makes for a tangy, slightly salty flavour, but it can be more extreme. *Miti hue* is a mild example: it's a thick, lumpy sauce made from fermented coconut meat. This sauce is savoury, not sweet, and delicious with taro, *uru* (breadfruit) and fish. *Taioro* is a breakfast dish made from grated coconut and sea-snail meat (or fish if snail is unavailable) that is left to ferment in a small amount of crab juice overnight resulting in a rich, salty-sweet mush. In the Marquesas, the basic dish is *popoi*, a sweet-and-sour dish that looks like a yellow paste. It consists of cooked *uru*, crushed in a mortar and mixed with a dollop or more of fermented *uru* pulp for flavour. But the pariah to many visitors is reeking, fetid *fafaru*. This dish is made with raw fish that has been briefly marinated in *mitifafaru*, seawater that has been infused with rotting fish for 10 days. The marination gives the fish a velvety, delectable texture and a tangy flavour – but the smell! *Fafaru* smells so strongly of old roadkill that eating it requires overcoming your strongest instincts for survival.

protected, turtle is still eaten in French Polynesia. You should categorically refuse to eat this endangered animal.

The most common accompaniments are coconut milk, which is made by grating the coconut meat and wringing it in a cloth, and *miti hue,* a slightly salty fermented sauce made of young coconut meat (see the boxed text, p53).

Among Chinese specialities, chow mein is the most popular. This fried noodle dish usually has pork and/or chicken in it, but vegetarians can always order a meat-free version. Pizza and pasta are also easy to find on the touristy islands.

Although you're not likely to find it served in restaurants, *punu pua'atoro* (canned corned beef) is Tahiti's answer to Spam. It's traditionally eaten with breadfruit and is probably one of the most frequently prepared dishes in French Polynesian homes.

Fruit & Vegetables

French Polynesia is dripping with tropical fruit, including mango, grapefruit, lime, watermelon, pineapple and banana. *Pamplemousse* (grapefruit) is the large, sweet, Southeast Asian variety. The rambutan, another Southeast Asian introduction, is a red spiny-skinned cousin of the lychee. Fruits on the high islands are seasonal; different ones will be available depending on when you're visiting. In the Tuamotus fresh produce is always scarce.

Vegetables are not a major component of Polynesian cuisine. *Uru* is a staple, and is eaten roasted or fried as chips. *Fei,* a plantain banana, is only eaten cooked and is much less sweet than a common banana. Taro root is usually boiled, as are sweet potato and manioc (cassava), but can also be fried as delicious chips. *Fafa* (taro leaves) are used to make *poulet fafa,* a stew with chicken and coconut milk. Carrots, Chinese cabbage, cabbage, tomatoes and bell peppers all make regular appearances in dishes like chow mein and *poisson cru.*

Desserts

A traditional Tahitian meal doesn't include dessert; the sweet things are simply served alongside the main meal. *Ipo* (boiled coconut bread) and *po'e* (baked, mashed fruit mixed with starch and doused with coconut milk) are the two most common sweet side dishes. *Faraoa coco* (coconut bread), *firifiri* (donuts) and *pai* (little turnovers filled with coconut, banana, guava or custard) are eaten for breakfast or as snacks.

When dessert is served Western style, it's usually fresh fruit or a fruit tart, but it's not hard to find more extravagant French cakes, mousses and confections in fine restaurants.

DRINKS
Nonalcoholic Drinks

Several delicious fruit juices are made locally, notably the Rotui brand. Freshly squeezed juices are sometimes available but are incredibly expensive. *Pape haari* (coconut water) is the healthiest, cheapest, most natural and thirst-quenching drink around. It is totally free of microbes and bacteria (if it has come straight from the coconut).

If you want a real coffee, order a *café expresso* (espresso coffee), otherwise you'll probably be served instant Nescafé. The further you get from the tourist hubs the further you get from espresso machines, so if you're an addict heading to the more isolated islands, prepare yourself for some instant coffees or some midmorning headaches (your best bet for an espresso is the bar of a top-end hotel).

Note that it is illegal and highly discouraged to bring local fruit and vegetables from Tahiti to islands in other archipelagos since you might also be bringing unwanted insect pests that could disrupt the balance of these fragile ecosystems.

Want to know everything there is to know about vanilla, plus find some great Tahitian recipes? Go to www.vanilla.com and the 'Vanilla Queen' (who ironically is from Santa Cruz, California) will give you a night's worth of reading.

The water inside a coconut is sterile and can be used in medical procedures.

TAHITI & FRENCH POLYNESIA'S TOP FIVE

Coco's Restaurant (p97), Tahiti Nui. The most posh French cuisine, with a view of Mo'orea.
Motu Moea – Restaurant la Plage (p120), Mo'orea. Swim or boat to isolated bliss.
Place Vaiete Roulottes (p91), Pape'ete. Get cheap, delicious food out of an eclectic collection of mobile food vans.
Restaurant Mauarii (p133), Huahine Iti. Scrumptious traditional Tahitian food, white sand and sunsets.
Villa Mahana (p162), Bora Bora. French-chef chic and six-table romantic.

Alcoholic Drinks

The local brand of *pia* (beer), Hinano, is sold everywhere and is available in glass 500mL bottles, 330mL and 500mL cans, and on tap. It is a fairly light, very drinkable beer. Foreign beers, notably Heineken, are also available. Allow at least 350 CFP for a beer in a bar or restaurant.

Most supermarkets stock red and white wines, imported from France. It can be excellent, but the tropical heat is a good wine's worst enemy, and you sometimes happen upon a crate of bottles that has spent time sitting in the sun at the port. Urgh! The cheapest (and nastiest) is boxed (cask) wine for around 450 CFP for 1L; it's possible to find a good French bottle for about 1000 CFP and up. Restaurants enjoy a tax reduction on alcohol, which makes it affordable (allow 1500 to 3000 CFP for a bottle).

After several years of research, Vin de Tahiti, Domaine Dominique Auroy has begun producing red, rosé and white wines from grapes grown on the atoll of Rangiroa (see p179). The result is a highly unusual wine that Dominique Auroy describes as having subtle flavours of *metua pua*, a Tahitian fern. Bottles are available in tourist boutiques for 4000 CFP and up.

The classic Tahitian holiday drink is the *maitai*, a yummy cocktail made with rum, fruit juices, coconut liqueur and, in some cases, Grand Marnier or Cointreau. This concoction is also available readymade as Tahiti Drink in 1L cartons. Go easy on it if you've had a long day in the sun.

Hinano, the fruit of the pandanus, was used in ancient times to make a fermented beverage – today it's the name of the local beer.

Alcohol is highly taxed and thus expensive in French Polynesia. Consider buying 2L (the maximum you're allowed to bring in to Tahiti) of your favourite booze at the duty free at your departure airport.

CELEBRATIONS

A Tahitian party – be it for a wedding, birthday, Christmas or just for the heck of it – is celebrated with copious amounts of food, drink and dancing. In general the food is cooked in a *hima'a* and the beer starts flowing early. The food never runs out and, unless it's a religious gathering, obscene amounts of alcohol are consumed. In smaller get-togethers the night fades to morning with the sounds of ukuleles and slurring vocals; at bigger celebrations there is usually a band that plays local hits while couples dance the Tahitian foxtrot.

WHERE TO EAT & DRINK

There is a wondrous array of restaurants on the island of Tahiti, where you can experience fine French cuisine, Vietnamese, even sushi, but the rest of French Polynesia has more limited options. The prices are fairly intimidating – expect to pay 1200 to 2000 CFP for a main in a midrange restaurant – but the food is very good. Most hotel restaurants host buffet and dance performances a few times a week, which usually cost around 8000 CFP. This may seem steep, but the dancers are generally of a very high standard, though the buffets can be hit or miss.

Cocktails in Tahiti by Richard Bondurant is a fun, picture-filled, drink recipe book that can help you re-create paradise via a martini glass once you get back home.

Quick Eats

A *snack* in French Polynesia is actually a little snack-bar-cum-café. These places are simple, cheap, and serve everything from sandwiches (made from French-style baguettes) and salads to *poisson cru* and meat or fish burgers.

For the cheapest, quickest fare with the most local clientele, head for a *roulotte* (mobile food van), with a kitchen inside and a fold-down counter along each side. The inventive use of eskies (coolers) allows the *roulottes* to whip up surprisingly good food in a flash. The nightly gathering of *roulottes* near the tourist office in Pape'ete is a real institution.

Self-Catering

Self-catering in French Polynesia can save you a lot of money; many budget and midrange places to stay have well-equipped kitchens. The Marché de Pape'ete (p84), in Pape'ete, is the heart and belly of French Polynesia. It opens at 5am, is laden with food from all the archipelagos and is great fun – but don't expect bargains. The best deals on fish, fruit and vegetables are found at roadside stalls found on most major islands.

Supermarkets of varying sizes are dotted around the islands. Some have dusty little collections of tins and packaged goods, while others, particularly those on Tahiti, Mo'orea and Ra'iatea, are very well equipped. The best supermarkets on Tahiti are the Carrefour chains (in Arue and Puna'auia). On other islands you're at the mercy of cargo-ship schedules.

European imports are heavily taxed, but a fresh baguette only costs about 50 CFP and a *pain au chocolat* (chocolate croissant) about 120 CFP.

VEGETARIANS & VEGANS

There are no vegetarian restaurants in French Polynesia, so self-catering is the best option. A few commonly served dishes like chow mein and salads can be tinkered with and made vegetarian but make it very clear to whoever is preparing the food just what it is that you don't want included.

EATING WITH KIDS

French Polynesian food is rarely spicy and, although children's portions are virtually unheard of, it's easy to find kid-friendly dishes on most menus. Don't expect to find booster seats or high chairs but do expect a welcoming atmosphere in most eateries. Tahitian food is traditionally eaten with the fingers; kids will love being able to really dig into dishes like *chevrettes*, *brochettes* (sheesh kebabs of meat or fish) or *poisson cru*. Western-style food is also available at most places.

For toddlers and babies, self-catering might be a simpler choice: jarred baby food and infant formula can be found even in remote areas. Polynesians love children and you should not be afraid to ask for assistance in finding certain foods or cooking facilities.

HABITS & CUSTOMS

Eating is central to both family and social life in French Polynesia. French, Tahitian and Chinese people converge on the concept of happiness through long meals in good company. In homes, lunch is usually a large meal while dinner is a bit lighter; in restaurants both lunch and dinner are copious although it's easier to eat light at lunch. Breakfast is classically French – baguettes with butter and jam served with coffee – but it's possible to find omelettes, fish and fruit on the menu in restaurants that open for breakfast. As in France, the bill is never brought to the table until it is asked for.

All restaurants in French Polynesia officially became nonsmoking areas in 2008 but you still might encounter the occasional cringer lighting up as if they owned the place.

Each edition of the *Saveur* magazine series, found in Tahitian bookshops, focuses on specific Polynesian ingredients like fish, local vegetables or poultry.

The chickens that you see everywhere don't belong to anyone and are rarely eaten. They are appreciated, though, for eating centipedes and other pesky insects.

DOS & DON'TS

■ Do eat Tahitian food with your fingers.

■ Do use a knife and fork for Western food.

■ Do greet men with a handshake and women with a kiss on each cheek.

■ Do take your shoes off before entering anyone's home.

■ Do take your own (large) bowl when ordering takeaway – you'll be given more food and use less plastic.

■ Don't tip unless there is a sign asking you to or the service was exceptional.

■ Don't forget to smile – it goes a long way in French Polynesia!

EAT YOUR WORDS
Useful Phrases

A table for two, please.

Une table pour deux, s'il vous plaît. · · · · · · · oon ta·bler poor der seel voo play

Do you have an English menu?

Est ce que vous avez un menu en anglais? · · · es·ker voo a·vay um mer·new on ong·glay

What's the speciality here?

Quelle est la spécialité ici? · · · · · · · · · · · kel ay la spay·sya·lee·tay ees·ee

I don't eat ...	*Je ne mange pas de ...*	zher ner monzh pa de ...
dairy produce	*produits laitiers*	pro·dwee lay·tyay
fish	*poisson*	pwa·son
meat	*viande*	vyond
pork	*porc*	por
poultry	*volaille*	la vo·lai
seafood	*fruits de mer*	frwee der mair

I'd like ...

Je voudrais ... · · · · · · · · · · · · · · · · · · zher voo·dray ...

The bill, please.

L'addition, s'il vous plaît. · · · · · · · · · · · la·dee·syo seel voo play

Thank you, the meal was excellent.

Merci, le repas était excellent. · · · · · · · · mair·see ler ray·pa e·tay ek·say·lon

Menu Decoder

brochette	bro·shet	sheesh kebab of beef heart, beef or fish
carpacio du thon	kar·pa·syo doo tonn	thinly sliced sashimi: quality raw tuna with a sprinkling of olive oil, salt and pepper and capers
casse-croûte	kas kroot	sandwich on a French-style baguette
chevrettes/crevettes	shay·vret/kray·vet	freshwater shrimp/freshwater prawns
chow mein	chow men	Chinese wheat noodles with carrot, cabbage, Chinese greens and chicken
ma'a tinito	ma te·nee·to	macaroni, red beans, rice vermicelli, Chinese greens and pork
nem	nem	spring rolls
poisson cru	pwa·son kroo	raw fish marinated in lemon then doused in coconut milk and mixed with tomato and cucumber
poulet citron	poo·lay see tron	battered and fried chicken with a lemony Chinese sauce
sashimi	sa·shee·mee	thinly sliced raw tuna served with a sauce
steak frites	stek freet	steak and chips
tartar du thon	tar·tair doo tonn	chopped raw tuna mixed with olive oil and a variety of seasonings and/or onion

Food Glossary

agneau	a·nyo	lamb
bière	bee·yair	beer
bœuf	berf	beef
café	ka·fay	coffee
café au lait	ka·fay o lay	coffee with milk
citron	see·tron	lemon
coco	ko·ko	coconut
eau	o	water
eau en bouteille	o om boo·tay	bottled water
jus de fruit	zhew der frwee	fruit juice
jus de fruit frais	zhew der frwee fray	fresh fruit juice
frit(e)	freet	fried
frites	freet	chips
glace	glas	ice cream
grillé(e)	gree·yay	grilled
lait	lay	milk
legumes	lay·gewm	vegetables
œuf	erf	egg
pâtes	pat	pasta
poisson	pwa·son	fish
poulet	poo·lay	chicken
riz	ree	rice
viande	vyond	meat
vin	vun	wine

Environment

It's impossible to talk about the French Polynesian landscape without sounding clichéd. From the lush slopes of the high islands, to the white-sand, palm-ruffled atolls with lagoons bluer than Billie Holiday, this is the place that stereotypic ideals of paradise come from.

THE LAND
Roughly halfway between Australia and California, the 118 islands of French Polynesia are scattered over an expanse of the Pacific Ocean stretching more than 2000km – an area about the size of Western Europe. Still, the islands and atolls make up a total land mass of barely 3500 sq km (less than one-third the size of the US state of Connecticut). Five archipelagos, the Society, Tuamotu, Marquesas, Austral and Gambier, divide the country into distinct geological and cultural areas.

High islands – think Tahiti, Mo'orea or Bora Bora – are essentially mountains rising out of the ocean that are often encircled by a barrier reef. A protected, shallow lagoon with that flashy blue colour of postcards and brochure fame is formed by the reef; beyond is the open ocean that fades to a deep, clear indigo.

The reefs are usually pierced by passes (waterways between the lagoon and ocean), some of which are wide and deep enough for boats to go through. The high islands often have ancient volcano craters, sharp peaks, knife-edged ridges and plateaux.

An atoll is not an island at all, but a ring of very old barrier reef that surrounds a now-sunken high island. Over time the reef was built up, eventually a few plants started to grow and mini-islands called *motu* were formed. These *motu,* which encircle the lagoon, reach a maximum height of 6m and are usually covered in low bushes and coconut palms. Most atolls are made up of any number of these rocky or sandy *motu,* which are separated by shallow *hoa* (channels) that link the inner lagoon to the ocean. Most atolls have at least one *hoa* that is deep enough for boats to pass through, in which case it is called a pass.

The Matarai'i I Ni'a on 20 November marks the beginning of the Polynesian season of abundance. The Matarii I Raro on 18 May is the beginning of the dry season.

WILDLIFE
The bulk of the Pacific's flora and fauna originated in Asia/Melanesia and spread east; the further east you travel, the less varied it becomes and French Polynesia is nearly as far in that direction as you can get. Don't come looking for wildlife safaris here unless they're underwater.

In French, *Plantes Utiles de Polynesie: Raau Tahiti* by Paul Petard is a collection of scientific and historical analyses of over 220 medicinal plants found throughout French Polynesia.

Land Animals
Basically, any fauna that couldn't swim, float or fly to French Polynesia has been introduced. The first Polynesians, knowing they would be settling new lands, brought pigs, chickens and dogs in their canoes. They also brought geckos and the small Polynesian rat, probably as stowaways. (The modern rat arrived with European explorers after stowing away on their ships.) The gecko, a small harmless, translucent lizard, remains Polynesia's most visible reptile. You'll often see it hovering just over the bed, hopefully about to munch a mosquito.

You'll surely see cockroaches, wasps and slow-moving millipedes. Mosquitos are an omnipresent nuisance and can transmit dengue fever when there are outbreaks. *Nono* (see the boxed text, p207) are particularly fierce and, although they are not disease carriers, their bites itch more and last longer than those of a mosquito – at least for most people. The only real land shark is the centipede, which can grow up to 20cm long, moves like lightning and has venom-injecting fangs that can cause swelling, bruising and pain for several hours. When in doubt, it's a good idea to shake out towels, clothes and shoes just in case.

The endemic bird life of French Polynesia is as fragile as it is fabulous. Of the 29 land species, 12 are introduced and have driven many local species to near extinction. The Society de Ornithology de Polynesie (SOP Manu) has embarked on a number of strategies to conserve and increase remaining populations. The 27 species of sea birds, including terns, noddies, frigates and boobies, make French Polynesia one of the richest tropical areas for marine species. The number of *kaveka* (sooty terns) nesting on 'Ua Huka has been estimated at nearly one million. In the Tuamotus, each atoll hosts a 'bird island' nesting ground.

> For information about French Polynesia's bird life check out www.manu.pf, the official site of SOP Manu, the Tahitian organisation for the protection of bird species.

Sea Animals

Any dismay about the lack of animal diversity on land is quickly made up for by the quantity of underwater species – it's all here. Every nook of reef provides a hiding place or shelter for an animal or plant. Unfortunately this is an exceedingly fragile environment and it receives little enforced protection.

At the top of the food chain, sharks are found in healthy numbers throughout the islands. The blacktip and whitetip reef sharks are the most common and pose little danger to anyone not carrying a bloody or dying fish (as many local spearfishermen do). They are easily recognised by the white or black tip on their dorsal fins (hence the names). More aggressive and sometimes unnervingly curious, the grey reef shark is common in the Tuamotus. It's a powerful, streamlined shark that reaches about 2m in length. Large sleeper or nurse sharks, distinguished by their broad head and oversized dorsal fins and tail, look daunting but generally keep to themselves on the bottom of channels and sandy banks.

Other larger creatures you are likely to encounter are graceful, open-mouthed, filter-feeding manta rays; smaller, spotted leopard rays; and whip-tailed stingrays that hide on the sandy sea floor. Five of the seven species of sea turtle make their home in French Polynesia. The two you are most likely to see are the green and hawksbill turtles, which often come to feed in the flourishing lagoons. Overfishing, egg hunting and beach destruction have radically diminished turtle numbers and they are now considered a protected species. You should never agree to eat turtle meat, which is highly illegal, sometimes poisonous, but still considered a delicacy on all the islands.

> Whales migrate off the coasts of French Polynesian islands between July and October but dolphins can be sighted year-round.

Marine mammal species are no strangers to the waters of French Polynesia; one-third of Pacific species call this home for at least part of the year. During the months of July to October, humpback whales can be seen primarily off the shores of Tahiti, Mo'orea and Rurutu. There are actually at least 24 species of whale that pass through French Polynesia but startlingly few are ever observed. Dolphins can be seen year-round, especially spinner dolphins, which often swim in the lagoons. Electra dolphins are a major attraction in Nuku Hiva where they gather in groups of several hundred, a phenomenon seen nowhere else in the world.

Hundreds of species of fish in all colours, shapes and sizes flutter about the reefs. Hidden in the coral crevices of the shelf, moray eels are among the more impressive species, their half-open mouths edged with fangs. Blue, green and pink parrotfish scrape the coral with their powerful beak-like mouths and *roi* (grouper) and *maito* (surgeonfish) sluggishly cruise past schools of edgy needlefish and sergeant majors. *Mahi mahi* (dorado), bonito, wahoo and tuna are fished in the open sea and make pleasing and regular appearances on Tahitian menus.

You are less likely to see shellfish, which hide in crevices and feed at night, but there's a host of species to be seen. Lobsters, slipper lobsters and crabs are found on the outer slopes of reefs or the bottom of caves and cliffs. The black-lipped pearl oyster has a flattened round shell that is striated black and grey. Only the small muscle is edible, but, because they are more valuable for creating pearls, they are not frequently eaten; the scalloplike edible part is called *korori*. *Pahua* (giant clams) have brightly coloured, velvety-looking mantles, which they draw in when threatened. The outer edges of the shells are crinkled. Porcelain and cat-eye kauri are valued by collectors but shells are so scarce in French Polynesia that it is not advised to take any living shells.

The comedians of the islands are hermit crabs, which can be drawn out of their hiding places any time by the smallest morsel of discarded food. In the Tuamotus the enormous and impressively colourful *kaveu* (coconut crab) feeds at night and is prized for its coconut-flavoured flesh. *Tupa* (land crabs), which are found in all the islands, dig holes in sandy areas and have an uncanny penchant for getting squashed by cars.

There are few real dangers in French Polynesian waters, but there are some species to be aware of. Cone shells have a needlelike stinger that protrudes from the hole at the cone's bottom; it can be deadly poisonous but you'd have to pick one up by its lower opening to get pricked. Purple pencil urchins live in crevices by day and dot the reefs at night – it's always a good idea to watch your feet since the spikes can cause extreme pain if you step on them. Urinating on the wounds helps ease the pain. The very well camouflaged stone fish is even more of a hazard and is quite prolific on coral reefs and rocky areas; if you do get stung, apply heat immediately and head for the hospital. Wearing plastic, waterproof sandals provides the best protection.

Plants

The fertile volcanic soils of French Polynesia's high islands nourish a luxuriant array of fruit trees, ornamental flowers, ferns and shrubs. Before human habitation the variety of vegetation was limited to the seeds and spores that could travel by means of wind, sea or bird droppings. Polynesians brought *uru* (breadfruit), coconut, taro and bananas, and early missionaries introduced sugarcane, cotton, pineapples, citrus fruits, coffee, vegetables and other staples. Over the years botanists and enthusiasts have brought in various tropical plant species, which have thrived in the favourable climate. Today visitors will encounter all the sumptuousness of a tropical paradise: papayas, star fruit, mangos, avocados, guavas, pomelos and rambutan grow among birds of paradise, hibiscus and allamanda.

Tahitians spend an enormous amount of time tending their gardens, which are full of bougainvillea, frangipani and invariably the *tiare*, a small, white, highly fragrant gardenia that is the symbol of French Polynesia. The significance of this flower runs deep. It is the first thing visitors are offered on arrival at Faa'a airport, it is used in many traditional medicines, as a perfume and is the classic flower to string as a *hei* (a flower crown or necklace) or wear behind your ear, perfuming the wearer with the scent of Tahiti.

The *uru* tree was the lifeline of ancient islanders, who used every part of the tree: the bark made *tapa* (paperlike cloth), the trunk was dug out for canoes, the roots and leaves used for medicine and of course the fruit was the dietary staple. The trees are majestically tall with large, glossy, deep-green leaves; the fruit is light green, slightly bumpy and about the size of a large cantaloupe. Taro is the secondary staple. The root vegetable comes in

Guide des Poissons de Tahiti et ses Îles (in French) is an exceptionally comprehensive, photo-filled encyclopedia of all the fish of French Polynesia.

The Tahitian language has at least seven words for the coconut; each describes a different stage of the nut's maturity.

The *tiare* flower has between five and nine petals – those with the most petals are thought to bring good luck.

purple and yellow varieties that sprout large elephant-ear leaves; the leaves of yellow taro resemble spinach when cooked and this is called *fafa*.

The valleys and lowlands of high islands are dominated by wild *purau* trees, relatives of the hibiscus. These fast-growing trees with yellow flowers that turn red right before falling off the branch were once extremely important to the islanders for *tapa* and for medicines. Today the trees are seen as weeds and are inevitably cleared from habitated land.

The atolls are a stark contrast to the lush high islands. Made up primarily of sand and coral rock, the land lacks the minerals to support much vegetation. Coconut palms are what appear to dominate the landscape but these are in fact introduced. On closer inspection, an endemic shrub, the red-barked *miki miki*, outwits even the wily coconut and can be seen sprouting out of knobs of sand scarcely peeking out of the sea. Adding grace and much-needed shade to the atolls is the grand *kahaia* tree with its large glossy leaves and fragrant white flowers.

> To stop your dive mask from fogging up, rub a flower from a *purau* tree on the interior glass then rinse it lightly in salt water.

ENVIRONMENTAL ISSUES

The environmental repercussions of French nuclear testing are still hotly debated. The view that Moruroa and Fangataufa were fissured by tests and that radioactivity has been allowed to escape was confirmed in 1999 when the French government admitted, for the first time, the existence of cracks in the atolls' coral cones. An independent investigation into the radioactive levels of inhabited, surrounding islands and atolls was launched in early 2005. So far, some evidence has been found of low-level activity in certain areas of the Gambiers but long-ranging conclusive evidence has yet to come forth. Many people who worked on the atolls are suffering with cancer and are battling the French government who claim (in most cases) that all necessary safety precautions were taken during the nuclear testing and the cancers are not related to the test site work. See p38 for more information.

Atolls and high islands are ecologically fragile and easily susceptible to damage, but French Polynesia has been slow to implement policies for

> The island of Tahiti is powered entirely by hydroelectricity and many people in the Tuamotus rely on solar power. Unfortunately the other islands use gas-guzzling generators.

NUTS ABOUT NONI

The most talked about fruit in Polynesia is the *noni* (sometimes called *nono* – not to be confused with the insect common in the Marquesas). It has long been used in traditional medicine to boost the immune system, to aid digestion, to add lustre to skin and hair and to increase mental clarity, and since the mid-1990s it has enjoyed enormous success in the American market.

Following work done by an American researcher, who is reported to have highlighted its anti-ageing virtues, a network was put in place to supply the American market with *noni* juice. Large numbers of Polynesians abandoned traditional agricultural activities to devote themselves to the much more lucrative activity of growing *noni*, which thrives in the wild. The crop is puréed and processed by the Morinda company on Tahiti and then shipped off to the USA. Morinda holds exclusive marketing rights to its special way of processing the fruit. Due to the distribution system known as pyramid selling, the price of the product may be increased 100-fold. Unfortunately buying prices have plummeted and now farmers are returning to taro and copra production.

Several companies produce *noni* juice for the local market and you can find 1L bottles in most markets. If you catch a virus on the plane or come down with travellers' diarrhoea, grab a fresh bottle from the refrigerator section of nearly any food shop and drink half a glass twice a day. It tastes awful and smells worse but there are sweetened varieties available that come mixed with lime, honey, grape juice, aloe or ginger, which make it go down easier. From our experience, this stuff lives up to the hype – it really helps snuff out colds, flu and tummy troubles if taken at the first signs of sickness. There are also a few brands that don't require refrigeration if you want to bring some home.

RESPONSIBLE TOURISM

Brochures may continue to paint French Polynesia as an unspoilt destination, but the environmental impact of some 200,000 visitors a year – a similar figure to the entire population of French Polynesia – cannot be swept under the carpet forever.

Although much of the development is low-rise and local style – thus avoiding the concrete-and-glass horrors of Hawaii – safe waste disposal, the recycling of materials and the use of solar power have until recently been the concern of the minority. 'Green' hotels are still fairly rare but are slowly emerging. Among the more conventional places to stay, consider staying in a locally owned hotel or guesthouse rather than a foreign-owned one. Although the foreign-owned companies provide valuable employment opportunities for locals, the profits do not stay on local shores.

environmental protection. Tourism is the region's main resource and focuses almost entirely on the natural heritage of the region, so French Polynesia has a strong incentive to protect its environment. Despite a limited number of 'green' establishments that are springing up, and the rigorous requirements of public buildings and hotels to blend in with the landscape, pollution is nonetheless steadily chipping away at the picture of paradise.

Although there are many low-lying atolls in French Polynesia, the effects of climate change, including rising sea level, have so far been minimal. Higher water temperatures are one of the biggest threats to the health of the country's coral reefs and, during El Niño years in particular (1998 was notable), huge amounts of coral die affecting the entire ecosystem.

The site for the French Polynesian Coral Reefs Initiative, www.ifrecor.pf (in French), supplies info about biological and social issues related to coral reefs, as well as news about upcoming events.

Protection of Fauna

Marine reserves in French Polynesia are few: Scilly and Bellingshausen (remote islands in the Leeward group of Society Islands) and eight small areas within Mo'orea's lagoon are the only ones protected by the country itself. Fakarava and its surrounding atolls (Aratika, Toau, Kauehi, Niau, Raraka and Taiaro) are a Unesco biosphere reserve. The only terrestrial reserves are the Marquesan Nature Reserves, which include the remote uninhabited islands of Motu One, Hatutu, Eiao and Motane. Several species are protected and there are limits placed on the fishing of some fish and crustaceans, particularly lobsters. Unfortunately fish continue to be caught indiscriminately and shells are still collected for decorative purposes. Although turtles are highly protected, they continue to be poached for their meat and their shells, which are used as ornaments.

Diving

One of the best destinations on Planet Scuba, French Polynesia offers sea-soned and novice divers the full slate: jaw-dropping topography, gin-clear visibility, year-round warm waters, glittering blue seas, high-voltage drift dives, close encounters with sharks, humpback whales and dolphins, and even one-of-a-kind sites such as the famed Tiputa Pass or Garuae Pass. Add the unbeatable bonus of having idyllic backdrops as you travel to and from the sites, and you'll have a fair view of the picture.

DIVING CONDITIONS

There are regularly optimal diving conditions throughout the year, except when the *maraamu* (trade wind) blows, from June to August, which produces choppy seas. Outstanding visibility is the norm – it runs to 40m and more, except when it has rained for several days, which washes out the islands and clouds the sea with runoff. The lack of pollution is an added bonus. Current conditions vary a lot, from imperceptible to strong.

Water temperatures range from a low of 26°C to a high of 29°C on most islands. You won't need anything more than a thin neoprene wetsuit. The only exception is the Australs, where water temperatures drop as low as 22°C during the coolest months (June to August), so at this time of year a 3mm wetsuit is recommended.

For detailed information on fish life in French Polynesia, read *Poissons de Tahiti et ses Îles* (published by Au Vent des Îles, www .auventdesiles.pf), with full-colour photos and English translations of fish names.

DIVE SITES

From Rurutu in the Australs to Fakarava in the Tuamotus or Hiva Oa in the Marquesas, you'll be spoilt for choice. Just as the individual islands have their distinct personalities, so the dive sites have their own hallmarks. Just take your pick!

SOCIETY ISLANDS
Tahiti

Although less charismatic than other French Polynesian islands, Tahiti shouldn't be sneezed at, with about 20 lagoon and ocean sites between Arue and Pa'ea, plus the odd wreck.

Should you need to brush up your skills, the **Aquarium**, off Faa'a airport's runway, is a good start. Multihued tropicals flitting among coral boulders scattered on a sandy floor in less than 10m, as well as two minor wrecks (an old Cessna aircraft and a cargo boat), make this site exciting. In the same area, the **Cargo Ship** and the **Catalina** refer to a shipwreck and an aircraft wreck. Of particular interest is the *Catalina,* a twin-engine WWII flying boat that was scuttled in 1964. The 15m structure is in fine condition, its right wing tip resting on the seabed at 20m. Overall there's nothing spectacular but it's very scenic.

Just outside the reef at Puna'auia, **St Etienne Drop-Off** is a perfect wall dive. Further south, don't miss the **Spring (La Source)**, a very atmospheric site featur-ing three towering coral mounts and a couple of freshwater springs bubbling up from the ocean floor. The **Turtles' Plateau** is another hot fave. As the name suggests, one or two curious turtles can be seen frolicking among divers. A pod of dolphins also frequents this site every morning. You'll see whitetip and blacktip sharks as well as Napoleons and moray eels at the **White Valley**, in about 20m.

On the north coast near Matavai Bay (Baie de Matavai), local divers swear by the **Faults of Arue**. This area features a good mix of gentle coral plateaus and steep drop-offs broken up by a series of fissures.

At the time of writing, there were no professional dive centres serving Tahiti Iti. See p77 for dive centres on Tahiti.

Mo'orea

A perfect introduction to more challenging dive sites in the Tuamotus, Mo'orea offers easy, relaxed diving, with a good balance of reef dives and shark dives. Most diving is focused at the entrances to Cook's Bay and Opunohu Bay, and off the northwestern corner of the island. Unlike those in neighbouring Tahiti, the reefs here do not drop off steeply, but slope gently away in a series of canyons and valleys. Sadly, corals are in a bad shape due to the crown-of-thorns starfish.

The **Tiki** has achieved cult status among shark lovers. Because of the site's long history of fish feeding, there are gangs of blacktip, grey and lemon sharks. **Opunohu Canyons/Eden Park** is famous for the many bulky lemon sharks (up to seven individuals) that regularly patrol the area, in about 20m.

Taotoi is another favourite, with a pleasant seascape. Watch for eagle rays passing through a nearby channel – up to a dozen can be seen gliding by if you're lucky.

Seasoned divers will enjoy the **Roses**. It features a vast expanse of *Montipora* coral that stretches as far as the eye can see. You might descend to 40m to hover over this gorgeous field for a closer look at the coral.

The dive centre based at the Sofitel Ia Ora uses different sites along the northeastern side of the island, including **Vaiare Pass** and **Temae**.

Sightings of wandering pods of dolphins are also frequently reported – the perfect end to any dive.

See p112 for dive centres on Mo'orea.

> A law was passed in 2006 to prohibit shark fishing and shark finning in French Polynesian waters.

Huahine

If you want relaxed diving, Huahine will appeal to you. Novice divers in particular will feel comfortable – the dive conditions are less challenging than anywhere else but still offer excellent fish action. There are some superb reef dives off Fare and near the airport, to the north of the island. A long-standing favourite, **Avapeihi (Fitii) Pass** is a five-minute boat ride from Fare. The highlight of the site is the dazzling aggregation of barracuda, snappers, trevallies and grey reef sharks. The best opportunity to spot predators is during an outgoing current, when they patrol the pass in search of drifting lagoon fish. The only drawback is the slightly reduced visibility, which averages about 20m.

> The only weak point of diving in French Polynesia is the lack of impressive wrecks.

SHARK FEEDING'S OUT, SMELLING'S IN

Shark feeding was a hugely popular activity at Mo'orea, Ra'iatea, Bora Bora and Manihi, but most dive centres have ceased doing it. 'The attitudes of divers have changed,' one dive instructor notes. 'Divers are now very nature-oriented and prefer to see sharks in their natural habitat, without any direct interaction with humans.' However, a number of dive instructors still use bait to guarantee shark sightings, but they don't feed them directly; the bait (usually tuna hunks) is put in a small cage that's placed on the sea floor to attract the sharks. At the end of the dive, the instructor releases the tuna hunks from the cage and the sharks swallow up the morsels. Though not completely environmentally friendly, this practice, locally called 'smelling', is much less controversial than shark feeding. If you're against it, do not hesitate to mention it to the dive operator.

DIVING IN TAHITI & FRENCH POLYNESIA

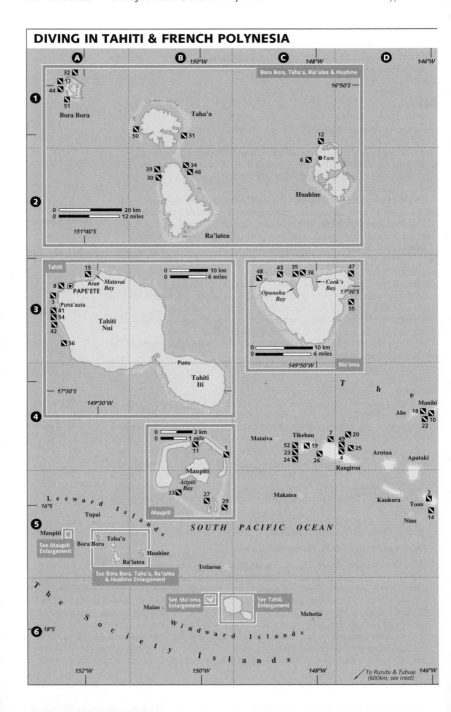

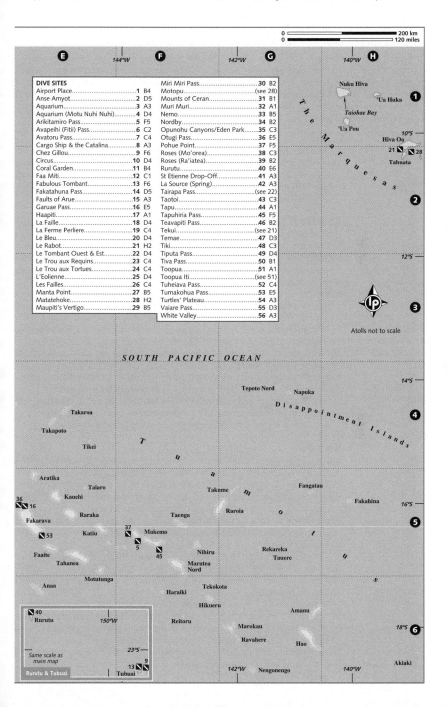

DIVE SITES

Airport Place	1	B4
Anse Amyot	2	D5
Aquarium	3	A3
Aquarium (Motu Nuhi Nuhi)	4	D4
Arikitamiro Pass	5	F5
Avapeihi (Fitii) Pass	6	C2
Avatoru Pass	7	C4
Cargo Ship & the Catalina	8	A3
Chez Gillou	9	F6
Circus	10	D4
Coral Garden	11	B4
Faa Miti	12	C1
Fabulous Tombant	13	F6
Fakatahuna Pass	14	D5
Faults of Arue	15	A3
Garuae Pass	16	E5
Haapiti	17	A1
La Faille	18	D4
La Ferme Perliere	19	C4
Le Bleu	20	D4
Le Rabot	21	H2
Le Tombant Ouest & Est	22	D4
Le Trou aux Requins	23	C4
Le Trou aux Tortues	24	C4
L'Eolienne	25	D4
Les Failles	26	C4
Manta Point	27	B5
Matatehoke	28	H2
Maupiti's Vertigo	29	B5
Miri Miri Pass	30	B2
Motopu	(see 28)	
Mounts of Ceran	31	B1
Muri Muri	32	A1
Nemo	33	B5
Nordby	34	B2
Opunohu Canyons/Eden Park	35	C3
Otugi Pass	36	E5
Pohue Point	37	F5
Roses (Mo'orea)	38	C3
Roses (Ra'iatea)	39	B2
Rurutu	40	E6
St Etienne Drop-Off	41	A3
La Source (Spring)	42	A3
Tairapa Pass	(see 22)	
Taotoi	43	C3
Tapu	44	A1
Tapuhiria Pass	45	F5
Teavapiti Pass	46	B2
Tekui	(see 21)	
Temae	47	D3
Tiki	48	C3
Tiputa Pass	49	D4
Tiva Pass	50	B1
Toopua	51	A1
Toopua Iti	(see 51)	
Tuheiava Pass	52	C4
Tumakohua Pass	53	E5
Turtles' Plateau	54	A3
Vaiare Pass	55	D3
White Valley	56	A3

REEFS UNDER THREAT: CROWN-OF-THORNS STARFISH INFESTATION

Several waves of the destructive crown-of-thorns starfish have caused extensive damage to many coral reefs in French Polynesia, especially in the Society Islands. This coral-eating starfish leaves only the white skeletons of coral behind them. 'We do our best to keep them at bay', says one dive master. 'We pick them up or we inject a poison in their body but, short of natural predators, it's hard to eradicate them.' Experts think that autoregulation could help diminish the population in the forthcoming years.

Another highlight, **Faa Miti**, just before the airstrip, features a series of atmospheric coral boulders laced with sand valleys at around 25m. Keep your eyes peeled for moray eels hiding in the recesses, stingrays buried in the sand, soldierfish, perch, surgeonfish and several species of butterflyfish.

See p129 for dive centres on Huahine.

Ra'iatea & Taha'a

One of the star attractions in Ra'iatea is the **Nordby**, the only real wreck dive in French Polynesia. She's easily accessible, right off the Raiatea Pearl Resort Hawaiki Nui, lying on her side on a sandy bottom, between 18m and 29m. This 50m vessel sank in August 1900 after a storm drove her ashore. She is relatively well preserved and can easily be penetrated. Look for the resident fish that hide in the darker parts, including groupers, soldierfish, Moorish idols, lionfish, a couple of moray eels and crustaceans. The *Nordby* is also encrusted with soft and hard species of coral. Visibility is not the strong point of this dive.

The destructive crown-of-thorns starfish is called *taramea* in Tahitian.

Teavapiti Pass is a must. As in all passes in French Polynesia, a strong tidal current runs through it, providing food for the little guys at the bottom of the food chain, who, in turn, attract middle- and upper-chain critters. Off the western coast, **Miri Miri Pass** has lots of fish action and delicate bunches of purple *Distichopora* coral. Seasoned divers will enjoy the **Roses**. At about 40m, the seabed is blanketed with gorgeous *Montipora* coral formations.

Off Taha'a, renowned sites include the **Mounts of Ceran** and the **Tiva Pass**, with a superb underwater terrain and a fine cast of reef fish and pelagics.

For dive centres on Ra'iatea and Taha'a, see p139 and p146.

Bora Bora

Surprisingly, there are only four to five sites that are regularly offered on this magical island, which means that some sites can feel a bit crowded.

Tapu is an exciting spot, although it tends to be pretty congested these days by hordes of snorkellers and divers. Sharks are the major attraction – a result of regular fish feeding. Apart from blacktip reef sharks, you'll certainly come across massive lemon sharks, usually found at around 25m. The reef is gently sloping and is studded with healthy coral formations that play host to a smorgasbord of reef species.

South of Teavanui Pass, **Toopua** and **Toopua Iti** are also well-regarded dive sites. Enjoy the channel where you can spot eagle rays, or explore the area's varied topography, with numerous canyons, gullies, corridors and swim-throughs.

In the mood for a thrill-packed dive? Ask for **Muri Muri**, also known as the White Valley, at the northern apex of the ring of islets encircling Bora Bora. Strong currents and regular feedings in the past ensure a respectable crowd of sharks, as well as trevallies, tuna and turtles. In the same area as Muri Muri, **Haapiti** is a relaxed dive along a sloping reef, with regular sightings of lemon sharks and blacktip reef sharks.

See p155 for dive centres on Bora Bora.

Maupiti

The novelty factor is Maupiti's main trump card. Diving started in 2008. Pure joy for divers of all levels: there are some truly amazing dive sites just a sandal shuffle away. Maupiti's signature dive is the aptly named **Manta Point**, in the lagoon. This cleaning station is visited by manta rays; small fish come out of the coral heads to scour the mantas of parasites, in less than 6m – thrilling!

Although the manta experience is the true clincher, you'll also find superb reef and wall dives along the east side of the island. For sheer wall diving, **Maupiti's Vertigo** is hard to rival. Another recommended site is **Airport Place**, near the airport *motu* (islet), where a sloping reef riddled with small chasms is shelter to lots of small species, along with the occasional pelagics, including barracudas and sharks.

In the lagoon, **Nemo** is an easy site, with coral pinnacles scattered over a sandy floor in less than 6m – the perfect place for beginners. Novice divers will also feel comfortable at the **Coral Garden**, with copious fish life and pinnacles blanketed in corals, a fin's stroke from Fare Paeao – Chez Jeanine.

There's no diving in Maupiti's single pass because the currents are too tricky to handle. At times, the dive boat can't exit the lagoon due to the large swells.

See p169 for the dive centre on Maupiti.

A manta ray cleaning station is the equivalent of a skin-care treatment for these majestic creatures.

THE TUAMOTUS
Rangiroa

Rangiroa is the stuff of legend, and one of the most charismatic dive areas in the South Pacific. It's brimming with adrenaline-pumping dive sites, and opportunities to approach big stuff just offshore. The weak points include the lack of diversity in terms of dive sites (just four sites are regularly offered by local dive centres) and the rather dull coral formations. But you don't come here for corals or reef species, you come here to see Mr Big!

With its amazing drift dives and dense concentration of pelagics, **Tiputa Pass** is almost a spiritual experience. Incredible rides are guaranteed every time, as are bewildering numbers of grey reef sharks at the entrance of the pass. Eagle rays, manta rays, dolphins, tuna, trevallies and hammerheads are also regularly seen. By outgoing current, **L'Eolienne**, along the outer reef, is regularly scheduled. **Avatoru Pass** is another not-to-be-missed site, with regular sightings of manta rays, as well as a few intimidating silvertips that are attracted by bait brought by the dive instructors. The **Aquarium**, located at Motu Nuhi Nuhi – a coral islet that stretches across Tiputa Pass

---

THE FIRST TIME

You've always fancied venturing underwater on a scuba dive? Now's your chance. French Polynesia is a perfect starting point for new divers, as the warm, turquoise water in the shallow lagoons is a forgiving training environment. Most resorts offer courses for beginners and employ experienced instructors, most of them competent in English.

Just about anyone in reasonably good health can sign up for an introductory dive (*baptême* in French), including children aged eight and over. It typically takes place in shallow (3m to 5m) water and lasts about 30 minutes. You're escorted by a divemaster.

If you choose to enrol in an Open Water course while in French Polynesia, count on it taking about three days, including classroom lectures and open-water training. Another option is to complete the classroom and pool sessions at home and perform the required Open Water dives in a PADI- or SSI-affiliated dive centre in French Polynesia. Once you're certified, your C-card is valid permanently and recognised all over the world. The greatest variety of instruction is found in the Society Islands.

THE BIG BLUE: INTERVIEW WITH ERIC LE BORGNE

Eric Le Borgne is a dive instructor and an expert on marine life in French Polynesia. He has dived numerous places across the world, but says that 'French Polynesia has no equivalent because big species, such as sharks, manta rays, turtles, barracudas and dolphins, are almost guaranteed, sometimes in one single dive. And most sites are suitable for novice divers. My favourite dive site is Tiputa Pass in Rangiroa. It's like visiting an underwater safari park. It's superior to Cocos Island in Costa Rica or the Galapagos because it's so easy to get to the site – it's only a five-minute boat ride.'

---

just inside the lagoon – is a favourite for novice divers, with a jumble of coral pinnacles providing a haven for a vast array of small critters in less than 10m.

And there's **Le Bleu**. Some dive centres take divers out into the open ocean. Then divers are positioned in about 15m of water, in the blue, while bait in a small cage is lowered in the midwater, attracting sharks from the depths. Thrilling!

See p180 for dive centres on Rangiroa.

Tikehau

Although it's less charismatic than neighbouring Rangiroa, Tikehau has its fair share of underwater delights and deserves attention for offering less-crowded dive sites. Most dives take place in or around **Tuheiava Pass**, 30 minutes by boat from Tuherahera village. Grey sharks, barracudas, trevallies and the usual reef species regularly cruise by. South of the pass you'll enjoy steep drop-offs at **Le Trou aux Requins** and **Le Trou aux Tortues**. Le Trou aux Requins features a tunnel that descends well into the reef; the entrance is at 57m, but you don't need to go that deep to see a congregation of sharks that usually hang around the entrance. The reef is peppered with fissures, ledges and overhangs.

The only site inside the lagoon is **La Ferme Perliere** (The Pearl Farm). It features a cleaning station where manta rays come to get scoured of parasites by little cleaner wrasses. Divers who remain quiet and don't touch or swim after the mantas (usually three to five individuals) are often able to observe this ritual up close, despite poor visibility.

See p189 for dive centres on Tikehau.

Manihi

Two live-aboards operate in French Polynesia: Aqua Polynésie (www.aquatiki .com) and Archipels Croisières (www.archipels .com). Both offer various trips in the Tuamotus and the Society Islands.

Some 175km northeast of Rangiroa, Manihi has only one pass, **Tairapa Pass**, with dive sites around it. With an outgoing current, you can dive the western exit of the pass at a place named **Le Tombant Ouest** or the eastern exit at **Le Tombant Est**, which both feature prolific fish life, including a few sharks, trevallies, barracudas and sea bream. Every year in May and June, masses of groupers come to breed here. When the tide is incoming, you start your dive with a brief exploration of Le Tombant Ouest or Le Tombant Est before letting yourself get carried by the current into the pass. Take time to explore the undercuts housing soldierfish, groupers and white-tip sharks. Manihi's most stunning site is the **Circus**, which refers to an area in the lagoon at the exit of the pass. Visibility doesn't exceed 15 metres, but this site is famous for the regular manta-ray encounters in less than 20m of water. Large boulders of dead coral scattered on a sandy floor serve as cleaner stations for these majestic giants. **La Faille** features a large fissure in the reef north of the pass. Fish feeding in Manihi usually takes place here.

See p193 for the dive centre on Manihi.

Fakarava

A 40-minute plane hop from Rangiroa, Fakarava is one of the most fascinating atolls in the Tuamotus, with a true sense of wilderness and frontier diving. There are only two dive areas, Garuae Pass at the northern end of the atoll and Tumakohua Pass at the southern end. Fakarava shares the same characteristics as Rangiroa, with the added appeal of much healthier coral formations. Pelagics are a bit less commonly encountered than in Rangiroa, though.

For atmosphere and fish action, the iconic **Garuae Pass** is hard to beat. Swimming through the intense cobalt blue *(moana)* water towards the entrance of this gigantic pass is an unsurpassable experience. Expect to come across hunting sharks, numerous reef fishes and, if you're lucky, manta rays. The dive usually finishes at Ali Baba Cavern, a large coral basin at 15m, replete with schooling fish. When the tide is going out, you dive along the outer reef, away from the current. Here you can find some really healthy coral gardens.

At the southern end of the atoll, the beauty of the **Tumakohua Pass** can bring tears to the eyes. At the entrance of the pass, you'll see a profusion of small and large reef fish, including bigeyes and marbled groupers (they breed here in July). Dozens of grey reef sharks (we counted 150 individuals on one single dive!) regularly pass by the right side of the pass, at 28m. Other attractions include white-sand gullies, where white-tip sharks usually lie, as well as healthy coral formations in the shallows at the end of the dive.

See p186 for dive centres on Fakarava.

Go to www.polynesia-diving.com for more information.

Toau

Toau is wilderness at its best. This atoll is almost uninhabited and absolutely pristine. There's no infrastructure but it's accessible from neighbouring Fakarava atoll. Fakarava's dive centres (p186) organise day trips there. Don't miss the opportunity to sample some sensational dives in the two fish-filled passes, **Fakatahuna Pass** and **Otugi Pass**. The former is accessible to all levels, while the latter is only suitable for advanced divers because of tricky currents.

Be sure to bookmark **Anse Amyot**, at the other side of the atoll, which is regarded as the Tuamotus' most spectacular wall dive, with several amphitheatre-shaped drop-offs that tumble to the abyss. Fish life is fairly poor, but it doesn't matter; it's the seascape that's the pull here.

Makemo

Makemo is still a secret, word-of-mouth destination for divers. If you venture this far in the central Tuamotus, you'll be rewarded with pristine sites, such as **Arikitamiro Pass**, a five-minute boat ride from the village. Sharks, Napoleon

---

RESPONSIBLE DIVING

The French Polynesian islands and atolls are ecologically vulnerable. By following these guidelines while diving, you can help preserve the ecology and beauty of the reefs:

- Encourage dive operators in their efforts to establish permanent moorings at appropriate dive sites.
- Practise and maintain proper buoyancy control.
- Avoid touching living marine organisms with your body and equipment.
- Take great care in underwater caves, as your air bubbles can damage fragile organisms.
- Minimise your disturbance of marine animals.
- Take home all your trash and any litter you may find as well.
- Never stand on corals, even if they look solid and robust.

wrasses, barracuda, tuna, groupers and the whole gamut of tropicals can be spotted here. As if that wasn't enough, the reef is perforated with canyons and swimthroughs and the corals are in good condition. The second pass, **Tapuhiria Pass**, is well worth the 90-minute boat ride from the village, with lots of fish action during tidal changes and a surreal atmosphere due to the remoteness of the site. **Pohue Point** is a virgin tract of reef about 45 minutes from the dive centre. It's overgrown with corals and has loads of medium and small fish. Tapuhiria Pass and Pohue Point are not dived very often, though, because of their remoteness.

See p196 for the dive centre on Makemo.

THE MARQUESAS

A two-hour flight from Rangiroa, the Marquesas open up a whole new world of diving. The main highlight is the dramatic seascape, with numerous drop-offs, caverns, arches and ledges, giving the sites a peculiarly sculpted look and an eerie atmosphere. To top it all off, the environment is still unspoiled. However, don't expect gin-clear waters. Since the Marquesas are devoid of any protective barrier reefs, the water is thick with plankton and visibility doesn't exceed 10m to 15m. You should also be prepared to cope with sometimes-difficult conditions to get to the sites.

'The main highlight of the Marquesas is the dramatic seascape, with numerous drop-offs, caverns, arches and ledges'

Nuku Hiva

Nuku Hiva's main claim to fame is the melon-headed whales *(Peponocephala electra)* that gather seemingly every day off the east coast. You don't dive with them, but you can snorkel with these graceful creatures – sheer delight, but keep in mind that the encounter cannot be guaranteed. See p205.

Sadly, diving is no longer available on Nuku Hiva. The local dive centre is open to TV crews and professionals only.

Hiva Oa

Here you can expect the unexpected. Most dive sites are located at the bottom of basaltic cliffs, at the southwestern part of the island. There are some protected bays and coves that are suitable for all levels of proficiency. **Le Rabot** is an underwater archaeological site, with dozens of old stone anchors lying on the seafloor, all encrusted with coral. The site was discovered by archaeologists in 2006. It also features an arch in about 25m and lots of reef species that flutter about big boulders. At **Tekui**, near Le Rabot, cameo appearances by manta rays spice up the diving.

The local dive centre also organises trips to Tahuata, across the Bordelais Canal. **Matatehoke** is famous for its dramatic seascape (boulders and a cascading drop-off) while **Motopu** refers to an exposed rocky promontory that acts as a magnet for predators (for advanced divers only).

See p221 for the dive centre on Hiva Oa.

THE AUSTRALS

The Australs are diveable year-round but bear in mind that water temperatures are noticeably cooler than anywhere else in French Polynesia – they can drop to about 22°C in July and August.

Rurutu

Rurutu is one of the most dependable locations in the world for close encounters with whales. From mid-July to October, several whales congregate around the island. Over the past decade or so, Raie Manta Club, one of the best-known dive operations in French Polynesia, has developed a program that allows snorkellers a reliable way to safely approach these behemoths.

HITTING THE UNDERWATER JACKPOT

If you're after something different, French Polynesia has a repertoire of once-in-a-lifetime experiences that will seduce even the most weathered divers.

Where to watch whales & dolphins?

The highlight of diving in Rurutu (Australs) is the humpback whales that come to the area to reproduce, calve and nurse from July to October. Unlike other popular whale-watching spots in the world, Rurutu still offers a wild experience. Under the guidance of a well-trained divemaster, snorkellers can actually get surprisingly close to these gentle giants. Unforgettable!

In Nuku Hiva (Marquesas) you'll have the unique opportunity to snorkel with melon-headed whales, a rare species of whales that look like oversized dolphins. They gather daily on the east side of the island. Tahiti, Mo'orea, Maupiti and Tubuai are also great spots to snorkel with whales. On Rangiroa, dolphins are regularly seen frolicking with divers in Tiputa Pass.

Where to get up close & personal with sharks?

If you're after close encounters with toothy critters, French Polynesia is the right place. Shark sightings are virtually guaranteed on any dive at Mo'orea, Huahine, Ra'iatea, Bora Bora, Rangiroa, Tikehau, Manihi, Makemo, Fakarava and Hiva Oa. In the Society Islands, sightings mostly consist of lemon sharks, blacktip reef sharks and grey sharks; in the Tuamotus, all kinds of sharks can be encountered, including tiger sharks. The Marquesas are famous for hammerhead sightings, though overfishing has taken its toll over the last few years.

Where to experience drift dives?

Drifting with the current is part and parcel of the dive experience in many of the sites in the Tuamotus. As the tide rises, enormous volumes of ocean water gush through the openings of the barrier reef (known as passes) to the lagoon, forming bottlenecks and creating strong currents. Outside the pass, divers drop into the flow and are sucked into the pass, surrounded by a procession of fish – a truly memorable experience. Make a beeline for Rangiroa, Fakarava, Toau, Manihi and Tikehau.

Where to swim or dive with manta rays?

French Polynesia is one of the best manta destinations in the world. They can easily be spotted in the passes of the Tuamotus and the Society Islands, as well as off the craggy shores of the Marquesas. But nothing beats the concentration of manta rays visiting cleaning stations where small fish come out of the coral heads to pluck parasites and dead skin cells off the mantas – a unique sight. Mantas stack or hover 'in line' to benefit from the services cleaner wrasses provide. Don't miss the cleaning stations on Maupiti, Tikehau and Manihi.

It's an ideal place because the fringing reef means that the whales come very close to the shore. Few experiences can compare with swimming with humpback whales in the open ocean.

During the rest of the year, the local dive centre offers classic dives near the passes.

See p230 for the dive centre on Rurutu.

Tubuai

This off-the-beaten-track island is a true gem with numerous untouched sites for those willing to venture away from the tourist areas. Another draw is the atmosphere: there's a true sense of eeriness and you'll have the sites to yourself. What makes the diving here so unique is the astounding quality of the coral (no crown-of-thorns starfish here!), the stellar visibility, the unique shades of blue (they are 'colder' than in other archipelagos) and the fairy-tale seascape, with lots of sandy canyons and convoluted coral pinnacles. The weak point is marine life, which is fairly limited.

DIVING & FLYING

Most divers who go to French Polynesia get there by plane. While it's fine to dive soon *after* flying, it's important to remember that your last dive should be completed at least 12 hours (some experts advise 24 hours) before your flight, to minimise the risk of residual nitrogen in the blood that can cause decompression injury. Careful attention to flight times is necessary in French Polynesia because so much of the interisland transportation is by air.

As in Rurutu, humpback whales also make regular appearances off the island from mid-July to October. It's pretty common to spot them during the boat rides to get to the dive sites.

There are about five dive sites, scattered off the northern section of the reef. A few favourites include **Chez Gillou**, with superb coral formations interspersed with sandy valleys, and the **Fabulous Tombant**, which refers to a drop-off peppered with chasms, small caves and chimneys. All sites are accessible to novice divers.

See p233 for the dive centre on Tubuai.

DIVE CENTRES

FACILITIES & SERVICES

There are about 30 professional dive centres in French Polynesia. All of them are affiliated to one or more internationally recognised certifying agencies (PADI, NAUI, CMAS, SSI). They offer a whole range of services and products, such as introductory dives (for children aged eight years and over, and adults), night dives, exploratory dives and certification programs. In general, you can expect well-maintained equipment, well-equipped facilities and friendly, knowledgeable staff members who can speak English. But like a hotel or a restaurant, each diving centre has its own style. On islands with several centres, do your research and opt for the one that best suits your expectations.

Dive centres are open year-round, most of them every day. All are land-based and many of them are attached to a hotel. They typically offer two to four dives a day. It's a good idea to book at least a day in advance.

Diving in French Polynesia is fairly expensive but there are multidive packages, which come much cheaper. Topdive dive centres have their own package that can be used in Tahiti, Mo'orea, Bora Bora and Fakarava.

Prices include equipment rental, so you don't need to bring all your gear.

Generally, dive operations (except for those on Tahiti) offer free pick-ups from your accommodation. Almost all dive centres accept credit cards.

There's one recompression chamber in Pape'ete. For more information on diving-related health issues, see p268.

DOCUMENTS

If you're a certified diver, bring your C-card; it's a good idea to have your dive logbook with you as well. Centres welcome certification from any training agency (CMAS, PADI, NAUI, SSI), but may ask you to do a checkout dive.

Divers with a C-card get a 15kg allowance on Air Tahiti flights.

HOW MUCH?

Introductory dive or single dive: 6000 CFP to 8500 CFP (including gear)

Open Water certification course: about 50,000 CFP

Tahiti

This probably isn't the island whose photograph was on your holiday brochure. No, there aren't any sweeping white-sand beaches, and vistas over a neon-blue lagoon are few and far between. Yet this is the heart of French Polynesia and it would be a shame to bypass the waterfall-laden, shadowy mountains, unpretentiously beautiful black-sand beaches and distinctly Polynesian buzz that make Tahiti a gem in its own right. Many people immediately hightail it out of Tahiti for the white-sand bliss of Mo'orea or Bora Bora so that ironically, the most accessible and well-known island of French Polynesia remains more off the beaten track than its far-flung sisters.

The island is very much centred on Pape'ete, the pint-sized chaotic capital with its traffic jams and smells of flowers, sweat and salt air. To islanders addicted to the city pace of life, this is the only place to be and they lap up the gritty nightlife, cinemas, music and endless array of food on hand.

While visiting Pape'ete is a must, it's the outdoor action outside the city and cultural offerings that woo visitors to extend their stay. Hike through archaeological sites, up never-ending river valleys and past coastlines dotted with wild passionfruit. In July catch the country's most spectacular festival, the percussion and dance-heavy Heiva, and from July to October go whale-watching with far fewer tourists than you'll find on Mo'orea. Year-round on Tahiti Iti there's a chance there will be big waves at Teahupoo and you can hire a boat to watch pro surfers tackle the break's cavernous tube up close.

HIGHLIGHTS

- Canyoning or hiking in the divinely lush and craggy interior inland from **Papenoo** (p77)
- Grabbing an ice-cold coconut to sip while perusing the colourful **Marché de Pape'ete** (p84)
- Watching the best of the best shake their hips and waggle their knees at the Heiva festival's **dance competitions** (p89) in July
- Taking a boat excursion past the road's end at **Teahupoo** (p104) to visit the remote and wild Fenua Aihere
- Dancing the night away with locals, surfers, sailors and transvestites in Pape'ete's rocking **nightclubs** (p93)

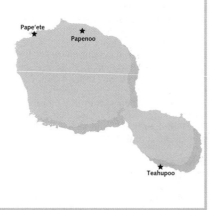

- POPULATION: 169,624
- AREA: 1045 SQ KM

TAHITI

History

Tahiti was not the first of the Society Islands to be populated in the Great Polynesian Migrations. Legends have the first settlers arriving in Tahiti from Ra'iatea, which was the most politically important island despite being much smaller than Tahiti.

Tahiti's importance increased as more and more European visitors made the island their preferred base, and it soon became a minor pawn in the European colonial game.

Tahiti's population is currently about 170,000, constituting more than 60% of French Polynesia's entire population. Tahiti is the economic, cultural and political centre of French Polynesia.

Geography & Geology

Tahiti is neatly divided into two circles connected by an isthmus: the larger and more populated Tahiti Nui (Big Tahiti) to the north-west and the smaller Tahiti Iti (Little Tahiti) to the southeast. The narrow coastal fringe of Tahiti Nui, where the vast majority of the population is concentrated, sweeps rapidly inwards and upwards to a jumble of soaring, green-clad mountain peaks.

A fringing reef encloses a narrow lagoon around much of the island, but parts of the coast, particularly along the north coast from Mahina through Papenoo to Tiarei, are unprotected. There are 33 passes through the reef, the most important of which is the Pape'ete Pass into Pape'ete's harbour. Less than 10km east is Matavai Bay (Baie de Matavai), the favourite anchorage point of many early explorers.

The mountainous centre of Tahiti Nui is effectively one huge crater, with the highest peak being Mt Orohena (2241m). A ridge runs northwest from the summit to Mt Aorai (2066m), and continues south to the spectacular rocky Diadème (1321m) then north to Mt Marau (1493m). A number of valleys run down to the coast from the mountains, the most impressive being the wide Papenoo Valley to the north. Tahiti Iti has its highest point at Mt Ronui (1332m).

Orientation

The *pointe kilométrique* (PK; kilometre point) markers start at zero in Pape'ete and increase in both a clockwise and an anticlockwise direction around Tahiti Nui until they meet at Taravao, the town at the isthmus that connects

Tahiti Nui with Tahiti Iti. Taravao is 54km from Pape'ete clockwise (via the east coast) and 60km anticlockwise (via the west coast). The counting starts again on Tahiti Iti, where the markers only go as far as the sealed road – remarkably, there's no road along the easternmost coast.

Activities

Whatever Tahiti lacks in beachlike postcard appeal, it sure makes up for with its huge array of fun stuff to do. If the following options don't sound thrilling enough, you could also take an aerial tour with **Polynesia Hélicoptères** (☎ 54 87 20; www.polynesia-helicopter.com). Twenty-minute flights cost from 20,000 CFP per person for four to five passengers. See also p103 for activities on Tahiti Iti.

BEACHES

Tahiti isn't as much of a beach destination as the outer islands but that doesn't mean you can't catch a few rays on the sand. The best stretches of white sand and decent snorkelling are between PK15 and PK21 on the west coast and there are public entries with parking at PK15, PK18 and PK18.5. Any Pa'ea-bound bus can drop you there. One of Tahiti's widest beaches is at Papara's Taharuu Beach (Map pp78–9; between PK38 and PK39), which has black sand, big surf and lots of local guys hanging out and drinking beer.

Three kilometres east of Pape'ete in Pira'e is a stretch of black-sand beach by Le Royal Tahitien hotel. There's also a nicer stretch of beach at Point Vénus (Map pp84–5; PK10). Little roadside beaches dot the rest of the island and as long as you don't have to walk through someone's property, feel free to take a dip. Tahiti Iti's best black-sand beaches are found in the villages of Tautira and Teahupoo.

CIRCLE THE ISLAND TOURS & 4WD EXCURSIONS

Taking a 'circle the island tour' can help you get your bearings and knock off most of the island's sights in one day. The following mini-buses take up to 10 passengers and charge 4500 CFP per person:

Adventure Eagle Tours (☎ 77 20 03)
Dave's VIP Tours (☎ 79 75 65; tahiti1viptours@yahoo .com) Dave is a super-friendly and knowledgeable American expat.

For more bumpy thrills take a 4WD to the island's centre around Lake Vaihiria. Full-day trips cost 6500 CFP per person and half-day trips are 4000 CFP; children under 10 are half-price and hotel pick-up is included. Our favourites:

Patrick Adventure (☎ 83 29 29; patrickadventure@mail.pf) Patrick knows his stuff and can also arrange custom tours.

Tahiti Safari Expeditions (☎ 42 14 15; www.tahiti-safari.com) This is the biggest operator and has reliable standards.

DIVING & WHALE-WATCHING
There are some excellent diving opportunities to be had in Tahiti and some dive shops also lead whale-watching tours between July and October when humpbacks swim near the coasts. For details about sites see p64. Dive centres on Tahiti include the following:

Aquatica Dive Centre (Map pp84-5; ☎ 53 34 96; www.aquatica-dive.com; Intercontinental Resort Tahiti) Also leads whale-watching, fishing and jet-ski tours.

Eleuthera Plongée (Map pp84-5; ☎ 42 49 29; www.dive-tahiti.com; Taina Marina, PK9, Puna'auia) A big outfit that also leads whale-watching excursions.

Fluid Dive Centre (Map pp84-5; ☎ 85 41 46, 70 83 75; Taina Marina)

Scuba Tek Tahiti (Map pp84-5; ☎ /fax 42 23 55; www.scubatek-tahiti.com; PK4, Arue) Also whale-watching tours.

Tahiti Charter Island (Map pp84-5; ☎ 41 38 33; www.tciplongees.com; Arue Marina) Whale- and dolphin-watching trips.

Tahiti Plongée (Map pp84-5; ☎ 41 00 62, 43 62 51; www.tahitiplongee.pf; PK7.5, Puna'auia)

Topdive (Map pp84-5; ☎ 86 49 06; www.topdive.com; Sheraton Hotel Tahiti) Leads whale-watching trips as well.

For whale-watching only, **La Vie En Blue** (Map pp84-5; ☎ 77 90 99; www.tahiti-whales.com; Moana Nui,

Puna'auia) leads trips for groups of two to four people. Day trips cost 1200 CFP per person if there are four people.

GOLF
Golf is all the rage with the nouveau riche of Tahiti and luckily they have the **Olivier Breaud International Golf Course of Atimaono** (Map pp78-9; ☎ 57 40 32; PK40.2, Papara; 9 holes 3500 CFP), a beautiful 18-hole par 72 course with some rather difficult par 3s. The Tahiti International Pro/Am is held around late July. Club rental is 2500 CFP.

HIKING & CANYONING
Hiking is taking off in Tahiti and canyoning (rappelling down waterfalls) is an even more exhilarating way to explore the interior. There are a handful of DIY hikes around the island, particularly the Fautaua Valley Trail and Mt Aorai (see p102), the trails from the Vaipahi Spring Gardens (p98) and around the Maroto if you are staying at the Relais de la Maroto (see p102), but for most other trails you'll need a guide. The best guided hiking spots are the Hitiaa Lava Tubes (p99) and the Te Pari Cliffs (p104). We recommend the following guides:

Mato-Nui Excursions (☎ 78 95 47; tmatonui@mail.pf; canyoning day trips per person 10,000 CFP) Mato really started the canyoning craze in Tahiti and has an overflow of energy and attitude. He leads hiking excursions and camping trips as well.

Syndicat des Guides de Randonnées de Polynésie Française (☎ 56 16 48; syndicatguides@hotmail.com) Has a comprehensive list of all the qualified guides and can make recommendations and help with bookings.

Tahiti Evasion (☎ 56 48 77; www.tahitievasion.com; all-day hikes per person from 5500 CFP) One of the most reputable operators in the country.

TAHITI

TAHITI

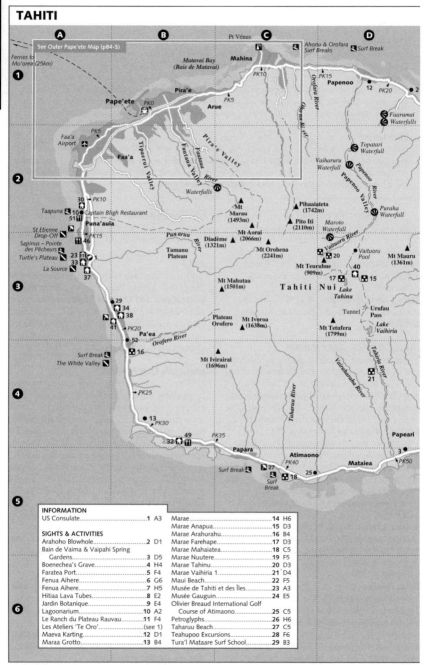

See Outer Pape'ete Map (p84-5)

Ferries to
Mo'orea (25km)

Pt Vénus

Matavai Bay
(Baie de Matavai)

Mahina

Ahonu & Orofara
Surf Breaks

Surf Break

PK10

PK15

Papenoo

12 PK20

2

Pira'e

Pape'ete

PK0

Arue

PK5

Faarumai
Waterfalls

Orofara River

Faa'a
Airport

PK5

Faa'a

Tipaerui Valley

Fautaua Valley

Fautaua River

Pira'e Valley

Waterfalls

Topatari
Waterfall

Vaiharuru
Waterfall

Papenoo

Papenoo
Valley

Puraha
Waterfall

30 PK10

Taapuna 10

Captain Bligh Restaurant

51 Puna'auia

St Etienne
Drop-Off

Sapinus – Pointe
des Pêcheurs

PK15

46

Turtle's Plateau

23

33

1

La Source

37

Pun aruu

Mt
Marau
(1493m)

Diadème
(1321m)

Tamanu
Plateau

Mt Aorai
(2066m)

Punaruu River

Pihaaiateta
(1742m)

Pito Iti
(2110m)

Maroto
Waterfall

Mt Orohena
(2241m)

Mt Teuruhue
(909m)

20

Vaituoru River

Vaituoru
Pool

Mt Mauru
(1361m)

40

17

15

Mt Mahutaa
(1501m)

Tahiti Nui

Lake
Tahinu

29

34

38

41

PK20

Pa'ea

52

16

Surf Break

The White Valley

Orofero River

Plateau
Orofero

Mt Ivoroa
(1638m)

Mt Ivirairai
(1696m)

Tunnel

Urufau
Pass

Mt Tetufera
(1799m)

Lake
Vaihiria

Taharuu River

Tahiria River

Vairaharaha River

21

PK25

13 PK30

32

49

PK35

Papara

Atimaono

PK40

Papeari

3

PK50

Mataiea

25

Surf Break

27

Taharuu Beach

18

Surf
Break

INFORMATION
US Consulate...............................1 A3

SIGHTS & ACTIVITIES
Arahoho Blowhole............................2 D1
Bain de Vaima & Vaipahi Spring
  Gardens.....................................3 D5
Boenechea's Grave.........................4 H4
Faratea Port...................................5 F4
Fenua Aihere..................................6 G6
Fenua Aihere..................................7 H5
Hitiaa Lava Tubes............................8 E2
Jardin Botanique.............................9 E4
Lagoonarium.................................10 A2
Le Ranch du Plateau Rauvau............11 F4
Les Ateliers 'Te Oro'....................(see 1)
Maeva Karting...............................12 D1
Maraa Grotto................................13 B4

Marae..14 H6
Marae Anapua..............................15 D3
Marae Arahurahu...........................16 B4
Marae Farehape.............................17 D3
Marae Mahaiatea............................18 C5
Marae Nuutere..............................19 F5
Marae Tahinu................................20 D3
Marae Vaihiria 1............................21 D4
Maui Beach...................................22 F5
Musée de Tahiti et des Îles...............23 A3
Musée Gauguin.............................24 E5
Olivier Breaud International Golf
  Course of Atimaono.....................25 C5
Petroglyphs..................................26 H6
Taharuu Beach..............................27 C5
Teahupoo Excursions......................28 F6
Tura'l Mataare Surf School...............29 B3

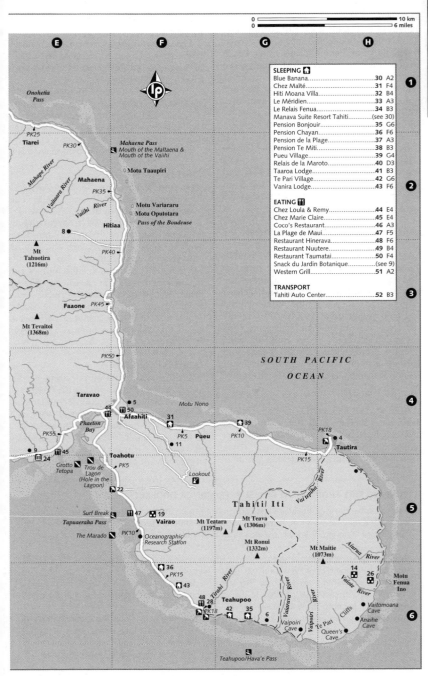

0 ——————————— 10 km
0 ——————————— 6 miles

SLEEPING 🏠
Blue Banana...........................**30** A2
Chez Maïté.............................**31** F4
Hiti Moana Villa......................**32** B4
Le Méridien...........................**33** A3
Le Relais Fenua.......................**34** B3
Manava Suite Resort Tahiti.......(see 30)
Pension Bonjouir......................**35** G6
Pension Chayan........................**36** F6
Pension de la Plage...................**37** A3
Pension Te Miti.......................**38** B3
Pueu Village..........................**39** G4
Relais de la Maroto...................**40** D3
Taaroa Lodge..........................**41** B3
Te Pari Village.......................**42** G6
Vanira Lodge..........................**43** F6

EATING 🍴
Chez Loula & Remy.....................**44** E4
Chez Marie Claire.....................**45** E4
Coco's Restaurant.....................**46** A3
La Plage de Maui......................**47** F5
Restaurant Hinerava...................**48** F6
Restaurant Nuutere....................**49** B4
Restaurant Taumatai...................**50** F4
Snack du Jardin Botanique.........(see 9)
Western Grill.........................**51** A2

TRANSPORT
Tahiti Auto Center....................**52** B3

Onohetia Pass

PK25
Tiarei PK30
Mahape River
Vaiaare River
Mahaena
PK35
Vaiihi River
Hitiaa
8 ●
▲ Mt
Tahuotira
(1216m)
PK40

Mahaena Pass
🏔 *Mouth of the Maltaena &
Mouth of the Vaiihi*
○ *Motu Taaupiri*

● *Motu Variararu*
● *Motu Oputotara*
Pass of the Boudeuse

Faaone PK45

▲ Mt Tevaitoi
(1368m)

PK50

S O U T H   P A C I F I C

O C E A N

Taravao ● 5
44
🏠 50
Afaahiti 31
Motu Nono
🏠 39
*Phaeton
Bay* PK5 **Pueu** PK10
PK55
🏔 4
Tautira
PK18
● 9 🏠 45
🏛 24 **Toahotu**
🏠 11

*Grotto
Tetopa* 🏠 *Trou de
Lagon
(Hole in the
Lagoon)* PK5
🏠 22

Lookout
PK15

🏠 47 🏠 19
Surf Break **Vairao**
Tapuaeraha Pass PK10
The Marado 🏠 *Oceanographic
Research Station*

T a h i t i   I t i

Mt Teatara
(1197m) Mt Teava
(1306m)

Mt Ronui
(1332m) ▲

Mt Maitie
(1073m) ▲

*Aiurua
River*

14
🏠 36 *Vaiote River* 26
PK15 🏠 43
48 28
Teahupoo
🏠 42 35
● 6 *Vaiparu
River*
*Vaitomoana
Cave*
**Motu
Fenua
Ino**

*Vaipoiri
Cave* *Ye Pari
Cliffs* *Anaihe
Cave*
*Queen's
Cave*

🏔 *Teahupoo/Hava'e Pass*

A B C D ... E F G H
1 2 3 4 5 6

SURFING

Polynesia is the birthplace of surfing, and Tahiti offers some fabulous beginner breaks, particularly at Papenoo and other beach breaks along the east coast. More advanced surfers can head to the Papara shore break and the reef breaks at Sapinus and Taapuna along the west coast and the big and small Vairao passes at Tahiti Iti. Tahiti's most famous and radical wave is at Hava'e Pass in Teahupoo on Tahiti Iti where there's a big international surf contest held each May; for details, see p104. In general the west coast waves break the biggest between May and October while the east coast is best from November to April – waves are fickle, so this isn't set in stone.

To paddle out for your first time or hone your skills, visit **Tura'I Mataare Surf School** (Map pp78-9; ☎ 41 91 37; surfschool@mail.pf; PK18.3; ⊗ Wed, Sat & Sun) on the mountain side of the road in Pa'ea. Half-day lessons including transfers and equipment are 5000 CFP. Courses are run by a qualified instructor and include equipment, transport to the different surfing spots and insurance. In Tahiti Iti equally qualified and super-friendly Doumé runs the much smaller, low-key **École Surf Iti Nui** (☎ 73 14 21; half-day lessons 3500 CFP) – classes go to spots around Tahiti Nui as well as Tahiti Iti and transport, equipment and insurance are included.

OTHER WATER ACTIVITIES

Tahiti Water Ski Club (☎ 45 39 36; www.tahitiskiclub .com) has introductory and advanced water-skiing and wakeboarding lessons. To try your hand at windsurfing, take a lesson at **Arue Sailing School** (Map pp84-5; ☎ 42 23 54). Call for prices.

For sea kayaking or 'hot-dogging' down a river in inflatable kayaks call **Aroha Pacific** (☎ 76 26 18; aroha-pacific@mail.pf; Mahina), which also leads hiking and canyoning excursions.

At the Intercontinental Resort Tahiti, the **Aquatica Dive Centre** (Map pp84-5; ☎ 53 34 96; www .aquatica-dive.com) has a long menu of water activities – from swimming with whales and dolphins to sunset catamaran cruises.

For sailboat charter information see p244.

Courses

Les Ateliers 'Te Oro' (Map pp78-9; ☎ 58 30 27; http:// danse-emergence.typepad.fr, in French; Tamanu Center Punaauia) offers two-, three- and five-day Tahitian dance workshops (from two to four hours per day) for adults and children from age 11. Courses are in French and English and special arrangements can be made for Japanese speakers. Group courses run throughout the year but you can also arrange private or individual courses. Prices depend on group size and the length of the course. The same school runs classes on Mo'orea as well (see p115). Reserve by email a few weeks in advance.

Tahiti for Children

Travelling with children is extremely easy in Tahiti. Any kid who loves the beach will love French Polynesia, and Polynesians absolutely love children. Just outside Pape'ete's urban sprawl, the **Lagoonarium** (Map pp78-9; ☎ 43 62 90; PK11; adult/child 500/300 CFP; ⊗ 9am-6pm) is a pleasant tourist trap with a meshed-in area of lagoon with a modest underwater viewing

---

SURFING TIPS FROM LOCAL PRO SURFER MANOA DROLLET

Manoa Drollet grew up in Papara and is considered to be the best of the best when it comes to surfing the massive waves at Teahupoo. In 2008 he came in second place at the Billabong Pro Surf Competition and is known around the world for his fearless Tahitian style.

Why Tahiti? For the weather and the variety of waves: beach break and reef break for all levels. But also everyone here is pretty welcoming and friendly.

Best time of year? I'd say March to May since the weather is good then, there's lots of swell and you can watch the best surfers in the world compete at the Billabong Pro. But really any time of year is good. There are always waves.

Any tips? If you're surfing a reef break go out with someone who knows the spot and don't go out if you're unsure of your level. Bring plenty of sunscreen and a long sleeve jersey to protect yourself from the sun and booties for walking on the reef. And if you can, make friends with someone who has a boat or expect to paddle a lot! But most importantly, enjoy yourself.

room; it's reached through a giant (though crumbling) concrete shark's mouth. The entrance to the Lagoonarium is part of the Captain Bligh Restaurant, and if you eat at the restaurant there's no charge to visit the Lagoonarium.

In Pape'ete, special child-oriented cultural and artistic shows take place in Parc Bougainville (p84), which also has a little playground. East of Pape'ete you'll find **Maeva Karting** (Map pp78-9; ☎ 82 87 36; maevakarting@mail .pf; ☽ 10am-6pm Wed-Sun), where children six years and older can race around two tracks on go-carts.

Kids will also dig the huge Galápagos tortoises at the 137-hectare **Jardin Botanique** (p98), on the far south coast of Tahiti Nui. It's also great fun exploring the walking paths winding through the garden, past ponds and palms, eels, crabs, ducks and chickens.

Getting Around
BUS

French Polynesia's once-famous *le trucks* have now, unfortunately, mostly gone to bus heaven. The 'real' air-con buses (still often referred to as *le trucks*) now, in theory, only stop at designated stops (with blue signs) and run to a timetable, but in reality the routes haven't changed and the drivers will usually stop if you wave them down.

Weekdays, buses around Pape'ete and along the west and north coasts operate roughly every 15 minutes from dawn until about 5.30pm except for the Pape'ete–Faa'a–Outumaoro line, which supposedly operates 24 hours but in reality gets very quiet after 10pm. Buses to Taravao run about every hour from around 5am to 5pm and buses to/from Teahupoo or Tautira run hourly (and sometimes less frequently) between 5am and 10am, plus one or two services towards Teahupoo and Tautira only (in the afternoon). At the weekend, particularly on Sunday, services are far less frequent. Fares for the shortest trips, from Pape'ete to a little beyond the airport, for example, start from 130 CFP (80 CFP for children and students); this fare rises to 250 CFP after 6pm. Outside this area, the prices are less clear. Out to about 20km from Pape'ete the fare will go up in stages to around 300 CFP; getting to Tahiti Iti costs 400 CFP.

Tahiti's buses have their route number and the final destination clearly marked.

There are basically three routes: greater Pape'ete, which is handy for the Pape'ete–Faa'a airport trip (catch this along Rue du Général de Gaulle); the east coast (catch this along Blvd Pomare); and the west coast (catch this along Rue du Maréchal Foch and Rue du Général de Gaulle). Both the east and west coast buses can be taken to reach Tahiti Iti.

CAR

Driving on Tahiti is quite straightforward and, although accident statistics are not encouraging, the traffic is fairly light once you get away from Pape'ete. Apart from on the Route de Dégagement Ouest (RDO) freeway out of Pape'ete to the west, the traffic saunters along at an island pace. As always, beware of children wandering on the road, and prepare yourself for a rather casual approach to overtaking. Don't leave anything on view in your car and always lock up; rental cars all have big orange stickers on them so local kids will know you're a tourist and will want to find out if you've left anything good inside.

For the price you'll be paying, you may be unpleasantly surprised by the standard of the hire cars and it costs even more if you want an automatic transmission.

Many of the following car-rental companies on Tahiti also have desks at the bigger hotels: **Avis** Faa'a airport (☎ 85 02 84); Pape'ete (Map pp86-7; ☎ 54 10 10; cnr Rue des Remparts & Av Georges Clémenceau)

Daniel Rent-a-Car (☎ 82 30 04; Faa'a airport)

Europcar Faa'a airport (☎ 86 60 61); Pape'ete (Map pp86-7; ☎ 45 24 24; cnr Av du Prince Hinoi & Rue des Remparts)

Hertz (☎ 82 55 86; Faa'a airport)

Tahiti Auto Center (Map pp78-9; ☎ 82 33 33; www .tahitiautocenter.pf; PK20.2, Pa'ea) Had the cheapest published rates at the time of writing.

Tahiti Rent-a-Car (☎ 81 94 00; Faa'a airport)

HITCHING

Hitching in Tahiti is relatively easy and usually quite safe, and you'll see both locals and *popaa* (Westerners) standing on the tarmac with their thumbs in the air. French Polynesia has low crime levels, but solo women could still encounter problems if getting in a car with men and should always use common sense. Avoid hitching on Friday and Saturday nights, when the roads are filled with alarmingly intoxicated drivers.

TAHITI

PARADISE ON THE CHEAP

If your budget doesn't allow for 50,000 CFP per night hotel rooms and 3000 CFP lunches, don't despair. In fact, getting outside of resort-land (even if you're staying at a resort) and trying out the less expensive, local-style options allows you to see a much more authentic side of Tahiti.

Best free sights Marché de Pape'ete (p84), Marae Arahurahu (p96), Maraa Grotto (p96) and Faarumai Waterfalls (p100).

Best free activities Hiking around Vaipahi Spring Gardens (p98), surfing (p80) or lounging and snorkelling on the beach (p76).

Best cheap eats Breakfast on baguettes and pastries from local grocery stores. Head back to the grocery store to buy 350 CFP sandwiches or takeaway prepared meals (usually around 800 CFP) for lunch – but get there by 11am before they sell out! In Pape'ete ask for half portions (usually around 600 CFP) at takeaway snack bars. For dinner get anything from a *roulotte* (mobile food van) on the Pape'ete waterfront (p91) or at random roadside locations around the island.

Cheap transport *Le trucks* (p81)! Hitching (though never entirely safe; p81) will give you the chance to meet locals.

PAPE'ETE

Metropolis this is not. Pape'ete is really just a medium-sized town (by Western standards) of moulding architecture with a lively port, lots of traffic and plenty of smiling faces to pull you through it all. You'll either get its compact chaos and colourful clutter or you'll run quickly from its grimy edges and lack of gorgeous vistas. Sip a cappuccino at a Parisian-style sidewalk cafe, shop the vibrant market for everything and anything (from pearls to bright *pareu* – sarongs), dine at a *roulotte* (mobile food van) in the balmy evening, or dance the night away with the beautiful people. All roads in French Polynesia eventually lead to Pape'ete, so you might as well scope it out.

Thanks to lots of effort by the image-conscious local government, Pape'ete's waterfront is receiving a major facelift that is helping to abate some of the disappointment that visitors used to feel when they first glimpsed the town. Sailboats are once again docking along portside Blvd Pomare, where you'll find paved walking paths that meander past blooming planter boxes and the occasional tree. While the traffic still buzzes by, it's an almost relaxing place for a stroll. By mid-2009 a manmade beach just northeast of To'ata Square should be completed but we'd advise against swimming in the polluted port waters.

HISTORY

Translated from Tahitian, Pape'ete's name literally means 'basket of water'. Historians theorise that this name is probably a reference to the springs where water was once collected.

In 1769, when James Cook anchored in Matavai Bay, there was no settlement in Pape'ete. Towards the end of the 18th century European visitors realised the value of its sheltered bay and easy access through the reef. London Missionary Society (LMS) missionaries arrived in Pape'ete in 1824 and the young Queen Pomare became a regular visitor to the growing town, which gradually swelled to become a religious and political centre.

Visiting whaling ships made Pape'ete an increasingly important port, and it was selected as the administrative headquarters for the new French protectorate in 1843. By 1860 the town had taken its present form, with a straggling European settlement between the waterfront and the street known as the Broom (now Rue du Commandant Destremeau, Rue du Général de Gaulle and Rue du Maréchal Foch).

Chinese merchants and shopkeepers also started to trickle into Pape'ete, but at the beginning of the 20th century the population was still less than 5000. A disastrous cyclone in 1906 and a German naval bombardment in 1914 took a toll, but during WWII population reached 10,000 and by the early 1960s it was over 20,000. The last few decades have seen the almost total destruction of the charming old colonial heart of Pape'ete.

ORIENTATION

The backbone of central Pape'ete is Blvd Pomare, which curves around an almost enclosed bay. This central district is easily covered on foot. Clustered around here and on the blocks back from Blvd Pomare are most of the central businesses, banks and restaurants, and some hotels. The Vaima Centre marks the centre of Pape'ete, and it's along this area of waterfront that the city throbs with life. The port zone, comprising Fare Ute and Motu Uta, is easily visible across the harbour to the north.

Greater Pape'ete forms a vast conurbation, squeezed between the mountains and the lagoon along the north coast of Tahiti. The westward sprawl of Pape'ete extends beyond the airport in the gritty suburb of Faa'a and on to Puna'auia. The coastal road westwards is complemented by the Route de Dégagement Ouest (RDO) freeway, which runs slightly inland, starting on the western edge of central Pape'ete and extending to Puna'auia before rejoining the coastal road.

On the other side of Pape'ete, Av du Prince Hinoi and Av Georges Clémenceau run east through the suburb of Pira'e, then join at Arue.

INFORMATION

The tourist office, main post office, the majority of the banks and the best bookshops are all clustered in Pape'ete.

Bookshops

Pape'ete has a few good bookshops, but the range in English is always poor. A good place to find English newspapers and magazines is at Faa'a international airport.

Librarie du Vaima (Map pp86-7; ☎ 45 57 57; Vaima Centre; 🕙 8.30am-6pm Mon-Fri, 8am-5pm Sat) A great bookshop with some ancient gems and a few new paperbacks in English.

Maison de la Presse (Map pp86-7; Blvd Pomare) This is the best choice in town for mags and news in English.

Odyssey (Map pp86-7; ☎ 50 13 15; 9 Place de la Cathédrale) It's huge but has only a small English section.

Emergency

Ambulance (☎ 15)
Hôtel de Police (Map pp86-7; Av Bruat)
Police (☎ 17)
Police Aux Frontières (Map pp86-7; Pl Vaiete)
SOS Infirmières (☎ 43 56 00)
SOS Médecins (☎ 42 34 56)

Internet Access

There are at least 10 cybercafes in central Pape'ete.

Tiki Copy (Map pp86-7; Rue Jeanne d'Arc; per min 12 CFP; 🕙 8am-5pm Mon-Fri, 8am-noon Sat) Slightly cheaper than the competition.

Tiki Soft C@fé (Map pp86-7; ☎ 88 93 98; per min 15 CFP) Frequented by a chic clientele.

Medical Services

Clinique Cardella (Map pp86-7; ☎ 42 81 90; Rue Anne-Marie Javouhey; 🕙 24hr) Private clinic behind the cathedral.

Clinique Paofai (Map pp86-7; ☎ 46 18 18; cnr Blvd Pomare & Rue du Lieutenant Varney; 🕙 24hr) Private clinic.

Mamao Hospital (Map pp86-7; ☎ 46 62 62, 24hr emergencies 42 01 01; Av Georges Clémenceau) The biggest hospital in French Polynesia, with good facilities and a range of medical specialities.

Money

There are banks (Banque Socredo, Banque de Tahiti and Banque de Polynésie) and ATMs scattered around Pape'ete and its suburbs. Banque Socredo and Banque de Polynésie have branches at Faa'a airport, where there's also an ATM. See p249 for general information on banks and changing money.

Most banks in Pape'ete change money and travellers cheques; the ATMs accept Visa and MasterCard. The following branches have ATMs.

Banque de Polynésie (Map pp86-7; Av Bruat; Rue du Général de Gaulle)

Banque de Tahiti (Map pp86-7; Rue Colette)

Banque Socredo (Map pp86-7; Blvd Pomare, Fare Tony)

Post

Post office (Map pp86-7; Blvd Pomare) Pape'ete's main post office is next to Parc Bougainville. For stamps and general postal services go upstairs from the Blvd Pomare entrance.

Tourist Information

In addition to the office listed here, there is an information desk at Faa'a airport.

Gie Tahiti Manava Visitor Information Centre (Map pp86-7; ☎ 50 57 12; www.tahiti-tourisme.com; Fare Manihini, Blvd Pomare; 🕙 7.30am-5pm Mon-Fri, 8am-noon Sat) Has heaps of information on all of French Polynesia. Although Mo'orea and Bora Bora have helpful tourist offices, the more remote islands don't, so if you have any queries, ask here.

SIGHTS

It's easy to get lost in Pape'ete and dumping the map and throwing caution to the trade winds is the best way to explore the town. Fortunately, the centre is so small that it's

TAHITI

OUTER PAPE'ETE

SIGHTS & ACTIVITIES
Aquatica Dive Centre	(see 12)
Arue Sailing School	(see 1)
Arue Yacht Club	1 D2
Bain Loti	2 D3
Cimetière Pomare	3 D2
Eleuthera Plongée	(see 9)
Fluid Dive Centre	(see 9)
House of James Norman Hall	4 D2
La Vie En Blue	5 B3
One Tree Hill	6 E1
Scuba Tek Tahiti	7 D2
Tahiti Charter Island	(see 1)
Tahiti Plongée	8 A3
Taina Marina	9 B3
Tomb of Pomare V	10 D2
Topdive	(see 15)

equally easy to find your way home again once you've stumbled across the sights.

Marché de Pape'ete

Load up on colourful *pareu* (sarongs), shell necklaces, woven hats and local produce at the famed Marché de Pape'ete (Pape'ete Market; Map pp86–7) – a Pape'ete must. It covers the whole block between Rue du 22 Septembre and Rue F Cardella, just one block back from Blvd Pomare. The most fun time to visit is early Sunday morning when local residents flock in. Dotted among the fruit, vegetables, meat and fish downstairs are little patisseries and lunchtime hawkers selling takeaway portions of *ma'a Tahiti* (traditional Tahitian food). Grab an ice-cold coconut at the door and then stroll upstairs to the knick-knacks, a local cafeteria-style restaurant with live music at lunchtime (most days) and a very good tattoo shop. Fish from other islands is on sale early in the day but the Tahitian catch does not appear until late afternoon. The place has lived through a tumultuous 250 years of cyclone damage and rebuilding and was even destroyed by German cruisers

in WWII. Today's airy structure was built in 1987.

Robert Wan Musée de la Perle

This **pearl museum** (Map pp86-7; Blvd Pomare; ☎ 46 15 55; admission free; ◷ 9.30am-5pm Mon-Sat, last entry 4.45pm) was created by pearl magnate Robert Wan with aims of luring visitors into his glamorous shop. It's a worthwhile, small and modern museum that covers all facets of the pearl-cultivating business. Explanations of the displays are in English and ogling Monsieur Wan's gorgeous, albeit uncommonly pricey, jewellery collection is almost as fun as the museum.

Parc Bougainville

A great spot to just chill out, Parc Bougainville (Bougainville Park; Map pp86-7) is a tropical oasis in the middle of the city. Lush and cool, it stretches from Blvd Pomare to Rue du Général de Gaulle and, not surprisingly, is fronted by a 1909 bust of the great French navigator. Frequent floral, cultural and artistic shows add to the appeal, and there's a children's playground.

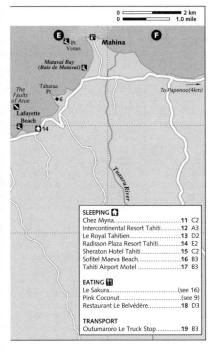

SLEEPING 🏠
Chez Myna.................................**11** C2
Intercontinental Resort Tahiti.......**12** A3
Le Royal Tahitien........................**13** D2
Radisson Plaza Resort Tahiti........**14** E2
Sheraton Hotel Tahiti..................**15** C2
Sofitel Maeva Beach...................**16** B3
Tahiti Airport Motel **17** B3

EATING 🍴
Le Sakura..............................(see 16)
Pink Coconut...........................(see 9)
Restaurant Le Belvédère...............**18** D3

TRANSPORT
Outumaroro Le Truck Stop.............**19** B3

To'ata Square

To'ata Square (Map pp86–7) is an evolving multi-use development project on Pape'ete's western edge. You can take the toddlers out for a stroller jaunt on paved walking paths through tropical floral gardens or visit on a romantic evening trip, sharing a quiet moment bathed in an artificial lantern's glow. The far end of the square is home to a 5000-seat pavilion, which is the scene of the July Heiva festivities (see p89 and boxed text, p48); it also hosts rock concerts throughout the year.

Cathédrale Notre-Dame

Taking pride of place in the centre of town is the Cathédrale Notre-Dame (Map pp86–7). The cathedral's story began in 1856, when plans were hatched for it to be built of stone imported from Australia, with a doorway carved out of granite from Mangareva in the Gambier Archipelago. Construction on the cathedral began, but then the money ran out; the original edifice was demolished in 1867, and a smaller cathedral was finally completed in 1875.

Temple Paofai

Although the Catholic cathedral is placed squarely in the town centre, Tahiti remains predominantly Protestant, a lasting legacy of the LMS missionaries. The large pink Temple Paofai (Map pp86–7) makes a colourful scene on Sunday morning, when it is bursting at the seams with a devout congregation dressed in white and belting out rousing *himene* (hymns). The church is on the site of the first Protestant church in Pape'ete, which was built in 1818.

Bain Loti

From east of the centre, the Route de Fautaua runs 2.5km inland to Bain Loti (Loti's Bath; Map pp84–5). It was here in Pierre Loti's 1880 novel *Le Mariage de Loti* (The Marriage of Loti) that the beautiful Rarahu, a 14-year-old Polynesian girl, met Loti (Frenchman Julien Viaud's pen name). This pool once supplied the town with drinking water, but now it's led through a concrete channel and surrounded by development. Nevertheless, it remains a favourite meeting place and swimming hole for locals. A bust of Pierre Loti overlooks the scene.

See p101 for details of the walk that leads inland from Bain Loti.

Administrative Buildings

The **Territorial Assembly** and other government buildings occupy **Place Tarahoi** (Map pp86–7), the former site of the Pomare palace. The termite-riddled 1883 palace was razed in 1960, but you can get an idea of what it looked like from the modern *mairie* (town hall), a few blocks east, which is built in a similar style. On Rue du Général de Gaulle, the assembly building is fronted by a **memorial to Pouvana'a a Oopa**, the late pro-independence figure of heroic proportions. The **High Commissioner's Residence** that stands to one side of the assembly building replaced the 1843 Palace of the Governor (those pesky termites again). Behind and between the two buildings is a freshwater spring. The pool is still known as the Bain de la Reine (Queen's Bathing Place), as the young Queen Pomare used to visit it. A more recent addition is the **Presidential Palace**, an imposing building used by the president.

To the west, along Av Bruat, is the **Ministère de la Culture** (☎ 50 15 01). There's an **exhibition space** (admission free; ☿ 7.30am–noon & 1.30–5pm) here that is worth a peek.

TAHITI

CENTRAL PAPE'ETE

Pape'ete Pass

Ⓐ Ⓑ Ⓒ Ⓓ

Q14

INFORMATION
Austrian Consulate............................1 D4
Banque de Polynésie & ATM.............2 E4
Banque de Polynésie & ATM.............3 F3
Banque de Tahiti & ATM....................4 F3
Banque Socredo & ATM......................5 F2
Banque Socredo & ATM...............(see 61)
Chilean Consulate..............................6 F3
Clinique Cardella...............................7 G3
Clinique Paofai..................................8 C5
Gie Tahiti Manava Visitors Information
  Centre...9 F3
Hôtel de Police................................10 E4
Librairie du Vaima...........................11 F3
Maison de la Presse.........................12 F2
Mamao Hospital...............................13 H2
Netherlands Consulate.....................14 D1
Odyssey...15 F3
Police aux Frontières.......................16 F3
Post Office.......................................17 E4
Service des Régies des Recettes.....(see 23)
Tiki Copy...18 F3
Tiki Soft C@fe...........................(see 59)

SIGHTS & ACTIVITIES
Cathédrale Notre-Dame....................19 F3
Government Buildings.......................20 E4
High Commissioner's Office..............21 E4
High Commissioner's Residence.......22 E4
Mairie (Town Hall)...........................23 F2
Marché de Pape'ete.........................24 F3
Ministère de la Culture.....................25 E5
Pouvana'a a Oopa Memorial............26 E4
Presidential Palace...........................27 F4
Robert Wan Musée de la Perle..........28 D4
Temple Paofai...................................29 D4
Territorial Assembly..........................30 E4
To'ata Square...................................31 C4

SLEEPING
Ahitea Lodge....................................32 H1
Fare Suisse......................................33 C5
Hotel Tahiti Nui...............................34 G2
Hôtel Le Mandarin...........................35 F2
Teamo Pension................................36 G3
Tiare Tahiti Noa Noa........................37 E3

EATING
Barrumundi......................................38 F3
Cafe de la Gare..........................(see 52)
L'Api'zzeria......................................39 D4
La Corbeille d'Eau............................40 C4
La Saladière.....................................41 F2
La Squadra......................................42 F4
Lou Pescadou...................................43 F4
Mango Café.....................................44 F3
Marché de Pape'ete....................(see 24)
Morrison's Café................................45 F3
New Port..46 E4
Patachoux..47 F3
Place Vaiete Roulottes......................48 F3
Polyself..49 F3
Restaurant Jimmy............................50 F2
Supermarché Champion....................51 C5

DRINKING
Café de la Gare...............................52 E3
Club 106..53 D4
Le Paradise Night.............................54 F1
Le Rétro...55 F3
Les 3 Brasseurs...............................56 F2
Piano Bar...57 F2
Royal Kikiriri....................................58 F2
Tiki Soft C@fé..................................59 G3
Ute Ute Café....................................60 F2

ENTERTAINMENT
Concorde....................................(see 11)
Hollywood..61 E3
Liberty...62 F3

SHOPPING
Aroma & Mano Salmon.....................63 F3
Galeries des Tropiques......................64 C4
Gallerie Winkler...............................65 F3
Mana'O Tattoo.................................66 F2
Marché de Pape'ete....................(see 24)
Olivier Creations...............................67 F3
Tahiti Music......................................68 F3
Vanilla Market..................................69 F2

TRANSPORT
Air Tahiti..70 F3
Air Tahiti Nui....................................71 G2
Avis..72 G2
Bus Stop...73 F3
Bus Stop...74 F2
Bus Stop...75 F3
Europcar...76 F2
Inter-Island Boat Quay......................77 E1
Mo'orea Ferry Quay..........................78 E1
Taxi Stand..79 F3
Taxi Stand..80 F3
Taxi Stand..81 F2

Motu Uta

Rue du Chef Teneporotoa

28
39
1
53

64 31
40
29
8
5

Rue du Commandant Destremeau
Rue du Lieutenant Varney
Blvd Pomare
Rue du Maré 1797
Rue Max 1797
Rue des Pollus Tahitiens

To Faa'a Airport
(5km)

33

Pape'ete's **mairie** is two blocks back from Blvd Pomare and a block north of Marché de Pape'ete. It was completed in 1990, in vague imitation of the old queen's palace.

House of James Norman Hall

Towards the outer edge of Pape'ete's urban sprawl in Arue is this lovely little replica of *Mutiny on the Bounty* co-author **James Norman Hall's house** (Map pp84-5; adult/child 600 CFP/free; 9am-4pm Mon-Sat). The house is in a shady garden and is decorated with Hall's original c 1920s furniture plus heaps of photos and memorabilia. It's on the mountain side of the road but parking is on the beach side – if you're heading away from Pape'ete you'll

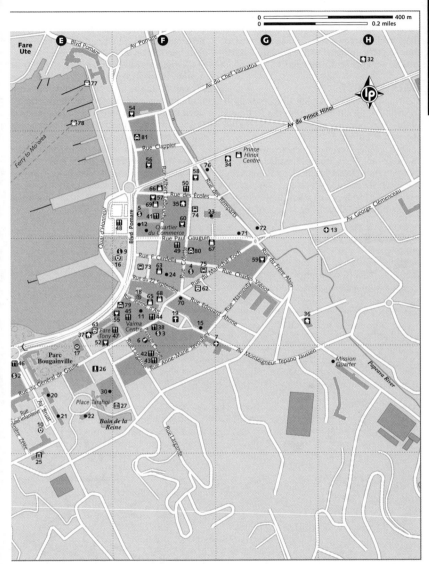

have to go around the roundabout to get to the parking lot. There's a small black-sand beach here where you can cool off after your visit.

Tomb of Pomare V

On Point Outuaiai in Arue, on the water's edge, signposted and just a short detour off the coastal road, is the tomb of the last of the Pomare family. The Tomb of Pomare V (Map pp84–5) looks like a stubby lighthouse made of coral boulders. It was actually built in 1879 for Queen Pomare IV, who died in 1877 after 50 years in power. Her ungrateful son, Pomare V, had her remains exhumed a few years later and when he died in 1891 it became his tomb.

TAHITI

Other Pomares are buried (or may be buried – their tombs are unmarked) in the **Cimetière Pomare** (Map pp84–5; PK5.4). A board at the cemetery indicates where Pomare I, II, III and IV are apparently interred.

WALKING TOUR

Central Pape'ete is compact, and lends itself to strolling. Ideally head off in the freshness of the early morning, or wait until the cool of the early evening.

Start a waterfront stroll from the west along the four-lane Blvd Pomare, shaded by overhanging trees. **To'ata Square** (1; p85), marking the westerly point of Pape'ete, is spacious, paved and a lovely place for strolling as long as it's not midday – there's not a speck of shade.

You can't miss central Pape'ete's imposing pink church, the **Temple Paofai** (2; p85); the missionaries would be rapt to see how busy the church is on a Sunday morning.

Across the road is a memorial to the great double canoe *Hokule'a,* which sailed from Hawaii to Tahiti in 1976. As you walk east there are racing *pirogues* (outrigger canoes) lined up under the trees like tadpoles. Local teams can be seen practising some afternoons and every Saturday morning.

On the inland side of the road is the **Robert Wan Musée de la Perle** (3; p84), where you can bask in the air-con before warming up again in the shady, green haven of **Parc Bougainville** (4; p84), further down the road.

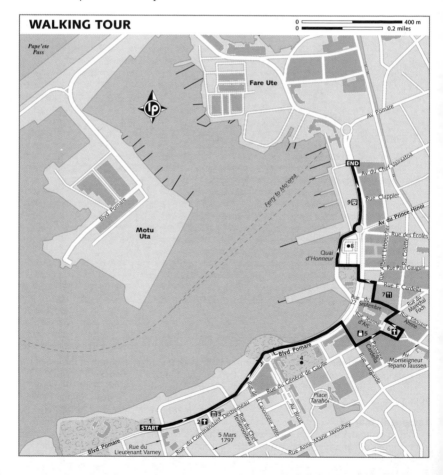

WALKING TOUR

TETIAROA: ATOLL OF BIRDS & BRANDOS

Bought by Marlon Brando in 1965 after he filmed *Mutiny on the Bounty* and fell in love with his Tahitian co-star Tarita Teriipia, the stunning atoll of Tetiaroa, 59km north of Tahiti, is in the process of major change. While Brando was alive, the atoll remained a bird preserve and housed only one small *pension* (guesthouse) where visitors could live like Robinson Crusoe in paradise. Brando, a pioneer in eco-tourism, always made it clear that he wished the island to remain preserved and that any development would have to be ecologically sound as well as aesthetically conforming to the atoll. Brando died in 2004 and by 2005 his estate executors had sold the rights to development to a major property developer in Tahiti for US$2 million. At the time of writing a luxury eco-resort to be called 'The Brando' was planned but legal snags had postponed the project indefinitely.

Air Moorea halted its service to the atoll in January 2004 stating that the Brandos' little *pension* owed the airline 40 million CFP and that the airstrip was not up to safety regulations. At the time of writing the only way to get to the island was by charter yacht, a few of which line up along the Pape'ete waterfront advertising lovely day trips to the atoll for around 13,000 CFP per person.

Continue along Blvd Pomare till you reach the **Vaima Centre (5)**, with shops, a few restaurants, an internet cafe and most of the airline offices. Stop here for a drink at the iconic yet pricey Le Rétro (p93), one of Pape'ete's best spots for people-watching.

Walk up the pedestrian-only road to Rue Jeanne d'Arc to the **Cathédrale Notre-Dame (6**; p85), built in 1875. This is a lovely cool spot for a quiet moment or two.

Following Rue du Général de Gaulle, turn left into Rue du 22 Septembre to the **Marché de Pape'ete (7**; p84). If it's lunchtime, head upstairs to see if the local band is playing.

If you stroll back towards Blvd Pomare, on the harbour side is the **Place Vaiete (8)**, which is home to multiple *roulottes* and occasional live-music performances at night but is quite peaceful during the day. There are plenty of public benches along here where you can sit and watch the world go by. On the inland side of Blvd Pomare, the seedy yet energetic (at night) **entertainment district (9)** starts just south of Av du Prince Hinoi and extends north past Av du Chef Vairaatoa. Stop here for another drink, at Les 3 Brasseurs (p93).

FESTIVALS & EVENTS

The **Heiva** festival in July is Pape'ete's biggest event. For details, see boxed text, p48. For other festivals and events see p247.

SLEEPING

Central Pape'ete is not the place to stay if you're looking for tranquillity or anything resembling a tourist brochure; the options on the outskirts of town offer more palm-fringed, beachlike choices. That said, city-side digs are a convenient base to explore the rest of the island and are the best places to stay if you want to enjoy the nightlife.

It's wise to reserve ahead during the Heiva festivities in July, when many hotels are completely booked out.

Unless otherwise noted all these places take credit cards.

Budget

Teamo Pension (Map pp86-7; ☎ 42 47 26; Rue du Pont-Neuf; dm/d 2500/7500 CFP; 🔀) It's a little depressing but cheap and sort of central. Rooms have private bathrooms and air-con while the dorm room has six beds. The shared kitchen is a plus.

Chez Myrna (Map pp84-5; ☎ 42 64 11; dammeyer .family@mail.pf; r with/without bathroom 7000/8000 CFP) Sparkling clean, tiny and friendly, Chez Myrna has simple rooms with breakfast included and there's an on-site snack bar and laundry services. No credit cards.

Ahitea Lodge (Map pp86-7; ☎ 53 13 53; pension .ahitea@mail.pf; Av Chef Vairaatoa; r incl breakfast from 8500 CFP; 🔀 🔁) The only budget option in town with a pool, this place is a real bargain. Rooms are big, bright and tiled and the best ones have sliding doors and small terraces. The cheapest rooms have shared bathroom and no air-con. There's a comfy lounge area, a communal kitchen and a garden around the pool. The location is quiet, but only a five-minute walk to the waterfront.

Midrange

our pick **Fare Suisse** (Map pp86-7; ☎ 42 00 30; www
.fare-suisse.com; dm 5500 CFP, d/f 10,000/15,000 CFP;
☒ ▣) Getting rave reviews from our read-
ers, this *pension* (guesthouse) is in a spotless
and stylish cement home in a quiet area right
in the centre of town. The tiled rooms are
simple but nicely decorated with bamboo furniture and are bright and airy. The best thing
about this place is the owner Beni who picks
guests up free of charge at the airport, lets
folks store their luggage and creates a super-
pleasant atmosphere with his helpfulness and
good humour. Beach transfers cost 1300 CFP
or Beni will drop you at a surf break with a
boogie board for 3000 CFP. Breakfast is an
extra 1200 CFP.

Tiare Tahiti Noa Noa (Map pp86-7; ☎ 50 01 00;
fax 43 68 47; Blvd Pomare; d from 12,000 CFP; ☒) This
clean hotel overlooks the water in the hub
of Pape'ete, but sadly is afflicted by the noise
of traffic. A somewhat kitschy favourite with
tour groups, it has a restaurant and excursion desk.

Tahiti Airport Motel (Map pp84-5; ☎ 50 40 00; www
.tahitiairportmotel.com; Faa'a; d/f 15,000/24,000 CFP; ☒ ▣)
Right across from Faa'a international airport
this would appear to be the most convenient
place to stay for a quick stopover, but there's
no shuttle so you have to drag your luggage
across the parking lot then up the short but
sometimes muddy hill. A two-minute taxi ride
here costs the same as to Pape'ete (2000 CFP).
Rooms are crisp, colourful and comfortable,
with TVs and fridges.

Sofitel Maeva Beach (Map pp84-5; ☎ 42 80 42; www
.sofitel.com; Maeva Beach; d 16,000-20,000 CFP; ☒ ▣ ☎)
With prices that nudge it into the midrange
category, this resort is one of the better deals
on the island. The '70s-style exterior could
use a facelift, but rooms, with sheer yellow
curtains, bright orange appliqué bedspreads
and lime-green countertops in the bathrooms, definitely have one of the happiest
colour schemes around (if you can handle it).
The pool is ordinary, but the semi-manmade
white-sand beach with Mo'orea smack dab
in the distance really makes you feel you are
on a tropical holiday. Le Sakura restaurant
(see p92) serves the best Japanese food this
side of Hawaii.

Le Royal Tahitien (Map pp84-5; ☎ 50 40 40; www.hotel
royaltahitien.com; r 18,000 CFP; ☒ ☎) The c 1975
tiki-tacky decor here might be leftover but
it's so well kept that it's become appealingly
retro and refreshingly unpretentious. Rooms
have Brady Bunch–style wood panelling,
olive-green carpet and burnt orange Formica
countertops but they're clean and the staff
are smiling. The grounds are stunning, with
flourishing mango trees, plumeria everywhere
and a pool with a cool fake waterfall, wood *tiki*
panels and plenty of foliage. The beach is a
skinny strip of black. Local musicians perform
on Friday and Saturday evenings and the place
can really rock with locals and tourists alike.
It's about 3km east of Pape'ete in Pira'e. Hunt
the internet for discounts.

Hotel le Mandarin (Map pp86-7; ☎ 50 33 50; www
.hotelmandarin.com; Rue Colette; r from 18,000 CFP; ☒ ▣)
Clean and with pretty hardwood floors and
colourful Polynesian bedspreads, this is one of
the city's better midrange bets. Central to the
quay and market, it also has a highly recommended restaurant attached.

Hotel Tahiti Nui (Map pp86-7; ☎ 50 33 50; www.hotel
tahitinui.com; r/ste 18,000/25,000 CFP; ☒ ▣ ☎) Not
yet open at the time of research, the Tahiti
Nui is a 90-room hotel right in the heart of
Pape'ete and 50 of the rooms are kitchen-
equipped suites. It's owned by the same folks
as Hotel le Mandarin but will be a step up in
luxury, with a pool and a business centre.

Top End

Luxury reigns supreme at these hotels, which
are all slightly outside Pape'ete or in the nearby
suburbs by the lagoon. Several times a week
these places offer Polynesian dance performances by the best groups on the island.

Radisson Plaza Resort Tahiti (Map pp84-5; ☎ 48 88
88; www.radisson.com/tahiti; r from 26,000 CFP; ☒ ▣ ☎)
East of Pape'ete is this elegant hotel on a
black-sand beach lined with almond trees
and fronted with Mo'orea views. The exterior
of the hotel looks like a common apartment
block but once you enter the minimalist-chic
lobby things get much better. Nearly all the
dark but tastefully designed rooms have a sea
view; angle for one on the upper floors for the
most privacy. Staff are particularly friendly
and there's a less ostentatious vibe here than
at Tahiti's other high-end resorts.

Sheraton Hotel Tahiti (Map pp84-5; ☎ 86 48 48;
www.starwoodtahiti.com; r from 33,000 CFP; ☒ ▣ ☎)
Despite its complete lack of beach, the
Sheraton is a lovely place for a short stay.
The lagoonside pool is fantastic, the hot tub
(creatively placed on top of a pile of rocks) has
awesome Mo'orea views and there's an over-

water restaurant and bar. Rooms are spacious and comfortable, but not super-swank.

Intercontinental Resort Tahiti (Map pp84–5; ☎ 86 51 10; www.tahiti.interconti.com; r/bungalows from 40,000/55,000 CFP; ✻ ▣ ☎) Hands down, this is the best luxury resort on the island. The Intercontinental (formerly Beachcomber) is as posh as Tahiti gets. Marble bathrooms, plush canopies and Mo'orea views from private balconies are standard both in the rooms and romantic over-water bungalows, which range from smallish to quite spacious. The two swimming pools are fabulous (one features a slick, cascading horizon) and the water-sports centre is the best on the island. On the downside, the beach here is artificial (it's made from imported white sand) and the lagoon is not nearly as translucent or dreamy as ones that you'll find on other islands.

EATING

Whatever you think of the capital, you're sure to have memorable eating experiences here. You can skip cuisines from French to Polynesian to Chinese and back again via Italian and Vietnamese – you couldn't possibly tire of dining in Pape'ete.

Ma'a Tahiti is often served as a special on Fridays at many budget and midrange places.

Unless otherwise noted, the following places all accept credit cards.

Budget

Self-catering is a breeze in Pape'ete. The market (p84) has fresh fish, fruit and vegies, and **Supermarché Champion** (Map pp86–7; Rue du Commandant Destremeau), close to the Temple Paofai, is handy if you're in the city centre.

Polyself (Map pp86–7; Rue Paul Gauguin; sandwiches from 150 CFP; mains 650–1100 CFP; ✻ breakfast & lunch) You can get breakfasts here such as as-you-like-them eggs as well as quick lunches of cheap sandwiches or pretty good Chinese and French-Tahitian food. It's all cafeteria-style point-and-slop service. You can also get takeaway but the air-con might entice you to take a seat.

ourpick **Place Vaiete Roulottes** (Pl Vaiete; treats from 200 CFP; mains from 800 CFP; ✻ dinner) The country's famous *roulottes* (literally 'caravans' in French, these are mobile food vans) are a wondrous gastronomic pleasure. These little stalls sizzle, fry and grill up a storm every evening from around 6pm; things don't quiet down until

well into the night. There are dozens of *roulottes* to choose from. Squeeze in next to that guy devouring his steak and chips and that woman relishing her chow mein. Get good thin-crust pizzas or everything and anything else from hamburgers to crêpes. Finish your meal with a Nutella-and-banana waffle. Live music livens the scene most weekend nights.

ourpick **Patachoux** (Map pp86–7; ☎ 83 72 82; sandwiches from 480 CFP; ✻ Mon-Sat) Takeaway sandwiches here are the deluxe version – fresh wholemeal or French bread stuffed with gourmet meats, fish and/or salads. Otherwise sit at the outdoor patio (on a lively pedestrian-only street) and order from an ever-changing menu of salads and fresh fish with international flair. Desserts like fruit tarts, mysterious creamy French pastries and a divine chocolate fondant from the bakery window are not to be missed.

La Saladière (Map pp86–7; ☎ 79 24 54; Quartier du Commerce; salads 700–1200 CFP, mains 1200–1800 CFP; ✻ 6am-3.30pm Mon-Fri) A gay-friendly and generally friendly stop for Tahitian (from 8am), American or Continental breakfasts (from 6am) or a meal-sized salad lunch – there's also hearty mains, panini and burgers. Seating is outdoors in a quiet pedestrian-only area.

Midrange

Restaurant Jimmy (Map pp86–7; ☎ 43 63 32; Rue Colette; dishes 1100–2000 CFP; ✻ lunch & dinner) Choose from Thai, Vietnamese or Chinese at this dimly lit local favourite. Thai mains are far from authentic but the rest of the menu is quite good. Take a table upstairs and try the *bo bun* salad (1300 CFP), a delicious creation of green salad, thin noodles and either grilled beef or chicken or Vietnamese spring rolls on top.

Lou Pescadou (Map pp86–7; ☎ 43 74 26; Rue Anne-Marie Javouhey; dishes 1100–3000 CFP; ✻ lunch & dinner) A Pape'ete institution, this cheery restaurant has hearty pizza and pasta dishes. It's authentic Italian, right down to the red-and-white check tablecloths and carafes of red wine. Service is fast and there are lots of vegie options. Check out the cartoons of owner Mario on the walls – these come from his signature newspaper ads through the years.

L'Api'zzeria (Map pp86–7; ☎ 42 98 30; Blvd Pomare; dishes 1000–2500 CFP; ✻ lunch & dinner) This semi-outdoor haven is often packed, the service is good and it's one of the few spots in town where you can get served an off-hour meal at

TAHITI

say, 4pm. The wood-fired thin-crust pizzas are very good, as are the pastas and salads.

Marché de Pape'ete (Map pp86-7; Marché de Pape'ete upstairs; mains 1200 CFP; ☺ breakfast & lunch) Grab one of the daily specials (usually couscous or a Tahitian-style stew) at the cafeteria-style counter and sit at a table in the heat of the market to enjoy regular live local music and plenty of local colour. *Ma'a Tahiti* is served on Fridays.

New Port (Map pp86-7; ☎ 42 76 52; Blvd Pomare; dishes 1400-2500 CFP; ☺ breakfast & lunch Mon-Sat) This place has the best sashimi in town. If you like or want to try raw fish in its many forms, order the *assiette* Newport (1800 CFP), which has a small portion of sashimi, *poisson cru* (raw fish) and *tartar du thon* so you can try them all. Otherwise there are plenty of cooked fish, meat dishes and salads to choose from.

Barrumundi (Map pp86-7; ☎ 42 05 35; Rue du Général de Gaulle; sushi plates from 250 CFP; mains from 1500 CFP; ☺ lunch Tue, lunch & dinner Wed-Sat) You get two restaurants in one at this place: a trendy nouveau-style sushi restaurant downstairs and a swanky French place upstairs. The excellent and creative sushi arrives via floating conveyer belt – you pay by the plate. Upstairs, tables have a view over the busy streets of Pape'ete. Both halves serve excellent cocktails (from 900 CFP).

Café de la Gare (Map pp86-7; ☎ 42 75 95; Rue du Général de Gaulle; dishes 1500-3000 CFP; ☺ lunch & dinner) This place has the feel of a true Parisian bistro – chic and packed. Ultra-tiny, it serves a menu of grilled meats and salads. Later the tables are cleared away and DJs spin house music for a trendy, young crowd well into the night (see opposite).

La Squadra (Map pp86-7; ☎ 41 32 14; Passage Cardella; dishes from 1500 CFP; ☺ lunch Mon-Sat, dinner Wed-Sun) A solid Italian restaurant; it has an extensive menu, with some less-traditional offerings and the usual assortment of hearty pasta dishes.

Top End

Restaurant Le Belvédère (Map pp84-5; ☎ 42 73 44; dishes 2000-5000 CFP; ☺ lunch & dinner) The views over Pape'ete are fantastic, particularly at sunset. Fondues are the speciality at this fine-dining restaurant, which is perched 600m above the city in Pira'e. Le Belvédère provides free transport from some hotels in Pape'ete at 11.45am, 4.30pm and 7pm. If you drive, take the first right after the Hamuta Total petrol station.

The 7km road to the restaurant is steep, winding and rugged towards the top.

Mango Café (Map pp86-7; ☎ 43 25 55; Rue Jeanne d'Arc; dishes 2500-4000 CFP; ☺ lunch Mon-Fri, dinner Tue-Sat) As far as decor goes, this Miami-style white and bright restaurant is as stylish as Pape'ete gets. The Tahitian nouveau-style menu here changes regularly but always has lots of locally inspired dishes such as *mahi mahi* (dorado fish) with *fafa* (taro leaves), coconut sauce and ginger (2500 CFP) or *magret de canard* (duck breast) with fresh mangoes (3500 CFP). The wine list is one of the best on the island and the owner (who used to teach about wine at the Culinary Academy in San Francisco) will often visit your table if you need a suggestion.

La Corbeille d'Eau (Map pp86-7; ☎ 43 77 14; Blvd Pomare; appetisers & dishes 2500-5000 CFP; ☺ lunch & dinner) There are no prices on the menu, but for the exceptional dining experience you get at this intimate French place you'll be happy to pay whatever it costs once the bill comes. There are only a handful of tables and the focus is on the food, which is prepared by one of Tahiti's best chefs. While local ingredients are often used, the experience is 100% French gastronomy.

our pick Le Sakura (Map pp84-5; ☎ 86 66 00; Sofitel Maeva Beach; teppanyaki 3500-7000 CFP; ☺ 6.30-9.30pm Tue-Sat) It's tucked away in an unlikely location at the Sofitel Maeva Beach, but this tiny Japanese teppanyaki grill restaurant is packed nightly with as many locals as tourists – reserve in advance. You eat at the bar while friendly chefs theatrically grill your choice of meats, fish and vegies right in front of you on an iron griddle. There's also good sushi (an assortment is 1500 CFP).

DRINKING

After a stay on other islands, where nightlife is just about nonexistent, Pape'ete could almost pass itself off as a city of wild abandon, though it only gets super-crazy on weekends.

On a balmy tropical evening the first question is where to go for a cold Hinano beer or a well-poured *maitai* (local cocktail). Many of the places along Blvd Pomare, the noisy nightlife strip, look pretty seedy, but they are frequented by plenty of local women and are generally safe for single female travellers (although you may be bothered by harmless suitors) – just don't go wandering up any dark alleys.

Bars & Pubs

The snazzy top-end hotels, such as the Sheraton Hotel Tahiti and the Intercontinental Resort Tahiti, all have bars where you can enjoy the ocean breezes and nibble the free peanuts.

Ute Ute Café (Map pp86-7; ☎ 53 46 46) Meaning 'red hot' in Tahitian, that's exactly what this place is right now. Decor is city lounge-style red and black and the coolest DJs and live bands play here. It also serves nouvelle cuisine (with dishes like prime rib with porcini mushrooms flambéed in Jack Daniels) that's just as hip as the café itself.

Morrison's Café (Map pp86-7; ☎ 42 78 61) Upstairs in the Vaima Centre is this popular spot for a drink. Rock and blues groups play several times a week and occasionally foreign DJs stop by for a spin.

Café de la Gare (Map pp86-7; ☎ 42 75 95; Rue du Général de Gaulle) Terribly chic, terribly French, it's an intimate spot for a classy cocktail with a popular happy hour that attracts the beautiful people and professional crowd.

Les 3 Brasseurs (Map pp86-7; Blvd Pomare) This congenial brewpub has excellent microbrewed beer on tap and a constant stream of locals and tourists wanting to sample it. Cover bands perform here at the weekend and you can also chow on some good French-style pub grub for lunch and dinner.

Le Rétro (Map pp86-7; ☎ 42 86 83; Blvd Pomare; ☯ lunch & dinner) It's overpriced with only so-so food (dishes 1500 to 3000 CFP), but the location, smack in the centre of Pape'ete in the Vaima Centre, is perhaps the best in town. It's full of attitude and atmosphere and is a great place to watch the world go by while sipping an espresso.

Tiki Soft C@fé (Map pp86-7; ☎ 88 93 98) DJs play music here on weekends; during the week it's a chilled-out internet cafe and coffee shop turned bar, where couples make small talk over the newspaper, fresh fruit juice or a strong *maitai*.

Nightclubs

Blvd Pomare is the main drag for nightclubs and discos. From the Tahitian waltz to European electronic music, it's all here. Dress codes are enforced and men in shorts or flip-flops will be turned away; women can get away with wearing as little as they like. Admission for men is between 1500 and 2000 CFP (which will usually include a free drink) but women can usually get in for free. Clubs typically close around 3am or 4am.

Le Paradise Night (Map pp86-7; Blvd Pomare; ☯ Wed-Sat) This is the classic, slightly kitsch Pape'ete bar-disco that attracts a mixed crowd of Polynesians and French.

Royal Kikiriri (Map pp86-7; ☎ 43 58 64; Rue Colette) A local favourite, the Royal Kikiriri showcases live music with its namesake band every night. Just about everyone gets asked to dance and you'll soon be swaying your hips in local foxtrot or *tamure* style. The 1500 CFP admission fee includes a drink at the weekend; entry is free other nights.

Mana Rock Café (Map pp86-7; Rue des Écoles; men 2000 CFP; ☯ Fri & Sat) Half the clientele here seem to be under 18 while the other half are visiting surfers and local hipsters. The pounding techno might make the head throb.

Piano Bar (Map pp86-7; Rue des Écoles; admission Fri & Sat 2000 CFP) A favourite with local transvestites this small club attracts a mixed clientele from French military to passing tourists – it's the classic, timeless seedy port bar and everyone gets their groove on. The music (techno, dance, local) isn't as important as the general atmosphere – snag a dark corner and soak it in. There's a drag show on Friday and Saturday nights around 2am and the weekend entry price includes a drink.

Club 106 (Map pp86-7; men 2000 CFP; ☯ Thu-Sat) The crowd is mostly on the other side of 30 and dances to '80s hits. The admission price includes a drink.

ENTERTAINMENT

From dance performances to French cinema, Pape'ete offers plenty of choices for those not interested in a night of bar-hopping.

Cinemas

The **Concorde** (Map pp86-7; ☎ 42 63 60; Rue du Général de Gaulle) in the Vaima Centre, **Hollywood** (Map pp86-7; ☎ 42 65 79; Rue Largarde) in the Fare Tony, and **Liberty** (Map pp86-7; ☎ 42 08 20; Rue du Maréchal Foch) all screen Hollywood blockbusters dubbed in French and the occasional French film. Screens are in poor shape and the sound systems are horrendous. Admission costs 1200 CFP.

Dance Performances

Tahiti is a good island for tapping your toes along to some of the best Polynesian dance and music groups, many of which appear several times a week in the big hotels. Those worried about cheesy, touristy performances can rest assured these groups are very professional and are enjoyed every bit as much by locals as by wide-eyed visitors. When held in the luxury hotels, these performances are often accompanied by a buffet (which usually costs around 8000 CFP), although parking yourself at the bar and ordering a drink will sometimes suffice. Check with the hotel reception desks at the Sheraton Hotel Tahiti, Intercontinental Resort Tahiti and Sofitel Maeva Beach about their programs and entrance policies. If you are in the region during the Heiva you'll be spoilt for choice – there are performances most nights (see p89 and boxed text, p48).

SHOPPING

In Pape'ete you can buy products from all over French Polynesia, including clothes, pearls and more pearls. For a truly great-smelling shopping experience check out the **Vanilla Market** (Map pp86-7; Quartier de Commerce; 9am-4pm Mon-Fri, 9am-noon Sat). Nearly everything in the shop is made from local vanilla; you can get whole pods (from 600 CFP for five) plus vanilla-infused honey, scented coconut cooking oil, incense, soaps and much more.

Art

Pape'ete is home to a number of art galleries. **Galerie des Tropiques** (Map pp86-7; ☎ 41 05 00; To'ata Sq) and **Olivier Creations** (Map pp86-7; ☎ 48 29 36; Rue Paul Gauguin) are recommended. **Gallerie Winkler** (Map pp86-7; ☎ 42 81 77; Rue Jeanne d'Arc) has an interesting mix of etchings, paintings and crockery.

Handicrafts

Upstairs in the Marché de Pape'ete (p84) you can wander for ages among the handicrafts. Wooden salad servers, fabric, wonderful homemade *monoi* (fragrant coconut oil), *pareu*, jewellery and even mother-of-pearl love-heart key rings can be purchased here. Watch out, though – anything that seems to be mass-produced probably is, in China, Indonesia or the Philippines.

There are heaps of craft and souvenir shops (of varying quality) along Blvd Pomare and Rue du Général de Gaulle and in the Fare Tony and Vaima Centre.

Music

Music shops where you can find local and Western music are dotted around Pape'ete. Try Tahiti Music, diagonally opposite the cathedral, which has a decent selection of CDs by local artists for around 3500 CFP; you can listen before you buy.

HOW TO BUY A PEARL

Pearl buying isn't as complicated as it looks. When shopping around look out for these qualities:

Shape Pearls come in various shapes from perfectly round or teardrop shaped (the two most expensive) to misshapen globs. Many pearls have rings etched around them (called *circlé*) that increase their artistic value but decrease their price.

Size Tahitian pearls start at around 7mm and go up from there (the biggest Tahitian pearl ever recorded is 25mm). The bigger they are, the pricier they are.

Colour From black to white to everything in between. Look for greens, pinks, silvers, golds, blues and purples. What you like is up to you.

Surface Quality Dimples, scrapes, cloudy spots and other imperfections decrease a pearl's value. A dull white spot anywhere means the pearl is of very low quality, so don't buy it.

Lustre How shiny is it? A high-quality pearl has a near liquid-looking surface.

Nacre Thickness This refers to the thickness of the layer of mother of pearl on top of the nucleus inside. Nacre wears away eventually so if the layer is too thin you'll be left with dull patches on your pearl, especially if you wear it a lot. The only way to determine nacre thickness is with an x-ray, so in many cases you simply can't know. Use common sense: if you buy cheap pearls in the 1000 CFP bin of shops, you're probably getting a thin-skinned pearl.

But the most important factor is do you like the pearl? Many people try so hard to determine how much a pearl is worth that they forget to take into account their own tastes. If you love it, buy it.

Pearls

There are so many jewellery shops and pearl specialists in Pape'ete that you have to be careful not to trip over them. Look around before buying, and consider purchasing a pearl here and getting it set at home (this will probably work out cheaper and ensures you get exactly what you want). Depending on the quality, you can by a single pearl for around 10,000 CFP (cheaper if you don't mind imperfections and much more expensive for something really outrageous); for a decent-quality ring you are looking at anywhere from 60,000 CFP. Also bear in mind that there are numerous pearl shops and pearl farms on the outer islands, so don't rush into purchasing.

Tattoos

So you really don't want to forget your trip to Tahiti? Try one of these recommended shops:
Aroma & Mano Salmon (Map pp86–7; ☎ Aroma 70 95 73, Mano 27 06 38; demonaroma@yahoo.com; Marché de Pape'ete) Popular shop with many styles available.
Mana'O Tattoo (Map pp86–7; ☎ 42 45 00; www .manaotattoo.com; 43 Rue Albert Leboucher) The four artists cater to tourists.

GETTING THERE & AWAY
Air

Faa'a airport (Map pp84–5; pronounced fa-ah-ah) is the aviation centre of French Polynesia. All international flights arrive here, and Air Tahiti and Air Moorea flights to the other islands leave from here. Flights within each archipelago hop from one island to the next, but many connections between archipelagos are via Faa'a.

International check-in desks are at the east end of the terminal. Air Tahiti's domestic check-in is at the west end; Air Moorea is in a separate small terminal slightly to the east of the main terminal.

For international flights to and from Tahiti, see p254; for general information about air travel within French Polynesia, see p258; and for connections to/from an island group or an individual island, see the relevant chapter or section.

AIRLINES

In Pape'ete, **Air Tahiti** (Map pp86–7; ☎ 86 42 42; Rue du Maréchal Foch; ☘ 7am-5pm Mon-Fri, 8-11am Sat) is at the intersection with Rue Edouard Ahnne. It also has an **office** (☘ 5am-5.30pm) in the domestic area of the airport.

For **Air Tahiti Nui** (Map pp86–7; ☎ 46 03 03; Pont de L'Est; ☘ 8am-5pm Mon-Fri, 8-11am Sat), the main office is between the Pae'ete Maire and the Pont de L'Est roundabout.

On Tahiti, **Air Moorea** (☎ 86 41 41) is based at Faa'a airport.

For international airline offices, see p254.

The following charter operators and helicopter services are available on Tahiti and are based at Faa'a airport:
Air Archipels (☎ 81 30 30)
Polynesia Hélicoptères (☎ 54 87 20)

Boat

All boats to other islands moor at the ferry quay (Map pp86–7) at the northern end of Blvd Pomare. Cruise ships and other interesting visitors moor at the Quai d'Honneur (Map pp86–7) close to the tourist office and the *capitainerie* (harbour master's office). The numerous cargo ships to the different archipelagos work from the Motu Uta port zone, to the north of the city (*le truck* route 3 from the *mairie*).

See p260 for general information on interisland ships, and the individual island chapters or sections for specific information on travel to/from those destinations.

GETTING AROUND

See p257 for information about car hire, buses and hitching in Tahiti.

To/From the Airport

Given that most flights into Faa'a arrive at an ungodly hour of the morning, and public transport stops around 10pm, Pape'ete joins that long list of places in the world where travellers pay exorbitant fees to get from the airport into town.

Taxis are expensive everywhere in French Polynesia, so if your hotel offers to collect you from the airport, jump at the chance. Otherwise, the taxi drive to central Pape'ete will set you back 2000 CFP during the day and 2500 CFP at night (8pm to 6am). Officially the taxis also charge an extra 100 CFP for baggage, but this is sometimes waived. At least drivers don't expect to be tipped.

If you arrive at a reasonable time of the day, you'll be able to catch any bus going towards town from the airport (northeast bound or to your left as you leave the airport), which will take you straight to the centre of Pape'ete in about 15 minutes for a flat fare of 130 CFP during the day and 250 CFP after 6pm (children cost 65 CFP; it's an extra 100 CFP for your baggage). Walk straight across the car park outside the airport, up the steps to street level and across the road to hail a city-bound *le truck*. From Pape'ete to the airport, take a bus heading to Faa'a and Outumaoro – the destination will be clearly posted on the front – from along Rue du Général de Gaulle.

Taxi

Taxis are so expensive that most visitors choose to ignore them (except when arriving at the airport late at night). Apart from the official government-established flat fares from the airport to most hotels, taxis are metered. Any trip of a reasonable length will approximate a day's car rental, so if you want wheels you may as well rent them (see p262).

All the big hotels have taxi ranks, and there are plenty of taxis in central Pape'ete.

AROUND TAHITI NUI

It's another world outside of Pape'ete; the sea is a deep blue, the jagged, green mountains frame the sky and cars putter along at 50km/h. While many people just zip around the 120km circuit taking everything in from their car windows, it's better to do as the locals do by taking it slow, stopping often and soaking in the incredible lushness. Smile because this is paradise.

WEST COAST

Tahiti Nui's west coast is busier and much more touristy than the island's eastern side. It has the greatest concentration of places to stay outside Pape'ete plus many of the museums and major sights.

Sights & Activities

Tahiti Nui has some interesting attractions; for more on regional activities including surfing, see p80.

MUSÉE DE TAHITI ET DES ÎLES

Only 15km from Pape'ete along the west coast, the excellent **Musée de Tahiti et des Îles** (Museum of Tahiti & Its Islands; Map pp78–9; ☎ 58 34 76; admission 1000 CFP; ☒ 9.30am-5.30pm Tue-Sun) is in

Puna'auia (below). The museum is divided into four sections: geography and natural history; pre-European culture; the European era; and outdoor exhibits. It's in a large garden and if you get tired of history, culture and art, you can wander out to the water's edge to watch the surfers at one of Tahiti's most popular breaks.

The museum is several hundred metres from the coastal road after the Punaruu bridge and just before the Temanu shopping centre. From Pape'ete, a Puna'auia *le truck* will drop you at the road junction. Check the last return trip time (usually 4.30pm or so).

PUNA'AUIA

There are good **beaches** between PK15 and PK21 (for more details, see p76). Puna'auia also has an excellent restaurant scene (see opposite). The most expensive homes on Tahiti are found along this stretch of coast, along the beach and high above the coast to better enjoy the breathtaking views across to Mo'orea. For divers, the St Etienne Drop-Off just outside the Puna'auia reef is a perfect wall dive.

MARAE ARAHURAHU & AROUND

Whether or not you believe in the powers of the *tiki* (sacred statue), it's hard to deny there is an amazing energy radiating from **Marae Arahurahu** (Map pp78–9; PK22.5) in the Pa'ea district. Tranquil, huge and beautifully maintained, the *marae* (traditional temple) is undoubtedly the best-looking one on the island and even rivals those on other islands.

The **Orofero River** (PK20), now a popular surfing site, was the spot where Pomare II fought the 1815 battle that reinstated him as ruler of Tahiti.

MARAA GROTTO

Lush gardens, overhung caverns, crystal-clear pools and ferny grottoes are all standard features at gorgeous **Maraa Grotto** (Map pp78–9; PK28.5). The fairytale park is found along the coastal road, and a manicured path runs throughout. It's a popular stop on round-the-island circuits, but also well worth visiting on your own.

Sleeping

There are a number of places to stay along the west coast, particularly around Puna'auia.

Compared with Pape'ete these places offer much more of a beach holiday type of experience.

Pension Te Miti (Map pp78-9; ☎ 58 48 61; www .pensiontemiti.com; PK18.6; dm 2500 CFP, r from 6500 CFP; 😎) Run by a young, friendly French couple, this lively place has a low-key backpacker vibe and is deservedly popular with young travellers. It's on the mountain side of the main road in Pa'ea, about 200m from the white-sand beach. Prices include breakfast. There's an equipped communal kitchen, a few bicycles for guests' use and a laundry service (500 CFP); 24-hour airport transfers are available for 1500 CFP per person. Credit cards accepted.

ourpick Taaroa Lodge (Map pp78-9; ☎ 58 39 21; www.taaroalodge.com; PK18; dm 2500 CFP, r 6000 CFP, bungalows 10,000 CFP) Right on the beach and a fabulous bargain, you'll have to book way in advance to get a bed here. Breakfast is included, and there are kitchen facilities and a friendly atmosphere. The lodge is owned by Ralph Stanford, an ex-longboard surfing champion of Tahiti and France.

Pension de la Plage (Map pp78-9; ☎ 45 56 12; www .pensiondelaplage.com; PK15.4; s/d/f 8000/9000/13,000 CFP; 😑 😎) Just across the road from Puna'auia's white-sand beach, this impeccably maintained place offers comfortable motel-style rooms in several gardenside buildings around a swimming pool. Each has tile floors and giant windows; some have kitchenettes. Breakfast is available for 900 CFP, dinner for 2500 CFP.

Le Relais Fenua (Map pp78-9; ☎ 45 01 98; www .relais-fenua.pf; PK18.25; r from 9500 CFP; 😎 😑 😎) A great option in Pa'ea, with clean and spacious rooms with TVs set around a little swimming pool. The lagoon is stumbling distance away, and there are a few affordable eating options just around the corner. Airport transfers cost 1500 CFP and breakfast costs 1000 CFP per person; prices go down in low season and for longer stays.

Manava Suite Resort Tahiti (Map pp78-9; ☎ 50 84 45; www.pearlresorts.com; PK10.8; 😎 😑 😎) Scheduled to open in April 2009, the Manava is run by the same people who manage the Pearl Resorts and will offer modern suites and studios, all with mini-kitchens. The infinity pool promises to be the biggest on Tahiti. Check the website for prices.

Le Méridien (Map pp78-9; ☎ 47 07 07; www .lemeridien.com; r from 38,000 CFP, bungalows 72,000 CFP; 😎 😑 😎) Le Méridien has truly lovely grounds dotted with lily ponds and fronted by a natural white-sand beach that has Mo'orea views – if you want a resort where you can swim in the lagoon this is your best bet. The rooms are a bit disappointing, with tiled floors and ageing furniture and bedspreads. The over-water bungalows, however, are stylishly built with hard woods and natural materials. We found the service here outstanding and the waterfront Carré restaurant has a great reputation. Dance performances with buffet take place on Friday nights.

Eating

Besides the following finer restaurants, there are plenty of tasty *roulottes* that open up along the roadside at night.

Western Grill (Map pp78-9; ☎ 41 30 56; PK12.6; mains 1500-2500 CFP; ⌚ lunch & dinner) Tired of raw fish? Tie your pony up at this saloon, complete with a Native American statue by the door and Western kitsch a go-go, for a good ol' American steak or burger and a beer. There are also creative but delicious interpretations of Mexican food available.

Pink Coconut (Map pp84-5; ☎ 41 22 23; Marina Taina; mains from 1600 CFP; ⌚ lunch & dinner) We love this lively spot located right on Marina Taina among the sailboats. Dine on French-inspired fare like delicious risotto with scallops and wild mushrooms or French-style shellfish platters. At night it's candlelit and there's sometimes live music and dancing on the weekends. Two other good, animated restaurants are also at this marina, so you can sort of bar-hop on weekends for a low-key night out.

Blue Banana (Map pp78-9; ☎ 41 22 24; PK11.2; dishes 2000-4000 CFP; ⌚ lunch & dinner Mon-Sat; 😎) Keeping on the psychedelic fruit theme, this hip new, lagoonside restaurant (it replaced the L'Auberge du Pacific) is heavenly romantic. The roof in the main dining room retracts, revealing a starry night-sky tableau. The food is as good as the ambience – feast on innovative French dishes (small portions but artistically presented) and fine French vintages from the air-conditioned cellar. Reservations recommended on weekends.

ourpick Coco's Restaurant (Map pp78-9; ☎ 58 21 08; PK16; dishes 2000-4500 CFP; ⌚ lunch & dinner) Dine in a gorgeous open plantation-style house bordered by a tropical garden that's framed

TAHITI

by coconut trees and looks out to Mo'orea. This is the sort of place that doesn't list prices on the menu and each dish is served under a silver dome so that everyone can unveil their meal at the same time. The fine food is very French, with lots of seafood options. Arguably Tahiti's swankiest and most romantic option.

SOUTH COAST

Moving further away from Pape'ete, the coastline from the village of Pa'ea to Taravao is much more quiet than the west coast from which it continues. Here you'll find a few interesting sights and some breathtaking diving (for details, see p64), as well as some decent places to sleep and eat.

Sights

The following sights are listed in an anticlockwise direction.

MARAE MAHAIATEA

Just east of the village of Papara, the Marae Mahaiatea (Map pp78–9) was the most magnificent *marae* on Tahiti at the time of Cook's first visit (according to Cook it measured 80m by 27m at its base, rising in 11 great steps to a height of 13m). Today the crumbling remains of the *marae* are still impressive for their sheer size.

Coming from Pape'ete, take the first turn towards the sea past the PK39 sign. Follow the road about half a kilometre all the way towards the coast. In the middle of the carpark area are the hidden massive remains of the *marae*.

MATAIEA

Between 1891 and 1893, Gauguin lived in Mataiea (Map pp78–9) where he produced works including *Two Women on the Beach, Woman with a Mango* and *Ia Orana Maria – Hail Mary*.

To the east of Mataiea, at PK47.5, is the turn-off for the rough track up to Lake Vaihiria, the Relais de la Maroto hotel and the north coast.

Heading towards Papara is the golf course at Atimaono at PK42 (p77), the site of the 1860s Terre Eugénie cotton plantation. Chinese workers were shipped in to supplant unwilling Polynesians, and descendants of the Chinese immigrants still live on the island today.

BAIN DE VAIMA & VAIPAHI SPRING GARDENS

Before the botanical gardens is Vaima Pool (Map pp78–9), where locals come from all over to bathe in the icy but exceptionally clear waters that are thought to have healing properties. Unfortunately, there are so many visitors here on weekends and holidays that the 'clean' pools can get filled with rubbish.

The Vaipahi Spring Gardens further along is a beautifully landscaped garden with a magnificent natural waterfall. There's a small network of hiking trails that lead from a signpost with a map up to more waterfalls and forests of *mape* (chestnut) and pine trees. The trails are well maintained but it's easy to get lost because they are not marked beyond the main sign. The longest loop takes a little over two hours to walk if you're in reasonable shape – and parts are pretty steep!

JARDIN BOTANIQUE & MUSÉE GAUGUIN

Tahiti's Jardin Botanique and the interesting Musée Gauguin share an entrance road and car park at PK51.2.

The 137-hectare **Jardin Botanique** (Botanical Gardens; Map pp78-9; admission 600 CFP; ☺ 9am-5pm) has walking paths that wind their way through the garden past ponds, palms and a superb *mape* forest. The gardens were founded in 1919 by an American, Harrison Smith, who introduced many plants to Tahiti including the large Southeast Asian pomelo known on Tahiti as *pamplemousse,* the French word for grapefruit. Unfortunately, Smith also introduced one or two botanical disasters that Tahiti could well have done without. Look out for the huge Galápagos tortoises. Mosquitoes in the gardens can be fierce.

The **Musée Gauguin** (Gauguin Museum; Map pp78-9; ☎ 57 10 58; admission 600 CFP; ☺ 9am-5pm) was preparing for renovations at the time of writing and is definitely worth a visit. Much of the text about Gauguin and his life is in English, and although the museum is dimly lit and there is a conspicuous lack of original works by Gauguin, there's a lovely natural setting. The museum gardens are home to three superb *tiki* from Raivavae in the Australs. *Tiki* do not like to be moved, and there are colourful stories about what happened to the men that moved these *tiki* here (they apparently died 'mysteriously' within weeks of the move). The huge *tiki* figure beside the walkway stands 2.2m high and weighs 900kg; it's a baby compared with the figure towards the waterfront, which stands 2.7m high and weighs 2110kg. You'll find a third, smaller figure beside the giant.

Sleeping & Eating

There are a few places to stay and dine on the south coast.

Hiti Moana Villa (Map pp78–9; ☎ 57 93 93; hiti moanavilla@mail.pf; PK32; bungalows from 9000 CFP; ▣) Impeccably clean bungalows set around a well-tended garden make this lagoonside spot in Papara a great option. There is no beach, but there is a pontoon for swimming and a small swimming pool. Bicycles, *pirogues* and kayaks can be rented. Airport transfers cost 1500 CFP per person each way. Credit cards accepted.

Chez Marie Claire (Map pp78–9; ☎ 57 44 69; PK53.1; mains 800-1800 CFP; ✆ lunch Wed-Sun, dinner nightly) It's amazing that a place this big out in the middle of nowhere can fill up nightly but Chez Marie Claire does. It's a basic open restaurant with red plastic chairs, an extensive and very good Chinese-Tahitian menu and lots of local atmosphere.

Snack du Jardin Botanique (Map pp78–9; ☎ 51 17 59; Botanical Gardens; mains 1800-2500 CFP; ✆ lunch daily) Skip the overpriced Restaurant Musée Gauguin that's actually not attached to the museum at all, and instead stop at this more humble beachside *snack* (snack bar) right in the Jardin Botanique parking lot. Dishes like grilled fish in vanilla coconut sauce, steaks and shellfish are some of our favourites on this coast and on Sundays there's a full authentic *ma'a Tahiti* for 3000 CFP.

Restaurant Nuutere (Map pp78–9; ☎ 57 41 15; PK32.5; dishes 2000-3500 CFP; ✆ Wed-Mon) You won't be able to miss the extravagantly painted facade at this great little restaurant. French specialities, cooked with local ingredients and some odd imported ones like ostrich or crocodile, are served in an intimate dining room. One speciality is the *korori* (pearl oyster meat) starter baked gratin-style in sea-snail shells. Don't expect fast service. Credit cards are accepted.

EAST COAST

The east coast is the quietest and most isolated section of Tahiti Nui. The road winds between cliffs and sea, and the views, deep into valleys and out along the reefless, jagged coast, are simply stunning. Sleeping and eating options

are limited on this coast, but it's a must-see for a day trip.

Sights & Activities

From lava tubes to waterfalls and a blowhole, the east coast has some seriously great natural attractions.

TARAVAO

Strategically situated at the narrow isthmus connecting Tahiti Nui with Tahiti Iti, the town of **Taravao** (PK54) has been a military base on and off since 1844, when the first French fort was established. The original fort was intended to forestall Tahitian guerrilla forces opposed to the French takeover from mounting operations against Tahiti Nui from Tahiti Iti. Today the **Faratea Port** (Map pp78–9), on the northeastern side of the isthmus, is being built to shift commercial sea trade from Pape'ete (which is getting gussied up for tourists) to Taravao.

From Taravao, roads run along the north and south coasts of Tahiti Iti. The central road into the Tahiti Iti plateau commences a short distance along a back road that links the north coast road with the south coast road. Although there is little of interest in the town, it does have shops, banks, petrol stations and a number of small restaurants (see p100).

HITIAA LAVA TUBES

These lava tubes (Map pp78–9) are elongated tunnels formed by the cooling and rapid hardening of lava. A river runs through the giant, wormlike caves so that hiking through them actually means lots of swimming in cold water. The hike can only be attempted when there's little or no chance of rain (you wouldn't want to be here during a flash flood) and it's imperative to have a guide (see p77).

You'll need a good torch (flashlight) and waterproof shoes for the three-hour hike/ swim. There are also a few areas that require climbing up rock faces but there's a rope to help you.

It is less than 15 minutes' walk from the parking area to the first tube, at 750m, which is around 100m long. The second tube is 300m long with two waterfalls. The third tube is the longest and darkest and, at about 100m in, it divides: the left fork continues about 300m to an exit, while the right fork leads to a large cave, complete with lake and waterfall.

FAARUMAI WATERFALLS

Through the village of Tiarei where the road swoops around a black-sand beach, you'll see a sign on the mountain side of the road for the exceedingly high Faarumai Waterfalls (Map pp78–9). Unfortunately you can't swim here anymore since a tourist was hit on the head by a falling rock, so bring mosquito repellent and just enjoy the view. It's a couple of hundred metres through a forest of *mape* trees to **Vaimahutu**, the first of the waterfalls. Another 20-minute stroll leads to the other two falls, **Haamarere Iti** and **Haamarere Rahi**, which stand almost side by side. You technically aren't supposed to swim here either, but many people do.

ARAHOHO BLOWHOLE

When the swell is big enough, huge sprays of water shoot out from the *trou du souffleur* (blowhole; Map pp78–9) by the road just before Tiarei at PK22, coming from Pape'ete. The blowhole is on the corner and there's a car park just beyond it; take care walking to the blowhole as there's a blind corner here. When the waves are right, the blow can be extremely strong – so forceful in fact that people have been swept right off the rock and out to sea.

Just past the blowhole is a fine sliver of black-sand beach, ideal for a picnic pause. There are sometimes fruit vendors here.

PAPENOO

At PK17, there's a popular **surf break** (Map pp78–9) just before the headland that signals the start of the small village of Papenoo. A long bridge crosses the Papenoo River at the far end of the village, and the 4WD route up the Papenoo Valley, cutting through the ancient crater rim to Relais de la Maroto, starts up the west side of the river. See opposite for more information about this magnificent route.

POINT VÉNUS & MATAVAI BAY

Part of Captain Cook's mission on his three-month sojourn in 1769 was to record the transit of Venus across the face of the sun in an attempt to calculate the distance between the sun and the earth. Point Vénus (Map pp78–9), the promontory that marks the eastern end of Matavai Bay, was the site of Cook's observatory.

Today Point Vénus is a popular beach stop. There are shady trees, a stretch of lawn, a black-sand beach, a couple of souvenir shops and an impressive **lighthouse** (1867). There is no sign to Point Vénus from the main road; just turn off at the Venus Star Supermarket in Mahina around PK10. It's about 1km from the road to the car park near the end of the point.

There is a **memorial** here to the first LMS Protestant missionaries, who made their landfall at Point Vénus on 4 March 1797.

ONE TREE HILL

At the top of the hill at around PK8, pull off to the lagoon side of the road and park in the lot that once belonged to Tahiti's very posh Hyatt Regency. From this crumbling site of the abandoned hotel you'll get sublime views all the way to Pape'ete, including the silhouette of Mo'orea in the distance. One Tree Hill (Map pp84–5) was named by Captain Cook who used it as a landmark. The hotel has been closed since 1998.

Sleeping & Eating

There is nowhere to stay on the east coast. Heading east out of Pape'ete, there are not many restaurants until you reach Taravao, although there are a few little *snacks*.

Chez Loula and Remy (Map pp78–9; ☎ 57 74 99; dishes 1500-2500 CFP; ✆ lunch & dinner) This family-run place in Taravao on the Tautira road serves an excellent array of French-style grilled meats and fish in boozy, congenial environs.

Restaurant Taumatai (Map pp78–9; ☎ 57 13 59; dishes 1500-2500 CFP; ✆ lunch & dinner Tue-Sat, lunch Sun) Grab a terrace table at this delightful little place right across the street from Loula and Remy, serving the town's best French and Tahitian food in an elegant garden setting. The restaurant is hidden behind a stone wall so it's a little hard to find.

INLAND

Archaeological remains, mossy, velvet-green mountains and fabulous hikes await you in Tahiti Nui's lush interior.

Sights & Activities

The best sights are reached on foot. This is a place to lace up the shoes and go for a hike.

MT MARAU

Across from Faa'a airport, a road signposted as Saint-Hilaire runs inland, under the RDO and up towards the summit of Mt Marau (1493m). It's possible to drive 10km to a height of 1441m, although the rough road requires a 4WD. The route reaches a *belvédère* (lookout) at 1241m. From the end of the road it is only a half-hour walk to the top of Mt Marau, from where there are superb views of the peaks around Tahiti Nui's central crater.

PAPENOO TO PAPEARI
Unfortunately, the wonderfully rugged 39km route that once ran all the way across the centre of Tahiti from Papenoo to Papeari is closed between Lake Vaihiria and the Relais de la Maroto. Fortunately you can still enjoy its splendours by going up one side or the other. This makes a great day trip by 4WD and presents a unique, 'lagoonless' view of Tahiti.

These central valleys once sheltered a dense population, and it was around here that the *Bounty* mutineers took refuge. When Christianity began to spread along the coastal regions, the Papenoo Valley became a last refuge for those faithful to the ancient Polynesian religion, and until 1846 it was also a shelter for the Tahitian rebel forces that opposed the French takeover. Archaeologist Kenneth Emory started the first systematic study of the valley's historic sites in 1925.

Specialised 4WD operators do the Papeari to Vaihiria route regularly (see p76). From the Relais de la Maroto (p102) on the Papenoo side, there are heaps of walking tracks.

Papenoo to the Relais de la Maroto
The 18km route from Papenoo on the north coast to the Relais de la Maroto follows the wide Papenoo Valley, the only valley to cut right through the ancient crater. The Papenoo River is the largest on Tahiti. In Papenoo, the turn-off is just past PK17; the track has its own PK markers. The **Topatari Waterfall**, at PK5, cascades down to the river. A little further up the valley the **Vaiharuru Waterfall** comes down from the west side and, further, the **Puraha Waterfall** from the east. At PK16 the track passes the **Vaituoru Pool** (Bassin Vaituoru) before reaching the Relais de la Maroto just past PK18.

Papeari to the Relais de la Maroto
Coming from the west, the turn-off on the south coast is at PK47.5, just beyond the Seventh-Day Adventist church and just before the Tahiria River bridge. At the time of research the road inland here was closed due to a barricade built by the area's residents but legal proceedings were under way to ensure that the road would remain accessible both to visitors and to Tahiti's hydroelectric company workers.

When it's open, the road runs directly inland for about 200m before taking a sign-posted sharp-left turn. From there the track follows the Tahiria River upstream to a small catchment lake (6.7km; 145m) and **Marae Vaihiria I** (7.5km; Map pp78–9). The extensive remains of the *marae* include an artificial canal, used to carry water through the site, which stretches up the hillside. The *marae* was in use from the 16th to the 19th century, and there are several informative noticeboards by the roadside and up the hill. Another *marae* is further down the valley, about 4km from the start of the cross-island road.

Continuing uphill (the road has been closed to cars from here for an indefinite period), there is a second small catchment lake (10km; 270m) before the road makes a very steep and winding climb to Lake Vaihiria (11.3km; 450m), the 200m-long tunnel (14.9km; 770m) and finally the Relais de la Maroto (20.7km). The 4WD track runs up the west side of Lake Vaihiria and there's a walking track that runs around the east shore.

Around the Relais de la Maroto
The Relais de la Maroto was originally built as accommodation quarters for workers on the hydroelectricity project that began in 1980. Ask at the reception desk for a map of walking trails in the area. The restored **Marae Farehape** site is almost directly below the ridge line on which the Relais de la Maroto perches; you can see an archery platform from where arrows were shot up the valley.

From the *marae*, a track climbs up to the Tahinu dam. A walking track skirts around the edge of the lake behind the dam to the **Marae Tahinu** archaeological sites, which are on both sides of the river. Another 4WD track starts from the dam and climbs up the Maroto Valley. A rough track turns off this route and leads to the top of the spectacular **Maroto Waterfall**.

The **Marae Anapua**, perched up above the Vainavenave dam, has been beautifully restored. The **Anapua Caves** are directly below the *marae* site, and can be reached on foot around the side of the dam or by the track around the valley side.

OTHER HIKES
Tahiti's interior is home to some of the most exquisite, and challenging, **hikes** in French

Polynesia. Or you can also take a 4WD tour (see p76).

One of the most pleasant and accessible walks on Tahiti, the **Fautaua Valley trail** doesn't require a guide, but you will need an access permit (adult/child 600/150 CFP). You can obtain one at the Pape'ete *mairie* at the **Service des Régies des Recettes** (Map pp86-7; ☎ 41 58 36); enter the building from Rue des Écoles.

To get to Fautaua Valley, follow Av du Prince Hinoi from the Pape'ete seafront for about 2km. At the third set of traffic lights, at the Total petrol station, turn right towards the mountains. You will pass in front of the Bain Loti (Loti Bath). Go straight ahead, as far as the Service de l'Hydraulique, where you hand in your access permit. The easy 4km walk to the Fachoda (Tearape) Bridge takes about an hour. After the bridge there's a rather steep climb, and after about 45 minutes you reach a superb viewpoint over Fautaua Waterfall. Another half an hour takes you to the summit of the waterfall, a prime swimming spot.

A bit further inland, **Mt Aorai** (2066m) is the third-highest peak on Tahiti and its ascent is one of the island's classic climbs. The path is clearly visible and well maintained, so you don't need a guide. It takes at least 4½ hours of steady walking to reach the top. It's possible to summit the peak and return in a day, but start at dawn because the summit tends to be covered in cloud after 11am. A better option is to spend the night in one of two simple shelters on the route. Each accommodates about 20 walkers, has electricity and is equipped with aluminium cisterns that are usually filled with drinkable rain water.

The Mt Aorai hike starts at Le Belvédère restaurant. From central Pape'ete take Av Georges Clémenceau and turn right at the intersection located 200m after the Total petrol station. Turn right again at the sign for Le Belvédère, which is 7km from the coast road.

The ascent of **Mt Orohena** (2241m), Tahiti's highest peak, is a tough two-day mission. You will have to contend with dense undergrowth, a crumbling ridge line and sometimes fierce winds. You will need to hire a guide to do this trek (for a list, see p77).

Sleeping & Eating

The only place to stay and eat is **Relais de la Maroto** (Map pp78-9; ☎ 57 90 29; maroto@mail.pf;

r 7000 CFP, bungalows from 9500 CFP), smack in the lush heart of the island. It has renovated but musty motel-style rooms and a few bungalows to choose from. The restaurant here is OK, although expensive, but the wine cellar is exceptional and there are regular wine-tasting evenings frequented by Tahiti's elite. Book ahead at the weekend.

Getting There & Away

A few companies organise trips across the island (see p76); you can also walk it in a few days or ride across on a mountain bike, if you've brought one. You can rent 4WDs; check the conditions of the track before you start out. In the rainy season this route can be truly perilous.

TAHITI ITI

Traditional Polynesian villages, beaches, archaeological sites and caves are all part of the alluring charm of Tahiti Iti. Unpretentious and beautiful, the smaller loop of Tahiti's figure eight quietly attracts independent, outdoorsy folk looking for a more authentic glimpse of Polynesia. More commonly called the Presqu'île, Tahiti Iti has made a bit of a name for itself in recent years thanks to the promotion of its famous wave at Teahupoo. But even though it has become famous because of surfing, there's much more to do in Tahiti Iti than ride the waves. Exceptional walks and abundant lack of commercialism are all perks.

SIGHTS

The best way to explore Tahiti Iti is to drive to the ends of both the north and south coast roads.

North-Coast Road

The coastal road from Taravao runs through Afaahiti to Pueu, past steep hills and numerous waterfalls, to the road's end at Tautira.

This stretch of coast is one of the least visited areas on the island, though historically things were different. In 1772 the Spanish captain Boenechea, who was leading the first missionary expedition to French Polynesia (see boxed text, p37), anchored his ship *Aguilla* about 10km beyond Tautira; Cook landed here in 1774; and many years later, in 1886, the writer Robert Louis Stevenson spent two months here. The landings of French Catholic missionaries at Tautira eventually led to the French takeover of Tahiti and the end of the Protestant monopoly.

The sealed road ends at Tautira, but you can bump along for another kilometre or two before the road becomes impassable to vehicles. A good **walking track** leads round the coast for another 10km or so before reaching the Te Pari Cliffs (see p104 for more details).

Tautira itself is a lovely village and unique on Tahiti as it's not clustered along one main road but has many small residential lanes that crisscross the town in a near grid. There's a sweeping black-sand beach (see right) at the edge of town and you can visit **Boenechea's grave** (Map pp78–9) in front of the Catholic Church in the centre of town.

Offshore close to Afaahiti is the stunning white-sand **Motu Nono**, a popular picnic spot for locals and tourist excursions.

Inland

There are two routes that climb to an inland **lookout** and can be combined to make a loop. In Afaahiti, at PK2.5, you'll find the turn-off by looking out for Le Ranch de Plateau Rauvau (see p104) horse stables signpost. The 7km road climbs through green fields, some home to very un-Tahitian-looking herds of cows, to the little covered lookout. The alternative route turns off the south-coast road at PK1.3 (turn inland at the grain factory, pass the high school and its football field then take a right at the stop sign). It meets the first route where the road forks, from where it's a short walk to the viewpoint. There are superb vistas across the isthmus of Taravao to the towering bulk of Tahiti Nui.

South-Coast Road

The south-coast road runs by beaches and bays to Vairao and the small village of Teahupoo before abruptly stopping at the Tirahi River at PK18. From the end of the road it is possible to walk about another 10km (although the quantity of vicious dogs from about 2km in on this stretch make this unadvisable) before the steep Te Pari Cliffs make the path too dangerous to attempt without a guide (for more on hiking in this area, see p104). Zane Grey, the American author, spent time here in the 1920s and described the beauty of the area in *Tales*

of Tahitian Waters. The Tapuaeraha Pass through the reef is the widest and deepest around Tahiti, but because of its remote position it's rarely used.

A signposted turn-off at PK9.5 leads a short distance inland to the rarely visited remains of **Marae Nuutere** (Map pp78–9), restored in 1994. There are three paved yards known as *tohua* (meeting places) with *ahu* (altars) at the end of them and large *turui* (seats) for *tahua* (priests) or *ari'i* (chiefs).

At Teahupoo's Tirahi River, park then cross the footbridge. From here it's a lovely five-minute walk through a shaded residential area and past lily ponds to a public beach with black sand and a few shady almond trees. There's good snorkelling out towards the pass here (see below).

ACTIVITIES

There are loads of activities to keep you occupied on Tahiti Iti.

Beaches

A picturesque strip of white sand, **Maui Beach** (PK8, Vairao) gets packed and noisy on weekends, but is peaceful during the week. It's right on the road but has shallow swimming, perfect for children, as well as deeper swimming and snorkelling off the reef. The black-sand beaches at PK18 in Teahupoo and PK6 in Pueu are good for boogie-boarding or surfing but can be rough for swimming. The black-sand beach in **Tautira** is often empty and offers good swimming.

From the sandy little peninsula about 500m beyond from the Teahupoo footbridge there are fantastic **coral gardens** just across the channel. If the current is too strong, don't attempt swimming here, but if it's calm, look both ways (lots of boats zip through here) and swim across the channel to the gardens and (if you're confident in the water) out the pass as far as the green channel marker.

For information on Tahiti Iti's world-famous surf breaks see p80; for diving see p77 and p64.

Boat Excursions

Probably the most fun you can have in a day on Tahiti Iti is by taking a boat excursion, which invariably includes a picnic lunch, a visit to Vaipoiri Cave and, if the weather permits, Te Pari. All *pensions* in the area can arrange excursions and the excellent tours from

TAHITI

Te Pari Village (see right) can be arranged even if you're not staying there.

The most professional independent boat operator is **Teahupoo Excursions** (Map pp78-9; ☎ 75 11 98; http://web.me.com/teahupooexcursion; 1hr/half day/full day for up to 6 people 5000/18,000/35,000 CFP) run by contagiously happy Michael. He organises à la carte tours or will shuttle folks out to the Teahupoo wave to watch surfing or to surf for 1000 CFP per person. Basically he'll organise anything that involves his boat.

Hiking & Horse Riding

A soggy but pretty 8km walk along the coast from the Teahupoo footbridge through several rivers brings you to **Vaipoiri Cave**. This coast, which is accessible only by boat or on foot, is called the **Fenua Aihere** (Map pp78–9), which literally means 'the bush country'. Although this walk is popular, there are a few aggressive unchained dogs along the way, making it a bit stressful. After about 7km signs direct you towards the mountain, through a *mape* forest and then up a hibiscus-covered hill to the cave. Inside, your eyes will adjust to the darkness and it's possible to swim to the back through the icy water. Boat excursions (see p103) also go to Vaipoiri Cave if you want to avoid the dogs and the sore legs.

From Vaipoiri Cave you can continue another 1.5km along the coast till you reach the **Te Pari Cliffs**. At this point the reef ends and the coastline becomes steep and gets pounded by waves when there's swell. It's possible to hike the entire 8km of this precarious coast dotted with archaeological treasures, wild passion-fruit, waterfalls and caves, but you can only do it in good weather and if the swell isn't too big. A guide is highly recommended both for safety and to help you discover all the very hidden gems found mostly off the trail. It takes two days to hike the whole Te Pari and camp is usually made in an airy and open beachside cave. It's an unforgettable experience. For a list of guides see p77.

On the northern half of Tahiti Iti towards Tautira, the coastline continues along from the Te Pari Cliffs another 10km or so through a second **Fenua Aihere**, till the paved road begins once again at Tautira village. Near the Vaiote River are some interesting **petroglyphs** (Map pp78–9) inscribed on coastal boulders and a series of *marae* inland in the valley. There are less growling dogs along this trail

and plenty of rivers and waterfalls waiting to be explored.

For horse riding, **Le Ranch du Plateau Rauvau** (Map pp78-9; ☎ 73 84 43; rides from 2000 CFP) offers guided rides to rarely visited points on the plateau with stunning views. It's best to reserve a few days in advance; there are no set hours.

FESTIVALS & EVENTS

The **Tahiti Billabong Pro** is held at Teahupoo every May. The famous surfing contest attracts the industry's best riders and draws surf fans and media from around the world.

SLEEPING & EATING

The south coast of Tahiti Iti has some of the best sleeping options on the whole island. You'll also eat well over here.

Pension Bonjouir (Map pp78-9; ☎ 77 89 69; www.bonjouir.com; r 7000 CFP, bungalows 11,500 CFP; ▣) Bonjouir is a nature-lover's paradise – it's surrounded by walks to waterfalls, swimming holes and caves and fronted by the clear lagoon. You'll need to take the shuttle boat from the dock at PK17 in Teahupoo (2500 CFP return) or walk about 40 minutes to get to this remote spot, but once you get here you may never want to leave. Accommodation is nothing fancy but is comfortable enough and has Tahitian flair. Bring mosquito repellent even though all the beds have nets. Half board is 4500 CFP and a few bungalows have their own kitchens. There's a young, fun and convivial vibe. Some travellers have complained of being charged for 'extras' they thought were free, so be clear with your hosts what the rates cover. You can also visit here for the day for 6000 CFP including boat transfers, a sandwich and free kayaks.

Te Pari Village (Map pp78-9; ☎ /fax 42 59 12; teparivillage@yahoo.fr; bungalows with full board per person 11,000 CFP) Ten minutes by boat from the Teahupoo pier, this option is in the middle of a magnificent coconut and fruit tree grove beside the lagoon and oozes tranquillity. The handful of simple wooden bungalows make a circle around tall red ginger flowers and the main eating area is a big Polynesian meeting hall–style building. It's not surprising that this place is a favourite location for meditation and yoga retreats. Prices include daily excursions and you can also go on the recommended excursions (lunch and transfers included) if you're not staying here for 5500 CFP. Whatever you do, it's a great deal.

our pick **Vanira Lodge** (Map pp78-9; ☎ 57 70 18; www.vaniralodge.com; d bungalows 13,000 CFP, f bungalows with kitchen 14,000 CFP; ☎) Our favourite *pension* in Tahiti, this place is up a steep driveway on a mini plateau with vast views of the lagoon, surf, village and myriad island colours. The seven bungalows are fabulously eclectic and are all built from some combination of bamboo, thatch, rustic planks of wood, glass, adobe, coral and rock. One of the newest bungalows has an earth roof that's bursting with flowers. Cosy nooks, hand-carved furniture, airy mezzanines and alfresco kitchens (in the five family-size bungalows that sleep four) are nice touches. There's tonnes of open space for kids as well as a little lily pond, a pool and fruit trees. Breakfast costs 1200 CFP, but you're on your own for other meals. Bikes and kayaks are free, but you'll need a car if you stay here.

Pension Chayan (Map pp78-9; ☎ 57 46 00; www .pensionchayantahiti.pf; PK14, Vairao; r from 15,000 CFP) Four sparkling concrete bungalows – all with mini-kitchens – nestle in a magnificent tropical garden complete with spectacular waterfall and natural bathing pool. Across the road there is a small black-sand beach for swimming. The owners are friendly and super helpful. This is a fantastic place to stay.

Restaurant Hinerava (Map pp78-9; ☎ 81 93 61; PK18; dishes 1200-2000 CFP; ☺ breakfast, lunch & dinner; ☎) At the end of the road in Teahupoo, this place was recently given a major facelift and is now a surprisingly classy place serving very good food. You can dine outside or inside in the air-con. There's a great selection of fish, meats and burger plates every day, *ma'a Tahiti* (2500 CFP) all day on Sundays, and daily specials such as *mahi mahi* in vanilla sauce or Moroccan-style couscous on other days of the week. The service is among the best on Tahiti.

La Plage de Maui (Map pp78-9; ☎ 74 71 74; mains around 2000 CFP; ☺ 10am-6pm) On the beach of the same name, this place looks like a shack inside and out but the food is Polynesian haute cuisine. We found the meals tasty, yet overpriced, but the position overlooking the lagoon is sublime. There are also cheaper burgers and such for the kids.

Also recommended on the very quiet north coast towards and around Tautira are:

Pueu Village (☎ 57 57 87; PK9.8, Pueu; bungalows from 9000 CFP) Very Tahitian Ma and Pa–style place with good bungalows.

Chez Maïté (☎ 57 18 24; www.chez-maithe.com; PK4.5, Afaahiti; s/d/tr 7000/7500/9500 CFP) Great for families, with a communal kitchen and beach access.

Mo'orea

Mo'orea is the stuff of fairytales. It's so beautiful you'll be rubbing your eyes at your first glimpse of it from Tahiti, and wondering if someone has slipped something mind-altering into your drink. Whether you arrive by ferry or plane, the loveliness of the island intensifies as you draw nearer. That turquoise lagoon that you were sure was Photoshopped in the brochure? It's better in real life. As you admire the near-vertical, emerald cliffs, you'll wonder if you are the luckiest person in the world. The short answer: yes.

Mo'orea has a healthy selection of top-end resorts, but it is also host to some of the best budget choices in French Polynesia, and midrangers will find an excellent choice of smaller hotels and beachfront family *pensions* (guesthouses). Catch up on your Zs on the skinny, white-sand beaches, frolic with rays and sharks, snorkel or dive through schools of fish over the never-ending quantity of coral, gorge yourself on stylishly prepared seafood, and just chill. If you need more action, learn to kite surf, take a hike, go on a whale- or dolphin-watching tour, rent a bike or go horseback riding.

While it is one of the most visited islands in French Polynesia, tourism is down and Mo'orea has been hit hard. When we visited, most hotels and *pensions* were half empty and a few had even dropped their prices to less than what they were three years ago. Yes, it's still expensive, but not as much as it used to be – and really, it's worth it.

HIGHLIGHTS

- Getting lost in the **Opunohu Bay and Valley** (p110), with its sparkling waters and ancient *marae* (traditional temples), breathtaking vistas and hidden walking paths

- Swimming to Motu Tiahura from Hauru Point for lunch and a cocktail at **Motu Moea – Restaurant la Plage** (p120)

- Sighting and maybe swimming with **whales and dolphins** (p113) from July to October

- Discovering the terrestrial pleasures of the island on a guided or independent **hike** (p113) into the outlandishly lush interior

- Feeling giddy while feeding the island's stingrays at **Stingray World** (p115) and being circled by reef sharks

■ POPULATION: 14,230	■ AREA: 53 SQ KM

HISTORY

The island's ancient name was Eimeo (sometimes spelled Aimeho). Some say that Mo'orea, which means 'yellow lizard', was the name of one of the island's ruling families, while others attribute this name to an image seen by a high priest while visiting the island.

Mo'orea was heavily populated before the Europeans arrived on its idyllic doorstep. Samuel Wallis was the first European to sight the island (1767), and he was soon followed by Louis-Antoine de Bougainville (1768) and James Cook (1769). The missionaries arrived on the scene in the early 1800s and made themselves at home, soon establishing their headquarters on the island. As elsewhere, European diseases and the introduction of weapons and alcohol had a disastrous effect on the population of Mo'orea, which declined during the 19th century.

Copra and vanilla were important crops in the past but these days Mo'orea is the pineapple-growing centre of French Polynesia. Tourism is the other major industry, but the island has managed to maintain a tranquillity that its more-developed neighbours, Tahiti and Bora Bora, lack.

GEOGRAPHY & GEOLOGY

Mo'orea is an extinct volcano. The magnificent Cook's Bay (Baie de Cook) and Opunohu Bay (Baie d'Opunohu) mark the floor of the ancient crater, and if you follow the trail from the Opunohu Valley up to Three Coconut Trees Pass, you stand very clearly on the edge of the old crater.

A reef encircles the island with a narrow and shallow lagoon. There are a number of passes through the reef, the biggest at Vaiare on the east coast.

Mo'orea is very mountainous, and its peaks are often theatrically draped in cloud. Mt Rotui (899m) tumbles into Opunohu Bay on one side and Cook's Bay on the other, only 2.5km apart. Mt Mouaputa (830m), which is known as the 'pierced mountain', is famed for the hole through its top.

There are pretty white-sand beaches at Hauru Point and Temae but nothing big and sweeping. The drawcard is the limpid, warm water of the vibrant lagoon.

ORIENTATION

The coastal road is about 60km around. Depending on your energy and fitness level, the circuit can be made by bicycle in one very long, sweaty day (there are, thankfully, few hills to tackle). The southern coast of the island is far more isolated and sees much less traffic.

The population of Mo'orea is concentrated in the villages around the coast. With its frenetic ferry quay, Vaiare is the busiest part of the island, but Afareaitu is the administrative headquarters.

Dense tourist development is in two strips: one from Maharepa down the eastern side of Cook's Bay to Paopao, the other around Hauru Point on the northwestern corner of the island. The airport is in the island's northeastern corner.

Adhering to French Polynesian logic, the *pointe kilométrique* (PK; kilometre point) markers start at PK0 at the airport and go around the coast in both clockwise and anticlockwise directions; they meet at Haapiti, which is at PK24 along the southern (clockwise) route and at PK37 along the northern (anticlockwise) route.

INFORMATION

Internet Access

It costs around 800 CFP an hour online. Some of the hotels also offer internet service as do the post offices.

Iguana Rock Café (Map p111; ☎ 56 17 16; ⏰ until midnight)

Maria@Tapas (Map p110; ☎ 55 01 70; mariatapas@mail.pf; PK5; ⏰ 8am-11pm Mon-Wed, 8am-1am Thu-Sat) Fast connections and friendly staff.

Top Phone Cyber Space (Map p110; ☎ 70 66 38; ⏰ 8am-5pm Mon-Fri, 8am-noon Sat) Slightly cheaper and across the street from Kaveka Hotel.

Medical Services

Moorea Hospital (Map p108; ☎ 56 23 23, 56 24 24) The only hospital is in Afareaitu.

Pharmacy (Map p110; ☎ 56 10 51; PK6.5; ⏰ 7.30am-noon & 2-6pm Mon-Fri, 8am-noon & 3.30-6pm Sat, 8-11am Sun & public holidays) In Maharepa, not far from the Centre Kikipa.

Pharmacy (Map p111; PK31; ⏰ Mon-Sat & Sun morning)

Money

The Banque Socredo across from the quay at Vaiare has an ATM. There are banks and ATMs clustered around the small shopping centre in Maharepa near PK6. In Le Petit Village (the Hauru Point shopping centre) there is a Banque de Polynésie (Map p111) and an ATM.

MO'OREA

lonelyplanet.com

MO'OREA

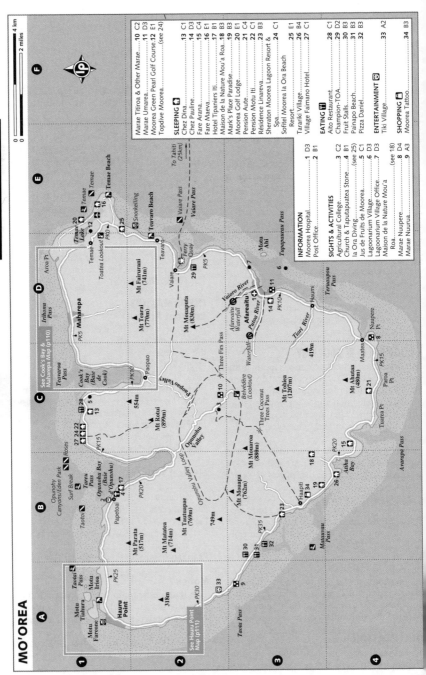

Marae Titiroa & Other Marae......10 C2
Marae Umarea...........................11 D3
Moorea Green Pearl Golf Course.12 E1
Topdive Moorea........................(see 24)

SLEEPING
Chez Dina.................................13 C1
Chez Pauline............................14 D3
Fare Arana...............................15 C4
Fare Maeva..............................16 E1
Hotel Tipaniers Iti......................17 B1
Maison de la Nature Mou'a Roa..18 B3
Mark's Place Paradise.................19 B3
Moorea Golf Lodge......................20 E1
Pension Aute............................21 C4
Pension Motu Iti.........................22 C1
Résidence Linareva......................23 B3
Sheraton Moorea Lagoon Resort &
 Spa.......................................24 C1
Sofitel Moorea Ia Ora Beach
 Resort....................................25 E1
Tarariki Village..........................26 B4
Village Faimano Hotel..................27 C1

EATING
Aito Restaurant.........................28 C1
Champion-TOA...........................29 D2
Fruit Stalls................................30 B3
Ia Ora Diving............................(see 25)
Jus de Fruits de Moorea...............5 C1
Pizza Daniel.............................32 B3

ENTERTAINMENT
Tiki Village...............................33 A2

SHOPPING
Moorea Tattoo...........................34 B3

INFORMATION
Moorea Hospital..........................1 D3
Post Office................................2 B1

SIGHTS & ACTIVITIES
Agricultural College......................3 C2
Church & Taputapuatea Stone........4 B1
Ia Ora Diving...........................(see 25)
Jus de Fruits de Moorea................5 C1
Lagoonarium Village.....................6 D3
Lagoonarium Village Office............7 D3
Maison de la Nature Mou'a
 Roa.....................................(see 18)
Marae Nuupere...........................8 D4
Marae Nuurua.............................9 A3

Post

Mo'orea has a post office in Maharepa and another in Papetoai, just before Hauru Point.
Post office (Map p110; 7.30am-noon & 1.30-4pm Mon-Thu, 7.30am-3pm Fri, 7.30-9.30am Sat) At the Maharepa shopping centre.

Tourist Information

Mo'orea Tourist Bureau (Map p111; ☎ 56 29 09; www.gomoorea.com; 8am-4pm Tue-Thu, 8am-3pm Fri, 8am-noon Sat) In front of Le Petit Village shopping centre. On Mondays, when it's closed, you can call ☎ 56 38 53 for information.

SIGHTS

The following circuit starts at the airport and moves in an anticlockwise direction, following the northern PK markers. For places to stay and eat in the following places, see p115 and p119.

Teavaro & Temae Beaches (PK1 to PK0)

The best beaches on the east coast, and the widest perhaps in all of French Polynesia, stretch from Teavaro round to the airport. The Sofitel Moorea Ia Ora Beach Resort occupies Teavaro Beach, where there's good snorkelling in the shallow water and out on the lagoon side of the fringing reef. The public section of Teavaro Beach just north of the Sofitel gets crowded on weekends.

A road on the lagoon side of the runway extends around **Temae Lake**, which is now home to the Moorea Green Pearl Golf Course (p115), but the route is cut off so it is not possible to rejoin the main coastal road, the airport or the entrance to the golf course.

Maharepa (PK4 to PK5)

The early-20th-century **Maison Blanche** (Map p110; PK5) is a fine example of a *fare vanira*, a plantation house from Mo'orea's vanilla-boom era. Located just past the Moorea Pearl Resort, the Maison Blanche is now a souvenir shop. It has a fairly typical selection of *pareu* (sarongs) and Balinese woodcarvings.

Cook's Bay to Paopao (PK6 to PK9)

The spectacular Cook's Bay is something of a misnomer because Cook actually anchored in Opunohu Bay. With Mt Rotui as a backdrop, Cook's Bay is a lovely stretch of water. There's no real centre to Cook's Bay; shops, restaurants and hotels are simply dotted along the road. As you head east, Cook's Bay merges with Maharepa.

At the base of Cook's Bay is the sleepy village of Paopao. There's the **old fish market** (Map p110) and a few shops here. Even though the fish market is no more, you can still see the wall mural painted by Mo'orea-based artist François Ravello.

Settlements are creeping up the Paopao Valley but the principal activity is still agriculture, with many hectares of pineapple plantations. The road leading inland from Paopao and Cook's Bay meets the Opunohu Valley road, just before the agricultural college and the walking track up to Three Coconut Trees Pass (see p114). A small *fare* at the agricultural college sells jams in local flavours and on occasion, ice cream. The road then continues inland and up to the *marae* (traditional temple) sites (see p112) and finally to the *belvédère* (lookout; p112) on the slopes of Mt Tohiea (1207m).

MO'OREA IN...

Two Days

Start by exploring the **Opunohu Valley** (p110) with its fascinating *marae* (traditional temples) and extraordinary views before the day gets too hot. Next head to **Hauru Point** (p110) with a detour to **Jus de Fruits de Moorea** (p110). Swim to **Motu Moea – Restaurant la Plage** (p120) for lunch then spend the rest of the day snorkelling and lounging on the beach. Finish with a night of French Polynesian entertainment and feasting at a **dance performance** (p121).

Fill day two with a **lagoon tour** (p115) and picnic lunch. After a long day in the sun, enjoy a quiet dinner at any of Mo'orea's fine restaurants.

Four Days

Start the third day with a morning **hike** or **horse ride** (p114). After lunch the afternoon is yours to lounge on the beach or explore the quiet southern part of the island.

On your last day on Mo'orea you could either take a **4WD tour** (p115) or go **whale-watching** (p113). Then spend the rest of the day soaking up the warm water and sunshine.

MO'OREA

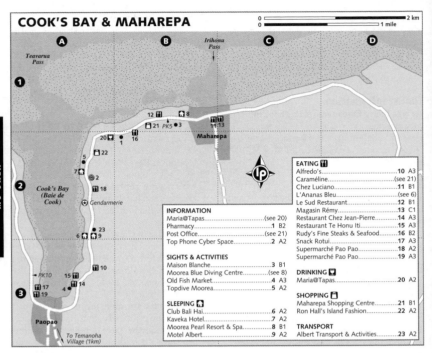

COOK'S BAY & MAHAREPA

INFORMATION
Maria@Tapas..................................(see 20)
Pharmacy...1 B2
Post Office.......................................(see 21)
Top Phone Cyber Space....................2 A2

SIGHTS & ACTIVITIES
Maison Blanche...................................3 B1
Moorea Blue Diving Centre............(see 8)
Old Fish Market.................................4 A3
Topdive Moorea.................................5 A2

SLEEPING
Club Bali Hai......................................6 A2
Kaveka Hotel......................................7 A2
Moorea Pearl Resort & Spa...............8 A2
Motel Albert.......................................9 A2

EATING
Alfredo's..10 A3
Caraméline.....................................(see 21)
Chez Luciano....................................11 B1
L'Ananas Bleu.................................(see 6)
Le Sud Restaurant............................12 B1
Magasin Rémy...................................13 C1
Restaurant Chez Jean-Pierre............14 A3
Restaurant Te Honu Iti.....................15 A3
Rudy's Fine Steaks & Seafood..........16 B2
Snack Rotui.......................................17 A3
Supermarché Pao Pao.......................18 A2
Supermarché Pao Pao.......................19 A3

DRINKING
Maria@Tapas....................................20 A2

SHOPPING
Maharepa Shopping Centre.............21 B1
Ron Hall's Island Fashion.................22 A2

TRANSPORT
Albert Transport & Activities............23 A2

Jus de Fruits de Moorea (PK11)

About 300m inland from the coastal road, the **Jus de Fruits de Moorea** (Map p108; ☎ 56 11 33; admission free; 🕑 8.30am-4.30pm Mon-Sat) is a welcome, thirst-quenching stop. The various fruit liqueurs are free to try but the juices are not (a carton of 100% pineapple juice is 320 CFP).

Opunohu Bay (PK14 to PK18)

Magnificent Opunohu Bay feels wonderfully fresh and isolated. The coastal road rounds Mt Rotui, and at about PK14 turns inland along the eastern side of Opunohu Bay. There is less development along here than around Cook's Bay, and it's one of the more tranquil and eye-catching spots on the island. Most of the Polynesian scenes in the 1984 movie *Bounty* were shot on Opunohu Bay.

At PK18, a road turns off inland along the Opunohu Valley to the valley *marae,* the *belvédère* (see p112) and the walking route to Three Coconut Trees Pass (see p114).

Papetoai (PK22)

A busy little village with a post office and a number of restaurants, Papetoai was es-tablished as the Pacific headquarters of the London Missionary Society (LMS) in 1811. In the 1870s, the missionaries constructed an octagonal **church** (Map p108) at Papetoai; today this is the oldest-standing European building in the South Pacific. As was often the case, the missionaries deliberately built this church atop an old *marae*. A single spike-like stone is the sole reminder of the ancient **Marae Taputapuatea**, dedicated to the god 'Oro.

Hauru Point (PK25 to PK30)

The coastal road rounds Hauru Point, the northwestern corner of the island, between PK25 and PK30. This is one of the island's major tourist enclaves. The tourist strip starts with the Intercontinental Moorea Resort & Spa at about PK25, and finishes at around PK31.

Hauru Point has one of the best **beaches** (Map p111) on the island, a narrow but sandy stretch that extends for about 5km. Immediately offshore are **Motu Tiahura** and **Motu Fareone**, attractive little islets so close to the shore you can easily swim out to them and enjoy fine snorkelling on the way. A little further east is the tiny **Motu Irioa**. Remember that the actual *motu* are private (although the littoral areas aren't).

Marae Nuurua (PK31.5)

Marae Nuurua (Map p108) is right on the water's edge, just past the end of a football field. There's an impressive wall of coral boulders and a restored three-level structure flanked by twin spiky, upright stones with clear **petroglyphs**. Despite neglect and its relatively populated setting, it's a very evocative ruin, overgrown with vegetation and surrounded by coconut trees.

Haapiti to Atiha Bay (PK30 to PK20)

The largest village on the west coast, Haapiti (Map p108) is home to the huge twin-towered Catholic **Église de la Sainte Famille**,

which is made of coral and lime. Haapiti's **Matauvau Pass** has a popular surf break.

Mo'orea's lazy west-coast atmosphere continues right round to Atiha Bay (Baie d'Atiha), a quiet fishing village that also attracts surfers.

Marae Nuupere (PK14)

Nuupere Point (Map p108) is immediately southeast of Maatea village, and the *marae* stands just 100m or so south of the point. All that remains is a massive coastal cairn of coral boulders, which is on private property. The property owner is not enthusiastic about visitors, so permission must be obtained before entering the property (ask at the tourist bureau, p109, in Hauru Point).

MO'OREA

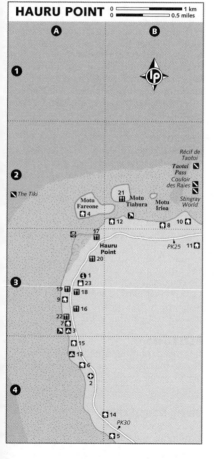

HAURU POINT

0 ——— 1 km
0 ——— 0.5 miles

INFORMATION	
Banque de Polynésie & ATM	(see 23)
Iguana Rock Café	(see 23)
Mo'orea Tourist Bureau	1 A3
Pharmacy	2 A4

SIGHTS & ACTIVITIES	
Aqua Blue	(see 10)
Bathy's Diving	(see 10)
Moorea Fun Dive	(see 13)
Scubapiti	(see 12)

SLEEPING	
Camping Chez Nelson	3 A3
Dream Island	4 A2
Fare Manuia	5 B4
Fare Miti	6 A4
Fare Vai Moana	7 A3
Fenua Mata'i'oa	8 B2
Hotel Hibiscus	9 A3
Intercontinental Moorea Resort & Spa	10 B2
Legends Resort	11 B3
Les Tipaniers Hotel & Restaurant	12 B2
Moorea Camping	13 A4
Tapu Lodge	14 B4
Teataura	15 A4

EATING	
A L'Heure du Sud	(see 23)
Bus Stop	16 A3
Chez Vina	17 A3
Fare Vai Moana	(see 7)
La Plantation	18 A3
Le Mayflower	19 A3
Le Motu	20 A3
Les Tipaniers Hotel & Restaurant	(see 12)
Motu Moea – Restaurant la Plage	21 B2
Restaurant Tumoana	22 A3

SHOPPING	
Le Petit Village	23 A3

TRANSPORT	
Europcar	(see 23)
Moorea Loca Boat	(see 9)

Afareaitu (PK10)

Afareaitu (Map p108) is the island's administrative centre, but don't blink or you'll miss it. Chez Pauline, the village's hotel, has a collection of ancient stone *tiki* (sacred statues) and other traditional artefacts. Only about 100m south of Chez Pauline is **Marae Umarea**, which is thought to date from around AD 900 and is the oldest *marae* on the island. Take the road that goes straight to the coast to see the *marae*, which is a long wall of coral boulders right along the waterfront.

Afareaitu's two **waterfalls** are a major island attraction (although they are but feeble trickles in winter). The trail to them begins from a 4WD track near the Ah Sing shop around PK9.

Vaiare (PK4)

The constant toing and froing of ferry boats and high-speed catamarans at the ferry quay, the busy market scene and the cars, taxis and *le trucks* (buses) shuttling visitors around render the 100m or so near the dock area the busiest patch of real estate on Mo'orea.

Vaiare is the starting point for the interesting walk across the ridge to Paopao and Cook's Bay; see opposite.

Paopao & Opunohu Valleys

From Mo'orea's two great bays, valleys sweep inland, meeting south of the coastal bulk of Mt Rotui. In the pre-European era the valleys were densely populated and the Opunohu Valley was dotted with *marae,* some of which have been restored and maintained. The great *marae* sites of Titiroa and Afareaito were extensively reconstructed by Dr Yoshihiko Shinoto in 1967. All *marae* seem to attract mosquitoes and these are no exception!

ARCHAEOLOGICAL SITES

The Opunohu Valley has some of the most important and numerous *marae* in French Polynesia. Unusually, you can walk to them along marked tracks and there are explanatory panels in French and English. The complex comprises a range of partially restored remains including family and communal *marae* as well as dwellings, archery platforms and other structures.

It's believed the valley was continuously inhabited for six centuries, and the oldest surviving structures date from the 13th century. This agricultural community reached its apogee in the 17th and 18th centuries. The first excavations date from 1925. In 1960, Roger Green carried out the most complete research on the area, and 500 structures have been inventoried. See the boxed text, p33, for more information on *marae*.

MARAE TITIROA & OTHER MARAE

Past the agricultural college, the valley road comes to a parking area beside the huge **Marae Titiroa** (Map p108), on the edge of a dense forest of magnificent *mape* (chestnut) trees. From the *marae* a walking track leads to the *tohua* (council platform), and two smaller *marae*.

From there the track continues to the **Marae Ahu-o-Mahine**, a more recent *marae* of round stones with an imposing three-stepped *ahu* (altar). You can cross the small stream running down the valley to other, more modest *marae*.

A short distance along the road from Marae Titiroa is **Marae Afareaito**. Although there is a walking path between the two, it is not easy to follow; the main road is an easier route. The large *marae* has a small, raised-terrace *ahu*, and back rests that were used by the priests. It is flanked by two crescent-shaped archery platforms.

BELVÉDÈRE

Beyond Marae Afareaito the road continues to climb steeply, winding its way up to the *belvédère*. This lookout offers superb views of Mt Rotui, which splits the two bays, and back to the towering mountains that rise in the centre of the island and once formed the southern rim of the ancient crater. West (right if you are facing inland) from behind the main parking area, a small trail winds around leading to the *marae*, from where you can loop back up to the parking lot again. Give yourself a good two hours to complete the not-well-marked loop (more if you get lost, which is easy) and look out for wild passionfruit growing in the bushes.

ACTIVITIES

It is wise to book activities as soon as you arrive on the island; contact organisers directly or check with your hotel or guesthouse. Many of the bigger hotels have activities desks.

Diving & Snorkelling

There are several beaches that are ideal for swimming, and you can even swim across to the handful of *motu* around Hauru Point. For **snorkelling**, join an organised lagoon tour or DIY around Hauru Point and its *motu* (p110), around the interior of the reef beyond Temae beach (p109) or just plop in anywhere the coral looks good (the water is usually so clear you can see the coral formations from the shore).

For a full day of snorkelling, you can also head to **Lagoonarium Village** (Map p108; ☎ 78 13 15; day pass adult/child 2500/2000 CFP). One of the best bargains around, a day pass gets you a boat shuttle to and from the small sandy *motu* surrounded by coral gardens and includes kayaks and snorkelling gear use. The best option for food is to bring a picnic lunch as there's both a barbecue and kitchen available, but you can order meals in advance if you call ahead. If you really love it here you can stay overnight for another 2500 CFP per person in the rustic bungalows. Taxi pick-up from your hotel or the ferry quay is available from 1500 CFP per person (or more depending on the distance).

If you want to experience diving but aren't quite sure it's for you, try **Aqua Blue** (Map p111; ☎ 56 53 53; aquablue_pf@hotmail.com; 6000 CFP) at the Intercontinental Moorea Resort & Spa. This outfit offers an excursion where you walk along the sea bed wearing a weighted helmet with air pumped into it. Since you actually walk on the bottom, you don't even need to be able to swim.

To the north of the island, there is some great **diving** for beginners and experienced divers (for details about sites see p65). Dive operators include the following:

Bathy's Diving (Map p111; ☎ 56 31 44; www.bathys .net; Intercontinental Moorea Resort & Spa)
Ia Ora Diving (Map p108; ☎ 55 12 12; www.iaora diving.pf; Sofitel Moorea Ia Ora Beach Resort)
Moorea Blue Diving Center (Map p110; ☎ 55 17 04; www.mooreabluediving.com; Moorea Pearl Resort & Spa)
Moorea Fun Dive (Map p111; ☎/fax 56 40 38; www .moorea-fundive.com; PK26.7) Near Moorea Camping.
Scubapiti (Map p111; ☎ 56 20 38, 78 03 52; www .scubapiti.com; Les Tipaniers Hotel & Restaurant) The only dive centre that doesn't engage in shark-feeding; see p65 for more information about this practice.
Topdive Moorea (☎ 56 17 32; www.topdive.com; Sheraton dive centre Map p108; Sheraton Moorea Lagoon Resort; Cook's Bay Map p110; Cook's Bay)

Whale- & Dolphin-Watching

This activity has exploded in recent years. You can count on finding dolphins year-round but

it's the whales, who migrate to Mo'orea from July to October, who draw in the crowds. If you're lucky you'll get to swim with the marine mammals but just seeing them in the water is a real thrill – trips cost 7900 CFP and kids under 12 are half price. We recommend:

Dolphin Quest (☎ 55 19 48; adult/child 20,000/12,000 CFP) If you want a calmer environment in which to commune with dolphins (or if you just get way too seasick to brave the boat!), try for a 'shallow-water encounter' with captive dolphins in an enclosure at the Intercontinental Moorea Resort & Spa. Snorkelling with dolphins is 19,000 CFP.
Dr Michael Poole (☎ 56 23 22, 77 50 07; www .drmichaelpoole.com; ☺ Mon & Thu) A world specialist on South Pacific marine mammals and an advocate for their protection, Dr Poole began the first whale-watching tours and continues to lead the best ones available.
Moorea Boat Tours (☎ 56 28 44; mooreaboattours@ mail.pf; ☺ daily) Run by an ex-employee of Michael Poole, these tours are lively, young and fun.

Surfing & Kite Surfing

The island's excellent surfing waves are for experienced to advanced surfers. The most popular spot is Haapiti (May to October; Map p108), which has the regularity and strength of reef waves with the security of a beach wave; plus it's pretty deep at the takeoff point. Other spots include Temae (year-round, depending on the winds), which is a difficult right-hander at a recess in the reef; Paopao (Cook's Bay) and Opunohu Bay (November to April) in a magnificent setting; and the expert-only left-hander at Intercontinental Moorea Resort & Spa (June to October), near the hotel's beach.

Kite surfing has become very popular on Mo'orea and on windy days you'll see dozens of kites whipping across the lagoon in front of the Intercontinental Moorea Resort & Spa. If you want to give it a go contact David at **Lakana Fly** (☎ 56 51 58, 70 96 71; 2hr course 1200 CFP), at Hauru Point, who offers beginner to advanced kite-surfing lessons for ages nine and up.

Hiking

Exhilarating hikes of varying difficulty tackle the lush inland area. Some of the trails are infrequently used and poorly marked, so it's wise to use a guide or get up-to-the-moment directions from your guesthouse.

VAIARE TO PAOPAO

This interesting and reasonably easy walk takes about two hours, starting from Vaiare and climbing to the ridge between Mt Tearai (770m) and Mt Mouaputa (830m) before dropping down into the valley and emerging at Paopao on Cook's Bay.

From the ferry quay in Vaiare, walk south across the first bridge and turn inland along the road beside the Chez Méno store. There are two intersections: take the right fork on both occasions. Don't take the next right turn but keep following the road, which deteriorates to a muddy track that climbs up above the south bank of the river. Do not follow the track to its conclusion; instead, look for a walking track, which turns off the track just before it becomes too narrow for a 4WD.

The walking track climbs steeply uphill and can be slippery after rain but, once found, it's easy to follow. Eventually the track emerges on the ridge between the two peaks. Follow the ridge uphill a short way to a rock with a wonderful view of Tahiti and of the pineapple plantations in the valley below. Towering above is the spectacular peak of Mt Mouaputa, the mountain with the 'hole' through it.

The track drops steeply, but handy vines and creepers make the descent fairly simple. The track passes through a thicket of bamboo and crosses a river before emerging on the flat valley floor.

THREE COCONUT TREES PASS

This climb is hard work but the pay-off is superb views from the ridge between Mt Mouaroa (880m) and Mt Tohiea (1207m). There are no longer three coconut trees up here – two were blown down in an early 1980s cyclone.

There are two ways to get to the pass. The more scenic way starts (by car if you have one) by turning right on a road right before the agricultural college on the road to the *belvédère* – look for the sign reading 'Vue de Roto Nui et du Marae' and a much smaller one with a pictogram of three coconut trees. You can park at the end of this 100m road.

The walking path, with its red trail markers, continues from the road then drops down to a small stream and climbs up the other side, through ferns, with the ridge and the coconut tree clearly visible to the right.

The route takes a sharp turn and drops steeply down to a wider river. Cross this river but don't go straight up the other side. The path now follows the river, and crosses it half-a-dozen times as it tumbles through a magnificent *mape* forest. Eventually the walking trail diverges from the river and heads up the hill. If you're uncertain whether you're still on the route, look for red markers. If you go far without them, you're lost.

Higher up the hill the markers seem to fade but bits of plastic tied to branches help. Clearings are the easiest places to get lost; each time you leave one, make sure you're on the right trail.

The final climb to the top of the knife-edge ridge is a real root-hanger, but you emerge from the undergrowth to unobstructed views on the way up. Follow the ridge to the right (west) for the best views over the bays (and all the way to Tetiaroa on a clear day).

Alternatively, you can hike up from the road leading inland towards La Maison de la Nature du Mou'a Roa (p118) from a small church (although it looks more like a school) near PK21 on the southwest side of the island. There's an electric box covered with red graffiti at the road's entrance. The road turns into a 4WD track and ends after 2.5km at La Maison de la Nature. From here Three Coconut Trees Pass is another 1km uphill on a well-marked track; you can ask at friendly La Maison de la Nature for directions.

OPUNOHU VALLEY LOOP

This one-day walk starts at Three Coconut Trees Pass then continues on. Follow the ridgeline through undergrowth of *mape* and *purau* (hibiscus) until you get to the *belvédère* (about 1½ hours). From there, it's about 45 minutes to Three Firs Pass, with superb views of Cook's Bay and Opunohu Bay as you face the ridge of Mt Rotui. This section presents no particular difficulties, apart from a short, steep rise just before the pass. The last stage is the return to the agricultural college, about 1¾ hours. After a steep descent you come to the basin of the caldera. Approaching the college you pass through banana plantations, a pine forest and coffee trees.

Horse Riding

Ranch Opunohu Valley (☎ 56 28 55; ranch_opu nohu_valley@yahoo.fr; rides 5000 CFP; ⊙ Tue-Sun) Two-hour guided rides into the island's interior are available mornings and afternoons.

Cycling

Mo'orea is a great island to cycle around. Doing the 60km circuit in a day is possible (depending on the state of your thighs), although tiring, particularly given the rather sorry state of the bikes available. Many of the hotels and several roadside stands have bikes for around 1000 to 2000 CFP for a full day.

Other Activities

Double-seater ATV 4WD buggies are a fun but expensive way to see some rugged interior areas. Two-hour tours are available from **ATV Moorea Tour** (☎ 56 16 60; www.atvmooreatours.pf; tours from 14,000 CFP).

Deep-sea fishing can be organised through **Moorea Fishing Charters** (☎ 77 02 19; half-day per person 18,000 CFP). There is a four-person minimum, but private and full-day tours can also be arranged.

Parasailing, water-skiing and wave-runner lagoon tours can be booked through **Mahana Tours** (☎ 56 20 44; tours 1500-3500 CFP).

The brand-new **Moorea Green Pearl Golf Course** (Map p108; ☎ 56 27 32; www.mooreagolf-resort.com; Temae) has 18 holes and is in full, scorching sun. The mountain behind is low and weedy and there's not much of a view of the sea but the lake is pretty enough. The course's hotel had hit a bureaucratic snare at the time of writing and building had been halted. We couldn't even get served a drink here when we passed.

COURSES

Les Ateliers 'Te Oro' (☎ 58 30 27; te.oro.danse@mail.pf; Painapo Beach) Tahitian dance courses for beginners or intermediate run every day except Wednesdays and Friday afternoons. Classes average three hours and include a lecture and a snack as well as some instruction on costume making. Courses are also taught sometimes at the Intercontinental Moorea Resort & Spa and regularly on Tahiti. See p80 for more details.

MO'OREA FOR CHILDREN

Don't hesitate to bring the whole family, as Mo'orea is particularly kid friendly. Many family-run bungalow operations (often on the beach) have kitchens and one to two bedrooms making them very reasonable as well as practical for families. If the kids ever tire of just splashing around, then hiking, horse riding and exploring the lagoon are fun activities.

La Maison de la Nature du Mou'a Roa (Map p108; www.lamaisondelanature.com; all-inclusive weekend per child 12,000 CFP) is superbly set up for children ages five to 16 and accepts foreign children

to many of its holiday camp programs that run throughout the year. Kids hike, learn about the local flora, build shelters, listen to local legends and have a grand old time. It's all in French, of course, but the owners speak some English and it's a great opportunity for kids to learn some French. See also p118.

TOURS
Lagoon Tours

The best way to discover Mo'orea's magnificent lagoon is by joining a lagoon excursion. Tours typically visit the two bays, stop to feed the sharks, feed and swim with the rays at Stingray World (Map p111), and picnic and snorkel on Motu Fareone. Plenty of operators are available for day-long tours that usually include lunch and cost around 7000 CFP; check at your accommodation.

4WD Tours

Several operators organise island tours aboard open 4WDs. There are complete tours of the island with visits to the archaeological sites in the Opunohu Valley, stops at the *belvédère* and the Afareaitu waterfalls, and visits to pineapple and vanilla plantations and the fruit-juice factory. The three-hour tours cost around 4000 CFP per person and are good value if you don't want to rent a car.

Albert Transport & Activities (☎ 56 13 53; alberttransport@mail.pf)

Inner Island Safari Tours (☎ 56 20 09; inner-saf@mail.pf)

What to Do on Moorea (☎ 56 57 66; www.magic moorea.com)

SLEEPING

Aaah, Mo'orea. There's no traffic (but plenty of roaring mosquitoes) and even the budget accommodation options have lovely garden settings.

Most accommodation is concentrated on the eastern side of Cook's Bay and around Hauru Point. Both these centres are very spread out; if you're staying at one end and want to eat at the other, it's not a case of just wandering a few steps along the road, although many restaurants will arrange to pick you up.

All top-end places and most of the mid-range options accept credit cards; many budget places don't.

Cook's Bay

Magnificent Cook's Bay does not have any beach, and so is the quieter, less touristy sister to Hauru Point.

Motel Albert (Map p110; ☎ 56 12 76; fax 56 58 58; r 5500 CFP, houses 10,500 CFP) An excellent budget choice, this place has a handful of ageing but well-maintained houses with open terraces, as well as a row of brightly decorated rooms with mini terraces closed in with mosquito screens. It's on the mountain side of the road in a lush garden. All options have kitchens and there's a minimum stay of three nights.

Kaveka Hotel (Map p110; ☎ 56 50 50; www.hotel kaveka.com; bungalows 13,500-26,500 CFP; 🏊) This place has bungalows with nice stained-glass detail, and is set in a well-tended garden. The hotel's restaurant is highly recommended.

Club Bali Hai (Map p110; ☎ 56 13 68; www.clubbalihai .com; d 16,000-27,000 CFP, bungalows 25,000-33,000 CFP; 🖥 🏊) Just across from Motel Albert is this stylish, breezy spot with views of Mt Rotui. There's a swimming pool, tennis court, boat dock and restaurant. This place is very popular with American travellers (many who have a time-share here), and you can still have a sundowner with Muk, one of the two remaining American 'Bali Hai boys' who built French Polynesia's first over-the-water bungalows.

Moorea Pearl Resort & Spa (Map p110; ☎ 50 84 52; www.pearlresorts.com; d 27,000-33,000 CFP, garden/ beach/over-water bungalows 46,000/39,000/69,000 CFP; 🏊 🖥 🏊) Occupying the site of the old Bali Hai Moorea, the infinity pool here is the island's best. The white-sand beach is smaller than those at other resorts but the Pearl's vibe is more intimate and very classy. If you're going to go for an over-the-water bungalow, take a premium one as these are over deeper, clearer water. The restaurant has a very good reputation even among locals, but skip the buffet.

Cook's Bay to Hauru Point

Chez Dina (Map p108; ☎ 56 10 39; www.pensiondinamoo rea.com; 2-/4-/5-person bungalows 7500/8500/9500 CFP) A friendly down-home Mo'orea sort of place, the kitchen-equipped bungalows here are kept spotlessly clean by the loving host family. It's on the mountain side of the road about 100m from the lagoon.

Hotel Tipaniers Iti (Map p108; ☎ 56 12 67; www.les tipaniers.com; bungalow d/q 8200/8950 CFP) Looking out over spectacular Opunohu Bay, this is a quiet spot with an over-the-water dock for lounging, but no beach. Bungalows are identical to those at the larger Les Tipaniers at Hauru Point. Guests can participate in the other hotel's activities, and a free shuttle runs to Les Tipaniers Hotel & Restaurant (opposite) in the evening.

Village Faimano Hotel (Map p108; ☎ 56 10 20; faimanodenis@mail.pf in French; bungalows 10,000-14,000 CFP) Old dartboards and woodcarvings hang haphazardly about this eclectically decorated place. It's quiet and on a lovely beach next to the Sheraton, but bungalows (which sleep one to four people or two to six and have kitchens) are getting pretty rundown. Reservations are for a three-night minimum and credit cards are accepted.

⭐ Pension Motu Iti (Map p108; ☎ 55 05 20; www.pensionmotuiti.com; dm 1700 CFP, garden/beach bungalows 10,500/12,000 CFP; 🖥) One of the best-value spots on Mo'orea, this place is impeccably friendly and clean. Waterfront rooms, which hover over the beach, could be considered a poor man's over-the-water bungalow and have views of sunrise and sunset. The dorms are airy (but not very social) with a view of the sea, and the beachside restaurant serves reasonably priced, tasty food.

Sheraton Moorea Lagoon Resort & Spa (Map p108; ☎ 55 11 11, reservations 86 48 49; www.sheraton moorea.com; garden/beach/over-water bungalows 38,000/60,000/91,000 CFP; 🏊 🖥 🏊) A lovely choice where we encountered bright, helpful service and lots of very happy guests; this is really one of Mo'orea's best resorts. The beach here is particularly splendid (with top snorkelling) and the activities desk is great – both of these aspects are important since the hotel is quite isolated from the main areas of the island. Breakfast is good but other meals aren't great value. Mandara Spa treatments can be enjoyed at the spa or in your room.

Hauru Point

Unlike Cook's Bay, Hauru Point has a beach. Though narrow, it's pretty spectacular with turquoise water, a few *motu* to swim to out front and good snorkelling.

Camping Chez Nelson (Map p111; ☎ 56 15 18; www .camping-nelson.pf; tent sites per person 1000 CFP, dm/d from 1600/4500 CFP, bungalows 5000 CFP; 🖥) A few trees and flowers would do great things for this bare-bones cheapy. As it is, it feels like a hot school-yard surrounded by flimsy huts. But what more do you need with that beach in front and a kitchen to cook in? Credit cards are accepted and management is understaffed but friendly.

Moorea Camping (Map p111; ☎ 56 14 47; fax 56 30 22; PK27.5; tent sites per person 1100 CFP, dm/d 1500/2500 CFP, bungalows 5000-9000 CFP) There are more plants and shade here than at Chez Nelson, but the accommodation looks like military barracks. However, the dorms are the island's cheapest, and you can cook at the waterfront kitchen and live on the beach. Reception is dry and to the point. Prices go down after three nights.

Teataura (Map p111; ☎ 56 22 01; tent sites per person 1000 CFP, q 8000 CFP) Owned by an elderly Tahitian couple and with an excellent, quiet location on the beach, these cosy rooms with kitchens are clean, well maintained and great value. Rooms sleep four but are fine for two and the garden is filled with flowers.

Fare Miti (Map p111; ☎ 21 65 59; mooreafaremiti@ yahoo.fr; 4-person garden/beach bungalows 11,000/13,000 CFP; 🖳) The outwardly attractive, round thatched bungalows here might be a little past their prime on the inside, but they are clean, and the location, on a quiet strip of Hauru beach, is divine.

Fare Manuia (Map p111; ☎ 56 26 17; kinarei@hot mail.com; 4-/6-person bungalows 12,000/16,000 CFP) Six bungalows are spaced out in a growing garden by a sunny stretch of beach. All have bathrooms with hot water, kitchens, TVs and large verandas. You'll find a washing machine, a *pirogue* (outrigger canoe) for free use and a kayak that can be rented. There's a two-night minimum stay.

Les Tipaniers Hotel & Restaurant (Map p111; ☎ 56 12 67; www.lestipaniers.com; bungalow with/without kitchen from 14,500/7500 CFP) It's a bustling hub of activity on this lovely knuckle of beach jutting out towards a coral-laden stretch of lagoon. Bungalows aren't going to win any architectural awards but are big, practical (most have kitchens and one to two bedrooms) and clean. It's a great spot for families and friends but not private enough for a honeymoon. The gardens are full of flowers and the restaurant is one of the best on Mo'orea (see above). Credit cards are accepted.

Hotel Hibiscus (Map p111; ☎ 56 12 20; www.hotel -hibiscus.pf; garden/beach bungalows 15,000/18,000 CFP; 🖾 🖳) Another good family choice, this hotel has 29 functional and slightly Spartan thatched-roof bungalows in a pleasant garden. They all have three beds, attached hot-water bathroom, groovy tie-dyed curtains, veranda and kitchen. Credit cards are accepted.

Fare Vai Moana (Map p111; ☎ /fax 56 17 14; www .fare-vaimoana.com; garden/beach bungalows 15,000/22,000 CFP) This upscale beachfront hotel is a more intimate and less expensive alternative to a resort. There are 13 very comfortable bungalows with refrigerator, mezzanine and bathroom with hot water; each accommodates up to four people but rates are for two people. Reserve well in advance for the choice ones on the beach. The restaurant (p120) overlooks the water and, though expensive, has an excellent reputation with French locals. Credit cards are accepted.

Tapu Lodge (Map p111; ☎ 55 20 55; www.tapulodge .com; 3- or 4-person units 15,900 CFP, 6-person units 26,500 CFP) These enormous, immaculate, modern units are more solid and stylish than you'll find anywhere else in this price range and have ocean views. They're close enough to the action of Hauru Point but far enough away to be very quiet. The welcoming management offers free trips out to the *motu* and rates are discounted for longer stays. Credit cards are accepted.

Fenua Mata'i'oa (Map p111; ☎ 55 00 25; www .fenua-mataioa.com; Village Tiahura; ste 30,000-60,000 CFP; 🖾 🖳 🖾) Behind an average-looking cement wall is this exceptionally serene option. The four sophisticated and exuberantly decorated suites are dripping with paintings, pillows, silks and antiques. Half board is an extra 10,000 CFP per person and the service is impeccable and personalised. It's the perfect spot for honeymooners. The only downside is that although the *pension* has lagoon access, there's no beach.

our pick Dream Island (Map p111; ☎ 56 38 81; www .dream-island.com; bungalows 35,000-53,000 CFP) A three-minute boat ride from Haapiti brings you to this superbly located, exclusive island paradise. The two houses/bungalows were built using local materials in authentic Polynesian style and are equipped with kitchens and phones. All manner of activities are offered by Kolka and his exceptionally charming family and you can even arrange to have your own personal chef (for a fee of course). There is a four-night minimum and credit cards are accepted.

Legends Resort (Map p111; ☎ 83 19 09; www.legends resort.fr; villas 37,400-91,200 CFP; 🖾 🖳 🖾) A new concept for Mo'orea, this brand new place combines the luxury of a resort with the practicality of a property rental. Each modern villa has gorgeous views over the lagoon (the resort is on a hill), its own kitchen and laundry areas, plus a private Jacuzzi on the generous terrace space. It's perfect for families as villas can sleep between four to six people, but also great for couples since the villas offer a high degree of privacy. A free shuttle service is available to a private *motu* where you can do the Mo'orea thing and lounge on the beach.

Intercontinental Moorea Resort & Spa (Map p111; ☎ 55 19 19; www.moorea.intercontinental.com; d 36,000 CFP; garden/beach/over-water bungalows 49,000/58,000/86,000 CFP; ❌ 🖳 🖳) Welcome to the biggest resort on Mo'orea, a sprawling, impersonal yet undeniably pretty spread of wooden bungalows set against turquoise water. Avoid over-the-water bungalows 601 to 603 and 501 to 506, which are positioned right next to the dolphin encounter where adults and children screech in delight to dolphin farting noises throughout the day. That said, there are lots of activities for children, making this a very family friendly resort, and gear like kayaks and snorkelling equipment are available free of charge. The spa here, Helene Spa, is the most respected on the island.

Haapiti to Afareaitu

Mark's Place Paradise (Map p108; ☎ 56 43 02, 78 93 65; www.marks-place-paradise.com; camping per person 1100 CFP, dm/bungalows from 2000/8000 CFP; 🖳) The open, well-planted garden, creative, cosy dorm bungalows and surfy/social atmosphere make this a good backpacker option on Mo'orea, but we've heard the odd grumble about variable service. It's away from the beach and just about everything else besides the Haapiti surf break, but bike and kayak rentals (1000 CFP per day) make getting around less of a chore. A handful of very cool private bungalows are also available (we love the one made of stone and colourful bottles) and credit cards are accepted.

Chez Pauline (Map p108; ☎ 56 11 26; d incl breakfast 6500 CFP) Opened by Pauline Teariki's mother in 1918, this was once the only hotel on the island; staying here gives you a glimpse into the Mo'orea of yesteryear. There are seven curtained rooms, sharing two bathrooms with cold water, and a handful of Pauline's adorable grandchildren animate the common areas. The restaurant specialises in Tahitian cuisine and there's an on-site museum.

our pick Tarariki Village (Map p108; ☎ 55 21 05; pensiontarariki@mail.pf; 2-/4-person bungalow 7500/12000 CFP, tree house 9500 CFP) The friendly, family atmosphere and quiet, beachside location make this the kind of place where you quickly lose track of the days. There are miniature cabins with two beds and a bathroom (cold water only), a bigger beachfront family bungalow and a Robinson Crusoe–style thatched bungalow perched in a tree. In the middle of the property

is a superb *fare potee* (open dining area), which is used as a communal kitchen. Kayaks are free for guests, there's a grocery store 300m away and bungalow prices drop after three nights.

La Maison de la Nature du Mou'a Roa (Map p108; ☎ 56 58 62; www.lamaisondelanature.com; half/full board per person 8700/9700 CFP) Completely off-the-beaten-track in the lush centre of the island, this place is a hiker's dream and perhaps the most environmentally conscious spot on the island. The colonial-style house with eight rooms (four to six beds in each) is painted bright yellow and mint green and looks like something straight out of a fairytale. Most of the time, the friendly staff are, in fact, running children's camps (see p115), but it's possible to arrange individual and group stays for adults and families. Call as far ahead as possible to arrange amazing outdoor adventures.

Fare Arana (Map p108; ☎ 56 44 03; www.farearana .com; d without/with air-con 9900/11,900 CFP; ❌ 🖳) This hilltop place is quite stylish. The gardens have a Southeast Asian flavour while the comfortable two-storey rooms have French touches. There are magnificent views, loads of flowers and convivial staff. Good-value packages including activities are often available on the website.

Pension Aute (Map p108; ☎ /fax 56 45 19; www.pen sionaute.com; bungalows 11,000-16,000 CFP) This *pension* has an amazing position on the wild southern side of the island and a variety of spacious bungalows for three to six people. All bungalows are very well equipped (they even have washing machines and TVs).

Résidence Linareva (Map p108; ☎ 55 05 65; www .linareva.com; 1-/2-/4-/6-person bungalows from 11,500/12,500/ 19,500/27,500 CFP; 🖳) This option has a wide variety of well-furnished bungalows in a lush garden by the beach and has a great reputation. Bicycles, *pirogues* and snorkelling equipment are all provided free of charge. If you don't mind the isolated location and the sometimes stand-offish reception, it's a great place to stay and is gay friendly. Credit cards are accepted.

Temae

Fare Maeva (Map p108; ☎ /fax 56 18 10; www.faremaeva moorea.com; bungalows 10,200 CFP) This charming, isolated place is dominated by coconut trees and coral gravel. All the tidy, artistically decorated bungalows have a bathroom and kitchen and the beach is only 200m away. Finding this place is quite a feat – follow the signs to the (now closed) Golden Nugget shop; Fare Maeva is about 150m further on.

Moorea Golf Lodge (Map p108; ☎ 55 08 55; www
.mooreagolflodge.pf; garden/beach bungalows 19,500/21,500
CFP; ☒) On a quiet strip of Temae beach (walk
five minutes to the better main beach) and only
100m from the golf course, three out of four of
these new pine bungalows sleep up to six people
(above rates are for a double, prices go up for
more people). All have equipped kitchens and
sun decks and meal service is available.

Sofitel Moorea Ia Ora Beach Resort (Map p108;
☎ 55 03 55; www.sofitel.com; beach/garden/over-water
bungalows from 58,000/31,000/76,000 CFP; ☒ ☐ ☒)
Stand-up applause is in order for the phenomenal remodel and overhaul (completed
in late 2006) of this now-excellent modern
Polynesian resort. It's on the best beach on
the island and the service is beyond anything
else we found on Mo'orea. We weren't crazy
about some of the 'modern touches' (bright
orange tables and digitalised Gauguin bed
headboards may be an acquired taste), but
overall the hotel is elegant and relaxing, and
the restaurant pricey but worth it.

EATING

Beach loungers beware: with all the rich,
exquisite food available at Mo'orea's restaurants you'll be packing home some extra
kilos. Cook's Bay and Hauru Point are the
dining epicentres.

Most places are open for lunch and dinner,
close around 9pm and accept credit cards unless otherwise noted.

Restaurants & Cafes
MAHAREPA & COOK'S BAY
Snack Rotui (Map p110; ☎ 56 18 16; PK9.5; mains from
700 CFP; ☺ closed Mon) For basic fare like chow
mein, *poulet citron* (lemon chicken) or an
assortment of cheap sandwiches, you can't
do better than this buzzing spot.

Caraméline (Map p110; ☎ 56 15 88; Maharepa shopping centre; breakfasts from 950 CFP, lunch mains from 1300
CFP; ☺ breakfast & lunch) Get all-day American-,
French- or Tahitian-style breakfasts, burgers,
pizzas, salads, ice-cream treats and more at
this affordable and popular cafe. Don't miss
the French-style coffee, pastries and crêpes.

L'Ananas Bleu (Map p110; ☎ 56 13 68; mains from
1000 CFP; ☺ breakfast & lunch daily, dinner Wed) On
the water in the Club Bali Hai, this place
has great snacks and light lunches. Catch the
dance show and à la carte seafood barbecue
(mains from 1900 CFP) Wednesday nights
at 6.30pm.

Le Sud Restaurant (Map p110; ☎ 56 42 95; lesud
.moorea@mail.pf; mains 1300-3000 CFP; ☺ lunch & dinner
Tue-Sat, lunch Sun) The airy French-plantation
decor and good food make this a winner
(though portions are a bit small) .

Restaurant Chez Jean-Pierre (Map p110; ☎ 56 18 51;
mains 1500-2500 CFP; ☺ lunch Mon, lunch & dinner Tue, Thu,
Fri & Sun, dinner Sat) This very Chinese place also
offers tofu and other vegetarian dishes on its
extensive menu.

Alfredo's (Map p110; ☎ 56 17 71; mains 1500-3000
CFP) A lively little Italian restaurant that has
forever been popular with travellers, but don't
expect particularly authentic Italian fare. The
good news is that there's often live music, even
during the week.

Restaurant Te Honu Iti (Map p110; ☎ 56 19 84; mains
1900-4200 CFP; ☺ lunch & dinner Thu-Tue) The terrace of
this place sits over the water, and at night the
water is lit up so you can watch rays and fish
swim below. The owner's original paintings
grace the walls, so you have something else
interesting to look at too, as you dine on exquisite osso bucco (2400 CFP), lobster (4200 CFP)
or an array of French-inspired dishes.

Chez Luciano (Map p110; ☎ 56 15 20; pizzas 2000
CFP) Catering to hungry French Polynesian
families, this place serves giant pizzas (plenty
of toppings) for five people for very reasonable prices. There's a cat-theme decor and the
chef lets out an occasional meow as he spices
his creations.

Rudy's Fine Steaks & Seafood (Map p110; ☎ 56 58
00; mains 2000-4500 CFP) The name says it all at
this new, hacienda-style eatery. Carnivores
will be particularly happy as they dine in
air-con bliss.

Aito Restaurant (Map p108; ☎ 56 45 52; mains
around 2500 CFP) Run by Corsican Jean-Baptiste,
who's a real character, and his wife Vanina,
this newly expanded lagoonside restaurant
is one of the musts on Mo'orea. The food is
French, Corsican and Tahitian, and the ambience is lively, breezy and boozy. Live music is
on Friday nights.

HAURU POINT
The strip along Hauru Point is teeming with
places to eat.

A L'Heure du Sud (Map p111; sandwiches 450-600 CFP;
☺ 10.30am-3.30pm Thu-Tue) A great variety of well-
stuffed sandwiches (think steak and barbecue
sauce stuffed in a baguette) are served at this
roulotte (mobile food van) in front of Le Petit
Village shopping centre. Cash only.

MO'OREA

MO'OREA

Le Motu (Map p111; mains 500-1900 CFP; 🕙 11am-8pm Mon-Sat) A great, Dairy Queen–style spot serving everything from salads and burgers to crêpes and pasta.

Restaurant Tumoana (Map p111; ☎ 56 37 60; mains 1000-2000 CFP) The decor is basic but the over-the-water location and local vibe more than make up for it. Expect simple yet yummy Tahitian-French grub and don't miss Friday and Sunday nights when there's live music and dancing.

La Plantation (Map p111; ☎ 56 45 10; mains 1100-3600 CFP) Lots of Cajun specialities as well as some of Mo'orea's best vegetarian dishes are available at this classy, white-clad, jazz-infused restaurant. There's often live music on Saturdays and the wine list and service are just as good as the food.

Pizza Daniel (Map p108; ☎ 56 39 95; PK34; pizzas 1300-1500 CFP; 🕙 closed Thu) Locals swear this little shack serves the best pizza on Mo'orea and we have to agree. Pull up a stool, order the thin-crust tuna pizza (with fresh tuna – delicious!), chat with the owner, then check out the eels in the adjacent stream.

Chez Vina (Map p111; ☎ 56 13 17; mains 1400-1800 CFP) With cement floors, bananas hanging in the foyer and a goat out back, this homey place has character as well as good, well-priced food. Try the specialty shrimp coconut curry (1800 CFP) or, for a real treat, show up for the Sunday all-you-can-eat *ma'a Tahiti* (traditional Tahitian food) banquet (3800 CFP) at noon.

our pick **Bus Stop** (Map p111; ☎ 56 41 19; mains 1600-2000 CFP; 🕙 lunch & dinner Thu-Tue) Ask any local and they'll cite this new place as their favourite restaurant. The seared tuna with vanilla sauce (1980 CFP) was the best dish we ate on Mo'orea and the giant loaf of fresh baked bread served with it did not go to waste. The fricassee of chicken and shrimp stew with turmeric (1800 CFP) is near island-famous as are the generous, luscious desserts.

Les Tipaniers Hotel & Restaurant (Map p111; ☎ 56 12 67; lunch 1200-1700 CFP, dinner 1600-3600 CFP) Breakfast and dinner are served at the beachside restaurant, but it's dinner at the less well located but elegant roadside restaurant that is truly to die for. Choose from dishes like filet of lamb with warm goat's cheese (1950 CFP) to fresh fish of the day with a choice of mango, vanilla, sea urchin (sounds weird, tastes great) or Mediterranean tomato sauces (1880 CFP).

Fare Vai Moana (Map p111; ☎ 56 17 14; mains 1700-3500 CFP) This eatery in the Fare Vai Moana hotel (p117) has a great beachside setting; the deck offers front-row seats for the sunset and there is sometimes live music. It's a favourite with French locals.

Painapo Beach (Map p108; ☎ 55 07 90; PK33; mains around 2000 CFP; 🕙 9am-3pm Thu-Mon) An all-in-one sort of place that offers gourmet food using local ingredients, a white-sand beach and occasional cultural demonstrations. You can't miss its huge (though falling apart) statue of a tattooed man holding a club at the entrance. There's usually a palm-weaving demonstration on Thursdays and a Tahitian feast on Sundays.

Le Mayflower (Map p111; ☎ 56 53 59; mains 2000-4000 CFP; 🕙 lunch & dinner Thu-Tue) Next to the Hotel Hibiscus, this deservedly popular French place is famous for its lobster ravioli.

MOTU TIAHURA

our pick **Motu Moea – Restaurant la Plage** (Map p111; ☎ 74 96 96; mains 1400-3000 CFP) This place has an idyllic setting on Motu Tiahura (also known as Motu Moea). The food is fresh and tasty, and fancy, fruity cocktails are also available. Take a dip (or swim back to whence you came) once you've digested your meal – this is the life! You can get a boat over to the *motu* (500 CFP) from Les Tipaniers Hotel & Restaurant or the Intercontinental Moorea Resort & Spa – or stuff your money in a ziplock plastic bag and swim.

Self-Catering

Self-catering on Mo'orea can save you heaps of cash and many places to stay have little kitchens. There are quite a few supermarkets and smaller shops around the island where you can buy fresh baguettes and basic supplies. However, it's not as easy as you'd hope to find fresh produce in Mo'orea's shops beyond lettuce and sad-looking tomatoes. Your best bet for local fruit is at roadside stands that pop up along the southwest coast between PK30 and PK35.

Champion-TOA (Map p108; 🕙 8am-8pm Mon-Sat, morning Sun) is the biggest supermarket and is about 500m south of the quay in Vaiare. Supermarché Pao Pao (Map p110) in Cook's Bay and Magasin Rémy (Map p110), near Chez Luciano, just east of PK5, are other supermarkets. Just over the bridge in Paopao is another supermarket.

The best way to buy fresh fish is directly from the fishermen who sell along the road in the afternoons, but you'll have to venture out of the main tourist areas to find them.

DRINKING & ENTERTAINMENT

Mo'orea is more the place to pay off a sleep debt than to kick up your heels. A boozy dinner and a dance performance is about as lively as things get. The big hotels have bars where all are welcome to whet their palates with a predinner drink and some restaurants host occasional live music.

A couple of times a week (usually on Wednesday and Saturday evenings) the bigger hotels organise Polynesian music and dance performances by local groups. These performances tend to be of a very high standard, so it's worth trying to catch one. Try Sofitel Moorea Ia Ora Beach Resort (p119), Intercontinental Moorea Resort & Spa (p118), Club Bali Hai (p116) and Moorea Pearl Resort (p116). Call the hotels for dates and times.

Maria@Tapas (Map p110; ☎ 55 01 70; ☻ 8am-11pm Mon-Wed, 8am-1am Thu-Sat; ☐) Order a (not-so-great) burrito and enjoy the music at this funky little Tex-Mex joint (mains 1000 CFP to 2000 CFP). You can check your email while you imbibe at the bar. It's best to reserve well in advance on nights when there is music (entry fee 500 CFP).

Tiki Village (Map p108; ☎ 55 02 50; www.tikivillage.pf; admission with lunch 1500 CFP, with/without dinner 8700/4400 CFP; ☻ lunch & day show Tue-Sat, dinner & night show Tue, Wed, Fri & Sat) This is a Tahitian cultural village where tourists can watch local people 'living' in the traditional way. The main draw is the spectacular 60-person evening dance performances (the biggest on the island). Daytime shows are an OK alternative but lack some of the intense energy you'll see at night.

SHOPPING

There are two small shopping centres on the island. The shopping centre (Map p110) in Maharepa has a few shops, some banks and the Librarie Kina Maharepa, which has a decent selection of magazines and one or two English-language newspapers.

Le Petit Village (Map p111) has various shops and souvenir outlets, a bank, a supermarket and a bookshop/newsagency. If you forgot your swimsuit, the best place to pick up a new one is at Ron Hall's Island Fashion (Map p110) in Cook's Bay.

The coastal road is littered with places selling *pareu* (some of them hand-painted), T-shirts, Balinese woodcarvings and other curios. There are also a number of places dotted around the island where artists display their work. Keep an eye out for signs along the coastal road.

Retail therapy cannot always be administered on Sunday, when many boutiques and jewellery shops close.

Black Pearls

Although no pearl farms are located on Mo'orea (no matter what anyone tells you), an increasingly large number of places around the island specialise in black pearls. Prices are generally the same as on Tahiti but you'll have to shop around. Often the smaller, less glamorous shops have the best deals while the bigger places have a greater variety of jewellery designs.

Tattoos

Unfortunately Mo'orea's two most famous resident tattoo artists, Chimé and Roonui, have left to ink different pastures. Our guess is they'll return someday, so ask around. Luckily, there's still James Samuela of **Moorea Tattoo** (Map p108; ☎ 76 42 60; www.mooreatattoo.com; PK32 Haapiti). James is one of the only artists who tattoos both the modern way (with a needle) and the ancient way (with a comb made from wild boar tusks). He's highly trained, young and professional.

GETTING THERE & AWAY

There's less than 20km of blue Pacific between Tahiti and Mo'orea, and getting from one island to the other is simplicity itself. At the quay in Pape'ete you can hop on one of the high-speed ferries and be on Mo'orea in less than half an hour. Or from the airport, catch an Air Moorea flight and be there in less than 10 minutes.

Air

Air Moorea (☎ Tahiti 86 41 41, Mo'orea 56 10 34; adult/child one way 2600/1800 CFP, after 5pm 4600/2700 CFP) Flights from Tahiti's Faa'a airport to Mo'orea leave about every half-hour; flights between 1pm and 3pm are 1800 CFP for both adults and children. At Faa'a airport, Air Moorea is in a separate small terminal, a short stroll to the east of the main terminal. See p122 for Mo'orea transport details.

Air Tahiti (☎ 86 42 42, weekends 86 41 84) Flies between Mo'orea and Bora Bora (18,400 CFP one way), Huahine (13,000 CFP one way) and Ra'iatea (13,000 CFP one way).

Boat

It's a breezy ride across the 'Sea of the Moon' between Tahiti and Mo'orea. First departures in the morning are usually around 6am; the last trips are in the afternoon at around 4.30pm or 5.30pm. All fares are 900 CFP each way.

The catamarans **Aremiti 5** (☎ Pape'ete 42 88 88, Mo'orea 56 31 10) and **Moorea Express** (☎ Pape'ete 82 47 47, Mo'orea 56 43 43) jet to and from Mo'orea in about 30 minutes six or more times daily. The bigger **Aremiti Ferry** (☎ Pape'ete 42 85 85, Mo'orea 56 31 10) and **Moorea Ferry** (☎ Pape'ete 45 00 30, Mo'orea 56 34 34) run about four times daily and take about 50 minutes to cross.

You can buy tickets at the ticket counter on the quay (Map p108) just a few minutes before departure. If you are bringing a car it's best to reserve in advance.

GETTING AROUND

Getting around Mo'orea without a car or bicycle is not that easy. Distances aren't great but are often a bit too far to walk. Bear in mind that many of the restaurants and quite a few pearl shops will pick you up for free or for a nominal fee if you call them. Hitching is never entirely safe but if you use good judgment it can be a decent way to get around Mo'orea – watch out particularly for drunk drivers.

To/From the Airport & Quay

Buses (300 CFP) meet all the catamaran arrivals and departures but not the bigger ferries. From the quay, one bus heads south (left) and the other north (right) and completes the island circuit, dropping you off wherever you and everyone else on board needs to stop. Mo'orea's taxis are notoriously expensive: from the airport to the Intercontinental Moorea Resort & Spa will cost about 4000 CFP.

Most hotels offer airport transfers. Air Mo'orea flights are met by a shuttle service costing 600 CFP (or 1100 CFP after 5pm) one way, per person to your hotel – book when you reserve your flight.

Bus

You can get around on the ferry port–bound buses (see above; 300 CFP) even if you aren't taking the catamaran. Hop on and tell the driver where you want to be let off. Buses usually stop at the Mo'orea Tourist Bureau (p109) at Hauru Point four to six times a day – ask inside for the current schedule, which changes frequently. Otherwise, just flag the bus down from the side of the road.

The big resorts offer private bus services to guests for 1500 CFP each way on a fixed schedule.

Boat

You can hire an outboard-powered boat – an ideal way to explore the lagoon and small *motu* – at **Moorea Loca Boat** (Map p111; ☎ 78 13 39; 2/4/8hr incl fuel 7000/9000/11,000 CFP), at the Hibiscus (p117) and Tipaniers hotels (p117). Peddle boats will also be available here by 2009.

Car

On Mo'orea having your own wheels is very useful but expensive. Car-rental operators can be found at the Vaiare ferry quay, at the airport and at some of the major hotels. Generally, you'll pay from around 9000/11,200 CFP for a half/full day including liability insurance and unlimited mileage. Try booking online for cheaper rates.

Albert Transport & Activities (Map p110; ☎ 56 19 28, 56 33 75) This place has prices that are generally lower than the international companies.

Avis (☎ 56 32 61, 56 32 68; fax 56 32 62) At the ferry quay at Vaiare, at the airport and at Club Bali Hai (p116).

Europcar Intercontinental Moorea Resort & Spa (Map p111; ☎ 56 19 50); Le Petit Village (Map p111; ☎ 56 34 00; fax 56 35 05); Sofitel Moorea Ia Ora Beach Resort (Map p108; ☎ 56 42 30); Vaiare (☎ 56 28 64) The main office is at Le Petit Village commercial centre. You can also find it at the ferry quay at Vaiare.

There are petrol stations located near the Vaiare ferry quay, close to the airport, beside Cook's Bay and at Le Petit Village on Hauru Point.

Scooter, Fun Car & Bicycle

Bikes can be rented or are sometimes offered for free by most hotels and *pensions*.

Europcar (Map p111; ☎ 56 34 00; fax 56 35 05) Europcar rents those funny little 'fun cars' for 8800 CFP for eight hours.

Tehotu Location (☎ 56 52 96; per 8/24hr 5500/6000 CFP) Located right at the ferry terminal; scooters are available here.

Taxi

It's not much more expensive to rent a car than to take a taxi from the airport or ferry quay to a hotel at Hauru Point. If you have to take a **taxi** (☎ 56 10 18), you can find one at the airport from 6am to 6pm.

Huahine

Huahine is immaculately tropical and effortlessly Polynesian. The mountains here are lower than those of Tahiti, Mo'orea and Ra'iatea so that land and sea feel brighter: the greens seem more vivid, the reds of the hibiscus flowers pop out at you and the turquoise of the lagoon almost vibrates with intensity. Exotically lush and scarcely developed, Huahine also differs from the drier, lagoon- and resort-dominated Bora Bora. This is an island to visit for extreme calm, communing with nature and a genuine taste of culture. You'll find one of the largest and best-maintained *marae* (traditional temple) complexes in the country, empty beaches and underwater thrills, but if you're looking for a party, head elsewhere. It's a fantastic choice for families or honeymooners looking for quiet, romantic evenings.

Huahine is actually two islands – Huahine Nui (Big Huahine) to the north and Huahine Iti (Little Huahine) to the south. According to oral history, this wasn't always the case. Polynesian legend has it that the split came after the god Hiro ploughed his mighty canoe into the land, cutting the place in two. The split is still evident today, not only because of the tiny gap that separates the two islands but also in their distinct personalities. Huahine Nui is more developed and noisy, home to the bustling little village of Fare and most of the main tourist and administrative facilities. Rugged and isolated, Huahine Iti offers the islands' best beaches, most wonderfully azure lagoons and a serene, get-away-from-it-all atmosphere.

HUAHINE

HIGHLIGHTS

- Lounging on Huahine Iti's picture-perfect lagoonside and *motu* **beaches** (p129)
- Shirking off the tourist crowd by taking the uphill *marae* walk at **Maeva** (p127)
- **Hiking** (p130) the island's rugged peaks for panoramic views over the island and lagoon
- Diving in the **Avapeihi (Fitii) Pass** (p65)
- Dining on *ma'a Tahiti* and the country's best shellfish at **Restaurant Mauarii** (p133)

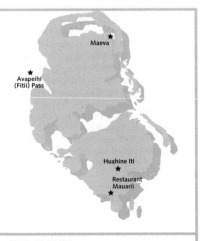

★ Maeva

★ Avapeihi (Fitii) Pass

Huahine Iti
★
Restaurant Mauarii
★

- POPULATION: 5741
- AREA: 75 SQ KM

POUVANA'A A OOPA – A TAHITIAN LEADER

French Polynesia's most famous politician was Pouvana'a a Oopa, who was born in Huahine in 1895 and went on to found the Rassemblement Démocratique des Populations Tahitiennes (RDPT; Democratic Assembly of Tahitian Populations) in 1949. For nearly 10 years he was at the forefront of local politics, opposing French colonial rule, denouncing capitalism and pushing for local employment in government and administrative posts. A man of the people and a devout Protestant, this charismatic leader was strongly supported by French Polynesians, who considered him a *metua* (father) figure.

It all fell apart in 1958 when a 'yes' vote in the referendum to remain linked to France desta-bilised the party. Pouvana'a a Oopa was blamed for the riots that shook Pape'ete on 10 and 11 October 1958 and he was exiled to France. Split by internal dissension, the RDPT was unable to mobilise against the nuclear-testing program in 1963, and was dissolved. Pouvana'a a Oopa was allowed to return to the Pacific in 1968 where he stayed until his death in 1977. Today he remains the pre-eminent Polynesian father figure, a man who made the all-powerful colonial structure tremble.

HISTORY

The rough English translation of the word Huahine is vagina, and although no one knows exactly where the name originated, historians theorise that it has something to do with the important role women played in this island's history – Huahine's ancient queens were highly respected rulers.

Europeans first arrived here in 1769, when James Cook and company landed on Huahine's shores. Polynesians inhabited the island for thousands of years before the *popaa* (Europeans) arrived: archaeological excava-tions to the north of Fare reveal some of the earliest traces of settlement in the Society Islands. Despite a hostile reception from the native inhabitants, Cook returned to Huahine twice, in 1774 and 1777. In 1808 a group of London Missionary Society (LMS) missionar-ies moved to Huahine to escape the turmoil on Tahiti. They remained for only a year but returned in 1818 to further the spread of Christianity in the region. Huahine supported the Pomares in the struggle against the French, and there were a number of clashes between 1846 and 1888, before French rule was eventu-ally accepted. Although the French kicked the English Protestant missionaries out, the island remains predominantly Protestant.

ORIENTATION

A sealed road follows the coast all the way around both islands and a series of *motu* (islets) stretch along the eastern shores. Lake Fauna Nui, actually an inlet from the sea, is on the north coast and almost cuts off the *motu*-like northern peninsula from the rest of Huahine

Nui. The reef fringes the north coast and there are only a few beaches on both islands.

Fare, the port and administrative centre, is on the west coast of Huahine Nui, 2.5km south of the airport. Faie and Maeva, on the east coast, and Fitii, on the west, are the other main settlements on Huahine Nui – although they are small and have no tourism infrastructure. There are four tiny villages on Huahine Iti: Haapu, Parea, Tefarerii and Maroe. The highest peaks are Mt Turi (669m) on Huahine Nui and Mt Pohue Rahi (462m) on Huahine Iti.

INFORMATION

There is a bank opposite the ferry quay in Fare and another on the bypass road running parallel to the main street; both have ATMs. Visiting yachties can obtain water from Pacific Blue Adventure (p129), on the quay.
Ao Api New World (Map p126; ☎ 68 70 99; per hr 900 CFP) Internet access with a view of Fare's port.
Huahine visitors information centre (Map p126; ☎ 68 78 81; ⏱ 7.30-11.30am Mon-Sat) On Fare's main street.
Medical centre (Map p126; ☎ 68 82 20) On the bypass road in Fare; handles minor emergencies.
Post office (Map p126) To the north of Fare towards the airport.
Video Shop Huahine (Map p126; ☎ 60 67 40; per hr 900 CFP; ⏱ 8.30am-noon & 4-8pm Mon-Sat, 5-8pm Sun) Internet access in Fare.

HUAHINE NUI

The following 60km circuit of the larger island starts in Fare and goes around the island in a clockwise direction.

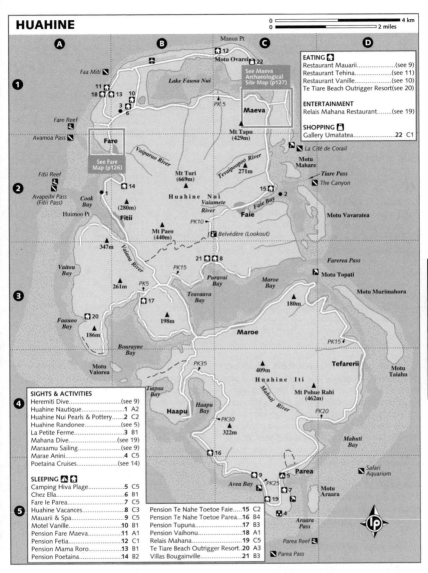

HUAHINE

0 ———— 4 km
0 ———— 2 miles

EATING
Restaurant Mauarii..................(see 9)
Restaurant Tehina.....................(see 11)
Restaurant Vanille......................(see 10)
Te Tiare Beach Outrigger Resort(see 20)

ENTERTAINMENT
Relais Mahana Restaurant........(see 19)

SHOPPING
Gallery Umatatea......................**22** C1

SIGHTS & ACTIVITIES
Heremiti Dive.............................(see 9)
Huahine Nautique........................**1** A2
Huahine Nui Pearls & Pottery......**2** C2
Huahine Randonee........................(see 5)
La Petite Ferme............................**3** B1
Mahana Dive...............................(see 19)
Maraamu Sailing..........................(see 9)
Marae Anini..................................**4** C5
Poetaina Cruises..........................(see 14)

SLEEPING
Camping Hiva Plage.....................**5** C5
Chez Ella......................................**6** B1
Fare le Parea................................**7** C5
Huahine Vacances.........................**8** C3
Mauarii & Spa...............................**9** C5
Motel Vanille................................**10** B1
Pension Fare Maeva.....................**11** A1
Pension Fetia...............................**12** C1
Pension Mama Roro......................**13** B1
Pension Poetaina.........................**14** B2

Pension Te Nahe Toetoe Faie.....**15** C2
Pension Te Nahe Toetoe Parea....**16** B4
Pension Tupuna..........................**17** B3
Pension Vaihonu.........................**18** A1
Relais Mahana..............................**19** C5
Te Tiare Beach Outrigger Resort..**20** A3
Villas Bougainville......................**21** B3

HUAHINE

Fare

A visit to tiny Fare almost feels like stepping back in time, so perfectly does it capture the image of a sleepy South Seas port. The air smells of hamburger grease and freshly caught fish, and vibrates with the pumping bass of Tahitian reggae. Women in brightly coloured straw hats catch up on the latest gossip over bottles of Hinano beer in breezy outdoor cafes and men talk shop on the quay while waiting for the boat to arrive. There's not a lot to do, but that's part of Fare's appeal. Check out the colourful little waterside market and the few creative boutiques, sign up for a dive or hire a ramshackle bicycle and just pedal around a bit.

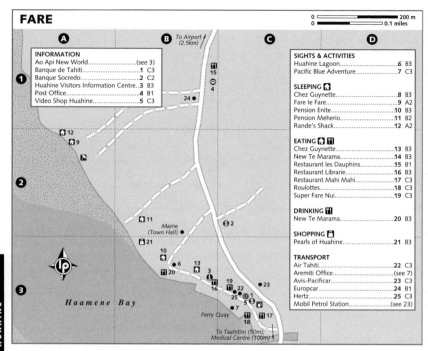

FARE

INFORMATION
Ao Api New World..........................(see 3)
Banque de Tahiti..............................1 C3
Banque Socredo...............................2 C2
Huahine Visitors Information Centre..3 B3
Post Office......................................4 B1
Video Shop Huahine.........................5 C3

SIGHTS & ACTIVITIES
Huahine Lagoon...............................6 B3
Pacific Blue Adventure......................7 C3

SLEEPING
Chez Guynette.................................8 B3
Fare Ie Fare.....................................9 A2
Pension Enite................................10 B3
Pension Meherio.............................11 B2
Rande's Shack................................12 A2

EATING
Chez Guynette...............................13 B3
New Te Marama..............................14 B3
Restaurant les Dauphins...................15 B1
Restaurant Librarie..........................16 B3
Restaurant Mahi Mahi.....................17 C3
Roulottes.......................................18 C3
Super Fare Nui................................19 C3

DRINKING
New Te Marama..............................20 B3

SHOPPING
Pearls of Huahine............................21 B3

TRANSPORT
Air Tahiti.......................................22 C3
Aremiti Office.............................(see 7)
Avis-Pacificar.................................23 C3
Europcar.......................................24 B1
Hertz..25 C3
Mobil Petrol Station....................(see 23)

Fare looks out over **Haamene Bay**, which has two passes to the sea: the northern Avamoa Pass is the main entry point for interisland shipping, while the Avapeihi Pass (Fitii Pass) to the south is a great diving site (see p65). Along the beach north of town, pearl farmer Ray Marks at **Pearls of Huahine** (Map p126; ☎ 72 09 96) sells beautiful pearls at excellent prices out of his home. Look for his sign.

Lake Fauna Nui & Fish Traps
The shallow expanse of Lake Fauna Nui (also known as Lake Maeva) is in fact an inlet from the sea. The land to the north of this is known as Motu Ovarei.

About 2km north of Fare the main sealed road runs along the inland side of Lake Fauna Nui. It's also possible to turn off to the airport and take the road on the ocean side of the lake and then return to the main part of the island by the bridge at Maeva village. If you take this route, don't miss a stop at **Gallery Umatatea** (Map p125; www.polynesiapaintings.com), where the exotic paintings of the highly respected artist Melanie Dupre are on display and prints are on sale. The gallery is open when the artist is home.

Beside the bridge coming off Motu Ovarei are a number of V-shaped fish traps, made from rocks. They have been here for centuries and some are still in use. The tips of the Vs point towards the ocean, the long stone arms emerging above the water level. As the fish are pulled towards the sea by the ebb tide they become trapped in the circular basin at the point of the V, where they are easily caught, usually by net or harpoon.

Maeva
Prior to European influence, Maeva was the seat of royal power on the island and *marae* are found along the shoreline, scattered among the modern buildings of the village and also up the slopes of Matairea (Pleasant Wind) Hill. Excavations and restoration of the site commenced in 1923; nearly 30 *marae* have since been located, more than half of which have been restored. The exceptional density of *marae* on the hillside has led to a theory that it was entirely inhabited by nobility and the families of the chiefs.

Maeva village is about 7km east of Fare. The fantastic walk around the site, along the water's edge and up Matairea Hill, takes around two hours and can be hot work, so take some drinking water as well as strong insect repellent.

FARE POTEE

Situated on the water's edge on the Fare side of Maeva, the *fare potee* (open traditional house) has a small **archaeological museum** (admission 500 CFP; 🕑 9am-4pm Mon-Fri). Around the site are 10 or more *marae,* some of which may date back to the 16th century. Flagstones cover a wide expanse of land along the shoreline.

MARAE WALK

This walk is a high point for anyone interested in archaeology, but be careful, since once on the hill, the trail isn't clearly marked. A signpost on the Fare side of Maeva points to the start of the hiking trail next to the public toilets. Take a right here through a hole in the **defence wall** then continue across the *marae* till you reach a well-cut trail lined with hibiscus on the left. It is thought that the defence wall was constructed in 1846, when French marines mounted an assault

on resistance forces. The trail soon enters dense forest and passes through patches of vanilla plantations, then crosses through a **fortification wall**. This second, older wall was built during the pre-European era, probably as protection against the warlike Bora Bora tribes.

A side path leads off to the multitiered complex of **Te Ana**, or Matairea Huiarii, draped up the hillside. This area includes *marae,* houses, agricultural terraces and other signs of habitation dating from AD 1300 to 1800, plus signs of an earlier settlement dating from around AD 900.

The side path winds through the forest to **Marae Tefano**, with a massive banyan tree overwhelming one end of the *ahu* (altar). Further on, a trail branches off to the left and runs slightly downhill to **Marae Matairea Rahi**. Once the principal *marae* at Maeva, where the most important island chief sat on his throne at major ceremonies, it was superseded by Marae Manunu, on the *motu* below. Also surviving are the foundations of a *fare atua* (god house), where images of gods were guarded day and night.

HUAHINE

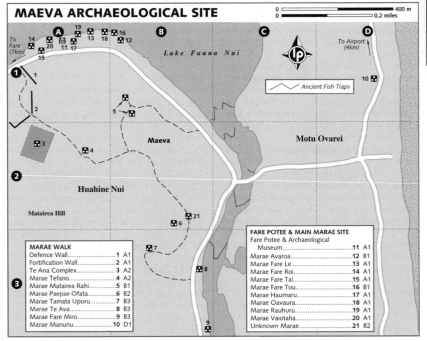

MAEVA ARCHAEOLOGICAL SITE

Lake Fauna Nui

To Fare (7km)

To Airport (4km)

Ancient Fish Traps

Maeva

Motu Ovarei

Huahine Nui

Matairea Hill

MARAE WALK	
Defence Wall	1 A1
Fortification Wall	2 A1
Te Ana Complex	3 A2
Marae Tefano	4 A2
Marae Matairea Rahi	5 B1
Marae Paepae Ofata	6 B2
Marae Tamata Uporu	7 B3
Marae Te Ava	8 B3
Marae Fare Miro	9 B3
Marae Manunu	10 D1

FARE POTEE & MAIN MARAE SITE	
Fare Potee & Archaeological Museum	11 A1
Marae Avaroa	12 B1
Marae Fare Le	13 A1
Marae Fare Roi	14 A1
Marae Fare Tai	15 A1
Marae Fare Tou	16 B1
Marae Haumaru	17 A1
Marae Oavaura	18 A1
Marae Rauhuru	19 A1
Marae Vaiotaha	20 A1
Unknown Marae	21 B2

> **ISLAND AGRICULTURE**
>
> Huahine is big on agriculture, with plenty of *faapu* (agricultural plots) of vanilla, grapefruit, *uru* (breadfruit), taro and pineapples. On the *motu* (islets), cantaloupe and *pastèque* (watermelons) are grown, often to sell in Pape'ete's market. Some village plantations look remarkably wild and neglected, but remember, every plant is private property and probably somebody's livelihood. Casually gathering fruit, in particular the prized pineapples, may result in an enraged villager emerging from the undergrowth with a large machete. Mangoes are one of the few exceptions: they fall from the trees and, delicious though they may be, often rot on the ground.

Nearby is another small part of the original **Marae Matairea Rahi** site. You can continue down this way (as the trail eventually emerges behind a house in the middle of the village) or retrace your steps to the main trail and continue to the turn-off to **Marae Paepae Ofata**, a steep climb above the main trail but worth the effort. The *marae* is like a large platform perched on the edge of the hill, with fine views down the hillside and across Motu Papiti to the outer lagoon, and down to the mouth of Lake Fauna Nui.

Return to the main path, which winds around the hillside to **Marae Tamata Uporu**, before dropping steeply down to the road. The path emerges just south of **Marae Te Ava**. A short walk south leads to **Marae Fare Miro**, which has some particularly good stonework and a fine setting.

A final *marae*, **Marae Manunu**, stands on the *motu*, across the bridge from the main Maeva complex. Manunu means 'eye of the north', and the massive structure stands 2m high, and measures 40m long and nearly 7m wide. It features a two-stepped *ahu* platform. (The only other such platform in the Leeward Islands is at Marae Anini, the community *marae* of Huahine Iti.) This *marae* was primarily dedicated to Tane, Huahine's own god of war and fishing.

Faie

The coast road turns inland beside narrow Faie Bay to the village of Faie. Huahine's famous **blue-eyed eels** can be seen in the river

downstream of the bridge – buy a can of sardines at the store here and handfeed them if you're brave enough. Inland from Faie it's a steep climb to the *belvédère* (lookout) on the slopes of Mt Turi. From this high point, the road drops even more steeply to the shores of Maroe Bay.

While in the area, visit **Huahine Nui Pearls & Pottery** (☎ 78 30 20; www.huahinepearlfarm.com; admission free; ☆ 10am-4pm). Peter Owen, the owner, is a potter as well as a pearl farmer and his work is shown in Pape'ete's galleries. His studio is on his pearl farm in the middle of the lagoon. From Faie a ferry departs for the studio every 15 minutes from 10am to 4pm. Upon arrival you'll be given a demonstration of pearl farming and have an opportunity to browse the collection of pearls inside the shop – they're particularly well priced.

Fitii

Just before completing the Huahine Nui circuit, the road passes through the Fitii district. This is an important agricultural area in the shadow of Mt Paeo (440m), where taro, vanilla and other crops are grown.

HUAHINE ITI

The smaller southern island features the best beaches, as well as some of Huahine's most imaginative accommodation. The following route circles the island in a clockwise direction.

East Coast

Dotted with the reminders of the god Hiro's splitting of the island in two, the village of **Maroe** sits on the southern side of Maroe Bay. You can spot the marks left by the god Hiro's paddle, the imprint of his finger, and even his rocky phallus. From here the coast road skirts across the mouth of a number of shallow inlets, looking across to Motu Murimahora, before coming to **Tefarerii** (House of the Kings). A century ago this small village was the home of Huahine's most powerful family. Today the inhabitants devote their time to fishing and growing watermelons and other produce on the nearby *motu*.

Marae Anini

Right on the southern tip of Huahine Iti, Marae Anini (Map p125) was a community *marae* made of massive coral blocks. The comparatively recent construction was dedicated to 'Oro (the god of war) and Hiro (the god of thieves and sailors). The 'Oro cult, with its human sacrifices, was virtually the last gasp for the old religion, which soon collapsed before the growing influence of Christianity.

There's a signpost from the coast road and the well-tended lagoonside setting is a lovely spot for a picnic.

West Coast

Some of the best **beaches** around Huahine are on the southern peninsula and along the western shore around Avea Bay. Further on, the road comes to a junction: left leads to the little village of **Haapu**; to the right, the road soon brings you back to the bridge and the completion of the island circuit.

ACTIVITIES

Relaxing is the favourite pastime in Huahine, followed by playing in the water or hiking through the jungle.

Water Activities

Fare has a pretty, sandy beach just north of the town. The wide, super-clear lagoon here drops off quickly, providing some truly great snorkelling amid stunning coral and dense fish populations. On the east coast, near the visitor car park at the now defunct Sofitel, you'll find La Cité de Corail, which offers more superb snorkelling among coral pinnacles and rich marine life only a few metres offshore. Motu Topati, at the entrance to Maroe Bay, is a magnificent site for snorkelling that's accessible by boat.

Around the hotel-and-guesthouse area of southwestern Huahine Iti, there's a beautiful white-sand beach and the lagoon here is very wide and good for swimming.

Huahine has some of the best and most consistent surf in French Polynesia, with left and right reef breaks best tackled by experienced surfers; see the boxed text, right. Local surfers can be very possessive, however, so be sure to be courteous in the waves, smile and say 'hi', don't show up in a big group and by all means, don't bring a camera. If you're cool and friendly, that's how you'll be treated too.

The lagoon around Huahine is one of those picture-perfect azure visions for which French Polynesia is famous, but to truly experience paradise you'll need to set sail for an untouched *motu* – the beaches are isolated and

> ### HUAHINE'S TOP SURF SPOTS
>
> - **Fare Reef break** (Year-round) The left here attracts the big names of world surfing. The right is also pretty good.
> - **Fitii Reef break** (Year-round) As with the left at Fare, this one is best when a southwest swell is running.
> - **Parea Reef break** (Year-round) Beautiful waves as long as the trade winds aren't blowing.

fantastic. To explore the lagoon and *motu* on your own, head to **Huahine Lagoon** (Map p126; ☎ 68 70 00; boat rental per 2/4/8hr 4500/7000/10,000 CFP) at the end of the main street in Fare. It hires out boats with outboard motors, as well as kayaks and bicycles. Nautical maps and scuba equipment are provided but you have to pay for fuel. There are no set hours, so just stop by and see if it's open.

On Huahine Iti, contact **Maraamu Sailing** (☎ 68 77 10; Mauarii & Spa; half-day boat rental 10,000 CFP) to hire a boat. The price includes fuel and fishing gear.

DIVING

Huahine has three scuba centres offering magnificent dives for all experience levels. **Mahana Dive** (☎ 73 07 17; www.mahanadive.com) in Fare is run by exuberant, English-speaking Annie and offers hands-on beginner dives as well as a slew of personalised trips for experienced divers. **Pacific Blue Adventure** (Map p126; ☎ 68 87 21; www.divehuahine.com; ☽ closed afternoon Sun) is a friendly centre on the quay at Fare. The newest centre is **Heremiti Dive** (Map p125; ☎ 27 90 57; www.heremitidive.com) at Mauarii & Spa on Huahine Iti.

For more information on diving off Huahine, see p65.

Horse Riding

To see the island from the back of a horse, visit **La Petite Ferme** (Map p125; ☎ 68 82 98; 1hr trips from 3000 CFP), on the main road between Fare and the airport. The two-hour ride along the beach, through coconut plantations and around the shore of Lake Fauna Nui is truly enchanting. Longer excursions include an all-day ride (12,000 CFP), during which you'll visit a vanilla plantation, and stop for a picnic lunch and snorkelling. The horses are suitable for all levels as well as for children.

HUAHINE

Hiking

There are no clearly marked trails on Huahine and the occasional paths in the interior grow over quickly if they're not maintained (which is usually the case) so DIY hikes are limited. The **marae walk** at Maeva (see p126) is the most interesting option; an alternative is the **3km trail** starting midway along the road between Fitii and the Hôtel Bellevue, which traverses a mountainous inland section of Huahine not far from the *belvédère*.

On Huahine Iti, a short **circuit walk**, easily done in an hour, starts from Parea – take the fork towards the interior just before the bridge. You cross a number of *faapu* (agricultural plots) before arriving back at Parea on the other side of the bridge.

For more serious hiking, including treks to the tops of either Mt Tapu on Huahine Nui or Mt Pohue Rahi on Huahine Iti, both of which offer sublime views of rolling mountains and the nearly fluorescent lagoon, contact Terii at **Huahine Randonee** (Map p125; ☎ 73 53 45; Camping Hiva Plage; half-day hikes per person incl transport, water & snacks 4500CFP). Terii has limited English skills but is extremely friendly and competent – if you speak French, Tahitian or Croatian he can tell you all about the local flora, history and archaeology.

TOURS

Lagoon Tours

Various lagoon tours are offered on Huahine, with stops for snorkelling, swimming, fish or shark feeding, a pearl-farm visit and a *motu* picnic. Departures are at around 9am or 10am, returning towards 4pm. A minimum number of participants are required, so book ahead.

The family-run company **Poetaina Cruises** (Map p125; ☎ 68 89 49; www.poetaina.com; tours from 6000 CFP) offers information and very friendly lagoon tours that include a *motu* picnic, a visit to a pearl farm, and French Polynesian song and dance performances.

Choose from jet skiing or outrigger-canoe trips at **Huahine Nautique** (Map p125; ☎ 68 83 15; www.huahine-nautique.com; tours from 8500 CFP). Both include picnics on the lagoon, stops for snorkelling and shark feeding, and also the chance to learn about the island's history.

Island Tours

There are numerous 4WD or minibus tours that offer a good overview of the island. They typically start in the morning or early afternoon and take three hours and a minimum number of participants (usually two) may be required. The tours cover the principal places of interest, including villages, archaeological sites, viewpoints, plantations, fish parks and handicraft outlets. None of the following have offices, but they'll pick you up from your hotel. All charge from 5000CFP.

Huahine Ecotour (☎ 68 81 69) Ask for the archaeology 'walk about', owner Paul's speciality.

Huahine Explorer (☎ 68 87 33) Run by Pension Vaihonu.

Huahine Land (☎ 68 89 21; www.huahineland.com) Has a fantastic reputation and offers a bit of everything.

SLEEPING

Most accommodation options are in and around Fare. Staying near the main village means easy access to facilities. Huahine Nui offers some of the best-value options in French Polynesia – prices are cheaper here than anywhere else in the Society Islands, and the quality is pretty good.

Huahine Iti's beaches do put Huahine Nui's to shame, but if you choose to stay on this side of the island and don't have a car, you'll have to rely on hitchhiking or your legs to get around. That said, most lodging options on Huahine Iti have on-site restaurants or guest kitchens and offer free bikes and kayaks for their clients.

Fare & Around

The places listed here are either right in town or a few kilometres to the north or south.

Chez Guynette (Map p126; ☎ 68 83 75; chezguynette@ mail.pf; dm 1800, s/d/t 4500/5500/6500 CFP) A Huahine institution and probably the most social place to stay in the whole country, this excellent-value place is on the main street opposite the beach. The seven simple but comfortable rooms have fans and bathrooms (with hot water). Dorms are spacious and clean (though not at all private), there's a big communal kitchen and the terrace restaurant has the best people-watching this side of Pape'ete. The new French owners are friendly, helpful and still starry-eyed that they actually get to live and work on Huahine. Book ahead – it's often full.

Pension Vaihonu (Map p125; ☎ 68 87 33; vaihonu@ mail.pf; dm/huts/houses 2000/5500/8500 CFP) A rustic little place overlooking a stretch of coral and sand beach which isn't swimmable, Vaihonu offers clean six-bed dorms with tiled floors, simple beachside huts or spacious two-storey homes with kitchens and hot-water bathrooms. Étienne, the friendly owner, speaks perfect English, bicycles are available and airport transfers are free.

Pension Meherio (Map p126; ☎ 60 61 35; s/d incl breakfast 7900/10,000 CFP) One of Fare's newest options run by Maohi poet and author Chantal Spitz' children, this is a great place to stay. Room exteriors are woven bamboo, interiors have lots of colourful local fabrics, there are plenty of plant-filled common areas and you're a stone's throw from Fare's nicest beach and snorkelling. Bikes, kayaks and snorkelling gear are free for guests.

Pension Mama Roro (Map p125; ☎ 68 84 82; houses from 8000 CFP) Tidy, local-style and functional, this place near the ocean especially appeals to families. Accommodation is in basic houses fully equipped with hot-water bathrooms, TVs and kitchen areas. Airport transfers are free but credit cards aren't accepted.

Chez Ella (Map p125; ☎ 68 73 07; d/q 8500/10,800 CFP) At the intersection of the coast road and the turn-off to the airport, Chez Ella has two houses with two bedrooms each and a chalet with mezzanine. They're comfortable and have a lounge area, TV, washing machine, refrigerator, kitchen and bathroom (with hot water).

Pension Poetaina (Map p125; ☎ /fax 68 89 49; www .poetaina.com; d from 9000 CFP; 🖭 🖳) The white cement house looks dismal from the outside, but inside you'll find big, clean rooms, a kitchen for self-catering and an upper-level dining terrace. The cheapest rooms share bathrooms and don't have air-con.

Pension Enite (Map p126; ☎ 68 82 37; s/d with half board 9500/17,000 CFP) Catering almost exclusively to return customers, the owner here requires you to reserve in advance. Known for its fabulous French cooking, this place has eight well-kept rooms and a small TV lounge. It's worth booking for the cuisine alone.

our pick **Pension Fetia** (Map p125; ☎ 72 09 50; bungalows incl breakfast 9000-20,000 CFP) Isolated out on Motu Ovarei, this is a place for a back-to-nature escape. The wide white-sand beach ends at some interesting coral formations that extend to a stretch of reef with waves crashing on it (not good for swimming). There's plenty of space and shade between the coconut palms and bougainvillea and a hammock is strung near the water's edge. The local

wood and bamboo constructed bungalows are huge and artistically designed with coral gravel floors and all have a semi-outdoor feel to them. Some have two levels and can sleep up to six people. All bungalows have equipped kitchens and mosquito nets and there's also a lovely waterfront restaurant that serves meals. Dinner costs 2500 CFP per day per person and airport transfers are free.

Rande's Shack (Map p126; ☎ 68 86 27; randesshack@ mail.pf; bungalows 10,000-15,000 CFP) Great for families and a long-time surfer favourite, American ex-pat Rande and his lovely Tahitian wife give a warm welcome and offer two great-value self-catering beachside houses, the larger of which sleeps up to six people. While the houses are nothing fancy, they're spotless, well maintained and ideally located on a small beach perfect for swimming and snorkelling, just a few minutes walk from Fare.

Motel Vanille (Map p125; ☎ 68 71 77; www.motel vanille.com; bungalows 10,500-17,300 CFP; 🖳) This pretty guesthouse is very popular and often fully booked. It features five local-style bungalows with bathrooms (with hot water), mosquito screens and small verandas, set around a swimming pool. Bicycles are available for guests' use. Half-board is an additional 2900 CFP per person and the restaurant here is quite good (see p133).

Pension Fare Maeva (Map p125; ☎ 68 75 53; www .fare-maeva.com; bungalows 12,800 CFP; 🖳) On a coral rock beach (not good for swimming), this place has 10 pleasant, well-kept bungalows sleeping two to four people, all with kitchens, private bathrooms (with hot water) and mosquito screens. New rooms, under construction at the time of writing, will be smaller, less expensive versions of the bungalows. There's a room-plus-car deal at 12,000 CFP (plus taxes) per day for two people. The good Restaurant Tehina (p133) is here around the small pool.

Fare le Fare (Map p126; ☎ 60 63 77; www.tahitisafari .com, in French; luxury tents 16,500 CFP) By far the most unusual sleeping option on Huahine, this fabulous find offers two giant African-themed luxury safari tents. Spacious and airy, the tents are uniquely decorated and ultracomfortable, featuring high ceilings, wooden floors, creative artwork and large beds with fluffy quilts. Right on a good swimming beach, the place has a funky, self-catering, gnarled-wood kitchen, and free snorkels, masks, kayaks and bicycles. There's also a sister set-up in Parea (see p132).

HUAHINE

Around Huahine Nui

Pension Te Nahe Toetoe Faie (Map p125; ☎ 68 71 43; www.pension-tenahetoetoe.net; s/d 3200/4500 CFP, bungalows 5500-8000 CFP) On a tiny piece of land right across from the pearl farm, digs here are either in tiny bungalows or in one of three small mezzanine rooms reached by a ladder. All choices are rather basic and lacking in privacy, but it's fabulous value. There's a communal kitchen, TV lounge, *pirogue* (outrigger canoes) and bikes to borrow, and free airport transfers. Meals can be arranged. The same owners run a similar place near Parea (see right).

Pension Tupuna (Map p125; ☎ 68 70 21; bungalows incl breakfast from 6500 CFP) On a relatively isolated private beach, this artistic guesthouse gets rave reviews from travellers. The four Polynesian-style bungalows, each with a private hot-water bathroom, are located in a lush tropical garden bursting with all sorts of exotic trees. The friendly owner is an amateur horticulturist, and happy to dish about the local ecology. Mostly organic meals (dinner 3000 CFP) are served family-style; kayaks and snorkelling equipment are free.

Te Tiare Beach Outrigger Resort (Map p125; ☎ 60 60 50; www.tetiarebeachresort.com; bungalows 42,000-90,000 CFP; ☒ ☐ ☒) Huahine's one true luxury resort is as low-key, intimate and pretty as the island itself. You'll need a boat to get here and the only sounds on the grounds are those of chirping birds – the staff even ride around on bikes to limit noise and pollution! The 41 bungalows (11 of which are over the lagoon) are not just posh and huge, they also blend into the environment. The on-site restaurant serves fine food at reasonable prices and we found the service stellar and the beach perfect for swimming. Regular boat shuttles to Fare are free for guests and there is a slew of activities on offer.

For longer-term villa rental for couples to bigger groups, including use of a car and a boat, contact **Villas Bougainville** (Map p125; ☎ 68 81 59; www.villas-bougainville.com/en/ile_f_en.htm; villas 20,500-32,500 CFP; ☒) or **Huahine Vacances** (Map p125; ☎ 68 73 63; www.huahinevacances.com; villas 17,500-27,500 CFP). Both are on the murky north shore of Maroe Bay and prices go down for longer stays.

Huahine Iti

The (marginally) smaller island has several ideally situated places as well as the most beautiful beaches and widest lagoon. No matter where you stay, prices are comparatively higher here than on Huahine Nui.

Camping Hiva Plage (Map p125; ☎ 68 89 50; campsites from 1200 CFP) Run by friendly Terii Tetumu, who is also Huahine's only licensed hiking guide (see p130), this place was still being constructed at the time of writing, but is in a great location on the beach near Parea.

Pension Te Nahe Toetoe Parea (Map p125; ☎ 68 71 43; www.pension-tenahetoetoe.net; campsite 1100 CFP, bungalows 7500-10,000 CFP) This is a better location than the Pension Te Nahe Toetoe Faie (see left) but it's on just as tiny a piece of land, is just as rustic and costs much more. You can also pitch a tent on a little plot of sand squashed between the road and the beach.

Mauarii & Spa (Map p125; ☎ 68 86 49; www.mauarii .com; r/bungalows from 7000/15,500 CFP; ☐) We think Mauarii is the hippest spot to stay on Huahine Iti – it's in a fabulous beachside location, has loads of activities on offer, tons of character, a hippyish little spa and one of the island's most-respected restaurants – but some travellers have complained that it tries so hard to exude shabby chic it sacrifices comfort. There are loads of different room-and-bungalow options, some fancier than others, but all crafted from local materials and enhanced with creative touches like polished oyster-shell shingles or knobbly wooden coffee tables. Book in advance as it's likely to be full.

Fare Ie Parea (Map p125; ☎ 60 63 77; www.tahiti safari.com, in French; luxury tents 16,500 CFP) The beach here is about on par with the Fare location (see p131) but there's an interesting *marae* (Taiharuru) on-site and it's much quieter over this side. Manager Marguerite is charming, helpful and adds some Polynesian flair. Tents are the same style as those at Fare Ie Fare.

Relais Mahana (Map p125; ☎ 68 81 54; www.relais mahana.com; r 28,000 CFP, bungalows 28,000-33,000 CFP; ☐ ☒) Totally renovated in 2007, this upscale hotel is on what's arguably the best beach on Huahine. Bungalow interiors are tastefully decorated with local art in soothing muted colours and all bathrooms (except in the rooms) have indoor-outdoor showers in private mini-gardens. Prices are very high for what you get and we've heard a few complaints about poor service, but this is an indisputably lovely spot. The restaurant gets bad marks but hosts some good Friday night dance performances (see p134) – luckily the very good restaurant at Mauarii & Spa is a short walk away.

EATING

Most of Huahine's places to eat are found near Fare. Around the rest of the island, eating options are limited to restaurants in *pensions* – some of which are fabulous – and casual *snack* eateries.

Fare & Around

The quayside *roulottes* (mobile food vans) are Huahine's best bargain for cheap eats. They operate from early morning until late at night. Huge portions of fish, chicken, burgers, steaks and chips are the order of the day, but there are also pizzas, crêpes, panini and ice cream. A meal typically costs 800 to 1500 CFP. If you're preparing your own meals, Fare has several well-stocked food shops, including the huge **Super Fare Nui** (Map p126; ✆ Mon-Sat, morning Sun), opposite the waterfront.

Chez Guynette (Map p126; ☎ 68 83 75; dishes 600-1500 CFP; ✆ breakfast & lunch) Fare's best coffee plus fresh fruit juices, breakfast dishes and light meals are served on a lively open-air terrace.

Restaurant Librairie (Map p126; ✆ 7am-late) Climb up the metal spiral staircase in downtown Fare to dine on light mains such as a variety of salads (from 700 CFP) or good breakfasts (from 1000 CFP). While you're up there, check out the bookstore that sells a few English titles including a small collection of cheap, used paperbacks.

Restaurant les Dauphins (Map p126; ☎ 68 78 84; dishes 1000-1500 CFP; ✆ lunch & dinner) This welcoming place serves traditional Polynesian-French food and is popular with locals. Fishing decor, with lots of nets scattered about, sets the ramshackle vibe.

Restaurant Tehina (Map p125; ☎ 68 75 53; dishes 1000-2500 CFP) Pension Fare Maeva's restaurant faces the sea and offers a varied and rather interesting day-long menu of fried tuna, tuna *carpaccio* (thinly sliced raw meat or fish), baked papaya and simple sandwiches.

Restaurant Mahi Mahi (Map p126; dishes 1000-3500 CFP; ✆ breakfast & lunch) Right in downtown Fare, this surf-style eatery has a live lobster tank (a meal of them is 3500 CFP) and a stunning mural on the wall of the namesake fish. The menu is creative with dishes like turkey curry with banana (1400 CFP), plenty of seafood, a great pastry counter, cocktails from 900 CFP and a good wine list. Yummy breakfasts are available from 900 CFP.

New Te Marara (Map p125; ☎ 68 70 81; dishes 1500-2000 CFP; ✆ lunch & dinner) In a great location right on the lagoon, this lively restaurant is a favourite local watering hole and the best place to eat around Fare. With polished oyster shells nailed to the walls and coloured lights strewn from the thatched ceiling, it has a beach-bar vibe and cooks a mean shrimp curry. The menu is meat- and seafood-based, portions are generous and dishes come with a choice of starch or vegetable on the side.

Restaurant Vanille (Map p125; ☎ 68 71 77; dishes 1500-2500 CFP; ✆ closed Mon) In the hotel of the same name (p131), this popular restaurant is a consistently good choice. The menu includes tasty French Polynesian–style tuna *chaud froid* (cold jellied tuna), tuna tartare with local honey and fish steaks.

Around the Island

Once you've left Fare there aren't too many places to eat, apart from the hotels and a few scattered, inexpensive *snack*.

Te Tiare Beach Outrigger Resort (Map p125; ☎ 60 60 50; mains around 2300 CFP; ✆ lunch) Depending on how business is doing, you might get charged 500 CFP each way to take the boat out here, but the beachfront cafe is an elegant and delicious option for a lunch of fish brochettes with mango chutney (2300 CFP) or a burger (1200 CFP).

our pick **Restaurant Mauarii** (Map p125; ☎ 68 86 49; dishes 1500-4500 CFP; ✆ lunch & dinner) Not only is this one of the only places in French Polynesia where you can consistently order *ma'a Tahiti* (traditional Tahitian food; see p53 for a description) à la carte, but it's also one of the only places you'll find the absolutely delectable local crab on the menu (from 3500 CFP – but worth it). For any shellfish, ask if it's fresh and don't order it if it's not since the crab especially can get a little funky. The setting is in a Polynesian-style hut overlooking an expanse of turquoise water. Definitely reserve here on the weekends when there is occasional entertainment at night.

DRINKING & ENTERTAINMENT

There are three ways to entertain yourself most nights on Huahine: curl up in bed with a bottle of Bordeaux and a trashy novel; cruise the Fare strip with your pals (blaring radio mandatory) and park by the quay with some Hinano; or head to Huahine's only bar.

New Te Marara (Map p126; ☎ 68 70 81) This restaurant and bar in Fare stays open until midnight and is *the* place to stay out in Huahine.

Linger over a fruity cocktail as the sun sinks low on the horizon or get rowdy over a few pitchers with friends old and new after the dinner crowd heads home.

Relais Mahana Restaurant (Map p125; ☎ 68 81 54; dance show with buffet 5100 CFP) Although the food here is no great shakes, the occasional Friday night 'mini dance shows' with buffet are good value and will keep you out past 8pm.

GETTING THERE & AWAY

Huahine, the first of the Leeward Islands, is 170km west of Tahiti and 35km east of Ra'iatea and Taha'a.

Air

Huahine's airport is 2.5km north of Fare. **Air Tahiti** (Map p126; ☎ 68 77 02; ⏲ 7.30-11.45am & 1.30-4.30pm Mon-Fri, 7.30-11.30am Sat) operates all flights and has an office on the main street in Fare, opposite the quay. Destinations include Pape'ete (11,000 CFP, 35 minutes, three to five daily), Ra'iatea (6000 CFP, 15 minutes, daily), Bora Bora (8000 CFP, 20 minutes, daily) and Mo'orea (13,000 CFP, 30 minutes, daily).

Boat

Inter-island cargo ships are another option, although less reliable. The *Vaeanu*, and *Hawaiki Nui* depart from Pape'ete and stop at Huahine (see p261 for more information).

GETTING AROUND
To/From the Airport

You could walk into town, but *pensions* and hotels in Fare will arrange taxi transfers (sometimes included in the tariff). It costs from 500 CFP to go to Fare and 1500 CFP to get to the south of the island.

Car

Huahine's three car-hire operators will deliver directly to the airport or to your hotel. Book ahead for long weekends, school vacations, Christmas and peak tourist seasons as there are sometimes not enough cars to go around. Hire periods of four, eight, 24 and 48 hours are offered, with or without unlimited mileage. If you intend to drive all the way around the island, unlimited mileage will probably be cheaper. It's worth asking about discounts and comparing the prices of the three agencies. Credit cards are accepted. There are two petrol stations in Fare.

Avis-Pacificar (☎ 68 73 34) Next to the Mobil petrol station in Fare, it also has a counter at the airport.

Europcar (☎ 68 82 59) The main agent is north of the centre of Fare near the post office; there are also counters at the airport and Relais Mahana.

Hertz (☎ 66 76 85) Right on the main strip in Fare, Hertz often has the best deals in town.

Scooter & Bicycle

You can hire bicycles from Europcar (above) or Huahine Lagoon (p129) for about 2000 CFP a day. For scooters, check with Europcar, which charges 6500 CFP for 24 hours or 5000 CFP for four hours.

Taxi

Public transport doesn't really exist. For taxis, call **Moe's Taxi** (☎ 72 80 60). Moe speaks perfect English and will take you anywhere on the island. Prices vary but are reasonable.

Ra'iatea & Taha'a

Ra'iatea and Taha'a are encircled by a common lagoon, but even though this wraps them up in the same package, you get two very different islands for the price of one. Ra'iatea is high, imposing and fiercely independent, has the second biggest town in French Polynesia after Pape'ete and is considered by many to be the spiritual seat of the Polynesian Triangle. Taha'a, on the other hand, has graceful low hills, is famous only for its sweet-scented vanilla and is arguably the quietest of the Society Islands. Neither island gets many tourists, making them the ideal place to explore a mysterious and wild-feeling Polynesia – unless of course you're going to Le Taha'a Private Island & Spa, which can even make some of Bora Bora's resorts seem humble.

The islands both have very few beaches and those that exist are only small strips that can get eaten up by the lagoon at high tide. Fortunately the reef is dotted with *motu*, white-sand gems that can fulfil anyone's dreams of a palm-fringed, blue-lagoon paradise. Within the vast lagoon itself is a never-ending aquarium perfect for diving, snorkelling, kayaking or just splashing around. On land the mountains, particularly on Ra'iatea, make you want to strap on your hiking boots in search of breezy vistas, waterfalls, untamed jungle and one of the world's rarest flowers, the *tiare apetahi*.

RA'IATEA & TAHA'A

HIGHLIGHTS

- Feeling the power of **Marae Taputapuatea** (p138), one of Polynesia's greatest spiritual centres
- Spending a day on Taha'a with an **island tour** (p146), exploring the fertile interior, glass-clear lagoon, pearl farms and vanilla plantations
- Kayaking to *motu* in either lagoon or up **Faaroa River** (p140), the country's only navigable waterway
- Oohing and aahing at Ra'iatea's imposingly lush coastline via **scooter** (p144)
- Diving through the technicolour underwater wonderland of **Teavapiti Pass** (p68)

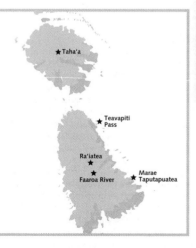

★ Taha'a

★ Teavapiti Pass

Ra'iatea ★

★ Faaroa River   ★ Marae Taputapuatea

RA'IATEA

pop 3568 / area 170 sq km

Ra'iatea is the second largest island of the Society Islands after Tahiti and is also the second most important economic centre, but its lack of beaches has left it to remain relatively off the tourist radar. Socially, the island is a lively hotchpotch of back-to-roots Polynesians, Chinese, French expats and surfers and yachties who never went home. What dominates here are the high, steep mountains and the vast, reef-fringed lagoon – the combination of the two are quite awe-striking and can make you forget that there's no beach. The capital Uturoa is a busy port, but explore the rest of the island and you'll find an intensely calm, back-to-nature reality.

According to oral history the great migration voyages to Hawaii and New Zealand commenced from Ra'iatea's Faaroa River, the only navigable river in French Polynesia. Ra'iatea was also home to Marae Taputapuatea, the most important traditional temple in Polynesia, which many believe still exudes power today. What is undeniable is that the island emanates a hard-to-pinpoint, mysterious energy that you won't feel anywhere else in French Polynesia – some love it, while it makes others feel continually uncomfortable.

As far as tourism goes, Ra'iatea is best known as French Polynesia's sailing and yachting centre, attracting hundreds of well-heeled water rats to its marinas each year. Surfers also are lured in by the perfect waves, but many are chased away by the aggressive vibe in the water.

HISTORY

Ra'iatea, known as Havai'iki Nui in ancient times, is the cultural, religious and historic centre of the Society Islands. According to legend, Ra'iatea and Taha'a were the first islands far to the northwest to be settled, probably by people from Samoa. It is said that Ra'iatea's first king was the legendary Hiro, who with his companions built the great canoes that sailed to Rarotonga and New Zealand.

Later Ra'iatea was a centre for the 'Oro (god of war) cult, which was in the process of replacing the earlier Ta'aroa (god of creation) cult when Europeans turned up and disrupted the entire Polynesian religious structure. At the time of James Cook's first Polynesian visit, Ra'iatea was probably under Bora Bora's control, and its chiefs were scattered far and wide.

Cook first came to the island on the *Endeavour* in 1769, when he anchored off Opoa. He returned in 1774 during his second Pacific voyage, and in 1777 he made a prolonged visit before sailing to Hawaii on his last voyage.

Protestant missionaries came to Ra'iatea in 1818 and it was from Ra'iatea that missionaries continued to Rarotonga in the Cook Islands in 1823 and to Samoa in 1830. Following the French takeover of Tahiti in 1842 was a long period of instability and fierce Ra'iatean resistance. It was not until 1888 that the French attempted a real takeover of the island and 1897 that troops were sent to put down the final Polynesian rebellion.

ORIENTATION

Ra'iatea is vaguely triangular in shape. A sealed road hugs the coast all the way around the island. *Pointe kilométrique* (PK; kilometre point) distances start in Uturoa near the *gendarmerie* (police station) and then run south to Faatemu Bay. The mountainous interior of the island includes the 800m-high Temehani Plateau and Mt Tefatua (1017m). The main range runs north to south for most of the length of the island, and the smaller ranges in the south are separated by a valley through which a road runs from Faaroa Bay to Faatemu Bay.

The airport, which also serves Taha'a, is on the northern tip of the island. The town of Uturoa extends southeast of the airport, and small villages are scattered across the rest of the island.

INFORMATION

The three French Polynesian banks have branches with ATMs in Uturoa. The following places are all found within Uturoa. There are two internet cafes in the *gare maritime* (boat terminal).

Hospital (Map p138; ☎ 60 08 01) Opposite the post office; offers emergency services.

Gendarmerie (Police Station; Map p138) Opposite the post office.

Post office (Map p138) North of the centre, towards the airport.

Raiatea visitors information centre (Map p138; ☎ 60 07 77; inforaiatea@mail.pf; ⏰ 8am-4pm Mon-Fri, 8am-3pm Sat, 9.30am-3pm Sun) In the *gare maritime* in Uturoa.

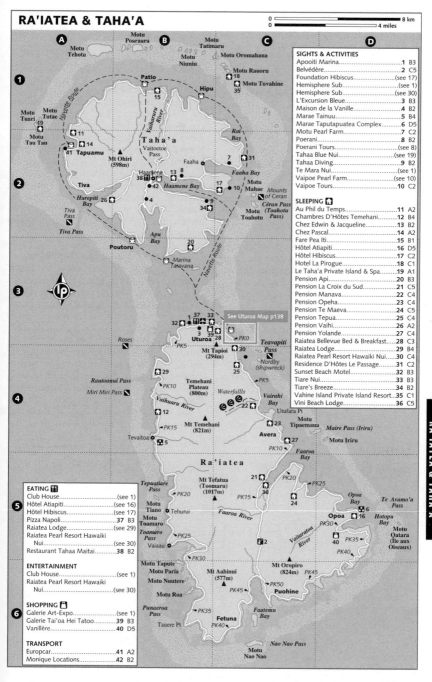

RA'IATEA & TAHA'A

0 — 8 km
0 — 4 miles

SIGHTS & ACTIVITIES

Apooiti Marina	1 B3
Belvédère	2 C5
Foundation Hibiscus	(see 17)
Hemisphere Sub	(see 1)
Hemisphere Sub	(see 30)
L'Excursion Bleue	3 B3
Maison de la Vanille	4 B2
Marae Tainuu	5 B4
Marae Taputapuatea Complex	6 D5
Motu Pearl Farm	7 C2
Poerani	8 B2
Poerani Tours	(see 8)
Tahaa Blue Nui	(see 19)
Tahaa Diving	9 B2
Te Mara Nui	(see 1)
Vaipoe Pearl Farm	(see 10)
Vaipoe Tours	10 C2

SLEEPING

Au Phil du Temps	11 A2
Chambres D'Hôtes Temehani	12 B4
Chez Edwin & Jacqueline	13 B2
Chez Pascal	14 A2
Fare Pea Iti	15 B1
Hôtel Atiapiti	16 D5
Hôtel Hibiscus	17 C2
Hotel La Pirogue	18 C1
Le Taha'a Private Island & Spa	19 A1
Pension Api	20 B3
Pension La Croix du Sud	21 C5
Pension Manava	22 C4
Pension Opeha	23 C4
Pension Te Maeva	24 C4
Pension Tepua	25 C4
Pension Vaihi	26 A2
Pension Yolande	27 C4
Raiatea Bellevue Bed & Breakfast	28 C3
Raiatea Lodge	29 B4
Raiatea Pearl Resort Hawaiki Nui	30 C4
Residence D'Hôtes Le Passage	31 C2
Sunset Beach Motel	32 B3
Tiare Nui	33 B3
Tiare's Breeze	34 B2
Vahine Island Private Island Resort	35 C1
Vini Beach Lodge	36 C5

EATING

Club House	(see 1)
Hôtel Atiapiti	(see 16)
Hôtel Hibiscus	(see 17)
Pizza Napoli	37 B3
Raiatea Lodge	(see 29)
Raiatea Pearl Resort Hawaiki Nui	(see 30)
Restaurant Tahaa Maitai	38 B2

ENTERTAINMENT

Club House	(see 1)
Raiatea Pearl Resort Hawaiki Nui	(see 30)

SHOPPING

Galerie Art-Expo	(see 1)
Galerie Tai'oa Hei Tatoo	39 B3
Vanillère	40 D5

TRANSPORT

Europcar	41 A2
Monique Locations	42 B2

RA'IATEA & TAHA'A

SIGHTS

We recommend hiring a vehicle (or, if you are in really good shape, a bicycle) and driving the 98km sealed-road circuit around Ra'iatea. Exploring the island this way not only gives you the opportunity to experience its wild natural beauty, but also gives a feel for its relaxed atmosphere.

In the south of the island, a short stretch of fine mountain road between Faaroa and Faatemu Bays takes you away from the coast and past an excellent lookout. Apart from places on the outskirts of Uturoa there is virtually nowhere along the way to buy lunch, so take a picnic.

The following sights are listed clockwise around the island.

Uturoa

Upon first glance you'd never guess this little place is French Polynesia's second largest town (after Pape'ete), but wander around and you'll catch its feisty buzz, especially on weekday mornings when you'll experience the only traffic jams outside of Tahiti. Meaning 'long mouth' in Tahitian, Uturoa has a reputation for being particularly gossipy but really it's just an old-fashioned place where men spend Saturdays sipping Hinano on the quay, local women get together to chat and tourists, fresh off cruise ships, scope out the pearl shops and colourful boutiques. Uturoa has a strong Chinese community, evidenced by the many Chinese shops and restaurants. Queen Pomare, exiled

from Tahiti in 1844 by the French takeover, took refuge in Vairahi, now swallowed up by the southward expansion of Uturoa. She remained there for three years before returning to Tahiti.

Uturoa to Faaroa Bay

Bustling Uturoa blends seamlessly into **Avera**, the site of the final battle between the French and local rebels. From here the road follows the contours of the narrow and magnificent **Faaroa Bay.** After going round the base of the bay and crossing Faaroa River, you reach the inland turn-off to the south coast.

From the turn-off, the road runs to a **belvédère** (lookout), with great views of Faaroa Bay, the coast and the surrounding mountains, before dropping down to the south-coast road.

Faaroa Bay to Marae Taputapuatea

If you don't take the turn-off to the south coast, the road winds around the lush south coast of Faaroa Bay and through the village of Opoa to **Marae Taputapuatea**. The most important *marae* (traditional temple) in French Polynesia, it looks out to Te Avamo'a (Sacred) Pass. Dedicated to 'Oro, the god of war who dominated 18th-century Polynesian religious beliefs, the *marae* sprawls extensively across Cape Matahira. It dates from the 17th century, when it replaced nearby Marae Vaearai, which was dedicated to Ta'aroa, the god of creation.

Despite its relatively short history, this *marae* assumed great importance in the

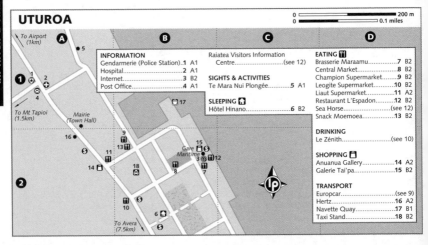

Polynesian religion. Any *marae* constructed on another island had to incorporate one of Taputapuatea's stones as a symbol of allegiance and spiritual lineage. This was the centre of spiritual power in Polynesia when the first Europeans arrived, and its influence was international: *ari'i* (chiefs) from all over the Maohi world, including the Australs, the Cook Islands and New Zealand, came here for important ceremonies.

The site encompasses a domestic, district and international *marae*. The main part of the site is a large paved platform with a long *ahu* (altar) stretching down one side. At the very end of the cape is the smaller **Marae Tauraa**, a *tapu* (taboo) enclosure with a tall 'stone of investiture', where young *ari'i* were enthroned. The lagoonside **Marae Hauviri** also has an upright stone, and the whole site is made of pieces of coral. The huge double canoes of royal pilgrims used to sail through the Te Avamo'a Pass en route to the *marae*.

The well-restored *marae* complex is an imposing sight, but unfortunately there is little explanation for visitors beyond some signboards that explain what a *marae* is, with nothing specific about Taputapuatea.

Marae Taputapuatea to Tevaitoa

The stretch of road from Marae Taputapuatea to Tevaitoa is the most remote part of Ra'iatea and it's here you'll really get a glimpse of the old spirit of the island. The road wriggles along the coast past agriculture and mucky beaches backed by blue lagoon. Before reaching the village of **Puohine** there's a long stretch where the steep green mountainsides are streaked with **waterfalls** during the wetter months of the year. The road follows the coast before reaching the village of **Fetuna**. During WWII, when the US military occupied Bora Bora, a landing strip was constructed here. **Motu Nao Nao**, just across from Fetuna, has a pleasant beach.

The sparsely inhabited coast continues all the way along to **Tevaitoa**, with vistas over the lagoon and some particularly large *motu* quite close to shore. In the middle of the village of Tevaitoa you'll find the island's oldest Protestant church, an architectural curiosity built smack on top of the magnificent **Marae Tainuu**. Behind the church the walls of the *marae* stretch for just over 50m, with some of the massive upright stones standing more than 4m high.

> **TIARE APETAHI: A RARE FLOWER ON A STRANGE ISLAND**
>
> Ra'iatea is home to one of the world's rarest flowers, the *tiare apetahi*. The endemic species is only found on the Temehani Plateau and although it's been attempted, it simply won't grow elsewhere. According to French Polynesian legend, the white flower's delicate petals represent the five fingers of a beautiful Tahitian girl who fell in love with a prince then died of a broken heart when she realised he'd never marry her. The petals close at night then open at dawn with a whisper of a crackle – the sound of the girl's heart breaking. You should be able to see the flower while hiking on the mountain – but note that it is strictly protected, so no picking.

Tevaitoa to Uturoa

You'll find the mega-bucks **Apooiti Marina** between Tevaitoa and Uturoa. With shops, a restaurant, a bar and a diving centre, it's a pleasant place to stop for a sunset cocktail or early dinner – especially appealing if you've been touring Ra'iatea via scooter. From the marina the road passes by the airport before circling back to Uturoa.

ACTIVITIES

Ra'iatea has the usual assortment of water-based activities, but it also offers plenty of great hiking opportunities in its mountainous interior. A handful of pearl farms are also open to the public and you can stop by and visit on your own or with a tour (see p140). At the time of writing the only horseback-riding operation on the island was closed, but ask around in case someone has started it up again.

Diving & Snorkelling

Ra'iatea has no beaches besides rare, skinny strips of sand – a hotel or guesthouse pontoon is your best bet for island-chilling or snorkelling. The reef *motu*, however, have splendid beaches and even more snorkelling. Ask at your accommodation about hiring a boat or joining a lagoon tour.

Ra'iatea has two diving centres. **Hemisphere Sub** (Map p137; ☎ 66 12 49; www.raiatea-diving.com), based at the Apooiti Marina, offers dives on the east and west coasts as well as around

RA'IATEA & TAHA'A

Taha'a; snorkelling trips to Teavapiti Pass are also possible. The centre also has a base at Raiatea Pearl Resort Hawaiki Nui. **Te Mara Nui Plongée** (Map p138; ☎ 66 11 88; www.temaranui.pf) is a small, locally recommended centre at the marina in Uturoa.

Both companies charge around 5500 CFP for a dive and provide transport from your hotel. There are about 10 dive sites along the east and west coasts and around Taha'a. Highlights include the superb Teavapiti Pass and the *Nordby*, the only real wreck dive in French Polynesia. For more information, see p68.

Another option is Uturoa-based **Polynésie Croisière** (☎ 28 60 06; www.polynesie-croisiere.com), which offers all-inclusive diving tours through the Leeward Islands on a scuba-equipped catamaran – if you want to do lots of diving, this is a very cost-effective choice. A three-day, three-night tour costs around 82,000 CFP per person in a group of five. Prices go up and down depending on how many guests are on-board and the length of the trip.

Yachting

Ra'iatea's central position in the Society Islands, and its fine lagoon, have helped make it the yacht-charter centre of French Polynesia. Most operations will offer whatever a customer demands and prepare fully stocked and equipped boats. Bare-boat charter rates vary seasonally (July to August is the high season). The following Ra'iatea-based companies are recommended:

Catamaran Tane Charter (☎ 66 16 87; www.raiatea .com/tane) Offers catamaran cruises in the Leeward Islands.

The Moorings (☎ 66 35 93; www.moorings.com) Has about 20 different boats; options include bare-boat charters, boat hire with skipper and host, or cabin charter to the Leeward Islands.

Sunsail (☎ 60 04 85; www.sunsail.com) Operates a variety of crewed cruises lasting from three days.

Tahiti Yacht Charter (☎ 45 04 00; www.tahiti yachtcharter.com)

Hiking

There are some good, though largely under-utilised, walking opportunities on Ra'iatea. Our favourite hike departs from Pension Manava (p142) and takes you past three **waterfalls**. Ask at the *pension* for directions to the trailhead. It's an easy stroll to the first waterfall (the smallest), which has a great swim-

ming hole, but the trail climbs steeply from here, with some tricky scrambles. After passing the second waterfall the trail follows the riverbed through a bamboo forest. The third waterfall is the most splendid – a 60m beauty with a fabulous swimming hole at its basin.

There are some interesting walks around **Temehani Plateau** (800m) at the northern end of the island. Accessible only by 4WD, the plateau is home to the *tiare apetahi,* a white gardenia endemic to Ra'iatea (see the boxed text, p139). You'll need a guide for these walks; the locals' favourite choice is **Eric Pelle** (☎ 66 49 54; hikes per person from 3600 CFP).

TOURS

Guided excursions are very popular in Ra'iatea and we definitely recommend doing one during your stay. Tours allow you to get out to those sandy *motu* and provide easy access to local pearl farms and vanilla plantations. Most tours actually spend the majority of their time on the island of Taha'a, but all the companies listed here pick up from the pier in Uturoa (to which your hotel will usually transport you for free). Tours generally involve travel by *pirogue* (outrigger canoe) and 4WD minibus, dividing their time between Taha'a's rugged interior and splendid lagoon.

Fruit tasting, a *motu* visit with snorkelling, pearl- and vanilla-farm visits, and a fabulous home-cooked lunch are highlights of the highly recommended lagoon and land tour run by Edwin at **Tahaa Tour Excursions** (☎ 65 62 18; tours 6500 CFP). Edwin also runs a *pension* if the tour entices you to go and stay on the island (see p147).

Dave of **Dave's Tours** (☎ 65 62 42; tours 8000 CFP) speaks a variety of languages and offers full-day tours of Ra'iatea and Taha'a that include pearl-farm and vanilla-plantation visits and stops for local-fruit tasting. Lunch is served on a *motu*, and you'll also have a chance to snorkel in Taha'a's beautiful coral garden.

Another good company, **L'Excursion Bleue** (Map p137; ☎ 66 10 90; www.tahaa.net; tours 9500 CFP) offers full-day tours of Taha'a entirely by boat that include drinks and lunch on a *motu*, snorkelling in the coral garden and pearl- and vanilla-farm visits. English guides.

For something completely unique, sign on with enthusiastic Hubert at **Lagon Aventure** (☎ 79 26 27; www.lagonaventure.com), who leads kayak tours (from 7500 CFP) not only to the dreamy *motu*, but also up the jungle-clad

Faaroa River – a real adventure. Take it a step further with overnight *motu* camping trips from 10,000 CFP per person. The company also does sailboat charters.

SLEEPING
Uturoa & Around
This is where the action is and, while the two out-of-town options are very pretty, you'll find more stunning scenery elsewhere around the island.

Raiatea Bellevue Bed & Breakfast (Map p137; ☎ 66 15 15; www.raiateabellevue-tahiti.com; r per person incl breakfast 4300 CFP; 🖳 🕱) Quiet and relaxing, this place is perched high above the northern side of Uturoa in a lush junglelike setting and features extraordinary views. The five small but tidy rooms have a bathroom (with hot water), TV, refrigerator and fan, and open onto a terrace beside a small swimming pool. Airport transfers cost 1000 CFP per person. Credit cards aren't accepted.

Tiare Nui (Map p137; ☎ 66 34 06; bungalow s/d 5900/6300 CFP) Bungalows here are tidy and pleasant but you'd only want to stay at this noisy roadside spot (adjacent to the Europcar parking lot) if you're on a serious budget and want to rent a car. A double bungalow including a 24-hour car rental is 11,900 CFP – quite a bargain.

Hôtel Hinano (Map p138; ☎ 66 13 13; www.hotel -hinano-tahiti.com, in French; s/d from 6500/7900 CFP; 🕱) The only hotel right in the centre of Uturoa, this place is overpriced compared to what's available elsewhere. Rooms are spacious and clean but they feel quite bare.

Raiatea Pearl Resort Hawaiki Nui (Map p137; ☎ 60 05 00; www.pearlresorts.com; r from 20,000 CFP, bungalows 31,000-42,000 CFP; 🕱 🖳 🕱) Ra'iatea's swankiest hotel has excellent service and stylish bungalows, but sadly its location, wedged between the road and the lagoon, isn't exactly stunning. That said, there is outrageous snorkelling in front (or off your own dock if you have an over-the-water bungalow) and you can paddle free kayaks out to the white-sand *motu* across the lagoon. Bikes and snorkels are available, and the bar and restaurant has a chummy, old South Seas feel to it.

East Coast
While the four establishments at Avera, on the east coast between PK6 and PK10 are still close to town, the other more-remote

options from Faaroa Bay to Opoa are in lush and wild-feeling surrounds.

Pension Te Maeva (Map p137; ☎ 66 37 28; www .temaeva.com; campsites per person 1200 CFP, bungalow incl breakfast 8800 CFP) The two older, cabin-style bungalows here are isolated high up a precarious road 7km north of Marae Taputapuatea. Each has outdoor equipped mini-kitchen, hot-water bathroom, fan, fridge and terrace. Prices include transfers. A new jungle-feeling camping area that is to have communal bathroom and kitchen was under construction at the time of writing. Bicycles are available for guests and you can also do your washing for 500 CFP. No credit cards.

OUR PICK Pension Tepua (Map p137; ☎ 66 33 00; www .tepua-raiatea.com; dm/s/d 2500/5000/7500 CFP, bungalows 10,000 CFP; 🖳 🕱) A social and pretty spot, this is one of the best budget options in the Society Islands. The owner speaks five languages, including perfect English, and happily dispenses his wealth of island information. Rooms are simple but clean and colourfully decorated, the dorms are spacious, and the bungalows sleep between four and six people and come with colourful Tahitian bedspreads, fridges, sinks and bathrooms. Adding to the laid-back ambience is the on-site bar and restaurant (as well as a communal kitchen), TV lounge, small pool and pontoon over the lagoon. Bike and kayak rental is available.

Pension Yolande (Map p137; ☎ 66 35 28; d 6000 CFP) Yolande, a charming Ra'iatea *mama*, keeps this cute-as-a-button place on a white-sand beach in shipshape. Not much English is spoken but good vibes abound and this place is a fabulous deal if you're looking for something that's really local style. Rooms all have sunken kitchens with adjacent hot-water bathrooms. Meals are available in a small *fare* facing the sea (breakfast 1000 CFP, full dinner 2500 CFP), kayaks are free and airport transfers cost 1300 CFP per group one way. No credit cards.

Pension La Croix du Sud (Southern Cross; Map p137; ☎ 66 27 55; d incl breakfast 7700 CFP) Set on a steep hill above Vini Beach Lodge, this *pension* offers some amazing views of the northern side of Faaroa Bay. There are three rooms all with private bathrooms and meals are served on a pleasant terrace overlooking the bay. Accommodation is all a bit flimsy and funky but it has plenty of Polynesian colour and charm. There are free bicycles for getting around but it's a long pedal to anywhere from this isolated

RA'IATEA & TAHA'A

spot. Airport transfers cost 1500 CFP per car load and credit cards aren't accepted.

Pension Manava (Map p137; ☎ 66 28 26; www.manava pension.com; d/f 8000/9400 CFP; 🖳) This is a super-friendly, well-managed place with spacious bungalows, all with kitchens, dotting a big, open garden. The huge two-bedroom family bungalow is great value for a group. The place offers free airport transfers and nightly trips to Restaurant L'Espadon in Uturoa; trips to Marae Taputapuatea (3500 CFP) and lagoon *pirogue* tours (6500 CFP) are also available. Credit cards aren't accepted.

Pension Opeha (Map p137; ☎ 66 19 48; www.pen sionopeha.pf; bungalows incl breakfast 10,000 CFP; 🔀 🖳) Not yet open when we passed, this brand new place has a handful of very white, very clean, kitchen-equipped bungalows, lined up in a row in a tiny, immaculate waterfront property.

Vini Beach Lodge (Map p137; ☎ 60 22 45; www.raiatea .com/vinibeach; bungalows 11,000-14,000 CFP; 🐾) A crisp and compact place overlooking Faaroa Bay, Vini Beach offers a collection of two-storey whitewashed bungalows, a tiled pool, a posh, covered communal deck area and a restaurant. The bungalows are spacious and classy, featuring kitchenettes, lovely cast-iron beds and porches with views of the bay and lush mountains. Try and get a sea-facing bungalow if you can. Airport transfers are 800 CFP per person return.

Hôtel Atiapiti (Map p137; ☎ 66 16 65; bungalows incl breakfast from 13,000 CFP) Besides having one of the better beaches (plus snorkelling) on the island, you'll get plenty of ancient Polynesian spiritual vibes here from Marae Taputapuatea right next door. Semi open-concept bungalows are decorated with bright, artistic flair (each is unique) and have mini kitchens and terraces, some of which are right on the beach. Add 2500 CFP per person for half board at the inviting country-style restaurant. Grab a free kayak or bike to explore the area. Airport transfers are 2500 CFP per person return.

West Coast

This coast isn't as lush as the east coast but is the best choice for surfers and is very lagoon-oriented.

our pick Sunset Beach Motel (Map p137; ☎ 66 33 47; www.raiatea.com/sunsetbeach; campsites per person 1500 CFP, bungalow s/d/tr/q 12,000/13,300/14,500/15,600 CFP) Just the location (on an expansive co-conut plantation lined by a skinny strip of white sand) alone would make this one of

Ra'iatea's best options, but the bungalows – which are perhaps better described as small homes – make this one of the best deals in the islands. It's a particularly great find for families as the kitchen-equipped bungalows comfortably sleep four and kids stay for half-price. *Pirogues* and pedal boats (which you can enjoy off the fantastic pontoon), bikes and airport transfers are free. The owners offer heaps of activities and the island's best camping is here.

Chambres D'Hôtes Temehani (Map p137; ☎ 66 12 88; www.vacances-tahiti.com; d incl breakfast 8500-9500 CFP, bungalows incl breakfast 10,500 CFP; 🖳) Two rooms decorated with handmade bedspreads and plenty of wood have a shared bathroom and are in the owner's beachfront home. A bungalow, planned at the time of writing, will be more private. Excellent French-Polynesian meals can be taken family style.

Raiatea Lodge (Map p137; ☎ 66 20 00; www.raiatea hotel.com; s/d/tr/q 12,000/15,000/19,000/28,000 CFP; 🔀 🖳 🐾) Under enthusiastic new manage-ment who have added much style and class to this boutique hotel, this is Ra'iatea's second-poshest place (after the Pearl Resort Hawaiki Nui). The colonial plantation-style building sits quietly at the back of a coconut plan-tation but you can still glimpse Bora Bora across the lagoon. Rooms are lovely, with hardwood floors, big terraces and heaps of comforts and mod-cons that are usually only found at French Polynesia's swankiest resorts. It's incredible value. The restaurant (mains from 1800 CFP) has a good reputation and the bar can get lively. Add 2200 CFP for return airport transfers. Bikes and kayaks (there's a lagoonside pontoon) are free and English is spoken.

EATING

In Ra'iatea you have a choice of eating pricey French fare or more affordable Chinese-Tahitian. You'll find small *snack*-style places and a few *roulottes* (mobile food vans that open mostly at night) dotted around the island.

Uturoa & Around

Uturoa has several well-stocked supermar-kets, open Monday to Saturday and some on Sunday morning. They include the Champion on the seafront and Leogite and Liaut on the main street. A handful of *roulottes* open at night along the waterfront strip at the north end of the marina.

Central Market (Map p138; ⏱ 5:30am-6pm Mon-Sat & 5am-9am Sun) Head to this small yet colourful local market for homemade *monoi* (fragrant coconut oil), flowers, fruits and vegies.

Snack Moemoea (Map p138; ☎ 66 39 84; dishes 600-1700 CFP; ⏱ breakfast & lunch) This is the most popular place in town with a large menu that features a variety of *poisson cru* (raw fish) options, as well as Chinese and French dishes. Those on a budget can also eat well – burgers, hot dogs and *croque-monsieur* (toasted ham-and-cheese sandwiches) are all around 1000 CFP.

Brasserie Maraamu (Map p138; ☎ 66 46 54; dishes 1000-1800 CFP; ⏱ lunch Mon-Sat, breakfast & dinner Mon-Fri) More Chinese than Moemoea, this is another immensely popular joint serving huge plates of reasonably priced food including a handful of tofu-based vegetarian options as well as steaks, poultry and fish. Hinano beer is on tap and breakfasts range from American eggs to Tahitian *poisson cru* and *firifiri* (doughnuts).

Pizza Napoli (Map p137; ☎ 66 10 77; dishes 1100-1600 CFP; ⏱ lunch & dinner) In a reed hut decorated with loads of flowers, this congenial pizzeria near the Europcar agency offers a long list of Italian dishes including pasta, wood-fired pizzas and meat and fish specials. The pasta dishes are quite good.

Sea Horse (Map p138; ☎ 66 16 34; dishes 1200-2100 CFP; ⏱ closed dinner Sun) With a fabulous location looking out on the lagoon from the *gare maritime*, Sea Horse is more upscale Chinese with plenty of soups and seafood on offer. It's elegant and romantic, and won't break the bank.

Restaurant L'Espadon (Map p138; ☎ 66 30 81; dishes from 1400 CFP; ⏱ lunch Mon-Fri, dinner Mon-Sat) Next to Sea Horse, the location here has half the view but the French food is more chic. The house speciality is swordfish with ginger although there are plenty of options like steaks and French-style salads to choose from. Live music on Friday nights draws in locals and tourists alike.

Club House (Map p137; ☎ 66 11 66; dishes 1500-3000 CFP; ⏱ lunch & dinner) The setting for this place is striking – a large, airy room overlooking the in Apooiti Marina. Unfortunately the French Polynesian cuisine doesn't quite live up to its inventive and stylish ambitions. Patrons can be picked up and dropped off for free as far as Sunset Beach Motel and Pension Manava.

Around the Island

Bring a picnic if you're travelling around the island as there aren't many opportunities to find a meal during the day. You can pick up cheap baguette sandwiches at small local shops around the island, but do so before noon when most close for siesta.

Raiatea Pearl Resort Hawaiki Nui (Map p137; ☎ 60 05 00; dishes 1500-3000 CFP) This resort restaurant has great water views and a friendly atmosphere, but the food is ordinary. The bar serves good cocktails for about 800 CFP.

`our pick` **Raiatea Lodge** (Map p137; ☎ 60 01 00; dishes from 1800 CFP; ⏱ lunch & dinner) There's still the ever-so-common grilled tuna steak with vanilla sauce, but when we passed, the owners (from Réunion Island) were planning to include specialities from around the world made using local ingredients. The semi-outdoor Zen-style setting is superb and is a great place for a drink as well as a meal.

Hôtel Atiapiti (Map p137; ☎ 66 16 65; set menu 2500-3200 CFP; ⏱ lunch) If you're a little peckish after visiting Marae Taputapuatea, head for the restaurant at this nearby hotel. The setting, facing the lagoon, is calm and pleasant and the cuisine makes the most of local ingredients. You have a choice of the full set menu, which includes entrée and dessert, or a simple set menu with either entrée or dessert.

DRINKING & ENTERTAINMENT

It's difficult to find a reason to stay up late on Ra'iatea, but try the following places.

Le Zénith (Map p138; admission women/men free/1500 CFP; ⏱ from 10pm Fri & Sat) On weekends Restaurant Moana, located above the Leogite Supermarket in Uturoa, metamorphoses into this disco. It's mainly popular with young locals.

Club House (Map p137; ☎ 66 11 66) A sunset drink at this place in the Apooiti Marina is mandatory. The restaurant (see left) may not serve the best food, but the mellow ambience – alfresco wooden benches set on lawns, or tables under a traditional thatched roof – is as fantastic as the sunset views.

Raiatea Pearl Resort Hawaiki Nui (Map p137; ☎ 60 05 00) The bar at this resort (p141) also offers great lagoon views, and stages weekly Polynesian dance performances – call for details on the prices.

SHOPPING

Uturoa has several well-stocked souvenir outlets, as well as some unique boutiques and excellent-value pearl shops.

Anuanua Gallery (Map p138; ☎ 66 12 66) This place features works by island craftspeople, including sculptures, pottery, paintings and mother-of-pearl objects.

Galerie Tai'oa (Map p138; ☎ 66 42 25) Sells a stunning collection of mostly Marquesan woodcarvings.

Galerie Art-Expo (Map p137; ☎ 66 11 83) Art-Expo, at Apooiti Marina, sells a wide variety of jewellery, clothes, decorative trinkets and wooden handicrafts – from mother-of-pearl belts to souvenir T-shirts.

Vanillère (Map p137; ☎ 66 15 61) One of the best places to buy all sorts of vanilla products; located at Hotopu Bay.

Hei Tattoo (Map p137; ☎ 76 30 25; haiputona_haiti@ yahoo.fr; Uturoa) Isidore Haiti specialises in Marquesan and tribal-style tattoos.

GETTING THERE & AWAY

Ra'iatea is 220km northwest of Tahiti and 40km southeast of Bora Bora.

Air

Air Tahiti (☎ 60 04 44; ☺ 7.30am-noon & 2-5.15pm Mon-Fri, 7.30-11.15am Sat, 2.30-5.15pm Sun) has an airport office. The airline operates direct flights from Tahiti (12,000 CFP, 40 minutes, eight daily) with connections via Mo'orea (13,000 CFP) and Huahine (5600 CFP). There are also direct flights to Bora Bora (6300 CFP, 20 minutes, daily) and Maupiti (6900 CFP, 20 minutes, three weekly).

Boat

Ra'iatea is separated from Taha'a by a 3km-wide channel.

TAHA'A

The *navette* (shuttle boat) services on the **Te Haere Maru IV, V & VI** (☎ 65 61 33) run between Uturoa and various stops on Taha'a – Marina Taravana, Poutoru, Tapuamu, Patio, Hipu and Haamene – twice a day. Services are all in the morning except one boat, which returns to Taha'a from Ra'iatea at around 5pm. You can buy tickets on board. There is no service on Saturday afternoon or Sunday. It takes less than 15 minutes to get from Uturoa to Marina Taravana, the closest stop on Taha'a; the one-way fare is 1000 CFP.

The **Tamarii Taha'a** (☎ 65 65 29) goes to the west coast of Taha'a twice daily from the Uturoa *navette* quay, at around 10.30am and 4.30pm, while the **Tamarii Taha'a II** operates the

same hours but to the east coast. It operates Monday to Friday and Saturday morning. The one-hour trip to Patio costs 1000 CFP.

There is also a **taxi-boat service** (☎ 65 65 30) between the two islands, which operates daily between 6am and 6pm. It costs 6000 CFP to go to southern Taha'a and 12,000 CFP to get to the north of the island (prices are per boat). You can be picked up at the airport or any of the accessible pontoons. Advance booking (24 hours) is required.

OTHER ISLANDS

The **Maupiti Express** (☎ 67 66 69) travels between Bora Bora, Taha'a and Ra'iatea. Four days a week it departs from Vaitape (Bora Bora) at 7am, arriving at Taha'a at 8.15am and at Uturoa at 8.45am. It leaves Uturoa on the same days at 4pm, stopping at Taha'a and arriving back at Bora Bora at 5.45pm. The one-way/return fare is 3500/4500 CFP; it costs 700 CFP to go from Ra'iatea to Taha'a.

The cargo ships *Vaeanu*, *Taporo VII* and *Hawaiki Nui* also make a stop at Ra'iatea; see p261.

GETTING AROUND

The options for getting around are to hire a car or hitchhike. Hitchhiking appears to be fairly accepted here because of the low-key tourism and lack of public transport. However, remember that there are always dangers associated with hitching.

To/From the Airport

There are taxis at the airport; the 3km trip into Uturoa costs 1300 CFP. Most island accommodation will pick you up if you have booked (although there may be a charge).

Bicycle & Scooter

Europcar (Map p138; ☎ 66 34 06; www.europcar.pf) hires out scooters for 6500 CFP for 24 hours. Some hotels and guesthouses hire out bicycles.

Boat

Europcar (Map p138; ☎ 66 34 06; www.europcar.pf) hires out boats with outboard motors for 10,000/12,000 CFP for eight/24 hours; they're the perfect way to explore the lagoon, but you need a boat license.

Car

The head office of **Europcar** (Map p138; ☎ 66 34 06; www.europcar.pf) is on the edge of Uturoa towards the airport; there are also desks at the airport and in the Raiatea Pearl Resort Hawaiki Nui. An economy car costs 7000 CFP for four hours and 11,000 CFP for 24 hours. Call to arrange a pick-up from your hotel.

Avis (☎ 66 20 00) has a desk at the airport and charges 9000 CFP per day for a similar model. **Hertz** (☎ 66 44 88), opposite the town hall in Uturoa, also charges 9000 CFP but sometimes offers better prices when business is down, and will deliver cars to the airport.

Taxi
There's a **taxi stand** (☎ 66 20 60) by the market, and taxis can also be found at the airport, but even the shortest trips don't cost less than 1300 CFP.

TAHA'A

pop 4845 / area 90 sq km
Roughly orchid shaped, Taha'a runs on two of the most pleasant things French Polynesia has to offer: vanilla and pearls. This befits the subtle and sweet personality of the island, where smiles are as common as hibiscus flowers and the scent of vanilla wafts through the air. For tourists, the main draw is the string of sandy *motu* to the north of the island where the silhouette of Bora Bora sits so close you could almost believe you were in the high-rolling neighbour's lagoon. You're not, of course. Taha'a is more a back-to-nature than a jet-set-tourist kind of haven, although it is becoming a more and more up-scale destination; Le Taha'a Private Island & Spa fancies itself the most exclusive resort in the country.

A sealed coast road encircles most of the island but traffic is very light and there is no public transport. Taha'a's easily navigable lagoon and safe anchorages make it a favourite for visiting yachties and day-trippers from Ra'iatea.

HISTORY
Taha'a was once known as Kuporu (Uporu). Since this traditional name also pops up in other Polynesian centres, historians have long speculated about a migratory connection between Taha'a and other Polynesian islands. For many years Taha'a lived in the shadow of Ra'iatea, its larger, stronger and more important neighbour, and at times

it played pawn in the struggles between Ra'iatea and the rulers of Bora Bora.

The first missionaries arrived from neighbouring Ra'iatea in 1822 and the island came under French control at the same time as Ra'iatea. Taha'a was once a centre for firewalking ceremonies, but this practice has now died out.

ORIENTATION
A 70km sealed road winds around the island and the population is concentrated in eight villages on the coast. Tapuamu has the main quay, Patio is the main town, and Haamene is where the roads around the southern and northern parts of the island meet, forming a figure eight. Apu Bay to the south, Haamene Bay to the east and Hurepiti Bay to the west offer sheltered anchorages.

INFORMATION
Taha'a's only reliably open bank is the Banque Socredo in Patio. There's internet access at the post offices in Patio and Haamene.

SIGHTS
It's possible to do the 70km circuit of the island as a bicycle day trip – the road is good, but there are a few steep stretches. PK markers start at Haamene and go anticlockwise around the northern half of the island, terminating at Patio at around PK25.

Starting from the Marina Taravana (the first *navette* stop if you're coming from Ra'iatea), the road follows the coast around Apu Bay. At the top of the bay there's a turn-off south to Poutoru; the main road leaves the coast and climbs up and over to the larger village of **Haamene**.

On the right of the road into Haamene is the **Maison de la Vanille** (Map p137; ☎ 65 67 27), a small family-run operation where you can see vanilla preparation and drying processes and also purchase vanilla pods. For more about vanilla cultivation, see the boxed text, p146.

A little further on the road climbs again, making a long sweeping ascent and descent to beautiful Hurepiti Bay and the village of **Tiva**, where you'll find several **pearl farms** by the coast. As you round the end of the bay, keep an eye out for the stunning silhouette of Bora Bora.

The island's main quay is located at **Tapuamu**, but **Patio**, further on, is the administrative centre of the island, with offices, a post office, a bank and shops. Continuing around

RA'IATEA & TAHA'A

VANILLA, VANILLA, VANILLA

Taha'a is accurately nicknamed 'the vanilla island', since three-quarters of French Polynesian vanilla (about 25 tons annually) is produced here. This is a far cry from the 150 to 200 tons produced a century ago, when vanilla cultivation flourished in the Society Islands.

Several vanilla farms are open to the public, and at these family-run operations you can buy vanilla pods at reasonable prices – about 1000 CFP for a dozen. You can also find out about the technique of 'marrying' the vanilla, a delicate operation in which the flowers are fertilised by hand because the insects that do the job in other regions are not found in French Polynesia. Nine months later the pods are put out to dry, and they turn brown over four to five months. They are then sorted and packed before being sold locally or exported.

Jacqueline Mama, a Taha'a vanilla farmer, gives us tips on buying and keeping vanilla pods: 'When you massage the bean with your fingers it should be flat. If the pod is puffed up at all it means that there is still moisture inside and your vanilla might mould when you get home. But the bean shouldn't be too dried out either – the outside should have some sheen, not look dry like wood. Once you buy your vanilla, keep it in an airtight place. Wrapping it tightly in plastic wrap usually does the job. If it starts to lose its sheen you can close it in a jar with a drop of rum to revive it.'

the coast, the road passes copra plantations before reaching **Faaha**. On the northern side of the bay you can visit **Motu Pearl Farm** (Map p137; ☎ 65 66 67), which has a small shop.

From the bay the road climbs over a headland and drops down to Haamene Bay. Alternatively, a dirt track turns off the coast road just beyond Patio and takes a direct route over the hills and down to Haamene. This road starts shortly after the village and although the first part is drivable, the second section needs a 4WD. It's really better as a walk or mountain-bike ride.

Where the coast road meets Haamene Bay, turn east to Hôtel Hibiscus and visit the **Foundation Hibiscus** (Map p137; ☎ 65 61 06), dedicated to saving turtles that have become entangled in local fishing nets. The hotel owner Léo buys the trapped turtles and keeps them in pens beside the hotel's pier. The turtles are fed every morning until they've grown large enough to be released.

From Hôtel Hibiscus the coast road goes around the northern side of the bay to Haamene, passing **Vaipoe Pearl Farm** (Map p137; ☎ 65 60 83; admission 100 CFP) and Rooverta Ebbs' **Poerani** (Map p137; ☎ 65 60 25; admission 100 CFP), where you can check out pearl grafting first hand. Mounted and unmounted pearls and mother-of-pearl are sold, although the prices aren't great.

ACTIVITIES

Taha'a has two dive centres, **Tahaa Blue Nui** (Map p137; ☎ 65 67 78, 60 84 00; www.bluenui.com), at Le

Taha'a Private Island & Spa (p148), and the independent **Tahaa Diving** (Map p137; ☎ 65 78 37; www.tahaa-diving.com), located near Tiare's Breeze. The dive centres on Ra'iatea regularly use the dive sites to the east of the island by Céran Pass, and will collect you from hotels in the south of Taha'a. See p139 for more details.

Like Ra'iatea, there are no real beaches on Taha'a and you have to go to the *motu* for swimming and snorkelling. Some guesthouses will drop you on a *motu* for the day or you can join an organised *pirogue* tour.

To organise a bit of game fishing, visit Hôtel Hibiscus (opposite). Prices vary, so ask when you ring.

Taha'a's interior is so dense it caters more to bushwalkers than hikers. The only real hiking trail into the interior follows a little-used 7km track across the centre of the island from Patio to Haamene and offers some dazzling views of Haamene Bay.

TOURS

Many tour operators are based in Taha'a but they also offer to pick up from Ra'iatea. Since Ra'iatea sees more tourists than Taha'a, we've listed the companies offering tours from both islands in the Ra'iatea section of this chapter (see p140). The places listed here are exclusive to Taha'a. Tours start at about 6500 CFP.

Poerani Tours (Map p137; ☎ 65 60 25)

Vaipoe Tours (Map p137; ☎ 65 60 83; Vaipoe Pearl Farm) Full-day lagoon tours.

Vanilla Tours (☎ 65 62 46) Ethno-botanic oriented and recommended.

SLEEPING

Taha'a's places to stay are dotted around the coast. It's wise to make reservations so you'll be collected from the appropriate village quay, or even the airport on Ra'iatea.

The Island

Chez Pascal (Map p137; ☎ 65 60 42; bungalows per person 3000 CFP, with breakfast/half board 3500/5000 CFP) Basic little bungalows here are decorated with lots of local fabrics, are kept spotlessly clean and have shared cold-water bathrooms. It's rootsy Polynesian style and meals are served in a restaurant where guests can also use the kitchen. You can't beat this place for the price. Bicycles and kayaks both cost 500 CFP for the day and *motu* transfers are 3000 CFP return. Transfers to/from the quay at Tapuamu are free.

Au Phil du Temps (Map p137; ☎ 65 64 19; www.pension -au-phil-du-temps.com; r/bungalows per person 5300/6300 CFP, per person half/full board 5300/8500 CFP) Kitted out with TVs, mosquito nets and private outside bathrooms, the local-style bungalows here are just a few metres from the lagoon and are very popular and well kept. Transfers to the airport cost 2000 CFP per person one way. No credit cards.

Pension Vaihi (Map p137; ☎ 65 62 02; bungalows 7000 CFP, per person half/full board 3000/4500 CFP) Head to this family guesthouse on the southern side of Hurepiti Bay for real isolation and tranquillity. The three spotless lagoonside bungalows come with bathrooms. To get here, ask the *navette* to drop you at the quay at Tiva, where the owners will pick you up. Bicycles can be hired for 1500 CFP.

Pension Api (Map p137; ☎ 65 69 88; jjwatip@mail.pf; r 8000 CFP, per person half board 4000 CFP) Near the sea, this *pension* offers two comfortable bungalow-style rooms. Each has a private bathroom, mosquito net and terrace. Breakfast is available for 600 CFP. To get here, take a *navette* to the quay and call the owners, who will come and pick you up. Free kayaks and bicycles are available for guests' use.

Hôtel Hibiscus (Map p137; ☎ 65 61 06; www.hibiscus tahaa.com; bungalows from 10,600 CFP, per person half board 4900 CFP) It's haphazardly run and there's a lot of drinking going on at the restaurant-bar, giving this hotel a boisterous, albeit unpredictable charm. Bungalows (some of which can sleep up to ten people) all have bathroom, terrace and fan and there are seven free boat moorings with dock access. Island tours, traditional fishing trips, *motu* picnics and even a

motu wedding can be organised. Bicycle hire costs 1000 CFP per day but kayaks are free.

Chez Edwin & Jacqueline (Map p137; ☎ 65 62 18; houses from 12,000 CFP; ☒) Good for independent types or families, these brand-new two-bedroom cement houses have big living rooms, TV, hot-water bathrooms and full kitchens. Friendly Edwin and Jacqueline will drive you to get groceries and you can check out the family vanilla plantation. Take an island tour with Edwin (see p140), explore the island on free bikes or just hang out by the pool.

Residence D'Hôtes Le Passage (Map p137; ☎ 65 66 75; www.tahitilepassage.com; bungalows with full board & activities per person 18,000 CFP; ☒ ☐ ☒) You get an all-inclusive package when you stay here (minus alcohol, which you can purchase), which is convenient since Taha'a can be hard to get around on your own and the food here has a great reputation. Cosy, stylish bungalows feel more like rooms and are clustered on a flowery hillside and linked by outdoor staircases; meals are served at a restaurant overlooking the sea. There's a pontoon for hanging out and snorkelling. Transfers from Ra'iatea cost 7000 CFP per person.

Tiare's Breeze (Map p137; ☎ 65 62 26; www.tiarebreeze .com; bungalows incl brunch 30,000 CFP; ☒ ☐) There's only one ultra-private hillside bungalow here but more are in the works. Plenty of deck space lets you lounge around and enjoy the view and great indoor/outdoor sound system, or you can trek down the hill to hang out in the posh over-the-water hang-out area on a pontoon. Everything is made with taste from local materials and you really feel in the lap of luxury. For meals you can cook in your own kitchen or the owner will drive you to nearby restaurants.

Fare Pea Iti (Map p137; ☎ 60 81 11; www.farepeaiti .pf; bungalows 30,000-36,000 CFP; ☐ ☒) This is a fabulously well-designed place with bungalows worthy of a shabby-chic spread in an architectural magazine; expect lots of bamboo, stonework and draped white fabrics. We love that the owner has stocked the place with everything you might need from torches and *monoi* to plush robes and slippers. Work out in the alfresco gym, and bliss out by the stylish pool or on the white-sand beach that looks out over the lagoon to palm-fringed *motu*. Our only gripe is that management seems gloomy compared to other hotels and *pensions* in the area – maybe we showed up on a bad day. Add 7300 CFP per person per day for half board;

it's expensive but the food is very good. Airport transfers are 8400 CFP return.

The Motu

Motu digs are set in private paradises that rival (and some would say exceed) the settings of Bora Bora's better resorts. As such, you'll be paying Bora Bora prices.

Hotel La Pirogue (Map p137; ☎ 60 81 45; www.hotel-la-pirogue.com; bungalows from 27,500 CFP, per person half board 6500 CFP; 🖥) If you want one of the country's best locations and enjoy natural environments (open, rustic, thatched-roof bungalows) more than hermetically sealed air-con rooms, head straight to this small, secluded *motu* resort. It's intimate and friendly, and appeals to couples looking for a bit of luxury without an exorbitant price tag – although it also caters to families. The restaurant has a varied menu and very good reputation (we'd suggest opting for half board). All sorts of activities can be arranged.

Vahine Island Private Island Resort (Map p137; ☎ 65 67 38; www.vahine-island.com; bungalows 50,000-67,000 CFP; 🖥) In a picturesque location with white-sand beaches and translucent water, this intimate, traveller-recommended resort has nine French Polynesian–style bungalows – three of which are perched over the lagoon. The bungalows are not ultraposh but they are lovingly decorated with bright Tahitian bedspreads, coral and shell adornments, and comfy hammocks on spacious wooden terraces. Add 10,500 CFP per person per day for half-board (recommended, as you are in the middle of nowhere). *Pirogues* and snorkelling equipment are available for free; lagoon tours and mountain-bike trips are organised. Airport transfers cost 7200 CFP per person return.

Le Taha'a Private Island & Spa (Map p137; ☎ 50 84 54; www.letahaa.com; bungalows from 104,000 CFP; 🍽 🖥 🏊) French Polynesia's only Relais & Chateaux resort aims to be the most exclusive resort in the country and we think it hits the mark. In an exceptional setting on Motu Tau Tau, if you don't have an over-the-water-bungalow facing either Taha'a or Bora Bora, you'll at least have your own pool. Every option is designed with luxurious creativity and offers space and a supreme level of privacy. Stairs cut into a tree in the main building lead up to a gourmet restaurant and cocktail bar, offering indoor and outdoor seating amid fabulous views. Le Taha'a is definitely a destination resort (it's very isolated and access to the mainland is expensive

and inconsistent) but the place offers enough activities to keep most guests entertained for days. Reach the resort by boat (10,000 CFP per person) or via private helicopter from Bora Bora (18,000 CFP per person).

EATING & DRINKING

There are shops in each village and a few *roulottes* open around the island at night, but the dining options are very limited. The *motu* resorts all have their own bars, but otherwise your drinking options are limited to the following two restaurants.

Hôtel Hibiscus (Map p137; ☎ 65 61 06; dishes 1200-3000 CFP; 🕑 lunch & dinner) This hotel restaurant has a solid reputation. A couple of good choices on the seafood-heavy menu include *mahi mahi* (dorado) and crab dishes. The bar gets quite busy at night, especially during the occasional Saturday-night performances.

Restaurant Tahaa Maitai (Map p137; ☎ 65 70 85; dishes 1500-3000 CFP; 🕑 lunch & dinner) Travellers recommend this restaurant right on Haamene Bay not only for its fabulous views but also for its delicious cuisine. The menu features lots of fresh seafood, local fruits and vegetables and delicious French desserts. There's also a long cocktail list, making this a popular local watering hole.

GETTING THERE & AWAY

There is no airport on Taha'a. The airport on Ra'iatea is only 15 minutes across the lagoon and some hotels will pick up guests from the airport or from the ferry quay at Uturoa on Ra'iatea.

See p144 for information on the *navette* service between Ra'iatea and Taha'a.

The **Maupiti Express** (☎ 67 66 99) operates on Monday, Wednesday and Friday between Bora Bora, Taha'a and Ra'iatea.

Interisland ships stop at Tapuamu on Taha'a en route from Ra'iatea to Bora Bora, but not on every voyage. If your trip doesn't stop at Taha'a it's easy enough to disembark at Uturoa and then take the *navette* service across.

GETTING AROUND

There is no public transport on Taha'a. If you are contemplating hitching, remember that traffic is very light. Hiring a car or bike are the only ways to see the island independently. The coast road is mostly sealed and in good condition. If you do decide to tackle it by bicycle keep in mind that there are some steep stretches on the south of the island that can be heavy going.

You can save money on Taha'a's ridiculously expensive car costs by hiring a scooter on Ra'iatea (see p144) and bringing it across on the *navette*. There are petrol stations in Patio and Tapuamu, which are open Monday to Saturday.

Residence D'Hôtes Le Passage (see p147) rents out Logans for 12,000 CFP for 24 hours.

Monique Locations (☎ 65 62 48), near the church in Haamene, hires out Citroën Saxos for 9000/11,000 CFP for eight/24 hours and bicycles for 1500 CFP for 24 hours.

Europcar (☎ 65 67 00; fax 65 68 08), at the Total petrol station at Tapuamu, has Fiat Pandas for 7000 CFP for four hours and 11,000 CFP for 24 hours.

RA'IATEA & TAHA'A

Bora Bora

This is it, this is the one. The arrival by plane says it all. From above, the promise of a wonderland is instantly made good: glinting turquoise sea and dazzlingly white sandy stretches of beach. Add sumptuous resorts in a sensational lagoon setting and indulgent gourmet dining in fancy restaurants and it's small wonder Bora Bora stakes a convincing claim to being a piece of paradise. This diva of an island is not only for unbridled pampering and romance, though; when you've finished sipping your *maitai,* check out diving, snorkelling, parasailing, walking under the sea and even hiking in the spectacular mountainous interior.

It's not all that rosy (well, turquoise), though. With, at the latest count, almost 700 over-water bungalows (compared with a few dozen 15 years ago) dotted over a fairly compact area, the sense of exclusivity is somewhat toned down now, and hedonists in search of a real escape have started turning their eyes to nearby Maupiti (but you didn't hear it from us). But so superior are its proportions that Bora Bora remains the stuff of legend, and nothing can beat a few days here to make the most of its pleasures and charms. And don't fret if your budget isn't in the four-figures-a-day category. A handful of quaint *pensions* and affordable midrange hotels beckon. They're not as ritzy, but you'll enjoy a slice of paradise nonetheless. Check in and chill out.

HIGHLIGHTS

- Discovering all the perks of a world-class resort on secluded **Motu Piti Aau** (p159) and recreating the *From Here to Eternity* kiss on your sundeck
- Hearing yourself scream 'Darling, it's magical' while ogling the stunning cerulean blue lagoon on a **boat tour** (p155)
- Seeing a bird's-eye view of the island on a scenic helicopter flight (p157) – pricey, but you deserve it
- Enjoying a romantic dinner with your partner in a gourmet **restaurant** (p162) on Matira Point
- **Diving** (p155) among harmless sharks at amazing sites such as Tapu and Muri Muri

Muri Muri

Tapu

Motu Piti Aau

Matira Point

Lagoon

- POPULATION: 5757
- AREA: 47 SQ KM

HISTORY

In ancient times, the island was known as Vava'u, perhaps supporting the theory that it was colonised by inhabitants from the Tongan island of the same name. According to local myth, the legendary Hiro, the first king of Ra'iatea, sent his son Ohatatama to rule Bora Bora.

Due to the shortage of flat ground on Bora Bora, land pressures created an unusually defensive population of fierce warriors. Only Huahine managed to resist the warriors of Bora Bora at their most expansive.

James Cook sighted Bora Bora in 1769 on his first voyage to French Polynesia, and a London Missionary Society (LMS) base was established on the island in 1820. Bora Bora supported Pomare in his push for supreme power over Tahiti, but resisted becoming a French protectorate (established over Tahiti in 1842) until the island was annexed in 1888.

During WWII a US supply base was established here, prompted by the bombing of Pearl Harbor in 1941. From early 1942 to mid-1946 Operation Bobcat transformed the island and, at its peak, up to 6000 men were stationed on Bora Bora. Today the runway on Motu Mute is the clearest (and most useful) reminder of those frenetic days. Eight massive 7in naval cannons were installed around the island during the war; all but one are still in place.

ORIENTATION

Bora Bora is spectacularly mountainous, rising to Mt Hue (619m), Mt Pahia (661m) and Mt Otemanu (727m). The main island stretches for about 9km from north to south and is about 4km in width at the widest point. A 32km road runs around the coast.

A wide, sheltered and navigable lagoon encircles the island, with sandy *motu* (islets) edging most of the outer reef. The Teavanui Pass on Bora Bora's western side is the only pass into the lagoon.

Vaitape is the main town, but Matira Point is the most developed spot. The quay for inter-island ships is at Farepiti, between Vaitape and Faanui. The airport is on Motu Mute at the northern extremity of the outer reef edge.

INFORMATION

All services are in Vaitape. There's a medical centre in Vaitape as well as numerous private doctors and a pharmacy.

Aloe Cafe (per hr 1600 CFP; 🕙 6am-6pm Mon-Sat) Internet access. Wi-fi is also available (same rates). At the back of a small shopping centre.

Banque de Polynésie (🕙 7.45-11.45am & 1.30-4.30pm Mon-Fri) Has an ATM and a 24-hour automatic exchange machine.

Banque de Tahiti (🕙 7.45-11.45am & 1.30-4.30pm Mon-Fri) Currency exchange, and has an ATM.

Banque Socredo (🕙 7.30-11.30am & 1.30-3.30pm Mon-Fri) Currency exchange, and has an ATM.

Bora Bora visitor information centre (☎ 67 76 36; info-bora-bora@mail.pf; 🕙 7.30am-4pm Mon-Fri) The office is on the quay at Vaitape and has pamphlets and other info. Mildly helpful.

Post office (🕙 7am-3pm Mon-Fri, 8-10am Sat) Internet access (with the Manaspot card, on sale at the counter).

SIGHTS

Bora Bora's 32km coast road hugs the shoreline almost all the way around the island and rarely rises above sea level. There aren't any overwhelming sights along the route bar Matira Beach, but it's great for a challenging day's bike ride (mere mortals may find themselves walking their bikes up the hill around Fitiiu Point on the east coast). Cars can also be easily hired, or you can join a 4WD tour. The following tour starts in Vaitape, going anticlockwise around the island.

Vaitape

If arriving by air you'll be transported from the Motu Mute airport to Vaitape, the island's main settlement. It's not the most evocative town, but it's the only place on Bora Bora that doesn't feel as if it were built exclusively for

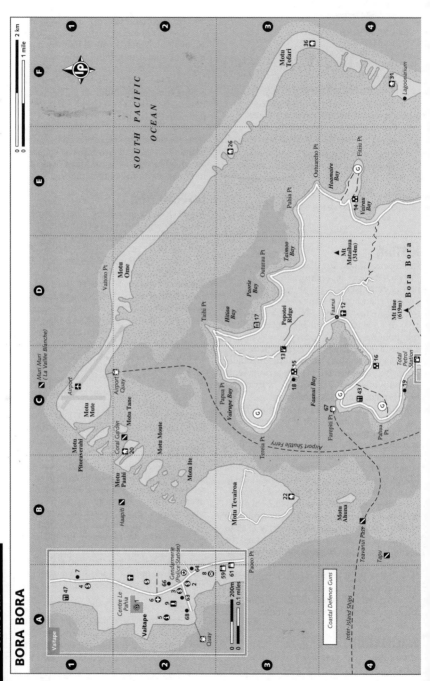

BORA BORA

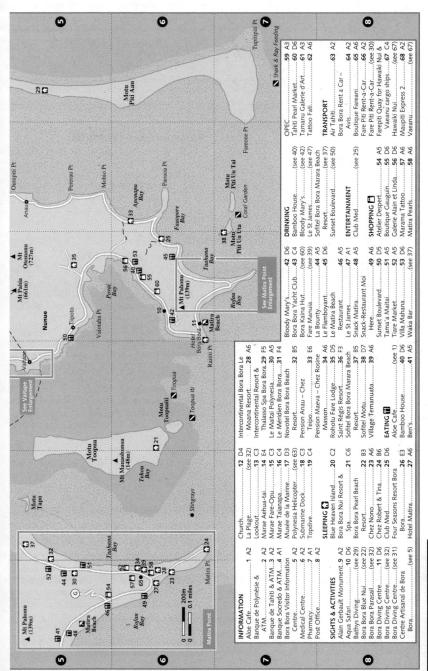

INFORMATION
Aloe Cafe.................................1 A2
Banque de Polynésie &
ATM......................................2 A2
Banque de Tahiti & ATM..3 A2
Banque Socredo & ATM....4 A1
Bora Bora Visitor Information
Centre..................................5 A2
Medical Centre....................6 A2
Pharmacy.............................7 A1
Post Office...........................8 A2

SIGHTS & ACTIVITIES
Alain Gerbault Monument.9 A2
Aqua Safari.........................10 D6
Bathys Diving..............(see 29)
Bora Bora Blue Nui.....(see 22)
Bora Bora Parasail.....(see 32)
Bora Diving Centre.........11 D6
Bora Diving Centre.....(see 32)
Bora Diving Centre.....(see 31)
Centre Artisanal de Bora
Bora...............................(see 5)

Church.................................12 D4
La Plage.........................(see 32)
Lookout................................13 C3
Marae Aehua-tai..............14 E4
Marae Fare-Opu................15 C3
Marae Taianapa.................16 C4
Musée de la Marine..........17 D3
Polynesia Helicopter....(see 63)
Submarine Dock.................18 C3
Topdive................................19 C4

SLEEPING
Blue Heaven Island...........20 C2
Bora Bora Nui Resort &
Spa....................................21 C6
Bora Bora Pearl Beach
Resort................................22 B3
Chez Nono.........................23 A6
Chez Robert & Tina..........24 B6
Club Med.............................25 D6
Hotel Matira......................26 E3
Centre Artisanal de Bora...27 A6

Intercontinental Bora Bora Le
Moana Resort....................28 A6
Intercontinental Resort &
Thalasso Spa Bora.........29 F5
Le Maitai Polynesia..........30 A5
Le Méridien Bora Bora......31 F4
Novotel Bora Bora Beach
Resort................................32 B5
Pension Anau – Chez
Teipo.................................33 E6
Pension Maeva – Chez Rosine
Masson...............................34 A6
Rohotu Fare Lodge...........35 D5
Saint Régis Resort............36 F3
Sofitel Bora Bora Marara Beach
Resort................................37 B5
Sofitel Motu......................38 D7
Village Temanuata............39 A6

EATING
Aloe Cafe......................(see 1)
Bamboo House...................40 D6
Ben's....................................41 A6

Bloody Mary's....................42 D6
Bora Bora Yacht Club........43 C4
Bora Kaina Hut............(see 60)
Fare Manuila.................(see 39)
La Bounty...........................44 A5
Le Flamboyant...................45 D6
Le Matira Beach
Restaurant.........................46 A5
Le St James........................47 A1
Snack Matira.....................48 A5
Snack-Restaurant Moi
Here....................................49 A6
Sunset Boulevard..............50 D5
Tama'a Maitai....................51 A5
Tiare Market......................52 A5
Villa Mahana.....................53 D6
Waka Bar......................(see 37)

DRINKING
Bamboo House..............(see 40)
Bloody Mary's...............(see 42)
Le St James...................(see 47)
Sofitel Bora Bora Marara Beach
Resort............................(see 37)
Sunset Boulevard.........(see 50)

ENTERTAINMENT
Club Med......................(see 25)

SHOPPING
Atelier Despert..................54 A5
Boutique Gauguin.............55 D6
Galerie Alain et Linda......56 D6
Marama Tattoo.................57 A6
Matira Pearls....................58 A6

OPEC..................................59 A3
Tahiti Pearl Market...........60 D6
Tamanu Galerie d'Art.......61 A2
Tattoo Fati.........................62 A6

TRANSPORT
Air Tahiti............................63 A2
Bora Bora Rent a Car –
Avis......................................(see 50)
Boutique Fareani..............64 A2
Fare Piti Rent-a-Car.........65 A6
Fare Piti Rent-a-Car.....(see 30)
Farepiti Quay for Hawaiki Nui &
Vaeanu cargo ships....(see 67)
Hawaiki Nui........................66 C4
Maupiti Express 2.............67 A2
Vaeanu..........................(see 67)

tourists. Vaitape is a great place to do a bit of shopping, take care of banking and internet needs and just get a feel for the way locals really live. Busy during the day, by late afternoon it becomes altogether sleepy, with *pétanque* (boules) players taking centre stage.

A **monument** to Alain Gerbault, who in 1923 was the first yachtsman to achieve a non-stop solo crossing of the Atlantic, stands at Vaitape quay. Gerbault lived on Bora Bora in the 1930s.

Matira Point & Around

Beyond the overland road, the coast road passes the Bamboo House restaurant and several shops. Further south, you'll find Bloody Mary's (p161), one of the island's most popular restaurants.

Luxurious Hotel Bora Bora (closed for renovation) at Raititi Point marks the start of easily accessible **Matira Beach**, Bora Bora's only real beach, which sweeps out to Matira Point. Along the road are several boutiques, *snacks* (snack bars), restaurants and places to stay. From the eastern edge of the Hotel Matira property a walking trail runs up the hill to a battery of **WWII coastal defence guns**. The hike takes about 10 minutes: a great way to stretch your legs.

On the eastern side of Matira Point is the classy Intercontinental Bora Bora Le Moana Resort. The hotel and a few *pensions* are down the road that runs out to Matira Point; the public beach along here is fabulous. The final leg of the annual Hawaiki Nui canoe race finishes right on the beach (see the boxed text, p45).

Matira Point to Anau

From Matira Point, the coast road passes a collection of busy little shops, restaurants and hotels. The road rounds the point and passes Club Med, then drops back down to the coast just before the fishing village of Anau, a rather strung-out affair.

Fitiiu Point

A fingerlike peninsula extending out into the lagoon, Fitiiu Point features several interesting sites, but they all take a bit of effort to find. Just as the road starts to climb, a track peels off and runs down to **Marae Aehua-tai**, on the water's edge. There are good views across the bay from the *marae* (traditional temple), with Mt Otemanu in the background.

Further up the hill there's a natural *marae* and two more **WWII coastal guns**. The walking

trail along the ridge starts behind the first house, at the sharp bend in the road. If anybody is around, ask permission to take the trail. The track terminates at, of all things, a scenic lagoonside garbage dump! Just before the dump a steep path runs uphill and emerges on the top of the ridge just before the gun site. From the site there are fine views out over the lagoon to the *motu*.

Haamaire Bay & Taimoo Bay

The road beyond Fitiiu Point traverses the most lightly populated stretch of coast as it rounds Haamaire and Taimoo Bays. The small, private **Musée de la Marine** (Marine Museum; ☎ 67 75 24; admission by donation) has a collection of model ships made by architect Bertrand Darasse. The opening hours are fairly haphazard, so you might like to call ahead.

Taihi Point to Farepiti Point

The north coast of the island around Taihi Point is sparsely populated. Just after the point, a steep and often muddy track climbs up to an old WWII radar station atop a ridge and on to a **lookout** above the village of Faanui.

At the end of Tereia Point, a rectangular concrete water tank marks the position of another **coastal gun**. There's no path; just clamber for a couple of minutes straight up the hill behind the tank.

Marae Fare-Opu is squeezed between the roadside and the water's edge. Two of the slabs are clearly marked with the turtle petroglyphs seen incised in stones at numerous other sites in the Society Islands.

Faanui Bay was the site of the US military base during WWII. Note the picturesque **church**, slightly inland. On the coastal road, the **Marae Taianapa** lies on private property on the edge of a coconut plantation, just off the mountain side of the road (ask around).

Farepiti Point to Pahua Point

Interisland ships dock at the rather drab Farepiti quay, which was built during WWII and is at the southwestern end of Faanui Bay.

Along the road from Farepiti Point to Pahua Point, one of the WWII defence guns can be seen silhouetted against the skyline. The road rounds the point, and two **coastal defence guns**, placed here to guard the shipping route into the lagoon, overlook the point. The route is not well marked, so ask around if you get lost.

ACTIVITIES

Ah, Bora Bora's lagoon. The stuff of dreams. How could you not be mesmerised by this stunning palette of sapphire, indigo and turquoise hues that mix together in modern-art abstractions? Small wonder it's the focus of most activities. Should you tire of water sports, there are a few options on land.

All operators listed below organise free pick-ups and drop-offs from hotels and *pensions*.

Swimming

Let's be frank: high hopes of sweeping expanses of silky sand might be dashed upon arrival on Bora Bora. Although the island boasts clear, aquamarine water and a brochure-esque appeal, it's not a beach holiday destination. You come here for the lagoon, less so for the beach. Even the best bits of beach are fairly narrow. The only 'real' beach is at Matira Point, which features a sandy spit of land. The beaches at most fancy hotels are artificial (in other words, the sand was extracted from the lagoon floor, which is not so eco-friendly). If you want to play sardines, you'll need to head to the *motu* to dabble in appealing palm-ruffled stretches of sand. Take a lagoon tour (right) or consider renting a boat to access them.

Diving & Snorkelling

Diving in the bath-warm waters of Bora Bora is amazing and features sloping reefs. Sharks, rays and other marine life abound, and can be seen in quite shallow waters in the lagoon, or outside the reef. Don't expect healthy coral gardens, though; the voracious crown-of-thorns starfish (*Acanthaster planci*) has taken its toll over the last few years, especially along the outside reef. Check out p68 for details about dive sites, which include the exciting Tapu (lemon sharks, anyone?) and, south of Teavanui Pass, Toopua and Toopua Iti. Bora Bora is also a great place to learn to dive.

There are five professional diving outfits on Bora Bora. They come with excellent reputations for equipment, safety and instruction. All offer free pick-ups from hotels and employ qualified, English-speaking staff. Expect to pay 7500 CFP to 8500 CFP for an introductory dive or a single dive, 14,500 CFP for a two-tank dive and from 50,000 CFP for a PADI Open Water course.

Bathys Diving (☎ 60 76 00; www.bathys-diving.com) At Intercontinental Resort & Thalasso Spa Bora Bora.

Bora Bora Blue Nui (☎ 67 79 07; www.bluenui.com) At Bora Bora Pearl Beach Resort.
Bora Diving Centre (☎ 67 71 84, 77 67 46; www .boradive.com) At Matira Point, at the Novotel Bora Bora and at Le Méridien Bora Bora.
Topdive (☎ 60 50 50; www.topdive.com) On the northern edge of Vaitape. Offers slightly cheaper rates.

No visit to Bora Bora would be complete without a bout of snorkelling. The lagoon seems to be tailored to the expectations of avid snorkellers, with gin-clear waters and a smattering of healthy coral gardens around. Schools of glittering fish and perhaps a stingray or a blacktip shark (fear not, they're harmless) are just a few of the regulars who are so used to snorkellers that many will go eyeball to face-mask with you (well, not the sharks!).

Apart from the coral garden that spreads around Hotel Bora Bora, the best snorkelling spots can't be reached from shore – you'll have to rent a boat or take a lagoon tour.

Lagoon Tours

Taking a cruise around Bora Bora's idyllic lagoon will be one of the highlights of your trip to French Polynesia and it's well worth the expense. Not only will these tours (sometimes pompously dubbed 'safaris') have you ooh and aah over the surreal hues of the lagoon, but you'll also see the island from a different angle.

Half- and full-day tours are available; it will cost about 6000 CFP to 7000 CFP for half-day trips and 9000 CFP for day trips, which typically run from 9am to 4pm. If you're staying at a fancy hotel, book a tour on your own as these places can tack on as much as 40% extra for the same excursion.

Competition is fierce among the various operators who provide trips on the lagoon and its surrounding *motu*, so don't hesitate to shop around. Ask what's included in a cruise, and which snorkelling and swimming spots are included. It's also worth checking whether the boats have a roof – you'll be spending all day under the sun, and ending up the colour of a crayfish could play havoc with your plans for romance.

Most tours bill themselves as 'safaris' because they include shark and ray feeding (they usually use tuna scraps), on top of snorkelling stops. Getting up close and personal with blacktip reef sharks and majestic stingrays in gin-clear water is an extraordinary experience,

---

EXPLORING THE LAGOON DIY-STYLE

Wanna escape the crowds and guided tours? It's high time for a DIY trip. If you prefer setting your own pace and fancy tootling around the lagoon yourself, consider exploring it in your own boat. La Plage (☎ 67 68 75, 28 48 66; laplage.bora@hotmail.com), based on the beach at the Novotel, rents small 6hp or 15hp four-seater motor boats that are easy to drive; no licence is required for the 6hp boats. A detailed map featuring the lagoon is provided, as well as life jackets. Plan on 15,000 CFP to 20,000 CFP per day for the boat, petrol and transfers included. Bring a picnic and your snorkelling gear.

Note that many of the *motu* belong to local families or have been bought by the luxury hotels: don't treat the land as yours to explore without permission. Ask La Plage about the areas you can access without a problem.

---

but whether or not these artificial encounters are a good idea is open to debate. On the one hand, it undeniably disrupts natural behaviour patterns; sharks and rays that grow dependent on 'free lunches' may unlearn vital survival skills. On the other hand, it's undoubtedly spectacular (and safe), and it's a good way to educate tourists. You be the judge.

All full-day tours provide a barbecued fish lunch on a *motu*. Most boats have snorkelling gear but it's not a bad idea to bring your own. Bring waterproof sandals, an underwater camera, a hat and sunscreen.

A few well-established operators:

Bora Bora Photo Lagoon (☎ 77 10 96; www .boraboraphotolagoon.com) Runs all kinds of tailor-made tours, such as 'Honeymoon Dream'.

Lagoonarium (☎ 67 71 34) Half- and full-day tours. Includes a visit to a 'lagoonarium' – a kind of mini underwater zoo, with turtles, sharks and rays.

Moana Adventure Tours (☎ 67 61 41, 78 27 37; www.moanatours.com) Half-day tours. Also offers personalised tours (four people maximum; 23,500 CFP per two hours) and honeymoon cruises.

Moana Reva Tours (☎ 67 60 27, 71 87 39)

Reef Discovery (☎ 76 43 43; www.boraborasnorkeling .com) Run by a dive instructor who arranges customised half-day tours (20,000 CFP for four people) with an emphasis on ecotourism (he doesn't dabble in shark or ray feeding and offers guided snorkelling trips on less crowded coral gardens). It's the only operator in Bora Bora that includes reef walks (and the chance to see the ocean side of the barrier reef).

Teiva Tours (☎ 67 64 26) Half-day tours (mornings only).

Teremoana Nono Tours (☎ 67 71 38; www.cheznono bora.com) Based at Chez Nono. Famous for its superb barbecue lunch.

Semisubmersible & Glass-Bottom Boats

For nondivers, **Bora Bora Submarine** (☎ 67 55 55, 74 99 99; www.boraborasubmarine.com; per adult 18,000-24,000 CFP) is a small (maximum six people) vessel that offers coral viewing (well, what's left of the coral) outside the barrier reef. The trip lasts 30 to 45 minutes and the vessel descends to depths of 35m. Departures are from Vaitape quay; pick-ups are also provided.

Moana Adventure Tours (☎ 67 41 41, 78 27 37; www.moanatours.com; per person 4000 CFP) runs glass-bottom trips three times a week. During the 1¼-hour outing, the boat chugs around the lagoon and you're bound to see tons of rainbow-coloured fish species. Great for children and senior travellers.

Prices include transfers from your hotel.

Undersea Walks

You're not able to swim but you want to walk along the seabed? Yes, it's possible. **Aqua Safari** (☎ 28 87 77, 75 20 22; www.aquasafari bora.com; trips 7800 CFP) provides the unique experience of walking underwater, wearing a diver's helmet and weight belt. Pumps on the boat above feed air to you during the 35-minute 'walk on the wet side', in less than 4m. Walks are available to everyone over the age of eight. It's very reassuring that a dive instructor accompanies you on your walk. Expect lots of tropical fish swirling around your body and, if you're lucky, stingrays. Perfect for families. Some environmentalists think that this activity might damage the seabed, but it takes place in a small area of sandy seabed, and is undoubtedly a good way to introduce nondivers to the wonders of the big blue.

Hiking

Not all the action is in the water on Bora Bora, and we suggest that you take the time to explore the island's spectacularly mountainous interior. Choked in thick forest and dominated by bulky basaltic mountains, the island's centre is virtually deserted and can only be reached by walking paths. You don't have to go very far before the comforts of your over-water bungalow start to feel a long, long way away.

A guide is essential as the paths are notoriously difficult to find and to follow. **Polynesia Island Tours** (☎ 29 66 60; half-/full-day walks 3500/6500 CFP) offers reputable guided tours. It's run by Azdine, a professional walking guide who conducts some interesting nature and cultural walks on the island and caters for all levels of fitness. He speaks passable English.

If you're really fit, you can try the arduous climb up to Mt Pahia, Bora Bora's iconic summit. It's a five- to six-hour hard-going return hike from Vaitape, with some difficult uphill scrambles and a few treacherous sections but…words fail us; if it's not covered in mist by the time you reach the summit (choose a clear day and start early), the panoramic views will be etched in your memory forever. Don't attempt to do this hike on your own because there have been instances of walkers getting lost and injured along the way. Arrange this hike with Polynesia Island Tours (count on 14,500 CFP). Wear suitable walking shoes and carry plenty of drinking water with you.

Four-Wheel-Drive Trips

A couple of operators organise island tours aboard open 4WDs. **Tupuna Mountain Safari** (☎ 67 75 06; trips 6600 CFP) and **Vavau Adventures** (☎ 60 38 30, 72 01 21; trips 6600 CFP) run half-day trips that visit American WWII sites along with locally important (and hard-to-find) archaeological areas and a few stops at lookouts. Guides are informative, providing interesting titbits on the island's flora and fauna. These tours are good value if you don't want to rent a car. Free pick-ups.

Parasailing

Picture yourself, comfortably seated, gracefully drifting at 100m above the multihued lagoon at Matira, feeling the caress of the trade winds on your face… Parasailing in Bora Bora is an unforgettable experience, and you don't even get wet! **Bora Bora Parasail** (☎ 70 56 62, 78 27 10; parasail@mail.pf), based at the Novotel Bora Bora Beach Resort, is a reputable outfit that offers 15-minute trips starting from 25,000 CFP for two (18,000 CFP for one). If you want to get high (literally), you can take the 300m-high trip. Free pick-ups.

Helicopter Tours

Take your beloved on a helicopter tour (preferably on a clear day), which offers pupil-dilating views of the lagoon and the tortured landscape of the main island. It's darn expensive, but (s)he'll never forget the thrill – neither will you – and it's worth every penny. Contact **Polynesia Helicopter** (☎ 67 62 59, 72 70 13; www.polynesia-helicopter .com; ☼ 7.30am-12.30pm & 1.30-4.30pm Mon-Thu, 7.30am-noon & 1.30-4pm Fri) in Vaitape. The 15-minute flight costs 18,000 CFP per person. For the full monty, you can book the 30-minute flight that takes in Bora Bora and Tupai (29,000 CFP). There are commentaries in English.

BORA BORA FOR CHILDREN

Though Bora Bora is a destination of choice for couples and honeymooners, there are plenty of things to keep the young whippersnappers entertained if you travel with your family. They can approach rays, inoffensive blacktip sharks and colourful fish in the lagoon. Matira Beach is also calm and fairly shallow in most places, which means it's quite safe for even young swimmers. Undersea walks (opposite) and a semisubmersible excursion (opposite) are also guaranteed to please the kids. And what about an introductory dive (provided they're over eight)?

SLEEPING

Glossy brochures and promotional literature focus on Bora Bora's ultraswish resorts, which are as luxurious and as expensive as the hype leads you to believe. Pure honeymoon, marriage and proposal territory (though not necessarily in that order). That said, there's a smattering of affordable *pensions* that have sprung up over the last two decades (and are still largely ignored by most first-time visitors).

Although places to stay can be found all around the island, as well as on the *motu,* the majority are concentrated along the southern coast. If you're travelling solo and looking to meet others, try a place near Matira Point. For more seclusion, head to the *motu.*

All the top-end and midrange places accept credit cards, but many of the budget places do not. Prices cited here include taxes.

West Coast

The following is the only quality option on the west coast. It lies approximately halfway between Vaitape and Matira Beach.

Rohotu Fare Lodge (☎ 70 77 99; www.rohotufare lodge.com; bungalows 19,000 CFP; ▣) A location scout's dream, this 'lodge' features three local-style, fully equipped bungalows cocooned in exotic gardens on the mountainside overlooking Povai Bay. You'll go giddy over the ever-so-slightly OTT interior, with a number of risqué statues in the bathrooms and kooky carvings. The two lagoon-view bungalows are the best, with stunning views over the bay. Perks include free transfers to Vaitape quay, free laundry service and free bikes. No beach nearby, but Matira Point is an easy bike ride away, or you can arrange transfer with Nir, your Israeli host, who speaks excellent English. If you don't fancy cooking, there's a number of restaurants nearby. Note: though it's only a hop and a skip from the coastal road, the access road is steep. Credit cards are accepted.

Matira Point & Around

Much of the island's accommodation is clustered around Matira Point, at the southern toe of Bora Bora. This area also features the island's best beach, as well as dive operators and tour companies.

BUDGET

They may lack the luxury of the top hotels, but there is a handful of little *pensions* around Matira Point that lay claim to the best sweep of beach on the main island. Many of the following places have cold water only; unusually for budget places, they all accept credit cards (except Pension Maeva).

Pension Maeva – Chez Rosine Masson (☎ 67 72 04; dm/d without bathroom 3700/7400 CFP) This ramshackle *pension* is a real find if you're working to a tight budget. Sure, the house creaks, the walls are paper thin and the mattresses sag, but the lagoonside setting is a delight. There are two rooms downstairs for one or two people, and three upstairs. A dorm-style room with three single beds is pleasant but obviously doesn't offer much privacy (there's no door and the walls don't make it to the ceilings). There's a shared lounge, kitchen and two bathrooms (one with hot water). There's an extra 400 CFP charge for one-night stays.

Chez Nono (☎ 67 71 38; nono.leverd@mail.pf; s/d without bathroom 6500/7500 CFP, bungalows 10,000-13,000 CFP) If you can secure one of the two round-shaped bungalows right on the beach, you'll be in seventh heaven. But if you end up in one of the six rooms – hot, overpriced and altogether claustrophobic – chances are you'll be disappointed. There are also two small bungalows, which are less attractive than the bigger ones, though still adequate. There's a communal kitchen, though on our visit its cleanliness was lacking. All told, it's all about location.

Chez Robert & Tina (☎ 67 72 92; pensionrobertettina@ mail.pf; d 8000-9200 CFP) Right on the point, this is surely one of the most divinely situated *pensions* in Bora Bora, especially if you score an upstairs room with a balcony. On a clear day, the views of the azure lagoon will subdue the most tormented of souls – guaranteed. Rooms are in three functional, fan-cooled homes, all with shared kitchen. A few rooms have private facilities. There's no direct beach access but Matira Beach is just a coconut's throw away. Don't expect a whole lotta love when checking in, but at these prices and in such a fabulous spot, nobody's complaining.

MIDRANGE

As you saunter into the midrange category, you can safely expect private bathrooms with hot water. Credit cards are accepted at all midrange places.

Village Temanuata (☎ 67 75 61; www.temanuata .com; bungalows from 16,000 CFP) On an island where affordable-but-beautiful hotels are a rarity, this midrange venture ideally positioned on Matira Point is a no-brainer. The 15 bungalows (including 'Temanuata Iti', which consists of five units that are on the mountainside, about one kilometre to the west) are well arranged but are tightly packed together on a grassy property overlooking a narrow stretch of beach. Only two units have full lagoon views.

Novotel Bora Bora Beach Resort (☎ 60 59 50; www .novotel.com; r from 19,000 CFP; ✷ ▣ ▣) If you're not desperate to stay in earshot of the sea, then this typical midrange hotel with no surprises up its sleeves represents perhaps the best value anywhere in the Matira area, especially if you can get a promotional deal (it shouldn't be a problem when it's slack). The reception, restaurants and pool are right by the beach; cross the coastal road and you'll find 70 rooms in a clutch of two-storey Polynesian-style blocks. They're scattered in a garden replete with colourful trees and flower blossom. Alas, no lagoon views.

Club Med (☎ 60 46 04; www.clubmed.com, bboccrec01@ clubmed.com; all-inclusive package per person from 20,000 CFP; ✷ ▣) Although Club Med caters mainly to honeymooning Americans on package tours, individuals are welcome if there's space available (no minimum stay). Sure, it doesn't have the all-out luxurious finesse of Bora's ritziest resorts, but when you factor in the setting and free perks – a fine stretch of private beach, the spacious bungalows, the themed buffet meals, all the booze you can drink, evening shows, *motu* excursions and snorkelling trips – this is actually a good deal.

Le Maitai Polynesia (☎ 60 30 00; www.hotelmaitai .com; r/bungalows from 20,000/30,000 CFP; ✷ ▣) While not as exclusive or as glam as its competitors, this sprawling resort is brilliant value, especially if you can score promotional rates. The over-water bungalows feature Polynesian designs but lack privacy (the coastal road passes just behind). Rooms across the road from the beach, in the hills amid lush jungle foliage, are impersonal but spotless.

TOP END

Hotel Matira (☎ 67 70 51, 60 58 40; www.hotel-matira .com; bungalows 22,000-37,000 CFP) Solid value, but there are a few (minor) drawbacks; the property is screened from the coastal road by an incongruous concrete wall and only the dearer bungalows have direct lagoon views. The bungalows themselves are dotted around manicured lawns and are comfortable and commodious, with large bedrooms, dark-wood furniture and the essential sun deck. And the beachfront setting is superb. Half board (7700 CFP per person) is available at nearby Fare Manuia (p162).

Sofitel Bora Bora Marara Beach Resort (☎ 60 55 00; www.sofitel.com; bungalows from 35,000 CFP; ✷ ▣ ✷) If only we could all look so good after a facelift. Still sexy in its mid-30s (the recent refurb certainly helped), this matriarch of the Bora Bora luxury hotel dynasty (it was originally built by filmmaker Dino De Laurentiis in 1977 to house Mia Farrow and the crew while shooting *Hurricane*) offers a wide range of facilities, including a pool, a small spa and a renowned Japanese restaurant. The bungalows come in a large range of categories, including beach units, garden units, over-water bungalows and the odd 'half over-water, half on the beach' bungalow. The catch? The whole complex is sandwiched between the coastal road and the lagoon, which doesn't exactly make it ideal for peace or privacy.

Intercontinental Bora Bora Le Moana Resort (☎ 60 49 00; www.borabora.interconti.com; bungalows from 70,000 CFP; ✷ ▣ ✷) No, you're not hallucinating, the location is real. The Moana Beach spreads along the eastern side of Matira Point, a glorious stretch of beach is right out front, the lagoon is divine and there's sensational snorkelling offshore. The over-water bungalows are in tip-top condition and come equipped with the mandatory glass window in the floor. The outdoor areas are tropical jungles, perfect for wandering. And best of all, though you're in an exclusive resort you don't feel cut off from the island. A perfect balance between luxury, seclusion and convenience. Some travellers have found the service a bit lackadaisical, though.

East Coast

The east coast is less built-up than the rest of the island.

Pension Anau – Chez Teipo (☎ 67 78 17; teipobora@ mail.pf; bungalow s/d 7200/10,500 CFP) The location sucks (the lagoon is muddy, there's no beach and it's a tad isolated) but the four bungalows are fully self-contained and wrapped in tropical foliage. Other precious perks include a fresh baguette every morning, tea/coffee facilities, big bathrooms with hot water, a nice decked area where you can work your suntan and free transfers from the Vaitape quay. Oh, and free bikes seriously increase your mobility. Overall, a fairly good deal. Credit cards are accepted.

The Motu

Nothing says romance like staying on an idyllic *motu* with someone you love. Here you can recreate the famous *From Here to Eternity* kiss without putting on a show for a dozen gawkers, with Bora Bora as a backdrop.

our pick **Blue Heaven Island** (☎ 72 42 11; www .blueheavenisland.com; bungalows 24,000 CFP) Simple hedonists will be hard-pressed to find a mellower spot to maroon themselves for a languid holiday. On (private) Motu Paahi, five wood-and-palm bungalows are dotted around a huge coconut grove. They're simple, clean and fully equipped. It's also eco-friendly: there's a solar-powered energy system, part of the food is grown organically and green waste is composted. Snorkel just offshore amid myriads of Technicolour fish, walk on the reef on the ocean side, glide on the lagoon in a kayak, or just chill out on your terrace with a cold Hinano in hand. And leave rejuvenated. Paradise found? You be the judge.

BORA BORA

Meals are optional (half board is about 8000 CFP per person), good English is spoken and payment is by cash only.

Sofitel Motu (☎ 60 56 00; www.sofitel.com; bungalows from 45,000 CFP; ✖ 🖳) This Sofitel strikes a good balance between luxury, seclusion, privacy (there are only 31 units) and convenience – on tiny Motu Piti Uu Uta, it's just five glorious minutes by boat from the main island, so you're not too far from the action (and you can use the facilities of the Sofitel Marara). The only dilemma: a well-appointed over-water bungalow or an elegant unit positioned on a greenery-shrouded hillside, with heavenly views of the lagoon? Due to its position, it gets plenty of sunshine, even late afternoon.

Bora Bora Pearl Beach Resort (☎ 60 52 00; www.pearlresorts.com; bungalows from 60,000 CFP; ✖ 🖳 🔊) A top-drawer hotel, but without the stiff upper lips. Of all Bora Bora's top-end options, the Pearl has the strongest Polynesian feel. The 80 units are all built from bamboo, thatch and wood and blend perfectly into the landscaped property. The over-water bungalows are lovely, but the garden suites, which come complete with their own swimming-pool, and the 10 beach suites, equipped with an outdoor Jacuzzi, will really win your heart over. Other highlights include the dazzling infinity pool and the tropical spa, where only Polynesian treatments are utilised. One grumble: the coral garden that spreads out near the over-water bungalows is manmade, which means that blocks of coral were extracted from their natural setting.

Bora Bora Nui Resort & Spa (☎ 60 33 00; www.boraboranui.com; bungalows from 70,000 CFP; ✖ 🖳 🔊) A splendid resort with suitably sky-high rates, the award-winning Bora Bora Nui Resort extends along a ravishing stretch of porcelain sand and boasts 120 glorious units, including over-water bungalows and lovely hillside villas, as well as top-notch amenities, including the obligatory glass-floor viewing panels in the over-water bungalows, infinity pool and a gourmet restaurant. Nestled in a grove overlooking the resort, the spa will make you go 'aah'. One quibble, though: there's no direct view of Bora Bora from this side of the *motu*, which is a bit frustrating.

Le Méridien Bora Bora (☎ 60 51 51; www.borabora.lemeridien.com; bungalows from 70,000 CFP; ✖ 🖳 🔊) Le Méridien is one of the best cures for winter blues – and the views of Mt Otemanu and the lagoon from your private terrace won't let you forget it. The vast glass floors in the over-water bungalows are mesmerising, the boat-shaped bar is fabulous and the infinity-edge pool is adorable. Le Méridien is strongly involved in sea-turtle protection work (it's not a gimmick; check out www.boraboraturtles.com), so guests have the added bonus of watching the rehabilitating turtles (and you can also 'adopt' a turtle). Though artificial, the beach has chalk-white sand and the water is so clear you can see fish darting about your feet. With 99 units, including 82 over-water bungalows, Le Méridien is certainly not a hideaway but it's in harmony with its surroundings.

Saint Régis Resort (☎ 60 78 88; www.stregis.com/borabora; bungalows from 90,000 CFP; ✖ 🖳 🔊) The Saint Régis is a bubble of exclusivity that will leave you speechless and never wanting to leave the premises. This is a romantic resort, extremely quiet and popular with couples. The 90 over-water and beach 'villas' (for these are not mere rooms at 145 sq metres for a standard!) have a gorgeous feel, with the use of lots of wood, quality furnishings and elegant textiles. You can also book in for a beauty treatment in the serene Miri Miri spa. The two restaurants are of a very high standard.

Four Seasons Resort Bora Bora (☎ 60 31 30; www.fourseasons.com/borabora; bungalows from 100,000 CFP; ✖ 🖳 🔊) Opened in 2008, the Four Seasons raised the bar again in the struggle for ultimate luxury on Bora Bora. The stadium-sized over-water bungalows are some of the most impressive in French Polynesia – each with its own sizeable pool on an enclosed deck overlooking the sea, with access to the lagoon down a staircase. The bedrooms and bathrooms are massive and both masterpieces of understatement despite including luxuries such as works of art adorning the walls, teak furnishings, high-quality linen and king-size beds. The international clientele is made up mainly of honeymooners and couples who spend the day by the pool and being treated at the spa, but it's also welcoming to families.

our pick Intercontinental Resort & Thalasso Spa Bora Bora (☎ 60 76 00; www.boraboraspa.interconti.com; bungalows from 100,000 CFP; ✖ 🖳 🔊) Phenomenal. Seen from above, the layout of the 80 over-water bungalows resembles two giant crab claws. Inside, it's no less impressive, with a Starck-inspired decor; think polished wood and chrome rather than exuberant Polynesian touches. Two highlights: the spa, possibly the most attractive on the island, and the seawater air-conditioning system, which is the pride of the hotel, and justifiably so – it saves 90% of the electricity consumed by a conventional cooling system of similar capacity. One weak point? Snorkelling is just average (the sea floor is sandy). Free shuttles to the Intercontinental Bora Bora Le Moana Resort.

EATING

There's a wide choice of restaurants on Bora Bora, from European gourmet dining to *roulottes* (food vans) and *snacks*. The largest concentration of eating places is between Vaitape and Matira Point. Most top-end hotels have an inhouse restaurant that's also open to nonguests. Other than the *snacks,* nearly all the independent restaurants, as well as some of the resort restaurants, offer free transport to and from your hotel (call ahead) and accept credit cards.

All the luxury hotels have dance performances with buffet dinners several times a week, costing around 7500 CFP to 9500 CFP.

Most restaurants firmly shut their doors at 9pm, so don't wait until late or you may go hungry.

West Coast

There are a few good places for breakfast, a snack or a cheap meal in Vaitape. There's a string of stalls along the main road that sell sandwiches, fruits and cold drinks. In the evening several *roulottes* take up position along the main road and serve simple dishes (1200 CFP to 1500 CFP). For self-caterers, there are several well-stocked supermarkets in town.

Aloe Cafe (☎ 67 78 88; mains 1000-2000 CFP; ⏰ breakfast & lunch Mon-Sat) A busy place right in the centre of Vaitape. Pastries are the reason to come, with a tempting choice of homemade treats such as coconut pies and chocolate croissants. It's also a good place for a light meal at lunchtime. Good breakfasts too (including one featuring pancakes, bacon and eggs).

Bloody Mary's (☎ 67 72 86; mains 1000-2700 CFP; ⏰ lunch & dinner Mon-Sat) Bloody Mary's isn't just a restaurant, it's an experience, especially at dinner. You walk on sand floors, sit on coconut stools under a thatched roof and are surrounded by exotic plants. The food impresses, too; you choose your meal from an extensive display at the entrance, with a presentation in English. Fish lovers will get a buzz here, with a tantalising array of lagoon fish and pelagics,

but dedicated carnivores are also well catered for, with meat cooked the American-barbecue way. A bit touristy, but it's a concept that has been cult since 1979, and it's a favourite with celebrities, so go with the flow.

Le St James (☎ 67 64 62; www.stjamesborabora.com; mains 1000-3600 CFP; ⏰ lunch & dinner Mon-Sat) Don't be deterred by the odd location – the place is hidden in the back of a small shopping centre in Vaitape – for once inside, you'll find French specialities with a bow to local ingredients, such as *blanc de volaille aux cèpes et riz à l'ananas* (poultry with cep mushrooms and rice with pineapple). Let the sea breeze whip through your hair while dining alfresco on the deck above the lagoon. Lunch is a tamer (and less expensive) affair, with salads, burgers and grilled fish.

Bora Kaina Hut (☎ 67 54 06; mains 1400-2600 CFP; ⏰ lunch & dinner Wed-Mon) The Kaina Hut ticks all the boxes for an idyllic island experience. Romantic interior with candlelit tables, wooden furniture and sand floor. Check. Well-presented food befitting the setting. Check. Attentive service and soothing soundtrack. Check. The oysters, mussels, lagoon fish or raw fish duo and tempura prawns sing of the sea, but don't miss the desserts (profiteroles with coconut and chocolate? More please).

Bamboo House (☎ 74 16 73; mains 1700-2000 CFP; ⏰ lunch & dinner Tue-Sat) Is it a lounge-bar? A restaurant? A disco? It doesn't matter – take a seat and sample honestly prepared dishes, or just grab a glass of something and nibble on tapas in exotic surrounds. No credit cards are accepted.

our pick **Sunset Boulevard** (☎ 67 57 67; mains 1700-3000 CFP; ⏰ dinner Tue-Sun) Easily the snazziest spot on Bora Bora at the time of writing. We're talking of two open-air, permanently moored boats as well as two decks in a tropical garden right by the lagoon. The emphasis is on local dishes with a contemporary twist; a few zesty treasures include 'BBQ King' (skewered fish and beef) and 'Humeur du Chef' (an assortment of sushi and sashimi).

Bora Bora Yacht Club (☎ 67 77 77; mains 1700-3000 CFP; ⏰ lunch & dinner) The Yacht Club delivers all the stereotypes expected for its location and name: a terrace overlooking the lagoon and fairly expensive fare in elegant (but not snooty) surrounds. The menu features all the usual suspects, with an emphasis on fish dishes. North of Vaitape.

BORA BORA

ourpick **Villa Mahana** (☎ 67 50 63; www.villa mahana.com; set menu €90-125; 🕑 dinner, closed Feb) Yes, the set menu has the potential to flag a red alert to Amex, but it's the top-end darling of Bora Bora. A true alchemist, the French chef Damien Rinaldi has got the magic formula right, fusing Mediterranean with Polynesian to create stunning cuisine. Will it be beef fillet with Provence herbs or pumpkin soup with vanilla and coconut milk? The choice is a challenge. Exquisite execution extends to the small dessert selection: the *fondant au chocolat* (chocolate cake) provides a flavour explosion. It's housed in a stylish villa reminiscent of Provence, with lots of ochre and yellow tones. Perfect for a romantic *tête à tête*, but be sure to book well in advance – there are only seven tables. No sign.

Matira Point & Around

The area around Matira Point offers the island's most varied eating options. Many of the fancy resorts have excellent restaurants, often offering very reasonably priced lunch menus.

Snack Matira (☎ 67 77 32; dishes 500-2000 CFP; 🕑 lunch Tue-Sun) This unfussy little eatery could hardly be better situated: it's right on the beach at Matira (think terrific lagoon views). The menu concentrates on simply prepared dishes as well as burgers and omelettes. Eat alfresco or grab your victuals and find your picnic spot on the beach.

Ben's (☎ 67 74 54; mains 600-1600 CFP; 🕑 lunch & dinner) Greasy burgers, inoffensive sandwiches, acceptable steaks, average quesadillas and bearable garlic bread: no wonder this well-positioned venture gets a loyal following of unfussy, penny-counting travellers.

Tama'a Maitai (☎ 60 30 00; mains 1000-2600 CFP; 🕑 lunch & dinner) A more mellow setting you'd be hard pressed to find. Part of Le Maitai Polynesia, Tama'a Maitai overlooks the beach and catches lots of breeze. All the usual suspects are featured on the menu including salads, pizza, fish and meat dishes, as well as a few vegetarian options.

Snack-Restaurant Moi Here (☎ 67 56 46; mains 1100-2600 CFP; 🕑 7am-8pm) It's the location that's the pull here, rather than the food. Burgers, salads, beef sirloin and fish dishes won't knock your socks off but you're right on the beach, with dizzying views of the turquoise lagoon.

Fare Manuia (☎ 67 68 08; mains 1200-3000 CFP; 🕑 breakfast, lunch & dinner) The hardest thing about eating at this local favourite is deciding between the excellent meat or fish dishes, crunchy salads, filling and delicious pasta and mouth-watering pizzas. Note to management: please dump those neon lights.

La Bounty (☎ 67 70 43; mains 1300-3000 CFP; 🕑 lunch & dinner) This buzzy restaurant in an open-air thatched-roof building is a good place to soak up the tropical climes and indulge in fine dining without breaking the bank. The sand-floor dining room is decorated with dense foliage, bamboo walls and wooden furniture. Alas, no lagoon views to speak of. The menu is eclectic and inventive – salads and *spaghetti au thon frais* (spaghetti with fresh tuna) sit happily alongside flavoursome thin-crust pizzas and even fondue.

Le Flamboyant (☎ 67 61 99; mains 1400-2900 CFP; 🕑 lunch Mon-Tue & Thu-Sat, dinner Thu-Tue) Le Flamboyant is a fine French-Polynesian eatery that's short on pretension and big on taste, especially at dinner (light meals only at lunchtime). The specialities on offer are always a treat, but the winner is the *uru* (breadfruit) gnocchi – memorable. How about dessert? The crumble with tropical fruits and taro ice cream has plenty of zing. Opt for the set menu – at 4000 CFP, it's a bargain.

ourpick **Le Matira Beach Restaurant** (☎ 67 53 79; mains 1500-4000 CFP; 🕑 lunch & dinner Fri-Wed) In this 'gourmet bistro', there are enough ambitiously poetic names to tempt the gourmand in you, such as *transparence de foie gras poêlé* (pan-fried foie gras). Lunch has a casual atmosphere, but dinner is a romantic affair. Another clincher is the agreeable terrace overlooking the beach. Pastry chef Nicolas forces tough choices upon you. Will it be his classic *crumble glacé* (iced crumble) or his intense *moelleux de banane au coeur coulant de chocolat noir* (banana cake with melted dark choc)? Life is brief; get both.

Sofitel Bora Bora Marara Beach Resort (p159) has several dining options, including the **Waka Bar** (☎ 60 55 00; mains 2000-3000 CFP; 🕑 Thu-Mon dinner), which serves excellent Japanese specialities.

Self-caterers can stock up the kitchenette at **Tiare Market** (🕑 6.30am-1.30pm & 3-7pm Mon-Sat, 6.30am-1pm & 3-6.30pm Sun), a local supermarket across from the Novotel Bora Bora. It's well stocked with all the necessities – from wine and fresh bread to sunscreen and toothpaste.

The Motu

Free shuttles, which generally operate until midnight, allow you to enjoy the restaurants at the luxury hotels on the *motu* around Bora Bora. These offer evening performances with dinner buffets several times a week. Reservations are advisable, and you may not be allowed over if the hotel is fully booked.

Recommending restaurants in these hotels is quite hard for it all depends on the culinary skills of the current chef. By popular opinion, the restaurants at Saint Régis Resort, Le Méridien Bora Bora and Intercontinental Resort & Thalasso Spa Bora Bora offered the best gourmet fare at the time of research. Anyway, you can't really go wrong at these places – their atmosphere is so wonderfully mellow and their setting so romantic that you're guaranteed to have a memorable lunch or evening out.

Dinner is usually a formal affair (no shorts and no thongs) with à la carte offerings, while lunch is more casual, with light snacks, salads and simple dishes. At dinner, expect to pay anything between 2400 CFP and 3000 CFP for a fish dish.

DRINKING

Frankly said, the bar scene is tame on Bora Bora. However, there are a few cool spots where you can cut loose over some sunset cocktails in pleasant surrounds, including Bamboo House (p161), Bloody Mary's (p161), the in-house bar at Sofitel Bora Bora Marara Beach Resort (p159), the Sunset Boulevard (p161) and Le St James (p161). They attract locals, expats and tourists alike for their funky ambience and relaxed vibe. There's sometimes live music at Bamboo House.

If it's just the setting you want to absorb, check out the bars in the big hotels. It will cost you from 1000 CFP for a cocktail, and some even have happy hours. The *motu* hotels offer free shuttle services, usually until about midnight.

ENTERTAINMENT

If there's one thing you absolutely have to check out while you're on Bora Bora it's a traditional dance show held in one of the luxury hotels. You can usually get in for the price of a drink at the bar, or for between 6500 CFP and 9000 CFP you can also feast on a buffet

---

WHEN THE ISLAND GOES WILD

Who said Bora Bora was tame? Locals recommend visiting in July, when the island goes wild for the Heiva. This festival takes place every year in July in Vaitape, on a big stage set up near the quay. It features a program of parades, dance, singing and sports contests, as well as beauty pageants and floral floats. It's said to be the best Heiva after the one held in Pape'ete (p48), and it's so festive that it's worth making your trip coincide with it.

The arrival of the Hawaiki Nui canoe race (p45) early November on Matira Beach is another indescribably cheerful event, with dozens of colourful *pirogues* (outrigger canoes) congregating on the beach.

---

dinner. There are performances two or three times a week; ask at the reception desks about the schedule and entry policy.

Other than that, nightlife is as restrained as it is on the other islands of French Polynesia. At the time of writing, the most 'happening' place was **Club Med** (☎ 60 46 04; admission 1500 CFP), which is open to nonguests at weekends for its 'Beach Party' and other themed evenings.

SHOPPING

There's no shortage of shops and boutiques on Bora Bora.

Black Pearls

Pearls, pearls, pearls. Black-pearl jewellery is sold in many places around Bora Bora, at prices that are often more expensive than in Tahiti. Most big names in the industry have opened a retail shop on Bora Bora. Given the fierce competition, sellers tend to be pushy and, of course, claim to be 'committed to finding you the highest quality pearls at the best possible prices'. An expert met in Tahiti suggested, 'If you're serious about buying a pearl, take your time to shop around and ignore any attempt at influencing you, and avoid buying pearls at the boutiques in the big hotels, as they're more expensive'.

A few places to check out (they're open daily from 9am to 5pm; free pick-ups can be arranged):

Matira Pearls (☎ 67 79 14; www.matirapearls.com) Sells mounted and loose pearls starting at 10,000 CFP and offers some creative pieces. It's run by two Americans so you won't have to worry about the language barrier.

OPEC (Office Polynésien d'Expertise et de Commercialisation; ☎ 67 61 62; www.opec-borabora.com) A longstanding boutique on the island. Nice designs.

Tahiti Pearl Market (☎ 60 38 60; www.tahitipearl market.com) Offers lots of choice, and competitive prices.

Souvenirs, Art & Crafts

Apart from pearls, shopping on Bora Bora tends to mean hopping between the many galleries and boutiques scattered around the island, or perhaps wrapping yourself in various brightly coloured *pareu* (sarongs). This is by no means an exhaustive list of the galleries and craft shops on Bora Bora; plenty of others can be found along the coastal road. They're open daily.

Atelier Despert (☎ 60 48 15; www.despert.com) Even if you can't afford to purchase the original paintings, it's worth stopping by this lovely little studio to chat with the charming artist and check out his latest work. Alain Despert only does originals (no prints), and his work has gained worldwide acclaim for its bold and bright patterns.

Tamanu Galerie d'Art (☎ 67 66 89) Loads of Polynesian art, along with the usual T-shirts, curios and pearls, are sold at this pretty special gallery just next to the post office in Vaitape.

Boutique Gauguin (☎ 67 76 67) This boutique sells some of the most artistic-looking *pareu* on the island and has a varied collection of clothes, crafts and sculptures.

Galerie Alain et Linda (☎ 67 70 32; www.borabora -art.com) About halfway between Vaitape and Matira Point, this gallery has a little bit of everything – including a mix of art, books, etchings and pottery.

In the tourist office by the Vaitape quay, Centre Artisanal de Bora Bora has lots of stalls selling *pareu*, basketwork and other crafts produced by island women.

Tattooists

For traditionally designed tattoos head to **Marama Tattoo** (☎ 72 03 75) or **Tattoo Fati** (☎ 67 50 84), both in Matira Point. Popular, sterile and reliable.

GETTING THERE & AWAY

Bora Bora is situated 270km northwest of Tahiti and can be reached by air or boat from there.

Air

Air Tahiti (☎ 67 70 35; Vaitape; ☼ 7.30-11.30am & 1.30-4.30pm Mon-Fri, 8-11am Sat) flies between Bora Bora and Tahiti (14,500 CFP, 45 minutes, up to 10 flights daily), Huahine (7000 CFP, 20 minutes, one to three flights daily), Mo'orea (18,400 CFP, one hour, one to three flights daily) and Ra'iatea (6300 CFP, 15 minutes, one to two flights daily). Air Tahiti also has direct flights from Bora Bora to the Tuamotus, with a very handy flight to Rangiroa (23,400 CFP, 1¼ hours, six flights weekly) and onward connections to other atolls, including Tikehau, Fakarava and Manihi.

Boat

Two cargo ships, the **Hawaiki Nui** (☎ in Papeete 54 99 54; contact@stim.pf) and the **Vaeanu** (☎ in Papeete 41 25 35), make two trips a week between Pape'ete and Bora Bora (via Huahine, Ra'iatea and Taha'a), leaving Pape'ete on Tuesday and Thursday around 4pm; they leave Bora Bora on Wednesday and Friday. It costs 1800 CFP on the deck or 5300 CFP in a cabin. Note that it's pretty difficult for tourists to get passage aboard the *Vaeanu* as it's usually booked out by locals. Both dock at the Farepiti quay, 3km north of Vaitape. See p260 for more information.

The **Maupiti Express 2** (☎ 67 66 69; www.maupiti express.com; Vaitape) runs between Bora Bora and Maupiti on Tuesday, Thursday and Saturday (3000/4000 CFP one way/return, 1¾ hours), departing the Vaitape quay for Maupiti at 8.30am; the return trip leaves Maupiti at 4pm on the same day, which makes it quite possible to visit Maupiti as a day trip from Bora Bora. The boat also serves Ra'iatea/Taha'a on Monday, Wednesday, Friday and Sunday (3000/4000 CFP one way/return, 1½ hours), departing for Ra'iatea and Taha'a at 7am on Monday, Wednesday and Friday and at 3pm on Sunday. Tickets can be bought on board or at the office on the Vaitape quay.

GETTING AROUND
To/From the Airport

Arriving on Bora Bora is dramatic. The airport is on Motu Mute, at the northern edge of the lagoon; transfers are offered to and from the Vaitape quay on two large catamaran ferries (included in the cost of your ticket). This makes for a wonderful free tour of the western side of the island! There's a regular bus from the quay to the hotels at Matira Point (500 CFP).

When leaving by air, you need to be at the quay at least 1¼ hours before the flight. The top hotels transfer their visitors directly to and from the airport; all other passengers are picked up at the quay by the catamaran ferries (the cost of this is included in the ticket).

Boat

Renting a boat is a heavenly way to explore the lagoon, and if you can get a few of you together, this is a cheaper option than the organised tours available. See p156 for more information.

Car & Bicycle

Cars and bikes can be rented for periods of four, eight and 24 hours. Cars cost from 12,000 CFP per 24 hours with unlimited mileage. Bikes cost 2000 CFP per 24 hours. The following can deliver directly to your hotel.

Bora Bora Rent a Car – Avis (☎ 67 70 03; www.avis-tahiti.com; ☉ 7.30am-5.30pm) Has its main office in the centre of Vaitape, as well as desks in several of the main hotels. Bike and car hire.

Fare Piti Rent-a-Car (☎ 67 65 28; ☉ 8am-noon & 1-6pm) In Vaitape and in Le Maitai Polynesia. Bike and car hire.

Many of the larger hotels have bikes available for guests. **Boutique Fareani** (Matira Point; ☉ Mon-Sat) also rents bikes for 1500 CFP per day.

There's a Total petrol station north of Vaitape, just before Topdive Bora Bora.

Maupiti

Close your eyes. And just imagine. You land on a strip of coral by the sea, you are garlanded at the traditional welcome with *tiare* by a smiling-eyed islander. There's a small, white-sand beach lapped by luxuriously warm waters, a shimmering lagoon with every hue from lapis lazuli to turquoise, white clouds billowing in a deep-blue sky, a perfect ring of islets girdled with sandbars, palm trees leaning over the shore and large coral gardens packed with rainbow-coloured species. Brochure material? No, just routine in Maupiti. Bora Bora's little sister, this impossibly scenic creation of basalt and coconut trees has all you need to throw your cares away.

Unlike its glamorous neighbour, Maupiti has managed to hold on to that slow-down-it's-the-South-Pacific feeling, and that's why it's gaining in popularity. There's only one road and virtually no cars, just bikes; there are no showy resorts, just a smattering of family-run *pensions*, which ensures your money goes straight into local pockets. In this *Bounty*-licious paradise, everything is small and personable, and that's the beauty of it.

Many visitors come here simply to relax, but if working your suntan ceases to do it for you, there are walks, lagoon excursions and snorkelling to keep you buzzing. And divers get spoiled too, with almost daily appearances of a corps de ballet of manta rays in the lagoon.

Try to visit both Bora Bora and Maupiti, because they perfectly complement each other. Thus, you'll get the full Polynesian picture – a subtle combination of glamour, sea-scented sensuality and barefoot tranquillity.

HIGHLIGHTS

- Exploring Maupiti's gin-clear lagoon while **snorkelling** (p169) with manta rays the size of a small car!
- Taking it real easy basking lizardlike on heavenly **Tereia Beach** (p168)
- Scaling up **Mt Teurafaatiu** (p169) and feasting your eyes on the 360-degree views of the translucent lagoon
- Reflecting on Maupiti's bizarre past while spotting well-preserved **petroglyphs** (p168)
- Finding your own paradise in a delightful guesthouse on a deserted islet (p170)

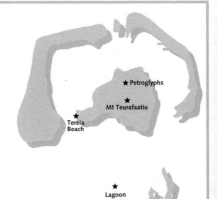

★ Petroglyphs

★ Mt Teurafaatiu

★ Tereia Beach

★ Lagoon

■ POPULATION: 1191   ■ AREA: 11 SQ KM

KNOW BEFORE YOU GO...

▪ Maupiti has no ATMs and credit cards are only accepted at a couple of *pensions*, so you'll need to bring enough cash to cover your entire bill, plus a little extra for surprise add-ons.

▪ Beware of tricky currents when snorkelling or kayaking near Onoiau Pass (where a few of the *pensions* are).

▪ The most enjoyable way to get around on the main island is by bicycle.

▪ Maupiti has no resorts; digs are in simple family guesthouses.

▪ Restaurants are also pretty much nonexistent, so unless you're the completely self-sufficient type, opt for *demi-pension* (half board) or *pension complète* (full board) at your guesthouse. It costs extra but the food is usually delicious and served family-style.

▪ Although you might be offered beverages throughout the day, don't expect these to be free, even if you're on a meal plan.

HISTORY

Dutch explorer Roggeveen is credited with the European 'discovery' of Maupiti in 1722, nearly 50 years before Wallis, Bougainville and Cook made their important landfalls on Tahiti. European missionaries were quick to follow, eventually succeeding in installing Protestantism as the major religion.

Bora Bora began to assert influence over Maupiti in the early 19th century; the power struggles continued throughout the century. French influence also reached the island during this period; missionaries and local chiefs continued to wield the most power until after WWII, when the French took over.

Maupiti has changed little over the last century; fruit crops grown on the *motu* (islets) are still major sources of income for the islanders. Copra production, heavily subsidised by the government, also remains important.

ORIENTATION & INFORMATION

From the air, Maupiti resembles a miniature Bora Bora – a *motu*-fringed aqua lagoon with a rocky, mountainous interior. A 10km road encircles the island. The main settlement is on the east coast. The primary shipping quay is on the southeastern corner of the island.

The high island mass is surrounded by a wide but shallow lagoon fringed with five *motu*, including Motu Tuanai, where the airport is located. There's only one pass, Onoiau, to the south.

To the north of the centre of the village the *mairie* (town hall), post office and Air Tahiti office are grouped together. There's no bank and no ATM, so bring a wad of cash.

THE MOTU

Maupiti's star attractions are its five idyllic *motu*, spits of sand and crushed coral dotted with swaying palms, and floating in the jade lagoon that surrounds the main island. Most travellers choose to stay on these fabulous islets, but the mainland *pensions* will happily organise day trips for around 3000 CFP per person if you're staying on the island. Besides acting as quiet retreats (perfect for sunbathing, swimming or simply reading a trashy novel), the *motu* also boast Maupiti's best beaches (though Tereia Beach, on the main island, is a very serious competitor).

Motu Paeao, at the northern end of the lagoon, is ideal for swimming and snorkelling.

There's an important melon-production plantation on **Motu Auira**. At low tide you can reach it from the mainland by wading across the lagoon – the water is warm and only waist high, but keep an eye out for rays.

Motu Tiapaa has beautiful, sandy, white beaches and good snorkelling on its ocean and lagoon sides. It's also the most developed *motu*, with several *pensions*, so it can seem crowded by Maupiti standards. If you have a kayak, however, you can paddle across to the completely isolated **Motu Pitihahei**, but be sure to steer way to the north of Onoiau Pass, which is very dangerous due to strong currents near the pass.

The airport and a few *pensions* are found on **Motu Tuanai**, another picture-friendly islet. However, the lagoon is shallow along this *motu*, which doesn't make it good for swimming.

THE MAIN ISLAND

The village spreads along the east coast and is dominated by a sharp ridge line running from

MAUPITI

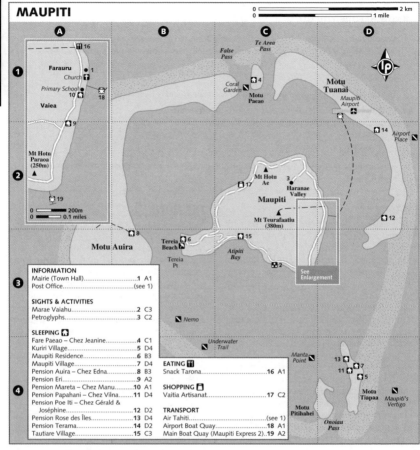

INFORMATION
Mairie (Town Hall).............................1 A1
Post Office.....................................(see 1)

SIGHTS & ACTIVITIES
Marae Vaiahu.................................2 C3
Petroglyphs....................................3 C2

SLEEPING
Fare Paeao – Chez Jeanine...............4 C1
Kuriri Village...................................5 D4
Maupiti Residence...........................6 B3
Maupiti Village................................7 D4
Pension Auira – Chez Edna...............8 B3
Pension Eri.....................................9 A2
Pension Mareta – Chez Manu..........10 A1
Pension Papahani – Chez Vilna........11 D4
Pension Poe Iti – Chez Gérald &
  Joséphine...................................12 D2
Pension Rose des Îles......................13 D4
Pension Terama..............................14 D2
Tautiare Village...............................15 C3

EATING
Snack Tarona..................................16 A1

SHOPPING
Vaitia Artisanat..............................17 C2

TRANSPORT
Air Tahiti....................................(see 1)
Airport Boat Quay...........................18 A1
Main Boat Quay (Maupiti Express 2)..19 A2

north to south. Neat houses, brightened with hibiscus, are strung along the road and they often have *uru* (breadfruit) trees shading the family tombs fronting many of them. Inland, the terrain climbs steeply up to the summit of Mt Teurafaatiu (380m).

The following tour starts in the village and proceeds around the island in an anticlockwise direction. It's a good idea to rent a bike as there's only one road and no traffic, plus the terrain is flat and distances are short (10km maximum for the complete loop around the island).

Petroglyphs
Maupiti has some interesting and easily viewed petroglyphs etched into boulders in a rocky riverbed. The biggest and most impressive is a turtle image on a flat boulder to the right of a placid spring. To reach the petroglyphs, head north out of the village and round the point before passing the basketball court near the church. You're now in the Haranae Valley; on the mountainside and just after a green house is a track heading inland. Follow it for 200m to a small pumping station, and then follow the rocky riverbed. After only 100m, on the left, you'll find the petroglyphs.

Tereia Beach
A more enchanting spot you'd be hard pressed to find. Fringed by a sparkling turquoise lagoon and backed by willowy palm trees, Tereia Beach is undisputedly the most beautiful spot

on the island. The lagoon is shallow, warm and crystal clear, and the bone-white beach is nearly all sand (no smashed coral or broken rock). There are no facilities or vendors here, just sand and sun. If you're with your sweetheart, come here at sunset; as the sunset sky deepens to orange, the spot becomes downright romantic.

From Tereia Beach it's easy to wade across the lagoon to Motu Auira during low tide.

Marae Vaiahu

History buffs will enjoy visiting Marae Vaiahu, Maupiti's most important *marae*, which features a large coastal site covered with coral slabs and a fish box. Made of four coral blocks set edgewise in the form of a rectangle, with a fifth serving as a lid, the box was used for ceremonial purposes to ensure successful fishing. Four fish kings are represented on the sides of the box. It's signposted, northwest of the main quay.

ACTIVITIES

For such a small island, there's quite a lot of options to keep you active on land and at sea.

Hiking

It's a fairly tough climb to reach **Mt Hotu Paraoa** (250m), the impressive rocky wall that looms above the village. On a clear day you can see all the way to Bora Bora. The trail begins near Pension Eri and is marked with painted arrows (although sometimes they can be a bit hard to find). There's one steep section where you'll need to use your hands to clamber up, and nearly the entire route is shaded. Count on one hour.

The ascent of **Mt Teurafaatiu** (380m) is even more vigorous, but the 360-degree panorama at the summit worth the effort. Ribbons of deep blue water flecked with turquoise and sapphire, islets girdled with brilliant scimitars of white sand, lagoons mottled with coral formations, and Bora Bora in the background… hallucinogenic. The track starts virtually opposite Snack Tarona and the climb is shaded for most of the way. The most difficult part is towards the end, with a climb up steep rock required to get to the ridge. Allow three hours for the return trip and be sure to bring plenty of drinking water.

It's best to go with a guide – contact your *pension* for securing one (about 3000 CFP).

ECO-SNORKELLING – THE 'UNDERWATER TRAIL'

The *sentier sous-marin* (underwater trail) set up in 2008 by **Maupiti Nautique** (☎ 67 83 80; www.maupiti-nautique.com) is an eco-friendly and informative approach to the lagoon. It consists of five buoys that were installed in an area to the south of the island. Each buoy is equipped with interpretative panels focusing on the lagoon ecosystem. You swim from one buoy to another under the guidance of the instructor, who'll be happy to answer your questions. It's a great chance to get really well acquainted with marine life. It costs 3000 CFP (snorkelling gear included) and lasts 1½ hours. Children over six are welcome.

Snorkelling, Kayaking & Lagoon Excursions

Maupiti's magnificent lagoon is gin-clear, bath-warm and filled with all manner of tropical marine life, from schools of butterflyfish and parrotfish to manta rays and banks of flame-coloured coral. The best **snorkelling** sites are the reefs stretching north of Onoiau Pass (but beware of the currents) and Motu Paeao. Most guesthouses have masks and snorkels you can borrow. The *pensions* also run lagoon tours that include stops for snorkelling. These trips cost between 3000 CFP and 5500 CFP, depending on their duration and whether a picnic is offered.

Sea kayaking is another popular activity of the DIY variety. Paddling around the quiet lagoon offers the chance to discover hidden coves, search for leopard and manta rays or just put down the oar, lie back and sunbathe. Most places to stay either rent or offer free sea kayaks for guests' use.

Maupiti Nautique (see below) also offers snorkelling trips to the manta rays' cleaning station.

Diving

At last, there's diving in Maupiti! There's one professional diving operator on the island, **Maupiti Nautique** (☎ 67 83 80; www.maupiti-nautique .com), which opened in 2008. And what diving: there aren't many places in the world where you can dive on a manta rays' cleaning station, where cleaner wrasses feed on parasites from the mantas' wings, in less than 6m of water.

'In principle, they're here every morning, but sightings can't be guaranteed,' advised the dive instructor. There are also outstanding dive sites outside the lagoon, but they aren't always accessible due to the strong currents and swell in the pass. See p69 for more information on diving on Maupiti.

Single dive trips or introductory dives cost 6000 CFP including gear and two-tank trips are 11,500 CFP. An open-water course costs 40,000 CFP. The dive-and-whale-watch combination is great value at 11,000 CFP. Cash only.

Whale & Dolphin Watching

Apparently, humpback whales find Maupiti attractive too. Every year during the austral winter, from mid-July to October, they frolic off Maupiti's barrier reef. Whale-watching trips are available through the local dive operator, **Maupiti Nautique** (☎ 67 83 80; www.maupiti -nautique.com). You may have the privilege of swimming right alongside these graceful giants, but don't stress them and follow the guide's instructions. Dolphins can be spotted all year round along the reef. A three-hour excursion costs 7000 CFP.

MAUPITI FOR CHILDREN

Bring the kids! Just focus on the outdoors: snorkelling and swimming (there are some really shallow waters, especially near Tereia Beach and Motu Tiapaa). The *sentier sousmarin* (p169) is accessible to children over six. Better yet, whale-watching trips are thrilling for all ages.

SLEEPING

Your biggest decision: staying on a *motu* or on the main island? For the full Robinson Crusoe experience, places on the *motu* are hard to beat. Be prepared to feel a bit captive, though, except if you're ready to paddle to the village or pay anything from 500 CFP to 1500 CFP for a transfer by boat. If island life is your top priority, stay on the main island. Better yet: combine the two options!

The Main Island

Guesthouses are all either right on the lagoon or very close to it, but only Maupiti Residence has a beach.

Pension Mareta – Chez Manu (☎ 67 82 32; chez manu@mail.pf; r per person without bathroom 3000 CFP) In this family-run venture in the centre of the village you won't pay very much and you won't get very much – a sort of win-win. The three rooms are threadbare and share a coldwater bathroom. Guests may use the cooking facilities for an extra 300 CFP or order a meal (about 2000 CFP). It might be noisy at weekends if a *bringue* (local party) is organised on the premises.

Pension Eri (☎ 67 81 29; r per person incl breakfast/ half board 3000/5000 CFP) Just a place to lay your head, with four smallish, no-frills rooms. A fan and a bed (alas, saggy mattress), and that's about it.

Tautiare Village (☎ 67 83 58; www.maupitiisland .com/tautiare/index.html; r per person incl breakfast/half board 6000/8500 CFP) An unfussy *pension* with an unpretentious appeal. Its dual attractions are its affordable rates and the spotlessness of the five adjoining rooms, equipped with big, hot-water bathrooms. They are set on grassy garden areas and face the lagoon, but don't get too excited: swimming is not *that* tempting here due to shallow (and sometimes murky) waters, but Tereia beach is just a 10-minute walk away.

Maupiti Residence (☎ 67 82 61; maupiti.residence@ mail.pf; bungalows 12,000-16,000 CFP; ⊠ 🖳) To all wannabe artists reading this: set your creative retreat here, because the location, right on Tereia Beach, is to die for. While hardly glitzy, the two villas (one more should have been built by the time you read this) contain enough room to accommodate a small troupe and exemplify functional simplicity with a living room, two bedrooms, a terrace that delivers full frontal lagoon views and a fully equipped kitchen. Perks include free bicycles and kayaks, hot water, DVD player, daily cleaning service, air-con (add 500 CFP), TV and washing machine, making this one of the best-value stays you'll have. You can order breakfast (1100 CFP) and have your lunch or dinner delivered to your bungalow. There's a 15% drop in price if you stay more than three nights. The secret's out, so book early. Credit cards are accepted.

The Motu

Places listed here offer plenty of remote and tropical tranquillity, but you'll need to arrange a trip to the mainland to visit a shop of any kind.

Pension Auira – Chez Edna (☎ /fax 67 80 26; Motu Auira; campsites per person 2000 CFP, bungalows with half board per person 7500-9000 CFP) This place has a split personality. Ramshackle and dusty are the words for the beach and garden bungalows; fabulous is the adjective that springs to mind when you see the location, right by a sandy beach lapped by topaz waters. Our verdict: a good bargain for those who have a tent, not so much so for those who bunk down in a bungalow.

Pension Rose des Îles (☎ 67 82 00, 70 50 70; Motu Tiapaa; campsites per person 2000 CFP, bungalows with half board per person 10,000-12,000 CFP) Run by a friendly French Polynesian couple, this *pension* offers two rustic bungalows made from woven palm fronds in a lovely location on the lagoon. They're not especially good value, given that mattresses are lumpy and bathrooms are shared, but the camping option is a good deal. The outdoor setting features small tables, hammocks and a profusion of plants and trees, as well as a few dogs that stick like leeches. Kayaks are available (it's an extra 500 CFP for campers).

Maupiti Village (☎ 67 80 08; Motu Tiapaa; dm/r/bungalows with full board per person 6000/7000/12,000 CFP) According to most travellers, the best part of staying here is the food, which is copious, varied and flavoursome, as well as the tip-top location on the ocean side of Motu Tiapaa. The charm ends there. Accommodation is clean but stark, with three particle-board rooms with a shared outside bathroom, a bare-bones six-bed dorm and two teensy cabins, all with flimsy mattresses. But if you can live with that, it's not a bad deal at theses prices, especially given that kayaks are free and you won't be inside much anyway.

Pension Terama (☎ 67 81 96, 71 03 33; http://maupiti .terama.over-blog.com; Motu Tuanai; r with half board per person 7000 CFP) An acceptable option if you want to base yourself on a *motu* without paying the hefty price tag. Run by an affable French-Tahitian couple, it exudes low-key vibes and features three basic rooms in the family home, with two communal bathrooms (one with bucket). There's also a very simple bungalow right on a little stretch of sand; lying on your bed you can see the glinting waters of the lagoon and the majestic silhouette of the main island. One drawback: the water's not deep enough for swimming, although free kayaks offer adequate compensation. Airport transfers are free.

Pension Poe Iti – Chez Gérald & Joséphine (☎ 74 58 76; maupitiexpress@mail.pf; Motu Tuanai; bungalows s/d 7500/8500 CFP; ☺) This desirable guesthouse

ticks all the right boxes, with a spiffing lagoon frontage, a small strip of beach, lofty views and four well-proportioned bungalows (with hot water) scattered in a well-tended property – not to mention green credentials (power is supplied by two windmills). Sunbathing is top-notch but swimming is not that enthralling, with very shallow waters; paddling to more idyllic swimming grounds expands your possibilities. When it comes to preparing Polynesian dishes for dinner, Joséphine, your gracious host, knows her stuff. Airport transfers, kayaks and snorkels are free.

Pension Papahani – Chez Vilna (☎ 60 15 35; pension papahani@hotmail.fr; Motu Tiapaa; bungalows with half board per person 9500-12,500 CFP) An atmosphere of dreamlike tranquillity characterises this well-run *pension* with a fab lagoon frontage. Your biggest quandary here: a bout of snorkelling (or kayaking) or a snooze on the white-sand beach under the swaying palms? The five bungalows blend perfectly into the tropical gardens. Try for one of the newer, slightly more expensive bungalows as the two units at the rear are a bit long in the tooth.

Kuriri Village (☎ 67 82 23, 74 54 54; www.maupiti -kuriri.com; Motu Tiapaa; bungalows with half board per person 12,500 CFP) Watch dolphins frolicking in the waves from a little wooden deck (with Bora Bora looming on the horizon), take a dip in the lagoon, read a book from the well-stocked library – it's a tough life at Kuriri Village, isn't it? A series of simply designed yet tastefully arranged bungalows is scattered amid lovely gardens and coconut palms. It's intimate and laid-back, and appeals to couples looking for a bit of style without an exorbitant price tag. The property opens onto the lagoon and the ocean – two different settings, two different atmospheres. As befits a French-run outfit, you can expect to eat divinely. Free kayaks and fishing rods.

Fare Paeao – Chez Jeanine (☎ 67 81 01; fare.pae .ao@mail.pf; Motu Paeao; s/d bungalows with half board 17,500/22,500 CFP) The inner real-estate agent in you will be crying out 'position, position, position' upon seeing the fabulous coral gardens and jade waters onto which this property edges – not to mention the soul-stirring sunsets. The six luminous and functional bungalows are sprinkled through gardens replete with fragrant shrubs of *tiare*. Guests can make use of the kayaks to explore the lagoon. Shame that it's significantly overpriced, especially considering what's available on the island.

MAUPITI

EATING

Most visitors opt for the half- or full-board options with their accommodation, and we'd highly recommend you do as well. In the village, several small shops sell basic supplies and soft drinks, but otherwise your options are limited to just one place.

Snack Tarona (☎ 67 82 46; dishes 900-1200 CFP; ☺ lunch & dinner) Just north of the village, this place comes recommended for its hearty portions of traditional French Polynesian dishes such as raw fish, tuna sashimi, braised beef, and pork with taro.

SHOPPING

You can find some quality souvenirs made from oyster shells, urchins and seashells as well as pearls at **Vaitia Artisanat** (☎ 67 83 23; ☺ daily), in the north of the main island (it's signposted).

GETTING THERE & AWAY

Maupiti is 320km west of Tahiti and 40km west of Bora Bora.

Air

Air Tahiti flies from Maupiti to Tahiti (15,500 CFP, 1½ hours, five flights weekly), Ra'iatea (7500 CFP, 25 minutes, three flights weekly) and Bora Bora (7000 CFP, 20 minutes, one or two flights weekly). The **Air Tahiti office** (☎ 67 15 05, 67 81 24; ☺ 8am-noon Mon-Fri) is in the village.

Boat

Because of strong currents and a tricky sand bar in the Onoiau Pass, the lagoon can only be navigated by smaller ships, which are often forced to wait for appropriate tidal conditions.

The **Maupiti Express 2** (☎ 67 66 69, 78 27 11; www.maupitiexpress.com) runs between Maupiti and Bora Bora on Tuesday, Thursday and Saturday (3000/4000 CFP one way/return). Leaving Vaitape (Bora Bora) at 8.30am, it arrives at Maupiti at 10.15am then departs for the return trip at 4pm, arriving back at Bora Bora at 5.45pm.

GETTING AROUND

If you've booked accommodation you'll be met at the airport, although some places charge for the trip (around 2500 CFP return).

It's simple to arrange a boat out to the *motu* from the village and vice versa. It costs 500 CFP to 1500 CFP to go from the main island to the *motu* and 3000 CFP to 5000 CFP for a lagoon excursion. All the *pensions* on the main land or *motu* can arrange these transfers.

Most *pensions* rent bikes for about 1000 CFP per day. Operators also wait on the quay when the *Maupiti Express 2* arrives at Maupiti.

The Tuamotus

Until you see a coral atoll with your own eyes you haven't experienced everything our great planet has to offer. According to Darwin's theory of atoll formation, these rings of coral are the barrier reefs of volcanic islands that sank to the bottom of the Pacific millions of years ago. Today the raised reefs (with an average elevation of just a few metres) sustain coconut palms, a variety of local trees and shrubs and hardy, sea-loving people known as the Paumotu. Life in the atolls is equal parts harsh and paradisiacal: hardly anything grows so there's little fruit or vegetables, the wind blows salty air over everything and the only drinking water is collected from the rain.

Yet the silence, the starry skies far from light pollution, the blinding-white beaches, intense blue lagoons, plentiful fresh fish, phenomenal diving and languid pace of life capture the hearts of nearly everyone who makes it out here. While an atoll is solid dry land, the small strips of coral squashed between the lagoon and the open ocean make you feel that you're somehow floating on the sea.

The vast archipelago is made up of 77 atolls scattered over an immense stretch of ocean 1500km northwest to southeast and 500km east to west. The closest islands are about 300km from Tahiti. With a total combined land area of only about 700 sq km, the rings of coral islets, known locally as *motu*, encircle an astounding 6000 sq km of sheltered lagoons. You can visit developed atolls like Rangiroa, Fakarava and Tikehau in complete luxury if you wish, or experience authentic Paumotu life (but with plumbing and plentiful food and water) on beauties like Ahe, Takapoto and Mataiva.

HIGHLIGHTS

- Trying to forget the movie *Jaws* while diving the sharky passes of **Rangiroa** (p180) and **Fakarava** (p186)

- Watching a lustrous dark pearl being 'birthed' from an oyster while visiting a pearl farm at **Manihi** (p192), **Ahe** (p193), **Takaroa** (p194) or **Fakarava** (p185)

- Walking along the endless swathes of pink- and white-sand beaches on **Tikehau** (p188)

- Biking through the coconut plantations and past the emerald lagoon of **Mataiva** (p191)

- Visiting the Tuamotus' spread of *marae* tucked in the bushes of **Takapoto** (p194)

History

Early Tuamotu history is a mystery. One theory is that the Paumotu people fled from the Leeward and Marquesas Islands following conflicts during the 14th, 15th and 16th centuries. Another theory is that the eastern Tuamotu were populated at the same time as the major Polynesian diaspora moved on from the Marquesas to the Gambier Archipelago and Easter Island, around 1000 AD.

European explorers were less than complimentary about the group – in 1616 Jacques Le Maire and Willem Schouten spoke of the 'Islands of Dogs', the 'Islands without End' and the 'Islands of Flies'. In 1722 Jacob Roggeveen called them the 'Pernicious Islands' and in 1768 French explorer Louis-Antoine de Bougainville dubbed them the 'Dangerous Archipelago'.

Thus the reputation of the group as an uninviting place was sealed and the Europeans turned their attention towards the more welcoming Society Islands.

Towards the end of the 18th century, around the time of first European contact, the ferocious warriors of Anaa Atoll spread terror across the whole region. Islanders from many atolls fled to Tahiti, where they were sheltered by the Pomares. Many of them were converted by the missionaries who were establishing themselves on Tahiti, and when the islanders returned to the Tuamotus in 1817 they brought Christianity with them.

Christian missionaries established copra production in the 1870s and by 1900 copra represented 40% of the total exports of the colony. Pearl diving and mother-of-pearl production both enjoyed a golden age around 1850.

From 1911 until 1966, phosphate mining on Makatea was the principal export activity not only for the Tuamotus but for all of French Polynesia. The population of other islands began to decline dramatically in the 1960s as copra production fell away and plastic buttons killed off the mother-of-pearl button business.

In the 1970s, when airstrips were built on many of the islands, the population decline was slowed and the group's economic prospects began to brighten. The flights back to Tahiti carried not only suntanned tourists but loads of fresh reef fish for the busy markets of Pape'ete.

The 1970s brought another far less congenial employment prospect to the Tuamotus when France's Centre d'Expérimentation du Pacifique (CEP) took over the central atoll of Hao and began to test nuclear weapons on the western atolls of Moruroa and Fangataufa (see p38).

Pearl culturing began in the 1980s and the atolls flourished with wealth and reverse migration from the late 1990s till around 2003 when pearl prices began to plummet. Today, on atolls such as Manihi and Tikehau, abandoned grafting houses dot the lagoon.

Culture

Hats off to these people, who managed to survive in the harsh conditions of atoll life long before the arrival of supply ships and canned goods. Fish are plentiful in the fertile lagoons, but farming a lump of coral with little water supply is a feat of exceptional ingenuity. To overcome the lack of water, people traditionally dug pits, sometimes stretching for hundreds of metres, down to the water table. These pits were then filled in with vegetable matter, an improvised compost that enabled the cultivation of taro, which was the staple. Direct supplies from Tahiti by schooners eventually made these systems obsolete but some islanders still make small pits for kitchen gardens.

Tuamotu life has always centred around the sea, and the people of the atolls are regarded as some of the best navigators and fishermen in Polynesia. Some people still speak a Paumotu dialect that is a variant of Tahitian, but Tahitian and French are quickly taking over.

Activities

You don't go to the Tuamotus for monuments or museums – activities are in the lagoons. Scuba diving is the number-one activity. Rangiroa, Tikehau, Manihi, Fakarava, Ahe and Makemo have dive centres, and dive cruises are a pricier but practical way to dive the Tuamotus – see the boxed text, p256.

You can visit the ubiquitous pearl farms, where you'll probably get to see the grafting operation. Some places to stay also have pearl farms.

Both spear and line fishing are available and you can also see fish parks, snorkel, explore archaeological sites and visit bird reserves on remote *motu*. Definitely bring a mask and snorkel.

There are numerous tourist operators, although hotels and *pensions* (guesthouses) often organise trips for guests. The best

THE TUAMOTUS

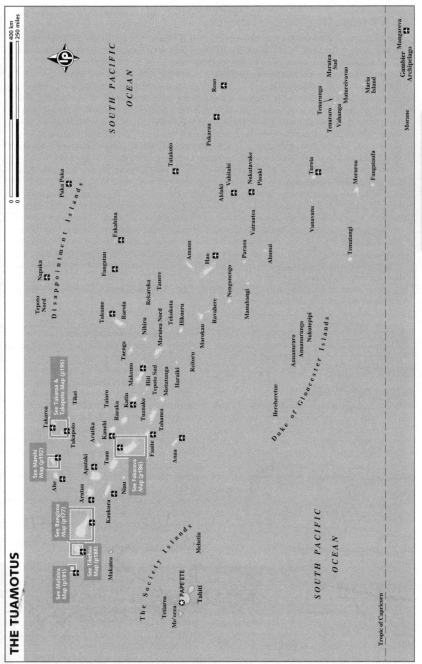

THE TUAMOTUS

BLACK PEARL, JEWEL OF THE TUAMOTUS

Black Tahitian pearls were once the black gold of the Tuamotus. Though farming officially began in the 1960s, the industry didn't have the technology to make it viable till the 1980s. For the next decade and a half the world market price for these 'rare' pearls was so high that many farmers became ridiculously rich ridiculously fast. By the year 2000 so many farmers had begun mass-producing that the market became saturated and prices began to drop. The situation worsened after the worldwide economic slump of 2001, and the price of pearls hit a low in 2003, with market prices often lower than the cost of production. Numerous small farms shut their doors. The market gradually bettered but with the world economic crisis in 2008 prices dropped even lower than in 2003. This time even large farms began to shut. With very little centralisation or government organisation, the future of pearling looks bleak. Yet for many it's the only livelihood they know, and they will grit their teeth and keep working to produce what are considered the world's most beautiful pearls. For buyers, there's never been a better time to purchase these stunning gems from the sea.

The Tahitian pearls that are 'farmed' are cultured; a cultured pearl is created by an operation called a graft. This is a highly specialised procedure in which a 6mm or larger shell ball (called a nucleus) is surgically inserted into the gonad of a host oyster. In the same incision, a small piece of mantle tissue (the organ that secretes mother of pearl) from a different oyster is inserted so that it touches the nucleus. In the gonad the mantle tissue activates a physiological process, much like a skin graft, and secretes mother-of-pearl around the shell nucleus. This culturing process takes approximately four years from the time the first oyster spawn are collected to the harvest of those oysters' first pearls.

For more information on pearl grafting go to www.pearl-guide.com/tahitian-pearl-farming .shtml; for buying tips, see the boxed text, p94.

---

beaches are often on remote *motu*. Operators will take you on picnic trips to these *motu*, or arrange to leave you there and collect you later.

Getting There & Away

The archipelago is accessible by plane; 31 atolls have airstrips and are served by Air Tahiti. Most of the traffic is to and from Pape'ete, but there are also connections with Bora Bora, the Marquesas and the Gambier Archipelago. Within the archipelago, Rangiroa and Hao are the principal flight hubs. If you're visiting an island, always give the Air Tahiti representative a contact address or phone number, as schedules are subject to change.

See p261 and individual Getting There & Away sections for details on how to reach the Tuamotus by cargo ship, and p244 for information on cruising yachts.

Getting Around

Outboard motorboat is how most people get around in the Tuamotus. Roads are often just crushed-coral tracks, perhaps a few kilometres long, linking the village to the airport or to the areas where copra is produced. Public transport usually does not exist. Ask at your hotel or *pension* about transport as they will usually be able to set you up with whatever you need.

Airports are sometimes near the villages, or sometimes on remote *motu* on the other side of the lagoon. If you have booked accommodation, your hosts will come and meet you but transfers are not necessarily free. If there is a charge it will depend on the distance travelled and the means of transport. Hitching (by car or boat) is possible as many islanders go to the airports for arrivals and departures, although there may not be room for you by the time all the freight is loaded! If you are given a ride, offer to help pay for petrol as it is quite expensive.

Bicycles and scooters are often used in the villages; some *pensions* rent them out or they can be hired from islanders.

RANGIROA

pop 3016 / lagoon area 1640 sq km

Rangiroa (rung-ee-roh-ah) is one of the biggest atolls in the world with a lagoon so vast that it could fit the entire island of Tahiti inside of it. While visitors coming directly from Bora Bora or Tahiti will probably find Rangi

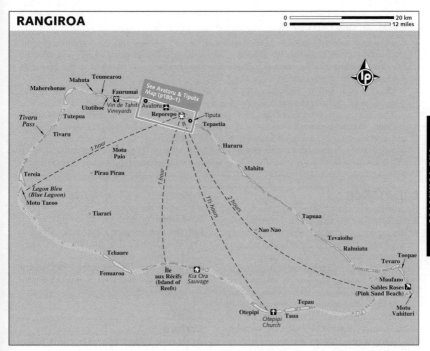

(as it's known to its friends) to be a low-key, middle-of-nowhere sort of a place, this is the big city for folks coming from anywhere else in the archipelago. With paved roads, a few stores, resorts, plentiful internet, and gourmet restaurants, there's really everything here you need – and in the Tuamotus, that's a really big deal! The main village of Avatoru, spread out between the two main passes, is where most people stay and this is very convenient if you've come here to dive as most sites will be just beyond your doorstep. For landlubbers the never-ending string of remote *motu* is the real draw and trips across the lagoon to the stunning Île aux Récifs (Island of Reefs; see p179) and Lagon Bleu (p179) are not to be missed. And then there's that funny little vineyard (see the boxed text, p179)…

A series of large swells has menaced the atoll's lagoon over the last several years and most of the white-sand beaches in the villages have been reduced to gravel-sand beaches. Even so, the stark whiteness of bleached coral against turquoise lagoon creates a bright, almost Grecian cocktail for the eyes and life in the lagoon has sprung back to its abundant norm. Expect to see sharks, sharks and more sharks.

HISTORY

Historically, Rangiroa has had to contend with two equally destructive threats: pirates and cyclones. At first, Rangiroa's inhabitants lived close to Motu Taeoo (Lagon Bleu), on the southwestern side of the atoll, until a cataclysm, probably a tsunami, destroyed these settlements around 1560.

Two centuries later, the population was settled around the three passes – Tivaru, Avatoru and Tiputa. Anaa warriors pillaged Rangiroa at the end of the 1770s; survivors were forced into exile on Tikehau and Tahiti. They returned to Rangiroa in the early 1820s and repopulated the atoll.

It was sighted in April 1616 by Dutchman Le Maire, but Rangiroa didn't receive European settlers – missionaries – until 1851.

Copra production played a vital economic role until it was overtaken by fishing, still an important industry. There's a handful of pearl farms on Rangi, and an oyster hatchery and school for pearl farmers and technicians.

FROM COCONUT TO COPRA

Copra (dried coconut meat for oil production) is found everywhere in the Tuamotus and the Marquesas. Rich in vegetable fat (palmitin), it's regularly collected by schooners and taken to Pape'ete. Crushed, heated, pressed and refined as oil, it is then sold to the food and cosmetics industries.

Copra production was introduced by the missionaries in the 1870s and has continued to develop and is still an essential economic activity all around French Polynesia.

The copra producers gather fallen coconuts from their plantations then split each nut with a machete. The half-nuts are then turned over and left in the sun for a few days. The meat is scooped out with a *pana* (scooping tool) from the shell, and the shavings placed on copra dryers (raised racks topped with a movable roof to protect them from rain) until completely desiccated. They are then packed in sacks, weighed and put in a hangar until a schooner arrives to collect them.

ORIENTATION

Rangiroa measures 75km from east to west and 25km from north to south. From the edge of the lagoon, it is impossible to see the opposite bank. The atoll's coral belt is no more than 300m wide, but the long circuit of islands, *motu* and *hoa* (channels) stretches for more than 200km. The lagoon opens to the ocean via three passes: Tivaru, Avatoru and Tiputa. The Tivaru Pass is narrow and shallow; the Avatoru and Tiputa Passes are each more than 200m wide. About 10km separates the Avatoru and Tiputa Passes.

Rangiroa has two villages. Avatoru is on a string of islets between Avatoru and Tiputa Passes. At the eastern end, beyond the Tiputa Pass, is the village of Tiputa. Most places to stay and eat are dotted along the string of islets east of Avatoru.

INFORMATION

You can buy telephone cards at the post offices, at some supermarkets and at a few souvenir boutiques. Internet connections are available at a handful of small internet shacks (usually for 300 CFP per minute), a few restaurants (p184), at the OPT office in Avatoru and increasingly at places of lodging.

Banque de Tahiti (☎ 96 85 52; Avatoru; ☷ 8-11am & 2-4pm Mon, Wed & Fri, 8-11.30am Tue & Thu) You can exchange currency and travellers cheques or withdraw cash with your credit card.

Banque Socredo Avatoru (☎ 96 85 63; ☷ 7am-3.30pm Mon-Thu, 7.30am-2.30pm Fri); Tiputa (☎ 96 75 57; ☷ 1.30-4pm Mon & Thu) Only the Avatoru office (next to the post office) has an ATM. Don't expect to change currency at the Tiputa branch.

Centre Médical Avatoru (☎ 96 03 75; Vaimate)

Centre Médical Rai Roa (☎ 96 04 44, 96 04 43; Avatoru) A private clinic operated by Dr Thirouard.

Dentist (☎ 93 13 13; Tevaiohie) Philippe Pujul is the only dentist in the Tuamotus.

Gendarmerie (police station; ☎ 96 73 61)

Pharmacie de Rangiroa (☎ 93 12 30; fax 93 12 36; ☷ 7am-12.30pm & 2.30-6.30pm Mon-Sat, 10.30am-12.30pm Sun)

Post office Avatoru (☷ 7am-noon & 1-3pm Mon-Thu, 7am-noon & 1-2pm Fri); Tiputa (☷ 7am-12.30pm Mon-Thu, to 11.30am Fri)

SIGHTS
Avatoru

Avatoru is a modern and bustling place by Tuamotu standards. There is a post office, a few banks and a supermarket with a decent selection of groceries. There are two churches, one Catholic and one Mormon, and a few little places to eat. A small site overlooking Tiputa Pass has been cleared so that visitors can watch the daily performances of dolphins that dance in the waves created by the outgoing current.

Tiputa

Around the middle of the day, you could pretty safely fire a gun along the main street in Tiputa and not hit anyone. It's a charming little village; getting a boat across the Tiputa Pass adds to the whole experience. Tiputa is the administrative centre that serves Rangiroa, Makatea, Tikehau and Mataiva. It has a *gendarmerie* with authority over several atolls. The village is also home to the Centre d'Études des Techniques Adaptées au Développement (Cetad), which trains young people for employment in the catering and hotel industries.

After the village the track continues east through coconut plantations until it's halted by the next *hoa*.

Lagon Vert

Lagon Vert (Green Lagoon) is only five minutes away from Avatoru by boat. It's a small yet strikingly pretty area and the residential houses along the beach only detract slightly from the natural beauty. It attracts fewer visitors than its blue counterpart, and so can make for a less touristy adventure.

Lagon Bleu

Lagon Bleu (Blue Lagoon; Map p177) is a popular spot about an hour away from Avatoru by boat. A string of *motu* and coral reefs has formed a natural pool on the edge of the main reef, a lagoon within a lagoon. Visitors go in large groups, but this detracts slightly from the heavenly white sand, ruffled coconut trees, and lapis lazuli water. The lagoon isn't deep and offers safe snorkelling among the myriad little fish, but don't expect much from the coral. Feasting on freshly barbecued fish, playing ukulele and feeding the sharks are usually on the itinerary. This is what many people visualise when imagining a Polynesian paradise.

Sables Roses

Sables Roses (Pink Sand Beach; Map p177), on the lagoon side near Motu Vahituri, is two hours from Avatoru by boat. Unfortunately the beach erodes away with large swells so it's hit-and-miss whether you'll find much of a beach or not. Pink sand is pretty, but not dramatically different from white sand – if you're fascinated by the idea, you should try and make a trip to Tikehau (p188), which has hundreds of more easily accessible pink-sand beaches. Still, this remote, less-visited Rangiroa site can be worth a visit for the voyage and isolation alone.

Île aux Récifs

South of the atoll, an hour by boat from Avatoru, Île aux Récifs (Island of Reefs; Map p177), also known as Motu Ai Ai, is an area dotted with raised *feo* (coral outcrops), weathered shapes chiselled by erosion into petrified silhouettes on the exterior reef. They stretch for several hundred metres, with basins and channels that make superb natural swimming pools. There's a good *hoa* for swimming and a picturesque coconut grove by the beach, which makes an ideal picnic spot. This is a great day trip, although it's quite popular so expect to see other groups. Don't even consider going here barefoot since the stunning formations are sharp as knives.

Otepipi

Otepipi (Map p177) is a *motu* on the south-eastern side of the atoll, about 1½ hours away

THE TUAMOTUS

CORAL WINE

A vineyard? On an atoll? While completely surreal, it's true. Vin de Tahiti has a 20-hectare vineyard planted on a palm-fringed *motu* about 10 minutes by boat from Avatoru village. It's not exactly organic: the coral-based soil is deficient and the water source (from a well squashed between two salty bodies of water) is not entirely reliable so it's taken quite a bit of technology to get the vines to their current healthy state.

Sébastien Thépenier, a leading French oenologist and winemaker for Vin de Tahiti (Map p177), tells us about these unusual wines:

What distinguishes Rangiroa wine from other wines in the world? This is the only atoll vineyard in the world making our wines, the only ones produced from coral soil.
What do experts think of the wines? Experts think that our wines have a real worldwide marketability and that they have a very unusual taste. The mineral flavour from the soil is the main characteristic.
Which of the wines is your favourite? My favourite is the coral white [apéritif] wine and the dry white that's aged in oak barrels. The fruity flavour of the coral white is unusual yet well balanced. The dry white is more complex with an oaky flavour and a mineral taste and ages nicely.
Do any Rangiroa restaurants serve the local wine? Yes, Vaimario, Novotel Rangiroa Beach Resort, Hotel Kia Ora and Rangiroa Lagoon Grill (see p184).

For more information and to taste the wines visit the Vin de Tahiti wine cellar in Avatoru (see p180). For more on Vin de Tahiti's history go to www.vindetahiti.pf.

THE TUAMOTUS

AVATORU & TIPUTA

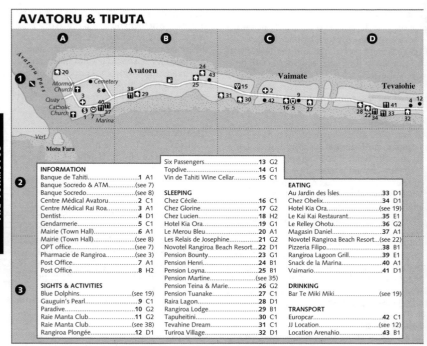

INFORMATION
Banque de Tahiti.............................1 A1
Banque Socredo & ATM...............(see 7)
Banque Socredo...........................(see 8)
Centre Médical Avatoru..................2 C1
Centre Médical Rai Roa...................3 A1
Dentist..4 D1
Gendarmerie.................................5 C1
Mairie (Town Hall).........................6 A1
Mairie (Town Hall)......................(see 8)
OPT office...................................(see 7)
Pharmacie de Rangiroa..................(see 3)
Post Office....................................7 A1
Post Office....................................8 H2

SIGHTS & ACTIVITIES
Blue Dolphins..............................(see 19)
Gauguin's Pearl.............................9 C1
Paradive.....................................10 G2
Raie Manta Club...........................11 G2
Raie Manta Club.........................(see 38)
Rangiroa Plongée..........................12 D1

Six Passengers.............................13 G2
Topdive......................................14 G1
Vin de Tahiti Wine Cellar...............15 C1

SLEEPING
Chez Cécile.................................16 C1
Chez Glorine................................17 G2
Chez Lucien.................................18 H2
Hotel Kia Ora...............................19 G1
Le Merou Bleu..............................20 A1
Les Relais de Josephine...................21 G2
Novotel Rangiroa Beach Resort.......22 D1
Pension Bounty............................23 G1
Pension Henri...............................24 B1
Pension Loyna...............................25 B1
Pension Martine..........................(see 35)
Pension Teina & Marie....................26 G2
Pension Tuanake...........................27 C1
Raira Lagon.................................28 D1
Rangiroa Lodge.............................29 B1
Tapuheitini.................................30 C1
Tevahine Dream............................31 C1
Turiroa Village..............................32 D1

EATING
Au Jardin des Îles..........................33 D1
Chez Obelix.................................34 D1
Hotel Kia Ora.............................(see 19)
Le Kai Kai Restaurant....................35 E1
Le Relley Ohotu............................36 G2
Magasin Daniel.............................37 A1
Novotel Rangiroa Beach Resort.....(see 22)
Pizzeria Filipo..............................38 B1
Rangiroa Lagoon Grill....................39 E1
Snack de la Marina.......................40 A1
Vaimario.....................................41 D1

DRINKING
Bar Te Miki Miki.........................(see 19)

TRANSPORT
Europcar....................................42 C1
JJ Location...............................(see 12)
Location Arenahio.........................43 B1

from Avatoru by boat. It once had a village, but some say illness forced the inhabitants to leave; others say it was a cyclone or tsunami. Only a church remains; religious retreats and pilgrimages are still made to the church periodically.

ACTIVITIES

The main activity on Rangiroa is **diving** and sharks are the big attraction. The dive centres provides equipment, and are happy to have two of you share a 10-dive pass; you'll pay around 6000/53,000 CFP for one/10 dives. For beginners, the Aquarium is an ideal spot to take a first dive: it's shallow, right in Tiputa Pass and thick with fish. Other sites include Nuhi Nuhi, Avatoru Pass, Mahuta and the stunning Les Failles; see p69 for details. Dive centres include the following.

Blue Dolphins (☎ /fax 96 03 01; www.bluedolphins .com; Hotel Kia Ora)
Paradive (☎ 96 05 55; www.chez.com/paradive)
Raie Manta Club (☎ 96 84 80; http://raiemantaclub .free.fr; Avatoru)
Rangiroa Plongée (☎ 27 57 82; Tevaiohie) Rangi's newest centre is traveller recommended.

Six Passengers (☎ /fax 96 02 60; www.the6passengers .com) About 500m east of Hotel Kia Ora.
Topdive (☎ /fax 96 05 60; www.topdive.com) About 300m from Hotel Kia Ora.

Snorkelling, with a guide or independently, is a great way to visit the lagoon. You can just grab a snorkel and splash around near your hotel or guesthouse (many of which provide snorkelling gear for guests). For guides, expect to pay around 4500 CFP for a three-hour snorkelling trip through the passes.

TOURS

Organised tours are really the only way of exploring the vast lagoon and, if you happen upon a nice group, make for a wonderful day. Most tours go to the opposite side of the lagoon from Avatoru, which takes at least an hour to cross and can be uncomfortable if the sea is rough. Usually a minimum of four to six people is required, but July and August can be so busy that it can be hard getting a place at all.

Snorkelling gear can be arranged, although you may have to pay for this. Full-day tours

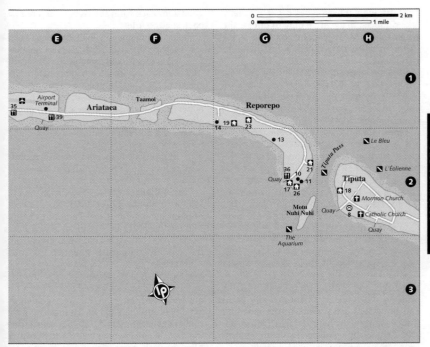

generally depart at 8.30am and return at 4pm and include a barbecue. Try to bargain for a reduced price for the kids, although many operators will not budge on this. When the weather's bad or the winds are too high, excursions are cancelled.

Trips to the Lagon Bleu or Île aux Récifs cost around 7500 CFP including lunch. An excursion to Sables Roses usually costs 10,000 CFP. Some companies take in two to three sites in one day but this makes for a less relaxing trip where you'll spend the bulk of your time travelling by boat. A few small companies offer snorkelling trips to Lagon Vert and the Aquarium dive sites – ask at your hotel or *pension*.

Gauguin's Pearl (☎ 93 11 30; Vaimate) Free tours are offered of the pearl farm directly next to the boutique. You can be picked up for free from your place of lodging.

Matahi Excursions (☎ 96 84 48; tours 2500 CFP; ☷ tours 9am & 2pm daily) Experience the lagoon without getting your feet wet on this glass-bottom boat tour.

Pa'ati Excursion (☎ 96 02 57) Standard well-run lagoon tours.

Te Reva Tane et Vahine (☎ 96 82 51) Offers some of the most popular lagoon tours and is highly recommended.

Vin de Tahiti (☎ 96 04 70; www.vindetahiti.pf; half-day tours per person 6000 CFP; ☷ Mon-Fri) Offers tours of striking vineyards on a *motu* and tastings back at the Avatoru wine cellar. Take home a bottle of wine from 4000 CFP.

Watergames (☎ 96 04 49) Does charter trips to the Lagon Vert and offers jet-ski tours from 12,000 CFP per hour for two people.

SLEEPING

Besides the three hotels, options on Rangiroa are family *pensions*, which range from rustic lodging with local families to posh and private lagoonside bungalows that are run like boutique hotels. While most are right on the lagoon, nearly none have sandy beaches, but they usually do have plenty of coral and good snorkelling, just steps from your bungalow.

Budget

Budget prices à la Rangiroa are still steep but most are with half board. Bungalows usually sleep two to three people, but there's generally at least one family bungalow available; children under 12 usually stay for half price. Budget places rarely have hot water, and although most places don't officially take campers, many are happy to offer a site when asked. Most places don't take credit cards. Except where noted, prices here are per person.

Rangiroa Lodge (☎ 96 82 13; http://rangiroa.lodge .free.fr; Avatoru; dm 2000 CFP, d with/without bathroom 5500/4500 CFP) Run by the Raie Manta dive club, this clean, barrackslike backpackers is Rangiroa's cheapest option.

Pension Loyna (☎/fax 96 82 09; www.pensionloyna .fr.st; Avatoru; r with half board 6000-7500 CFP) Lovely, clean *pension*. Cheaper rooms are in the owner's home (without bathroom); several rooms with bathroom and new two-bed-room family bungalows with bathroom are out the back. The ocean is 100m away, but the warm welcome and high standards more than make up for this.

Pension Teina & Marie (☎ 96 03 94; pensionteina simone@caramail.com; Reporepo; r with half board 6500-7500 CFP, campsites 1000 CFP) Great views of Tiputa Pass and a friendly, laid-back atmosphere make this one of the best budget, no-frills options. The food is phenomenally good and nonguests can reserve in the morning if they want to eat here at night (worth the effort especially if lobster is on the menu). Campers have use of bathroom facilities.

Chez Lucien (☎ 96 73 55; pensionlucien@mail.pf; Tiputa Village; bungalows with half board 7000 CFP) Run by grandma and grandpa, Chez Lucien is the only place to stay on the Tiputa side of the pass. It graces a little white beach shaded by a huge, and quite famous, 100-year-old tree. There are three spacious bungalows, one ac-commodating up to seven people, with mez-zanine and bathroom. Return transfers to the airport cost 1000 CFP per person. If you stay for a minimum of three nights, Lucien will take you for a free picnic on a *motu*.

Turiroa Village (☎/fax 96 04 27; pension.turiroa@ mail.pf; Tevaiohie; bungalows with/without bathroom 8500/ 6500 CFP) Cheery *pension* with lots of family bungalows sleeping four people and one double. Some of the bungalows have their own kitchens but there's also a communal kitchen available. It's clean and shipshape.

Chez Glorine (☎ 96 04 05; pensionglorine@mail.pf; Reporepo; bungalows with half board 7500 CFP) On the lagoon corner of Tiputa Pass, right next to Teina & Marie, Chez Glorine is another spot renowned for its good food – unfortunately it's frequently closed so make sure you call ahead to reserve. The tiny bungalows are a

good 20m back from the lagoon but are in a cool, shady garden.

Pension Bounty (☎/fax 96 05 22; www.pension-bounty .com; Reporepo; r with breakfast 7500 CFP; 🖳) In a wonder-ful location about 100m from the Kia Ora beach (the best on Avatoru), the owners here really go out of their way to make sure their guests have everything they need. Lodging is in rooms rather than bungalows, but these are exception-ally clean, cool and modern, have mosquito screens and hot water. Dinner is available (add 3500 CFP per person) but you also have your own equipped kitchen and nearby restaurants offer pick-up. English, Spanish and Italian are spoken and this place accepts credit cards.

Pension Martine (☎ 96 02 53; tetua.martine@mail.pf; Tevaiohie; r with half board 7500-8500 CFP) Needs a coat of paint but retains a real Paumotu charm. The owners also run a pearl farm and have a small pearl boutique across the street from the *pension*. Credit cards accepted.

Chez Cécile (☎ 96 05 06; Vaimate; bungalow with half board 8500 CFP) A very pleasant place with rela-tively new and spacious wood bungalows with hot-water bathrooms in a flowery garden. A handful of smaller, older tiled bungalows have cold-water bathrooms. All the bungalows line the 'beach', which is actually a breakwater filled in with coral gravel, but there's de-cent swimming access and it's pretty. Credit cards accepted.

Midrange

You can pay with a credit card in most of the midrange bracket.

Pension Henri (☎/fax 96 82 67; http://henri.sejour.n -rangiroa.com; Avatoru; s/d/tr bungalow with breakfast 11,000/15,000/16,000 CFP) The rustic-chic bunga-lows and French-Tahitian owners give this place a hip vibe. All bungalows are large, with hot-water bathrooms and a terrace and face the ocean side of the atoll with its crashing waves, exposed reef to walk on and some swaying coconut palms. Three bungalows have kitchens and can sleep up to six peo-ple. For half board add another 2700 CFP per person.

Pension Tuanake (☎ 96 04 45; www.sitetuanake.fr.st; Vaimate; s/d/tr with half board 10,500/16,000/21,000 CFP; 🖳) A cross between a family-run place and a hotel. Two small bungalows are for three people and two bungalows for six people. It's clean, organised and set in a coconut planta-tion on the coral gravel–lined lagoon. The food is great.

Tapuheitini (☎ 96 04 07; www.rangiroa-dream.com; Avatoru; s/d with half board 11,500/18,000 CFP) A clean little set-up of three brand-new bungalows all with mosquito nets, fan and fridge. The owners here also offer tours to their private *motu*, half an hour away by boat, where they will occasionally bring campers.

Raira Lagon (☎ 96 04 23; www.raira-lagon.pf; Tevaiohie; bungalows with half board per person from 11,000 CFP; ❌ 🖳) Feeling even less family-run than Pension Tuanake but still retaining a friendly vibe, this place has 10 fan-cooled bungalows spread throughout a garden fringed by one of the better beaches in the area. The restaurant balcony faces the lagoon and serves large, buffet-style breakfasts in lieu of the usual bread and coffee and has reasonably priced cocktails in the evening.

our pick **Le Merou Bleu** (☎ 79 16 82; www .merou-bleu.com, in French; Avatoru; s/d/tr with half board from 11,500/21,000/32,000 CFP; 🖳) An outstanding option in a magical garden setting right on Avatoru Pass in front of the surf break. Bungalows are creatively made from woven coconut thatch and other natural materials but manage to maintain a good level of comfort, have hot water, good mosquito nets and lovely terraces perfect for lounging. Plans for an oceanside Jacuzzi are in the pipeline. Credit cards are not accepted.

Tevahine Dream (☎ 93 12 75; www.tevahinedream .com; Avatoru; bungalow with half board per person 12,500 CFP, house per day for up to 4 people 25,000 CFP) We love these spacious new bungalows designed in a Zen-meets-Polynesia style, which are dripping with wood and draping white fabrics. Bathrooms are mini oases with ferns and coral gravel. Three bungalows are intimate and sleep two to three but there's also a whole-house option, complete with a kitchen that can sleep up to six people – and the bathroom is so big you could all shower at the same time! Prices include bikes, kayaks and a car tour. The beach is coral gravel (good for snorkelling) and there's a little dipping pool up by the eating terrace and bar. This place is planning on accepting credit cards, but check before you arrive.

Top End

Whip out the credit card and deal with the damage when you get home.

Les Relais de Josephine (☎ /fax 96 02 00; http:// relaisjosephine.free.fr; Reporepo; s/d/tr bungalow with half board 20,000/32,000/39,000 CFP; 🖳) The setting of this very French interpretation of the Polynesian *pension,* in full view of the dancing dolphins on Tiputa Pass, is arguably the prettiest in the Avatoru area and the luxurious Euro-Balinese design makes it feel luxurious. Lounging on the deck here is a truly decadent experience, as is dining on the elegant French-style food made from local ingredients. Nonguests can reserve early in the day for lunch or dinner.

Novotel Rangiroa Beach Resort (☎ 86 66 66; www.novotel.com; Tevaiohie; bungalows 23,000-38,000 CFP; ❌) A step down from the luxury of the Kia Ora but a notch above the midrange group, bungalows here aren't memorable but are certainly comfortable. The best part of the hotel is the grounds, covered in swaying palms and flowers and highlighted by a little lily pond. There's not really a beach but there is a pontoon and the restaurant serves good food and has lagoon views (though some readers have complained about slow service). There are a handful of rooms designed for disabled guests.

Kia Ora Sauvage (Map p177; ☎ 96 03 84; www.hotel kiaora.com; bungalows with full board per person 47,000 CFP) This is Hotel Kia Ora's 'savage' sister, on Motu Avearahi, about an hour away by boat. The beach setting is stunning and there's a maximum of 10 guests at any time. At night, the whole place is lit by candlelight and oil lamps. It's the ultimate escape, an uncommonly elegant way to play Crusoe and just about everyone who stays here raves that it was one of the best vacations they ever had. Price includes return boat transfers and full board, which is compulsory; minimum stay of two nights.

Hotel Kia Ora (☎ 96 03 84; www.hotelkiaora.com; Reporepo; bungalows 39,000-80,000 CFP; ❌ 🖳 🖳) The biggest resort in the Tuamotus and the priciest option on Rangiroa is undeniably plush. It has an old-school feel to it: the lounge looks like someplace your grandpa liked to smoke cigars and the small pool is lined with 1980s-style blue tiles. Bungalows are dotted around a magnificent coconut plantation situated on the best beach around Avatoru.

EATING

Most visitors opt for half board at their *pension* and wherever you stay you can expect copious meals involving plenty of fresh fish. There are also good restaurants and a few offer free pick-up from Avatoru. If you do have a mode of transportation, you can also book a meal at some of the *pensions* that are well respected for their cuisine; these include Pension Loyna, Pension Teina & Marie, Chez Glorine and Les Relais de Josephine (see Sleeping, p181). Be sure to notify your *pension* that morning if you plan to eat elsewhere for dinner.

All restaurants and *snacks* (snack bars) are open lunch and dinner unless otherwise noted; hotel restaurants are open for breakfast as well.

Restaurants

Vaimario (☎ 96 05 96; Tevaiohie; mains 2500-3000 CFP; ☺ closed Tue) Feast on anything from pizza to grilled fish. Try the specialities of giant clams in coconut milk (2300 CFP) or trevally with ginger and lychee (2100 CFP). Free transfers are offered and there's a decent wine list and spirits.

Rangiroa Lagoon Grill (☎ 96 04 10; Tevaiohie; ☺ closed Mon) A new, highly recommended option right on the water that serves a more classic version of French food including lots of grilled meat dishes (as well as fish) and even a real French cheese platter. Offers pick-up service.

Le Kai Kai Restaurant (☎ 96 03 39; Tevaiohie; lunch 350-1000 CFP, dinner mains 1300-2000 CFP; ☺ closed Wed; ▣) French garden restaurant, with simple lunch and more elaborate dinner menus including a set option (there's a set menu for children). Evening cocktails are available and transfers from your Avatoru *pension* or hotel are free.

Novotel Rangiroa Beach Resort (☎ /fax 86 66 66; Tevaiohie; lunches from 950 CFP, dinner mains 1900-3000 CFP) French cooking using local products creates an appetising menu at dinner. Light meals, pizzas and American lunch plates (around 1500 CFP) with sandwiches and burgers are offered at lunch.

Hotel Kia Ora (☎ 96 03 84; Reporepo; appetisers 900-1500 CFP, mains 2500-4000 CFP) As fancy as Rangiroan cuisine gets. The over-water restaurant and bar is lovely. Lunch (appetisers 1300 to 1600 CFP, mains 1400 to 2500 CFP) is cheaper than the evening version. Wednesday and Sunday there's a buffet and Polynesian dance performance (5000 CFP).

Cafés & Snack Bars

Each village has a few *snacks*; you can eat in or order takeaway. There's also a café at the airport that opens before every flight.

Le Relley Ohotu (Reporepo; burgers 500-800 CFP, mains 1000-1500 CFP) A buzzing *snack* opposite Chez Glorine, overlooking the water. The servings are diver sized and the fish is fresh.

Pizzeria Filipo (☎ 73 76 20; Avatoru; appetisers 650-1200 CFP, pizzas 1000-1500 CFP) Here's a great little place right near Rangiroa Lodge. The food is delicious (try the daily specials for around 1200 CFP); the pizzas are huge, and the whole place is as clean as a whistle.

Snack de la Marina (☎ 96 85 64; Avatoru; mains 1000-2000 CFP; ☺ closed lunch Sun) A local favourite that serves excellent, fresh food in massive portions. Light eaters can order single fish *brochettes* (300 CFP each) or big side orders of salad, fries and more (also 300 CFP each). For dessert try hot delicious *gaufres* (Belgian-style waffles; from 400 CFP) with a choice of sweet toppings.

Chez Obelix (Tevaiohie; mains 1000-2000 CFP; ☺ 8am-10pm; ▣) Although there's nothing out of the ordinary on the menu and the roadside setting isn't spectacular, travellers and locals rave about the excellent food here. A big portrait of Obelix inspires you to stuff your belly.

Self-Catering

Self-catering on Rangiroa is possible, but in most shops you'll only find canned goods and such. Avatoru has a few supermarkets, the best being **Magasin Daniel** (☺ closed 11.45am-2.30pm), which is near the post office in Avatoru, and there are a few little grocery stores in sleepy Tiputa. Supermarkets are generally open Monday to Saturday, and close for lunch.

Au Jardin des Îsles (Tevaiohie; ☺ 6am-noon & 4-6pm Mon-Fri, 4-6pm Sat) For fruit and veggies stop at this roadside stall, which has a selection of imported fruit like apples (around 580 CFP per kilo) and some other produce from around French Polynesia and Rangiroa. They're not exactly giving the food away but prices are only marginally more expensive than in Pape'ete.

DRINKING & ENTERTAINMENT

The roosters might make a racket all night long, but most people are well and truly slumbering by 10.30pm.

The only real island entertainment is the twice-weekly buffet with traditional dance organised by Hotel Kia Ora (p183). It's possible to skip the buffet and just have a drink in the bar if you want to catch the entertainment.

The bar here, Bar Te Miki Miki, closes at 11pm.

GETTING THERE & AWAY
Air
The airport is smack in between Avatoru (to the west) and Tiputa (to the east). **Air Tahiti** (☎ 93 11 00, 96 05 77; ☼ 7.30am-12.30pm & 1.30-6.30pm Mon-Sat) has an office inside the airport.

Rangiroa is connected by air to Tahiti, Bora Bora, the Marquesas and other atolls in the Tuamotus. There are several flights daily between Pape'ete and Rangiroa (one hour). There is also a weekly flight from Rangiroa to Nuku Hiva (Marquesas).

One-way fares on offer include Pape'ete–Rangiroa 16,500 CFP, Bora Bora–Rangiroa 24,000 CFP, Rangiroa–Tikehau 6000 CFP and Rangiroa–Fakarava 6000 CFP (see p258 for more details).

Boat
The *Mareva Nui* and *Saint-Xavier Maris-Stella* are the only cargo ships serving Rangiroa that take passengers besides the *Aranui,* which stops on Rangiroa on its way back from the Marquesas.

For details, see p260.

GETTING AROUND
A sealed road runs the 10km from Avatoru village at the western end of the string of islets to the Tiputa Pass, at the eastern extremity. There's no public transport on Rangiroa, but there's a rather casual approach to hitchhiking (which is never entirely safe, although you'd be unlikely to run into problems on Rangiroa) where if you're walking along in the hot sun, someone will often stop and offer you a ride. Slightly more reliable is **Ignace Tupahiroa** (☎ 77 28 02) who runs a minibus between the Tiputa and Avatoru Passes several times a day (unscheduled) and will take you anywhere for 500 CFP. He starts at the Tiputa Marina and ends at the Avatoru Marina but you can flag him down anywhere in between. He also meets all arriving flights at the airport.

The easiest way to get around is to hire a bicycle or a scooter (as it's hardly worth getting a car). The road is not lit at night, which makes getting around without a car in the evenings virtually impossible.

There are regular boats (1000 CFP return) that cross the pass separating the Avatoru islets from Tiputa village; taking a bicycle over costs 500 CFP extra.

To/From the Airport
If you have booked accommodation, your hosts will be at the airport to welcome you. If your *pension* is near the hotel, transfers will probably be free; places further away tend to charge (ask when you book). Otherwise snag Ignace Tupahiroa (see left) before he leaves.

Rentals
Europcar (☎ 96 03 28; Vaimate; ☼ 7.30am-6pm) rents cars from 7000/8500 CFP for a half/full day; 'fun cars', those curious little three-wheeler devices, rent for 5500/6500 CFP; and scooters cost 4500/5500 CFP. Credit cards are accepted. Several guesthouses work with Europcar and have bicycles and scooters at the same rates.

Location Arenahio (☎ 96 82 45; ☼ 7.30am-6pm Mon-Sat) hires out cars for 6500/8500 CFP for a half/full day; scooters are 4500/5500 CFP and bicycles 800/1500 CFP. Credit cards are accepted.

JJ Location (☎ 27 57 82; Tevaiohie) rents scooters for 1500 CFP per hour or 4000/5500 CFP for a half/full day and bikes for 800/1500 CFP for a half/full day.

Hotel Kia Ora (p183) also rents out bicycles and scooters.

NORTHERN TUAMOTUS

If you can visit any of these atolls do it. You'll find an enthusiastic Polynesian welcome and can plunge headlong into authentic Paumotu life. If you need luxury, there are resorts on Tikehau and Manihi plus a handful of swish family *pensions* throughout the archipelago. There are also some great, more rustic, budget options that allow you to really see the local side of island life.

The northern group includes Makatea, southwest of Rangiroa; Tikehau and Mataiva in the west; and Manihi and Ahe in the northeast.

To the east are Takaroa and Takapoto, and to the southeast the giant Fakarava competes in size with Rangiroa. Anaa is a small atoll further south and Makemo is just east from there.

FAKARAVA
pop 699 / lagoon area 1121 sq km

Fakarava might be the second-largest atoll in the Tuamotus (after Rangiroa) but it can

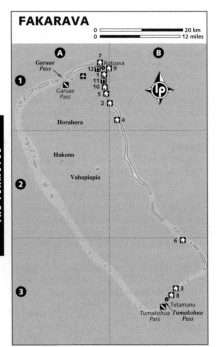

FAKARAVA

```
0 ————————— 20 km
0 ————————— 12 miles
```

SIGHTS & ACTIVITIES
Fakarava Diving Center	(see 5)
Tetamanu Diving	(see 8)
Topdive	(see 2)

SLEEPING
Havaiki Pearl Guesthouse	**1** A1
Hôtel Maitai Dream Fakarava	**2** A1
Motu Aito Paradise	**3** B3
Pension Kiria	**4** B1
Pension Paparara	**5** A1
Raimiti	**6** B3
Relais Marama	**7** A1
Tetamanu Village	**8** B3
Tokerau Village	(see 2)
Vahitu Dream	**9** A1
Vaiama Village	(see 5)
Veke Veke Village	**10** A1

EATING
Snack Chez Elda	**11** A1
Snack Te Anuanua	**12** A1

Fakarava Diving Center (☎ 93 40 75; www.fakarava -diving-center.com) At Pension Paparara.

Te Ava Nui (☎ 98 42 50, 98 43 50, 79 69 50; www .divingfakarava.com; Rotoava)

Tetamanu Diving Center (☎ 77 10 06; www.tetama nuvillage.pf) At Tetamanu Village.

Topdive (☎ 98 43 23, 73 38 22; www.topdive.com) At Hôtel Maitai Dream Fakarava.

claim Garuae Pass, in the north of the atoll, as the widest pass in all of French Polynesia. It also has a second pass, Tumakohua in the far south, that the locals reckon is the most beautiful in the Tuamotus and it's hard not to agree. The atoll's particularly diverse ecosystem has made it a Unesco-protected area.

Most islanders live in **Rotoava** village at the northeastern end, 4km east of the airport. Aside from Rangiroa's Avatoru, this is the most developed and busy town in the Tuamotus but it's still pretty quiet by most people's standards. A handful of inhabitants also live in **Tetamanu** village, on the edge of the southern pass, which is as backwater as backwater gets.

Activities
Visits to pearl farms and picnics plus snorkelling on idyllic *motu* are the order of the day – half-day boat excursions start at 9500 CFP per person. A bike ride around the village gives you time to peruse the pearl boutiques.

Fakarava has amazing diving in the Garuae and Tumakohua Passes (for details, see p71) and dive operators here can organise day trips to pristine Toau. The four operators:

Fakarava is also on the program for several dive-cruise operators and the *Aranui 3* (see the boxed text, p203).

Sleeping
ROTOAVA & AROUND
The following places are near or relatively near the airport and northern pass and unless otherwise noted are on gorgeous white sandy beaches, have cold-water bathrooms, don't take credit cards and offer free airport transfers. All offer kayaks and bikes for hire or for free.

Relais Marama (☎ /fax 98 42 51; www.relais .marama.com; campsites per person 2000 CFP, bungalow s/ d 5000/9000 CFP; ▫) On the ocean side of the *motu* at Rotoava, behind the *mairie* (town hall), this good-value, backpackerlike option has eight basic but pleasant and immaculate bungalows with shared bathroom. All prices include breakfast and for other meals you can use the communal kitchen or go to nearby eateries. Campers share the same facilities as the bungalows.

Vahitu Dream (☎ 98 42 63; vaihitudream@mail .pf; r with breakfast per person 4500 CFP, r with half board per person 7500 CFP) The most simple option on

Fakarava is based in Rotoava village and offers five rooms with shared bathroom in a family home. It's a friendly atmosphere, is just across the street from the lagoon and the fishing trips (from 5500 CFP/per person) have a great reputation.

Pension Paparara (☎ /fax 98 42 66; www.fakarava -divelodge.com; s/d/tr bungalow half board without bathroom 9500/17,000/24,000 CFP, s/d/tr bungalow half board 16,000/20,000/29,000 CFP) You have two options here: one of two small but wonderfully organic 'Robinson *fare*' that are right on the water and share a cold-water bathroom, or more comfortable but still artistic beachside bungalows with private bathrooms. There's an on-site dive centre and Fakarava Locations rents bikes and scooters from here. The owners are young and dynamic, serve good food and accept credit cards.

Vaiama Village (☎ /fax 98 41 13; www.fakaravavaiama .com; bungalow s/d/tr/q with half board 11,000/18,000/26,00 0/33,000 CFP) One basic two-storey house sleeps five people while three smaller and prettier coconut thatch bungalows sleep two. All have attached bathrooms with coral gravel floors and big ferns for a tropical oasis effect. The site is gorgeous and there's a pontoon and good snorkelling out front. It's a family atmosphere and airport transfers cost 1000 CFP return.

Pension Kiria (☎ 83 41 05; pensionkiria@mail.pf; s/d bungalows with half board 11,000/19,000 CFP) Each of the four bungalows here is made from coconut thatch and a variety of local materials – each is different to the others and exceptionally beautiful. The attached bathrooms are filled with ferns and the grounds are covered in coral gravel, which keeps the place especially tidy (and no sand in your bed) – there's a little sandy beach beyond the coral, however. The smiles of the owners stand out even by Paumotu standards. Airport transfers are 2000 CFP return.

Havaiki Pearl Guesthouse (☎ 93 40 16; www .havaiki.com; s/d with half board 11,500/18,000 CFP; 💻) This is the liveliest *pension* on Fakarava and the ambience is like a small hotel. Bungalows are basic wooden structures but they're all well decorated with local fabrics and have good mosquito nets. The restaurant serves meals to guests and nonguests with plenty of options including lunchtime hot sandwiches from 500 CFP and cocktails for around 1100 CFP. Breakfast is a buffet with lots of options beyond the standard bread and jam. Also on offer here is an interesting activity the owner

calls 'pearl fishing'; for 3000 CFP you can dive down and pick a grafted oyster, open it then keep the pearl you find inside. Credit cards are accepted, good English is spoken and airport transfers cost between 1000 and 2000 CFP.

Tokerau Village (☎ 98 41 09, 71 30 46; tokerauvillage@ mail.pf; bungalow s/d with half board 12,000/22,000 CFP) This is the most upscale and comfortable *pension* on Fakarava and its relatively low prices make it a real bargain. Flora the owner spends her days fine-tuning the garden and making sure there's not a speck of dust in any of the four large, modern wood bungalows. Each unit has a big terrace, mosquito net, TV and sleeps up to three people. The food is creative, delicious and usually involves vegetables as well as fresh fish. Credit cards are accepted, some English is spoken and the whole place runs on solar energy.

Veke Veke Village (☎ 98 42 80; www.pension -fakarava.com; bungalows s/d with half board 13,000/19,000 CFP) Choose between two family-sized semi-over-the-water bungalows or two smaller bungalows with coral gravel floors right on the beach. All options are on the old side but are well kept and there's a brand new dining area that has beautiful sunset views over the lagoon. It's an exquisite spot and the management is very friendly. Airport transfers are 1000 CFP return and credit cards are accepted.

Hôtel Maitai Dream Fakarava (☎ 43 08 83; www.hotel maitai.com; bungalows 27,000-38,000 CFP; 🏊 💻) With 27 classy wooden bungalows, a restaurant and numerous activities on offer, this is the biggest and most luxurious option on Fakarava. The beach is good and there's a particularly picturesque pontoon but the hotel is understaffed, beds lack mosquito nets and the garden needs some TLC. Add 7000 CFP per person for half board. Credit cards accepted.

TETAMANU & AROUND
At the other end of Fakarava, near Tumakohua Pass and a two-hour boat ride from the airport, is the village of Tetamanu (population six). The three options listed here can easily fulfil any fantasies of being stranded, alone, on a desert island.

Motu Aito Paradise (☎ /fax 41 29 00; www.fakarava .org; r with full board per person 14,000 CFP) This *pension* is a feat of artistic ingenuity. The *motu* is really nothing special, but the owners have built such beautiful coconut-thatch structures and planted enough flowers that they've transformed the land into something spectacular.

Tasty meals, taken with the other guests, are served in a large, interior communal area or in a covered area at the lagoon's edge, though some hungry divers have reported there's sometimes not enough food to go around. Prices are for a three-night minimum stay and include daily excursions and airport transfers.

Raimiti (☎ 55 05 65; www.raimiti.com; s/d bungalow with full board for 2 nights from 47,000/84,000 CFP) Travellers enthuse about this Crusoe-chic and very isolated spot with only two bungalows (one wooden with hot water and a more rustic thatch, one with cold-water bathroom) – romance anyone? Meals are excellent, especially considering the location, and are served either in a lagoonside, shell-fringed hut or under the stars. Oil lamps light the scene at night and during the day, if you're not off on an organised activity, you can walk for hours along the empty lagoon or exterior reef. Prices include transfers and activities and credit cards are accepted.

Tetamanu Village (☎ 43 92 40; tetamanuvillage@ mail.pf; r with full board per person per 3/4/5 days 48,000/58,000/61,000 CFP) This place is a real heart-breaker. It is in a superb setting on a white-sand beach overlooking the stunning Tumakohua Pass. Unfortunately, we've heard reports of unreliable service, which can be worrisome in such a remote setting. There's a dive centre here and credit cards are accepted.

Eating

The two *snacks* are open for lunch and dinner and offer free pick-up from all the *pensions* at the north of the island.

Snack Te Anuanua (☎ 98 41 58; Rotoava; mains 1200-2900 CFP) One of the pleasures of Fakarava is eating at this surprisingly chic restaurant with sea views, good music and even better food. The boutique, open during lunch hours sells beautiful *pareu* (sarong-type garment) and some creative pearl jewellery.

Snack Chez Elda (☎ 98 41 33; mains 1000-1300 CFP) Simple meals are served at this lagoonside place. Call ahead to make sure it's open.

Getting There & Away

The atoll is 488km east-northeast of Tahiti and southeast of Rangiroa.

The airport is 4km west of Rotoava. **Air Tahiti** (☎ 67 70 35, 67 70 85; www.airtahiti.pf) flies from Pape'ete to Fakarava every day (18,000 CFP one way), three times a week to/from

Bora Bora (27,000 CFP), twice weekly from Fakarava to Rangiroa to (5200 CFP) and Manihi (11,000 CFP) and once weekly to Hiva Oa in the Marquesas (28,000 CFP).

The *Saint-Xavier Maris-Stella*, *Cobia III* and *Mareva Nui* stop at Fakarava and take passengers.

Getting Around

A scheduled visit by former French president Jacques Chirac (he never actually showed up) brought funding to pave a 20km road from the airport to the southeast side of the atoll. It's a long haul cycling this in the hot sun; some *pensions* will drop you off at the far end so you can pedal back to town.

TIKEHAU

pop 407 / lagoon area 461 sq km

This is our favourite atoll in the Tuamotus for its unparalleled beauty, endless beaches and low-key yet reasonably developed tourist infrastructure. Time has eroded the ring of coral into sweeping, twisting *motu* of white and pink sands that engulf little bays, craggy nooks and the lagoon, which is one of the world's best natural swimming pools. The lagoon is as blue as any you'll find in French Polynesia, the beaches are out of this world and the pass houses an exceptional abundance of fish.

Most islanders live in Tuherahera village, in the southwest of the atoll, leaving the majority of the paradisiacal *motu* untouched. People live from copra production, fishing and, increas-

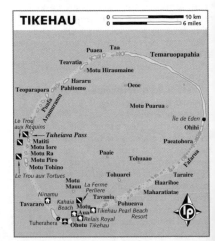

ingly, tourism. With regular flights and cargo ships, it's a well-stocked and well-tended place where everyone has a reason to be smiling.

The roughly oval-shaped atoll is 26km on its longest axis. It's cut by Tuheiava Pass in the west and by more than 100 *hoa*.

Information

There is no bank or ATM on Tikehau and at the time of research very little public internet was available – although many *pensions* were talking about getting it. The Tuherahera **post office** (7.30-9.30am Mon, Wed & Fri, to 11am Tue & Thu) has fax facilities and sells phonecards that you can use at the phone box in front.

Sights & Activities

Tuherahera is a pretty village, bursting with *uru* (breadfruit), coconut trees, bougainvillea and hibiscus. There is an uncommon variety of faiths including Catholic, Sanito, Seventh-Day Adventist and Protestant, all of which have their own church.

Lagoon excursions are the easiest way to explore the magnificent lagoon. Regular stops include a visit to the rocky **Motu Puarua** (Île aux Oiseaux, or Bird Island) where several species of ground-nesting birds including brown noddies and *uaau* (red-footed boobies) are easily spotted. Another interesting stop is at **Île de Eden**, an establishment of the Church of the New Testament, which has created a vibrant, organic garden in the infertile sands of its superb *motu* – they also have a fish park filled with blue jacks and *uluwati* (giant trevally). A last stop is usually a barbecue picnic on one of many idyllic *motu*. Pensions generally organise excursions, sometimes through an outside operator, and trips cost from 7000 to 7500 CFP per person.

Tuheiava Pass, to the west of the atoll, about 30 minutes by boat from Tuherahera village, is another fantastic site that is worth a visit. Unfortunately, it's hard to get anyone to take you there unless you're going to dive it with one of the clubs or are staying at Ninamu (see p190).

Jacques Cousteau, on his one of his expeditions to Tikehau, stated that it had the densest fish populations of all the atolls on the planet, so **scuba diving** and **snorkelling** are obviously recommended activities. There are also great drop-offs at Le Trou aux Requins and Maama; see p70 for details about sites. Dive centres include **Raie Manta Club** (/fax 96 22 53; http://raie mantaclub.free.fr) at Tikehau Village (p190), and

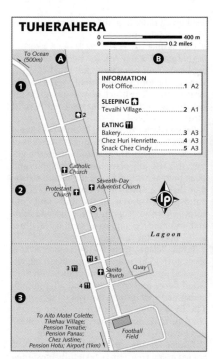

Tikehau Blue Nui (/fax 96 22 40, 96 23 00; www.bluenui .com) at Tikehau Pearl Beach Resort (p190).

Sleeping

All *pensions* on Tikehau are on white-sand beaches and serve meals. Prices quoted include transfers to the airport as well as taxes. Unless otherwise noted they have private cold-water bathrooms, don't take credit cards and the prices listed are per person. In general, add 1000 to 1500 CFP per person if you want full board; kids under 12 are charged half price for everything. While every option has either mosquito screens on the windows or mosquito nets, and all offer mosquito coils, come well armed with repellent.

TUHERAHERA VILLAGE & AROUND

Options here are near the village and airport and are lined up along the lagoon side of the *motu*.

Pension Panau (/fax 96 22 99; bungalows with half board 6000 CFP) This is the least expensive place on Tikehau, and the most simple, but with that million dollar beach in front, you won't

THE TUAMOTUS

need much more than the friendly family vibe to keep you happy.

Chez Justine (☎ 96 22 87, 72 02 44; r & bungalows with half board 8000 CFP) Ask for one of the three big beachfront bungalows here that cost the same as the four simple, small rooms tucked away behind. The beach is spacious, great for swimming and has a volleyball net. Credit cards are accepted.

Pension Hotu (☎ /fax 96 22 89; bungalows with half board 8500 CFP) On one of the nicest stretches of beach, and the furthest *pension* from the village, this friendly place has five spacious and clean bungalows that have a little more artistic flair than the others in this price bracket, via hand-painted *pareu* on the walls and cool coral and wood decoration. Kayaks and mineral water are free and basic sanitary facilities are available for campers.

Tevaihi Village (☎ /fax 96 23 04; bungalows with half board 8500 CFP) This is the only *pension* in the village and the four newish bungalows with their wood floors and colourful *tifaifai* (appliqué) bedspreads, are among the best on this *motu*. The beach here is fronted by some craggy coral formations but there's OK swimming just beyond. Credit cards are accepted.

Pension Tematie (☎ /fax 96 22 65; bungalows with half board 9000 CFP) Three tastefully designed hexagonal bungalows with cement floors and lots of windows sit in garden shaded by ironwood trees on a small beach. There's one bigger family bungalow that can sleep five or six people. It's run by a friendly French and Tahitian couple.

Aito Motel Colette (☎ 96 22 47, 74 85 77; fax 96 23 07; bungalows with half/full board 14,000/17,000 CFP) Stylish, wooden bungalows on stilts with coconut thatch roofs share the fetching beach with neighbour Tikehau Village. The beachside eating area is decked out in shells and woven palm fronds and the food is good but some travellers have complained that the service is lacking. It offers no more than most family *pensions* so the hefty price tag makes it poor value.

Tikehau Village (☎ 96 22 86; tikehauvillage@mail.pf; s/d/f bungalows with half board 15,000/22,000/34,000 CFP) Tikehau's biggest *pension* got a stylish facelift in 2007 and the eight beachfront bungalows are now dripping with thatch, varnished local wood and coral stonework – plus the bathrooms have hot water. The shady terraces look out over white-sand and turquoise-lagoon bliss. The restaurant area is one of the prettiest spots around, overlooking the water with cool breezes and a social vibe – nonguests are welcome. There are kayaks for guests' use and an on-site dive centre. Credit cards are accepted and English is spoken.

PRIVATE MOTU

Kahaia Beach (☎ 96 22 77; fax 96 22 81; bungalows with half board 7500 CFP) The bungalows here are in a deplorable state but Peta, the owner, often whips out his ukulele at night and soon everyone's singing on the beach, eating fresh fish and not thinking about the holes in the roofs. You can also camp here, but there are no real facilities. It's just across a small waterway from the Tuherahera *motu*.

Ninamu (Billabongteahupoo@mail.pf) Still under construction when we passed, this Australian-run place was already looking like one of the most photo-worthy and eco-conscious places to stay in the Tuamotus. On a private white-and pink-sand *motu* near the pass, the massive bungalows are built from gnarled hunks of wood, coral stonework and coconut thatch. The restaurant is another Crusoe-with-style masterpiece with a stage for bands and a professional kitchen ready for a willing chef. Everything is powered by wind and sun and toilets are self-composting (and smell as fresh as any resort's septic ones). Let's hope the service is as stellar as the surrounds.

Relais Royal Tikehau (☎ 96 23 37; www.royal tikehau.com in French; s/d with half board 16,000/24,000 CFP, s/d bungalow with half board from 21,000/31,000 CFP; 🖥) A hop over from the Kahaia Beach *motu*, this immaculate and lovingly tended place is a great alternative if you can't afford the Tikehau Pearl Beach Resort. Bungalows are big and comfy and decorated with Polynesian taste – think lots of ruffles and bright colours. Rooms are smaller, and have neither the views nor the cooling breezes that the bungalows have. The whole place is run on solar and wind power, the charming hosts speak English and it's about a 20-minute walk across some shallow waterways to the village. When Peta from Kahaia Beach, next door, doesn't have guests (which is often) he comes and plays music here instead. At the time of research it was also the only place on Tikehau where you could check the internet (for a whopping 500 CFP for 15 minutes).

Tikehau Pearl Beach Resort (☎ 96 23 00; www .pearlresorts.com; bungalows 48,000-83,000 CFP; 🍽 🖥) We love this resort not only for its stunning position between endless swathes of white- and pink-sand beaches and bright blue waters, but also because it makes an effort to be environmentally and socially responsible – a huge percentage of the village is employed here and the director tries to keep energy use and impact to a minimum. Walk for hours along empty beaches, spend the day in the water or take off on one of many offered water activities. There are free shuttle boats to the village five times a day. The over-the-water suites offer the extra bonus of privacy and are so big and exquisitely designed that you might never want to leave your private dock. All options except the over-the-water standard bungalows have air-con. Credit cards are accepted.

Eating

Chez Huri Henriette (⏲ 6am-noon & 2-7pm daily) is a general store, and on certain days of the week you can get coconut pastries from the village's only *boulangerie* (bakery) a few doors down. **Snack Chez Cindy** (☎ 96 22 67; mains 1200-1400 CFP; ⏲ lunch Sun-Fri, dinner Sat-Thu), the only snack bar in town, serves massive portions of good *poisson cru* (raw fish), *steak frites* (steak and chips), chow mein and more. To eat lighter order a 500 CFP burger.

Nonguests can also grab a table at Tikehau Village (opposite) or call for the shuttle times to lunch at the swanky **Tikehau Pearl Beach Resort** (⏲ noon-2.30pm; opposite).

Getting There & Away

The airport is about 1km east of the village entrance. **Air Tahiti** (☎ 96 22 66) has seven flights a week between Pape'ete and Tikehau (17,000 CFP). There are also several flights between Bora Bora and Tikehau (24,000 CFP). The five-days-a-week Tikehau–Rangiroa flight costs 5500 CFP.

The *Mareva Nui* and *Saint-Xavier Maris-Stella* are the only cargo ships that offer transport to Tikehau.

Getting Around

A 10km track goes around Tuherahera, and passes by the airport. Bicycles can be hired (600/1200 CFP per half/full day) at your *pension* or if you stay at Chez Justine they're free.

MATAIVA

pop 235 / lagoon area 25 sq km

Despite the limited tourist infrastructure, this tiny atoll provides a delightful escape holiday

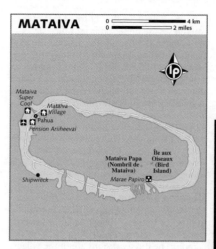

and is becoming one of the more popular spots in the archipelago. There are superb and easily accessible beaches, numerous snorkelling spots, lots of fish and one of the few noteworthy archaeological sites in the Tuamotus.

The structure of the Mataiva lagoon gives it an unusual appearance: the coral heads create walls 50m to 300m wide that form about 70 basins with a maximum depth of 10m. Seen from the plane it looks like a mosaic of greens.

Plans to mine the lagoon for its phosphate deposits have been halted due to the community's determined opposition but the Tahitian government is still pushing for mining rights. The accessible part is estimated to contain 12 million tonnes, enough for 10 to 15 years of mining.

The village of Pahua is divided by a pass a few metres wide and no deeper than 1.5m, suitable only for very small boats. A bridge spans the pass and links the two parts of the village.

Information

There is no bank on the atoll. Pahua has two shops and a post office, south of the bridge. The post office has a fax service and sells phonecards. There are card-operated telephone booths next to the post office and at the airport.

Sights & Activities

Marae Papiro is a well-kept *marae* (traditional temple) on the edge of a *hoa*, about 14km from the village. In the centre of this *marae*, you can see the stone seat from which, according to legend, the giant Tu guarded the pass against invasion. In the south, along the edge of the lagoon, there are gorgeous **beaches**.

Île aux Oiseaux (Bird Island), to the east of the lagoon, is a crescent-shaped coral spit covered in small shrubs. It is a favourite nesting place for *oio* (brown noddies), *tara* (great crested terns) and red-footed boobies.

Don't miss the chance to help fishermen catch fish in one of the numerous **fish parks** around the lagoon and the pass. Sorted, scaled and gutted, the fish are sold in the village.

Sleeping & Eating

The people of Pahua hope that an increasing number of tourists will dissuade the government from setting up drilling sites on the lagoon. The three *pensions* are in the village. Prices are per person per day and include taxes and airport transfers. No credit cards.

Pension Ariiheevai (☎ 76 73 23, 96 32 50; fax 96 32 46; bungalows with full board & excursions 8000 CFP; ✷) This place is one of the best deals in the Tuamotus. Alphonsine, the owner, lovingly tends the six huge bungalows all on the edge of the white-sand-fringed emerald lagoon. The food is great and there are plenty of activities offered including flower-garland making, picnics at Marae Papiro and visits to the bird *motu* or the fish park. Kayaks and bikes are free. Reserve in advance!

Mataiva Village (☎ /fax 96 32 95; campsites for 1/2 people 1500/2500 CFP; s/d bungalows with full board from 7500/14,000 CFP; ✷) Eight comfortable bungalows grace the pass but there's not really a beach. Three have fully equipped kitchens and kayaks are 1000 CFP per day and bikes 500 CFP. Campers are welcome.

Mataiva Super Cool (☎ 96 32 53, 28 79 15; fax 96 32 92; bungalows with full board incl excursions 8500-10,000 CFP) On the other side of the bridge, to the south, this place has four comfy bungalows with cold-water bathrooms and terraces overlooking the pass. Kayaks and bikes are free.

Apart from the *pensions* there's really nowhere to eat, although there are several small shops with basic food supplies.

Getting There & Away

Mataiva is 350km northeast of Tahiti and 100km west of Rangiroa.

The proprietor of the Mataiva Village is the local representative of **Air Tahiti** (☎ 96 32

48). There are two Pape'ete–Mataiva flights (17,000 CFP one way) a week, and one flight to/from Rangiroa (5900 CFP one way).

Mataiva is on the routes of the *Mareva Nui* and *Saint-Xavier Maris-Stella*.

Getting Around

A track goes almost all the way around the island through the middle of the coconut plantation for about 28km.

Cycling is an excellent way of getting to Marae Papiro. The *pensions* rent bicycles for about 1000 CFP per day.

The *pensions* organise trips to the various sites by motorboat and by car, costing about 3000 CFP for the day, including a picnic.

MANIHI

pop 1239 / lagoon area 192 sq km

Considered the birthplace of the Tahitian pearl industry, Manihi is a classically gorgeous atoll with one deep pass (Tairapa) in the southwest and great fishing. Since pearl prices began to plummet around 2000 (see the boxed text, p176), approximately 50 farms have gone out of business but there are still about eight family-run and three industrial pearl farms dotted around the lagoon. Manihi is now eclipsed by its quiet neighbour Ahe in terms of numbers of pearls produced but it's still a great place to visit a pearl farm and maybe buy the pearl of your dreams.

Shaped like an ellipse, the atoll is 28km long and 8km wide. The best beaches and

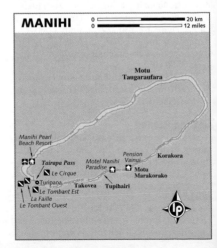

picnic spots are at the south of the lagoon where white sand, ruffled palms and sapphire waters make for the perfect escape. The not-very-pretty village of Turipaoa takes about five minutes to wander round but is a good place to get a sense for atoll life.

There are a number of magnificent diving sites near the pass, including Tairapa Pass and Le Tombant. See p70 for details. The dive centre **Manihi Blue Nui** (☎ /fax 96 42 17, 96 42 73; www.bluenui.com) operates from the Manihi Pearl Beach Resort.

Information

There is no bank on the atoll, but the Manihi Pearl Beach Resort (right) and Libre Service Jean-Marie, near the marina, may be able to change money. The post office is in Turipaoa village opposite the marina. There are card-operated telephone booths at the post office, the airport and Manihi Pearl Beach Resort. Turipaoa also has an infirmary.

Sleeping & Eating

Manihi offers three distinct options, each on private *motu*, which cater to different levels of independence. All are great places for families and accept credit cards. Apart from the *pensions* and hotels, there are hardly any places to eat. In Turipaoa, there's a well-stocked shop, Libre Service Jean-Marie, near the marina and another smaller shop at the quay on the pass.

Pension Vainui (☎ 96 42 89; www.pensionvainui.com; r with full board per person 12,000 CFP) East of the village and about a half-hour boat ride from the airport, this all-inclusive *pension* has eight very funky rooms without bathrooms. There is not much privacy here but the site is one of the best on the atoll, the welcome is friendly and the food is copious and well prepared. Rates include well-organised daily excursions but airport transfers cost 1000 CFP round trip.

Motel Nanihi Paradise (☎ 96 41 54; www.nanihi paradise.com; 1/2 r in bungalow without meals 14,000/21,000 CFP, whole bungalow with full board per person 13,500 CFP) On a tiny *motu*, this place has two clean, flower-bedecked, two-bedroom bungalows with fully equipped kitchen and luminous, well-designed bathrooms. Excursions are offered to pearl farms (2600 CFP), there are lagoon tours (4000 CFP) and diving can be organised through Manihi Blue Nui dive centre. Round-trip airport transfers for stays under three nights are 2100 CFP.

Manihi Pearl Beach Resort (☎ 96 42 73, in Pape'ete 43 16 10; fax 96 42 72, in Pape'ete 43 17 86; beach/over-water bungalows 31,000/67,000 CFP; 🖳 🖭) An exceptionally well-run resort, this place feels like a superluxurious summer camp for honeymooners. A slew of daily activities on offer ranges from village visits to deep-sea fishing and on Wednesday night the bar manager offers a free star-watching talk. Of course you could just as easily spend the day enjoying the little beach, the comfort of your plush bungalow and the very good restaurant.

Getting There & Away

The representative of **Air Tahiti** (☎ 96 43 34, flight days 96 42 71) is in Turipaoa but on flight days will be at the airport. There are almost daily flights between Pape'ete and Manihi (20,000 CFP one way), direct or via Ahe, Tikehau or Rangiroa (11,000 CFP one way). There's also a twice-weekly flight to Fakarava (11,000 CFP one way).

The *Mareva Nui* and *Saint-Xavier Maris-Stella* service Manihi and accept passengers.

Getting Around

The only track on Manihi links Motu Taugaraufara to the airport, covering a total distance of only about 9km. The Manihi Pearl Beach Resort rents bicycles for around 1000 CFP per day but you can't get too far and the road is barren and shadeless.

All sleeping options offer airport transfers and the *pensions* will organise transport if you want to dive with Manihi Blue Nui dive club (left).

AHE

pop 377 / lagoon area 170 sq km

Although Ahe is the biggest pearl-producing atoll in the Tuamotus, its 20km-long by 10km-wide ring of coral is less developed than many other surrounding atolls because of its geography. The atoll's only pass, Tiareroa (Long Flower), is at the northwest of the atoll while the village of Tenukupara is in the far southwest and the airport is at the northern extremity. This means that just getting to the airport from the village takes over an hour! Still, the atoll's beauty draws in a large number of yachties between May and August and the two *pensions* here are among the best in the archipelago. It's a great place to experience the unadorned charm of the Tuamotus and to buy pearls.

Sleeping & Eating

The following places are run by solar power.

Chez Raita (☎ /fax 96 44 53; www.ahedream.com, in French; bungalows with half/full board per person 7500/9500 CFP) Owned by the local fireman and his family, this friendly *pension* is on a white-sand *motu* on the east side of the atoll. We've had enthusiastic reports from readers who claimed that staying here was a highlight of their world travels. Picnic excursions to Tenukupara village and other *motu* are offered from 4100 to 7000 CFP per person. Line fishing in the lagoon is 1200 CFP per person.

Cocoperle Lodge (☎ /fax 96 44 08; www.cocoperle lodge.com; bungalows with half/full board per person from 11,000/13,000 CFP; 💻) An eco-boutique hotel that's a step up in organisation from your standard family *pension*, Franco-Polynesian-run Cocoperle Lodge gets consistently great reviews from travellers. In a coconut plantation facing the lagoon, six well-decorated bungalows made with local materials have either attached or shared bathroom (all with hot water), fan and mosquito screens; those with attached bathroom can sleep a family of four. Excellent meals are served in a *fare* by the lagoon and the bar is open all day. Excursions to the nearby bird *motu* or to a pearl farm cost 1000 CFP and there's a whole menu of other free and paid activities on offer. The lodge packs its rubbish to Pape'ete for proper disposal and is a member of the Reef Check program (see p252). At the time of research the hotel was planning to open a dive club early in 2009 – check its regularly updated website for news on this. Credit cards are accepted, and English and some Italian are spoken.

Getting There & Away

Air Tahiti flies from Pape'ete to Ahe four days weekly (20,000 CFP one way). Twice-weekly flights to Manihi are 6000 CFP one way.

The *Saint-Xavier Maris-Stella* and *Mareva Nui* service Ahe.

TAKAROA

pop 1023 / lagoon area 113 sq km

Of the Takaroa-Takapoto pair, Takaroa is the more populous and prosperous (it's one of the biggest pearl producers in the country) but has less to offer tourists beyond snorkelling, pearl farm visits and a beach-laden Paumotu setting. (Good luck getting a beer here, since the population is 90% Mormon.) The atoll is 27km long by 6km wide and has one pass,

Teauonae, in the southwest. The only village, Teavaroa, is on a round *motu* at the pass and is home to the largest meteorological station in the northern Tuamotus.

First seen by European eyes in 1616 by Le Maire, Takaroa (literally, Long Chin) and its close neighbour, Takapoto, have been called the King George Islands on marine maps (but not elsewhere) ever since Byron's visit in 1765.

Sleeping & Eating

Poerangi Village (☎ 98 23 82; poerangivillage@mail.pf; bungalows with half/full board per person from 8000/9500 CFP) Poerangi literally means 'pearls of heaven' and guests may think it's a good description. It's on the south side of the pass, 10 minutes by boat from the village. There are three bungalows with bathroom (cold water only), one with a kitchenette. Rates include airport transfers. Meals including local specialities are served in the *fare potee*, where there's also a bar. Various activities are offered, including kayaking (free), snorkelling, fishing trips, visits to pearl farms and various excursions on the atoll.

For meals, apart from the *pension* there's one *snack* in the village as well as a few small shops.

Getting There & Away

Takaroa is 575km northeast of Pape'ete and less than 100km east of Manihi.

The airport is 2.5km northeast of the village. The office of the Air Tahiti representative is in the village. There are five weekly flights from Pape'ete to Takaroa (22,000 CFP); the trip takes just over 1½ hours. Although most flights stop in Takapoto, Air Tahiti does not offer this flight.

The *Mareva Nui* and *Saint-Xavier Maris-Stella* stop at the atoll and take passengers.

Getting Around

The only track goes from the village to Paul Yu's pearl farm, through the airport – about 10km.

TAKAPOTO

pop 485 / lagoon area 102 sq km

Takapoto (literally, Short Chin), 9km south of Takaroa, is one of the friendliest atolls in the Tuamotus and is also home to an impressive number of ancient *marae* (a rarity in this archipelago). The 20km-long and 6km-wide lagoon has white- and pink-sand beaches that

THE TUAMOTUS

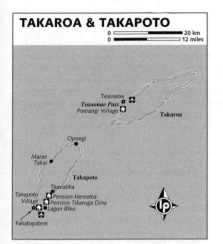

TAKAROA & TAKAPOTO

0 ——————— 20 km
0 ——————— 12 miles

Teavaroa
Teauonae Pass
Poerangi Village

Takaroa

Opongi

Marae
Takai

Takapoto

Teavatika

Takapoto Village
Pension Hereatea
Pension Tikaruga Dina
Lagon Bleu

Fakatopatere

rival Tikehau's and a lagoon that couldn't possibly be a more intense shade of blue. Because it doesn't have a pass there are few sharks and the sandy bottom, though ideal for swimming, isn't great for snorkelling.

The second pearl farm in the Tuamotus was built on this atoll in the late 1960s and pearling flourished till prices crashed around 2003. Today the residents have turned mostly back to copra (convenient since there is an uncommon quantity of mature coconut palms on the atoll) but a few small pearl farms are still running.

The atoll has been the subject of multidisciplinary studies since 1974 under the auspices of Unesco's Man & Biosphere (MAB) program and today the EVAAM (Établissement pour la Valorisation des Activités Aquacoles et Maritimes), at the edge of Fakatopatere village, continues research on pearl oysters and pearl farming.

Information

There is no bank or internet on the atoll. The Fakatopatere post office, next to the *mairie,* offers fax facilities and phonecards but internet installation had been stalled when we passed. There are card-operated telephones in front of the *mairie,* at the marina and at the airport. The community clinic is also next to the post office.

Sights & Activities

The little village of **Fakatopatere** has a surprising number of interesting vestiges including two **bronze cannons** that villagers claim have been proven to be from one of Roggeveen's ships, the *Africanishe Queen,* which sunk off Takapoto in 1722. Another **18th-century mobile cannon** is stuck on the reef and can be seen from Takapoto's new oceanside **marina.**

Takapoto has many idyllic **beaches** but the pink-sand **Lagon Bleu** about 1km north of the village is one of the best for the view and for swimming. Another gorgeous spot is **Teavatika,** a small fish park built of coral blocks in a *hoa,* where there are always a few locals net fishing. It's at the end of the northward-bound coral track, about 9km from the village.

Some 20 ancient *marae* are found dotted around the atoll and have the densest concentration at **Opongi,** the site of the old village at the far north. At Fakatopatere is a **marae** where boys were circumcised in ancient times (near the cemetery) and about 2km north of here is the small **Hikuragi** where it's thought (though disputed) that young virgins were deflowered. Also reachable by road is small, crumbling **Marae Takai,** approximately 15km from Fakatopatere towards the west (on the lagoon side just after the first bridge), which is thought to have been a funeral site.

Sleeping & Eating

There are two little shops in Fakatopatere plus a *boulangerie* that sells baguettes (except on the days when Mama Tepui makes her fresh coconut bread). The following *pension* prices are for half board per person. No-one takes credit cards and showers are cold.

Pension Tikaruga Dina (☎ 98 64 26, 28 90 75; www
.pensiondinamoorea.pf; bungalows 6000 CFP) Two two-storey chalet-style bungalows look out over the sublime lagoon and a pontoon with a converted grafting shack bungalow at the end of it. The two connected bathrooms are outside the bungalows and are a long walk if you're staying on the pontoon. It has a welcoming local-style atmosphere and is solar powered.

Takapoto Village (☎ 98 65 44; bungalows 6500 CFP) Takaroa's oldest *pension* has two big bungalows at the edge of the village on a very good, but busy (with dogs, kids and locals, not sun-worshippers) beach. It was getting a fresh coat of paint when we passed and guests can expect to be immersed in the day-to-day life of the owners, the charming Toti family.

Pension Hereatea (☎ 77 49 37; bungalows 11,000 CFP) Greener, tidier and fresher feeling

THE TUAMOTUS

THE TUAMOTUS

WOKING THE DOG

Traditionally, dog was consumed in all of the archipelagos of French Polynesia but today it's generally cooked up in a hush-hush manner and mostly on smaller, more remote islands particularly in the Tuamotus. The dogs that are done in are usually the ones that cause trouble – that steal things or bite people – but upsets do occur when someone eats someone else's beloved pet. In very rare cases, dogs are bred to be food. While many outsiders find this practice horrific, remember that there are no sterilisation services on the islands and even on Tahiti getting a dog spayed costs around 32,000 CFP. Frying up a 'bad' dog occasionally keeps the canine population in check, makes life better for the 'good' dogs and adds a little pizazz to a fish-heavy diet.

---

than the competition, the three tiny pink bungalows hover at the edge of a skinny, palm-shaded beach. There's a big, very well-equipped communal kitchen for making lunch but guests are encouraged to take half board. It's solar run, has a few fresh vegetables grown by the manager, and is a great place to stay.

Snack-Resto Veronica (✿ breakfast, lunch & dinner Thu-Tue) Takapoto's only *snack*. Get heaping portions of the usual suspects: chow mein, steak and fries and *poisson cru*.

Getting There & Away

Takapoto is 560km northeast of Pape'ete and less than 100km east of Manihi.

The airfield is behind the village. Air Tahiti has three weekly Pape'ete–Takapoto flights that cost 20,000 CFP one way.

The *Saint-Xavier Maris-Stella* and *Mareva Nui* stop at Takapoto and take passengers.

Getting Around

From the village, a crushed coral track runs about 9km northeast to the fish park and northwest 15km out. The ideal way to explore the atoll is by bicycle but watch out for mean dogs. Picnics on deserted *motu*, reached by speedboat, cost between 3500 and 8000 CFP depending on who you ask or if anyone really feels like going.

MAKEMO

pop 914 / lagoon area 620 sq km

Spectacular undersea landscapes, pristine *motu* and an off-the-beaten-track charm make Makemo an ideal destination for anyone looking for an authentic Paumotu experience. The opening of the professionally run dive centre Scubamakemo (at Scuba Makemo; see right) will surely attract visitors, but for now it's a sleepy and lightly visited escape.

Pouheva village is an administrative and school centre for the central Tuamotus. Still, there is no bank, just a little post office near the quay. All the *pensions* organise lagoon excursions (from 6000 CFP per person) that visit the old village site and the two passes.

See p71 for details about dive sites, including the pristine Arikamiro Pass.

Sleeping & Eating

Don't expect anything glamorous in Makemo but the welcome is friendly. No-one takes credit cards.

Scuba Makemo (☎ /fax 98 03 08, 78 49 13; makemo dive@mail.pf; bungalows with full board per person 7500 CFP) Ludovic, the manager of the dive centre Scubamakemo and the local fireman, also rents out two bungalows with attached bathroom. The bungalows are about 25m from the lagoon and are simple but clean. Meals are local-style and tasty.

Teanuanua Beach Pearls (☎ 78 23 23, 78 99 10; fax 98 02 19; s/d with full board 14,000/28,000 CFP) This place, 24km from the village, is completely isolated. Owned by French Tahitian pearl farmers, it has nine cement bungalows on stilts on a pretty beach – bathrooms are communal. The food here is exceptional considering the isolation, but we've had reports that the owners are often more concerned with their pearls than their visitors. There are mountain bikes for hire (500 CFP) as well as a car (8000 CFP), and kayaks are free.

Getting There & Around

The airport is 9km by a paved road from the village – if you have reserved at a *pension* they will collect you free of charge.

Air Tahiti flies to Makemo three times a week from Pape'ete (22,000 CFP one way) and once a week to Anaa (9500 CFP one way) and Hao (13,000 CFP one way). The cargo ships *Hotu Maru* and *Kura Ora II* and *III* serve the atoll.

ANAA
pop 639 / lagoon area 184 sq km
Anaa, which used to be densely populated, became known for its ferocious warring inhabitants, who extended their domination over the northern part of the archipelago, pillaging the atolls they conquered. Today, the calmness and tranquillity of the atoll and its people make this hard to imagine. Anaa Atoll is just 28km long and 5km wide and it doesn't have a pass.

The inhabitants live off fishing and copra production and it is gaining note from tourists for its saltwater fly-fishing opportunities.

Sleeping
Chez Louise (☎ 98 32 25; bungalow with half/full board 4500/6000 CFP) Has one simple chalet near the lagoon.

Pension Toku Kaiga (☎ 98 32 69; flyfishing.anaa@hotmail.com; bungalow or r with half/full board per person 7000/9000 CFP) Offers a choice between a bungalow and a fully-equipped 'chalet' in the village or a room in a house near the airport. Bicycles are available and airport transfers are included. Some fly-fishing tours use this place for a base.

Getting There & Away
Anaa is 450km east of Pape'ete. There are Pape'ete–Anaa flights twice a week (18,000 CFP one way) and Hao–Anaa flights every

Monday for 17,000 CFP via Makemo. It's also on the shipping routes of the *Kura Ora II* and *III*.

SOUTHERN & EASTERN TUAMOTUS

If not for the presence of the infamous Centre d'Expérimentation du Pacifique (CEP) conducting nuclear-testing operations (see Moruroa, p198), this totally isolated region would have remained forgotten to the outside world.

Cultured-pearl and copra production and fishing are the major industries of these islands. Hao is the regional centre. The smallest atolls in the archipelago are in this region; some, such as Nukutavake, Pinaki and Akiaki, are barely 5 sq km. Tourist facilities are rare and so are visitors.

HAO
pop 1613 / lagoon area 609 sq km
Affected by the unfortunate destiny of Moruroa and Fangataufa, Hao experienced growth from the 1960s onwards as an administrative and transit centre for the CEP. For a short time the French agents convicted of sinking the *Rainbow Warrior* served here (see the boxed text, p39). Its state-of-the-art infrastructure includes a 3300m runway built to handle the military transport planes. When atmospheric tests were conducted, there were

---

THE RISE & FALL OF MAKATEA

It's difficult to imagine an island in the Tuamotus covered in mining installations with more than 1000 workers, but for 50 years Makatea (population 94; area 30 sq km) made French Polynesia an industrial centre. The only high island in the Tuamotus, Makatea is a bean-shaped plateau with 80m-high cliffs forming its outer edge. These cliffs used to be a barrier reef and the plateau was once the basin of a lagoon, where vast amounts of phosphate accumulated.

The phosphate was discovered at the end of the 19th century and the Compagnie Française des Phosphates d'Océanie (CFPO) was created in 1908 to exploit the deposit. Infrastructure appeared from nowhere including a rail network, schools, a cinema, churches and shops. Until the early 1950s labour came largely from Asia.

With 3071 inhabitants in 1962, Makatea was the most populated island in the Tuamotus with phosphate being the core of the French Polynesian economy. From 12,000 tonnes in 1911, the extraction rate rose to 251,000 tonnes in 1929 and 400,000 tonnes in 1960, a record year.

By 1966, when the reserves were depleted, nearly 11 million tonnes of phosphate had been torn from the island. In the space of a few weeks, the workers packed everything up and the island became a ghost town. Today only a few people live on Makatea, making their living from copra and *kaveu* (coconut crabs).

up to 5000 people busy on the atoll. Hao has a middle school and a medical centre in Otepa, in the northeast.

Chez Amélie (☎ 97 03 42; dantzer@mail.pf; r per person 8500 CFP; ☒), in Otepa, is owned by Amélie Danzer, the local Air Tahiti representative. It has four rooms with air conditioning, in a house with attached bathroom (with hot water).

Air Tahiti flies from Pape'ete to Hao (2½ hours) four times a week for 26,000 CFP. There are flights once a week to Makemo (13,000 CFP), Anaa (17,000 CFP) and Mangareva (25,000 CFP). There are irregular connections from Hao to Takume, Fangatau, Fakahina, Tatakoto, Tureia, Vahitahi, Nukutavake, Pukarua and Reao. Inquire at Air Tahiti about flight schedules.

The *Nuku Hau, Kura Ora II* and *III* stop at Hao.

MORUROA
pop 20 / lagoon area 324 sq km

Ill-fated Moruroa, 1250km southeast of Tahiti, will forever be synonymous with nuclear testing and the catastrophe of the Greenpeace ship *Rainbow Warrior* (see the boxed text, p39). 'Discovered' in 1792 by the Englishman Matthew Weatherhead, it is 28km long and 11km wide, and has only one pass.

Moruroa was chosen for the tests because of its isolation from inhabited zones and its suitability for the necessary infrastructure. It was equipped with ultramodern electricity-production installations, a desalinisation plant and an airport for large aircraft. The atoll was ceded to the French state in 1964. With the final tests, jurisdiction was returned to the French Polynesian government and the installations were dismantled. Today there's just a small contingent of French legionnaires.

The Marquesas

Grand, brooding, powerful and charismatic. That pretty much sums up the Marquesas. Here, nature's fingers have dug deep grooves and fluted sharp edges, sculpting intricate jewels that jut up dramatically from the cobalt blue ocean. Waterfalls taller than skyscrapers trickle down vertical canyons; the ocean thrashes towering sea cliffs; sharp basalt pinnacles project from emerald forests; amphitheatre-like valleys cloaked in greenery are reminiscent of the *Raiders of the Lost Ark;* and scalloped bays are blanketed with desert arcs of white or black sand.

This art gallery is all outdoors. Some of the most inspirational hikes and rides in French Polynesia are found here, allowing walkers and horseback riders the opportunity to explore Nuku Hiva's convoluted hinterland. Those who want to get wet can snorkel with melon-headed whales or dive along the craggy shores of Hiva Oa and Tahuata. Bird-watchers can be kept occupied for days, too.

Don't expect sweeping bone-white beaches, tranquil turquoise lagoons, swanky resorts and Cancun-style nightlife – the Marquesas are not a beach holiday destination. With only a smattering of *pensions* (guesthouses) and just two hotels, they're rather an ecotourism dream.

In everything from cuisine and dances to language and crafts, the Marquesas do feel different from the rest of French Polynesia, and that's part of their appeal. Despite the trappings of Western influence (read: mobile phones), their cultural uniqueness is overwhelming. They also make for a mind-boggling open-air museum, with plenty of sites dating from pre-European times, all shrouded with a palpable historical aura.

THE MARQUESAS

HIGHLIGHTS

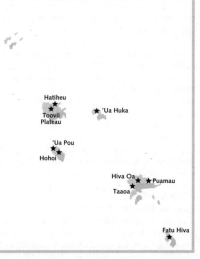

- Forgetting what day it is and realising the internet is really just a frivolous modern convenience on hard-to-reach **Fatu Hiva** (p225)

- Living out your Indiana Jones fantasies while wandering flabbergasted amid *tiki* (sacred sculptures) petroglyphs, and sacred sites at **Puamau** (p222), **Taaoa** (p222), **Hohoi** (p217) and **Hatiheu** (p208)

- **Clip-clopping** (p205 and p220) across the verdant Toovii Plateau or Hiva Oa's fecund interior

- Gazing down impenetrable valleys while **hiking** (p205 and p220) across the Nuku Hiva or Hiva Oa heartlands

- Experiencing timeless traditional village life on **'Ua Huka** (p211) or **'Ua Pou** (p214), lodging in homestays and meeting master carvers

Hatiheu
Toovii
Plateau
'Ua Huka
'Ua Pou
Hohoi
Hiva Oa
Puamau
Taaoa
Fatu Hiva

THE MARQUESAS

NORTHERN GROUP & SOUTHERN GROUP

The Marquesas are divided into two groups. The northern group consists of three main inhabited islands – Nuku Hiva, 'Ua Huka and 'Ua Pou – and the deserted *motu* (islets) further to the north: Hatu Iti (Motu Iti), Eiao, Hatutu (Hatutaa), Motu One (Sand Island) and the Clark Sandbank. The southern group comprises three inhabited islands – Hiva Oa, Tahuata and Fatu Hiva – and the four deserted islands of Motane (Mohotani), Fatu Huku, Terihi and Thomasset Rock.

History

Among the first islands to be settled by the Polynesians during the great South Pacific migrations, the Marquesas served as a dispersal point for the whole Polynesian triangle from Hawaii to Easter Island and New Zealand. Estimates of the islands' colonisation vary from prehistory to between AD 300 and 600.

The Marquesas' isolation was broken in 1595 when Spanish navigator Alvaro de Mendaña y Neira sighted Fatu Hiva by pure chance. Mendaña's fleet then sailed along past Motane and Hiva Oa, and anchored for around 10 days in Vaitahu Bay on Tahuata. Mendaña christened these four islands Las Marquesas de Mendoza in honour of his sponsor, the viceroy of Peru, García Hurtado de Mendoza.

In 1774 James Cook lingered for four days on Tahuata during his second voyage. Ingraham, the American commander of the *Hope,* 'discovered' the northern group of the Marquesas in 1791, arriving slightly ahead of Frenchman Étienne Marchand, whose merchant vessel took on fresh supplies at Tahuata and then landed on 'Ua Pou. In 1797 William Crook, a young Protestant pastor with the London Missionary Society (LMS), landed on Tahuata, but his attempts at evangelism were unsuccessful.

French interest in the region grew as a means of countering English expansion in the Pacific. After a reconnaissance voyage in 1838, Rear Admiral Abel Dupetit-Thouars took possession of Tahuata in 1842 in the name of French King Louis-Philippe.

Under the French yoke, the Marquesas almost fell into oblivion – the French administration preferred to develop Pape'ete on Tahiti, which they thought had a more strategic value. Only the Catholic missionaries, who had been active since their arrival on Tahuata in 1838, persevered, and Catholicism became, and still is, firmly entrenched in the Marquesas.

Upon contact with Western influences, the foundations of Marquesan society collapsed. Whaling crews brought alcohol, firearms and syphilis. In a stunning decline the population plummeted from around 18,000 in 1842 to 5264 in 1887, and 2096 in 1926.

In the 20th century the Marquesas were made famous by Hiva Oa residents Paul Gauguin and Belgian singer Jacques Brel (see boxed text, p220). Slow but sure development of infrastructure has helped lessen the archipelago's isolation, while archaeological surveys are uncovering a culture that was lost only a comparatively short while ago. There's now a growing interest in this fantastic island group, whose ecotourist potential is still intact.

Culture

One of the highlights of a visit to the Marquesas is the culture, which is still alive. The Marquesans have their own dances (the Haka Manu or the Dance of the Pig will make your spine tingle) and their own language, and they

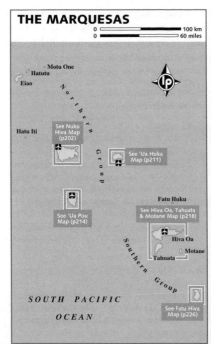

KNOW BEFORE YOU GO

- The Marquesas are not a beach holiday destination
- There are neither ritzy hotels nor spas, just a handful of small-scale, low-key hotels and *pensions* (guesthouses), of good standard
- ATMs as well as reliable internet access are available only on Nuku Hiva, Hiva Oa and 'Ua Pou
- Diving is only available on Hiva Oa
- Bring your boots – activities are nature-oriented (hiking, horse riding, bird-watching)
- An absolute minimum of 10 days is required if you plan to visit the two main islands (Nuku Hiva and Hiva Oa) plus one secondary island ('Ua Pou, 'Ua Huka, Tahuata or Fatu Hiva)
- For culture vultures, lots of archaeological sites beckon, but most of them are yet to restored

rank among the best tattooists in Polynesia. One recognised expert working on the field on 'Ua Huka described it as 'a dream-come-true for archaeologists', and the only place in French Polynesia where the past is almost palpable thanks to a wealth of archaeological remains, many of which are unexplored or lying hidden in the undergrowth. Fortunately, some of them have been neatly restored. See the boxed text, p210 for more details. If you find a good guide, fascinating details such as *ua ma* (pits that stored and fermented breadfruit), ancient prison pits, tattooing areas, sacrificial bone dumps, hidden petroglyphs and much more will be pointed out to you. Bear in mind, however, that this isn't ancient Egypt, and that the lack of explanatory signs and documentation is frustrating.

Getting There & Away
AIR
Nuku Hiva and Hiva Oa are well connected with Tahiti, with almost daily direct flights from Pape'ete. There's also a once-weekly direct flight from Rangiroa in the Tuamotus to Nuku Hiva (but there is no return flight back to Rangiroa from the Marquesas). Flights to 'Ua Huka via Nuku Hiva run four days a week and 'Ua Pou has flights six days a week via Nuku Hiva or Hiva Oa.

Note that the Marquesas are half an hour ahead of Tahiti time.

BOAT
The *Taporo IX* and *Aranui* service the Marquesas, departing from Pape'ete and travelling via the Tuamotus (Fakarava and/or Rangiroa). The *Aranui* does about 16 trips a year. Note that the *Taporo IX* doesn't take passengers. See also p262.

Getting Around
Given the lack of public transport, it's still a bit of an adventure to get around the Marquesas, but that can be part of the fun.

BETWEEN ISLANDS
The easiest and quickest way to island-hop within the archipelago is by regular Air Tahiti flights. *Bonitiers* ('skipjack boats') can be individually chartered and you can hop on the cargo ship *Aranui* if your timing is right (ask about arrival dates). Tahuata and Fatu Hiva are only accessible by boat and it takes some ingenuity to organise this. See the individual islands' Getting There & Away sections for more information.

ON THE ISLANDS
Guides and taxis are the main modes of transport for getting around the islands' web of 4WD tracks (and, increasingly, surfaced roads). It is possible to rent your own vehicle on Nuku Hiva and Hiva Oa. On Tahuata, Fatu Hiva and 'Ua Pou, you'll have to charter a 4WD with driver.

Chartering a *bonitier* or a speedboat is sometimes a more convenient option for travelling between two villages but, unless you share expenses with other travellers, it will cost you an arm and a leg.

NUKU HIVA

pop 2632 / area 340 sq km
The wow factor kicks in fast when you land on the airstrip at Terre Déserte (Desert Land) at Nuku Hiva's northwestern tip and head for Taiohae, the 'capital' of the Marquesas. The 4WD transfer along innumerable twists and

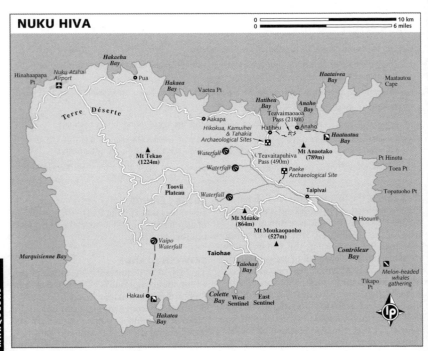

NUKU HIVA

0   10 km
0   6 miles

THE MARQUESAS

turns offers drama, seemingly around every other bend, with stunning landscapes and explosive vistas. This huge (the second largest in French Polynesia after Tahiti), sparsely populated island boasts a fantastic terrain, with razor-edged basaltic cliffs pounded by crashing waves, deep bays blessed with Robinson Crusoe–like beaches, dramatic waterfalls and timeless valleys that feel like the end of the world.

Nuku Hiva has good infrastructure (by Marquesan standards) and is heaven for ecotourists and for those wanting a diverse range of activities. Horse riding is topnotch and there's exceptional hiking, too. Sadly, diving is no longer available but if you want to snorkel 'with' a pod of melon-headed whales, Nuku Hiva is your answer. And culture? The island has a gobsmacking portfolio of archaeological sites, with more *tiki* and *tohua* (open-air gathering places) than you can count, and there are some beautiful handicrafts available.

With daily flights from Pape'ete and good connections to other islands in the archipelago, you have no excuse not to spend at least

three (preferably four) days here to do the island justice.

History

The American Joseph Ingraham was the first Westerner lucky enough to see Nuku Hiva, in 1791. During the first half of the 19th century sandalwood merchants and whalers put into port in Taiohae Bay. Catholic missionaries reached the island in 1839 and the religion took hold when the archipelago was seized by the French in 1842. During the second half of the 19th century the island was ravaged by diseases introduced by Europeans. The knowledge and culture lost has never been fully regained.

TAIOHAE
pop 1700

The first glimpse of Taiohae after the one-hour journey from the airport at Terre Déserte will take your breath away. Nestled at the base of soaring mountains, the town deploys itself along a perfectly crescent-shaped bay. On a clear day, the jagged peaks of 'Ua Pou loom on the horizon. While it's the Marquesas' 'capital', Taiohae oozes the kind of sunny languor you'd associate with the tropics, and it's easy to wind down a few gears here. Spend your Sunday morning in church, take a stroll along the seafront, meet a few woodcarvers and toss back a cool Hinano on a beach at sundown. Taiohae also offers useful services, including a tourist office, ATMs, internet access, a few shops and a handful of accommodation options. This is the obvious place to base yourself in Nuku Hiva.

Information

Banque Socredo (☎ 92 03 63; ⏰ 7.30-11.30am & 1.30-4pm Mon-Fri) Currency exchange, as well as two ATMs.
Hospital (☎ 91 20 00) Around 100m from the post office. Has a dentist, too. Each village also has basic medical services.

Moetai Marine (☎ 92 07 50; ⏰ 8am-5pm Mon-Fri) On the quay. Has internet access (900 CFP per hour), laundry service (1000 CFP) and can help yachties with formalities.
Post office (⏰ 7-11.30am & noon-3.30pm Mon-Thu, 7-11.30am & noon-2.30pm Fri) Internet access (with the Manaspot card, available at the counter). Has an ATM.
Tourist office (☎ 92 03 73; marquises@mail.pf; ⏰ 7.30am-4pm Mon-Fri) Has a few brochures and can help with simple queries. See also www.marquises.pf.

Sights

The most striking building is **Notre-Dame Cathedral of the Marquesas Islands**, built from wood and stones on a former sacred site venerated by the ancient Marquesans. The stones come from the archipelago's six inhabited islands.

THE ARANUI

If there's an iconic trip in French Polynesia, it must be on the *Aranui*. For nearly 25 years, this 104m boat has been the umbilical cord between Tahiti and the Marquesas and a hot favourite with tourists. Noted one tourist: 'It's a winning formula, because it's both a freighter and a passenger vessel, and you get an overview of the archipelago in a relatively short time at a fraction of what you'd pay if you had to do it independently; it's also a sustainable approach, because you get to know the island life.' Its 14-day voyage, departing from Pape'ete, takes it to one or two atolls in the Tuamotus and the six inhabited islands of the Marquesas. There are 16 trips per year.

The *Aranui* has been supplying the remote islands of the Marquesas since 1984 and that is still its primary mission. The front half of the *Aranui* looks just like any other cargo boat of its size, with two cranes and holds for all types of goods. The back, however, is like a cruise ship, with cabins, several decks and a small swimming pool. There's nothing glitzy about it – everything is simple and functional. Unless you're on a yacht, there's simply no other way to visit so many islands in the Marquesas (along with two Tuamotu atolls thrown in as a bonus) in such a short period. Note that this is an organised journey; if you don't like to be tied to a schedule or forced to live with a group, it may not be for you.

There are four classes of accommodation, from large cabins with balcony, double bed and bathroom (€4500 to €4800 per person) to dorm-style beds with shared bathroom facilities (€2000 per person). All the accommodation has air-con. There's also a rather Spartan deck class used by islanders, for whom the ship is their local transport. Prices include all meals and taxes for a 14-day trip from Pape'ete. It is also possible to join the *Aranui* on Nuku Hiva for eight days in the Marquesas. Foreigners are not supposed to use deck class, but if you are just going from one island to the next and there's room, there shouldn't be a problem. Contact the tour guides at the stopovers and count on paying about 4000 CFP from one island in the Marquesas to another.

The stops are tied up with the loading and unloading of freight, a major event on the islands. While the ship is unloading and loading, passengers make excursions ashore, which typically include picnics, scuba diving, snorkelling, 4WD trips to archaeological sites and remote villages, and horse-riding excursions. Stops are made at craft centres where you can meet craftspeople and make purchases. There are no nights spent ashore; all shore visits last just a day or half-day and include multilingual guides. European and North American art history experts, archaeologists and ethnologists are invited on the cruise, providing cultural insights.

Bookings are essential and peak periods (July, August and December) are booked up months in advance. Contact your travel agency; or the shipowner, **Compagnie Polynésienne de Transport Maritime** (CPTM; ☎ Pape'ete 42 62 42, 43 48 89; www.aranui.com), directly.

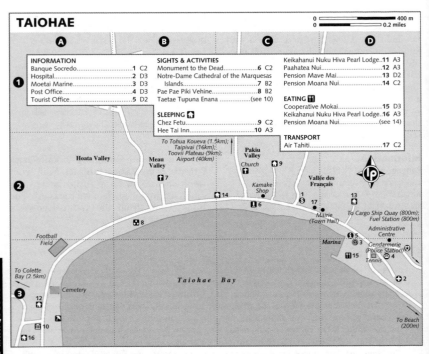

TAIOHAE

0 _____ 400 m
0 _____ 0.2 miles

INFORMATION
Banque Socredo.............................1 C2
Hospital..2 D3
Moetai Marine...............................3 D3
Post Office......................................4 D3
Tourist Office.................................5 D2

SIGHTS & ACTIVITIES
Monument to the Dead...................6 C2
Notre-Dame Cathedral of the Marquesas
 Islands..7 B2
Pae Pae Piki Vehine........................8 B2
Taetae Tupuna Enana ....(see 10)

SLEEPING
Chez Fetu......................................9 C2
Hee Tai Inn..................................10 A3

Keikahanui Nuku Hiva Pearl Lodge..11 A3
Paahatea Nui.................................12 A3
Pension Mave Mai..........................13 D2
Pension Moana Nui........................14 C2

EATING
Cooperative Mokai.........................15 D3
Keikahanui Nuku Hiva Pearl Lodge..16 A3
Pension Moana Nui...................(see 14)

TRANSPORT
Air Tahiti......................................17 C2

To Tohua Koueva (1.5km);
Taipivai (16km);
Toovii Plateau (9km);
Airport (40km)

Hoata Valley

Meau Valley

Pakiu Valley

Church

Kamake Shop

Vallée des Français

Mairie (Town Hall)

To Cargo Ship Quay (800m);
Fuel Station (800m)

Administrative Centre

Marina

Gendarmerie (Police Station)

Tennis

Football Field

To Colette Bay (2.5km)

Cemetery

Taiohae Bay

To Beach (200m)

On the seafront, opposite the Kamake shop, is the **Monument to the Dead**, an obelisk fronted by a cannon constructed in honour of Étienne Marchand.

Marking the centre of town is the **Pae Pae Piki Vehine**, also known as Temehea. Rebuilt for the 1989 Marquesas Festival, this *pae pae* (traditional meeting platform) contains modern sculptures and a dozen magnificent *tiki* made by the island's sculptors and by artisans from Easter Island. Its central, breezy location makes it a popular hang-out for local kids.

The massive **Tohua Koueva** is just over 1km up the Pakiu Valley on the Taipivai road, and 700m along a dirt track. Turn east from the main road at the gravel-making machine then go past the poorly situated garbage dump by the river. It's believed that this extensive communal site, with its paved esplanade, belonged to the war chief Pakoko, who was killed by the French in 1845. Today it is a peaceful spot full of banyan trees and flowers. All the stone carvings are contemporary.

If you're into **beaches**, you can try the one near the post office or the one near

Keikahanui Nuku Hiva Pearl Lodge, but none are too attractive.

The little museum **Taetae Tupuna Enana** (☎ 92 03 82; admission free; ✆ 8-11.30am & 2-5pm Mon-Fri, 8-11.30am Sat) has a few documents and artefacts focusing on traditional Marquesan culture. It's at the Hee Tai Inn.

Want to see the base camp for *Survivor Marquesas* (2002)? Head to **Colette Bay**, about 3.5km from Taiohae. Take the track going up to the Keikahanui Nuku Hiva Pearl Lodge, at the western side of the bay. Instead of branching left to the hotel, keep right and continue for about 2km. The track climbs along the western side of the cove and descends to the beach at Colette Bay. It's ideal for a gentle stroll (or a picnic) with your beloved, but bring plenty of insect repellent if you don't want to lose him or her!

Activities

Short of scuba diving (sadly, the local dive centre caters to TV crews and professionals only), hiking and horseback riding are eco-friendly ways to experience the island's wild beauty.

HIKING

To date, hiking is *the* very best Nuku Hiva has to offer, and it's dizzying (literally). We're not talking about crowded, waymarked trails crisscrossing the island, but a couple of exceptional walks that take in some awe-inspiring viewpoints, without another traveller in sight, guaranteed. A guide is essential because trails are not marked and it's easy to get lost.

Marquises Rando (☎ 92 07 13, 29 53 31; www.marquises rando.com in French) is run by a professional guide who offers three topnotch hikes for all levels:

Tehaatiki – explore the ridges around the southeastern part of Taiohae Bay. Magnificent views of the bay and the coastline, with 'Ua Pou looming in the distance. Few shady areas. Cost is 6600 CFP. About five to six hours, moderate.

Peaks and cliffs near Aakapa and Hatiheu – a very scenic hike. Starting from Toovii Plateau, the path snakes its way through a primary forest on the plateau, with a mix of huge ferns, shrubs, rivulets and gnarled trees. Hold on to your hat as you approach viewpoints right on the plateau rim – the view over the Aakapa peaks and the northern coastline will be etched in your memory forever. It's mostly flat and shady. Keep an eye out for endemic birds, including the Marquesan imperial pigeon and the white-capped fruit dove. Cost is 8400 CFP and includes transfers, water, fruits and biscuits. About six hours, moderate.

Big Z – an altogether different atmosphere. This part of the island is barren. You start at an altitude of about 1000m and follow a volcanic ridge to the west. Highlights include a lookout over a 'hidden valley', featuring snaggle-toothed peaks tangled together. The hike ends at a rocky spur that directly overlooks the iconic Hakaui Valley (p206) – hair-raising. Expect to see wild goats, white-capped fruit doves and white-tailed tropic birds. No shade, but lots of breeze. Cost is from 10,000 CFP, including transfers, water, fruits and biscuits. About six hours, moderate.

Other excellent walking options include the hikes to the Vaipo Waterfall (p206), Colette Bay (opposite) and from Hatiheu to Anaho (p209). All hikes are weather-dependent.

HORSE RIDING

Horse riding is another good way to soak up the drop-dead-gorgeous scenery. In Taiohae, **Sabine Teikiteetini** (☎ 92 01 56, 25 35 13; half-day rides incl transfers 8000 CFP) is a qualified guide who can arrange lovely rides on Toovii Plateau. You don't need any riding experience, as Sabine caters to all levels of proficiency. Rides last about three hours. In Hatiheu contact Yvonne Katupa at Chez Yvonne (p209).

WHALE WATCHING

At sea, Nuku Hiva's main claim to fame is a bewildering whale gathering 'event'. Dozens (and at times, hundreds) of melon-headed whales *(Peponocephala electra)* congregate off the east coast in the morning. They usually stay at the surface, vertically or horizontally, sometimes playing, sometimes basking motionless. Observing these graceful creatures is a thrilling experience. If you're game, you can snorkel with them (but don't attempt to touch them). Though their habits remain largely unknown, some experts think that the east coast is their resting area during the day. The site itself is impressive, since it's anywhere between 300m and 1km off the coast, in a deep-blue sea (still game to snorkel?). While an encounter is not guaranteed, the operator claims a success rate of 70%.

One proviso: the 45-minute journey to get to the site, along Nuku Hiva's pounded sea cliffs, can be a nightmare if the sea is choppy. How do you say 'seasick' in Marquesan?

Whale-watching excursions are run by **Marquises Plaisance** (☎ 92 08 75, 73 23 48; e.bastard@ mail.pf; half-day cruise for 2 people 16,000 CFP). Prices include snorkelling gear.

Tours

The hotels and some *pensions* (guesthouses) organise tours. You can also contact **Jocelyne Henua Enana Tours** (☎ 92 00 52; www.marquisesvoyages .com.pf in French). Jocelyne knows just about everything there is to know about Nuku Hiva. She is one of the only guides available on Sundays, speaks English and takes credit cards.

Sleeping

Chez Fetu (☎ 92 03 66; r per person 2000 CFP) The fully equipped bungalow has seen its fair share of bodies (and bugs), the beds sag and the furnishings should be dumped at a flea market, but it still fits the bill if you keep your expectations in check. It's in a leafy spot about 200m up a small dirt path that starts at the western side of the Kamake shop. You can pick up fruits in the garden (mangoes!).

Paahatea Nui (☎ 92 00 97; paahateanui@mail.pf; r/bungalows per person incl breakfast 3200/5500 CFP) The good people at Paahatea Nui – husband Justin and wife Julienne – are not setting out to win any 'best in its class' awards with their establishment but the virtue is that it's kept in tip-top shape and you'll be made to feel at home. The three rooms in the main house (try for room 2, which has private facilities) are clean and come equipped with firm mattresses. The six bungalows are not well spaced out but the garden, overflowing with blossoming tropical flowers, ensures you're sealed off from your neighbours. No meals are available except breakfast but you can use the kitchen. There's a small beach across the road.

Pension Moana Nui (☎ 92 03 30; pensionmoananui@ mail.pf; s incl breakfast/half board 6500/9000 CFP; d incl breakfast/half board 9400/15,000 CFP; ✕ ▣) All eight rooms are clean, well organised (air-con, a small balcony, private facilities, hot shower, free wi-fi, daily cleaning) and utilitarian – perfect for the budget-conscious traveller who's not looking for fancy trimmings. It also has the bonus of a good restaurant on the premises and views of the bay (rooms 1 and 2 are the best in this department), not to mention a handy location. The affable owner, Charles Mombaerts, is helpful if you need to rent a car or book activities. Credit cards are accepted.

Pension Mave Mai (☎ 92 08 10; pension-mavemai@ mail.pf; s/d 7000/8000 CFP; ✕) Peacefully reposed over sloping grounds above the marina, this guesthouse features eight rooms in a two-storey motel-style building. They're not terribly Polynesian, but they're light and well appointed, with private facilities (hot water) and air-con, as well as a kitchenette in two of the rooms. The real draw is the small terrace (or balcony upstairs) overlooking the bay. The place can feel a bit deserted during the day because the owner doesn't live on the premises. There's an on-site restaurant (half-board costs 3000 CFP) with ample views. Credit cards are accepted.

ourpick Hee Tai Inn (☎ 92 03 82; rose.corser@mail.pf; s/d 8500/10,500 CFP; ✕ ▣) This place was almost finished when this book went to print and it should be one of the most reliable hotels on Nuku Hiva, with eight comfy rooms and a wide range of amenities. It's run by Rose Corser, an American lady who fell for Nuku Hiva a long time ago, so English-speaking visitors will feel right at home here. It's at the western tip of the bay, beneath the Keikahanui Nuku Hiva Pearl Lodge.

Keikahanui Nuku Hiva Pearl Lodge (☎ 92 07 10; www.pearlresorts.com; bungalows 30,000-45,000 CFP; ✕ ▣ ▣) Nuku Hiva's only upmarket option, the Keikahanui occupies a wonderfully peaceful domain at the western tip of the bay. Digs are in 20 Polynesian-style bungalows hidden in a sea of greenery, on a hillside. They are commodious and decked out with *tapa* (cloth made from beaten bark and decorated with traditional designs) and woodcarved panels. Plus, each bungalow has a private balcony with a simply eye-popping view over the bay. Need more? There's a sweet swimming pool (the size of a teacup, though), a bar and a restaurant. The ethos here is one of relaxation, so don't expect late-night revelry. Wi-fi.

Eating

Cooperative Mokai (mains 800-1000 CFP; ✕ breakfast & lunch Mon-Fri) At this little place right on the quay you can fuel up with simple dishes such as raw fish, sandwiches and fruits.

Pension Moana Nui (☎ 92 03 30; mains 1500-2900 CFP; ✕ lunch & dinner Mon-Sat) This is where all heads turn when it comes to a well-priced meal in an attractive setting on the seafront. Basking in a convivial buzz, the restaurant at this hotel has an eclectic menu, from osso bucco to fish fillet with meunière sauce. Or go troppo and opt for a pizza cooked in a wood-fired oven (evenings only). Credit cards are accepted.

Keikahanui Nuku Hiva Pearl Lodge (☎ 92 07 10; mains 1300-3000 CFP; ✕ lunch & dinner) Chef Erick Lafond has assembled a knockout dinner menu at this upscale hotel, which sees quality local ingredients fused with Gallic know-how. Rejoicings begin with, say, broccoli quiche, followed by rosewood-smoked swordfish and pumpkin mousse. His desserts are elegant. Crème brûlée with coconut? We'll take it. Bag a table on the terrace and savour the views of the bay and the twinkling stars. Light meals are available at lunchtime. Credit cards are accepted.

You'll find several well-stocked supermarkets on the seafront, as well as a bakery and a few *roulottes* (mobile food vans) – your best bargain for cheap eats.

HAKAUI VALLEY

Of all the marvels that Nuku Hiva offers, few equal the awe-inspiring majesty and raw power of the Hakaui Valley, which slices through the basaltic landmass, west of the island. On either side of the canyon, vertical walls rise to nearly 800m and **Vaipo Waterfall**, the highest in French Polynesia at 350m, plummets into a natural swimming pool at the end of the valley. It's not the Niagara Falls, though; in the drier months the volume of the falls lessens and can be reduced to a mere trickle. Refrain from taking a dip because of falling rocks.

The Hakaui Valley is also of strong historical interest. The valley was once the fiefdom of King Te Moana and Queen Vaekehu, and the ancient royal road follows the river past numerous ancient sites, namely *pae pae* and *tohua*, hidden behind a tangle of vegetation.

From Taiohae, the valley can be reached by speedboat (about 30 minutes). From Hakaui Bay, where the boat anchors, allow about 2½ hours to reach the waterfall on foot, on a flat path which follows the river (be prepared to get wet) and includes stretches of the ancient paved royal road. Back to Hakaui Bay, walk 100m east to the magnificent **Hakatea Bay**. It's fringed with a long beach (yeah!) but there are *nono* (gnats; boo!). Bring lots of repellent (see the boxed text, below).

Marquises Plaisance (☎ 92 08 75, 73 23 48; e.bastard@mail.pf) is a reliable operator that can arrange guided trips to the waterfall and Hakatea Bay. It costs 13,500 CFP for two people for the full-day excursion, but no picnic is provided.

TOOVII PLATEAU

'Where am I?' is probably what you'll be wondering on reaching Toovii Plateau, which spreads out at an average altitude of 800m at the heart of the island. With its conifer forests and vast pastures where cattle graze, it looks like it's straight out of a Brothers Grimm fairy tale. The mountain setting and cooler climate can be a very welcome change from the muggy coastal areas. At times, ghostly mists add a touch of the bizarre. Toovii used to supply the whole archipelago with meat, dairy produce and timber, but serves now as a playground for various eco-activities including horse riding (p205) and hiking (p205).

NONO A GOGO

Even the hardiest of adventurers can be brought to their knees (and the edges of their fingernails) by the nearly invisible but undeniably hostile *nono*. Cover yourself in lightweight trousers and long-sleeve shirts and whip out the jungle juice. This little gnat's bites can leave welts that itch like no other. Fortunately, they are found almost uniquely on beaches and are not disease carriers.

HAVE YOUR KAIKAI & ASK FOR IT TOO

Don't *'ia orana'* or *'maururu'* anyone out here – the Marquesan language is surprisingly different from Tahitian. A little effort with some simple words will be greatly appreciated by the local people.

Te Henua Enana	'The land of men' – the Marquesan name for their islands
kaoha	hello
apae	goodbye
koutau	thank you
kaikai	food, to eat
kaikai metai	enjoy your meal
kanahau	good, delicious, beautiful

TAIPIVAI

Here's a riddle: who was on board the American whaler *Acushnet*, which put in at Taiohae in July 1842, jumped ship, spent three weeks at Taipivai and wrote his unusual experiences in *Typee* (1846)? Answer: Herman Melville (you know, who also wrote *Moby Dick* and *Billy Budd*).

Forget about stories of fierce warriors and cannibals – now Taipivai is a charming village that carpets the floor of a river valley and its affable inhabitants will welcome you with a smile. At the eastern end of the village the river rushes into the majestic **Contrôleur Bay**.

The main reason to stop in Taipivai is to visit the **Paeke archaeological site**, which lies on a hillside at the exit of the village on the way to Hatiheu (the path that leads to the site is not signed, so ask around). It features two well-preserved *me'ae* (traditional sacred sites) flanked by a set of brick-coloured *tiki*. The *me'ae* further up the hill has a pit into which human remains were thrown. From the main road, it's a 15-minute walk uphill on a well-maintained path.

It takes about half an hour by 4WD on a paved road in good condition to reach Taipivai from Taiohae.

HOOUMI

Colourful houses, well-groomed gardens, a small church… The atmosphere is chilled out to the max in this charming hamlet. Who would guess that it was once inhabited by the Teavaaki, one of the fiercest tribes of Nuku Hiva?

THE MARQUESAS

HATIHEU

Hatiheu is a graceful little village dominated by a crescent of black sand, soaring peaks and immaculate, colourful gardens; it's no wonder that Robert Louis Stevenson succumbed to its charms when he passed through in 1888. On one of the peaks to the west, at a height of 300m, is a white statue of the Virgin Mary, erected in 1872.

From Taipivai, follow the main road 7.5km as it climbs to the impressive Teavaitapuhiva Pass (490m), from which there are magnificent views over Hatiheu Bay.

Sights

Hatiheu's archaeological sites are of highly historical significance but there aren't any explanatory signs. It makes sense to hire a knowledgeable guide. Contact **Jocelyne Henua Enana Tours** (☎ 92 08 32, 74 42 23; www.marquises voyages.com.pf) in Taiohae or Rose Corser, the American lady who runs Hee Tai Inn in Taiohae (p206). Prices depend on the size of the party.

HIKOKUA ARCHAEOLOGICAL SITE

One of the most powerful archaeological sites in the Marquesas, Hikokua was discovered by the archaeologist Robert Suggs in 1957 and has been restored and maintained by Hatiheu locals since 1987. It dates from around AD 1250 and was in use until the 1800s.

The vast, central, rectangular esplanade *(tohua)* was used for dance performances at community festivals. It's flanked by tiers of small flat basalt blocks that were once used as steps for the spectators.

On the terrace stand two modern stone carvings by a local artist, and a flat rock that was used for various purposes, including solo dances and rituals associated with puberty.

Near the centre of the esplanade are nine Christian tombs. They probably date from the time of the first missionaries' arrival, after the abandonment of the site.

The platform at the bottom, on the northern side of the esplanade towards the ocean, was the *tuu,* or ceremonial activity centre. It was on this *tuu* that sacrifices and displaying of the victims' bodies took place. The chief's residence stood at the northeast corner of the esplanade.

KAMUIHEI & TAHAKIA ARCHAEOLOGICAL SITES

About 300m towards Taipivai from the Hikokua site, these two connecting sites make up the largest excavated archaeological area of Nuku Hiva. A team led by the archaeologist Pierre Ottino began restoration in 1998.

The importance and sheer number of these structures testify to the dense population this valley once sheltered. The site is spectacular and eerie; with its large moss-covered basalt rocks and huge banyans, the largest of which has been estimated to be over 600 years old, the whole place exudes *mana* (spiritual power).

At the foot of the largest banyan is a deep pit, presumably dug for the remains of sacrifices or for taboo objects. Other pits are scattered about the site; these are mostly *ua ma*, which stocked the all-important breadfruit. A little higher are two large rocks about 2.5m high by 3m wide and decorated with petroglyphs that represent turtles, fish and the eyes of a *tiki,* along with human figures. It's estimated that the valley contains more than 500 other petroglyphs like these.

On the other side of the track is the restored *tohua* Tahakia, one of the biggest in the Marquesas, as well as some *pae pae.*

DID YOU SAY ARCHAEOLOGY?

The Marquesas are a superb open-air museum but they remain largely underrated when it comes to archaeological sites. According to French archaeologist Pierre Ottino, who has contributed to numerous restorations in the Marquesas over the last two decades: 'The Marquesas can't compete with Easter Island in terms of proportions, but they boast much more diversity, and the sites are more closely linked to their environment. In the Marquesas, we have statues, gathering places, ceremonial centres and houses, all set within varied and powerful landscapes. Truth is, archaeological sites in the Marquesas are overshadowed by the idyllic seascapes and turquoise lagoons in the Tuamotus or the Society Islands, for which Polynesia is so famous. On Easter Island, it's a different story; cultural sites come first in the mind of tourists.'

Activities

In search of a complete escape? Walk to Anaho (about 1¼ hours; see below) and Haatuatua (another 30 minutes). Horse riding can be organised through Chez Yvonne (about 5000 CFP; below).

Sleeping & Eating

Chez Yvonne – Restaurant Hinakonui (☎ 92 02 97; hinakonui@mail.pf; bungalows incl breakfast s/d 5000/7000 CFP, with half board 8000/12,000 CFP; mains 1600-3000 CFP; ☻ lunch & dinner Mon-Sat, by reservation) Hmm, just recalling the lobster flambéed with whisky makes us drool. The goat with coconut milk is another palate-pleaser in this authentic Marquesan restaurant run by Yvonne Katupa, a well-known personality on the island. Bookings are recommended, otherwise you might find the kitchen closed if there aren't enough customers. It's a relaxing spot, with an open-air thatched terrace opening onto the seafront. Sadly, the five boxy bungalows are starting to show their age, with saggy mattresses and sombre bathrooms, but the location, on a grassy property facing the bay, is fantastic. However, they're convenient enough to flop down for the night and set off early in the morning for Anaho.

ANAHO & HAATUATUA

One of the best-kept secrets in the Marquesas is the sublime little village of Anaho, where it's hard to feel connected with the outside world. It's a terrific place to kick off your shoes for a few days in a fabulous setting, and the fact that it's only accessible by speedboat (15 minutes from Hatiheu; 7000 CFP) or a little less than 1½ hours by foot (also from Hatiheu) adds to the sense of seclusion. A few families make their living harvesting copra among the swaying coconut plantations; there is a tiny chapel and not much else. It's a popular anchorage for visiting yachts and, with the only coral reef on Nuku Hiva, the bay is lagoonlike and inviting. Small wonder that back in 1888 Robert Louis Stevenson was inspired to write many pages eulogising its unsettling beauty.

Take the paved road at the end of Hatiheu up towards the valley. About 300m uphill there's a small clearing and a well-marked trail to the left. From the **Teavaimaoaoa Pass** (218m), reached after about 45 minutes, Anaho Bay appears like a mirage. Both the ascent from Hatiheu and descent to Anaho are quite steep but the track is in good condition and is well marked. Bring mosquito repellent and plenty of water.

If Anaho's not enough for you, head to **Haatuatua Bay**, a 30-minute stroll to the east, on an easy-to-follow trail. A crescent-shaped bay fringed with a yellow scimitar of sand, framed by lofty volcanic ridges, is bound to satiate any contemplative mind. Just you, the caress of the sea breeze, the sand in your toes…and a few wicked *nono* to mar the experience!

Sleeping & Eating

Be sure to book your accommodation – Anaho is quite popular with weekending families from Taiohae. Coming from the airport, take a taxi to Hatiheu (4000 CFP), then walk or take a speedboat (7000 CFP).

Te Pua Hinako (☎ 92 04 14; r with half board per person 4600 CFP) Absolutely no frills here, but you'll be bowled over by the faaabulous setting, a coconut's throw from the seashore. It features two rooms with shared bathroom (no door, just a curtain). The food is reputedly good – ask for the octopus in coconut milk.

Kao Tiae (☎ 92 00 08; bungalows per person with half board 5000 CFP) It's more or less the same story at Kao Tiae, just behind Te Pua Hinako, except that you'll bunk down in very simple bungalows with no direct bay views. The beds are thin, which is a drag if you have a bad back. But the grandeur of Mother Nature offers ample compensation – not to mention the delicious local food.

GETTING THERE & AWAY
Air

Find the office for **Air Tahiti** (☎ 91 02 25, 92 01 45; ☻ 8am-noon & 2-4pm Mon-Fri) in the centre of Taiohae.

There are up to nine weekly flights between Pape'ete and Nuku Hiva (28,000 CFP one way, three hours). There is also one direct flight per week from Rangiroa to Nuku Hiva but no service going back to Rangiroa (28,000 CFP one way, 2½ hours).

Within the Marquesas there are five to seven weekly flights from Nuku Hiva to Hiva Oa (11,000 CFP one way), and four to six flights per week from Nuku Hiva to 'Ua Huka and 'Ua Pou (both cost 7000 CFP one way). These flights connect with the Pape'ete flights through Nuku Hiva.

Boat

The *Aranui* (see the boxed text, p203) stops at Taiohae and Taipivai.

THE MARQUESAS

ARCHAEOLOGY IN THE MARQUESAS – LEARN YOUR BASICS

You don't need to have a PhD to appreciate the archaeological remains that are typical of the Marquesas but a few explanations will greatly enhance your trip.

Tohua

The *tohua* refers to a paved rectangular platform with several tiers of basalt block rows on either side. The *tohua* were used as meeting places and also hosted festivals and dance performances. Flat boulders form a sort of stage on which solo dances took place, and which was also used by young chiefs to show off their tattoos.

A few not-to-be-missed *tohua* include the recently restored *tohua* Mauia on 'Ua Pou (p217), *tohua* Upeke on Hiva Oa (p222) and *tohua* Hikokua on Nuku Hiva (p208).

Me'ae

The *me'ae* is the Marquesan equivalent of the Tahitian *marae*. *Me'ae* are religious sites built from basalt blocks placed side by side and piled up. Generally found in the valleys and away from secular places, the *me'ae* was the sacred precinct par excellence and was a place of worship, burial and human sacrifices. It was strictly *tapu* (forbidden); access was restricted to a few priests or chiefs endowed with *mana* (spiritual power). *Me'ae* were also used for cannibalistic rituals. They were generally built near a banyan, a sacred tree. Don't miss the *me'ae* at lipona on Hiva Oa (p222).

Pae Pae

Pae pae are platforms of stone blocks, on which *ha'e* (human habitations) were built from native plants and wood. The *pae pae* was divided into two sections. The front level was reserved for daily activities, while the back section, which was covered and slightly raised, served as a sleeping area. The roof was made of leaves from the *uru* tree and coconut palm. Only the stone foundations have survived; the vegetation and wooden structures have been destroyed.

Foundations of *pae pae* are ubiquitous in the Marquesas. Some modern houses are even built on them!

Tiki

One of the Marquesas' most pervasive images, the enigmatic *tiki* are carved humanlike statues, the height of which varies from a few dozen centimetres to almost 3m (they're definitely shorter than the monumental *moai* on Easter Island). Since they were generally erected on or near a holy place, experts believe *tiki* had a religious and symbolic function, possibly representing deified clan ancestors. They also marked the boundaries of places that were *tapu*. The highly stylised mouth and eyes are the most striking features; the mouth is represented by a long and narrow rectangle, while the eyes are large concentric circles. Sculpted in the form of statues, *tiki* were also carved in bas-relief, on weapons, paddles and dugout canoes. According to many locals, some *tiki* are still possessed of *mana* and have a potential for evil that can manifest itself if they are moved or handled.

The best-preserved *tiki* can be found on Hiva Oa (p222 and p223), Nuku Hiva (p207) and 'Ua Huka (opposite).

Petroglyphs

Lovely petroglyphs! They are designs carved on stones. They feature sharks, turtles, whales, outrigger canoes, facial features, geometric patterns… An ancient work of art? Possibly, according to local experts. The most impressive petroglyphs are found on Fatu Hiva (p226), Hiva Oa (p219) and 'Ua Huka (p212).

GETTING AROUND

Slowly but surely the roads of Nuku Hiva are being paved. At the time of writing a sealed road ran from Taiohae to within a few kilometres of the airport and almost to the Teavaitapuhiva Pass.

To/From the Airport

It takes at least 1¼ hours to reach the airport from Taiohae along a winding road (it should be sealed by the time you read this), longer if it has rained and the ground is muddy – and it's only 18km as the crow flies!

Licensed 4WD taxis that carry four to six people generally wait for each flight. It is nevertheless wise to book through your hotel or *pension*. Transfers to Taiohae cost 4000 CFP per person.

4WD

You can rent 4WDs with or without a driver. Taxi drivers and some lodgings will make excursions.

From Taiohae, the vehicle (which will take four passengers) with a driver costs around 12,000 CFP to Taipivai and 20,000 CFP to Hatiheu.

4WDs without driver can be rented from 12,000 to 16,000 CFP per day. Rates include insurance and unlimited mileage but not petrol. The following operators can deliver directly to your hotel or *pension*:

Europcar (☎ 92 04 89, 72 02 65)
Nuku Rent A Car (☎ 92 06 91, 73 51 67)
Pension Moana Nui (☎ 92 03 30; pensionmoananui@ mail.pf)

'UA HUKA

pop 582 / area 83 sq km
Call it an injustice or misinformation, but 'Ua Huka falls off most travellers' radars. All the better for you: this low-key, less-visited island remains something of a 'secret' and you'll probably have it all to yourself. Here's your chance to buy carvings from master carvers, zigzag up the flanks of an extinct volcano to reach mysterious archaeological sites tucked away in the jungle, take a boat excursion to intriguing offshore islets and delve right into Marquesan life, with the added appeal of a few epicurean indulgences (will it be lobsters or *kaveka* (sooty tern)–egg omelettes today?).

There are only three villages, and after a day or two the community seems to absorb you like a giant, friendly sponge; this is the kind of place that tempts you to do as Gauguin did and devote your life to art and nature. But shhh, that's just between you and us…

INFORMATION

Infrastructure is very limited on 'Ua Huka. There is no bank. The post office is in Vaipaee, next to the museum. Each village has an infirmary or first-aid post.

SIGHTS
Vaipaee

The island's main town is at the end of a very deep, narrow inlet, about 1km long and rightly named Invisible Bay.

Next to the mayor's office, the little **museum** (admission free) features pestles, *tiki*, finely carved sculptures, *pahu* (drums), jewellery and period photos as well as a *ha'e* (traditional house). Donations are appreciated. Hours are erratic; ask at the mayor's office.

The **arboretum** (admission free; ☽ Mon-Sat) is halfway between Vaipaee and Hane. The fact that so many species have adapted to the dry Marquesan soil opens up great possibilities for local agriculture. The species best adapted to the climate are used for reforestation where the vegetation has been destroyed by wild goats and horses.

Hane

Experts believe that the first Polynesian settlement on the Marquesas was here, tucked away in a bay protected on the east by the impressive Motu Hane.

The white house on the seafront contains the craft centre as well as a modest **marine museum** (admission free), which shows the evolution of traditional *pirogues* (outrigger canoes) as well as hooks used for shark fishing. Ask around for someone to help you get the key.

The number-one reason to stop in Hane is the **Meiaute archaeological site**, higher up in the valley. It includes three, 1m-high, red-tuff *tiki* that watch over a group of stone structures,

'UA HUKA
0 — 10 km
0 — 6 miles

Haunanu Pt
Vaikivi Petroglyphs
Hitikau (855m) ▲
Meiaute Archaeological Site
Tetutu Pt
Arboretum
Hane
Hokatu
Vaipaee
Hatuana
Haavei Bay
Motu Hemeni
Motu Teuaua
Motu Papa
Motu Hane

MARQUESAN HANDICRAFTS

If there is one place in French Polynesia where it's really possible to spend some cash, it's the Marquesas. *Tiki* (sacred sculptures), pestles, *umete* (bowls), adzes, spears, clubs, fish hooks and other items are carved from rosewood, *tou* (dark, hard-grained wood), bone or volcanic stone. These treasures are pieces of art, items you will keep for a lifetime. Less-expensive buys include seed necklaces and *umu hei,* an assortment of fragrant plant material such as ylang-ylang, vanilla, pieces of pineapple covered in sandalwood powder, and various other fruits and plants, held together with a plant fibre. Fatu Hiva prides itself on being the only island in French Polynesia to have perpetuated the manufacture of *tapa* (cloth made from beaten bark and decorated with traditional designs).

In most villages there is a small *fare artisanal* (craft centre) where you can shop around. They may open only when requested or when the *Aranui* is in port. It's also well worth approaching craftspeople directly. Some work is done to order only, so if you stay several days on an island it's worth making a visit as soon as you arrive.

Bring enough cash because you cannot pay by credit card. Prices may be relatively high but they're still lower than in Pape'ete and are well worth it for the time and artistic effort put into the works. Expect to pay at least 1500 to 2000 CFP for a small *tapa* piece (up to 10,000 CFP for a piece 1m long), 3000 CFP for a small 15cm *tiki* (and up to 100,000 CFP for a large one) and 5000 CFP for a bowl or plate of about 50cm. Bargaining is not a Pacific tradition so don't expect to be able to beat the prices down very much.

---

pae pae and *me'ae,* which are partly overgrown. Two of these *tiki* have projecting ears, one has legs and a phallus, while the other two have only a head and trunk. The clearing forms a natural lookout with magnificent views of Hane Bay on one side and the caldera on the other. It's a 25-minute walk from Auberge Hitikau (see p214). You don't really need a guide to get there; follow the main road inland, until you reach a concrete stairway on your right, 30m after a sharp bend. Climb the steep hill to the *pae pae*. A little higher up, in a clearing, you will find the *tiki*. If you're not sure, villagers will be happy to point you in the right direction.

Hokatu

Everybody loves Hokatu – it's so mellow. And very scenic: about 3km east of Hane, it lies in a sheltered bay edged with a pebble beach pounded with frothy azure seas and offers direct views of imposing, sugar-loafed Motu Hane. On the waterfront there's a small **petroglyph museum** (admission free) that displays well-presented photographs of the petroglyphs around the island.

Motu Teuaua & Motu Hemeni

If Alfred Hitchcock's *The Birds* scared you, then stop reading, or be prepared to relive a scene from the movie. Thousands of *kaveka* nest year-round on the islets of

Hemeni and **Teuaua**, near the southwestern point of 'Ua Huka, and they lay thousands of eggs daily.

Access to Hemeni is prohibited in order to protect the species. Teuaua, the neighbouring islet (also known as Île aux Oiseaux or Bird Island), is accessible by speedboat when the sea is calm. You can accompany the islanders when they gather the eggs (which are considered a delicacy). It's not for the faint-hearted, because you'll need to jump on to a rocky ledge and clamber up the rock using a permanently fixed rope. As you approach the nests, the *kaveka* become extremely angry and their cries deafening. The bravest birds start swooping at you.

If, despite all this, the experience still attracts you, wear a hat.

Motu Papa

This island, ideal for picnicking and snorkelling (no *nono*), is just offshore from the airport. It is a large, treeless block of volcanic rock that, at low tide, has a wide rocky ledge where you can sit. Speedboats can't motor up to the side so you'll have to swim about 50m to the edge. It's only possible to visit this islet when the sea is calm.

Vaikivi Petroglyphs

This little-visited archaeological site on the Vaikivi Plateau is well worth the detour, if only for the walk or horse ride to get there (see below). The petroglyphs represent an outrigger canoe, a human face and various geometric designs.

ACTIVITIES
Walking
From Hane, it's a memorable three-hour walk inland to the Vaikivi Petroglyphs (opposite). A guide is essential because the trail is unmarked. From Hane, a steep path wiggles up to the edge of the caldera, from which you'll get cardiac-arresting views of Hane Bay (plan on one hour from Hane). Then it's an easier walk to the petroglyphs (another two hours or so), well inland, amid a variety of landscapes – from thick vegetation to tree ferns and a dramatic finish of hacking through pandanus. Ask at your *pension* for a guide; the usual cost is about 5000 CFP, picnic included.

There are several shorter walks: any chunk of the coastal route between Haavei Bay to the west and Hokatu to the east offers jaw-dropping views. Another recommended walk is from Vaipaee to the lunar landscapes of an area called 'the small crater' (about two hours return).

Horse Riding
Riding is a popular activity on 'Ua Huka. A fantastic ride is from Vaipaee to Hane, passing the arboretum, airport and windswept plateaus before reaching the coastal road, which plunges down towards Hane.

If you want to explore the fecund interior and reach a secluded archaeological site, then nothing beats the ride from Hane to Vaikivi Petroglyphs (opposite).

Horse-riding trips can be organised through your *pension*. A ride typically costs 5000 CFP for a half day or 10,000 CFP for a full day, including a guide.

SLEEPING & EATING
Considering the small number of visitors, 'Ua Huka has a lot of *pensions*, but only Le Reve Marquisien and Chez Maurice et Delphine receive a regular trickle of visitors. Airport transfers are 2000 CFP return and excursions by boat, 4WD and horse are often organised. With no bank on 'Ua Huka, no-one could accept credit cards even if they wanted to.

our pick **Chez Maurice et Delphine** (☎ /fax 92 60 55; Hokatu; s/d with half board 7000/14,000 CFP) You're going to love this: five well-arranged (but simply built) bungalows on a little knoll on the village outskirts, with sweeping views of Hokatu Bay and Motu Hane (and, if you're lucky, dolphins frolicking offshore). Delightful hosts: Maurice is a master carver (his living room resembles a craft museum) and he'll be happy to teach guests some of his techniques, while his wife Delphine (who can get by in English) is adept at preparing delicious Marquesan meals and flower garlands. Try to book the bungalow Mata Otemanu, which boasts a perfect position – lying on your bed you can see the bay and

THE MARQUESAS

WATCHING BIRDLIFE

Philippe Raust, president of the association Manu ('birds' in Tahitian), whom we met on Fatu Hiva with two birdwatchers, rates the Marquesas as 'a top birding hot spot in Polynesia, with rare, endemic species, some of which are classified as endangered'. Twitchers, polish your binoculars or your 400mm lens and keep your eyes peeled for the following feathered creatures:

Marquesan swiftlet (*Collocalia ocista*) – throughout the archipelago
White-capped fruit dove (*Ptilinopus dupetithouarsii*) – throughout the archipelago
Marquesan reed warbler (*Acrocephalus mendanae*) – throughout the archipelago
Marquesan kingfisher (*Todiramphus godeffroyi*) – Tahuata
Iphis monarch (*Pomarea iphis*) – 'Ua Huka
Fatu Hiva monarch (*Pomarea whitneyi*) – Fatu Hiva
Ultramarine lorikeets (*Vini ultramarina*) – 'Ua Huka
Marquesan imperial pigeon (*Ducula galeata*) – Nuku Hiva and 'Ua Huka
Marquesan ground dove (*Gallicolumba rubescens*) – Hatutu and Fatu Huku
Marquesan (Motane) monarch (*Pomarea mendanae motanensis*) – Motane

For more information, go to www.manu.pf and www.birdlife.org.

the ocean. Mattresses are thin but they should have been changed by the time you read this.

Le Reve Marquisien (☎ 79 10 52; revemarquisien@ mail.pf; Vaipaee; s/d with half board 15,000/19,000 CFP) Scene: a secluded clearing at the far end of the village, surrounded by a lush coconut grove. Soundtrack: birds twitching in the jungle. Close up: totally relaxed, you're sipping a fruit juice on your private terrace. Le Reve Marquisien is a perfect escape hatch. The four bungalows are of high standard, with wooden floors, firm beds, hot water and TV. Our only quibble is that it feels a bit too isolated (if a 2km walk down to Vaipaee worries you, then reconsider now). Transfers are included.

Other options:

Chez Alexis Scallamera (☎ /fax 92 60 19, 79 09 48; Vaipaee; r per person 2000-4000 CFP; 🏊) Two home-style rooms without bathroom (cold water only) right in the thick of the owners' sprawling home. Rooms lack intimacy, but sport tip-top mattresses.

Mana Tupuna Village (☎ /fax 92 60 08; Vaipaee; s/d with half board 7000/13,000 CFP) Three local-style bungalows on stilts, perched on the side of a flowery hill. Beautiful views over the valley below. Hot water. An acceptable plan B if Le Reve Marquisien and Chez Maurice et Delphine are full.

Auberge Hitikau (☎ /fax 92 61 74; Hane; s/d with half board 5200/10,400 CFP) The only option in Hane. Three threadbare rooms without bathroom (cold water).

GETTING THERE & AWAY

Four days a week a 20-seater plane flies from Nuku Hiva to 'Ua Huka (7000 CFP one way) and back, connecting with the Pape'ete–Nuku Hiva flight (31,000 CFP Pape'ete to 'Ua Huka one way). There's also one direct 'Ua Huka–Atuona (Hiva Oa) return flight per week. Contact the **Air Tahiti representative** (☎ 92 60 85) in Vaipaee.

The *Aranui* (see the boxed text, p203) stops at 'Ua Huka.

GETTING AROUND

A surprisingly good 13km road links Vaipaee to Hokatu via Hane.

'Ua Huka's airport is on an arid plateau midway between Vaipaee and Hane. Most *pensions* charge 2000 CFP return for airport transfers.

The *pension* owners have 4WDs and can take you to visit the island's villages (about 5000 CFP per day).

'UA POU

pop 2110 / area 125 sq km

Approaching 'Ua Pou by plane is an exhilarating experience. Buffeted by crosswinds, the plane drones towards a thin ribbon of tar sandwiched between the slopes of steep mountains. Its wings twitch frantically up and down a few times before the wheels finally hit the tarmac – pheeww!

This aerial approach is a perfect introduction to 'Ua Pou's fascinating geology. What you'll see is a collection of 12 pointy pinnacles that seem to soar like missiles from the basaltic shield. Almost constantly shrouded in swirling mist and flecked by bright sunlight, they form one of the Marquesas' most enduring images. Completing this natural tableau of otherworldly proportions are a few oasislike valleys bursting with tropical plants as well as a handful of tempting beaches.

'Ua Pou's jewel-like natural setting will frame everything you do here, from hiking and horse riding across the island to visiting secluded hamlets. For culture buffs, the island musters up a handful of powerful

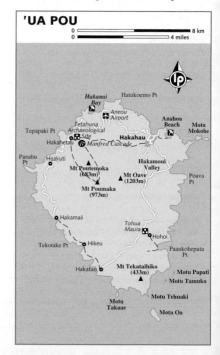

'UA POU

Hakanai Bay
Hatukoemo Pt
Aneou Airport
Anahoa Beach
Motu Mokohe
Tepapaki Pt
Tetahuna Archaeological Site
Hakahau
Hakahetau
Manfred Cascade
Panahu Pt
Haakuti
Hakamoui Valley
Mt Poutemoka (683m)
Mt Oave (1203m)
Poava Pt
Mt Poumaka (973m)
Hakamaii
Tohua Mauia
Hohoi
Tekotake Pt
Hikeu
Paaukoheputa Pt
Hakataō
Mt Tekataihiko (433m)
Motu Papati
Motu Tamuko
Motu Takaae
Motu Tehuaki
Motu Oa

archaeological sites, including two *tohua* that were neatly restored for the Marquesas Arts Festival of 2007, hosted by 'Ua Pou (see the boxed text, p216).

HAKAHAU

'Ua Pou's largest settlement, Hakahau has few charms of its own but it's blessed with a photogenic location. A huge bite chomped out of the fretted coastline of 'Ua Pou's northern coast, Hakahau Bay resembles a giant mouth about to swallow up its prey, with the iconic basalt peaks in the background. Hakahau is a relaxed coastal town blessed with a sweeping black-sand beach – fairly suitable for a dip – and wicked waves that keep local surfers happy.

With a couple of *pensions* and useful services, it's a convenient base.

Information

There's a small medical centre with a doctor and dentist in the south of the village.

Banque Socredo (☎ 92 53 63; ☯ 7.30am-noon & 1-3pm Mon-Fri) Currency exchange, as well as an ATM.

Post office (☯ 7-11.30am & 12.15-3pm Mon-Thu, 7-11.30am & 12.15-2pm Fri, 7-11.30am Sat) On the seafront. Internet access (with the Manaspot card, on sale at the counter). Has an ATM.

Sights

Inside the **Catholic church**, you'll find some fantastic woodcarvings of religious figures with a distinctly Marquesan touch.

For a beautiful view of **Hakahau Bay** head east from Restaurant-Pension Pukuéé along a track until you reach a small pass. At the pass, take the right fork and climb steeply for about 10 minutes until you reach a small flight of steps leading to a white cross, which you can see from the quay.

From Hakahau, it's a 30-minute walk east to deserted **Anahoa Beach**. From the Hakahau quay, follow the sign for Restaurant-Pension Pukuéé and continue along the paved road beyond the restaurant.

Activities

If you want to work off any extra pounds gained at Pension-Restaurant Pukuéé, you can simply walk along the 4WD tracks that connect the villages (but there's no shade). For deeper exploration, it's advisable to hire a **walking** guide since it's easy to get lost. Ask at your *pension*. A full-day guided walk is

about 7000 CFP for two. Recommended hikes include the cross-island path from Hakahau to Hakahetau (about three hours) and the more challenging Poumaka loop (about four hours). Both hikes afford hauntingly beautiful panoramas of the iconic basaltic 'pillars' that jab the skyline.

Horse riding can also be organised – contact any of the *pensions* – but be aware that there's no professional guide on 'Ua Pou.

Sleeping & Eating

Pension Vehine (☎ 92 50 63, 70 84 32; fax 92 53 21; r or bungalows incl breakfast/half board per person 4500/6500 CFP) In the centre of Hakahau, this *pension* offers two simple rooms with shared bathroom in a house and two beautifully finished bungalows in the garden (alas, no views). Meals are served at Snack Vehine, the family's restaurant.

Chez Dora (☎ 92 53 69; r incl breakfast/half board per person 5000/7000 CFP, bungalows incl breakfast/half board per person 7000/9000 CFP) At the far end of the village. This is a mixed bag. The three rooms with shared bathroom in the owners' house have nothing to excite the senses (and might be noisy if the whole family is around) but will do the trick if you have an eye on the bank balance. More charming are the two standalone bungalows in the garden.

Restaurant-Pension Pukuéé (☎ 92 50 83, 72 90 08; pukuee@mail.pf; r with half board per person 8600 CFP; ☒) Reliable, friendly and fabulously sited on a hillside with swoony views of Hakahau Bay. Restaurant-Pension Pukuéé garners points for daring to do something a bit different, as the layout attests: the four smallish, no-frills rooms with shared bathrooms (hot water) occupy an all-wood house that resembles a chalet (couples, take note: the walls don't make it to the ceilings), and there's a little pool surrounded by eye-soothing greenery. Owner Jérôme is great with excursion organisation and logistics and well versed in ecotourism. Jérôme's wife, Elisa, is a genuine cordon-bleu cook and will treat you with the freshest island ingredients (vegetables, local fish and other seafood) at dinner (2700 CFP). Laundry service is available. Wi-fi.

Snack Vehine (☎ 92 50 63; mains 1100-1500 CFP; ☯ lunch & dinner Mon-Sat) A mango's throw from Pension Vehine, this casual eatery is your spot for chow mein, grilled or raw fish, and steaks.

THE MARQUESAS ARTS FESTIVAL

Powerful, grandiose, visceral – words do little justice to the Marquesas' premier festival, which lasts about one week and is held once every four years, usually in December, either on 'Ua Pou, Nuku Hiva or Hiva Oa. It's so colourful that it's definitely worth timing your trip around it. The last edition was held in December 2007 on 'Ua Pou, so you'll have to wait until December 2011 for the next one on Nuku Hiva. If you don't have the patience, 'mini festivals' are held on the smaller islands (on Fatu Hiva in 2009) in between two 'big' festivals.

The Marquesas Arts Festival revolves around a series of music, dance and cultural contests, with dance performances being the highlights. Groups from all the Marquesan islands demonstrate their skills at traditional dances, including the spine-tingling Haka Manu (Bird's Dance) and Haka Pua (Dance of the Pig). Groups from other Polynesian archipelagos are invited and they join the contests too. Most dancing contests take place on restored archaeological sites, which strengthens the visual appeal of the performances. Events also include traditional Marquesan meal preparations as well as arts and crafts displays.

The Marquesas Arts Festival is your top chance to immerse yourself in traditional Marquesan culture. All islanders take it very seriously. As one organiser said, 'It's not folklore; for us, it's a way to preserve our identity and transmit our traditions to the younger generations'. Book your Air Tahiti flight a few months in advance.

HAKANAI

Shortly after the airport at Aneou, **Hakanai Bay** appears like a mirage from around a sharp bend: a long curve of wave-lashed beach, and the only footprints to be seen other than your own are those of crabs and insects (except at weekends, when locals enjoy picnics here). It has been named Plage aux Requins (Shark Beach) because of (wait for it…) the sharks that are occasionally seen in the cove (it's safe for a dip nonetheless).

HAKAHETAU

This tranquil village springs up like an oasis after driving along the dusty track. There aren't many things to see, but the addictive peaceful atmosphere could hold you captive longer than expected.

At the northern entrance of the village there's a large flat stone that you can walk out onto to see a view of the village and bay. It's now used to dry copra but in ancient times it had the more grisly job of drying human remains before they were transported in a *pirogue* up the mountain for 'burial'.

About 150m further towards the village a sign marks the mountainside track to **Manfred Cascade**. Follow this 4WD track for 1.5km up to a footpath on the right. The waterfall is about 300m from here. It has a deep round bathing pool that looks like something out of a tonic-drink advert. On the way to the Cascade, at the far end of the village, make a beeline for the **Tetahuna archaeological site**. This grandiose *tohua* was restored in 2007 and hosted numerous dance and cultural performances during the Marquesas Arts Festival that was held in 'Ua Pou in 2007.

Sleeping & Eating

Pension Leydj (☎ 92 53 19; r incl breakfast/half board per person 3500/5500 CFP) In a plum setting on a hill at the edge of Hakahetau, this mellow *pension* offers clean, well-swept yet impersonal rooms at a nice price. Bathrooms (cold water) are shared. Owner Tony is a renowned master carver and the living room is like a small art gallery – you won't find a better place to buy high-quality souvenirs. His spouse Célestine can cook some seriously good Marquesan meals. Various excursions can be organised.

HAAKUTI

One street links the stone church, built on a *pae pae* at the top of the village, with the tiny, sea-swept quay some 600m below.

HAKAMAII

At the end of the 4WD track, this one-street village stretches along the Kahioa River. The facade of the town's stone church, facing the ocean, has unusual yellow, blue and red wooden panels that are meant to imitate stained-glass windows.

A path running up the hill next to the church leads up to a ridge for some fantastic views.

HOHOI

Tranquillity reigns supreme in this little charmer about 12km southeast from Hakahau, and nobody's complaining. Apart from its lovely setting and peaceful ambience, Hohoi is a definite must-see for culture vultures. Situated above the village, the magnificent **Tohua Mauia** comprises a huge L-shaped stone platform and numerous *pae pae* dotted around the main complex. The whole area was restored in 2007 and hosted memorable dance and cultural performances during the Marquesas Festival in December 2007. Even if your interest in ruins is only slight, the enchanting setting and the almost mystical hush are reason enough to come here.

Further down in the village, look for the pagoda-shaped Catholic church. Continue down to the beach; if you are lucky, you might come across *pierres fleuries* (flowering stones) – pieces of phonolite that have crystallised to form amber-coloured flower shapes.

GETTING THERE & AWAY
Air

There is an office for **Air Tahiti** (☎ 91 52 25; ☒ 7.30am-noon & 1.30-3.30pm Mon-Fri) in Hakahau.

There are flights six days a week on a 20-seater plane from Nuku Hiva to 'Ua Pou (7000 CFP one way), connecting with the Pape'ete–Nuku Hiva flight (Pape'ete to 'Ua Pou costs 32,000 CFP one way). There are also two to three weekly flights from Hiva Oa to 'Ua Pou (8200 CFP one way).

Boat

The *Aranui* (see the boxed text, p203) stops at Hakahau and Hakahetau.

GETTING AROUND

One dirt 4WD track runs most of the way around the island, with the only inaccessible bit being the section between Hakamaii and Hakatao.

The airport is at Aneou, about 10km west of Hakahau. Your hosts will come to collect you if you have booked accommodation; it usually costs 2000 CFP per person return.

Ask at your *pension* about hiring a 4WD with driver; expect to pay 15,000 CFP to go as far as Hakamaii. Each route is nearly a full-day round trip from Hakahau with stops at points of interest.

HIVA OA

pop 1991 / area 320 sq km

What a beauty! Scenery- and atmosphere-wise, Hiva Oa is worthy of an Oscar. This serpentine island is a picturesque mix of lush jungle, sea-smashed coastal cliffs and towering volcanic peaks. Many of the bays that fret the coastline make wonderful photo ops with their combinations of indigo water, white- or black-sand or pebble-stubbled foreshores and nodding palms – not to mention a smattering of typical Marquesan hamlets where time has stood still.

But wait! There's more to Hiva Oa than grandiose landscapes and laid-back vibes. Pre-European history is achingly prominent here, with a collection of enigmatic archaeological sites scattered in the jungle, including the most intriguing *tiki* in French Polynesia, which will give you plenty to ponder.

By far the best way to experience Hiva Oa is to visit the island's far-flung corners on horseback or by foot (or, for those who want some creature comforts, by 4WD), and soak up sublime views of the wild geography. Divers will get a buzz in the prolific waters along the shores of Hiva Oa.

Hiva Oa is also the optimal launching pad for exploring Tahuata and Fatu Hiva.

One thing is sure: after a few days here, you'll understand why the artist Paul Gauguin and the Belgian singer Jacques Brel chose to call it home.

ATUONA & AROUND
pop 1300

Atuona is the southern group's administrative capital and one of the Marquesas' most attractive settlements. Nestled at the mouth of a lovely bay, it's framed by forested mountains that rise steeply up behind it to converge on a crenellated central ridge. It's the only town with any sort of bustle (by Marquesan standards) on Hiva Oa, and has a small selection of restaurants and guesthouses. Neat, modern houses cling like limpets to a rocky peninsula that separates the town centre from the majestic Tahauku Bay to the east, a favourite anchoring place among yachties.

Atuona is particularly famous for having been once home to Gauguin and Belgian singer Jacques Brel (1929–78), whose memories are kept alive by a regular trickle of visitors.

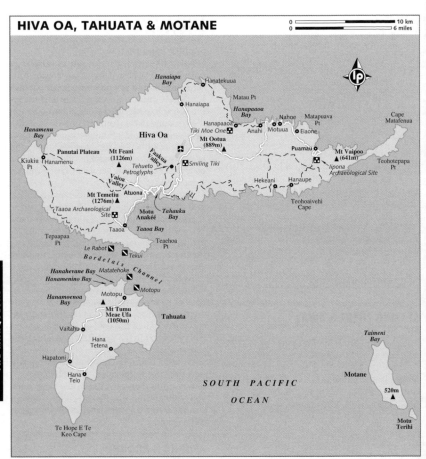

HIVA OA, TAHUATA & MOTANE

0 — 10 km
0 — 6 miles

Information

Banque Socredo (☎ 92 73 54; ⏱ 7.30-11.30am & 1.30-4pm Mon-Fri) Currency exchange. Has a 24-hour ATM.

Hospital Small but well equipped; it's behind the mayor's office.

Post office (⏱ 7.30-11.30am & 1.30-4.30pm Mon-Thu, 7.30-11.30am & 1.30-3.30pm Fri, 7.30-8.30am Sat) Internet access (with the Manaspot card, available at the counter). Has an ATM, too.

Tourism office (☎ 92 78 93; www.maquises-hivaoa .org.pf; ⏱ 8am-noon & 1-3pm Mon-Fri) Right in the centre. Hands out useful brochures and sells sketch maps of most tourist sites (100 CFP).

Sights

For Gauguin fans (see the boxed text, p220), a visit to the refurbished **Espace Culturel Paul Gauguin** (adult/child 600/300 CFP; ⏱ 8-11am & 2-5pm Mon-Thu, 7.30am-2.30pm Fri, 8-11am Sat) is a must. Don't get too excited, though; you won't find any originals, just digital copies of his work. The detailed signs in English are very informative. Once you've done a full round of the paintings, timeline and literature, head outside and have a look at the Maison du Jouir (House of Pleasure), a replica of Gauguin's own house. Behind the Espace Culturel Paul Gauguin you'll find a big aircraft hangar that houses the **Centre Jacques Brel** (adult/child 500/250 CFP; ⏱ 8-11am & 2-3pm Mon-Thu, 7.30am-2.30pm Fri, 8-11am Sat). In the centre is Brel's plane, *Jojo*; posters tracing the musician's life adorn the walls and his music plays dreamily over the sound system. For more on Brel's life, see the boxed text, p220.

Another must-see for Gauguin and Brel devotees (as well as for romantics and art lovers) is the **Calvaire Cemetery**, perched on a hill overlooking Atuona. You will find this frangipani-filled graveyard an appropriately colourful place for Paul Gauguin's tomb. While most of the tombs are marked with white crosses, Gauguin's is a simple round stone with his name painted in white. Right behind, a replica of the statue *Oviri* (meaning 'wild') stands guard. Jacques Brel's grave is in the lower part of the cemetery, near the access steps, on the left. The gravestone, lovingly planted with flowers, is adorned with a medallion depicting the singer with his female companion, Madly.

To get there, head north on the road just east of the *gendarmerie*. Continue for about 600m until you reach a fork in the road and follow the sign to the cemetery 100m further on. It takes about 20 minutes on foot.

Restored for the 1991 Marquesas Arts Festival, the **tohua Pepeu** faces Banque Socredo in the centre of town. It's used today as a festivities centre for the town, where dances and cultural activities are performed.

The **Catholic church**, right in the centre, is also worth a peek for its elegant architecture.

Anyone with an interest in ancient Marquesan civilisation shouldn't leave Atuona without a visit to the **Tehueto petroglyphs**. Hidden high up in the Tahauku Valley, they are a good walk from Atuona but it's usually quite overgrown and the path is confusing; we suggest hiring a guide (ask at your *pension* or contact Alain Tricas; see p220). You'll find a massive rock with prolific carvings on two sides, including stylised human figures. Then follow the trail that leads up a small hill to an overgrown *tohua* sporting a *tiki* carved in bas relief in the side of the stone platform (you can't miss it).

And now, Hiva Oa's most bizarre statue. The **Smiling Tiki** (no joke) can be found near the road to the airport, about 10km from Atuona. About 1m in height, it stands alone in a clearing. Its two clearly outlined eyes resemble big glasses, and its curved lips suggest a smile. Honestly, this *tiki* looks like a puppet that you just want to hug! To find it (no sign), ask your hosts to draw you a sketch or ask for the little sketch map that's on sale at the tourism office (it's surprisingly reliable).

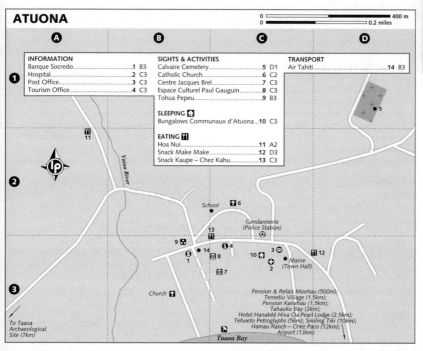

IN THE STEPS OF PAUL GAUGUIN & JACQUES BREL

For many people (especially the French), the Marquesas are closely associated with painter Paul Gauguin (1848–1903) and singer-songwriter Jacques Brel (1929–78). Both were won over by the archipelago's powerful landscapes and serenity, and both chose to live out their lives on Hiva Oa. They rest in the Calvaire Cemetery (p219), which has become something of a pilgrimage site for numerous devotees.

The evocative paintings of Paul Gauguin are largely responsible for Polynesia's enduring reputation as a paradise lost. Constantly in search of an escape, he first voyaged to Brittany, Martinique and Provence, but this was still not enough to appease his tormented mind. In a letter to the painter Odilon Redon in 1890, he wrote: 'I am going to Tahiti and hope to finish my life there. I consider that my art…is just a seed and I hope to cultivate it there for myself, in its primitive and wild state.' In Mataiea on Tahiti, where the Musée Gauguin now stands, he concentrated on capturing images of daily life and, in 1892 and 1893, experienced an intensely productive period. Exuberant settings and flamboyant colours, with yellows, reds and blues predominating, increasingly pervaded the artist's painting.

Gauguin sold few canvases and was impoverished. He sailed for France in 1893 and in November of that year a large exhibition devoted solely to his work opened in Paris. He embarked on writing a narrative, *Noa Noa*, inspired by his Tahitian period and designed to make the public understand his work. But short of any recognition, he set off for the South Seas once again in 1895.

His most powerful compositions, *Te Arii Vahine* (The Royal Woman; 1896), *Nevermore* (1897) and *Where Do We Come From? What Are We? Where Are We Going?* (1897), date from this second and final stay in Polynesia, which was marked by illness and distress. After a failed suicide attempt, Gauguin took refuge on Hiva Oa in the Marquesas, where he defended the inhabitants against the colonial administration and the all-powerful Catholic Church. Although weakened, he did not stop writing, drawing, sculpting and painting, and it was during this period that he produced one of his most beautiful nudes, *Barbaric Tales* (1902). Gauguin died in May 1903.

Ironically, Belgian-born artist (and a legend in France and in Belgium) Jacques Brel was as iconoclastic as Gauguin and he derided the flaws of society in his powerful songs. In an attempt to escape media pressure, he set out to sail around the world on the *Askoy*, his private ketch, accompanied by his female companion, Madly, from Guadeloupe. In November 1975 they arrived at Atuona and, seduced by its serenity, they never left. In 1976 Brel and Madly set up a small home on the hillside above the village. He equipped himself with *Jojo*, a Beechcraft airplane in which he travelled between the islands of the northern group and as far as Pape'ete. Jacques Brel and Madly became involved in village life and were well liked by the locals. From time to time the artist would perform medical evacuations to Pape'ete in his plane. Jacques Brel died of cancer in October 1978 at the age of 48. His last song, 'Les Marquises' (The Marquesas), resounds as a vibrant homage to this generous place. His tomb is near that of Paulo (as Brel referred to Gauguin).

Activities

HIKING

There are some truly excellent hiking possibilities on Hiva Oa. Given the lack of a waymarked trail, a guide is strongly recommended (except if you stay on easy-to-follow 4WD tracks). **Alain Tricas** (☎ 20 40 90) is a competent guide who can customise hikes in the wildest areas of the Taaoa Valley, starting from the *tohua* Upeke archaeological site (p222). The highlights are the incredible views of the valley and the southern part of the island. He can also guide you to the Tehueto petroglyphs (p219) and charges 1000 CFP per hour (per person), with a maximum of 8000 CFP per day. Another professional guide is **Henry Bonno** (☎ 92 74 44). Transfers can be arranged.

HORSE RIDING

Seeing Hiva Oa from the saddle is a typical Hiva Oa experience and a low-impact way to imbibe the majestic scenery. A network of trails leading to some of the most beautiful sites can be explored on horseback. **Hamau Ranch – Chez Paco** (☎ 92 70 57, 28 68 21; hamauranch@mail.pf; rides 7000-14,000 CFP) organises three-hour jaunts on the plateau near the airport. No previous experience is necessary. The ultimate is a full-day ride to Hanatekuua Bay, to the north of the island, along undulating ridges and the coastline. Riders must be at least six years old. Transfers can be arranged.

DIVING
When you're talking great dive spots in French Polynesia, Hiva Oa doesn't immediately come to mind, and it's a shame. Hiva Oa certainly is not possessed of dazzling tropical reefs (there's no barrier reef and no turquoise lagoon in the Marquesas, remember), but there are many excellent diving sites along the crumpled coastline of Hiva Oa and Tahuata. And there's only one dive boat: yours.

The only dive centre in the Marquesas, **SubAtuona** (☎ 92 70 88, 27 05 24; eric.lelyonnais@wanadoo.fr; Atuona) offers personalised tours and a wealth of experience in Marquesan waters. Including all gear, the cost of a single/two-tank dive is 7000/13,000 CFP (minimum two divers). SubAtuona also offers day trips to Tahuata that combine one dive and a tour of Tahuata's main villages. The price is 15,000 CFP and includes a picnic on a secluded beach. Payment is by cash only. For details of dive sites in the area, see p72.

BOAT EXCURSIONS TO TAHUATA
Taking a boat excursion to nearby Tahuata (p224) will be one of the main highlights of your visit to Hiva Oa and it's well worth the expense (especially given the lack of reliable boat services to Tahuata). **SubAtuona** (☎ 92 70 88, 27 05 24; eric.lelyonnais@wanadoo.fr; Atuona; full-day tours 11,000 CFP) can arrange day trips to Tahuata. They typically stop to visit Hapatoni and Vaitahu and picnic in Hanamenino Bay.

Sleeping
Accommodation options on Hiva Oa are fairly limited. There's only one budget place, and at the other end of the scale only Hanakéé Pearl Resort qualifies as luxurious. In between is a handful of quality guesthouses that meet the requirements of most visitors. All places are in Atuona, bar one in Puamau. Unless otherwise noted, credit cards are accepted.

Bungalows Communaux d'Atuona (☎ 92 73 32; fax 92 74 95; bungalows 3000 CFP) An obvious choice for thrifty travellers. In theory, the seven bungalows with bathroom (cold water) and kitchenette, next to the *mairie* (town hall), are reserved for officials, but they can be let to tourists depending on availability. Pluses:

affordable, well located, serviceable. Minuses: crude and sticky hot (no fans are provided). Credit cards are not accepted. For booking, call the *mairie* between 7.30am and 11.30am or 1.30pm and 4.30pm Monday to Friday.

our pick **Temetiu Village** (☎ 91 70 60; www.temetiu village.com; bungalows standard s/d 7000/8900 CFP, large 9200 CFP; ☐ ☎) Seeking a stress-melting cocoon in Hiva Oa with homely qualities, efficient hosts and a big dollop of atmosphere without an exorbitant price tag? This well-run *pension* has all the key ingredients, with four recent, shiny-clean bungalows perched scenically on a lush hillside, each enjoying wraparound views of Tahauku Bay. There are also two older (and slightly cheaper) bungalows but they show signs of wear and tear and lack the wow factor. After a long day's *tiki*-seeing, nothing beats a dip in the small pool. The food here is a definite plus (see p222).

Pension Moehau (☎ 92 72 69; www.relaismoe hau.pf; s/d incl breakfast 8100/12,000 CFP, with half board 11,100/18,200 CFP) Please call an architect! While the front rooms are light-filled and face a bay-view terrace, those at the back face the dark hill behind. The moral of the story: ask for an oceanside room (especially rooms 2 and 3). All rooms are scrupulously clean, amply sized and well appointed (hot water, fan and plump bedding) but they lack charm. There's a good restaurant downstairs.

Pension Kanahau (☎ 91 71 31, 70 16 26; http://pension kanahau.com; s/d 10,000/12,000 CFP; ☐) Tania, your gracious host, does a superb job in keeping her place shipshape. Location-wise, this *pension* plays in the same league as nearby Temetiu Village, with a flower-filled garden and stupendous views of Tahauku Bay and the mountain amphitheatre. The four bungalows are well furnished, spacious and sparkling clean (hot water is available); two units are equipped with cooking facilities (add 1000 CFP). The catch? Except breakfast (1100 CFP), Tania no longer offers meals, but she does drive guests to town for lunch or dinner and takes them back to the *pension*, for free. No credit cards are accepted, but you can pay in dollars or euros. There's a 15% drop in price if you stay more than three nights. Wi-fi.

Hotel Hanakéé Hiva Oa Pearl Lodge (☎ 92 75 87; www.pearlresorts.com; bungalows 23,000-40,000 CFP; ☒ ☐ ☎) Recipe for romance: take a film-set-worthy location (a secluded property on a mound overlooking Tahauku Bay, with Mt Temetiu as a backdrop). Add 14 well-designed bungalows adorned with fancy touches and lots of tropical flowers. Bake in the Marquesan heat by the pool, stir in a refreshing sea breeze, crack open a bottle of wine, and you have a deliciously sexy hotel. Wi-fi.

Eating

In Atuona, you will find several well-stocked grocery stores.

Snack Make Make (☎ 92 74 26; mains 800-2500 CFP; ☽ lunch & dinner Mon-Sat) You wouldn't guess it from the unprepossessing surrounds, but this place boasts an eclectic menu, from Chinese specialities and fish dishes to goat and mussels. Gourmet it's not; tasty and inexpensive it is.

Snack Kaupe – Chez Kahu (☎ 92 71 61; mains 1000-1700 CFP; ☽ lunch Sun-Fri, dinner daily) Blink and you'll miss this discreet venture conveniently positioned across from Espace Culturel Paul Gauguin (no sign). No culinary extravaganza here, just a few classics faultlessly prepared (grilled sirloin, grilled fish, shrimps with tomato sauce). Kahu himself is something of a star in the Marquesas – he's one of the best Haka Manu (Bird's Dance) dancers.

Relais Moehau (☎ 92 72 69; mains 1400-2300 CFP; ☽ lunch & dinner) It might feel weird to sit down for a pizza on a South Pacific island, but the fish pizza is too flavoursome to ignore (at dinner only). Other headliners include *chaud froid de thon* (cooked tuna served cold), grilled wahoo and raw shrimps with coconut sauce. Pity about the tiled dining room, which is yawn-inducing.

Hotel Hanakéé Hiva Oa Pearl Lodge (☎ 92 75 87; mains 1500-2800 CFP; ☽ lunch & dinner) Probably the number-one spot for fine dining in Hiva Oa, and certainly the most suitable place for a *moment à deux*. The sweeping views from the terrace are impressive enough, but the excellent French-influenced cuisine is better still, and makes imaginative use of the island's rich produce.

Hoa Nui (☎ 92 73 63; set menu 2700 CFP; ☽ lunch & dinner, by reservation only) Hidden amid a jungle-like foliage, this modest eatery specialises in Marquesan cuisine (think pork, fish, seafood or goat), though the desserts are disappointing. Chinese specialities are sometimes offered, too, but are much more ordinary.

Temetiu Village (☎ 91 70 60; set menu 3000 CFP; ☽ lunch & dinner, by reservation) What's the draw here? The panoramic views from the open-air dining room? The convivial atmosphere or the delectable (and copious) Marquesan specialities? Come and see for yourself. Credit cards are accepted.

TAAOA

This site doesn't have the impressive *tiki*, as at Iipona (see below), but its sheer size makes it just as interesting. The location is certainly impressive: backed by jagged green mountains high in an uninhabited valley and surrounded by thick overhanging trees (including huge banyan trees), it's not hard to imagine the power such sacred sites once had for the pre-Christian islanders. On arrival at the site, you will find yourself facing a vast *tohua* built on several levels. Continue for 100m and, on the right, is a well-preserved *tiki* more than 1m in height sitting on a platform. From a distance it looks like a plain block of basalt, but as you get closer you can clearly pick out the contours of the eyes and mouth – thrilling!

It is a short 7km from Atuona.

PUAMAU

Chances are great that you'll come here to visit the Iipona archaeological site lying on the outskirts of the village. Puamau itself is a delightful, timeless village that occupies a coastal plain bordered by a vast amphitheatre of mountains.

Sights

IIPONA ARCHAEOLOGICAL SITE

No, it's not just another stone platform, but one of the best-preserved archaeological sites in French Polynesia and probably the star attraction of Hiva Oa. It's not Easter Island, but you'll be moved by the eeriness of the site and impressed by the five monumental tiki – it pulsates with *mana*.

As you advance towards the first platform, you'll first notice the reclining Tiki Maki Taua Pepe, representing a woman lying on her stomach, her head stretched out and arms pointing to the sky. Experts believe she represents a woman giving birth. The petroglyphs on the pedestal represent dogs but their meaning is unknown.

And now, **Tiki Takaii**, at 2.67m the largest *tiki* in French Polynesia; it's named after a warrior chief renowned for his strength. Tiki Te Tovae E Noho is to the left of Takaii, on a lower platform. Less finely worked than the others, its upper torso is hard to make out and the head has disappeared. Note that its hands each have six fingers. Further back stands Tiki Fau Poe. Measuring about 1.8m, it is sitting with its legs stretched out, a position typical of women when they work in the fields. Experts believe it to be Takaii's wife. Tiki Manuiotaa is in complete contrast to the others: less massive, its proportions are harmonious and balanced. The hands are clearly recognisable, as is its female sex. It was decapitated but its head has been replaced by archaeologists.

Known to ethnologists and archaeologists in the 1800s, the Iipona (Oipona) site was extensively restored in 1991 by French archaeologists Pierre and Marie-Noëlle Garanger-Ottino.

To reach the site from Puamau, follow the track directly back from the seafront, next to the football ground, and continue for about 1.5km. You will need to pay 300 CFP to the person who maintains and guards the site.

TOHUA PEHE KUA
On the property of the Chez Marie-Antoinette, shortly before the Iipona site, is a small graveyard with the tomb of the valley's last chief and his partner, who died early in the 20th century. One of the four tombs at the site is flanked by two *tiki*. You'll also find an imposing *pae pae*.

Sleeping & Eating
Chez Marie-Antoinette (☎ 92 72 27; d with half board per person 6000 CFP) The only option outside Atuona looks tired, but it's a convenient port of call for those who want to spend some time in the Puamau area. Two bare but acceptable double rooms with shared bathroom (cold water only) are available. The *tohua* Peke Kua (above) is in its grounds. The real hit is the tasty Marquesan food (fresh fish, goat, pork). Nonguests on a day trip from Atuona usually have lunch here (by reservation only). Credit cards are not accepted.

HANAPAAOA & SURROUNDING HAMLETS
It's a winding but scenic 1½-hour journey by 4WD to wild and beautiful Hanapaaoa from Atuona. The track passes the airport and splits shortly after; the first turn-off goes to Hanaiapa, and the second leads to Hanapaaoa.

In Hanapaaoa, ask a local to take you to the **Tiki Moe One**, hidden in a forest on a hillside.

One of the quirkiest statues in the Marquesas, it features a carved crown around the head and is said to be endowed with a strong *mana*. It's modestly sized at under 1m in height. According to legend, the inhabitants used to take it down to the beach every year where they bathed it and coated it with *monoi* (fragrant oil) before putting it back in place.

From Hanapaaoa, you can get to **Anahi** and **Nahoe**, two end-of-the-world hamlets to the west. Hold on to your hat – now the real fun begins! The 4WD track snakes along the coast, offering ethereal vistas around every other bend. Even control freaks might prefer the passenger seat, to fully absorb the awesome panorama splayed below – indigo blue ocean, plunging cliffs, stunning bays. Oh, and watch out for stray goats! It's not a road trip for the faint-hearted. Be prudent (don't attempt it in wet weather), take your time and you'll enjoy one of the Marquesas' most spectacular drives. Or you can hire a car with driver.

HANAIAPA
Picturesquely cradled by striking mountains carpeted with shrubs and coconut trees, Hanaiapa is a gem. Stretching for more than 1km along a single street, this neat and flower-filled village really feels like the end of the line. The majestic Hanaiapa Bay is fringed with a pebble beach. An imposing rock sits in the middle of the bay.

At the entrance of the village (coming from Atuona), about 200m off the main road, to the right, you'll find some well-preserved **petroglyphs**. A big boulder sports elaborate geometric patterns.

Hanaiapa is a cul-de-sac, but you can walk to the hamlet of Hanatekuua – a little path follows the coastline.

If you're looking for souvenirs, it's not a bad idea to stop at **Jean & Nadine Oberlin** (☎ 92 76 34), a couple from Alsace who fell in love with Hanaiapa long ago. They make lovely *tapa* (with a contemporary twist) as well as engraved calabashes. Their house (and workshop) is right at the entrance of the village, about 200m from the turn-off to the petroglyphs (look for the 'Artisanat' sign).

GETTING THERE & AWAY
Air
There are flights from Atuona to Pape'ete, Nuku Hiva, 'Ua Pou and 'Ua Huka (via

Nuku Hiva). Pape'ete–Atuona return flights go seven times a week, direct or via Nuku Hiva (32,000 CFP one way). There are five to seven Atuona–Nuku Hiva return flights a week (11,000 CFP one way), two to three Atuona–'Ua Pou return flights a week (8200 CFP one way) and one 'Ua Huka–Atuona return flight per week (8200 CFP).

Air Tahiti (☎ 92 70 90; ⏲ 7.30-11.30am & 1.30-4.30pm Mon-Fri) has an office in Atuona. Credit cards are accepted.

Boat
The *Aranui* (see the boxed text, p203) stops at Atuona and Puamau and, less frequently, at Hanapaaoa and Hanaiapa.

To get to Tahuata, you can take the twice-weekly communal *bonitier* (when it's not out of order) from Atuona (2000 CFP one way, one hour) or charter a private boat and share the costs with any other passengers (about 20,000 CFP from Atuona to Vaitahu). If you stay at Pension Amatea on Tahuata (opposite), the owner can organise transport for 15,000 CFP.

Getting Around
TO/FROM THE AIRPORT
The airport is 13km from Atuona. If you have booked your accommodation, your host will come and collect you for about 3500 CFP return.

CAR
Excursions by 4WD cost about 8000 CFP to Taaoa, 10,000 CFP to Hanaiapa, 17,000 CFP to Puamau and 20,000 CFP to Hanapaaoa – these prices are for the full car (four people). For information, contact *pension* owners.

Atuona Rent-a-Car (☎ 92 76 07, 72 17 17) and **Hiva Oa Location** (☎ 91 70 60, 24 65 05) rent 4WDs without driver for about 13,000 CFP per day, with unlimited mileage and insurance included.

TAHUATA

pop 671 / area 70 sq km
Just as lush but not as steep, Tahuata is Hiva Oa's shy little sister. Separated from Hiva Oa by the 4km-wide Bordelais Channel, it is the smallest inhabited island in the archipelago. It won't be long before you're smitten by the island's mellow tranquillity and laid-back lifestyle.

Most travellers visit Tahuata on a day tour from Hiva Oa, which is a shame as it deserves a couple of days to do it justice. So stretch that

schedule and put on your explorer's hat – you'll need it. It's a great place to meet the bone carvers and tattoo artists at work, splash about on a deserted beach, explore the archaeological sites and take a horse-riding trip. Diving is also available (from Hiva Oa).

History
Catholicism was introduced in Vaitahu between 1797 and 1838, and the island was a bridgehead for the evangelisation of the Marquesas.

In 1842 Captain Abel-Nicolas Dupetit-Thouars forced his former ally, Chief Iotete of Tahuata, to sign the treaty of annexation by France. Realising that he had been duped, Iotete later opposed the transfer, but his rebellion was crushed by the French. It was also during this period that the island's reserves of sandalwood were plundered.

Information
Tourist infrastructures are as scarce as hens teeth on Tahuata. Bring cash, as there is no bank. The post office is in Vaitahu.

SIGHTS
Vaitahu
This tiny village, built against the steep slopes of the central ridge, retains a few vestiges of its stormy past. On the seafront stands a modest **memorial** topped by a rusty anchor, recalling the first meeting between Admiral Dupetit-Thouars and Chief Iotete in 1838.

Next to the post office, there is a tiny **museum** (admission free) with some archaeological items including fish hooks and stone pestles.

On the hill that dominates the village to the south are a few remains of a building known as the **French Fort**, which is in ruins. There are sweeping views from the ridge.

The monumental stone **Catholic church** is opposite the seafront. Financed by the Vatican and opened with great pomp and ceremony in 1988, it recalls the importance of Tahuata in the evangelisation of the archipelago. The church has beautiful stained-glass windows and some interesting woodcarvings.

Vaitahu is a good place to have a wander. Copra-drying sheds are dotted here and there, and brightly coloured traditional *vaka* (outrigger canoes) line the shore.

In Vaitahu try to meet Edwin Tii, Félix Fii and Teiki Barsinas, three renowned wood and bone carvers. They are also tattooists (see also the boxed text, opposite).

THE MARQUESAS

Hapatoni

Hapatoni curves around a wide bay and is accessible by boat in less than 15 minutes from Vaitahu, or by a track.

The **royal road** is the village's main attraction. Built on a dyke on the orders of Queen Vaekehu II in the 19th century, this paved road, lined with 100-year-old tamanu trees, extends along the shore. At the promontory a path leads up to a lookout, marked by a cross, with a magnificent view of the bay.

If you want a well-informed guide, ask for Liliane Teikipupuni. She will also take you to the craft centre where you will be able to shop around.

Beaches

Lucky yachties! They can anchor in idyllic **Hanamoenoa Bay**. Other soul-stirring bays lined with a ribbon of white sand include **Hanahevane** and **Hanamenino**.

ACTIVITIES

The track that joins Vaitahu and Motopu in the northeast, a distance of about 17km, is suitable for **horse riding**. Ask the locals about hiring a mount.

Divers, gear up – there's topnotch action along the coast. **Diving** is arranged through SubAtuona in Hiva Oa (see p221).

SLEEPING & EATING

Good news for indecisive travellers: Tahuata has only one place to stay, **Pension Amatea** (☎ 92 92 84, 76 24 90; r per person with half board 7000 CFP), in Vaitahu. It's secure and well maintained, with helpful hosts and a good location near the seafront. The four rooms share bathrooms. Marguerite, the owner, can help arrange any activity and also transportation to and from Tahuata.

Every village has one or two small shops.

GETTING THERE & AWAY

Don't rely on the communal *bonitier,* which normally runs a twice-weekly Vaitahu–Atuona ferry service (4000 CFP return, one hour each way), as it's frequently out of order. Your best bet is to contact Pension Amatea (see left), which can help arrange passage with private boats (about 15,000 CFP per boatload).

Another option is to board the *Aranui* (see the boxed text, p203) at Hiva Oa.

A convenient option is to take an excursion from Hiva Oa. **SubAtuona** (☎ 92 70 88, 27 05 24) charges 11,000 CFP per person for a day trip (minimum four persons), which includes visits of Hapatoni, Vaitahu and a picnic on a beach at Hanamenino.

GETTING AROUND

A 17km track, accessible to 4WD vehicles, crosses the island's interior to link Vaitahu with Motopu and Vaitahu with Hapatoni. It costs 15,000 CFP for a day's hire with driver.

Hapatoni is less than 15 minutes from Vaitahu by speedboat. It costs about 6000 CFP to hire a boat between Vaitahu and Hapatoni, and 7000 to 10,000 CFP between Vaitahu and Hanahevane Bay.

FATU HIVA

pop 562 / area 80 sq km

As far away from the rest of the world as it's possible to get in these modern times (despite mobile phones and satellite TVs), Fatu Hiva is the Marquesas' frontier and a marvellous 'stop the world and get off' place. For travellers

---

GETTING A TATTOO

Fancy looking like a fierce Marquesan *toa* (warrior) or a queen, thanks to indelible geometric patterns on your chest/shoulder/butt/neck/ankles/arms (take your pick)? Think about getting tattooed. Marquesan tattooists rank among the best in the South Pacific. Ironically, most Marquesan tattooists are not in the Marquesas, but work either on more touristy islands in French Polynesia (especially Tahiti, Mo'orea and Bora Bora) or abroad. On Nuku Hiva, ask for Brice Tattoo or Jean-Yves Tamarii (who divides his time between Nuku Hiva and another tattoo shop on Mo'orea); on Hiva Oa, Santos Nazario has a good reputation. The most charismatic tattooists are certainly Teiki Barsinas and Felix Fii; you'll meet them on Tahuata. 'I show my portfolio to tourists', says Jean-Yves Tamarii, 'so that they have an idea of my style and patterns. No two tattooists do the same designs. It's a bit of a work of art.' They all work to high-quality standards and use sterile needles. See p51 for more information.

FATU HIVA

0   8 km
0   4 miles

Teaite
Hoe Pt

Tevaii Pt

(820m) ▲

*Bay of Virgins
(Baie des Verges)*   Hanavave

Cape Matautu

Ouia

Matakoo Pt

Omoa

Mt Tauaouoho
(1125m) ▲

Tataaihoa Pt

Teae Pt

who relish the idea of getting marooned for a few days, this hard-to-reach island way off most people's radar (bar yachties) is hard to beat. When arriving by boat (there's no landing strip), expect a visual shock: wrinkled cliffs tumble into the ocean and splendid bays, including the iconic Bay of Virgins, indent the coastline.

There are only two villages, one good *pension* and one dirt track, so there are plenty of opportunities to move into slow gear. For some cultural sustenance, a couple of giant petroglyphs – the biggest in French Polynesia – hidden in the forest beckon.

It's a bit challenging to get to Fatu Hiva, but for those who do brave the perils of unreliable boat services we'll only make one guarantee: your stay will be memorable.

INFORMATION

Bring a stash of cash – there's no bank on the island and credit cards are not accepted. There is a post office in Omoa.

SIGHTS
Omoa

Time moves at a crawl in Omoa. The most striking monument is the Catholic **church**, with its red roof, white facade and slender spire. It makes a colourful scene on Sunday morning, when it's bursting at the seams with a devout congregation neatly dressed and belting out rousing *himene* (hymns). Travellers are welcome to join and show their singing skills.

Omoa is famous for its two **giant petroglyphs**, in two different locations. The first site is easily accessed after a 10-minute walk from the main road (ask around) and features a huge fish (probably a dorado) as well as a few small anthropomorphic designs inscribed on big basaltic boulders. The second site is a 20-minute walk from Chez Lionel Cantois (below) and is hidden in fairy-tale bushland. It has a clearly outlined whale incised on a big slab – an eerie sight. To get there, you'll need a guide (Lionel will be happy to show you the site).

Hanavave

Be prepared to get dewy-eyed. When the setting sun bounces purple halos off the towering basaltic cones of **Bay of Virgins**, at the mouth of a steep-sided valley, with a cluster of yachts at anchor, it's a hallucinatory wonderland. We say 'cones' because we're prudish. Truth is, they resemble giant phalluses protruding out of the ocean. This risqué natural tableau was originally (and aptly) named Baie des Verges in French (Bay of Penises). Outraged, the missionaries promptly added a redeeming 'i' to make the name Baie des Vierges (Bay of Virgins).

Should you feel overburdened with naughty thoughts, you can confess your sins inside the town's small, sober church, then admire the elaborate wooden altar.

ACTIVITIES

Most activities on Fatu Hiva are of the DIY variety, including **walking** and **horse riding**. Why not follow the 17km-long track that links the two villages via the interior? The four-hour walk is not too difficult and you can't get lost. The first part of the walk goes up the Omoa Valley along a cliff-top path with sweeping views over the village below. The trail then crosses through the island's interior. It's a steep descent to Hanavave and there's not much shade along the way, but the views of the village and the dramatic coastline are so terrific that all thoughts of aching legs will be forgotten. You can also horse-ride it – ask at your *pension*.

SLEEPING & EATING

The only accommodation options are in Omoa.

ourpick Chez Lionel Cantois (☎ 92 81 84, 70 03 71; chezlionel@mail.pf; s/d incl breakfast 5000/6000 CFP, bungalow incl breakfast 9000 CFP; dinner 2000 CFP) Hands down

THE MARQUESAS

the best *pension* on the island, at the far end of Omoa. Basking in familial warmth, it has an air of *Little House on the Prairie*. Empathetic Lionel, a Norman who is a mine of local information (his English is passable), can take you virtually anywhere on the island, while his Marquesan wife Bernadette is an adept cook. The well-equipped bungalow with bathroom (hot water) in the manicured garden is as cosy as a bird's nest but, if funds are short, the two rooms in the owners' house cut the mustard (the walls don't make it to the ceilings, though). Not a bad place to get stuck on Fatu Hiva (fear not, Lionel will help you arrange transportation back to Hiva Oa).

Chez Norma Ropati (☎ 92 80 13; r per person with half board 4200 CFP) An acceptable fallback, with four boxy and rather darkish rooms with shared bathroom (cold water).

GETTING THERE & AWAY

Fatu Hiva is the most difficult island to get to in the Marquesas, but sorting out transport is manageable if you're flexible. The easiest option is the communal *bonitier* (pray it's not out of service), which usually runs on Tuesday from Hanavave and Omoa to Atuona (same-day return) and costs 4000 CFP one way. The crossing takes anything between three and five hours, depending on the sea conditions. The journey can be uncomfortable if the sea is choppy (this author knows what he's talking about!). You can also find out if charters are being organised during your stay and you may be able to share the costs. But there's no regular service; it all depends on the needs of locals (going to Hiva Oa for medical consultation or to catch the plane etc). Another option is to hop on the *Aranui* (see the boxed text, p203) when it stops at Atuona, Omoa or Hanavave.

If you've got the dough, you can charter a private *bonitier* (about 55,000 CFP for the whole boat).

If you're desperate, contact Lionel at Chez Lionel Cantois (opposite), who's well clued up on the subject and claims that he 'can always find a solution'.

GETTING AROUND

The only dirt road is 17km long and links Hanavave with Omoa, but it's quicker (and cheaper) to hire a speedboat to travel between the two villages (about 7000 CFP per boat).

Inquire at your *pension* about renting a 4WD; expect to pay 15,000 CFP a day with driver.

The Australs

Isolated and straddling the Tropic of Capricorn, the magnificent and pristine Austral Islands are arguably French Polynesia's most underrated destination. The climate here is temperate – and sometimes downright chilly – but everything else befitting of a tropical paradise is here: flower-filled jungles, sharp peaks, outrageously blue water and genuinely friendly people. The islands here have had less of a history with Europeans and less influx from the outside world, so have kept their culture and delicious local-style cuisine alive. Pandanus weaving is still a mainstay and these crafted items are greatly sought after by islanders in other archipelagos.

The islands are wonderfully varied, from the limestone caverns of Rurutu and the Bora Bora–like lagoon of Raivavae to the fertile slopes and windy bays of Tubuai. The climate means that peaches and carrots grow alongside banana trees and vast taro plantations and it's not too hot to bike or hike all day long if you want. Whales visit the coastlines from July through October every year and Rurutu, with its lack of a fringing reef and clear waters, has become world renowned as a place to swim with the graceful mammals. In Rimatara the wildlife is on land: the red, green, yellow and blue Rimatara lorikeet draws in adventurous birders looking to add a rare species to their repertoire. If you tire of the present, the past is highly visible everywhere through the remains of great *marae* (traditional temples), some preserved while others lie hidden in the bush.

THE AUSTRALS

HIGHLIGHTS

- Swimming with awe-inspiring humpback whales at **Rurutu** (p231)
- *Motu*-hopping in the radiant **Raivavae lagoon** (p234) and picnicking on local specialities
- Hiking to peaks on each of the islands including the ancient *pa* (hilltop fortresses) on **Rapa Iti** (p237)
- Imagining the glorious past of **Tubuai** (p232) while visiting its unique *marae*
- Exploring the surreal caves and caverns of **Rurutu** (p230)

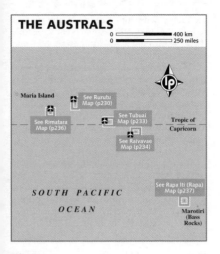

THE AUSTRALS

giant stone *tiki* and bowls were gradually pillaged and taken away to be displayed in museums far from the quiet islands from which they came. Today the Australs are renowned for their mats, hats and baskets woven from pandanus.

Getting There & Away

Air Tahiti flies to Rururu and Tubuai four days a week and to Raivavae and Rimatara three days a week. One-way fares include Tahiti–Rururu (19,500 CFP), Tahiti–Tubuai (21,500 CFP), Tahiti–Raivavae or Tahiti–Rimatara (24,000 CFP), Rururu–Tubuai or Tubuai–Raivavae (10,000 CFP), and Rururu–Rimatara (8000 CFP). You can also add an 'Australs Extension,' which includes Raivavae, Rururu and Tubuai to some Air Tahiti air passes (see p260) for 27,000 CFP – a real bargain.

Getting to Rapa, over 1000km south of Tahiti, is an adventure. The cargo ship *Tuhaa Pae II* arrives weekly to the Australs, but stops off at Rapa only once every two months or more; see p262 for details.

RURURU

pop 2098 / area 36 sq km

If it weren't so darned expensive to get here, Rururu would surely be one of French Polynesia's premier destinations. Because of the island's geology (see the boxed text, p235) there is a variety of terrain rarely seen in the islands. Vertical limestone cliffs pockmarked with caves line the coast, while the volcanic interior is a fertile, mind-bogglingly abundant jungle. While there's very little fringing reef, there are plenty of white-sand beaches and bright-blue swimming areas close to shore. In our opinion it's a near-perfect tropical paradise – it just gets a bit nippy sometimes.

History

The Australs were the last of the Polynesian islands to be settled; the first arrivals were believed to be from Tahiti between 1000 and 1300 AD. Cook first saw Rururu in 1769, Gayangos and Varela 'found' Raivavae in 1775, Cook was back to make the first landing on Tubuai in 1777 and Vancouver 'found' Rapa in 1791. It wasn't until Captain Samuel Pinder Henry chanced upon Rimatara in 1811 that the last of the islands came to European attention.

Apart from a colourful chapter in the *Bounty* saga, when the mutineers unsuccessfully tried to establish themselves on Tubuai, contact with Europeans and the Western world was limited until the late 19th and 20th centuries. This long period, during which English missionaries (or more frequently their native representatives) held sway, has ensured that Protestantism remains strong to this day.

Culture

Nearly all of French Polynesia was ravaged by disease at the onset of European contact, but the reverberation is felt most strongly in the Australs. During the islands' prime, before most of the population had been killed off by a series of imported maladies, the Australs produced some of the finest art known in the Pacific. The statue of the Rururu ancestor god A'a on display at the British Museum in London is one of the most important surviving Polynesian wood carvings. Canoe paddles,

---

KNOW BEFORE YOU GO...

- Raivavae, Rimatara and Rapa don't have banks or ATMs
- Many businesses don't accept credit cards
- There are very few restaurants, so you'll probably need to take at least half board at your *pension* (guesthouse)
- Expect some cold nights – or even days – if you visit between May and December

THE AUSTRALS

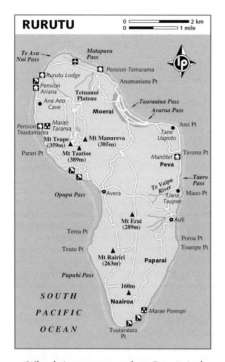

RURURU

Te Ava Nui Pass
Matapueu Pass
Rurutu Lodge
Pension Temarama
Anamaniana Pt
Pension Ariana
Tetuanui Plateau
Ana Aeo Cave
Tauraatua Pass
Moerai
Avarua Pass
Pension Teautamatea
Marae Tararoa
Arei Pt
Mt Teape (359m)
Mt Manureva (385m)
Tane Uapoto
Parari Pt
Mt Taatioe (389m)
Manôtel
Tavenu Pt
Peva
Te Voipa River
Taero Pass
Opupu Pass
Avera
Tiana Taupee
Mauo Pt
Mt Erai (289m)
Auti
Terea Pt
Poroa Pt
Teutu Pt
Toarepe Pt
Mt Rairiri (263m)
Paparai
Pupuhi Pass
160m
SOUTH
Naairoa
PACIFIC
Marae Poreopi
OCEAN
Toataratara Pt

SOUTH PACIFIC OCEAN

What brings most people to Rurutu is the whales. During July to October it's commonplace to see a mother and baby humpback gliding along close to shore with a small boatful of divers swimming around them. When the whales aren't around, there are plenty of other activities on offer: explore the interior on horseback, on foot or by 4WD, learn to weave a pandanus basket or just enjoy the utter peacefulness and friendliness of the locals.

Cook sailed past Rurutu in 1769 during his first voyage, but the islanders' hostile reception prevented him from landing. There was little contact with Europeans until well into the 19th century, when the London Missionary Society (LMS) sent native teachers to establish a mission. Christianity quickly took hold and European diseases arrived at much the same time.

Orientation & Information

Rurutu has a circumference of about 32km, but the road cuts inland through the mountains, making the island feel much bigger. Apart from the Moerai to Marae Tararoa

section, which is practically flat, the route is so hilly that biking the island is only possible if you've brought a good mountain bike and have thighs of steel.

Of the three main coastal villages, Moerai is the largest, with the island's only dock, plus a post office, bank, medical centre, pharmacy and several shops. A sealed road runs about a third of the way around the island, linking the airport with Moerai and Auti. Another sealed road climbs over the centre of the island to link Moerai with Avera, the third village.

There is an ATM inside the **Banque Socredo** (7.30-11.30am & 1.30-4.30pm Mon-Fri) in Moerai. The **post office** (7am-3pm Mon-Thu, to 2pm Fri), which has an outdoor ATM and public internet post, is nearby and the *gendarmerie* (police station) is at the southern end of town.

Sights

Turning right out of the main village of Moerai, you'll find a large roadside cavern with stalactites and stalagmites, called **Tane Uapoto**. Traditionally this cave was used to salt (for preservation) and divide whale meat among the islanders. Just beyond the cave there's a whale-watching platform. About 3km from here is another cavern that's accessible from the road called **Tiana Taupee**.

At the southern end of the island, near Toataratara Point, is the small **Marae Poreopi**, and a series of beautiful little **beaches** that run east of the point.

Behind Pension Teautamatea on the west side of the island are the well-preserved remains of **Marae Tararoa**, the *marae* of the last Rurutu royal family. At one time this *marae* was only a small part of the larger and now destroyed Marae Vitaria, which stretched for over 1km.

Another 500m north from the *marae*, there's a signposted track going to the right that leads to the huge **Ana Aeo Cave**. Today the locals have also dubbed it the Mitterrand Cave since President François Mitterrand visited here in 1990. This cave, with its massive, oozy-looking stalactites and stalagmites, is the most stunning on the island.

Activities

Raie Manta Club (96 85 60, 72 31 45; raiemantaclub@ mail.pf; half day 10,000 CFP) has been offering very professional whale-watching tours for over nine years. They also offer exploration dives

RURUTU, ISLAND OF WHALES

There are few activities in the world as fantastic as the opportunity to swim with humpback whales. Rururu, which has been nicknamed Island of Whales, actually has fewer of these mammals visiting its coastlines each year than Mo'orea or Tahiti. What makes this an ideal place to see them is the absence of a lagoon, which causes the whales to come closer to shore. The incredible visibility makes the experience all the more impressive.

The whales come to Rururu from around late July to mid-October to reproduce before heading back to the icy waters of the Antarctic. There are no promises that you will see any, but the best chance of seeing the whales is in August and September. *Pensions* fill quickly around this time.

Whale-watching trips are open to all – the dive club will even pull unconfident swimmers along on a boogie board if it's not too rough; see opposite for more information.

around the coast (see p72 for details about dive sites).

All *pensions* offer worthwhile half-day **island tours** for around 3500 CFP, usually with guides who are very knowledgeable about the history of the island (see below for contact details).

For **horse riding**, contact Viriamu at Pension Teautamatea (right). Superb trips, suitable for all levels, pass some stunning viewpoints in the island's interior (5000 CFP for a half day).

Reti Mii (☎ 25 97 08), leads half-day **hiking tours** and **cave tours** to some otherwise hard-to-access caves for 3000 CFP. Unfortunately if it's raining even a little bit, these areas get too slippery and Reti has to cancel the trip.

Those interested in learning how to weave pandanus baskets can take a short class with **Dorian** (☎ 93 03 50; per hr 2500 CFP).

The island's interior is perfect for **walking**. A network of tracks crisscrosses the Tetuanui Plateau (200m), leading to the peaks of Taatioe (389m), Manureva (385m) and Teape (359m). You can also walk the cross-island road between Moerai and Avera.

Sleeping & Eating

Unless otherwise mentioned, credit cards are not accepted.

Home Sweet Home (☎ 77 76 87; magasin.sinn.rururu@ mail.pf; r per person incl breakfast 5300 CFP; 🖳) These are the most luxurious three rooms in the Australs, although they are very much in the (charming) owner's home. There's a Southeast Asian flair of design, you can use the kitchen and washing machine and the best room has a Jacuzzi tub. It's right in Moerai above the owner's grocery store on the waterfront.

Pension Ariana (☎ 94 06 69; fax 94 07 14; pension ariana@mail.pf; s/d 4000/5000 CFP, bungalow s/d 4500/5500 CFP, half/full board per person 3500/5500 CFP; 🖳) In a labyrinth of lush gardens and coconut palms

descending to a private white-sand beach, this *pension* has four rooms in its main building with shared bathroom, and seven rustic, colourful bungalows with private bathroom. The owner Ariana is a real character and true Rururu mama, who keeps her staff and guests in good order.

Heiata Nui (☎ 94 05 82; chambresdhotesheiatanui@ mail.pf; s/d/t 5000/6000/7000 CFP, s/d/tr with half board 8500/12,500/17,500 CFP; 🖳) Right in the heart of Moerai, this brand-new place run by an adorable older Rururu couple has big, modern tiled rooms in a cosy house. Meals are served at Snack Paulette near the port (see p232), which the owners run as well, but because the *pension* is right in town you could theoretically eat elsewhere too.

Pension Temarama (☎ 93 02 80, 72 30 20; fax 93 02 81; pensiontemarama@mail.pf; s/d 4500/6000 CFP, half/full board per person 4000/5000 CFP; 🐾 🖳) Near the airport, this option has eight rooms with bathrooms in a big white house. Although the setting is nothing special and the building is not particularly Polynesian, it's spotlessly clean, the welcome is warm and the food has a good reputation. Credit cards accepted.

Pension Teautamatea (☎ /fax 93 02 93; teauta matea@mail.pf; s/d/tr/q with half board 8300/13,000/ 17,700/22,400 CFP; 🖳) Run by a British-Rururu couple, the cosy rooms here are artistically decorated in a Polynesian-meets-European-countryside chic. It's in a stunning setting in front of Marae Tararoa and just across the road from one of Rururu's best beaches. Excellent English is spoken.

our pick Manôtel (☎ 93 02 26; fax 93 02 25; manotel @mail.pf; s/d/t bungalow with half board per person 11,100/15,600/20,200 CFP; 🖳) The exceptionally well-run Manôtel has four very pretty and stylish bungalows with fan, good bathroom and particularly inviting terraces; it's across

THE AUSTRALS

the road from a long stretch of white beach near Peva. The garden is blooming with colours and the owner runs some of the best island tours around. Four new bungalows with kitchen facilities were planned at the time of writing. Credit cards accepted.

Rurutu Lodge (☎ 94 02 15, 79 09 01; rurutulodge@mail .pf; bungalow s/d/tr with half board from 11,000/17,200/21,200 CFP; 🖳) This is the closest thing you'll find to a hotel in the Australs, run by the Raie Manta diving club. You won't get much of a connection with the locals here but it's pleasantly designed, has flower-filled gardens and a lovely beach. There are occasional Saturday-night buffet and dance performances (3000 CFP), which are pretty much the only thing you'll ever find to do at night on Rurutu – everyone on the island is invited. Credit cards accepted.

Tiare Hinano (☎ 77 55 24; mains from 900 CFP; 🕑 10.30am-8:30pm Mon-Sat) A Chinese chef straight from China whips up surprisingly good and authentically Eastern grub as well as local favourites.

Snack Chez Paulette (mains 900-1000 CFP; 🕑 lunch & dinner) This place has no sign and is hidden behind a gate right across from the boat quay in Moerai. Regular *snack* fare is offered plus a few extras like stuffed peppers and chocolate crêpes.

Shopping

Rurutu is known for its woven pandanus hats, bags and mats. The shop at the airport is open to coincide with flights, but you might find better deals at Hei Pae Ore, an artisanal shop right near the mayor's office in Moerai or at artisanal shops in the other two villages. Ask to stop at one if you take a 4WD island tour.

Getting There & Around

Rurutu, about 600km south of Tahiti, is served by regular flights. **Air Tahiti** (☎ 94 03 57) has an office at the airport, which is open before and after each flight.

If you've booked accommodation you'll be picked up at the airport (sometimes for a fee of 500 to 1000 CFP round trip). Most *pensions* rent out bicycles for 1000 to 1600 CFP a day. Pension Temarama and the Total Station in Moerai rent 4WDs for 12,000 CFP per day.

TUBUAI

pop 1979 / area 45 sq km

With its spreading, fertile plains, low hills and temperate climate, Tubuai is not only the fruit bowl and veggie bin of French Polynesia, but it's also rich ground for archaeology. Munch a fresh carrot or apple while you explore the island's *marae* – some hidden by weeds, others scarcely restored – and try to imagine life here a few hundred years ago.

Tubuai is the largest of the Austral Islands, and the administrative centre of the archipelago. With an average of 300 days of wind per year, it could also become a mecca for kitesurfing and windsurfing.

Locals are proud to tell visitors about the *Bounty* mutineers who tried, unsuccessfully, to establish themselves on Tubuai in 1789 and were met with such hostility that they were forced to leave. From 1822 the LMS dispatched to the island native teachers who met with a more gentle welcome although today the island has a growing Mormon population.

European diseases started to afflict the islanders around the time of evangelism, and by 1828 the population reportedly plummeted from 3000 to less than 300.

Orientation & Information

Tubuai is the only French Polynesian island that is completely encircled by a sandy beach. Two mountain ranges slope down to the flat plains by the sea and a low-lying central region bisects the two. A cross-island road connects Mataura and Mahu. The island is surrounded by a wide, shallow lagoon with an outer reef dotted with a handful of *motu* (islets) at its eastern end.

Mataura, about 4km east of the airport, is the main village and has a post office with public internet and an outside ATM, a **Banque Socredo** (🕑 7-11.30am & 1.30-4pm Mon-Fri) with an ATM outside, a basic hospital and a supermarket. A few smaller stores are dotted round the island.

Sights

Over 200 *marae* have been found in Tubuai and the few that have been cleared are among the most fascinating in the country. You'll need a guide to access the following sites (contact Pension Viateanui, p234, or Raroata Dream opposite). **Raitoru** and **Haunarei Marae** are two connected *marae* that were for birthing and umbilical cord–cutting ceremonies respectively. Nearby is **Marae Hariitaata**, which once served as a meeting place for chiefs.

At **Vaitauarii** are the remains of a site dedicated to tattooing Tubuai royalty. Until 2007 it was believed that the ancient Tubuai people were not tattooed but now this site, along with

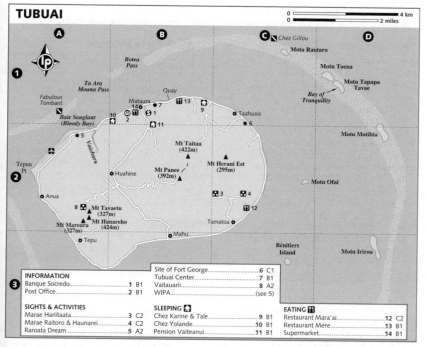

INFORMATION	
Banque Socredo	**1** B1
Post Office	**2** B1

SIGHTS & ACTIVITIES	
Marae Hariitaata	**3** C2
Marae Raitoro & Haunarei	**4** C2
Raroata Dream	**5** A2
Site of Fort George	**6** C1
Tubuai Center	**7** B1
Vaitauarii	**8** A2
WIPA	(see 5)

SLEEPING	
Chez Karine & Tale	**9** B1
Chez Yolande	**10** B1
Pension Vaiteanui	**11** B1

EATING	
Restaurant Mara'ai	**12** C2
Restaurant Mere	**13** B1
Supermarket	**14** B1

shell tattoo combs found on the island, have confirmed otherwise.

The *Bounty* is remembered by a sign on the northeastern corner of the island marking the site of **Fort George**, where the mutineers attempted to set up camp for two months in 1789.

If you head towards the airport from Moerai you will see a small reef pass that opens onto a white-sand beach. This was the site where the mutineers massacred Tubuai warriors, and the bay has been dubbed **Baie Sanglant** (Bloody Bay) after the spilled blood that turned the turquoise lagoon to a deep red.

Activities

WIPA (☎ /fax 95 07 12; maletdoom@mail.pf), run by effervescent Wilson Doom, has a kitesurfing and windsurfing club but you'll need to bring your own equipment.

The excellent, locally run dive centre **La Bonne Bouteille** (☎ /fax 95 08 41; www.labonnebouteille plongee.com, in French) offers diving (6500 CFP per dive) as well as whale watching or swimming with whales (8000 CFP). See p73 for details about dive sites.

Lagoon tours offered by the *pensions* cost about 7000 CFP per person, with a picnic provided, and are great if the sun is shining. **Island tours** (2500 CFP) take about three hours, visiting the island's fecund interior as well as some hidden and overgrown *marae*. Very interesting **marae tours** (2500 CFP), best for history buffs, take three hours and visit the *marae* described on opposite.

There are several good **walking** opportunities, the best being to the summit of Mt Taitaa (422m). The route is signposted along the cross-island road and the return journey takes about three hours. The easiest way up is from the trailhead near Pension Vaiteanui (p234).

Sleeping & Eating

Come prepared for mosquitoes and don't count on using credit cards.

Raroata Dream (☎ 95 07 12; maletdoom@mail.pf; r with half/full board per person 4400/6600 CFP; ☐) Great for families or kitesurfers, the Doom family offers two rooms with shared bathroom in their cosy and artistically decorated home.

Chez Karine & Tale (☎ 93 23 49; s/d 5000/8000 CFP) The two completely equipped and spacious bungalows are homey and clean. Breakfast is included in the price but you are on your own for other meals.

Pension Vaiteanui (☎ /fax 93 22 40; bodinm@mail.pf; s/d with half board 7600/10,300 CFP; 🖥) This well-run, centrally located *pension* on the cross-island road has five rooms with bathroom. All activities can be organised, French-inspired meals are very good and it also has a pizzeria.

Chez Yolande (☎ /fax 95 05 52; s/d with half board per person 8500 CFP) Right by the sea in Mataura, this place has six immaculate rooms with bathroom in a modern and functional house. The upstairs rooms are the most private.

Restaurant Mere (☎ 95 04 17; mains 900-1000 CFP; 🕑 lunch & dinner Mon-Sat) There's a lengthy menu but only three items were available when we ate here. It's a cramped dining area but the food is copious and hearty.

Restaurant Mara'ai (☎ 95 08 32; mains 850-1100 CFP; 🕑 lunch & dinner) The best dining option on Tubuai, eat under a palm-frond roof on the sand on gourmet (for Tubuai) specialities like seared tuna.

There is one supermarket in Mataura, plus a scattering of smaller stores and snack bars around the island. The best deals on fresh produce are from roadside stalls.

Getting There & Around

Tubuai is 600km south of Tahiti. **Air Tahiti** (☎ 95 04 76) has an office at the airport. Cargo ships enter through the large passes on the northwestern edge of the reef and dock at Mataura.

Airport transfers are free if you have booked accommodation. Cycling the flat 25km of coast road is a pleasant way to pass a few hours. Bicycles can be rented at **Tubuai Center** (half/full day 800/1350 CFP; 🕑 8am-12pm & 1.30-5pm Mon-Fri) near Mataura, and Pension Vaiteanui and Chez Yolande have cars (about 5000 CFP per day) for clients' use.

RAIVAVAE

pop 1049 / area 16 sq km

Visitors to Raivavae (ra-ee-va-va-eh) rave that this is what Bora Bora must have been like 50 or even 75 years ago. This is a paradise not only because of the sweeping blue lagoon, idyllic white-sand *motu* or the green mountainous interior dominated by square-topped

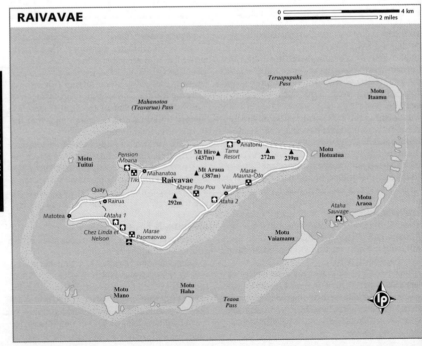

RAIVAVAE

MAKATEA

A *makatea* is a geological phenomenon that takes Darwin's theory of atoll formation one step further. Volcanic islands gradually grow coral reefs around them that form small islets, as is visible at Bora Bora, Mo'orea and Raivavae. Over time, the volcanic cones sink, forming atolls, such as those found in the Tuamotus. A *makatea* is formed by the added jolt of nearby volcanic activity that causes the sea floor to buckle and forces the sunken volcanic cone and its surrounding coral islets up to the surface. This forms a hilly, volcanic island walled in by a fossilised coral limestone shell.

Mt Hiro (437m), but the warm Polynesian welcome and traditional way of life you'll find here is one of the most authentic and heart-warming in all of French Polynesia. Foodies will appreciate the excellent traditional food (arguably the best in the country) on offer at nearly all the *pensions*. Amazingly, the island receives only a small trickle of tourists.

The quay is at Rairua, as well as a post office (home to the island's only public internet post), infirmary and *gendarmerie*. Little stores everywhere along the coast road are well stocked with canned goods but there is little fresh produce available.

History

Captain Thomas Gayangos of Spain was the first European to land on Raivavae when he stopped there in 1775 en route to Peru. The island was ceded to Pomare II of Tahiti in 1819, and then became a French protectorate in 1842.

In 1826 the same European fever that had devastated the island of Tubuai reached Raivavae and killed almost the entire population. Of 3000 inhabitants, only about 100 people survived, and the island's cultural and seafaring traditions were all but wiped out.

Archaeological Sites

Most of Raivavae's *marae* have either been destroyed or simply forgotten in the bush. **Marae Paomaovao**, across the street from the airport, is falling down after having been restored a few years back, but better care has been given to **Marae Mauna-Oto** on the east coast. This *marae* is also known as the 'princess *marae*' because of the tomb near the entrance where a little girl is

buried – some say she was a princess. Another well-maintained *marae*, **Marae Pou Pou**, can be found about 1km from the Vaiuru entrance of the cross-island road.

Raivavae is most famous for its two giant stone *tiki*, which are now displayed in museums on Tahiti (one at the Musée Gauguin and the other at the Musée de Tahiti et des Îles), although plans have been made (and broken then made again) to bring them back to Raiavavae. The only verifiable remaining **tiki** on the island stands neglected and overgrown in a private garden just to the west of Mahanatoa.

Sleeping

All *pensions* offer excursions to *motu* (2500 CFP to 6000 CFP) and hikes up steep Mt Hiro (2500 CFP), plus a tour of the island by car and free bikes. People will laugh at you if you ask to use a credit card.

Pension Moana (☎ /fax 95 42 66; r 3000 CFP, half/full board per person 3000/5500 CFP) The three rooms and shared bathroom are very rustic (as in the shower is a bucket) but the site, on a secluded peninsula, is fantastic. Grandma cooks up local treats for guests and is a respected hat weaver.

Pension Ataha (☎ /fax 95 43 69; r per person 3500 CFP, Ataha Sauvage per person 1500 CFP, half/full board per person 3500/5500 CFP) Ataha has three options: a secluded three-room house west of the airport, a more convivial three-room house east of the airport (all rooms have shared bathroom and equipped kitchen) and Ataha Sauvage, a rustic hut on stilts situated alone on a *motu* of white sand. Odile and Terani, the warm and happy owners, serve excellent *ma'a Tahiti* at the *pension* or bring it out by boat to the *motu*.

our pick **Chez Linda et Nelson** (☎ /fax 95 44 25; pensionchezlinda@hotmail.fr; Rairua; s/d with half board 7000/10,000 CFP, s/d bungalows with half board 10,000/12,500 CFP) This is a well-kept place with three Polynesian-style bungalows with private bathrooms and three rooms in an immaculate house with shared bathroom. Linda the young owner, is one of the nicest people in the world, cooks delicious traditional food and takes great care of her guests.

Tama Resort (☎ /fax 95 42 52; s/d/tr with half board 8500/13,000/17,000 CFP, s/d/tr with full board 10,000/16,000/22,000) Three clean, coconut-thatched bungalows with bathrooms sit on one of Raivavae's best beaches; there are also three comfortable rooms with shared bathroom in the family's home and a secluded yet comfortable bungalow out on a white-sand *motu* (meals are delivered). A few more gardenside bungalows are planned. The local-style food and welcome here is extraordinary and excellent English is spoken.

Getting There & Away

Raivavae is about 650km southeast of Tahiti and 200km southeast of Tubuai. Air Tahiti operates flights to/from Pape'ete three days a week, sometimes via Tubuai. The ship *Tuhaa Pae II* comes by about twice a month.

RIMATARA

pop 791 / area 8 sq km

Tiny Rimatara is a rough circle measuring 4km in diameter, rising to Mt Uahu (Mt Vahu; 83m) in the centre. Air Tahiti began servicing the island in 2006 but it has yet to get under the tourist radar. The exception is birders, who visit in search of the rare and exquisitely coloured Rimatara lorikeet – locally known as the *ura*. An estimated 740 of the birds are said to inhabit the island.

Rimatara looks like a mini Rurutu and is circled by a fringing reef and beautiful white-sand beaches. It's the most densely populated of the Austral Islands with three small villages, **Anapoto**, **Amaru** and **Mutua Ura**. Pandanus work and shell necklaces, plus the plantations, support the islanders, who have preserved their own distinct dialect.

Rimatara was the last of the Australs to be 'discovered', in 1811. The first native missionary

teachers came to the island in 1821 and within two years the entire population of 300 had been converted to Christianity.

There are only two *pensions* as yet, both in Amaru.

Chez Utia Mania (☎ 94 43 10; r per person 3000 CFP) A more basic option in Amaru village, this place is only several metres from the beach. The three rooms share a clean hot-water bathroom and there's a common area with TV. More excellent local-style food is available here for 1000 CFP per meal. The owner Mania can take you bird-watching.

Pension Ue Ue (☎ 94 42 88, 74 66 13; utia.claudine@mail.pf; bungalows with half board s/d 8000/12,000 CFP) Open in July 2008, this is the most comfortable option. There's no view, but the four modern bungalows all with hot-water bathrooms, terraces and fans, are in a lovely garden with a pair of caged Rimatara lorikeets to liven it up a bit. Expect delicious *ma'a Tahiti* made from local ingredients. Add 2000 CFP for full board and 1000 CFP per day to hire a bike.

Getting There & Away

Rimatara is located about 600km southwest of Tahiti and 150km west of Rurutu. Air Tahiti flies to/from Pape'ete sometimes via Rurutu three times a week.

RAPA ITI (RAPA)

pop 521 / area 22 sq km

Rapa is French Polynesia's most remote and isolated island – its nearest inhabited neighbour, Raivavae, is over 500km away. This far south there are no coral reefs and no coconut palms, and the temperature can drop as low as 5°C in winter.

Of its soaring and jagged-edged peaks, six reach over 400m, the highest being Mt Perau (650m). The island is known as Rapa Iti (Little Rapa) to distinguish it from Rapa Nui (Big Rapa, the Polynesian name for Easter Island) but everyone just calls it 'Rapa'. The population is concentrated in the villages of Haurei and Area, which are on opposite sides of Haurei Bay. They are generally linked by boat as there is only a rough road around the bay.

History

From a crowded 2000 at first European contact around 1816, Rapa's population plummeted to a mere 150 people by 1864. During

RIMATARA

0 —————— 2 km
0 —————— 1 mile

Teruahu Pt

Anapoto

Airport

Amaru

Hiava Pass

Plateau Oromana

▲ Mt Uahu (83m)

Iririiroa Pt

Mutua Ura

Virgin Bay (Baie des Vierges)

THE AUSTRALS

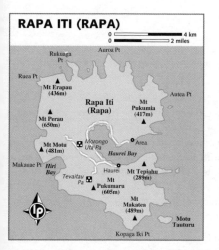

RAPA ITI (RAPA)

When steamships began to operate across the Pacific, a coaling station was established on Rapa Iti for ships crossing the Pacific Ocean. In an attempt to combat the English influence in Polynesia, the French annexed Rapa Iti.

Archaeological Sites

Between Haurei and Hiri Bays, **Morongo Uta Pa** is the best preserved of Rapa Iti's ancient *pa* and was restored by a crew including Thor Heyerdahl in 1956. The great *pa* has terraces separated by deep moats around the central fortress, which has a perimeter of over 300m and is overlooked by a double-pyramid watchtower.

Directly overlooking Haurei is the **Tevaitau Pa**, restored in 1960. Other *pa* can be found along the mountain ridge and at the passes from one valley to another.

Sleeping

Chez Cerdand Faraire (☎ 95 72 84; r per night/month 5500/65,000 CFP), in Haurei, is the only *pension* on the island.

Getting There & Away

Rapa Iti is more than 1000km southeast of Tahiti and more than 500km beyond Raivavae. The *Tuhaa Pae II* usually calls at Rapa Iti between once a month and, more likely, once every three months.

this same dismal period, Peruvian slaving ships raided the islands. The men of Rapa Iti seized one of the ships, sailed it to Tahiti and demanded that the French take action. The Peruvians attempted to return over 300 of the Polynesians they had enslaved, but the vast majority died en route; the handful of survivors who landed on Rapa Iti brought a smallpox epidemic with them, which decimated the rest of the population.

THE AUSTRALS

The Gambier Archipelago

All the makings of an island holiday paradise can be found in the jaw-droppingly beautiful Gambier Archipelago, but it's so far away (about 1700km southeast from Tahiti) and expensive to get to that it remains one of the least developed regions in French Polynesia. The geology here is unique: one reef, complete with sandy *motu* (islets), encircles a small archipelago of lush high islands dotting an exquisitely blue lagoon that's as clear as air. Adding to the allure, the Gambier is the cradle of Polynesian Catholicism and houses some of the most eerie and interesting post-European structures in the country. Today the archipelago is famous for its lustrous and colourful pearls.

Administratively and geologically, the islands are linked to the Tuamotu Archipelago, but because of the vast cultural and linguistic differences and because the islands are volcanic rather than coral atolls, the islands are generally considered to be their own group.

HIGHLIGHTS

- Taking a lagoon and island tour to **Taravai** and **Aukena** (p241)
- Marvelling at the crumbling **Cathédrale Saint-Michel** (p240) of Rikitea
- Relaxing on the **beaches** of Aukena (p241) and the other outer islands – some of the best in French Polynesia
- Hiking up **Mt Duff** (p240) for extraordinary views over the entire archipelago
- Marvelling over detailed and artistically carved oyster shells at the **Camika CED** (p240) in Rikitea

★ Mt Duff   ★ Rikitea

★ Aukena

★ Taravai

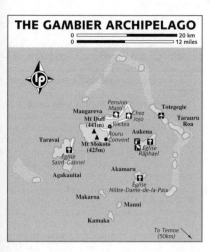

THE GAMBIER ARCHIPELAGO

History

The Gambiers were populated in three waves from the 10th to the 13th centuries, and they may have been a stopping point on the Polynesian migration routes to New Zealand or Easter Island.

The Sacred Heart Congregation, the first Catholic mission in French Polynesia, was established here in 1834 and Father Honoré Laval and his assistant François Caret became virtual rulers of the archipelago. Laval ran the islands like his own personal fiefdom until persistent complaints about his behaviour led to his exile on Tahiti in 1871.

Laval built roads, a huge cathedral, nine churches and chapels, monuments, lookout towers, quays and numerous buildings. Unfortunately, at the same time, the people of the Gambier Archipelago simply died out. When Laval arrived the population may have been 5000 to 6000, but by 1887 the population had dropped to 463 and only recently has it once again passed 1000.

What role Laval played in this disaster is an open question. One view is that imported European diseases annihilated the population, and that Laval was merely an observer. The opposite view is that Laval wiped out native culture and then worked the islanders to death constructing overambitious monuments to his beliefs.

Moruroa (see p38) lies just 400km northwest of Mangareva and between 1966 and 1974, when above-ground nuclear tests were conducted, the population of the island was herded into fallout shelters (now demolished) if winds threatened to blow towards the Gambier. Mateo Pakaiti remembers staying in a shelter twice as a child: 'Our livestock died and once I got so sick afterwards that my parents thought I was going to die too,' he says.

Today Mangareva is known for producing some of the finest and most colourful pearls in Polynesia, as well as engraved oyster shells.

Culture

Early European explorers noted the absence of outrigger canoes when they passed Mangareva. Peter H Buck, an ethnologist from New Zealand who studied the Gambiers in 1930, formulated the hypothesis that, because of the geography of the islands, people didn't need outriggers and did all their day-to-day activities using rafts. The only time outriggers were used was in warfare. When Te Ma-teoa, the grandfather of the last king of Mangareva, won supreme leadership he forbade the construction of outriggers, since any attempt to build them would be in anticipation of war. Visitors from Tahiti and the Tuamotus later reintroduced the outrigger canoe to the Gambiers.

Geography

The polygon-shaped lagoon is protected by a 90km coral reef. Along the northern half there are 25 *motu* but the southern half of the reef is partly submerged.

Within this massive lagoon are 10 volcanic islands. Only a handful of people live on the islands other than Mangareva, which is 8km long and measures only 1.5km across at its narrowest point, but is still the archipelago's largest. The highest peaks are Mt Duff (441m) and Mt Mokoto (425m). The three other larger islands are Taravai, Aukena and Akamaru. About 50km southeast is the small island of Temoe.

Getting There & Around

Air Tahiti (☎ 97 82 65; Rikitea; ✆ 8am-2pm Mon & Fri, to 9am Tue & every other Sat, to 10am Wed) flies to the

KNOW BEFORE YOU GO

- The Gambier Islands are one hour ahead of Tahiti
- There are no banks or ATMs, so bring lots of cash
- It gets chilly here, so pack warm clothes

THE GAMBIER ARCHIPELAGO

Gambier Archipelago on Tuesdays and every other Saturday. A return flight from Pape'ete costs 57,000 CFP and takes about 3½ hours. During the school holidays another flight is added, usually via Hao.

From Tahiti the cargo ship *Nuku Hau* is the only one serving the Gambier that takes passengers and it sails once a month; see p261 for details.

The airport is on Motu Totegegie, on the northeastern side of the lagoon. A communal ferry from Mangareva meets every flight; the journey takes 45 minutes and costs 500 CFP.

On Mangareva there is a small network of walking tracks and the island is small enough that you could easily walk the whole island. It's possible to bike around as well, but parts are very steep and only a few stretches are paved.

MANGAREVA

The bulk of the population live on Mangareva, in and around the miniscule, fruit tree–fringed village of **Rikitea**. In the upper part of the town stands the whitewashed **Cathédrale Saint-Michel** (Cathedral of St Michael), built between 1839 and 1848, which was Laval's most ambitious project. While still imposing (the building can accommodate 1200 people – more than the population of the island today), the church was closed at the time of research and was scheduled for a US$2 million restoration. Jacques Sauvage, the 88-year-old guardian, has the key and sometimes lets people inside – ask through your *pension* or at the *gendarmerie*. In the meantime, mass is being held in the unsightly **salle d'omnisport** (sports complex) at the north of town.

Various other Laval constructions can be found in the village, including the coastal watchtowers and the turret, which are all that remain of the 'palace' Laval built for the island's last king, Maputeao. At the instigation of Laval, Maputeao changed his name to Gregoria Stanislas, and there's a memorial to him in **Cimetière Saint-Pierre**. The eerily beautiful remains of **Couvent Rouru** (Rouru Convent), which once housed 60 nuns, stands south of the cemetery and is quickly getting engulfed by weeds. It's said that Laval hid the entire female population of the island in the convent whenever whaling ships paid a visit.

To check out Mangareva's famous mother-of-pearl carvings, head to the **Camika CED** (the carving school; ☎ 97 82 89; ☯ 8am-3pm Mon-Fri), just downhill to the left from the intersection above Cathédrale Saint-Michel, where you can watch students as they engrave shells. You can buy finished products including small pendants and barrettes at the on-site shop. Prices for an engraved shell start at around 4000 CFP.

A well-maintained hiking trail to **Mt Duff** is signposted about 2km north of Rikitea and it's about a 1½-hour climb to the peak from this point. Look for the stones at the top from where the ancient Mangarevans would scan the horizon for weather and/or incoming boats.

Sleeping & Eating

Only one *pension* in Mangareva and some small shops in the village accept credit cards. All the *pensions* can help organise daylong lagoon and island tours for 5000 CFP to 8500 CFP per person.

Chez Jojo (☎ /fax 97 82 61; r with half board per person 8000 CFP, bungalows s/d with half board 13,000/20,000 CFP) The two bungalows are perched over the turquoise lagoon, but you're a bit isolated at 5km from Rikitea. There's also one clean room with shared bathroom in the owner's house. The local-style food is excellent and there are bikes and kayaks available for hire. Jojo also runs the biggest *snack*-style eatery in Rikitea.

Pension Maro'i (☎ 97 84 62; btqhinarau@hotmail.com; bungalows with breakfast 9500 CFP) Mangareva's newest option has four immaculate bungalows laid out on a grassy, fruit tree–studded lawn lined with a white beach. This is the only place that accepts credit cards and it's on the opposite side of the island from Rikitea. Meals (2200 CFP) are available.

Tara Etu Kura (☎ 97 83 25; Rikitea; bungalow with breakfast 9500 CFP) Good for those wanting quiet, the lone bungalow here sleeps three and feels like a fairy-tale forest cottage. It's on a tiny white beach and the elderly owners are charming. Meals (2500 CFP) are also available.

Chez Bianca & Benoît (☎ /fax 97 83 76; Rikitea; s/d with half board 10,000/16,500 CFP, bungalows s/d with half board 17,000/22,000 CFP; ☯ closed Jun) Big bungalows sleep three to four people and have bamboo woven walls and decks with views over Rikitea and the lagoon. This is a central location with dynamic owners and good food.

Pizzatomic (☎ 97 83 09; Rikitea; pizzas from 1000 CFP; ☯ 5.15-9pm Fri-Sun) Next door to the now-bulldozed fallout shelter, get glowing-hot pizzas to eat in or take away.

TARAVAI & AUKENA

Taravai had a population of 2000 when the missionaries arrived, but today only about five people live here. The 1868 **Église Saint-Gabriel** (Church of St Gabriel), with its gorgeous shell decoration, is well maintained and has a decaying, picturesque arch that welcomes you from the shore. Five distinct colours of sand can be found on the island's beaches.

Aukena also has reminders of the missionary period, including the 1839 **Église Saint-Raphaël** (Church of St Raphael) and the hexagonal **lookout tower**, still used as a landmark, on the southwestern tip of the island. The white-sand beach leading to the tower is one of the prettiest in all of French Polynesia.

AKAMARU & TEMOE

Akamaru was the first island to be visited by Laval and his majestic, 1841 **Église Nôtre-Dame-de-la-Paix** (Our Lady of Peace Church) still stands on the sparsely inhabited island. The family that lives around the church keeps it shipshape and groups from Mangareva occasionally come over to hold services.

The remote island of Temoe, 50km southeast of Akamaru, has a **marae** with some Marquesan features, leading to theories that Marquesans may have paused here en route to Easter Island. Temoe was populated until 1838, when the missionaries shifted the inhabitants to Mangareva. In 1934 James Norman Hall, co-author of *Mutiny on the Bounty,* was shipwrecked on the island.

Directory

CONTENTS

Accommodation	242
Activities	244
Business Hours	245
Children	245
Climate Charts	246
Customs	246
Dangers & Annoyances	246
Discount Cards	247
Embassies & Consulates	247
Festivals & Events	247
Food	248
Gay & Lesbian Travellers	248
Holidays	248
Insurance	248
Internet Access	248
Legal Matters	248
Maps	249
Money	249
Post	250
Shopping	250
Telephone	251
Time	251
Tourist Information	251
Travellers with Disabilities	252
Visas	252
Volunteering	252
Women Travellers	253
Work	253

ACCOMMODATION

Glossy brochures focus on the idyllic overwater bungalows, but French Polynesia actually has a wide range of accommodation options – from camping upwards. Whatever the category, however, the price-to-quality ratio is invariably discouraging. It's not necessarily that standards are low; it's just that the prices visitors are charged are so damn high they have a right to expect much more. The most basic, ramshackle room in a family home can cost as much as a three-star, amenity-packed hotel in Los Angeles. Then again, you're not paying to be pampered; French Polynesia is all about the oh-so-irresistible real estate. So if you're in the market to rent a slice of paradise, you might as well stop fingering those worry beads. Throw common sense to the wind and deal with the credit-card damage when you get home.

Most hotels and resorts, and all *pensions* (guesthouses), quote their rates in French Polynesian francs, although the high-end places will usually also list the price in euros and US dollars.

French Polynesia's high season runs between June and September, and during the Christmas holidays; prices jump and many favourite places are booked out well in advance at these times. The majority of French Polynesia's accommodation is in bungalows. Unless otherwise stated, the prices listed in this book are for two-person bungalows. Many bungalows can actually sleep between four and six, and extra guests are generally charged a per-person supplement of between 1000 and 2000 CFP. Children under 12 almost always stay for half-price. Some places offer half- and full-board options; in these cases the prices quoted will usually be per person. In this guide we place accommodation costing less than 10,000 CFP a night in the budget category, 10,000 CFP to 20,000 CFP in the midrange category and over 20,000 CFP in the top end. Taxes, which include the TVA (*taxe sur la valeur ajoutée*; value-added tax, 5%), a 5% government tax and the *taxe de séjour* (a daily tax of 50 CFP to 150 CFP per person) are included in our listed prices. Watch out, though, because many places will quote you before-tax prices, only to surprise you with a rather hefty list of add-ons at the end of your stay.

Camping & Hostels

Camping options come and go around French Polynesia, but generally it's a matter

---

BOOK YOUR STAY ONLINE

For more accommodation reviews and recommendations by Lonely Planet authors, check out the online booking service at www.lonelyplanet.com/hotels. You'll find the true, insider lowdown on the best places to stay. Reviews are thorough and independent. Best of all, you can book online.

PRACTICALITIES

▦ The weekly English-language tourist paper *Tahiti Beach Press* includes some local news coverage. If you read French, there are two Tahitian dailies, *Les Nouvelles de Tahiti* and *La Dépêche de Tahiti*.

▦ There are about 10 independent radio stations that broadcast music programs with news flashes in French and Tahitian along with the occasional interview. Among the best-known stations are Tiare FM (the pioneer nongovernmental radio station), Radio Bleue, Radio Maohi, Te Reo o Tefana (a pro-independence station), Radio 1, NRJ and RFO-Radio Polynésie.

▦ Radio France Outre-Mer (RFO) has two TV channels: Télépolynése and Tempo. TNTV is the satellite carrier and has its own channel as well.

▦ The video format in French Polynesia is Secam, but videos made for tourists are generally also available in PAL and NTSC.

▦ French Polynesia uses 220V, 60Hz electricity, although some deluxe hotels may have 110V supply for electric shavers. Sockets are French style, requiring a plug with two round pins.

▦ French Polynesia follows the international metric system.

---

of guesthouses having areas where you can pitch your tent and allowing use of the facilities; you'll pay anywhere from around 1200 CFP to 2500 CFP per person. Camping is possible on Tahiti, Mo'orea, Huahine, Ra'iatea, Bora Bora, Maupiti, Rangiroa, Tikehau and Mataiva. You may need to re-think camping if it's raining too hard. Also, make sure your tent is mosquito-proof or lather yourself in repellent. Some guesthouses have dorm beds ranging from 2000 CFP to 3500 CFP per person per night.

Hotels

There is a glut of midrange hotels on the more touristy islands, but on remote islands it's sometimes either five-star glamour or *pensions* (which range from rudimentary to very comfortable) and not much in between. Most midrange places have a restaurant on site and you'll typically pay from around 10,000 CFP to 40,000 CFP per night for a bungalow; almost all hotels in this category accept credit cards.

Pensions

Pensions are a godsend for travellers who baulk at the prices of the big hotels. These little establishments, generally family-run affairs, are great places to meet locals and other travellers. At the lower end of the scale, brace yourself for cold showers, lumpy pillows and thin walls, but lap up the charm, interesting discussions and artistic touches that are often part and parcel of the *pension* experience.

Upmarket versions can be private, have lots of amenities and be downright comfortable.

Many *pensions* offer (and sometimes insist upon) half board (or *demi-pension*), which usually means breakfast and dinner. Full board means all meals are included. In many cases, the food is great and, on less touristy islands, there might not be other options available anyway. It can cost anything from 4500 CFP to 9000 CFP per person per day, although prices vary widely from island to island. Young children are often allowed to stay for free, and children up to about 12 usually pay half-price.

Think ahead in terms of money, as many *pensions* do not take credit cards.

Resorts

If you are ever going to pamper yourself silly, French Polynesia is a great place to do it. The sumptuous luxury hotels often manage to blend their opulent bungalows into the natural setting. Some of the top hotels are on isolated *motu* (islets), and can only be reached by boat. Four- and five-star hotels are found on Tahiti, Mo'orea, Bora Bora, Huahine, Ra'iatea, Taha'a, Rangiroa, Hiva Oa, Manihi and Nuku Hiva. You can expect restaurants, bars, a swimming pool, a shop or two and a well-organised activities desk. Most of the bigger hotels put on a Polynesian dance performance, often with buffet meal, a few times a week. Glass-bottomed coffee tables, which look straight down into the lagoon, have become standard features of the over-water bungalows. The prices are just as dazzling: expect to pay from 45,000 CFP to 250,000 CFP a night, not including meals.

ACTIVITIES

French Polynesia's exceptional natural heritage lends itself to a range of leisure activities. Scuba diving and snorkelling are the main activities (see the Diving chapter, p64), but sailing is also very popular. Increasing numbers of surfers are sampling the islands' excellent reef breaks, while the jagged relief of the high islands makes for some absolutely superb walking and horse riding.

Cycling

On many islands it is possible to rent bicycles, which are the perfect means to get around. The rough roads leading into the interior are great for mountain bikes, should you decide to bring one with you from home.

Hiking

The high islands offer superb walks but the tracks are sometimes unmarked and are hard to follow: it's often necessary to hire a guide. Tahiti and Mo'orea are the main islands for walking, but there are also good walks on Ra'iatea, Bora Bora and Maupiti. Several new trails on Nuku Hiva in the Marquesas are well maintained. During the rainy season (November to April) the paths can be dangerous and even impassable.

Horse Riding

There are equestrian centres in the Society Islands on Tahiti, Mo'orea, Huahine and Bora Bora. Most places offer short jaunts and longer excursions that explore the island interiors. Horses are an important part of life in the Marquesas, and there are various places to rent them, with or without a guide; you can also horse ride on Rurutu in the Australs.

Surfing

Polynesia was the birthplace of *horue* (surfing), and in recent years there has been a major resurgence of local interest. Tahiti in particular has surf shops and a local surfing scene. The island is home to Teahupoo, one of the most powerful waves in the world and the site of the Tahiti Billabong Pro competition each year. Tahiti, Mo'orea Ra'iatea and Huahine are the main islands for surfing,

but Tikehau in the Tuamotus also has a good surfing spot.

In general, there are good conditions on the north and east coasts from November to April and on the west and south coasts for the other half of the year – but these distinctions are really theoretical.

Access to the shore breaks is generally easy from the coast roads. You may need to find a boat to take you out to the reef breaks, or resign yourself to doing a lot of paddling. For more information and a message board on surfing in French Polynesia, check out the Tahiti page at www.globalsurfers.com.

Like surfers anywhere in the world, French Polynesians can be possessive of *their* waves, especially if you paddle in like you own the place. If you want to enjoy the surf, observe all the usual rules of surfing etiquette, give way to local surfers and smile and say hello. On Huahine and Ra'iatea, don't even think of taking surf pictures or of arriving at the wave in a big group – this is a sure-fire way to get punched, and we're not kidding.

There are several surf shops in Pape'ete. Elsewhere, the local surf shops all have boogie-board equipment as well as short boards and traditional surfboards. You certainly don't need a wetsuit in the warm waters of French Polynesia, but a lycra vest will protect you from the sun.

For more info on Tahiti's best surfing spots, see p80. For Mo'orea, see p113, and for the top surfing spots in Huahine, see p129. The only surfing schools are on Tahiti; see p80 for details.

Yachting

Renting a yacht can be a fine way to explore French Polynesia, and you can choose from a bare-boat charter (which you sail yourself) or a cabin on a fully crewed luxury boat. Ra'iatea is the main yachting base in French Polynesia, although there are a number of yacht-charter operations around the islands with a flotilla of modern monohulls and catamarans. Cruises on a crewed yacht will usually include tour programs at the stops en route, and dive cruises are also possible.

The following are some of the companies offering cruises and charter boats.

Atara Royal (☎ 79 22 40; www.motoryachtcharter tahiti.com) Luxury, dive-equipped motor cruiser based in Ra'iatea that visits the Leeward, Tuamotu and Marquesas Archipelagos.

Aqua Polynésie (☎ 73 47 31; www.aquapolynesie .com) Luxurious 14m catamarans with crewed cruises around the Leeward Islands and the Tuamotus, and a boat specially equipped for dive cruises. Departures are from Bora Bora, Nuku Hiva (Marquesas) or Fakarava (Tuamotus).

Archipels Croisières (☎ 56 36 39; www.archipels.com) Reasonably priced crewed cruises to the Leeward Islands and the Tuamotus on deluxe 18m catamarans. Departures are from Rangiroa (Tuamotus), Mo'orea or Pape'ete.

L'Escapade (☎ 72 85 31; www.escapade-voile.com) Sail on a 14m monohull to Tetiaroa, the Society and Tuamotu Islands from Tahiti.

MoeMoea Nui (☎ 70 74 04; www.marquise-croisiere .com) Cruise the Marquesas with this Nuku Hiva–based 14m catamaran.

Moorings (☎ 66 35 93; www.moorings.com) Twenty different options, including bare-boat charters, hire with skipper and host, or cabin charters. It's based at Apooiti Marina at Ra'iatea and offers cruises to the Society and Tuamotu Islands.

Polynésie Croisière (☎ 28 60 06; www.polynesie -croisiere.com) Scuba specialist catamarans based on Ra'iatea offering a host of cruises to the Leeward Islands.

Sailing Huahine Voile (☎ 68 72 49; www.sailing-hua hine.com) This operation, based on Huahine, has monohulls and offers cruises in the Leeward Islands and the Tuamotus.

Sun Sail (☎ 60 04 85; www.sunsail.com) Based at the Stardust Marina on Ra'iatea, this operation offers bare-boat charters, hire with skipper and/or host, and cabin charter. About 20 boats of a variety of types are available for hire. Cruises are in the Leeward Islands and the Tuamotus.

Tahiti Yacht Charter (☎ 45 04 00; www.tahitiyacht charter.com) Catamarans and monohulls; bare-boat charter or hire with skipper and host. Cruises are possible in all the archipelagos. Vessels depart to the Society, Tuamotu and Marquesas Islands from Ra'iatea and Tahiti.

Wanda Charter (☎ 25 12 38; www.charterwanda.com) Based at Ra'iatea, this monohull cruises the Leeward Islands.

It's often possible to pick up crewing positions on yachts, particularly if you have had some relevant sailing experience. Check notice boards in popular restaurants and at the yacht clubs on Tahiti, Ra'iatea, Bora Bora and other popular yachting stops. Yacht owners have to complete complex paperwork when making crew changes, so make sure your own papers are in order.

The yacht owner will want to vet potential crew members, but it's equally important to check the boat and crew you are considering joining. Readers have suggested that the Marquesas is probably not the ideal place to join a boat; it's the first arrival point for yachts from North America so many first timers are getting off and keeping their feet on land!

BUSINESS HOURS

The opening hours for banks vary from branch to branch but are typically from 8am to noon and 1.30pm to 5pm Monday to Thursday, and 8am to noon and 1pm to 3pm on Friday. Shops and offices normally open around 7.30am, close for lunch from 11.30am to 1.30pm and shut around 5pm, Monday to Friday. On Saturday, shops are typically open between 7.30am and 11.30am; almost everything (except a few grocery stores and boutiques on the more touristy islands) is closed on Sunday. Restaurant hours vary according to the type of food served and the clientele. Most places open around 10.30am, however, and stay open until about 11pm.

CHILDREN

Fire the babysitter and bring the kids: French Polynesia is a fantastic destination to explore with children. There are no major health concerns, the climate is good and the food is easy to navigate. Plus, children are very much a part of public life in Polynesia.

Practicalities

Ensure vaccinations are up to date before you leave and that you have health records with you. Make sure that your repatriation insurance also covers your child.

Consider bringing a baby carrier, and pack light clothes that cover the whole body. Total-block sunscreen is almost as important as your passport and tickets (it is readily available in French Polynesia, but is very expensive); nappies (diapers) are also available but are pricey (2000 CFP for 38 nappies!).

The water is completely safe to drink in Pape'ete, and other select areas of Tahiti, on Bora Bora and on Tubuai, but you may like to buy bottled water anyway. On the other islands you will all be dependent on bottled water. Remember to encourage your child to drink frequently.

There are medical facilities located everywhere in French Polynesia. Mamao Hospital in Pape'ete has a modern paediatric department but outer-island facilities will be limited.

You will have priority when boarding Air Tahiti aircraft. The Carte Famille (Family

DIRECTORY

Card), which costs 2000 CFP, entitles you to significant reductions on some flights (see p258 for details). At hotels and guesthouses, children under 12 generally pay only 50% of the adult rate; very young children usually stay for free.

Lonely Planet's *Travel with Children* is an excellent before-you-go resource containing general tips on vacationing with the kiddies.

CLIMATE CHARTS

French Polynesia is tropical and humid but with nearly constant sea breezes it rarely gets uncomfortably hot. The coolest and driest months are May to October and the hottest, wettest months are January through March. April, November and December can go wet and hot or can be cool and dry depending on the year. For further information on choosing the best time of the year for visiting French Polynesia, see p22.

CUSTOMS

The duty-free allowance for visitors entering French Polynesia includes 200 cigarettes or 50 cigars, 2L of spirits or wine, two cameras and 10 rolls of unexposed film, one video camera and 50mL of perfume. No live animals can be imported (if they're on a yacht they must stay on board) and certification is required for plants. For information on customs regulations for yachts, see p252.

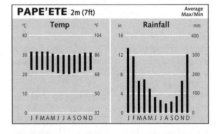

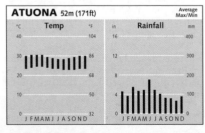

DANGERS & ANNOYANCES

French Polynesia is not a particularly dangerous or annoying destination, which is all the more reason to go there.

Although it's rarely a problem for travellers, French Polynesian men like their beer, particularly at festivals and feasts. There are two points to remember: some French Polynesians are not good drunks and most of them are probably bigger than you. The locally grown marijuana, known as *pakalolo*, is very prevalent although technically illegal.

You're unlikely to be kept awake by late-night revelry anywhere except in the heart of Pape'ete, but the roosters are another matter. A nonstop symphony can 'entertain' you until the early hours (when roosters are supposed to make a racket) and then some of them duly begin all over again.

French Polynesia may not have malaria, but the mosquitoes are hell-bent on sucking blood anyway. They are tolerable during the cooler season from May to October but can be a real bother in the hotter, wetter months. The tiny *nono* (gnats) are found around the whole country but are particularly bad in the Marquesas Islands (see the boxed text, p207). Expect to see a couple of giant cockroaches that can sometimes make their way into even the most clean and sealed rooms. This book makes a great weapon to squash them with.

Swimming in French Polynesia usually means staying within the calm, protected waters of a lagoon, but swimmers should always be aware of tides and currents, and particularly when tides whip out of the lagoon and through a pass into the open sea. Wearing amphibious footwear will protect you against French Polynesia's biggest danger, the stonefish (see p268).

Although early explorers all complained about the French Polynesian propensity for theft, it's a lesser problem today. This is not to say that your camera won't disappear if you leave it lying around on the beach, but even busy Pape'ete is relatively safe compared with cities in the USA and Europe. If you have valuables and you are staying in a more expensive hotel, it's probably wise to use the hotel safe. Don't leave anything of value in a rental car.

Violence is also rarely a problem in French Polynesia. As in any city, if you're out on the town in Pape'ete don't go wandering off into dark alleyways late at night or you might stumble on drunks or methed-out teens looking for a fight.

DISCOUNT CARDS

Older travellers and those under 25 qualify for travel discounts in French Polynesia. If you are over 60, Air Tahiti offers a Carte Marama (Third Age Card), and if you are under 25 you can get a Carte Jeune (Youth Card); either costs 1000 CFP and allow substantial reductions on Air Tahiti flights (see p258 for details).

EMBASSIES & CONSULATES
Consulates in French Polynesia

Given that French Polynesia is not an independent country, there are no foreign embassies, only consulates, and many countries are represented in Pape'ete by honorary consuls.

The following consulates and diplomatic representatives are all on Tahiti. Many are just single representatives and do not have official offices so you'll have to call them.

Australia & Canada (Map pp86-7; ☎ 46 88 53; service@mobil.pf; BP 9068, Pape'ete)

Austria, Switzerland & Leichtenstein (Map pp86-7; ☎ 43 91 14; paulmaetztahiti@mail.pf; Rue Cannonière Zélée, BP 4560, Pape'ete)

Chile, Brazil, Paraguay, Argentina & Bolivia (Map pp86-7; ☎ 43 89 19; c.chilepapeete@mail.pf; BP 952, Pape'ete)

China (☎ 45 61 79; BP 4495, Pape'ete)

Denmark (☎ 54 04 54; c.girard@groupavocats.pf; BP 548, Pape'ete)

Germany (☎ 42 99 94; BP 452, Pira'e)

Great Britain (☎ 70 63 82; BP 50009, Pira'e)

Italy (☎ 43 45 01; consolato_polinesia@yahoo.fr; BP 380 412, Tamanu)

Israel (☎ 42 41 00; consulisrael@mail.pf; BP 37, Pape'ete)

Japan (☎ 45 45 45; nippon@mail.pf; BP 342, Pape'ete)

Korea (☎ 43 64 75; bbaudry@mail.pf; BP 2061, Pape'ete)

Netherlands (Map pp86-7; ☎ 42 49 37; htt@mail.pf; Mobil Bldg, Fare Ute, BP 2804, Pape'ete)

New Zealand (Map pp86-7; ☎ 54 07 40; nzcgnou@offratel.nc; c/- Air New Zealand, Vaima Centre, BP 73, Pape'ete)

Norway (☎ 42 89 72; amitahiti@mail.pf; BP 274, Pape'ete)

Spain (☎ 77 85 40; mlpromotion@mail.pf; BP 186, Pape'ete)

Sweden (☎ 47 54 75; jacques.solari@sopadep.pf; BP 1617, Pape'ete)

United States (Map pp78-9; ☎ 42 65 35; usconsul @mail.pf; US Info, Centre Tamanu, Puna'auia BP 10765, 98711 Pa'ea)

FESTIVALS & EVENTS

French Polynesia has festivals for all occasions, with a few pretty bizarre offerings.

Late January to Mid-February
Chinese New Year The date changes each year (it's based on the Chinese lunar calendar) but the celebrations always include dancing, martial-arts displays and fireworks.

March
Arrival of the First Missionaries Commemorated on 5 March, the landing is re-enacted at Point Vénus on Tahiti; there are celebrations on Tahiti and Mo'orea.

April & May
Beauty Contests Lots of contests are held around the Society Islands in April and May, leading up to the Miss Tahiti and Miss Heiva i Tahiti contests (inquire at a tourist office). There are also Mr Tahiti contests.
Matarii I Raro Traditional festivities mark the beginning of the dry period on May 18th.
Tahiti Billabong Pro Held at Teahupoo on Tahiti Iti, the famous surfing contest attracts the industry's best riders and draws surf fans and media from around the world.

Late June to Early July
Tahiti International Golf Open A four-day championship held at the Olivier Bréaud Golf Course on Tahiti.

July
Heiva i Tahiti Held in Pape'ete, French Polynesia's most important festival lasts an entire month and is so impressive it's almost worth timing your trip around it. See p48 for details.

October
Stone-Fishing Contest This traditional contest takes place on Bora Bora during the first half of October.
Carnival Held in Pape'ete in late October, this features parades of floats decked with flowers.
Hawaiki Nui Canoe Race French Polynesia's major sporting event of the year, this is a three-day *pirogue* (canoe) race from Huahine to Ra'iatea, Taha'a and Bora Bora. For more info, see the boxed text, p45.

November
Matari'i I Ni'a November 20th marks the beginning of the Polynesia 'season of abundance'. There are often cultural ceremonies at *marae* (traditional temples) in Tahiti at this time – check at your hotel or *pension*.

December
Tiare Tahiti Days A festival celebrating the national flower – the ubiquitous but delightful *tiare*. Events take place all around French Polynesia on 1 December.

Marquesas Festival This arts festival celebrating Marquesan identity is held every four years.

FOOD

With the exception of Tahiti and Mo'orea, restaurants are so few and far between in French Polynesia that we have listed them by location rather than price. However, where we do use price breakdowns, we've placed dishes costing less than 1200 CFP in the budget category, 1200 CFP to 2000 CFP in the midrange category and over 2000 CFP in the top end. See the Food & Drink chapter (p53) for thorough descriptions of the cuisine and the types of restaurants you'll find in French Polynesia.

GAY & LESBIAN TRAVELLERS

French laws concerning homosexuality prevail in French Polynesia, which means there is no legal discrimination against homosexual activity. Homophobia in French Polynesia is uncommon, although open displays of affection in public should be avoided. French Polynesia does feel remarkably heterosexual, given the preponderance of honeymooning couples, but you will meet lots of *mahu* (men living as women) working in restaurants and hotels. For gay package tours check out http://tahiti-tourisme.com/specials/tahitigay vacations.asp and for the best transvestite action head to the Piano Bar in Pape'ete (p93).

Te Anuanua o Te Fenua (Gay, Lesbian & Bisexual Association of French Polynesia; ☎ 77 31 11) was formed in 1997 and is based on Tahiti.

HOLIDAYS

Public holidays, when all businesses and government offices close, include the following.

New Year's Day 1 January
Arrival of the First Missionaries 5 March
Easter March/April
May Day 1 May
VE Day 8 May
Ascension Late May
Pentecost & Pentecost Monday Early June
Internal Autonomy Day 29 June
Bastille Day 14 July
Assumption 15 August
All Saints' Day 1 November
Armistice Day 11 November
Christmas Day 25 December

INSURANCE

A travel-insurance policy to cover theft, loss and medical problems is vital. There is a wide variety of policies available and your travel agent will have recommendations. Some policies offer different medical-expense options, but the higher ones are chiefly for countries such as the USA, which has extremely high medical costs.

Some policies specifically exclude 'dangerous activities', which can include scuba diving, motorcycling and even trekking. If such activities are on your agenda, you obviously don't want that sort of policy.

You may prefer a policy that pays doctors or hospitals directly rather than requiring you to pay on the spot and claim later. If you have to claim later, make sure you keep all documentation. Some policies ask you to call (reverse charges) a centre in your home country where an immediate assessment of your problem is made.

Check the small print: for example, does the policy cover ambulances and an emergency flight home? If you have to stretch out you will need two seats and somebody has to pay for them!

Worldwide travel insurance is available at www.lonelyplanet.com/travel_services. You can buy, extend and claim online any time – even if you're already on the road.

INTERNET ACCESS

Surfing in French Polynesia has always been something you do with a surfboard, but the internet is gaining its fans as well. Internet cafés can be found on all the major islands – although the ones on the smaller islands often have only ancient computers and slow connections. Most post offices also have internet posts. Many top-end hotels offer internet access to their guests (sometimes at ridiculously high prices), and access elsewhere is fairly straightforward. You'll generally pay around 900 CFP per hour.

If you're toting your own computer through the Society, Marquesas or Austral Islands, consider buying from the local post office a pre-paid **Mana Pass** (1/3/10 hr denominations 990/2000/5300 CFP) that allows you to access the internet at 'Mana Spots' (wi-fi zones) located in post offices and at some hotels, restaurants and public areas. Check the website www.manaspot.pf for current locations.

LEGAL MATTERS

French Polynesia is a part of France, and is thus subject to that country's penal system.

The police rarely hassle foreigners, especially tourists. On the smaller islands, the police presence is usually limited to one or two officers, who close up shop around 6pm. Drink driving is a real problem on the larger islands, and police sometimes set up checkpoints on Tahiti, Ra'iatea and Mo'orea.

MAPS

The map *Tahiti Archipel de la Société* (IGN No 3615), at a scale of 1:100,000, is readily available in Pape'ete and from map specialists abroad. It covers the Society Archipelago and is the one really useful map for travellers. IGN also publishes maps at 1:50,000 for each island in the archipelago, although these are harder to track down. The SHOM navy maps of the Tuamotus are the best available; for the Marquesas there are SHOM maps and IGN maps at 1:50,000 for Hiva Oa, Nuku Hiva and 'Ua Pou.

MONEY

The unit of currency in French Polynesia is the *cours de franc Pacifique* (CFP; Pacific franc), referred to simply as 'the franc'. There are coins of 1, 2, 5, 10, 20, 50 and 100 CFP, and notes of 500, 1000, 5000 and 10,000 CFP. The CFP is pegged to the euro.

There are fairly hefty bank charges for changing money and travellers cheques in French Polynesia. You generally pay at least a 500 CFP commission on travellers cheques and to exchange cash, although exchange rates do vary from bank to bank; if you have time, shop around to find the best rate. A better idea is to use ATMs. See the inside front cover for an exchange-rate table and p22 for info on costs.

ATMs

Known as *distributeurs automatiques de billets* or DABs in French, ATMs will give you cash via Visa, MasterCard, Cirrus or Maestro networks. International cards generally work only at ATMs associated with Banque Socredo; luckily most islands have at least one of these. You'll need a four-digit pin number.

The exchange rate on these transactions is usually better than what you get with travellers cheques, and the charge your own bank makes on these withdrawals (typically about US$5) is far less than you'll be charged by banks in French Polynesia for changing money or travellers cheques.

ATMs can be found dotted around Tahiti, but they're less common on other islands. Mo'orea, Huahine, Ra'iatea, Bora Bora and Rangiroa have ATMs (there are no ATMS in Maupiti, and Rangiroa has the only ATM in the Tuamotus). On Nuku Hiva, 'Ua Pou and Hiva Oa in the Marquesas, and on Rurutu and Tubuai in the Australs, there are ATMs inside the Socredo agencies. There's a Socredo ATM at Faa'a International Airport.

Banks

There are three major banks operating in French Polynesia: Banque de Tahiti, Banque de Polynésie and Banque Socredo.

Most banks are concentrated in Pape'ete and the more populous islands of Mo'orea, Ra'iatea and Bora Bora. All the main islands in the Society group, apart from Maupiti, have at least one banking agency. In the Tuamotus, only Rangiroa has a permanent banking service. In the Marquesas there are Socredo agencies on 'Ua Pou, Nuku Hiva and Hiva Oa. In the Australs group, Rurutu and Tubuai have some banking services.

Banking hours vary from branch to branch but are typically from 8am to noon and 1.30pm to 5pm Monday to Thursday, and 8am to noon and 1pm to 3pm on Friday. Some branches in Pape'ete do not close for the traditional French Polynesian lunch break, and a handful of Tahitian branches open on Saturday morning. The Banque de Polynésie has banking facilities at Pape'ete's Faa'a airport for flight arrivals.

Credit Cards

All top-end and midrange hotels, restaurants, jewellery shops, dive centres and the bigger supermarkets accept credit cards, sometimes exclusively Visa or MasterCard (although American Express is gaining ground), but they usually require a 2000 CFP minimum purchase. You can also pay for Air Tahiti flights with a card. Most budget guesthouses and many tour operators don't accept credit cards.

Tipping

Tipping is not a part of life in French Polynesia. The price quoted is the price you are expected to pay, which certainly simplifies things. In special circumstances, such as an excellent tour or great service by the hotel cleaning crew, a tip is appreciated.

DIRECTORY

POST

The postal system in French Polynesia is generally quite efficient, and there are modern post offices on all the main islands. Mail to Europe, the USA and Australia takes about a week. Postcards or letters weighing up to 20g cost 85 CFP to France, 120 CFP to anywhere else.

French Polynesian stamps are often beautiful but massive; something to think about when writing on a tiny postcard!

Post offices are generally open from around 7.30am to 4pm Monday to Friday, although the main post office in Pape'ete has longer opening hours and the post office at Faa'a airport is also open from 6.30am to 10am Saturday and Sunday.

Mail on more populated islands is usually addressed to a *boîte postale* (BP; post office box). If you want to receive mail, ask for it to be addressed to you care of poste restante at the appropriate post office; on smaller islands just your name and the island will do.

Fed-Ex (☎ 45 36 45; PK 2.5 Faa'a) and **DHL Express** (☎ 83 73 73; across from Faa'a International Airport) have offices in Pape'ete. If you need to send something fast from the outer islands they can usually help out – although it will probably involve sending the item by freight on Air Tahiti so that the Fed-Ex or DHL agent can pick it up at Faa'a International Airport.

SHOPPING

There are plenty of art-and-craft shops waiting to lure you in, but beware of local souvenirs that aren't local at all – many woodcarvings, even those with Bora Bora neatly painted on them, come from Bali. Nevertheless, French Polynesia does have some excellent local crafts, many of which can be found on Tahiti, especially in the Marché de Pape'ete.

There are duty-free shopping facilities in Pape'ete and at Faa'a airport, with the usual liquor, tobacco and perfume discounts, but the prices are not very exciting by international standards.

Stamp collectors will be excited by the interesting and very colourful stamps on sale. The Centre Philatelique is next door to the main post office in Pape'ete.

Bargaining

Bargaining is not a part of life in French Polynesia. The only exception to this is for black pearls, for which some discounts may be offered; you may also be able to bargain when buying craft work directly from an artist (Marquesan sculptures, for example), but don't force it too hard or you'll insult the artist.

Black Pearls

Black pearls – surely a gal's second-best friend – are cultivated in the Tuamotus, the Leeward Islands and the Gambier Archipelago. You can visit the pearl farms in the Tuamotus, particularly on Rangiroa, and there are jewellery shops and black-pearl specialists all over Pape'ete and on other touristy islands – we found some of the best deals for quality pieces in Ra'iatea. The pearls can be bought both mounted and unmounted. Allow anywhere from 1500 CFP to 200,000 CFP and more for a single pearl.

Clothing & Decoration

Hats, bags and mats of woven pandanus are among the best examples of a true local craft. The best work is said to come from the Australs. *Tapa* is a traditional nonwoven fabric made from the bark of *uru* (breadfruit), banyan or paper mulberry trees. Fabric from Europe superseded *tapa* long ago, but it is still made on Fatu Hiva in the Marquesas and can be bought in Pape'ete.

Tifaifai are large, brilliantly coloured appliqué bed spreads, usually decorated with stylised flower or fruit designs. Each family has its own special designs and the best examples are hand-sewn – which can take two to four months! Expect to pay between 35,000 CFP and 75,000 CFP.

The *pareu* is a single piece of cloth, colourfully decorated and usually worn by women – although it's equally appropriate for men. It costs about 1500 CFP to 2500 CFP, but beware that *pareu* are often imported from Asia.

French Polynesia's favourite beauty product, *monoi* (fragrant oil), is used as moisturising oil, soap, shampoo, sunscreen and perfume. You'll pay around 450 CFP for a bottle, and this blend of coconut oil perfumed with flowers makes a great present. Unfortunately it tends to solidify in colder climates.

Music

French Polynesian song has developed into a sort of island country-and-western music, with melancholic tales of lost love and day-to-day life set to the accompaniment of guitar and ukulele. It's easy on the ear and very catchy – and if you stay at any of the luxury resorts you'll usually hear so much of it you'll likely be inclined to purchase a CD or two (for some ideas see the boxed text, p49). There are a number of music shops in and around Pape'ete where you can find local and international music.

Painting & Sculpture

A number of interesting Polynesian and European artists work in French Polynesia, and their work is on display in galleries and little studios on Tahiti, Mo'orea and Bora Bora. Originals and high-quality prints and posters are available.

Sculpture and woodcarving, in fine wood and in stone or bone, are particularly renowned in the Marquesas. Here you'll find local craft centres where you can see local artists' work, although you can also approach the artists directly. *Tiki* (sacred sculpture), *umete* (traditional wooden bowls), trunks, spears and personal adornments are the most popular items.

Specialist galleries in Pape'ete also sell sculptors' work, but at higher prices. Twice a year Marquesan sculptors have an exhibition and sale in the Territorial Assembly in Pape'ete, usually in June and November.

Tattoos

Tattooed flesh abounds in French Polynesia, on locals and travellers alike. Given that everyone is so tanned, and nobody wears much clothing, they usually look great. Before you launch in and get one though, have a think about how it will look in 20 years' time, in winter. If you're still keen, there are plenty of places to choose from. See p51 for more information.

TELEPHONE

The public telephone system in French Polynesia is widespread and, when it comes to international calls, rather expensive. Public phone boxes can be found even in surprisingly remote locations, and all use the same phonecards. You are able to buy phonecards from post offices, newsagencies, shops and even some supermarkets. Phonecards are available in 1000 CFP, 2000 CFP and 5000 CFP denominations.

There are no area codes in French Polynesia. Local phone calls cost 34 CFP for two and a half minutes at normal tariff rates. If you're calling from a mobile phone the rate you get will depend on your service plan.

Mobile phone services operate on 900 GSM and 98% of the inhabited islands have cellular coverage. SIM cards are available for 5000 CFP at most post offices on main islands bearing a 'Vini' sign and this price includes one hour of local minutes. Additional minutes can be purchased from 1000 CFP, also at the post office (Tahiti is your best bet as outer islands run out of these). Many foreign mobile services have coverage in Tahiti but roaming fees are usually quite high.

If you want to call a phone number in French Polynesia from overseas, dial the international access number, then ☎ 689 (Tahiti's international dialling code), then the local number.

To call overseas from French Polynesia dial ☎ 00, then your country code, the area code (dropping any leading 0) and the local number. If you have any difficulty, call **information** (☎ 3612).

If you want to make a reverse-charge call, ask for *un appel payable a l'arrivée*.

TIME

French Polynesia is 10 hours behind London, two to three hours behind Los Angeles and three hours ahead of Sydney; the region is just two hours east of the International Date Line. The Marquesas are a half hour ahead of the rest of French Polynesia (noon on Tahiti is 12.30pm in the Marquesas). Make sure that you check your flight schedules carefully: Air Tahiti departures and arrivals in the Marquesas may run on Tahiti time.

TOURIST INFORMATION

The main tourist office is the **Gie Tahiti Manava visitors information centre** (☎ 50 57 00; www.tahiti-tourisme.com; Fare Manihini, Blvd Pomare; ❥ 7.30am-5pm Mon-Fri, 8am-noon Sat & public holidays) in the centre of Pape'ete. This office has information about the whole of French Polynesia, and has helpful staff. The more touristy islands generally have some sort of tourist office or counter, but they vary widely in usefulness and dependability.

For information before you leave home, contact **Tahiti Tourisme** (☎ 50 57 00; www.tahiti-tourisme.com), which shares the building with the visitors bureau. Information about Tahiti Tourisme office locations and phone numbers around the world, as well as a slew of

DIRECTORY

international websites, can be found on the website.

TRAVELLERS WITH DISABILITIES

With narrow flights of steps on boats, high steps on *le trucks* (public buses) and difficult boarding facilities on Air Tahiti aircraft, French Polynesia resembles a tropical obstacle course for those with restricted mobility. What's more, hotels and guesthouses are not used to receiving guests with disabilities, and nautical and open-air activities are geared for the able-bodied. However, all new hotels and public buildings must conform to certain standards, so change is happening.

Those who are not put off by these obstacles can contact **Te Nui o Te Huma, La Fédération des Handicapés de Polynésie** (Polynesian Federation for the Handicapped; ☎ 43 30 62) for more information.

VISAS

Everyone needs a passport to visit French Polynesia. The regulations are much the same as for France: if you need a visa to visit France then you'll need one to visit French Polynesia. Anyone from an EU country can stay for up to three months without a visa, as can Australians and citizens of a number of other European countries, including Switzerland.

Citizens of Argentina, Canada, Chile, Japan, Mexico, New Zealand, the USA and some other European countries are able to stay for up to one month without a visa. Other nationalities need a visa, which can be applied for at French Embassies.

Apart from permanent residents and French citizens, all visitors to French Polynesia need to have an onward or return ticket.

Visa Extensions

It's possible to extend a month-long visa exemption for two more months but it can be tricky. Tahiti's Immigration Department states it's best to get an extended visa at a French Embassy before arrival but we have found that this requires heaps of time and paperwork and even then requests are often refused. Better to try at the **Police aux Frontières** (Frontier Police; ☎ 42 40 74; pafport@mail.pf; ☑ airport office 8am-noon & 2-5pm Mon-Fri, Pape'ete office 7.30am-noon & 2-5pm Mon-Fri), at Faa'a airport and next to the Manava visitors information centre in Pape'ete, at least one week before the visa or exemption expires. Dress nice and smile big. An extension costs 3500 CFP.

Stays by foreign visitors may not exceed three months. For longer periods, you must apply to the French consular authorities in your own country for a residence permit; you cannot lodge your application from French Polynesia (see opposite for information on work permits) unless you have a sponsor or get married.

Formalities for Yachts

In addition to presenting the certificate of ownership of the vessel, sailors are subject to the same passport and visa requirements as travellers arriving by air or by cruise ship. Unless you have a return air ticket, you are required to provide a banking guarantee of repatriation equivalent to the price of an airline ticket to your country of origin.

Yachties must advise the **Police aux Frontières** (Frontier Police; ☑ 7.30am-noon & 2-5pm Mon-Fri), next to the tourist office in Pape'ete, of their final departure. If your first port of call is not Pape'ete, it must be a port with a *gendarmerie* (police station): Afareaitu (Mo'orea), Uturoa (Ra'iatea), Fare (Huahine), Vaitape (Bora Bora), Taiohae (Nuku Hiva, Marquesas), Hakahau ('Ua Pou, Marquesas), Atuona (Hiva Oa, Marquesas), Mataura (Tubuai, Australs), Moerai (Rurutu, Australs), Rairua (Raivavae, Australs), Avatoru (Rangiroa, Tuamotus) or Rikitea (Mangareva, Gambiers). The *gendarmerie* must be advised of each arrival and departure, and of any change of crew.

Before arriving at the port of Pape'ete, announce your arrival on channel 12. You can anchor at the quay or the beach, but there are no reserved places. Next, you'll need to report to the **capitainerie** (harbour master's office; ☑ 7-11.30am & 1-4pm Mon-Thu, 7-11.30am & 1-3pm Fri), in the same building as the Police aux Frontières, and complete an arrival declaration.

VOLUNTEERING

Generally volunteering opportunities in French Polynesia are set up for residents or long-term visitors. Still, you could contact the following organisations to find out if they need a hand and/or make a donation (which is probably the better plan of action).

Fenua Animalia (☎ 42 34 23; www.fenua-animalia .org) Tahiti's much-needed animal-protection organisation is gaining momentum and doing a great job.

Reef Check (www.reefcheck.org) Active in French Polynesia; write to the California headquarters for volunteering opportunities.

Te Honu Tea (☎ 57 97 32; www.tehonutea.fr, in French) Actively studies and protects sea turtles as well as their habitat.

WOMEN TRAVELLERS

French Polynesia is a great place for solo women to explore. Local women are very much a part of public life in the region, and it's not unusual to see Polynesian women out drinking beer together or walking alone, so you will probably feel pretty comfortable following suit.

It is a sad reality that women are still required to exercise care, particularly at night, but this is the case worldwide. Some women have commented on being the object of unwanted interest in parts of French Polynesia, but this attention is on the whole harmless, although annoying. As with anywhere in the world, give drunks and their beer breath a wide berth.

Perhaps it's the locals getting their own back after centuries of leering European men ogling Polynesian women, but there is reportedly a 'tradition' of Peeping Toms in French Polynesia, mainly in the outer islands. Take special care in places that seem to offer opportunities for spying on guests, particularly in the showers, and make sure your room is secure.

WORK

French citizens aren't required to comply with any formalities but for everyone else, even other EU citizens (with the exception of those with very specialised skills), it's difficult to work in French Polynesia. Unless you're a pearl grafter, a Chinese chef or a banking executive, you stand little chance. Authorisation to take up paid employment is subject to the granting of a temporary-residence permit, issued by the French state, and a work permit, issued by the territory.

Transport

CONTENTS

Getting There & Away	**254**
Entering the Country	254
Air	254
Sea	257
Getting Around	**258**
Air	258
Bicycle	260
Boat	260
Local Transport	262

GETTING THERE & AWAY

ENTERING THE COUNTRY

Entry procedures for French Polynesia are straightforward. You'll have to show your passport, with any visa (see p252) you may have obtained beforehand. You'll also need to present completed arrival and departure cards, usually distributed on the incoming flight. You may also be asked to show proof of a return airline ticket – Polynesians don't want to share their paradise with you forever.

You do not have to fill in a customs declaration on arrival unless you have imported goods to declare, in which case you can get the proper form from customs officials at the point of entry.

AIR

Most visitors arrive by air. Faa'a airport, on Tahiti, is the only international airport in French Polynesia. There is no departure tax within French Polynesia.

Airports & Airlines

The **Faa'a International Airport** (PPT; ☎ 86 60 61; www.tahiti-aeroport.pf) is on Pape'ete's outskirts, 5km west of the capital. International check-in desks are at the terminal's eastern end.

A number of international airlines serve French Polynesia from different parts of the world. The following airlines have offices in Pape'ete:

Aircalin (Air Caledonie International; airline code SB; ☎ 85 09 04; www.aircalin.nc; hub Noumea International Airport, New Caledonia)

Air France (airline code AF; ☎ 47 47 47; www.airfrance .com; hub Orly Airport, Paris) Code share with Air Tahiti Nui.

Air New Zealand (airline code NZ; ☎ 54 07 47; www .airnz.com; hub Auckland International Airport, Auckland) Code share with Air Tahiti Nui.

Air Tahiti Nui (airline code TN; ☎ 45 55 55; www .airtahiti.com; hub Faa'a International Airport, Tahiti)

Hawaiian Airlines (airline code HA; ☎ 42 15 00; www .hawaiianair.com; hub Honolulu International Airport, Honolulu)

Japan Airlines (airline code JL; ☎ 50 70 65; www.jal .com, jal@southpacificrepresentation.pf, ; hub Narita International Airport, Tokyo) Code share with Air Tahiti Nui.

LanChile (airline code LA; ☎ 42 64 55; www.lan.com; hub Santiago International Airport, Santiago)

Qantas Airways (airline code QF; ☎ 43 06 65; www .qantas.com; hub Kingsford Smith Airport, Sydney) Code share with Air Tahiti Nui.

Tickets

Tickets can be purchased cheaply on the internet and many airlines offer better fares to web surfers. Online ticket sales work well if you're doing a simple one-way or return trip on specified dates. However, online fare generators are no substitute for a travel agent who knows all about special deals, has strategies for avoiding layovers (very helpful for French Polynesia, which is so far away from *anywhere*) and can offer advice on everything from which airline has the best vegetarian food to the best travel insurance to bundle with your ticket.

You may find the cheapest flights are advertised by obscure agencies. Most such firms are honest and solvent, but there are some

---

THINGS CHANGE...

The information in this chapter is particularly vulnerable to change. Check directly with the airline or a travel agent to make sure you understand how a fare (and ticket you may buy) works and be aware of the security requirements for international travel. Shop carefully. The details given in this chapter should be regarded as pointers and are not a substitute for your own careful, up-to-date research.

CLIMATE CHANGE & TRAVEL

Climate change is a serious threat to the ecosystems that humans rely upon, and air travel is the fastest-growing contributor to the problem. Lonely Planet regards travel, overall, as a global benefit, but believes we all have a responsibility to limit our personal impact on global warming.

Flying & Climate Change

Pretty much every form of motor travel generates CO_2 (the main cause of human-induced climate change) but planes are far and away the worst offenders, not just because of the sheer distances they allow us to travel, but because they release greenhouse gases high into the atmosphere. The statistics are frightening: two people taking a return flight between Europe and the US will contribute as much to climate change as an average household's gas and electricity consumption over a whole year.

Carbon Offset Schemes

Climatecare.org and other websites use 'carbon calculators' that allow jetsetters to offset the greenhouse gases they are responsible for with contributions to energy-saving projects and other climate-friendly initiatives in the developing world – including projects in India, Honduras, Kazakhstan and Uganda.

Lonely Planet, together with Rough Guides and other concerned partners in the travel industry, supports the carbon-offset scheme run by climatecare.org. Lonely Planet offsets all of its staff and author travel.

For more information check out our website: lonelyplanet.com.

---

rogue fly-by-night outfits around. Paying by credit card generally offers protection, as most card issuers provide refunds if you can prove you didn't get what you paid for. Agents who accept only cash should hand over the tickets straight away and not tell you to 'come back tomorrow'. After you've made a booking or paid your deposit, call the airline and confirm that the booking was made.

If you purchase a ticket and then later would like to make changes to your route or get a refund, you will need to contact the original travel agent. Airlines issue refunds only to the purchaser of a ticket, which is usually the travel agent or online booking site that bought your ticket on your behalf. Many travellers change their routes halfway through their trips, so make sure that you think carefully before you go ahead and buy a ticket that is not easily refunded or changed.

Booking flights in and out of Tahiti during the high season (June to September and over Christmas) can be difficult and more expensive – book well in advance.

Good online booking agencies for Tahiti:
- www.expedia.com
- www.orbitz.com
- www.travelocity.com

INTERCONTINENTAL (RTW) TICKETS

If you're travelling to multiple countries, a round-the-world (RTW) ticket – where you pay a discounted price for several connections – may be the most economical choice.

A Circle Pacific ticket is similar to a RTW ticket but is cheaper and covers a more limited region. This ticket uses a combination of airlines to connect Australia, New Zealand, North America and Asia, with a variety of stopover options in the Pacific islands. Generally, Circle Pacific fares are a better deal from the USA and Asia than from Australia.

Online companies that can arrange RTW and Circle Pacific tickets:
- www.airbrokers.com
- www.airstop.be
- www.airtreks.com
- www.aroundtheworlds.com
- www.oneworld.com

Asia

Air Tahiti Nui operates flights between Japan (Tokyo and Osaka) and Pape'ete. Return flights from Tokyo start at US$1900. From other parts of Asia, the simplest connection is via Australia or New Zealand.

A good travel agent in Japan is **No 1 Travel** (☎ 03 3205 6073; www.no1-tr avel.com).

TRANSPORT

PACKAGE-TOUR PARADISE

French Polynesia lends itself to the package tour. Given the high price of flights to the region, and the often astronomical price of accommodation once there, a package tour can work out to be a financial godsend. On the downside, package tours don't give much leeway to explore at will. Although most tours offer the opportunity to visit more than one island, you will have to prebook one hotel for each destination before departure (meaning do your homework in advance – you can't swap resorts halfway through if you're not happy).

There's a variety of tour packages available from travel agents in all Western countries, and some online booking agents also offer special deals. If you want more than a straightforward combo package, a good travel agent is essential – they can negotiate better prices at the larger hotels, handle Air Tahiti bookings for your domestic flights once in French Polynesia and have your schedule finalised before you arrive. In addition to the traditional travel operators, there are agencies that specialise in diving tours. These packages typically include flights, accommodation, diving fee and diving tours.

A great list of packages available from several different agencies with departures from around the world is available on the **Air Tahiti Nui** (www.airtahitinui.com) website.

Tahiti specialists in the USA include **Tahiti Legends** (☎ 800 200 1214; www.tahitilegends.com) and **Tahiti Vacations** (☎ 800 553 3477; www.tahitivacation.com). Packages for seven nights start at US$1900 on Mo'orea and US$2600 on Bora Bora.

In Australia **Hideaway Holidays** (☎ 02-9743 0253; www.hideawayholidays.com.au) is a respected South Pacific specialist that offers heaps of flight-and-accommodation deals to Tahiti. Seven-night packages from Sydney to Tahiti start at A$2300.

In the UK **Audley Travel** (☎ 01993 838 830; www.audleytravel.com) arranges packages to French Polynesia. Ten-day packages start at £2400 to Tahiti and £3000 to Bora Bora.

For stays in family *pensions* (guesthouses) or small hotels you can book packages from www.easytahiti.com and www.islandsadventures.com.

Australia & New Zealand

All flights from Australia to Pape'ete are via Auckland. In Auckland, Qantas Airways flights connect with either Air Tahiti Nui or Polynesian Airlines for the Auckland–Pape'ete leg. Fares increase considerably in the high season (June to September and over Christmas). From Sydney expect to pay about A$1050/1500 for a return trip in the low/high season with either Qantas or Air New Zealand.

As in Australia, fares from New Zealand increase during high season. From Auckland return fares start at NZ$850/1250 in low/high season. Both Air New Zealand and Qantas/Air Tahiti Nui offer connecting flights from Pape'ete to Los Angeles.

Many Australians choose to travel to French Polynesia on a package tour; see the boxed text, above.

Other Pacific Islands

There are regular connections between French Polynesia and New Zealand, New Caledonia, the Cook Islands (on Air Tahiti once a week) and Hawaii. Island-hopping around the Pacific is not difficult, but because some flights only operate once a week or every few days you may be faced with some scheduling problems if your time is limited.

South America

LanChile operates flights between Santiago and Pape'ete; one flight a week has a stopover on Easter Island. Return fares cost around US$2200.

UK & Continental Europe

Air New Zealand (from London and Frankfurt), Air France and Air Tahiti Nui have flights to Pape'ete via Los Angeles. Return fares from Paris and Frankfurt start at around €1800; return fares from London start at around £1400 in the low season. From other destinations in Europe the easiest option is to travel to one of these cities and connect with flights to Pape'ete. Some recommended agencies across Europe are listed following.

FRANCE

Anyway (☎ 0892 893 892; www.anyway.fr)
Lastminute (☎ 0892 705 000; www.lastminute.fr)
Nouvelles Frontieres (☎ 0825 000 747; www.nouvelles-frontieres.fr)

GERMANY
Expedia (www.expedia.com)
Just Travel (☎ 089 747 3330; www.justtravel.de)
STA Travel (☎ 01805 456; www.statravel.de)

UK
Discount air-travel ads appear in *Time Out,* the *Evening Standard* and the free magazine *TNT.*
Flightbookers (☎ 0870 010 7000; www.ebookers.com)
Trailfinders (☎ 0845 058 5858; www.trailfinders.co.uk)
Travel Bag (☎ 0870 890 1456; www.travelbag.co.uk)

USA & Canada

Coming from the USA you can either fly direct from Los Angeles to Pape'ete or go via Honolulu (fare differences vary greatly depending on the season). Air New Zealand and Qantas do a code share with Air Tahiti Nui on this route, and Air France and Air Tahiti Nui flights from Paris to Pape'ete go via Los Angeles. Return fares from Los Angeles to Pape'ete range from around US$1200 to US$1800. If you are starting your trip in Honolulu, return fares from Honolulu to Pape'ete start from US$1020 in the low season (January to May) and US$2250 in the high season (November to December).

If you are interested in exploring other parts of the Pacific, Air New Zealand also offers deals that allows four stopovers – Honolulu, Nadi (Fiji), Pape'ete and Rarotonga – en route to Auckland. Check with Air New Zealand or your travel agent for ticket options and fares.

There are no direct flights from Canada, so you will need to go via Honolulu or the US West Coast. Return fares from Vancouver via Los Angeles start from C$2500 in the low season.

If you'd like to book your flight and hotel as a package, see the boxed text, opposite.

SEA
Cruise Ships

Getting to French Polynesia by sea can be a real challenge, although cruise ships from the USA and Australia occasionally pass through for a day or so. Another possibility by sea is to travel with the US-based **Society Expeditions** (☎ 206-728 9400, 800 548 8669; www.societyexpeditions.com), which has regular sailings aboard the *World Discoverer* between Tahiti, Pitcairn and Easter Islands. Departures are from Los Angeles and fares start at US$7000 per person.

Yacht

Travelling to French Polynesia by yacht is eminently feasible. Yachts heading across the Pacific from North America, Australia or New Zealand are often looking for crew and, if you're in the right place at the right time, it's often possible to pick up a ride. It's also possible to pick up crewing positions once in French Polynesia. Sailing experience will definitely score extra points, but so will the ability to cook soup when the boat's keeled over and waves are crashing through the hatch.

On the eastern side of the Pacific, try the yacht clubs in San Diego, Los Angeles, San Francisco or Honolulu. On the western side, Auckland, Sydney and Cairns are good places to try. Look for notices pinned to bulletin boards in yacht clubs and yachting-equipment shops, and post your own notice offering to crew. Another great resource is the **Latitude 38** (www.latitude38.com) crew list where you can post yourself as a potential crew member and peruse ships that are looking for crew.

Ideally you should do some sailing with the boat before you actually set off. A month from the next landfall is not the time to discover that you can't bear the crew or that the ogre of seasickness is always by your side.

It takes about a month to sail from the US West Coast to Hawaii and another month south from there to the Marquesas; with stops, another month takes you west to Tahiti and the Society Islands. Then it's another long leg southwest to Australia or New Zealand.

There are distinct seasons for sailing across the Pacific in order to avoid cyclones. Late September to October and January to March are the usual departure times from the USA. Yachts tend to set off from Australia and New Zealand after the cyclone season, around March and April.

GETTING AROUND

Getting around French Polynesia is half the fun. There are regular and affordable connections between the larger islands by boat (wonderfully languorous) and aeroplane (dramatic and scenic). Getting to the remote islands can be time-consuming and difficult, but never boring.

On some islands there are paved roads, *le truck* (bus) services and myriad car-rental companies; on others there are rough dirt or

TRANSPORT

coral tracks and public transport is unheard of. Generally, your best bet is to rent a car or, even better, a bicycle and be controller of your own destiny.

AIR

There are some (expensive) charter operators with small aircraft and helicopters, but essentially flying within French Polynesia means **Air Tahiti** (☎ 86 42 42; www.airtahiti.aero) and its associate **Air Moorea** (☎ 86 41 41; www.airmoorea.com). Air Tahiti flies to 41 islands in all five of the major island groups. Window seats on its modern fleet of high-wing turboprop aircraft offer great views, but for the nervous flyer these flights can be rather hairraising. Air Moorea is the secondary airline, operating smaller aircraft between Tahiti and Mo'orea. Note that Pape'ete is very much the hub for flights within French Polynesia and, with only a few exceptions, you'll generally have to pass through Pape'ete between island groups.

Flight frequencies ebb and flow with the seasons, and extra flights are scheduled in the July–August peak season. Air Tahiti publishes a useful flight-schedule booklet, which is essential reading for anyone planning a complex trip around the islands. If you are making reservations from afar, you can reserve online and pay by credit card.

Note that Air Tahiti and Air Tahiti Nui are different airlines: Air Tahiti Nui is the international carrier, while Air Tahiti operates domestic flights only.

Air Routes in French Polynesia

See the specific chapters for information on fares between the various islands of French Polynesia – we've listed only general routes in this section. Because distances to the remote islands are so great, some of the full fares are quite high and the cheapest way to visit a number of islands by air is to buy one of Air Tahiti's air passes (see opposite).

THE SOCIETY ISLANDS

From Pape'ete there are direct flights every half-hour or so to Mo'orea and several times a day to other major islands in the group, except for Maupiti, where connections are less frequent (about five a week). There are daily connections on most routes between Mo'orea, Huahine, Ra'iatea and Bora Bora. On some routes, such as the busy Pape'ete-Bora Bora connection, there are up to eight flights a day in the high season. The Society Islands are quite close together and the longest nonstop flight (between Pape'ete and Bora Bora) takes only 45 minutes. Other flights, such as the speedy trip between Pape'ete and Mo'orea, may be as short as seven minutes.

THE TUAMOTUS

Air Tahiti divides the Tuamotus into the busier, touristy northern Tuamotus (Ahe, Apataki, Arutua, Faaite, Fakarava, Kauehi, Manihi, Mataiva, Napuka, Rangiroa, Tikehau, Takapoto, Takaroa) and the much less frequented eastern Tuamotus (Anaa, Fakahina, Fangataufa, Hao, Makemo, Nukutavake, Puka Puka, Pukarua, Reao, Takume, Tatakoto, Tureia, Vahitahi). The Gambier Archipelago is reached via the eastern Tuamotus.

Rangiroa is the main flight centre in the Tuamotus, with between one and five flights to/from Pape'ete daily (one hour). Three days a week one flight continues on to Manihi. Other flights from Pape'ete, either direct or

---

DISCOUNT CARDS

Air Tahiti has several cards available that let you buy tickets at reduced prices, depending on whether the flight is blue, white or red. If you're under 25, the Carte Jeune (Youth Card) gives you a 50% reduction on blue flights and 30% on white flights. If you're over 60, a Carte Marama (Third Age Card) gives you 50% and 30% reductions respectively. A Carte Famille (Family Card) provides family members with a 50% (adult) and 75% (child) discount on blue flights, 30% and 50% on white flights and 10% and 50% on red flights.

The Carte Jeune and Carte Marama cost 1000 CFP and require a passport-type photo and your passport or other form of identification; the Carte Famille costs 2000 CFP and requires photos of the parents and birth certificates or passports for the children – just having them listed in your passport isn't enough.

These cards are issued on the spot, but are only available in French Polynesia.

DOMESTIC AIR ROUTES

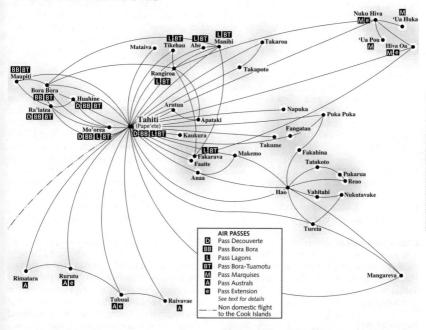

AIR PASSES

D	Pass Decouverte
BB	Pass Bora Bora
L	Pass Lagons
BT	Pass Bora-Tuamotu
M	Pass Marquises
A	Pass Australs
e	Pass Extension
	See text for details
-----	Non domestic flight to the Cook Islands

via Rangiroa, include Apataki, Arutua, Anaa, Fakarava, Ahe, Makemo, Mataiva, Takaroa, Takapoto and Tikehau.

Apart from Tahiti the only Society Island with a direct connection to the Tuamotus is Bora Bora. There's one daily Bora Bora–Rangiroa flight (from which you can easily connect to Manihi or Fakarava) and a weekly flight from Rangiroa to Nuku Hiva (and on to Atuona on Hiva Oa) in the Marquesas.

THE MARQUESAS

Flights to the Marquesas are usually direct from Pape'ete (about three hours), but some are via Rangiroa and a few are via Bora Bora. There are daily flights to Nuku Hiva, some of which continue on to Hiva Oa. From Nuku Hiva there are daily to 'Ua Pou, and four flights weekly to 'Ua Huka.

THE AUSTRALS

Air Tahiti has six flights weekly from Pape'ete to Rurutu (1½ hours) and Tubuai. There are also flights three days a week to Raivavae and Rimatara that stop in Tubuai and Rurutu before continuing back to Pape'ete.

THE GAMBIER ARCHIPELAGO

There is one flight every Tuesday to Mangareva from Pape'ete (about 3½ hours) and one flight every other Saturday.

CHARTER FLIGHTS

Both based at Faa'a airport, **Air Archipels** (☎ 81 30 30) can arrange charter flights with small aircraft to any destination in French Polynesia. **Polynesia Hélicoptères** (☎ 54 87 20; www.polynesia-helicopter.com) is also at the airport and organises helicopter charters (around 18,000 CFP for 20 minutes; minimum of four people required).

Air Passes

There are six island-hopping air passes offering inclusive fares to a number of islands.

Travel must commence in Pape'ete and you cannot connect back to Pape'ete till the end of the pass. You are only allowed one stopover on each island, but you can transit an island if the flight number does not change. If you stop at an island to change flights, it counts as a stopover.

Passes are valid for a maximum of 28 days and all flights (except Pape'ete–Mo'orea or

Mo'orea–Pape'ete) must be booked when you buy your pass. You can use either Air Tahiti or Air Moorea on the Pape'ete–Mo'orea sector. Once you have taken the first flight on the pass the routing cannot be changed and the fare is nonrefundable. The children's fares are for kids 12 and under.

You can extend the Society Islands and Tuamotu Islands passes to include the Marquesas (Nuku Hiva and Hiva Oa) for an extra 49,000/28,000 CFP per adult/child fare. An extension to the passes to the Australs (Rurutu, Raivavae, and Tubuai) costs 29,000/18,000 CFP.

PASS DECOUVERTE
The Passe Decouverte (Discovery Pass; adult/child 27,000/17,000 CFP) is the most basic pass and allows visits to Mo'orea, Ra'iatea and Huahine from Pape'ete.

PASS BORA BORA
The Passe Bora Bora (Bora Bora Pass; adult/child 37,000/22,000 CFP) allows you to visit the six main islands in the Society group: Tahiti, Mo'orea, Huahine, Ra'iatea, Bora Bora and Maupiti.

PASS LAGONS
The Passe Lagons (Lagoons Pass; adult/child 41,000/24,000 CFP) allows you to frolic in the vast lagoons of Mo'orea, Rangiroa, Tikehau, Manihi, Ahe and Fakarava.

PASS BORA–TUAMOTU
This pass (adult/child 52,000/29,000 CFP) allows you to enjoy the high islands of Mo'orea, Huahine, Ra'iatea, Bora Bora, Maupiti before heading to the atolls of Rangiroa, Tikehau, Manihi, Ahe and Fakarava.

PASS MARQUISES
Visit wild and ancient Nuku Hiva, Hiva Oa, 'Ua Pou and 'Ua Huka for adult/child 64,000/36,000 CFP.

PASS AUSTRALS
With a Pass Australs you can enjoy the cool climates of Rurutu, Tubuai, Raivavae and Rimatara for adult/child 49,000/28,000 CFP.

BICYCLE
Cycling around the islands of French Polynesia is a sheer pleasure, particularly if it's not too hot. The distances are rarely great, the traf-

fic is rarely heavy (except in Tahiti) and the roads are rarely hilly. Bikes can be rented on many of the islands for about 1500 CFP a day, but you may find yourself riding an antique. Consider bringing your own bike if you are a really keen cyclist. Bicycles are accepted on all the interisland boats.

BOAT
Boat travel within the Society group isn't as easy as you'd hope unless you're only going to Mo'orea or taking a cruise or sailboat. A number of companies shuttle back and forth between Tahiti and Mo'orea each day; other routes between the islands are less frequent but served at least twice a week by cargo vessels.

In the other archipelagos travel by boat is more difficult. If you are short on time and keen to travel beyond the Society Islands you may need to consider flying at least some of the way.

Cargo ships, also known as *goélettes* or schooners, are principally involved in freight transport. Some take passengers, however, and for those who want to get off the beaten trail such a voyage can, depending on the circumstances, be anything from a memorable experience to an outright nightmare. The level of comfort is rudimentary: some ships don't have passenger cabins and you have to travel 'deck class', providing your own bedding to unroll on the deck and all your own meals. You will get wet and cold. And then there's seasickness… At the same time, the connection with the locals and the sheer street cred of travelling this way can make it worth it for a select few.

A notice posted at Chez Guynette in Huahine sums up the cargo-ship schedules: 'The boats arrive when they are here and leave when they are ready.'

Cruise Ship
At the other end of the spectrum from rudimentary cargo ships are the luxury cruise ships that operate in the Society Islands. These ships are incredibly stylish and comfortable, and offer shore excursions at each stop – this is a long way from the leaky copra boats of traditional interisland travel.

Managed by **Bora Bora Pearl Cruises** (☎ 43 43 03; www.boraborapearlcruises.com), the *Haumana* is a magnificent 36m catamaran that accommodates up to 60 people and does three- or four-day cruises between Bora Bora, Ra'iatea and Taha'a. The *Tia Moana* and *Tu Moana,* both also managed by Bora Bora cruises, offer seven-day cruises in the Society Islands.

You may see the enormous *Paul Gauguin* (seven-day voyages), Princess Cruises' *Tahitian Princess* (10-day cruises) or the 'tall ship' *Star Flyer* (seven- to 11-day cruises) anchored in Pape'ete. They depart Pape'ete to visit the Society islands and sometimes an atoll or two in the Tuamotus.

For a more intimate cruising experience **Archipels Croisieres** (☎ 55 36 39; www.archipels.com) has five eight-person catamarans that cruise the Society Islands and Tuamotus. It's a full-service experience with all meals and activities.

See **Tahiti Tourisme** (www.tahiti-tourisme.com) for more information about cruising.

Ferry & Cargo Ship
THE SOCIETY ISLANDS
It takes between half an hour and an hour to travel between Tahiti and Mo'orea, depending on which company you go with. The car ferries, such as those run by Moorea Ferry, are slower than the high-speed ferries, which take only passengers, motorcycles and bicycles. The **Aremiti 5** (☎ Pape'ete 42 88 88, Mo'orea 56 31 10) and the **Moorea Express** (☎ Pape'ete 82 47 47, Mo'orea 56 43 43) jet between Tahiti and Mo'orea six or more times daily between 6am and 4.30pm. The trip takes about 30 minutes; fares are 900 CFP. You can buy tickets at the ticket counter on the quay just a few minutes before departure.

Vaeanu (☎ 41 25 35) operates the Pape'ete–Huahine–Ra'iatea–Taha'a–Bora Bora round trip, leaving Pape'ete on Tuesday and Thursday at 5pm. It sets out from Bora Bora on Wednesday and Friday. The Huahine and Ra'iatea arrivals are in the middle of the night (most guesthouse owners will not pick you up). Reservations are advisable and the one-way tariff to any of the islands to/from Pape'ete is 2000 CFP. The office is at the Motu Uta port area in Pape'ete, near the *Aranui* office; take *le truck* 3 from the *mairie* (town hall).

Hawaiki Nui (☎ 54 99 54) also travels the Society Islands circuit on a similar schedule and has two departures a week (Tuesday and Thursday at 4pm; deck/cabin per person 2000/5500 CFP).

The **Maupiti Express** (☎ 67 66 69) makes regular trips between Bora Bora and Maupiti

(one way 3500 CFP) and Bora Bora to Taha'a and Ra'iatea (one way 3500 CFP). The boat departs the Vaitape quay in Bora Bora for Maupiti at 8.30am on Tuesday, Thursday and Saturday; the return trip leaves Maupiti at 4pm on the same day. Tickets can be purchased at the quay.

THE TUAMOTUS & GAMBIER
The cargo vessels that serve the Tuamotus and Gambier Archipelagos are true lifelines. Only the following take passengers (others take only freight) but their main purpose is to transport goods and petrol and the standard of comfort is generally basic. Because of insurance changes in recent years the costs of travelling by boat to these islands has increased and is not much less than flying. Still, this is the way to go if you're looking for adventure, have plenty of time on your hands and are hoping to leave a softer carbon footprint.

The routes and fares mentioned here are just an indication and are subject to change. The offices are all in the Motu Uta port area in Pape'ete (take *le truck* 3 from the *mairie*).

The **Cobia III** (☎ 43 36 43; ☯ office 7.30am-3.30pm Mon-Fri, 8-11am Sat) is a small boat (think lots more wave movement) that travels Pape'ete–Kaukura–Arutua–Apataki–Aratika–Toau–Fakarava–Pape'ete once a week; there are no cabins and no meals are served. The fare is about 6000 CFP.

The **Saint-Xavier Maris-Stella** (☎ 42 23 58; ☯ office 7.30-11am & 1.30-4pm Mon-Fri) travels a circuit from Pape'ete every 15 days, taking in Mataiva, Tikehau, Rangiroa, Ahe, Manihi, Takaroa, Takapoto, Arutua, Apataki, Kaukura, Toau, Fakarava, Kauehi, Raraka and Niau. Departing from Pape'ete, allow 7500/10,000 CFP for deck-class/air-conditioned cabin to Rangiroa, 8500/15,000 CFP to Manihi and 10,000/17,000 CFP to Fakarava. Meals are included. This is the most comfortable option for the Tuamotus but it's still pretty grubby.

The **Nuku Hau** (☎ 54 99 54; ☯ office 7.30am-4pm Mon-Fri) travels Pape'ete–Rikitea–Marutea Sud–Maturei Vavao–Tenararo–Tenarunga–Vahanga–Pape'ete every 25 days. It costs around 10,000 CFP on the deck. Contact the captain directly for reservations.

The **Mareva Nui** (☎ 42 25 53; ☯ office 7.30-11.30am & 1.30-5pm Mon-Thu) runs a circuit from Pape'ete taking in Makatea, Mataiva, Tikehau, Rangiroa, Ahe, Manihi, Takaroa, Takapoto, Raraka, Kauehi, Aratika, Taiaro, Fakarava,

Arutua, Apataki, Niau, Toau and Kaukura. Fares vary from 10,000 to 15,000 CFP (including meals) for a bunk on deck; the complete trip takes eight days.

The **Kura Ora II** and **Kura Ora III** (☎ 45 55 45; ☻ office 7.30am-3pm Mon-Thu) do a trip every 15 days to the remote atolls of the central and eastern Tuamotus, including Anaa, Hao and Makemo. Deck-class prices cost from around 7000 CFP, depending on the distance travelled, plus around 2500 CFP per person per day for meals. The complete trip takes about three weeks.

THE MARQUESAS

The **Aranui** (☎ 42 62 40; www.aranui.com) is a veritable institution, taking freight and passengers on 16 trips a year from Pape'ete (see the boxed text, p203). The only other cargo ship, the *Taporo IX*, won't take passengers.

THE AUSTRALS

Services between the Society Islands and the Australs are limited, so make sure you plan ahead. While you'll need plenty of time to travel this way, it will save you lots of money.

The 60m *Tuhaa Pae II* leaves Pape'ete for the Australs three times a month. It stops at Rurutu and Tubuai on every trip, Rimatara and Raivavae twice a month, Rapa once every two months and Maria Island in the Gambiers very occasionally.

You can choose between berths and air-con cabins. From Pape'ete to Rurutu, Rimatara or Tubuai a berth/air-con cabin costs 6000/8500 CFP; to Raivavae it costs 8500/12,000 CFP. Three meals add another 3500 CFP per day. The **Tuhaa Pae II office** (☎ 50 96 09, 41 36 06; snathp@ mail.pf) is in Pape'ete's Motu Uta, between the *Kura Ora* and *Mareva Nui* offices.

Yacht

French Polynesia is an enormously popular yachting destination, as the international line-up of yachts along the Pape'ete waterfront testifies. It's also possible to rent a yacht in French Polynesia (see p244).

LOCAL TRANSPORT

Most islands in the Society group have one road that hugs the coast all the way around. Tahiti (where there is even a stretch of freeway), Mo'orea, Bora Bora, Ra'iatea, Taha'a and Huahine have paved and reasonably well-maintained roads. On all of these islands,

tracks leading inland are often rough-and-ready and almost always require a 4WD.

There are far more boats than land vehicles in the Tuamotus, although there is a sealed road running the length of Rangiroa's major island – all 10km of it!

Outside the towns there are hardly any sealed roads in the Marquesas. Tracks, suitable for 4WDs only, connect the villages although slowly bits and pieces are being paved.

Sealed roads encircle both Tubuai and Raivavae in the Australs, and there are reasonable stretches of sealed road on Rurutu. Otherwise, roads in the Australs archipelago are fairly limited and little transport is available.

Bus

French Polynesia doesn't have much of a public transportation system; Tahiti is the only island where public transport is even an option. The colourful, old *le trucks* (trucks with bench seats in the back for passengers) have now been almost entirely replaced by a more modern fleet of air-con buses, though some still run in and around Pape'ete. Buses (often still called *le trucks*) stop at designated spots (marked with a blue sign) and supposedly run on a schedule – although times are hardly regular. Although there are official *le truck* stops, complete with blue signs, they are rather difficult to spot, and *le trucks* will generally stop anywhere sensible for anybody who hails them. Note that you pay at the end of your trip and that for many routes there is a set fare, irrespective of distance.

Car & Scooter

If you want to explore the larger islands of the Society group at your own pace, it may be worth renting a car or scooter, particularly given the price of taxis and the dismal state of public transport outside Pape'ete.

DRIVING LICENCE

Car-rental agencies in French Polynesia only ask to see your national driving licence, so an international driving licence is unnecessary.

HIRE

There are many different car-rental agencies on the more touristy islands, but the prices really don't vary much: compared with rental costs in the rest of the world, prices are high. For a small car expect to pay from 7000 CFP a day including unlimited kilometres and basic insurance – and that's not even including petrol. On some islands (Taha'a comes to mind) rentals start at 12,000 CFP, and on Tahiti, good luck finding a rental under 10,000 CFP per day. Rates drop slightly from the third day onwards.

Fortunately, the cars available are pretty economical and you won't cover too many kilometres, no matter how hard you try. Off-road excursions into the interior are usually off limits to anything other than a 4WD.

Most places offer four-, eight- and 24-hour rates, as well as two- and three-day rentals. At certain times of the year (July, August and New Year's Eve) it's wise to book vehicles a few days in advance although at any time of year reserving in advance helps ensure that you get one in the price bracket you are hoping for.

You'll need a credit card, of course.

On Tahiti you will find the major international car-rental agencies such as Avis, Budget, Europcar and Hertz. On other islands such as Mo'orea, Huahine, Ra'iatea and Bora Bora, as well as on Rangiroa in the Tuamotus, the market is divided up between Avis and Europcar. Smaller local agencies exist on some islands, but the rates are almost as high.

You can hire a car on Rurutu in the Australs, but in the Marquesas rental vehicles are mainly 4WDs with a driver. Rental without a driver is possible only on Atuona (Hiva Oa) and Taiohae (Nuku Hiva).

Avis and Europcar rent scooters on a number of islands. It's a good way of getting around the small islands, but bear in mind you won't be wearing protective gear, so this is probably not the place to learn to ride a scooter. You'll pay around 6000 CFP a day. After numerous accidents there are no rental scooters on Tahiti.

ROAD RULES

Driving is on the right-hand side in French Polynesia. Although the accident statistics are pretty grim, driving here is not difficult, and the traffic is light almost everywhere apart from the busy coastal strip around Pape'ete on Tahiti. However, the overtaking habits of locals can sometimes get the heart rate up. Beware of drunk drivers at night, and of pedestrians and children who may not be used to traffic, particularly in more remote locations. Sometimes dodging sauntering dogs and chickens makes driving in Tahiti feel like a video game – take it slow.

Hitching

Hitching (*auto-stop* in French) is a widely accepted – and generally safe – way of getting around the islands in French Polynesia, and you'll see locals and travellers alike standing with their thumbs out on the roadside. Of course, hitching is never entirely safe, but if you're going to hitch, French Polynesia is an easy place to start – usually you'll never have to wait more than 15 or 20 minutes for a ride, plus you'll meet some interesting folks. Always take the necessary precautions and use your judgement before jumping into a car; drunk drivers are probably your biggest problem. It's not recommended for women to hitch alone.

TRANSPORT

Health

CONTENTS

Before You Go	**264**
Insurance	264
Recommended Vaccinations	264
Medical Checklist	264
Internet Resources	265
Further Reading	265
In Transit	**265**
Deep Vein Thrombosis (DVT)	265
Jet Lag & Motion Sickness	265
In French Polynesia	**266**
Availability & Cost of Health Care	266
Infectious Diseases	266
Traveller's Diarrhoea	267
Environmental Hazards	267
Travel with Children	269
Women's Health	269

You probably have less chance of getting sick in French Polynesia than in any major international city. There's no malaria, land snakes, poisonous spiders or crocodiles, and cold and flu bugs are brought in from elsewhere. Mosquitoes do exist in quantity, however, and dengue fever will be a concern when there is an outbreak. Your biggest worry will be sunburn and avoiding infection in minor cuts and scrapes. Health facilities in the country are generally of a good standard but some less-populated islands will have little to no medical services.

BEFORE YOU GO

Prevention is the key to staying healthy while overseas. A little planning before departure, particularly for pre-existing illnesses, will save you a lot of trouble later. Make sure you see your dentist before a long trip, carry a spare pair of contact lenses and glasses, and take your optical prescription with you. Bring medications in their original, clearly labelled containers. A signed and dated letter from your physician, describing your medical conditions and medications, including generic names, is also a good idea. If carrying syringes or needles, be sure to have a physician's letter documenting their medical necessity.

INSURANCE

If your health insurance does not cover you for medical expenses abroad, consider supplemental insurance. (Check the Travel Services section of www.lonelyplanet.com for more information.) Find out in advance if your insurance plan will make payments directly to providers or reimburse you later for overseas health expenditures. (In French Polynesia doctors will often expect payment in cash; see opposite for details.)

If you are an EU citizen you have the same rights in French Polynesia as you do in France; remember to fill in the EU Form E111 before leaving home. It is still best to have private health-insurance coverage. Serious illness or injury may require evacuation, eg from an outer island to Tahiti or even from Tahiti to a major city such as Los Angeles or Auckland; make sure that your health insurance has provision for evacuation. Under these circumstances hospitals accept direct payment from major international insurers, but for all other health costs cash up front is usually required.

RECOMMENDED VACCINATIONS

The World Health Organization (WHO) recommends that all travellers should be covered for diphtheria, tetanus, measles, mumps, rubella and polio, regardless of their destination. Since most vaccines don't produce immunity until at least two weeks after they're given, make sure you visit a physician at least six weeks before departure. A recent influenza vaccination is always a good idea when travelling. If you have not had chicken pox (varicella) consider being vaccinated.

MEDICAL CHECKLIST

It is a very good idea to carry a medical and first-aid kit with you, to help yourself in the case of minor illness or injury. Following is a list of items you should consider packing:

- antibiotics (prescription only), eg ciprofloxacin (Ciproxin) or norfloxacin (Utinor; Noroxin)
- antibiotic plus steroid eardrops (prescription only), eg Sofradex, Kenacort Otic
- antidiarrhoeal drugs, eg loperamide
- acetaminophen (paracetamol) or aspirin

- anti-inflammatory drugs, eg ibuprofen
- antihistamines (for hay fever and allergic reactions)
- antibacterial ointment, eg Bactroban for cuts and abrasions (prescription only)
- antigiardia tablets such as tinidazole (prescription only)
- steroid cream or hydrocortisone cream (for allergic rashes)
- bandages, gauze, gauze rolls, waterproof dressings
- adhesive or paper tape
- scissors, safety pins, tweezers
- thermometer
- pocket knife
- DEET-containing insect repellent for the skin
- Permethrin-containing insect spray for clothing, tents and bed nets
- sun block
- oral rehydration salts, eg Gastrolyte, Diarolyte, Replyte
- iodine tablets (for water purification)
- syringes and sterile needles, and intravenous fluids if travelling in very remote areas

Note that aspirin should not be used for fever because it can cause haemorrhage in dengue fever. Also, don't take the scissors, tweezers or pocket knife in your carry-on luggage.

INTERNET RESOURCES

There is a wealth of travel-health advice on the internet. For further information, **LonelyPlanet .com** (www.lonelyplanet.com) is a good place to start. The World Health Organization (WHO) produces a superb text called *International Travel and Health,* which is revised annually. It is no longer published in book form but is available online at no cost at www.who. int/ith.

Other websites of general interest:

Centers for Disease Control and Prevention (www .cdc.gov)

Fit for Travel (www.fitfortravel.scot.nhs.uk) Up-to-date information about outbreaks, very user-friendly.

MD Travel Health (www.mdtravelhealth.com) Provides complete travel health recommendations for every country, updated daily, at no cost.

Travel Doctor (www.traveldoctor.com.au) An Australasian site, similar to Fit for Travel.

It's also a good idea to consult your government's travel-health website before your departure.

Australia (www.dfat.gov.au/travel)
Canada (www.phac-aspc.gc.ca)
New Zealand (www.mfat.govt.nz/travel)
UK (http://nhs.uk/Healthcareabroad)
USA (www.cdc.gov/travel)

FURTHER READING

Good options for further reading include Lonely Planet's *Travel with Children*; *Healthy Travel Australia, New Zealand and the Pacific* by Dr Isabelle Young; and *Your Child's Health Abroad: A Manual for Travelling Parents* by Dr Jane Wilson-Howarth and Matthew Ellis.

IN TRANSIT

DEEP VEIN THROMBOSIS (DVT)

Blood clots may form in the legs during plane flights, chiefly because of prolonged immobility. And the longer the flight, the greater the risk. The chief symptom of DVT is swelling of or pain in the foot, ankle or calf, usually but not always on just one side. When a blood clot travels to the lungs, it may cause chest pain and breathing difficulties. Travellers with any of these symptoms should immediately seek medical attention.

To prevent the development of DVT on long flights you should walk about the cabin, contract the leg muscles while sitting, drink plenty of fluids and avoid alcohol and tobacco.

JET LAG & MOTION SICKNESS

To avoid jet lag (common when crossing more than five time zones) try drinking plenty of nonalcoholic fluids and eating light meals. Upon arrival, get exposure to natural sunlight and readjust your schedule (for meals, sleep and so on) as soon as possible.

Antihistamines such as dimenhydrinate (Dramamine) and meclizine (Antivert, Bonine) are usually the first choice for treating motion sickness. A herbal alternative is ginger.

IN FRENCH POLYNESIA

AVAILABILITY & COST OF HEALTH CARE

French Polynesia has doctors in private practice, and standard hospital and laboratory facilities with consultants in the major specialities – internal medicine, obstetrics/gynaecology, orthopaedics, ophthalmology,

HEALTH

paediatrics, pathology, psychiatry and general surgery. Private dentists, opticians and pharmacies are also available. The outer islands, of course, have more basic services.

Private consultation and private hospital fees are approximately equivalent to Australian costs. It costs from 3500 CFP to see a GP; specialists are more expensive and anywhere you go, the waiting times can be very long. Direct payment is required everywhere except where a specific arrangement is made, eg in the case of evacuation or where prolonged hospital stay is necessary; your insurer will need to be contacted by you. Although most of the larger hospitals are coming into line in accepting credit cards, there will be difficulty with the more remote small medical facilities. Doctors will accept credit cards but prefer cash, and not all credit cards are acceptable – check with the relevant company beforehand. If a credit card is not accepted you should be able to arrange cash on credit through the local banking system.

Most commonly used medications are available. Private pharmacies are not allowed by law to dispense listed drugs without a prescription from a locally registered practitioner, but many will do so for travellers if shown the container. While the container should preferably specify the generic name of the drug, this has become much less of a problem with the use of internet search engines. Asthma inhalers and most anti-inflammatories are available over the counter.

It's best to have a sufficient supply of a regularly taken drug as a particular brand may not be available and sometimes quantities can be limited. This applies particularly to psychotropic drugs like antidepressants, antipsychotics, anti-epileptics or mood elevators. Insulin is available even in smaller centres, but you cannot guarantee getting a particular brand, combination or preferred administration method. If you have been prescribed 'the very latest' oral antidiabetic or antihypertensive make sure you have enough for the duration of your travel.

Except in the remote, poorly staffed clinics, the standard of medical and dental care is generally quite good even if facilities are not sophisticated. The overall risk of illness for a normally healthy person is low. The most common problems are diarrhoeal upsets, viral sore throats, and ear and skin infections, all of which can mostly be treated with self-medication. For serious symptoms, eg sustained fever, or chest or abdominal pains, it is best to go to the nearest clinic or private practitioner in the first instance.

INFECTIOUS DISEASES

Despite the long list, the realistic risks to visitors from infectious diseases are very low.

Dengue Fever

Dengue fever is a viral disease spread by the bite of a day-biting mosquito. It causes a feverish illness with headache and severe muscle pains similar to those experienced with a bad, prolonged attack of influenza. Another name is 'break bone fever' and that's what it feels like. Danger signs include prolonged vomiting, blood in the vomit and a blotchy rash. There is no preventive vaccine and mosquito bites should be avoided whenever possible. Self-treatment involves paracetamol, fluids and rest. Do not use aspirin. Haemorrhagic dengue has been reported only occasionally, manifested by signs of bruising, bleeding and shock, and it requires immediate medical care.

Eosinophilic Meningitis

A very rare illness manifested by scattered abnormal skin sensations, fever and sometimes by the meningitis symptoms (headache, vomiting, confusion, neck and spine stiffness), eosinophilic meningitis is caused by a microscopic parasite – the rat lungworm – that contaminates raw food. There is no proven specific treatment, but symptoms may require hospitalisation. For prevention pay strict attention to advice on food and drink.

Hepatitis A

This is a viral disease, causing liver inflammation and spread by contaminated food or water. Fever, nausea, debility and jaundice (yellow coloration of the skin, eyes and urine) occur and recovery is slow. Most people recover completely but it can be dangerous to people with other forms of liver disease, the elderly and sometimes to pregnant women towards the end of pregnancy. Food is contaminated by food preparers, handlers or servers, and by flies. There is no specific treatment. The vaccine is close to 100% protective.

Hepatitis B

This is a viral disease causing liver inflammation, but it is much more serious than hepatitis A and frequently goes on to cause chronic liver disease and even cancer. It is spread, like HIV, by mixing body fluids, ie by sexual intercourse, contaminated needles or accidental blood contamination. Treatment is complex and specialised but vaccination is highly effective.

Hepatitis C

A viral disease similar to hepatitis B, and causing liver inflammation, which can go on to chronic liver disease or result in a symptomless carrier state. It's spread almost entirely by blood contamination from shared needles or contaminated needles used for tattooing or body piercing. Treatment is complex and specialised. There is no vaccine available.

HIV/AIDS

The incidence of HIV infection is on the rise in the whole region. It is fast becoming a problem in French Polynesia although it is not talked about much. Safe-sex practice is essential at all times. Blood-transfusion laboratories do tests for HIV.

Leptospirosis

Also known as Weil's disease, leptospirosis produces fever, headache, jaundice and, later, kidney failure. It is caused by a spirochaete organism found in water contaminated by rat and pig urine. The organism penetrates skin, so swimming in flooded areas or in rivers near pig farms is a risky practice. If diagnosed early it is cured with penicillin. This disease is often confused with dengue fever; if you have blood in your urine consider leptospirosis, which is considerably more serious.

Typhoid Fever

A bacterial infection acquired from contaminated food or water. The germ can be transmitted by food handlers or flies, and can be present in inadequately cooked shellfish. It causes fever, debility and late-onset diarrhoea. Untreated it can produce delirium and is occasionally fatal, but the infection is curable with antibiotics. Vaccination is moderately effective, but care with eating and drinking is equally important. It is extremely rare in French Polynesia.

TRAVELLER'S DIARRHOEA

Diarrhoea is caused by viruses, bacteria or parasites present in contaminated food or water. In temperate climates the cause is usually viral, but in the tropics bacteria or parasites are more usual. If you develop diarrhoea, be sure to drink plenty of fluids, preferably an oral rehydration solution (eg Diarolyte, Gastrolyte, Replyte). A few loose stools don't require treatment, but if you start having more than four or five stools a day, you should start taking an antibiotic (usually a quinolone drug) and an antidiarrhoeal agent (such as Loperamide). If diarrhoea is bloody, persists for more than 72 hours or is accompanied by fever, shaking, chills or severe abdominal pain you should seek medical attention. Giardiasis is a particular form of persistent, although not 'explosive', diarrhoea caused by a parasite present in contaminated water. One dose (four tablets) of tinidazole usually cures the infection.

To prevent diarrhoea pay strict attention to the precautions regarding food and water as described on p268.

ENVIRONMENTAL HAZARDS

Threats to health from animals and insects are rare indeed but you need to be aware of them.

Bites & Stings

JELLYFISH

The blue-coloured Indo-Pacific 'man o' war' is found in all waters but is rare in French Polynesia. If in the unlikely event you see these floating in the water or stranded on the beach it is wiser not to go in. The sting is very painful. Treatment involves ice packs and vinegar; do not use alcohol. Smaller cubomedusae are abundant and are found particularly on still, overcast days. They usually produce only uncomfortably irritating stings but rarely can cause generalised symptoms, especially in someone with poorly controlled heart disease.

POISONOUS CONE SHELLS

Poisonous cone shells abound along shallow coral reefs. Stings can be avoided by handling the shell at its blunt end only and preferably using gloves. Stings mainly cause local reactions; nausea, faintness, palpitations or difficulty in breathing flag the need for medical attention.

HEALTH

SEA SNAKES

As in all tropical waters, sea snakes may be seen around coral reefs although they are very rare in French Polynesia. Unprovoked, sea snakes are extremely unlikely to attack and their fangs will not penetrate a wetsuit. First-aid treatment consists of compression bandaging and splinting of the affected limb. Antivenin is effective, but may have to be flown in. Only about 10% of sea-snake bites cause serious poisoning.

STONE FISH

These are very well camouflaged and are quite prolific on coral reefs and rocky areas, making them one of the country's main health concerns. If you do get stung apply heat immediately and head for the hospital. Wearing plastic, waterproof sandals provides the best protection.

Coral Ear

This is a commonly used name for inflammation of the ear canal. It has nothing to do with coral but is caused by water entering the canal, activating fungal spores resulting in secondary bacterial infection and inflammation. It usually starts after swimming, but can be reactivated by water dripping into the ear canal after a shower, especially if long, wet hair lies over the ear opening. Apparently trivial, it can be very, very painful and can spoil a holiday. Apart from diarrhoea it is the most common reason for tourists to consult a doctor. Self-treatment with an antibiotic-plus-steroid eardrop preparation (eg Sofradex, Kenacort Otic) is very effective. Stay out of the water until the pain and itch have gone.

Coral Cuts

Cuts and abrasions from dead coral cause no more trouble than similar injuries from any other sort of rock, but live coral can cause prolonged infection. If you injure yourself on live coral don't wait until later to treat it. Get out of the water as soon as possible, cleanse the wound thoroughly (getting out all the little bits of coral), apply an antiseptic and cover with a waterproof dressing. Then get back in the water if you want to.

Diving Hazards

Because the region has wonderful opportunities for scuba diving, the temptation to spend longer-than-safe times at relatively shallow depths is great and is probably the main cause of decompression illness (the 'bends'). Early pains may not be severe and may be attributed to other causes, but any muscle or joint pain after scuba diving must be suspect. Privately run compression chambers are available on Tahiti but transport to a chamber can be difficult. Supply of oxygen to the chambers is sometimes a problem. Even experienced divers should check with organisations like **DAN** (Divers' Alert Network; www.diversdalertnetwork.org) about the current site and status of compression chambers, and insurance to cover costs both for local treatment and evacuation. Novice divers must be especially careful. If you have not taken out insurance before leaving home you may be able to do so online with DAN.

Food & Water

The municipal water supply in Pape'ete and other large towns can be trusted, but elsewhere avoid untreated tap water. In some areas the only fresh water available may be rainwater collected in tanks, and this should be boiled. Food in restaurants, particularly resort restaurants, is safe.

FISH POISONING

Ciguatera is a form of poisoning that affects otherwise safe and edible fish unpredictably. Poisoning is characterised by stomach upsets, itching, faintness, slow pulse and bizarre inverted sensations, eg cold feeling hot and vice versa. Ciguatera has been reported in many carnivorous reef fish, especially barracuda and very large jack but also red snapper and napoleon fish; in French Polynesia it sometimes occurs in the smaller reef fish as well and this will vary from island to island. There is no safe test to determine whether a fish is poisonous or not. Although local knowledge is not entirely reliable, it is reasonable to eat what the locals are eating. However, fish caught after times of reef destruction, eg after a major hurricane, are more likely to be poisonous. Treatment consists of rehydration and if the pulse is very slow, medication may be needed. Healthy adults will make a complete recovery, although disturbed sensation may persist for some weeks.

Heat

French Polynesia lies within the tropics, so it is hot and frequently humid.

HEAT EXHAUSTION

Heat exhaustion is actually a state of dehydration associated to a greater or lesser extent with salt loss. Salt is lost through sweating, making it easy to become dehydrated without realising it. Thirst is a late sign. Small children and old people are especially vulnerable. For adults, heat exhaustion is prevented by drinking at least 3L of water per day, and more if actively exercising. Children need about 1.5L to 2.5L per day. Salt-replacement solutions are useful since muscle weakness and cramps are due to salt as well as water loss and can be made worse by drinking water alone. The powders used for treating dehydration due to diarrhoea are just as effective when it is due to heat exhaustion. Apart from commercial solutions, a reasonable drink consists of a good pinch of salt to a pint (0.5L) of water. Salt tablets can result in too much salt being taken in, causing headaches and confusion.

HEAT STROKE

When the cooling effect of sweating fails, heat stroke ensues. This is a dangerous and emergency condition characterised not only by muscle weakness and exhaustion, but by mental confusion. Skin will be hot and dry. If this occurs, 'put the fire out' by cooling the body with water on the outside and cold drinks for the inside. Seek medical help as a follow-up anyway, but urgently if the person can't drink.

SUNBURN

It should go without saying that exposure to the ultraviolet (UV) rays of the sun causes burning of the skin with the accompanying misery (together with the long-term danger of skin cancer), but experience shows reminders are necessary. The time of highest risk is between 11am and 3pm, and remember that cloud cover does not block out UV rays. The Australian 'slip, slop, slap' slogan is a useful mantra – slip on a T-shirt or blouse, slop on a sunscreen lotion of at least 15-plus rating, and slap on a hat. Treat sunburn like any other burn – cool, wet dressings are best. Severe swelling may respond to a cortisone cream.

TRAVEL WITH CHILDREN

For young children, it is dengue fever that could pose a problem. The disease tends to come in epidemics, mainly in the hotter, wetter months, so it should be possible to plan holidays accordingly.

WOMEN'S HEALTH

Tampons and pads are readily available in main centres but do not rely on getting them if you travel to one of the outer islands. Dengue fever, especially in the first three months of pregnancy, poses a hazard because of fever but otherwise there is no reason why a normal pregnancy should prevent travel to the region. However, as a general principle, immunisation in the first three months of pregnancy is not recommended.

HEALTH

Language

CONTENTS

Tahitian & French	**270**
Tahitian	270
French	271
Useful Words & Phrases	271

TAHITIAN & FRENCH

Tahitian and French are the official languages of French Polynesia, but Tahitian is spoken more than it is written. Although French dominates, many of those working in the tourist industry can speak some English; once you venture to the more remote and less touristy islands where the Tahitian dialects are spoken, it's definitely useful to know some French. The Polynesians have given their French a wonderful island lilt. Fortunately, bad French is readily accepted in French Polynesia – wheel out that old school French and see how you go. For more extensive Tahitian-language tips, pick up a copy of Lonely Planet's *South Pacific Phrasebook*, which also includes a useful section on Pacific French.

TAHITIAN

Tahitian (also known as Maohi) belongs to the group of Polynesian languages that includes Samoan, Maori, Hawaiian, Rarotongan and Tongan. There are several dialects of Tahitian, including the Tuamotan or Paumotan dialect of the Tuamotus, the Marquesan dialect of the Marquesas and the Mangarevan dialect of the Gambier Archipelago. It was the spread of Christianity through French Polynesia that helped to make Tahitian, the variety spoken on Tahiti, the most widespread dialect.

Few Tahitian words have managed to make their way into English or any other languages. The two familiar exceptions are 'tattoo' from the Tahitian *tatau* and 'taboo' from the Tahitian *tabu* (or *tapu*).

Tahitian grammar is pleasantly uncomplicated. There are no genders, declensions, conjugations or auxiliaries, and plural forms are denoted solely by the article: the definite article (the) is *te* in the singular and *te mau* in the plural. The notions of past, present and future are expressed by using prefixes or suffixes with the verb. A single word in Tahitian can be a verb, adjective or noun, eg *inu* can mean 'to drink', 'a drink' or 'drinkable', according to the context.

Tahitian & the Modern World

Although Tahitian borrowed a number of terms from English during the earlier years, it was not simply content to borrow or adopt terms for items new or unknown to Tahitian culture. Tahitians are a most resourceful people who use their own rich language to derive terms for words generated by modern technology. Some of the terms that have come into being are very colourful and expressive. (The word *ra'a* in some terms listed below is used as a grammatical marker.)

accelerator	*ha'a pūai ra'a pereo'o* (make-power-vehicle)
aeroplane	*manu reva* (bird-space)
airport	*tahua manu reva* (field-bird-space)
ambulance	*pereo'o ma'i* (vehicle-sick)
bank	*fare moni* (house-money)
bar	*fare inu ra'a* (house-drink)
battery	*'ōfa'i mōrī pata* (stone-light-switch on)
bedroom	*piha ta'oto* (room-sleep)
bicycle	*pereo'o tāta'ahi* (vehicle-pedal)
bra	*tāpe'a tītī* (hold-breast)
camera	*pata hoho'a* (click-image)
can-opener	*pātia punu* (stab-container)
car	*pereo'o uira* (vehicle-lightning)
cathedral	*fare pure ra'a rahi* (house-pray-big)
cheese	*pata-pa'ari* (butter-hard)
dentist	*taote niho* (doctor-tooth)
drawer	*'āfata 'ume* (box-pull)
fork	*pātia mā'a* (spear-food)
glasses	*titi'a mata* (filter-eye)
goat	*pua'a niho* (pig-tooth)
horse	*pua'a horo fenua* (pig-run-ground)
hose	*uaua pipi tiare* (rubber-water-flower)
hospital	*fare ma'i* (house-sick)
motorcycle	*pereo'o tāta'ahi uira* (vehicle-pedal-lightning)
office	*piha pāpa'i ra'a parau* (room-write-word)
post office	*fare rata* (house-letter)
refrigerator	*'āfata fa'a to'eto'e ra'a* (box-make-cold)
submarine	*pahī hopu moana* (ship-dive-ocean)

telephone	*niuniu paraparau* (wire-speak)
television	*'āfata teata na'ina'i* (box-cinema-small)
toilet	*fate iti* (house-small)

Pronunciation

Tahitian isn't a difficult language for English speakers to pronounce, as most Tahitian sounds are also found in English. Likewise, the Tahitian alphabet, devised in the 19th century, is fairly simple to use.

As with all other Polynesian languages, there are five vowels, pronounced much as they are in Italian or Spanish:

a	as in 'father'
e	between the 'e' in 'bet' and in 'they'
i	as in 'marine'
o	as the 'o' in 'more'
u	as the 'oo' in 'zoo'

Tahitian and most other Pacific languages have a second series of long vowels. The 'shape' of these is the same as their shorter counterparts, but they are held for approximately twice as long. You can get an idea of this concept by comparing the pronunciation of English 'icy' and 'I see' – both are distinguished only by the length of the final vowel sound. Long vowels are indicated in this language guide by a macron over the vowel (ā, ē, ī, ō and ū).

Consonants are pronounced much as they are in English, with a few modifications.

h	as in 'house' or as the 'sh' in 'shoe' when preceded by **i** and followed by **o**, eg *iho* (only/just)
p	as in 'sponge', not as the 'p' in 'path' (ie not followed by a puff of breath)
r	often rolled as is common in Scottish or Spanish
t	as in 'stand', not as the 't' in 'talk' (ie not followed by a puff of breath)
'	glottal stop. This sound occurs between two vowels and is like the sound you hear between the words 'uh-oh'. In Tahitian, this sound isn't indicated in the normal spelling (with a few minor exceptions), since native speakers know where they occur. Foreigners, however, aren't so lucky. In this language guide the glottal stop is indicated by the apostrophe (').

FRENCH

All French nouns are either masculine or feminine, and adjectives change their form to agree with the noun. In the following list of words and phrases, only the singular version of nouns and adjectives is given.

Basic French vowels are pronounced the same way they are in Tahitian, but there are a few other rules of pronunciation worth remembering:

ai	as the 'e' in 'pet'. Any following single consonant is usually silent.
eau/au	as the 'au' in 'caught' but shorter
ll	as 'y', eg *billet* (ticket), pronounced 'bee-yeh'
ch	always pronounced as 'sh'
qu	as 'k'
r	pronounced from the back of the throat

There is a distinction between **u** (as in *tu*) and **ou** (as in *tout*). For both sounds, the lips are rounded and pushed forward, but for the 'u' sound try to say 'ee' while keeping the lips pursed. The 'ou' sound is pronounced as the 'oo' in 'cook'.

For nasal vowels the breath escapes partly through the nose. They occur where a syllable ends in a single **n** or **m**; the **n** or **m** is silent but indicates the nasalisation of the preceding vowel.

USEFUL WORDS & PHRASES

English French	Tahitian
Hello/Good morning.	
Bonjour.	*Ia ora na, nana.*
Goodbye.	
Au revoir.	*Pārahi, nana.*
Welcome.	
Bienvenue.	*Maeva, mānava.*
How are you?	
Ça va?	*E aha te huru?*
My name is ...	
Je m'appelle ...	*To'u i'oa 'o ...*
Thank you.	
Merci.	*Māuruuru.*
Pardon?	
Comment?	*E aha?*
Excuse me/Sorry.	
Pardon.	*E'e, aue ho'i e.*
No problem/Don't worry.	
Pas de problème.	*Aita pe'ape'a.*

Yes.
Oui. — *E, 'oia.*

No.
Non. — *Aita.*

Good luck!
Bon courage! — *Fa'aitoito!*

I don't understand.
Je ne comprends pas. — *Aita i ta'a ia'u.*

How much?
Combien? — *E hia moni?*

How many?
Combien? — *E hia?*

Where is ...?
Où est ...? — *Tei hea ...?*

When?
Quand? — *Afea?*

What time is it?
Quelle heure est-il? — *E aha te hora i teie nei?*

Cheers! (for drinking)
Santé! — *Manuia!*

I'm ill.
Je suis malade. — *E ma'i to'u.*

In the following nouns, the French definite article ('the' in English) is included for gender reference purposes.

address
l'adresse — *vahi nohoraa*

bank
la banque — *fare moni*

bathroom
la salle de bain — *piha pape*

beach
la plage — *tahatai*

bed
le lit — *ro'i*

beer
la bière — *pia*

bicycle
le vélo — *pereo'o tāta'ahi*

boat
le bateau — *poti*

breakfast
le petit déjeuner — *tafe poipoi*

bus
l'autobus — *pereo'o mata'eina'a*

car
la voiture — *pereo'o uira*

chemist/pharmacy
la pharmacie — *fare ra'au*

coffee
le café — *taofe*

country
le pays — *fenua*

day
le jour — *ao*

embassy
l'ambassade — *fare tonitera rahi*

film (camera)
la pellicule — *firimu*

food
la nourriture — *ma'a*

map
le plan — *hoho'a fenua*

menu
la carte — *tāpura mā'a*

money
l'argent — *moni*

now
maintenant — *i teie nei*

parents (extended family)
les parents — *fēti'i*

plantation
la plantation — *fa'a'apu*

police station
la gendarmerie — *fare mūto'i*

restaurant
le restaurant — *fare tāmā'ara'a*

room
la chambre — *piha*

shop
le magasin — *fare toa*

telephone
le téléphone — *niuniu paraparau*

that
cela — *terā*

today
aujourd'hui — *j teie nei mahana*

tomorrow
demain — *ānānahi*

tonight
ce soir — *i teie pō*

water
l'eau — *pape*

1	un	hō'ē
2	deux	piti
3	trois	toru
4	quatre	māha
5	cinq	pae
6	six	ono
7	sept	hitu
8	huit	va'u
9	neuf	iva
10	dix	'ahuru
20	vingt	piti 'ahuru
100	cent	hō'ē hānere
1000	mille	hō'ē tauatini
10,000	dix mille	hō'ē 'ahuru tauatini
1,000,000	un million	hō'ē mirioni

Glossary

ahu – altar in a *marae;* in the *marae* of French Polynesia the *ahu* was generally a pyramid shape
aparima – dance with hand gestures
ari'i – high chief of the ancient Polynesian aristocracy; literally, 'king'
Assemblée de Polynésie Française – Assembly of French Polynesia
atoll – type of low island created by *coral* rising above sea level as an island gradually sinks; postcard atolls consist of a chain of small islands and reef enclosing a *lagoon;* see also *low island*
atua – god or gods

barrier reef – *coral* reef forming a barrier between the shoreline and the open sea but separated from the land by a *lagoon*
belvédère – lookout
bonitier – whaleboat or skipjack boat; used for fishing and for transferring passengers and cargo from ship to shore on islands that have no wharf or quay
boules – see *pétanque*
BP – *boîte postale;* post-office box
breadfruit – see *uru*

capitainerie – harbourmaster's office
caldera – volcano crater
CEP – Centre d'Expérimentation du Pacifique; the French nuclear-testing program
CFP – Cour de Franc Pacifique, usually known as *franc cour pacifique;* currency of French Polynesia
ciguatera – malady caused by eating infected reef fish
CMAS – Confédération Mondiale des Activités Sub-aquatiques; scuba-diving qualification; the Francophile equivalent of *PADI*
copra – dried coconut meat, used to make an oil
coral – animal of the coelenterate group which, given the right conditions of water clarity, depth and temperature, grows to form a reef
cyclone – tropical storm rotating around a low-pressure 'eye'; 'typhoon' in the Pacific, 'hurricane' in the Caribbean

demi-pension – see *half board*
demi – person of Polynesian-European or Polynesian-Chinese descent

faapu – small cultivated field
fare – traditional Polynesian house; hotel bungalow
fare atua – house for the gods on *marae;* actually a small chest in the form of a statue

fare potee – chief's house or community meeting place; open dining-room of a restaurant or hotel
fenua – country or region of origin
feo – coral outcrop
fetii – extended family
fringing reef – *coral* reef immediately alongside the shoreline, not separated from the shore by a lagoon as with a *barrier reef*
full board – bed and all meals (French: *pension complète*); see also *half board*

gendarmerie – police station

ha'e – traditional Marquesan house
half board – bed, breakfast and lunch or dinner (French: *demi-pension);* see also *full board*
hei – garland of flowers
heiva – celebration or festival; the Heiva is a huge festival of Polynesian culture (mainly dance) that takes place on Tahiti in July
high island – island created by volcanic action or geological upheaval; see also *low island*
hima'a – underground oven used for cooking traditional Polynesian food
himene – Tahitian-language hymn
Hiro – god of thieves who features in many Polynesian legends
hoa – shallow channel across the outer reef of an atoll, normally carrying water into or out of the central lagoon only at unusually high tides or when large swells are running; see also *pass*

kaina – Polynesian; Polynesian person; local; see also *popaa*
kaveka – sooty tern
kaveu – coconut crab

lagoon – calm waters enclosed by a reef; may be an enclosed area encircled by a *barrier reef* (eg Rangiroa and Tetiaroa) with or without *motu,* or may surround a *high island* (eg Bora Bora and Tahiti)
lagoon side – on the lagoon side of the coast road (not necessarily right by the lagoon); see also *mountain side*
le truck – public 'bus'; a truck with bench seats that operates a buslike service
leeward – downwind; sheltered from the prevailing winds; see also *windward*
LMS – London Missionary Society; pioneering Protestant missionary organisation in Polynesia
low island – island created by the growth and erosion of *coral* or by the complete erosion of a *high island;* see also *atoll*

ma'a – food
ma'a Tahiti – Tahitian or Polynesian food; Tahitian buffet
mahi mahi – dorado; one of the most popular eating fish in French Polynesia
mahu – transvestite or female impersonator; see also *raerae*
mairie – town hall
maitai – local cocktail made with rum, pineapple, grenadine and lime juices, coconut liqueur and, sometimes, Grand Marnier or Cointreau
makatea – *coral island* that has been thrust above sea level by a geological disturbance (eg Rurutu, and Makatea in the Tuamotus)
mana – spiritual or supernatural power
manahune – peasant class or common people of pre-European Polynesia
manu – bird
ma'o – shark (French: *requin*)
Maohi – Polynesian
mape – Polynesian 'chestnut' tree
maraamu – southeast trade wind that blows from June to August
marae – traditional Polynesian sacred site generally constructed with an *ahu* at one end; see also *me'ae*
me'ae – Marquesan word for *marae*
Melanesia – islands of the western Pacific; Papua New Guinea, the Solomons, Vanuatu, New Caledonia and Fiji
Micronesia – islands of the northwest Pacific including the Mariana, Caroline and Marshall groups, Kiribati and Nauru
monoi – coconut oil perfumed with the *tiare* flower and/or other substances
motu – small islet in a lagoon, either along the outer reef of an *atoll* or on a reef around a *high island*
mountain side – on the mountain side of the coast road (not necessarily up in the mountains); see also *lagoon side*

nacre – mother-of-pearl; iridescent substance secreted by pearl oysters to form the inner layer of the shell; shell of a pearl oyster
navette – shuttle boat
niau – sheets of plaited coconut-palm leaves, used for roof thatching
noni – yellowish fruit with therapeutic properties, grown in the Marquesas and popular in the USA; also known as *nono*
nono – very annoying biting gnat found on some beaches and particularly prevalent in the Marquesas
nucleus – small sphere, made from shells found in the Mississippi River in the USA, which is introduced into the gonads of the pearl oyster to produce a cultured pearl

'Oro – god of war; the cult that was superseding the Ta'aroa cult when the first Europeans arrived

pa – hilltop fortress
PADI – Professional Association of Dive Instructors; the most popular international scuba-diving qualification
pae pae – paved floor of a pre-European house; traditional meeting platform
pahu – drum
pahua – giant clam
pamplemousse – grapefruit
pandanus – palm tree with aerial roots; the leaves are used for weaving hats, mats and bags
pareu – traditional sarong-like garment
pass – channel allowing passage into the lagoon through the outer reef of an atoll or the barrier reef around a high island; see also *hoa*
pension – guesthouse
pension complète – see *full board*
pétanque – French game in which metal balls are thrown to land as near as possible to a target ball; also known as *boules*
petroglyph – carving on a stone or rock
pirogue – outrigger canoe (Tahitian: *va'a*)
PK – *pointe kilométrique;* distance markers found along the roads of some French Polynesian islands
Polynesia – islands of the central and southeastern Pacific, including French Polynesia, Samoa, Tonga, New Zealand and the Cook Islands
popaa – European or Westerner; see also *kaina*
pu – conch shell
purau – hibiscus

raerae – *mahu;* sometimes applied to *mahu* who are transsexual or homosexual, rather than just cross-dressers
requin – shark (Tahitian: *ma'o*)
roulotte – mobile diner; a food van operating as a snack bar

seaward – side of an *atoll,* island or *motu* that faces the sea rather than the *lagoon*
snack – snack bar

Ta'aroa – supreme Polynesian god whose cult was being superseded by worship of 'Oro, god of war, at the time of the European arrival
tabu – alternative spelling of *tapu*
tahua – faith healer; priest of the ancient Polynesian religion
tamure – hip-jiggling version of traditional Polynesian dance
tapa – cloth made from beaten bark and decorated with traditional designs; worn by the people of pre-European Polynesia
tapu – sacred or forbidden; the English word 'taboo' comes from *tapu* or *tabu*
taro – root vegetable; a Polynesian staple food

tatau – tattoo; although tattoos were also known in Japan, it was on Tahiti that European sailors first discovered them and added the word to European vocabularies

taxe de séjour – accommodation tax

tiare – fragrant white gardenia endemic to the Pacific; the flower has become symbolic of Tahiti

tifaifai – colourful appliquéd or patchwork material used as blankets, bedspreads or cushion covers

ti'i – Society Islands term for the Marquesan word *tiki*

tiki – humanlike sacred sculpture usually made of wood or stone and sometimes standing more than 2m high; once found on many *marae*

tohua – meeting place or a place for festival gathering in pre-European Polynesia but especially in the Marquesas

tou – *Cordia subcordata;* tree, common in the Marquesas, that produces a dark, hard, grained wood popular with carvers

tupapau – irritating spirit ghosts of the ancient Polynesian religion, still much feared

TVA – *taxe sur la valeur ajoutée;* a tax added to accommodation rates

tuu – ceremonial activities centre in the Marquesas

ua ma – Marquesan food pit

umete – traditional Tahitian wooden dish or bowl

uru – breadfruit; starchy staple food of Polynesia that grows on a tree as a football-sized fruit (French: *arbre à pain*)

va'a – outrigger canoe (French: *pirogue*)

vahine – woman

vanira – vanilla

windward – facing prevailing winds; see also *leeward*

The Authors

CELESTE BRASH

Celeste first visited French Polynesia in 1991, fell in love with her now husband, as well as Polynesian culture, and moved to the country permanently in 1995. Her first five years were spent living off fish and coconuts on a pearl farm on a remote atoll sans plumbing, telephone or airstrip, but now she calls the more modern island of Tahiti home. Her award-winning travel stories have appeared in *Travelers' Tales* books and her travel articles have appeared in publications including *Los Angeles Times* and *Islands* magazine. She has written over a dozen Lonely Planet guides, but she considers the *Tahiti & French Polynesia* guide to be her *pièce de résistance*. For this edition Celeste wrote the front- and endmatter chapters (except Diving), Tahiti, Mo'orea, Huahine, Ra'iatea & Taha'a, the Tuamotus, the Australs and the Gambier Archipelago.

JEAN-BERNARD CARILLET

A Paris-based journalist and photographer, Jean-Bernard is a die-hard Polynesia lover, a diving instructor and a Polynesian dance aficionado. He has travelled the length and breadth of French Polynesia for nearly 15 years now – this assignment was his eighth trip to the *fenua*. So far, he has explored 28 islands in the five archipelagos, on land and at sea, from the heights of the Society Islands and the Marquesas to the depths of the Tuamotus' atolls, as well as the most remote corners of the Austral and Gambier Archipelagos.

Jean-Bernard has contributed to many Lonely Planet titles, both in French and in English, and has coordinated Lonely Planet's *Diving & Snorkeling Tahiti & French Polynesia*. For this edition Jean-Bernard wrote the Diving, Bora Bora, Maupiti and Marquesas chapters.

Behind the Scenes

THIS BOOK

This 8th edition was written by Celeste Brash and Jean-Bernard Carillet. The previous edition was written by Becca Blond and Celeste Brash; Jean-Bernard Carillet wrote the Diving chapter. This guidebook was commissioned in Lonely Planet's Melbourne office, and produced by the following:

Commissioning Editors Judith Bamber, Suzannah Shwer
Coordinating Editor Rosie Nicholson
Coordinating Cartographer Andras Bogdanovits
Coordinating Layout Designer Cara Smith
Managing Editor Bruce Evans
Managing Cartographer David Connolly
Managing Layout Designer Laura Jane
Assisting Editors Jackey Coyle, Anne Mulvaney, Gabrielle Stephanos
Cover Designer Pepi Bluck
Project Manager Ruth Cosgrove
Language Content Coordinator Quentin Frayne

Thanks to Glenn Beanland, Jessica Boland, Lucy Birchley, Melanie Dankel, Sally Darmody, Jennifer Garrett, Chris Girdler, Nicole Hansen, Naomi Stephens

THANKS
CELESTE BRASH

Most thanks to my kids Jasmine and Tevai and my husband Josh for putting up with my absences with the same good humour you always do. Big thanks to Joel House on Huahine, Edwin and Jacqueline on Taha'a, to Ben and Hinano on Rurutu, Lily and Ralph and family on Ra'iatea, Mateo Pakaiti and Jacques Sauvage on Mangareva, Eleanor on Raivavae, Suzanne and Marie-Helen on Takapoto, Cathy Campbell on Mo'orea, and to Manoa Drollet, Bibi Jorge and Magali Verducci on Tahiti. Professional help was given by Tehani at Tahiti Tourisme plus the always great Lonely Planet in-house gang, especially Judith Bamber. This book wouldn't be what it is without the excellent input, collaboration and first-edition text base written by author/superhero Jean-Bernard Carillet.

JEAN-BERNARD CARILLET

Heaps of thanks to Lonely Planet's Suzannah and Judith for their trust. In French Polynesia, a heartfelt *māuruuru roa* goes out to Yan and Vai and *fetii*, who are my family and guardian angels. I felt so much at home in Mahina. A big thanks also to all diving staff (and colleagues) and to all the people who helped out and made this trip so enlightening, including Verly, Maire, Moearii, Eric, Jean-Christophe, Ronald, Laurent, Fred, Helene, Pierre, Jean-Yves and Alex, among others.

A huge *merci beaucoup* to Celeste, coordinating author extraordinaire, with whom I share the

---

THE LONELY PLANET STORY

Fresh from an epic journey across Europe, Asia and Australia in 1972, Tony and Maureen Wheeler sat at their kitchen table stapling together notes. The first Lonely Planet guidebook, *Across Asia on the Cheap*, was born.

Travellers snapped up the guides. Inspired by their success, the Wheelers began publishing books to Southeast Asia, India and beyond. Demand was prodigious, and the Wheelers expanded the business rapidly to keep up. Over the years, Lonely Planet extended its coverage to every country and into the virtual world via lonelyplanet.com and the Thorn Tree message board.

As Lonely Planet became a globally loved brand, Tony and Maureen received several offers for the company. But it wasn't until 2007 that they found a partner whom they trusted to remain true to the company's principles of travelling widely, treading lightly and giving sustainably. In October of that year, BBC Worldwide acquired a 75% share in the company, pledging to uphold Lonely Planet's commitment to independent travel, trustworthy advice and editorial independence.

Today, Lonely Planet has offices in Melbourne, London and Oakland, with over 500 staff members and 300 authors. Tony and Maureen are still actively involved with Lonely Planet. They're travelling more often than ever, and they're devoting their spare time to charitable projects. And the company is still driven by the philosophy of *Across Asia on the Cheap*: 'All you've got to do is decide to go and the hardest part is over. So go!'

same passion for Polynesia – thanks again for your efficient liaising.

And how could I forget my daughter Eva, who shared some of my Polynesian adventures and gives direction to my otherwise roving life?

OUR READERS

Many thanks to the travellers who used the last edition and wrote to us with helpful hints, useful advice and interesting anecdotes:

Stefan Arf, Michael Bentall, Karen & Rob Braithwaite, Steve Brosnan, Tom Daley, Flo Detour, Eileen Dietrich, Matthew Durling, Patrick Garcia, Peggy Haworth, Olaf Jacob, Laurent Juan De Mendoza, Nikoleta Kanelli, Amy & Hyon Kim, Marco Kunz, Victoria Lam, Ruth Lockhart, Rodrigues Lopes, Ulrike Luebcke, Roxolana Marmash, Claudia Meier, Troels Munk, Edith & Doug Naegele, Jaroslaw Olszewski, Scott Ripley, John Roeg, Folker Rudolph, Herma Rudolph, Andrew Southcott, Insa Thiele, Kim Van Zanden

ACKNOWLEDGMENTS

Many thanks to the following for the use of their content:

Globe on title page ©Mountain High Maps 1993 Digital Wisdom, Inc.

Internal photographs: Douglas Peebles Photography/Alamy p13; Photo Resource Hawaii/Alamy p16 (#2); Shiyana Thenabadu/Alamy p11. All other photographs by Lonely Planet Images, and by Michael Aw p8 (#2); Jean-Bernard Carillet p6 (#1 & 2), p7, p11 (#3), p12, p13 (#3), p14 (#2); Mark Daffey p10; Josh Humbert p15, p16 (#1); Uros Ravbar p9; Merten Snijders p5, p8 (#1), p14 (#1).

Index

4WD tours
  Bora Bora 157
  Huahine 130
  Mo'orea 115
  Ra'iatea 140
  Tahiti 76-7

A
accommodation 24, 242-4, *see also individual locations*
activities 29, 244-5, *see also individual activities*
Afareaitu 112
Ahe 193-4
air travel
  air tickets 254-5
  airlines 254
  airports 254
  carbon offset 255
  deep vein thrombosis (DVT) 265
  domestic air passes 259
  jet lag 265
  to/from French Polynesia 254-7
  within French Polynesia 258-60
Akamaru 241
Amaru 236
Anaa 197
Anahi 223
Anaho 209
Anapoto 236
animals 59-61, *see also individual species*
Arahoho blowhole 100
Aranui 203
archaeological sites, see also *marae, petroglyphs, tiki*
  Hikokua (Marquesas) 208
  Iipona (Marquesas) 222-3, **13**
  Kamuihei (Marquesas) 208
  key features 210
  Maeva (Huahine) 127, **127**
  Meiaute (Marquesas) 211
  Paeke (Marquesas) 207
  Raivavae 235
  Rapa Iti (Rapa) 237
  Taaoa (Marquesas) 222

Tahakia (Marquesas) 208
Tetahuna (Marquesas) 216
'Ua Huka (Marquesas) 212-3
archaeology 30, 208, 210
architecture 48-9
art galleries 126
arts 46-52
Atiha Bay 111
ATMs 249
Atuona 217-22, **219**
Aukena 241
Australs 228-37, **229**
Avatoru 178, **180-1**

B
Bain de Vaima 98
Bain Loti 85
banks 249
bargaining 250
beaches
  Bora Bora 154, 155, **6**
  Huahine 129
  Manihi 192
  Mataiva 192
  Maupiti 167, 168-9, **6**
  Mo'orea 109, 110
  Nuku Hiva 207
  Rangiroa 179
  Tahiti 76, 100, 103
  Tahuata 225
  Takapoto 194, 195
  'Ua Pou 215, 216
beauty pageants 44
beer 55
bicycle travel, *see* cycling
birds 60
bird-watching
  Marquesas 213
  Mataiva 192
  Rimatara 236
  Tikehau 189
  'Ua Huka 212
boat travel, *see also* boat trips, kayaking, lagoon tours, sailing
  to/from French Polynesia 257
  within French Polynesia 203, 260
boat trips, *see also* kayaking, lagoon tours, sailing
  Bora Bora 156

Fakarava 186
Hiva Oa 221
Huahine 129
Marquesas 203
Nuku Hiva 207
Ra'iatea 140
Tahiti 103-4
'Ua Huka 212
Boenechea, Don Domingo de 37, 102, 103
books 23-5, *see also* literature
  anthropology 37, 44
  arts 50
  drinks 55
  food 53
  health 265
  history 31, 32, 34, 35
  marine life 64
  plants 59
  surfing 45
Bora Bora 150-65, **152-3**, **6**
  accommodation 157-61
  activities 155-7
  attractions 151-4
  children, travel with 157
  diving 68, 155
  drinking 163
  entertainment 161, 163
  food 161-3
  history 151
  information 151
  itineraries 26
  shopping 163-4
  travel to/from 164
  travel within 164-5
Bougainville, Louis-Antoine de 34
Bounty 36, 51, 232, 233
Brel, Jacques 218, 219, 220
bus travel 262
bushwalking, *see* hiking
business hours 245

C
canyoning 77
car travel 262-3
carbon offset 255
cargo ships, *see* boat travel
cathedrals, *see* churches & cathedrals

000 Map pages
000 Photograph pages

caves
    Ana Aeo Cave (Australs) 230
    Anapua Caves (Tahiti) 101
    Tane Uapoto (Australs) 230
    Tiana Taupee (Australs) 230
    Vaipoiri Cave (Tahiti) 104
cell phones 251
cemeteries, *see also* tombs
    Calvaire Cemetery 219
    Cimetière Pomare 88
children, travel with 245
    Bora Bora 157
    food 56
    health 269
    Maupiti 170
    Mo'orea 115
    Tahiti 80
churches & cathedrals
    Cathédrale Notre-Dame (Tahiti) 85
    Cathédrale Saint-Michel (Gambier
        Archipelago) 240
    Église de la Sainte Famille
        (Mo'orea) 111
    Église Nôtre-Dame-de-la-Paix
        (Gambier Archipelago) 241
    Église Saint-Gabriel (Gambier
        Archipelago) 241
    Notre-Dame Cathedral of the
        Marquesas Islands (Marquesas)
        203
    Papetoai church (Mo'orea) 110
    Temple Paofai (Tahiti) 85
    Vaitahu Catholic church
        (Marquesas) 224
cinema 51, 52
climate 22, 246
climate change 255
clothing 49-50
Colette Bay 204
cone shells 61, 267
consulates 247
Contrôleur Bay 207
Cook, James 34, 35, 100
Cook's Bay 109, **110**
copra 178
coral cuts 268
coral ear 268
costs 22-3
    diving 74
    food 55
courses
    dance 80, 115
    diving 69
credit cards 249
crown-of-thorns starfish 68

cruise ships, *see* boat travel
culture 32, 41-52
customs 46, 56, 57
customs regulations 246
cycling 244, 260
    Mo'orea 114-15
    Taha'a 145

D
dance 46-7, **14**
    courses 80, 115
dance performances
    Bora Bora 161
    Mo'orea 121
    Tahiti 93-4
dangers, *see* safe travel
deep vein thrombosis (DVT) 265
disabilities, travellers with 252
diving 64-74, **66-7**
    Bora Bora 68, 155
    conditions 64
    costs 74
    courses 69
    facilities 74
    Fakarava 71, 186
    Hiva Oa 72, 221
    Huahine 65, 129
    internet resources 70, 71
    Makemo 71-2
    Manihi 70, 193
    Maupiti 69, 169-70, **9**
    Mo'orea 65, 112-13
    Nuku Hiva 72
    Ra'iatea 68, 139-40, **8**
    Rangiroa 69, 180, **8**
    responsible diving 71
    Rurutu 72, 230
    safety 74, 268
    services 74
    Taha'a 68, 146
    Tahiti 64-5, 77
    Tikehau 70, 189
    Toau 71
    Tubuai 73-4, 233
dolphin watching 73
    Maupiti 170
    Mo'orea 113
    Rangiroa 178
    Tahiti 77
dolphins 60
drinks 54-5, *see also* beer, *maitai*,
    wine
driving licences 262
driving, *see* car travel

E
economy 43
electricity 243
embassies 247
emergencies, *see* inside front cover
environmental issues 62-3
    crown-of-thorns starfish 68
    nuclear testing 38, 62, 198
    shark feeding 65
environmental organisations 146, 252
exchange rates, *see* inside front cover
ethnicity 43-5

F
Faaroa Bay 138
Faie 128
Fakarava 71, 185-8, **186**
Fakatopatere 195
Fangataufa 38, 39, 62
Fare 125-6, **126**
Fatu Hiva 225-7, **226**
ferries, *see* boat travel
festivals & events 247-8, *see also*
    sports
    Festival International du Film
        Documentaire Océanien 52
    Heiva 48, **14**
    Marquesas Arts Festival 216
    Tattoonesia 51
Fetuna 139
fishing
    Mataiva 192
    Mo'orea 115
    Taha'a 146
Flosse, Gaston 40
food 53-8, 248, 268
French 271-2

G
Gambier Archipelago 28, 238-41, **239**
Gauguin, Paul 98, 218, 219, 220
gay travellers 248
geology 59, 235
golf
    Mo'orea 115
    Tahiti 77

H
Haakuti 216
Haamene 145
Haamene Bay 126
Haapiti 111
Haatuatua 209
Hakahau 215

Hakahetau 216
Hakamaii 216
Hakanai Bay 216
Hakatea Bay 207
Hakaui Valley 206-7
Hanaiapa 223
Hanapaaoa 223
Hanavave 226
handicrafts 50, 250
    Bora Bora 164
    Mangareva 240
    Marquesas 212
    Tahiti 94
Hane 211-12
Hao 197-8
Hapatoni 225
Hatiheu 208-9
Hauru Point 110-11, **111**
health 264-9
Heiva 48, 14
helicopter services
    Bora Bora 157
    Tahiti 76
Heyerdahl, Thor 25, 32, 237
hiking 244
    Bora Bora 156-7
    Fatu Hiva 226
    Hitiaa lava tubes 99
    Hiva Oa 220
    Huahine 130
    Mangareva 241
    Maupiti 169
    Mo'orea 113-14
    Nuku Hiva 205, 207
    Ra'iatea 140
    Raivavae 235, 11
    Rurutu 231
    Taha'a 146
    Tahiti 77, 100-2, 104, 10
    Tubuai 233
    'Ua Huka 213
    'Ua Pou 215
historic buildings 31
    House of James Norman Hall 86
    Maison Blanche 109
history 31-40
hitching 263
Hitiaa lava tubes 99
Hiva Oa 72, 217-24, **218**
Hohoi 217
Hokatu 212

holidays 22, 248
Hooumi 207
horse riding 244
    Fatu Hiva 226
    Hiva Oa 220
    Huahine 129
    Mo'orea 114
    Nuku Hiva 205, 209
    Rurutu 231
    Tahiti 104
    Tahuata 225
    'Ua Huka 213
    'Ua Pou 215
hotels 243
Huahine 123-34, **125**
    accommodation 130-2
    activities 129-30
    diving 65, 129
    drinking 133-4
    entertainment 133-4
    food 133
    history 124
    itineraries 26
    tours 130
    travel to/from 134
    travel within 134

I
Île aux Récifs 179
insurance
    car 262-3
    health 264
    travel 248
internet access 248
internet resources
    accommodation 242
    air tickets 255
    culture 32, 41, 50
    current affairs 40
    diving 70, 71
    environment 63
    food 54
    health 265
    history 32
    tourist information 25
    wildlife 60
itineraries 26-30
    adventure activities 29, **29**
    archaeological sites 30, **30**
    Australs 28, **28**
    Bora Bora 26, **26**
    ecotravel 30, **30**
    Gambier Archipelago 28, **28**
    honeymooning 29, **29**

Huahine 26, **26**
    lagoons 27, **27**
    Mo'orea 26, 109, **26**
    Tahiti 77

J
jellyfish 267
jet lag 265

K
kayaking
    Huahine 129
    Maupiti 169
    Ra'iatea 140
    Tahiti 80
kite surfing 113, 233

L
Lagon Bleu 179
Lagon Vert 179
lagoon tours 27
    Bora Bora 155-6
    Fakarava 186
    Huahine 130
    Makemo 196
    Maupiti 169
    Mo'orea 115
    Ra'iatea 140
    Rangiroa 180
    Taha'a 146
    Tikehau 189
    Tubuai 233
Lake Fauna Nui 126
language 57-8, 207, 270-2
legal matters 248-9
lesbian travellers 248
literature 24, 48, *see also* books

M
Maeva 126-8, **127**
Maharepa 109
mahu 42
maitai 55
Makatea 197
makatea 235
Makemo 71-2, 196-7
Mangareva 240, 241
Manihi 70, 192-3, **192**
manta rays 60, 73, 9
maps 249
marae 33
Marae Aehua-tai (Bora Bora) 154
Marae Afareaito (Mo'orea) 112

Marae Ahu-o-Mahine (Mo'orea) 112
Marae Anapua (Tahiti) 101
Marae Anini (Huahine) 128-9
Marae Fare-Opu (Bora Bora) 154
Marae Fare Miro (Huahine) 128
Marae Farehape (Tahiti) 101
Marae Hariitaata (Australs) 232
Marae Haunarei (Australs) 232
Marae Mahaiatea (Tahiti) 98
Marae Manunu (Huahine)128
Marae Matairea Rahi (Huahine) 127-8
Marae Mauna-Oto (Australs) 235
Marae Nuupere (Mo'orea) 111
Marae Nuurua (Mo'orea) 111
Marae Nuutere (Tahiti) 103
Marae Paepae Ofata (Huahine) 128
Marae Paomaovao (Australs) 235
Marae Papiro (Tuamotus) 191
Marae Pou Pou (Australs) 235
Marae Raitoru (Australs) 232
Marae Tahinu (Tahiti) 101
Marae Taianapa (Bora Bora)154
Marae Tainuu (Ra'iatea) 139
Marae Takai (Tuamotus) 195
Marae Tamata Uporu (Huahine) 128
Marae Taputapuatea (Ra'iatea) 138, 13
Marae Tararoa (Australs) 230
Marae Te Ava (Huahine) 128
Marae Tefano (Huahine) 127
Marae Titiroa (Mo'orea) 112
Marae Umarea (Mo'orea) 112
Marae Vaiahu (Maupiti) 169
Marae Vaihiria I (Tahiti) 101
Marché de Pape'ete 84
marine animals 60-1, 64, 8, 9, *see also
    individual species*
marine reserves 63
markets 84
Maroe 128
Marquesan language 207
Marquesas 199-227, **200**
Marquesas Arts Festival 216
Mataiea 98
Mataiva 191-2, **191**
Matavai Bay 100
Maupiti 166-72, **168**, 6
    accommodation 170-1
    activities 169-70
    attractions 167-9
    children, travel with 170
    diving 69, 169-70, 9
    food 172
    history 167
    information 167
    shopping 172

travel to/from 172
travel within 172
measures 243
medical services 265-6
metric conversions, *see inside front cover*
mobile phones 251
money 22-3, 247, 249, 258, *see also
    inside front cover*
monoi 50
Mo'orea 106-22, **108**
    activities 112-15
    attractions 109-12
    children, travel with 115
    courses 115
    diving 65, 112-13
    drinking 121
    entertainment 121
    food 119-21
    history 107
    internet access 107
    itineraries 26, 109
    shopping 121
    tourist information 109
    tours 115
    travel to/from 121-2
    travel within 122
Moruroa 38, 39, 62, 198
mosquitoes 246
motorcycle travel, *see* scooter
    travel
Motu Ai Ai 179
Motu Auira 167
Motu Fareone 110
Motu Hemeni 212
Motu Irioa 110
Motu Nao Nao 139
Motu Nono 103
Motu Paeao 167
Motu Papa 212
Motu Pitihahei 167
Motu Puarua 189
Motu Teuaua 212
Motu Tiahura 110
Motu Tiapaa 167
Motu Tuanai 167
Mt Aorai 102
Mt Hiro 235, 11
Mt Marau 100-1
Mt Orohena 102
museums
    Centre Jacques Brel (Marquesas) 218
    Espace Culturel Paul Gauguin
        (Marquesas) 218
    Maeva archaeological museum
        (Huahine) 127

Musée de la Marine (Bora Bora) 154
Musée de Tahiti et des Îles
    (Tahiti) 96
Musée Gauguin (Tahiti) 98
Robert Wan Musée de la Perle
    (Tahiti) 84
Taetae Tupuna Enana (Marquesas)
    204
music 47-8, 49
Mutua Ura 236

N
Nahoe 223
nature reserves 63
newspapers 243
noni 62
nono 246
nuclear testing 38, 62, 198
Nuku Hiva 72, 201-11, **202**

O
Omoa 226, 12
Opunohu Bay 110
Opunohu Valley 112, 114
Otepipi 179-80

P
package tours 256
Pae Pae Piki Vehine 204
painting 49, 251
Paopao 109
Paopao Valley 112
Pape'ete 82-96, **84-5**, **86-7**
    accommodation 89-91
    attractions 83-8
    drinking 92-3
    emergency services 83
    entertainment 93-4
    festivals & events 89
    food 91-2
    shopping 94-5
    tourist information 83
    travel to/from 95
    travel within 95-6
    walking tour 88-9, **88**
Papeari 101
Papenoo 100, 101
Papetoai 110
parasailing 157
parks & gardens
    Jardin Botanique (Tahiti) 98
    Maraa Grotto (Tahiti) 96
    Parc Bougainville (Tahiti) 84
    Vaipahi Spring Gardens (Tahiti) 98

passports 254, *see also* visas
Patio 145
pearls 94, 176, 250, **15**
    Huahine 126, 128
    Mo'orea 121
    Taha'a 145, 146
    Tahiti 84, 95
    Tuamotus 181
pensions 243
petroglyphs
    Fatu Hiva 226, **12**
    Hiva Oa 219, 223
    Maupiti 168
    Tahiti 104
    'Ua Huka 212
phosphate mining 197
plants 59, 61
Point Vénus 100
poisonous cone shells 267
politics 20, 21, 40
Pomares 36-8
population 43
postal services 250
Pouheva 196
Pouvana'a a Oopa 124
Puamau 222-3
Puna'auia 96
Puohine 139

R
Ra'iatea 136-45, **137**
    accommodation 141-2
    activities 139-40
    attractions 138-9
    diving 68, 139-40, **8**
    drinking 143
    entertainment 143
    food 142-3
    history 136
    shopping 143-4
    tours 140-1
    travel to/from 144
    travel within 144-5
radio 243
raerae 42
Rainbow Warrior 39
Raivavae 234-6, **234**, **11**
Rangiroa 176-85, **177**
    accommodation 181-3
    activities 180
    attractions 178-80

000 Map pages
000 Photograph pages

diving 69, 180, **8**
drinking 184-5
entertainment 184-5
food 183-4
history 177
information 178
travel to/from 185
travel within 185
Rapa Iti (Rapa) 236-7, **237**
religion 45-6
resorts 24, 243-4
responsible travel 23, 63
    carbon offset 255
    diving 71
    itineraries 30
restaurants 55
Rikitea 240
Rimatara 236
Rimatara lorikeet 236
Rotoava 186
Rurutu 72, 229-32, **230**

S
safe travel 246-7
    diving 74, 268
    hitching 263
    swimming 246
sailing 244-5, 257
    Huahine 129
    Ra'iatea 140
    visas 252
scooter travel 262-3
sculpture 251
sea snakes 268
shark feeding 65
sharks 60, **8**
shopping 250-1
snorkelling
    Bora Bora 155
    Huahine 129
    Maupiti 169
    Mo'orea 112-13
    Ra'iatea 139-40
    Rangiroa 180
    Taha'a 146
    Tikehau 189
Song, Gaston Tong 40
sports 45
    Hawaiki Nui Canoe Race
        45
    Raid Painapo 45
    Raid Tahiti 45
    Tahiti Billabong Pro 104
stone fish 268

surfing 45, 80, 244, **16**
    Huahine 129
    Mo'orea 111, 113
    Tahiti 80, 100, 104, **16**
swimming safely 246

T
Taha'a 145-9, **137**
    accommodation 147-8
    activities 146
    attractions 145-6
    diving 68, 146
    food 148
    history 145
    tours 146
    travel to/from 148
    travel within 148-9
Tahiti 64-5, 75-105, **78-9**, **10**, **16**
Tahiti Billabong Pro 104
Tahitian 270-1
Tahuata 221, 224-5
Taiohae 202-6, **204**
Taipivai 207
Takapoto 194-6, **195**
Takaroa 194, **195**
tapa 50
tapu 46
Tapuamu 145
Taravai 241
Taravao 99
tattoos 51, 225, 251, **15**
    Bora Bora 164
    Marquesas 225
    Mo'orea 121
    Tahiti 95
Tautira 103
taxes 23
Te Pari Cliffs 104, **10**
Teahupoo 80, **16**
Tefarerii 128
telephone services 251
Temaru, Oscar 40
Temoe 241
Tetamanu 186
Tetiaroa 89
Tevaitoa 139
theft 246
Three Coconut Trees Pass 114
tiare apetahi 50, 139 , **11**
Tikehau 70, 188-91, **188**, **7**
tiki
    Hiva Oa 219, 223
    Hiva Ova 222, **13**
    Raivavae 235

time 251
tipping 249
Tiputa 178
Toau 71
Tohua Koueva 204
Tohua Mauia 217
tombs, *see also* cemeteries
    Pomare V 87
    Tohua Pehe Kua 223
Toovii Plateau 207
tourist information 25, 251-2
tours 256, *see also* 4WD tours, boat
    trips, lagoon tours, package tours
    Huahine 130
    Nuku Hiva 205, 207, 208
    Rangiroa 180-1
    Rurutu 231
    Taha'a 146
    Tahiti 76-105
    Tahuata 225
    Tubuai 233
travel to/from French Polynesia 254-67
travel within French Polynesia 257-63
trekking, *see* hiking
Tuamotus 173-98, **175**
Tubuai 73-4, 232-4, **233**
Tuheiava Pass 189
Tuherahera 189
turtles 60, 146
TV 243

U
'Ua Huka 211-14, **211**
'Ua Pou 214-17, **214**
undersea walks 156
uru 61
Uturoa 138, **138**

V
vacations 22, 248
vaccinations 264
Vaiare 112
Vaipaee 211
Vaitahu 224
Vaitape 151-4
vanilla 54, 146
    Ra'iatea 140
    Taha'a 145
    Tahiti 94
vegetarian travellers 56
video systems 243
visas 252, *see also* passports
volunteering 252

W
walking, *see* hiking
Wallis, Samuel 33
waterfalls
    Afareaitu (Mo'orea) 112
    Faarumai Waterfalls (Tahiti) 100
    Manfred Cascade (Marquesas)
    216
    Opunohu Valley (Mo'orea) 112
    Vaipo Waterfall (Marquesas)
    206
watersports
    Huahine 129
    Mo'orea 115
    Tahiti 80
    Tubuai 233
weather 22, 246
websites, *see* internet resources
weights 243
whale watching 73
    Maupiti 170
    Mo'orea 113
    Nuku Hiva 205
    Rurutu 230, 231
    Tahiti 77
    Tubuai 233
whales 60, 231
wildlife 59-62
wine 55, 179
women travellers 253
women's health 269
woodcarving 49
work 253

MAP LEGEND

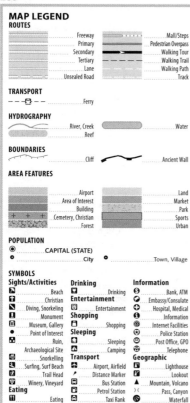

ROUTES

Freeway		Mall/Steps
Primary		Pedestrian Overpass
Secondary		Walking Tour
Tertiary		Walking Trail
Lane		Walking Path
Unsealed Road		Track

TRANSPORT
Ferry

HYDROGRAPHY
River, Creek
Reef
Water

BOUNDARIES
Cliff
Ancient Wall

AREA FEATURES
Airport
Area of Interest
Building
Cemetery, Christian
Forest
Land
Market
Park
Sports
Urban

POPULATION
CAPITAL (STATE)
City
Town, Village

SYMBOLS

Sights/Activities
Beach
Christian
Diving, Snorkeling
Monument
Museum, Gallery
Point of Interest
Ruin
Archaeological Site
Snorkelling
Surfing, Surf Beach
Trail Head
Winery, Vineyard
Eating
Eating

Drinking
Drinking
Entertainment
Entertainment
Shopping
Shopping
Sleeping
Sleeping
Camping
Transport
Airport, Airfield
Distance Marker
Bus Station
Petrol Station
Taxi Rank

Information
Bank, ATM
Embassy/Consulate
Hospital, Medical
Information
Internet Facilities
Police Station
Post Office, GPO
Telephone
Geographic
Lighthouse
Lookout
Mountain, Volcano
Pass, Canyon
Waterfall

LONELY PLANET OFFICES

Australia
Head Office
Locked Bag 1, Footscray, Victoria 3011
☎ 03 8379 8000, fax 03 8379 8111
talk2us@lonelyplanet.com.au

USA
150 Linden St, Oakland, CA 94607
☎ 510 250 6400, toll free 800 275 8555
fax 510 893 8572
info@lonelyplanet.com

UK
2nd fl, 186 City Rd,
London EC1V 2NT
☎ 020 7106 2100, fax 020 7106 2101
go@lonelyplanet.co.uk

Published by Lonely Planet Publications Pty Ltd
ABN 36 005 607 983

© Lonely Planet Publications Pty Ltd 2009

© photographers as indicated 2009

Cover photograph: Firedancer, Tiki Village, Mo'orea, French Polynesia/
Holger Leue/LOOK Die Bildagentur der Fotografen GmbH/Photolibrary

Many of the images in this guide are available for licensing from
Lonely Planet Images: www.lonelyplanetimages.com.

Printed by Hang Tai Printing Company.
Printed in China.

MIX
Paper from
responsible sources
FSC™ C021741
www.fsc.org